TURNER CLASSIC MOVIES

International Film Guide
2008

the definitive annual review of world cinema

edited by Ian Haydn Smith

44th edition

WALLFLOWER PRESS

LONDON & NEW YORK

61st
Film Festival Locarno
6–16 | 8 | 2008

Festival internazionale del film Locarno
Via Ciseri 23, CH-6601 Locarno
t +41 (0)91 756 21 21, f +41 (0)91 756 21 49
info@pardo.ch, www.pardo.ch

Main sponsors:

 UBS AET Azienda Elettrica Ticinese   MANOR  swisscom

Contents

Editor
Ian Haydn Smith
Publisher
Yoram Allon, Wallflower Press
Founding Editor
Peter Cowie
Consultant Editor
Daniel Rosenthal
Editorial Assistants
Katerina Andreakou, Anne Hudson,
Matthew Winston
Business Manager
Sara Tyler
International Advertising Manager
Sara Tyler
Europe, Film Festivals
tel: +44 (0)1349 854931
saraifg@aol.com
International Sales Consultants
Voula Georgakakou
Greece
tel: +30 210 729 2793
vgeo@artfree.org
Lisa Ray
Far East, Middle East, South Africa
tel: +44 (0)7798 662955
l.ray@hotmail.com
Design
Elsa Mathern
Photo Consultants
The Kobal Collection
tel: +44 (0)20 7624 3300
www.picturedesk.com

Wallflower Press
6 Market Place
London
W1W 8AF
tel: +44 (0)20 7436 9494
info@wallflowerpress.co.uk
www.wallflowerpress.co.uk

ISBN 978-1-905674-61-9

A catalogue record for this book is available
from the British Library

Copyright © 2008 Wallflower Publishing Ltd

Printed and bound in Poland
produced by Polskabook

For information on sales and distribution
in all territories worldwide, please contact
Wallflower Press on info@wallflowerpress.co.uk

FILM MAKING WITHOUT THE STRESS.

International Liaison

Afghanistan: Sandra Schäfer
Algeria: Roy Armes
Argentina: Alfredo Friedlander
Armenia: Susanna Harutyunyan
Australia: Peter Thompson
Austria: Gunnar Landsgesell
Bangladesh: Ahmed Muztaba Zamal
Belarus: Andrei Rasinski
Belgium: Erik Martens
Benin: Roy Armes
Bolivia: José Sánchez-H.
Bosnia & Herzegovina: Rada Sesić
Brazil: Nelson Hoineff & Leonardo
  Luiz Ferreira
Bulgaria: Pavlina Jeleva
Burkina Faso: Roy Armes
Cameroon: Roy Armes
Canada: Tom McSorley
Chad: Roy Armes
Chile: Andrea Osorio Klenner
China: Sen-lun Yu
Colombia: Jaime E. Manrique &
  Pedro Adrián Zuluaga
Costa Rica: Maria Lourdes Cortés
Croatia: Tomislav Kurelec
Cuba: Jorge Yglesias
Cyprus: Ninos-Fenek Mikelidis
Czech Republic: Eva Zaoralová
Denmark: Jacob Neiiendam
Ecuador: Gabriela Alemán
Egypt: Fawzi Soliman
Estonia: Jaan Ruus
Fiji: Lorenzo Codelli
Finland: Antti Selkokari

France: Michel Ciment
Georgia: Nino Ekvtimishvili
Germany: Andrea Dittgen
Greece: Ninos-Fenek Mikelidis
Guatemala: Maria Lourdes Cortés
Hong Kong: Tim Youngs
Hungary: Eddie Cockrell
Iceland: Freyr Gigja Gunnarsson
India: Uma da Cunha
Indonesia: Lisabona Rahman
Iran: Jamal Omid
Ireland: Michael Dwyer
Israel: Dan Fainaru
Italy: Lorenzo Codelli
Ivory Coast: Roy Armes
Japan: Tomomi Katsuta
Kazakhstan: Gulnara Abikeyeva
Kenya: Ogova Ondego
Kyrgystan: Gulnara Abikeyeva
Latvia: Andris Rozenbergs
Malta: Daniel Rosenthal
Mauritania: Roy Armes
Mexico: Carlos Bonfil
Morocco: Roy Armes
Namibia: Martin P. Botha
Nepal: Prabesh Subedi
Netherlands: Leo Bankersen
New Zealand: Peter Calder
Nigeria: Steve Ayorinde
Norway: Trond Olav Svendsen
Pakistan: Aijaz Gul
Panama: Maria Lourdes Cortés
Paraguay: Alfredo Friedlander &
  Jorge Jellinek

Peru: Isaac Léon Frías
Philippines: Tessa Jazmines
Poland: Barbara Hollender
Portugal: Martin Dale
Puerto Rico: Raúl Ríos-Díaz
Romania: Cristina Corciovescu
Russia: Kirill Razlogov
Rwanda: Ogova Ondego
Senegal: Roy Armes
Serbia & Montenegro: Goran
  Gocić
Singapore: Yvonne Ng
Slovakia: Miro Ulman
Slovenia: Ziva Emersić
South Africa: Martin P. Botha
South Korea: Nikki J.Y. Lee
Spain: Jonathan Holland
Sri Lanka: Tissa Abeysekara
Sweden: Gunnar Rehlin
Switzerland: Marcy Goldberg
Taiwan: David Frazier
Tajikistan: Gulnara Abikeyeva
Tanzania: Ogova Ondego
Thailand: Anchalee Chaiworaporn
Tunisia: Roy Armes
Turkey: Atilla Dorsay
Uganda: Ogova Ondego
Ukraine: Volodymyr Voytenko
United Kingdom: Philip Kemp
United States: Eddie Cockrell
Urugay: Jorge Jellinek
Uzbekistan: Gulnara Abikeyeva
Venezuela: Martha Escalona Zerpa
Zimbabwe: Martin P. Botha

Front Cover
*Tony Leung Chiu Wai and Wei Tang are the lovers in Ang Lee's adaptation of Eileen Chang's novella **Lust, Caution** (Se, jie). The film won the Golden Lion at the 2007 Venice International Film Festival. Image courtesy of Focus Features.*

Notes from the Editor

Something old, something new...

The *International Film Guide* returns after a brief hiatus with its 44th edition. A few things have changed since 2006. It has a new publisher (Wallflower Press) and a new sponsor in the form of Turner Classic Movies (TCM). And, of course, a new editor. It is both a pleasure and a somewhat daunting task to fit into the shoes of predecessors who each year successfully brought the cinemas from around the world into one single volume, and this edition also presents the cinematic output of 98 countries.

The last year has seen the passing of many filmmakers and individuals who played an important role in the film industry. With the death of Ingmar Bergman and Michelangelo Antonioni, much was written about the end of serious cinema. There is no denying that over the last few decades there has been a shift away from the environment that encouraged such great directors. However, such arguments appear redundant when faced with the growing number of directors who have only begun to show their potential: Nuri Bilge Ceylan, Carlos Reygadas, Paul Thomas Anderson, Cristian Mungiu, Valeska Grisebach, Fatih Akin... And the list goes on.

In the first of our 'Directors of the Year' profiles, Eddie Cockrell focuses on Fatih Akin, the vanguard of a remarkable renaissance in German cinema. This renaissance – and the history behind it – is discussed in detail by Shane Danielsen in our 'Country Focus' section. Germany has played a crucial part in the development of modern cinema and this piece offers an illuminating account of its past, present and what might be a very rosy future.

Romania is also one of the vital cinemas at the moment, with the films of Corneliu

Ian Haydn Smith

Porumboiu, Catalin Mitulescu and the late Cristian Nemescu winning awards at countless international festivals. This culminated in the country's first Palme d'Or, for Cristian Mungiu's remarkable *4 Months, 3 Weeks & 2 Days*. However, the domestic situation is not so good, writes Christina Corciovescu. Audiences have little time for local fare, opting instead for the latest Hollywood blockbuster. Cristian Mungiu was forced to go on the road with a 'caravan cinema' in order to screen his film to his home audience.

Romania is not alone in this problem. Sen-lun Yu identifies a similar issue in China. There, the template of the Hollywood blockbuster has been developed for home audiences at the expense of serious cinema. Another 'Director of the Year', Jia Zhangke, might win a Golden Lion at Venice, but the greater challenge is to convince domestic audiences to pay to see his films when *The Banquet* and *Curse of the Golden Flower* are screening next door.

In some countries, the problem is not the choice of films available but the lack of a cinema in which to screen them. Steve

Ayorinde reports on an ingenious plan by four Nigerian directors to make their films available through bank branches across the country. As with so many countries, Hollywood has a stranglehold on distribution and exhibition; however, local filmmakers are engaging with digital technology and finding alternative ways to ensure their films are seen.

Piracy remains rife around the world, crippling some film industries. Although laws have been introduced to combat it, in too many countries authorities have yet to enforce them. Jonathan Holland reports that in Spain 43% of the population download pirated films with the result that Sogecine, Spain's most successful production company over the last ten years, announced that it was halting film production.

Documentary continues to be an important feature on the cinematic landscape, with the number of festivals increasing and the profiles of those well established never as clear as they are now. Hannah Patterson highlights a number of trends in recent documentaries, from the conflict in Iraq to the blurring of the line between fact and fiction; nowhere more clear than in Nick Broomfield *Battle for Haditha* and Brian De Palma's *Redacted*, the controversial film by mainstream American director Brian de Palma.

And what of Hollywood? The bad hasn't improved, but the good appears to have increased. The reference point for many remains the last golden age of American cinema, the 1970s. *The Assassination of Jesse James by the Coward Robert Ford* draws heavily on the work of Terrence Malick yet asserts its own original take on the outlaw myth, while *Michael Clayton*, *Zodiac*, and *The Good Shepherd* prove that there were still a few conspiracy theories worth exploring. Elsewhere, *There Will Be Blood*, *The Bourne Ultimatum*, *Knocked Up* and *The Painted Veil* all point to an industry willing, occasionally at least, to accept that audiences will stomach more intelligent films. And if they won't, there's always *Transformers*.

With cinema increasingly regarded as the ancillary market and home entertainment where revenue generation really hits the jackpot, Brad Stevens provides an account of how the DVD market has developed, offering audiences the chance to revisit lost classics and discover titles that may never have reached our screens. What will replace the DVD is currently anyone's guess, but like the state of cinema globally, changes these days happen fast.

***

A brief note about this 44th edition of the *International Film Guide*. As there was no edition last year, each country report not only includes a round-up of 2007 but also a brief summary of select titles and events from 2006, highlighting cinema activity and industry news, thus ensuring a smooth flow between the last edition and this new incarnation.

Finally, a word of thanks to TCM whose passion for championing classic cinema around the world mirrors the *International Film Guide*'s role in continuing to be the definitive annual survey of contemporary global cinema.

WORLDWIDE BOX OFFICE 2007

	$m
1. *Pirates of the Caribbean: At World's End*	$958.4
2. *Harry Potter and the Order of the Phoenix*	$937.0
3. *Spider-man 3*	$885.4
4. *Shrek the Third*	$791.4
5. *Transformers*	$701.1
6. *Ratatouille*	$615.9
7. *The Simpson's Movie*	$525.5
8. *300*	$456.6
9. *The Bourne Ultimatum*	$440.9
10. *Live Free or Die Hard*	$377.5

source: worldwideboxoffice.com

TURNER CLASSIC MOVIES

TCM **CLASSIC SHORTS** 2008
FILM COMPETITION

THE SEARCH FOR THE FILM-MAKERS OF THE FUTURE LAUNCHES MAY 2008

Fancy yourself as the next Scorsese or Hitchcock?
Then enter your short film into the TCM Classic Shorts Competition.

This annual event is recognised as one of Europe's most prestigious short film
competitions and is open to entrants from the UK, Europe, Middle East and Africa.

Why Enter?
• First prize - £5,000; Second prize - £3,000; Third prize - £2,000.

• Judged by some of the most prominent names in the film and media industry, with new judges chosen annually.

• Official Award Ceremony held as part of the internationally recognised BFI London Film Festival in October.

• Promotion of your work on movie channel TCM and extensive PR exposure by TCM.

• A highly valuable stepping stone to anyone beginning a career in film-making.

How to Enter?
Go to **tcmclassicshorts.com** for entry forms and full rules and regulations. Short films must have been completed
between 1st August 2007 and 31st July 2008. The 2008 competition officially launches 1st May 2008.

Who Can Enter?
Open to entrants from Europe, Middle East and Africa. For further details of the countries that are eligible for entry
go to **tcmclassicshorts.com**

Film channel TCM is available via cable, satellite and digital terrestrial in over 35 million households throughout Europe, Middle East
and Africa with 8 regional versions in 11 different languages.

TCMONLINE.CO.UK   **TCMCLASSICSHORTS.COM**

Welcome from TCM

Tuning in to the world of film...

Turner Classic Movies (TCM) is a 24-hour cable, satellite and digital terrestrial film channel operating as part of the Time Warner Group. In 1994 it launched in the US, followed by the UK, Europe, the Middle East and Africa in 1999. TCM offers viewers the opportunity to escape to a world of film and enjoy a vast range of unforgettable movies from all genres. Broadening the cinematic experience, viewers can enhance their enjoyment of the world's most popular art form, with exclusive documentaries, interviews with Hollywood insiders and a front-row seat at international film events.

Throughout its global operation TCM sees the importance of keeping Hollywood's classic heritage alive and relevant to contemporary audiences. The channel invests substantial funds into original documentaries and its star profile, *Brando*, a joint US and EMEA production, screened at numerous international film festivals, enjoying a debut at Cannes and an Emmy nomination. TCM's documentaries focus on revealing the true characters behind some of the twentieth century's most influential personalities, including Steve McQueen, Greta Garbo and John Ford. The exclusive OFF SET interviews also feature on TCM, an ongoing series of 30-minute interviews showcasing a host of movie stars, entertainers and directors, who discuss their love of the movies, screen icons and filmmakers that have inspired their own careers. Contributors have included Carrie Fisher, Billy Crystal, George Clooney, Anthony Minghella, Samuel L. Jackson, Greta Scacchi, Michael Douglas, Imelda Staunton and Michael Caine.

Supporting the film industry at its grass roots is also key for the channel, which strives to champion the next wave of filmmakers through a continued presence at international film festivals. In the past year, as well as premiering its original documentaries, the channel had a presence at film festivals across the globe, from the hugely influential Tokyo Film Festival to the 'most northern international film festival', in Tromsø, Norway. TCM has also partnered with film festivals at Cannes, Berlin, London and Krakow, and sponsored the Public Award at the San Sebastián Film Festival.

In 2000, TCM launched *TCM Classic Shorts*, an annual short film competition offering the largest financial reward for filmmakers engaged in this form. Initially a UK-only event, it has since opened its doors to Europe, the Middle East and Africa in an attempt to find and nurture up-and-coming talent. *TCM Classic Shorts* is supported by some of the most prestigious names in the industry who give their valuable time to help judge the competition; past judges have included Dame Helen Mirren, Lasse Hallström, Lord Puttnam, Kate Winslet, Sir Alan Parker, Ridley Scott, Bernardo Bertolucci, Ewan McGregor, Jude Law, Gurinder Chadha, Terry Gilliam and Imelda Staunton. The competition launches every year in May, with its official awards ceremony held as part of the London Film Festival in the autumn.

TCM is proud to be the title sponsor for the *International Film Guide*, and is confident that this unique annual publication will continue to provide invaluable industry information on, and extend the knowledge and appreciation of, contemporary global cinema in all its diverse forms.

TURNER CLASSIC MOVIES

Directors of the Year

Fatih Akin by Eddie Cockrell

On the cold Sunday afternoon in February 2004 during which he surprised just about everyone by winning the Golden Bear at the Berlin Film Festival for *Head-On* (*Gegen die wand*), his fourth fiction feature as director, German-born Turkish writer-director Fatih Akin was, to put it politely, ecstatic. Shortly after the awards ceremony, alone in the middle of the Marlene Dietrich Platz outside the festival headquarters in central Berlin, three revellers could be seen whooping it up. Intrepid partygoers from the previous night? On closer inspection, the three were Akin, friend and frequent co-star Birol Ünel, and lead actress Sibel Kekilli. Their glee was infectious; passing close by, an observer couldn't help but feel that these three were genuinely, giddily, appealingly thunderstruck by the achievement.

Three years and a few months later, upon receiving the award for Best Screenplay at the 2007 Cannes Film Festival's for his fifth fiction feature, *The Edge of Heaven* (*Auf der anderen Seite* – literally, 'on the other side'), Akin thanked his wife and crew before proclaiming, 'I have one message for Turkey: all is one, united we stand, divided we fall'.

At the same festival, *The Edge of Heaven* also won the Ecumenical Prize and was praised by that jury as 'the story of the intersecting destinies in Germany and Turkey of men and women from different backgrounds. It makes the viewer aware of the pain and complexity of the loss of cultural identity and relationships, as well as the valuable cultural exchanges, transitions and cohabitations possible between these two worlds. Three other major themes are the difficulties of parent/child relationships, the costs of sacrifice and complex issues of reconciliation.'

Clearly, the time is right for the ascension of 34-year-old Fatih Akin. Much more than a talented and perceptive writer-director, he brings an articulate, compassionate vision of the conundrum that is the contemporary migrant experience to his films. Call it a benevolent look at multicultural challenges in today's world from a card-carrying insider. By most accounts affable and outspoken in equal measure, his films thrum with the urgent business of full lives being lived, even as cultural divides are grappled with.

When asked if immigrants should drop their traditions in favour of assimilation, Akin's answer symbolises the tension in his art: 'The answer is somewhere in between,' he said. 'Me, personally, I stand in opposition to tradition, but I am also loyal to tradition. I don't say everything is wrong. I don't believe in that. I would like to keep a lot of stuff from the Turkish heritage; some things I would not like to keep because I don't accept them. I was born in Germany, went to German school. To try to keep the respect, that is very important to me.'

Fatih Akin was born on 25 August 1973 in Hamburg, Germany. The son of Turkish parents, he exhibited an early aptitude for writing and storytelling. He began studying visual communication at Hamburg's College of Fine Art in 1994. The next year, his first short film, *Sensin… You're the One!* (*Sensin… du bist es!*), received the audience award at his hometown's short film festival. In 1996, his second short work, *Weed* (*Getuerkt*), picked up three international awards. Slice-of-life dramedies about streetwise Turks in Hamburg, both shorts exhibit the delicate balance of grim reality and heart-on-the-sleeve passion that informs his later work. They also marked the first collaboration with brother Cem Akin, as well as actors Mehmet Kurtulus and Idil Üner.

Short Sharp Shock

Fond of Martin Scorsese's maxim, 'I'm always searching for a master', Akin clearly modelled his 1998 feature debut, *Short Sharp Shock* (*Kurz und schmerzlos*), on that director's own *Mean Streets* (1973). The film follows the adventures of a multi-ethnic trio of youths in contemporary Hamburg: Turk Gabriel (Kurtulus), Greek Costa (Adam Bousdoukos) and loose-cannon Serb Bobby (Aleksandar Jovanovic). When Gabriel tries to save Costa and Bobby from the dangerous appeal of thug life, he imperils his own dream of relocating to Turkey to run a seaside restaurant. Enthusing on the film's energy from its Locarno festival premiere, *Variety* critic Derek Elley, perhaps the first high-profile champion of Akin's work, declared 'German cinema gets its first real *Boyz N the Hood*' with this 'punchy, gritty tale' in which 'well-defined personalities … maintain interest, rather than the rap-style visual trimmings'. *Short Sharp Shock* won Locarno's Bronze Leopard and the Bavarian Film Award for Best Young Director.

True to his rapidly developing form, Akin followed his startling debut with what Elley rightly called the 'impressive career swerve' of *In July* (*Im Juli*, 2000), a romantic comedy that nevertheless manages to continue the director's ongoing fascination with cultural tension. Facing a summer of doing nothing, stodgy student teacher Daniel Bannier (*Run Lola Run*'s Moritz Bleibtreu) follows the sun by impulsively pursuing the mysterious and beautiful Melek (Idil Üner again) from Hamburg to Istanbul, with secret soulmate Juli (Christiane Paul) in tow. As the pair chart a course along the Danube River, they experience a series of strange encounters, with a crafty trucker (Jochen Nickel), some really good weed, a hip Turk (Kurtulus again) with a body in his trunk, affable Romanian border guards (Akin and his brother Cem) and the enigmatic beauty and self-proclaimed 'ex-Yugo', Luna (Branka Katic). After a wild chase through Budapest – during which his Hungarian pursuer runs out of gas – Daniel finally discovers his inevitable destiny on the Bosphorus. A box office hit, Akin's second feature is a sunny screwball surprise that breathes fresh life into the German road movie

In July

and showcases the spectacular chemistry of the dreadlocked Paul and Cary Grant-ish Bleibtreu. 'You're in love?' someone asks our smitten hero early on. 'Cool. Tell me about it.' With this sparkling romantic adventure, Akin does just that.

In July

Already evident in Akin's work is a narrative fluidity that belies the detailed and episodic nature of his stories. For his third feature, Akin stretched himself yet again, this time to tell the story of a southern Italian family who emigrate to Germany. Deciding in 1964 that their fortunes lie elsewhere, the Amato family leave their Italian village for the industrial Ruhr town of Duisburg. When father Romano (Gigi Savoia) tires of work in the mines, mother Rosa (Antonella Attili) decides to open an Italian restaurant, which they name after their hometown – Solino. The eventual success of the enterprise is played out against the rivalry of the grown-up siblings, Gigi (Barnaby Metschurat), an aspiring filmmaker, and the more macho Giancarlo (Moritz Bleibtreu

Solino

again). It's always a pleasure to watch a young filmmaker gradually expand his horizons and focus his talent, and *Solino* (2002) is a mature, thoughtful, compassionate story of emigration, perseverance and the vital importance of family.

Solino won the Best Screenplay for Ruth Toma (who went on to pen *The White Massai* and *Emma's Bliss*, among others) at the Bavarian Film Awards, as well as a prize from the Guild of German Art House Cinemas.

As skilled as Akin had become in such a short period of time, few were prepared for the emotional wallop that is *Head-On*. Made as the first film under his production banner, Corazon International, it seems both of a piece with his previous work and a breathtakingly confident step forward.

Head-On

Following an obviously long-standing path of self-destructive behaviour, 40-year-old Cahit (Birol Ünel again) concludes a night of drinking and fighting by driving his old car head-on into the wall of a building. He is placed under observation at a psychiatric clinic, where a well-meaning doctor (played by Hermann Lause) quotes cult band The The to his incredulous patient: 'If you can't change the world, change your world.' After that meeting, he's approached by another patient, Sibel (Sibel Kekilli), who asks him to marry her. A charming, effervescent, nascent free spirit, Sibel yearns to break free from the suffocating control of her devout parents (played by Aysel Iscan and Demir Gokgol) and wild-eyed, overprotective brother (Cem Akin again). So desperate that she tries to slash her wrists, her offer to Cahit is to marry, but live separate lives. Initially reluctant, Cahit allows himself to be cleaned up, and under the tutelage of pal Seref (Guven Kirac) he manages to persuade Şibel's suspicious family that he's legit.

After their traditional marriage, she takes to her freedom like a duck to water. In addition to her drinking and drug-taking, Sibel gets her navel pierced and drags Cahit to clubs, where he usually passes out and she leaves with a different man each time. Cahit is comfortable with the arrangement for a few months, content to have a clean flat for once and enjoying rough sex with occasional lover Maren (Catrin Striebeck), who takes Sibel on at her hair salon.

Drawing strength from her love of life, Cahit falls for Sibel and, in a jealous rage, kills one of her one-night-stands who had dared taunt him about his affections for his wife. As Cahit is about to enter prison, Sibel realises she loves him. Moving to Istanbul, staying with hotel-worker pal Selma (Meltem Cumbul), Sibel degrades herself to the point where she's viciously beaten and stabbed. Upon his release from prison, a reformed Cahit travels to Istanbul and, through Selma, finds Sibel, who has since begun a new life.

Akin imbues a story that sounds conventional and convoluted on the page with the best of his previous work. *Head-On* possesses the nervous, low-life energy of *Short Sharp Shock*, the leisurely yet logical plotting and careful attention to character detail of *Solino*, and just enough of the quirky, life-affirming humour found in *In July* to ensure that the grief these two cause each other on their way to love and mutual respect remains a riveting experience for the viewer. Akin quite clearly relishes the chance to dive deep into Turkish culture and the problematic issues of identity and cultural pride faced by Turks who either move to or are born in Germany. The dreary, multi-culti, working-class district of Hamburg-Altona is

a far cry from the sunny beauty of Istanbul, where Cahit is startled to discover his Turkish cabbie actually hails from Bavaria.

Ünel, who has appeared in all Akin's features except *Solino*, brings an appealing ferocity to Cahit. Newcomer Kekilli, discovered by Akin after they exhausted their search for what his producers called 'young women who speak Turkish fluently and are ready to get undressed in front of the camera', has a lithe beauty and a natural relationship with the lens. Frequent collaborator and co-producer Mehmet Kurtulus plays a bartender who exploits Sibel during her debasement in Istanbul.

Head-On

Winning Berlin's Golden Bear was only the beginning for *Head-On*, which subsequently earned Akin the European Film Award for Best Feature, the German Camera Award, a sweep of the German Film Awards, Spain's Goya for Best European Film, the Best Foreign Language Film Award from America's National Society of Film Critics, and numerous other regional festival plaudits.

'I put so much into the making of *Head-On*,' Akin explains in the international press-kit for his newest feature, *The Edge of Heaven*, 'that when I finished, I had no idea what to do next … Ironically, to make matters worse, *Head-On* became a big success for me … I felt pressure to come up with something better.'

That 'something better' is what Derek Elley calls 'an utterly assured, profoundly moving, superbly-cast drama in which the lives and

The Edge of Heaven

emotional arcs of six people – four Turks
and two Germans – criss-cross through love
and tragedy'. Hamburg University professor
Nejat (Baki Davrak), at first faintly bemused
to find his father involved with a hard-as-nails
Turkish prostitute, Yeter (Nursel Köse), is
horrified when tragedy strikes and his father
accidentally kills her.

Partly out of curiosity and partly to assuage his
guilt, Nejat sets off to Istanbul to find Yeter's
daughter Ayten (Nurgül Yesilçay). Unbeknownst
to him, she's a political activist befriended
by Lotte (Patrycia Ziolkowska), the liberated
daughter of more conservative and middle-
class Susanne (Hanna Schygulla).

Blurring the lines between the personal, social
and political, each character's journey has them
cross boundaries both physical and emotional.
Yet unlike many films that set up chance
meetings and coincidences among a stable of
protagonists, The Edge of Heaven never feels
forced, rushed, or as schematic as such films
can in lesser hands.

'To really grow up,' Akin says, 'I felt I had
to make three films. Call it a trilogy if you

The Edge of Heaven

want to, but it's basically three films that
belong together because of their themes
of love, death and evil. Head-On was about
love. The Edge of Heaven is about death …
Something is still missing that will be in the
third film about evil. I just feel like I have to
tell something to the end. These three films
are kind of my homework, then I can move
on. Maybe move on to genre films; film noir,
western, even horror…'

Subsequent to its warm reception at
Cannes, where many critics had tipped it
to win the Palme d'Or, The Edge of Heaven
was chosen as Germany's official entry
into the 2007 foreign film Academy Award
sweepstakes, prompting another example of
the filmmaker's self-depracating humour: 'I'm
extremely happy,' he told Variety. 'What luck
that Tom Tykwer filmed Perfume in English.'
Interestingly, Akin is represented twice in
the 'best foreign film' field, having also co-
produced, through Corazon International,
Turkey's official entry, Takva: A Man's Fear of
God, directed by Ozer Kiziltan.

Crossing the Bridge: The Sound of Istanbul

Befitting a filmmaker of international stature,
Akin has branched out into documentary,
screenwriting and even acting. His
documentary films include an hour-long
profile of his Turkish parents, We Forgot to
Go Back (Denk ich an Deutschland: Wir haben
vergessen zurueckzukehren, 2000), as well
as the feature-length music film Crossing the
Bridge: The Sound of Istanbul (2005), which

Kebab Connection

provided much of the inspiration for *The Edge of Heaven*.

Collaborating once again with Toma, Akin wrote the box office hit *Kebab Connection* (2005), which has travelled little beyond Germany, but is a mischievous throwback to the rowdier humour of *In July*. Hamburg-born Ibrahim 'Ibo' Secmez (Denis Moschitto) aspires to make the first German kung-fu movie. Though stymied by actual plot details, he's already got a killer title: 'Lethal Fist of the Yellow Avenger'. To hone his craft, Ibo has made a razzle-dazzle cinema ad – 'for two fistfuls of doner' runs the tagline – for Kebab Connection, the fast-food stand run by his uncle, Ahmet (Hasan Ali Mete), in direct competition with the Greek joint across the street, owned by the equally determined Kirianis (Adnan Maral) and his seductive daughter Stella (Tatjana Velimirov). Ibo's plans are derailed, however, when his lovely and mature German girlfriend Titzi (Nora Tschirner) becomes pregnant. Titzi herself is determined to be accepted at drama school, practising *Romeo and Juliet* incessantly with her roommate, Nadine (Paula Paul). Are Ibo's strict but eager Turkish parents ready for such a grandchild? Is Ibo ready for fatherhood? And is Hamburg ready for Ibo?

Kebab Connection continues a bold new chapter in German film, where tensions over nationality and religion are relieved and bridged by good old-fashioned, politically incorrect, belly laughs.

Akin was also approached to direct a five-minute segment for the portmanteau film *Visions of Europe* (2005). His black-and-white song cycle, once again starring Üner, harnesses poet Heinrich Heine's 'The Evil Old Songs' ('Die boesen alten lieder') to condemn fascism and war. 'I see a film a day,' he told one writer, 'and hope to make films that reflect upon cinema my entire life.'

In addition to taking small parts in all his films up until *In July*, Akin has acted in a handful of German television programmes, was a voice in Oliver Hirschbiegel's *The Experiment* (*Das Experiment*, 2001) and has appeared in small roles in films by friends.

Around the time *The Edge of Heaven* was selected for Cannes, Akin was working on a documentary about a controversial landfill planned for his grandmother's village, Camburnu, in the tea-growing region close to the Turkish coast of the Black Sea. Provisionally titled *Garbage in the Garden of Eden*, it is a project in which Akin has invested a great deal of passion. 'If we can step up enough pressure for the project to be halted, there could be a happy ending,' the crusading Akin told an interviewer in Istanbul. 'But it could also end in tragedy, with the death of the village ... I've been fighting together with its inhabitants for the past two years. I think the only chance the village has is political pressure from abroad. There's no place for [Turkey] in the European Union if it can't sort out its environmental problems.'

In the summer of 2007, Akin was investigated by police in Hamburg for allegedly breaking a law forbidding the display of Nazi symbols on clothing. He appeared on a film set wearing a t-shirt emblazoned with a swastika in place of the 's' in the word 'Bush'. In an interview with the German newspaper, *Spiegel*, Akin made his feelings clear: 'Bush's policy is comparable with that of the Third Reich. I think that under Bush, Hollywood has begun making certain films at the request of the Pentagon to normalise things like torture and Guantanamo.

I'm convinced the Bush administration wants a third world war. I think they're fascists.'

Akin and wife Monique welcomed their first child, a son, in 2005. He continues to live in Hamburg, and has most recently been linked to the Chinatown section of the portmanteau film, *New York, I Love You* (2008), a sequel of sorts to the popular 2006 compilation *Paris, je t'aime*. Akin also maintains a high festival profile, having served on the competition juries at both Berlin and Cannes.

Yet despite his rapid ascendancy over the past dozen years, Akin is anything but complacent. The viewer senses that the palpable tension between entertainment and social concerns will only intensify in future films: 'The times are too irritating, too disturbing at the moment for me to be able to ignore [politics] in my art,' he recently told one interviewer. But then: 'First of all, I want to entertain. That's my job, I'm a storyteller.' A mere five fiction films into a career that promises as much as it delivers, it's abundantly clear that Fatih Akin loves his work.

EDDIE COCKRELL is a *Variety* film critic and freelance programming consultant who, when not reviewing from festivals in Europe and Canada, splits his time between Maryland and Sydney.

Fatih Akin filmography

[feature film directing credits only]

1998
KURZ UND SCHMERZLOS
(Short Sharp Shock)
Script: Fatih Akin. Photography: Frank Barbian. Production Design: Guido Amin Fahim. Editing: Andrew Bird. Players: Mehmet Kurtulus (Gabriel), Aleksandar Jovanovic (Bobby), Adam Bousdoukos (Costa), Regula Grauwiller (Alice), Idil Üner (Ceyda), Ralph Herforth (Muhamer). Produced by Daniel Blum, Stefan Shcubert, Ralph Schwingel. 100 mins

2000
IM JULI
(In July)
Script: Fatih Akin. Photography: Pierre Aïm. Editing: Andrew Bird. Players: Moritz Bleibtreu (Daniel Bannier), Christiane Paul (Juli), Mehmet Kurtulus (Isa), Idil Üner (Melek), Jochen Nickel (Leo), Branka Katic (Luna), Birol Ünel (Club Doyen), Sandra Borgmann (Marion). Produced by Stefan Shcubert, Ralph Schwingel. 99 mins

2002
SOLINO
Script: Ruth Toma. Photography: Rainer Klausmann. Production Design: Bettina Schmidt. Editing: Andrew Bird. Players: Christian Tashe (Jos Vater), Barnaby Metschurat (Gigi), Tiziana Lodato (Ada), Antonella Attili (Rosa), Moritz Bleibtrau (Giancarlo). Produced by by Hejo Emans, Stefan Schubert, Ralph Schwingel. 124 mins

2004
GEGEN DIE WAND
(Head-On)
Script: Fatih Akin. Photography: Rainer Klausmann. Production Design: Tamo Kunz. Editing: Andrew Bird. Players: Birol Ünel (Cahit Tomruk), Sibel Kekilli (Sibel), Catrin Striebeck (Maren), Meltem Cumbul (Selma), Zarah McKenzie (Barfrau in der Fabrik), Stefan Gebelhoff (Nico). Produced by Stefan Shcubert, Ralph Schwingel. 121 mins

2005
CROSSING THE BRIDGE:
THE SOUND OF ISTANBUL
Script: Fatih Akin. Photography: Hervé Dieu. Editing: Andrew Bird.

Players: Alexander Hacke, the bands Baba Zula, Orient Expressions, Duman, Replikas, Istanbul Style Breakers, Siyasiyabend. Produced by FA, Sandra Harzer, Christian Kux, Klaus Maeck, Andreas Thiel. 90 mins

2007
AUF DER ANDEREN SEITE
(The Edge of Heaven)
Script: Fatih Akin. Photography: Rainer Klausmann. Production Design: Tamo Kunz, Sirma Bradley. Editing: Andrew Bird. Players: Nurgül Yesilçay (Ayten Öztürk), Baki Davrak (Nejat Aksu), Tuncel Kurtiz (Ali Aksu), Hanna Schygulla (Susanne Staub), Patrycia Ziolkowska (Lotte Staub), Nursel Köse (Yeter). Produced by FA, Klaus Maeck, Andreas Thiel. 122 mins

Susanne Bier by Mette Hjort

S usanne Bier is one of the most significant Danish directors to have appeared on the international festival circuit in recent years. Known amongst Nordic colleagues for her razor-sharp mind, unrelenting professionalism, determination, charisma and sense of humour, Bier has directed ten feature films since she graduated from the Danish National Film School in 1987 with her short film *Island of the Blessed* (*De saliges ø*). There is every reason to believe that this energetic and still relatively young director is well on her way to establishing herself, internationally and not only on a European level, as one of the most accomplished women filmmakers of her generation.

Bier's background and career

Bier was born in Copenhagen on 15 April 1960. She came to film via an unusual route; having first embarked on studies focusing on comparative religion and set design at the University of Jerusalem, she subsequently pursued architecture in London, before applying for admission to the competitive Danish National Film School. Her interest in built environments, and particularly in the people who inhabit them, is evident in *Like It Never Was Before* (*Pensionat Oskar*, 1995), which begins with striking images of immaculately maintained suburban dwellings and goes on to explore the acrimonious relationships of those who live inside them. Religion plays a key role in *Island of the Blessed* as well as in the thriller *Credo* (*Sekten*, 1997), which takes a close look at cults and the psychological dynamics that make them possible. And in her first feature film, the Swedish/Danish co-production, *Freud flyttar hemifrån...* (1991), Bier draws on her Jewish background to explore the clash between orthodox and secular conceptions of Judaism.

In a country where cultural and ethnic homogeneity was the norm until recently, Bier's Jewish background and cosmopolitan outlook set her apart from her peers; not surprisingly, these aspects of her identity also inform her driving concerns. When queried about her self-understanding as both a woman and a (Danish) filmmaker, Bier is always quick to point out that she is more preoccupied with attitudes towards outsiders, with cultural conflicts and with the impact of globalisation on national cultures than she is with a set of readily recognisable feminist or national themes. While Bier draws on popular Danish genres, such as the 'folk comedy' (*folkekomedie*), she sees herself as taking a certain distance in her work from what she regards as the Scandinavian tradition of naturalistic cinematic representation, involving an overly literal-minded or straightforward correlation between inner sentiment and its external expression. Her films feature characters whose emotional turmoil is presented in anything but a stereotypical way. In *Freud flyttar hemifrån...*, for example, Rosha (Ghita Nørby), a vital yet domineering and neurotic Jewish mother and Holocaust survivor, expresses her fear of dying in one scene by clutching her handbag as she sits, motionless, in a hospital bed. Instead of tears or emotional outpourings, Bier uses Rosha's stillness to convey to viewers an inner torment barely under control.

Unlike Thomas Vinterberg, who achieved international recognition early, with *The Celebration* (*Festen*, 1998), but arguably failed to cope with its many challenges, Bier's career path has been more gradual. In 1999, she achieved a major breakthrough with the Danish romantic comedy, *The One and Only* (*Den eneste ene*), which attracted an audience of over 840,000 in Denmark alone and cemented Bier's reputation as a filmmaker with a strong commitment to making popular but also intelligent films. She has successfully tried her hand at a number of European co-productions, including *Brothers* (*Brødre*, 2004) and *After the Wedding* (*Efter brylluppet*, 2006). Produced by DreamWorks and featuring Halle Berry and Benicio del Toro, Bier's most recent film, *Things We Lost in the Fire* (2007), marks her move into English-language filmmaking.

Brothers

Bier is currently associated with Peter Aalbæk Jensen and Lars von Trier's Zentropa, where she is considered the company's most bankable director. Indeed, Bier is often evoked as the director most likely to secure Zentropa's financial situation in the future. Her place within the Zentropa scheme of things rests

Open Hearts

on the international response to her work, starting with the Dogme film *Open Hearts* (*Elsker dig for evigt*, 2002). A key factor here, as Bier herself notes, has been her tendency to explore questions of loss and compromise in various contexts, be it the conflict in Afghanistan (*Brothers*) or poverty in developing countries (*After the Wedding*). Having now moved into English-language film production with *Things We Lost in the Fire*, Bier finds herself with a significantly expanded range of opportunities as she embarks on the next stage of her career as a filmmaker.

Families, erotic longings and fate

Bier's oeuvre reveals a consistent pre-occupation with the family, eroticism and the choices that human beings make as they respond to fateful events or encounters. Her films are character-driven rather than plot-driven and relationships, of a familial and often erotic nature, lie at the heart of most of them. Foregrounding the perspective of the neurotic psychology student, tellingly nicknamed 'Freud', the melancholic yet humorous *Freud flyttar hemifrån...*, explores the effects of parental trauma (and the tangled dependencies it provokes) on the next generation. While Bier has never made explicit reference to psychoanalysis in interviews, her films are rife with Freudian themes. Desire and sexuality figure prominently in the film: sex is recommended by a sibling as a cure for Freud's various psychosomatic symptoms; his brother, David (Philip Zandén), struggles to gain parental acceptance of his homosexuality;

and his sister, Deborah (Jessica Zandén), tries hard to maintain a commitment to orthodox beliefs as the passions of her former, and far more permissive self, resurface during a visit to Sweden from Israel.

The focus on family and erotic longing reappears in Bier's next two features, *Family Matters* (*Det bli'r i familien*, 1994) and *Like It Never Was Before*. In *Family Matters*, Swedish cook Jan Borelius (Philip Zandén again) has sex with the lovely Constanca (Ana Padrão) who, unbeknownst to him at the time, is his sister. Separated at a young age because of the tumultuous life of their mother Lilli (played again by Ghita Nørby), and fatefully brought together by Jan's desire to find his birth mother, the young adults are initially traumatised when they realise they are siblings. However, they subsequently affirm their incestuous desire, physically and publicly, in front of both their mother and Håkon Borelius (Ernst-Hugo Järegård), the man who adopted and raised Jan. What is striking is that Bier seems to be making a case for the legitimacy of incestuous desire under certain circumstances, thereby echoing the Freudian thought that the functional bases for taboos can disappear with time.

Like It Never Was Before focuses on a once idealistic and creative husband, Rune Runeberg (Loa Falkman), who finds himself sexually frustrated and bullied after years of marriage. He breaks free from the stifling attitudes of his conformist and careerist wife Gunnel (Stina Ekblad) through an almost accidental homoerotic relationship with the fire-breathing magician Petrus (Simon Norrthon) during a family holiday at a seaside resort. Opting to pursue the path of authenticity and to embrace his new sexual identity, Rune leaves the middle-class home that appeared so ominously normal and functional at the outset of the film. Gunnel's hysterical response to Rune's decision is to create a bonfire outside her suburban home, using many of the material possessions from which he has effectively freed himself and

in which her libido has been tragically over-invested.

The thriller *Credo* is once again about erotic longing, but this time in the context of a social arrangement that stands as a perversion of the family, and of the kind of intimacy and sense of belonging that this institution ideally provides. The film features Sofie Gråbøl and Ellen Hillingsø, two of contemporary Danish cinema's most prominent actresses, as women who become ensnared in the sexually exploitative practices of a cult. Their attempts to extricate themselves from the hypnotic powers and physical abuse of the cult's leaders provide key elements of suspense. At the same time, these endeavours offer an opportunity to reflect on the nature of the libidinal desires that are opportunistically mobilised by the cult, making its existence possible in the first place.

Bier's breakthrough hit, *The One and Only*, is a humorous reflection on family dynamics seen through a series of mismatched relationships that are eventually put right by a chance encounter and a deadly but convenient accident. Sus (Sidse Babett Knudsen), a feisty beautician, discovers that her Italian lover Sonny, with whom she is expecting a child, has been unfaithful to her. Niller (Niels Olsen), a kitchen installer, is married to the overbearing Lizzie (Søs Egelind). The two meet and fall in love when Niller arrives at Sus and Sonny's home to install a new kitchen. When Lizzie is killed by a car on her way to purchase milk for her newly adopted daughter, Mgala (Vanessa Gouri), Niller decides to pursue Sus, successfully courting her in an operating room where she is preparing to undergo an abortion. The film ends with a celebration of the kind of non-traditional family arrangement that is increasingly familiar to contemporary Danes: Sus marries Niller, and will give birth to Sonny's baby, who will grow up as Niller's child and be the sibling of a girl from Burkina Faso.

Open Hearts, *Brothers*, *After the Wedding* and *Things We Lost in the Fire* are thought-provoking dramas that look at the role of chance in human life and at the impact of tragic events that lie beyond our control. The Dogme film *Open Hearts* reflects the director's response to the events of 9/11. The film is about the way in which lives can be transformed beyond recognition by a single fateful event; in this case a car accident that paralyses the newly engaged Joachim (Nikolaj Lie Kaas) and brings his needy and emotionally vulnerable fiancé Cæcilie (Sonja Richter) into contact with the doctor, Niels (Mads Mikkelsen), whose wife Marie (Paprika Steen) was at the wheel of the speeding car that hit Joachim. Bier has talked about the affair that develops between Cæcilie and Niels (and especially about the latter's decision to walk away from a solid family life) in terms of her resistance to the idea that the family must take priority over all other values and must be defended at all costs. *Open Hearts* takes issue, then, with the kind of 'for better or worse' reasoning that lies at the heart of traditional concepts of the family. In this manner, the film invites reflection on, and indeed acceptance of, the relevant institution's necessary vulnerabilities in the face of life's inevitable contingencies.

Brothers

In *Brothers* the family unit is perturbed by the murderous actions that father and husband Michael (Ulrich Thomsen) undertakes against his will while on military duty in Afghanistan, and by the psychological transformation he undergoes as a result of having to live with the memory of his actions. The film features a stellar performance by Connie Nielsen in her

first Danish film, as Michael's wife Sarah, and equally remarkable performances by Lie Kaas and Thomsen, the two very different brothers who desire her. The film screened at the San Sebastián, Toronto, Sundance and London film festivals, and received nominations for a number of European Film Awards.

After the Wedding

In *After the Wedding*, fateful change is linked to terminal illness. The ethical issue that concerns Bier is the extent to which a dying person is justified in using his wealth and power to manipulate those closest and dearest to him into a new family arrangement that is to become operative after his death. Jørgen's (Rolf Lassgård) scheme succeeds, as his matchmaking, we are left to assume, brings his wife and her former lover together, puts his daughter in contact with her biological father, and produces a new father for the young children who will initially be rendered fatherless by his death. Yet the question remains whether such scheming can be justified, even when the consequences have to be judged positively. *After the Wedding* reached the final round in the competition for the Academy Award for Best Foreign Language Film in 2007, eventually losing to Florian Henckel von Donnersmark's *The Lives of Others* (*Das Leben der Anderen*).

In *Things We Lost in the Fire*, unexpected loss and its implications for the family are once again the main concern. When Brian Burke (David Duchovny) dies as a result of senseless street violence, his widow, Audrey Burke (Halle Berry), invites his best friend, Jerry Sunborne (Benicio del Toro), a recovering heroin addict, to live with her and her two children. Underpinning the narrative is the development of Audrey and Jerry's relationship; whether she will come to understand what her husband saw in Jerry, and will become romantically involved with him. Of Bier's films, this American production received by far the most mixed reviews. Critics took issue with the film's many extreme close-ups, with its melodramatic elements and with its strong sense of generic predictability. Most critics did, however, praise Benicio del Toro's performance as Jerry, and some saw valuable continuities between *Things We Lost in the Fire* and Bier's earlier works.

Things We Lost in the Fire

Creative teams

Bier's films are the result of collaborations that date back to her early days as a filmmaker. Most important amongst these is Bier's long-term collaboration with editor Pernille Bech Christensen. An important element of the negotiations for *Things We Lost in the Fire* concerned Bier's insistence on Bech Christensen's participation in the film, and on Zentropa's Film Town in Avedøre as the base where the editing would take place. That the continued collaboration with a long-trusted colleague can provide crucial levels of confidence is clearly evident in the film's production history. When DreamWorks objected to Bier and Bech Christensen's decision to opt for a-chronological editing, the two Danish film professionals insisted on their creative choice, confident that they were right not only because they interpreted the test audience results in exactly the same way, but because they had a long history of judicious and jointly made decisions behind them.

Another recurrent figure in Bier's creative universe is one of Danish cinema's most productive and talented scriptwriters, Anders Thomas Jensen, whose trademark acerbic wit was somewhat tempered by Bier's influence in the scripts for *Open Hearts*, *Brothers* and *After the Wedding*. *The One and Only*, one of Danish cinema's most successful films, saw Bier collaborating with Kim Fupz Aakeson, another extraordinarily talented scriptwriter who, together with Jensen, can lay claim to having scripted the vast majority (some sixty films between them) of films associated with the New Danish Cinema.

Zentropa's Peter Aalbæk Jensen produced Bier's diploma film and served as executive producer for all of her Zentropa productions. Sisse Graum Jørgensen, who worked on *Open Hearts* as producer Vibeke Windeløv's assistant, went on to produce *Brothers* and *After the Wedding*.

Whereas Bier collaborated with a number of different cinematographers during the early part of her career, her most recent productions show the influence of Morten Søborg, who provided the camerawork for *Once in a Lifetime* (*Livet är en schlager*, 2000), *Open Hearts*, *Brothers* and *After the Wedding*, the last three characterised by extreme close-ups intended, according to Bier, to punctuate the unfolding narrative with moments of almost poetic abstraction.

Swedish composer Johan Söderqvist has scored no fewer than six of Bier's ten feature films to date (*Freud flyttar hemifrån...*, *Family Matters*, *Like It Never Was Before*, *Brothers*, *After the Wedding*, *Things We Lost in the Fire*), and Jesper Winge Leisner has provided original compositions for three of the others (*Once in a Lifetime*, *The One and Only*, *Open Hearts*).

Bier has often drawn on the same actors over the years and clearly develops strong relationships with them, in part as a result of the somewhat unorthodox, but apparently amusing and effective, methods she employs to help them assume their roles. She spends a lot of time, for example, browsing and shopping for clothes with her actors, the idea being that a character's wardrobe choices provide a particularly useful point of entry to the character's personality. Ghita Nørby played leading roles in *Freud flyttar hemifrån...* and *Family Matters*. And in *Credo* Nørby has a smaller part as a wealthy, cold and controlling mother-in-law. Sidse Babett Knudsen, one of the stars of the New Danish Cinema, owes much of her success to her role as Sus in *The One and Only*. In *After the Wedding*, Bier again teamed up with Babett Knudsen, casting her as Helene, the soon-to-be-widowed wife of the terminally ill multi-millionaire, Jørgen. Mads Mikkelsen, whose stardom transcends his local context, delivers a superb performance as the adulterous doctor Niels in *Open Hearts*, and his contribution to *After the Wedding*, as the idealistic but by no means always responsible Jacob, is no less remarkable. Swedish Stina Ekblad provides outstanding performances as a self-involved bourgeoise in *Like It Never Was Before* and as the controlling wife of sect leader Dr Lack in *Credo*. Philip Zandén figures centrally in *Freud flyttar hemifrån...* and in *Family Matters*, and has smaller parts in *Credo*, *Open Hearts* and the short film, *A Letter to Jonas* (1991).

Many other names could be mentioned, but the ones listed here serve to make the point that Bier's work as a director relies on a tight network of associates, in which friendship and trust are important factors. Given that directorial success tends to propel individuals rather than entire groups to a new level in the international film industry, the challenge for Bier will undoubtedly involve negotiating the many uncertainties that the possible loss of a much trusted community entails. While many a small-nation filmmaker has failed to meet the challenges that exist at the border between national and international filmmaking, there is every reason to believe that Bier will rise to the occasion.

METTE HJORT is Professor and Director of Visual Studies at Lingnan University in Hong Kong, and a Leverhulme Visiting Professor of Film Studies at St Andrews University, Scotland.

Susanne Bier filmography

[feature film directing credits only]

1991
FREUD FLYTTAR HEMIFRÅN
Script: Marianne Goldman. Photography: Erik Zappon. Editing: Pernille Bech Christensen. Production design: Ulla Kassius. Players: Ghita Nørby (Rosha Cohen), Gunilla Röör (Freud), Palle Granditsky (Ruben Cohen), Philip Zandén (David Cohen), Jessica Zandén (Deborah Cohen), Peter Andersson (Adrian), Stina Ekblad (nurse). Produced by Peter Kroponin, Nina Crone (Crone Film Produktion A/S). 103 mins

1994
DET BLI'R I FAMILIEN
(Family Matters)
Script: Lars Kjeldgård, Philip Zandén. Photography: Erik Zappon. Editing: Pernille Bech Christensen. Production design: Birgitte Mellentin, Niels Sejer. Players: Philip Zandén (Jan), Ghita Nørby (Jan's mother), Ernst-Hugo Järegård (Håkon Borelius), Ana Padrão (Constanca), Anna Wing (the grandmother). Produced by Vibeke Windeløv, Peter Aalbæk Jensen, Waldemar Bergendahl, Kerstin Bonnier, Lars Kolvig, Joaquim Pinto. 98 mins

1995
PENSIONAT OSKAR
(Like It Never Was Before)
Script: Jonas Gardell. Photography: Kjell Lagerroos. Editing: Pernille Bech Christensen. Production design: Eva Norén. Players: Loa Falkman (Rune Runeberg), Stina Ekblad (Gunnel Runeberg), Simon Norrthon (Petrus), Philip Zandén (superintendent), Sif Ruud (Evelyn), Ghita Nørby (Hjördis). Produced by Stefan Baron. 108 mins

1997
SEKTEN (Credo)
Script: Peter Asmussen, Susanne Bier, Jakob Grønlykke, based

on Juliane Preisler's novel Dyr. Photography: Göran Nilsson. Editing: Per K. Kirkegaard, Jacob Thuesen. Production design: Eva Norén. Players: Sofie Gråbøl (Mona), Ellen Hillingsø (Anne), Sverre Anker Ousdal (Dr. Lack), Stina Ekblad (Karen), Ghita Nørby (mother in law). Produced by Peter Aalbæk Jensen, Ib Tardini, Vibeke Windeløv (Zentropa Entertainments). 87 mins

1999
DEN ENESTE ENE
(The One and Only)
Script: Kim Fupz Aakeson, based on idea by Susanne Bier. Photography: Jens Schlosser. Editing: Pernille Bech Christensen, Mogens H. Christiansen. Production design: Eva Norén. Players: Sidse Babett Knudsen (Sus), Niels Olsen (Niller), Sas Egelind (Lizzie), Rafael Edholm (Sonny), Paprika Steen (Stella), Sofie Gråbøl (Mulle), Lars Kaalund (Knud), Vanessa Gouri (Mgala), Hella Joof (adoption lady). Produced by Thomas Heinesen, Bo Christensen (Metronome Productions A/S). 100 mins

2000
LIVET ÄR EN SCHLAGER
(Once in a Lifetime)
Script: Jonas Gardell. Photography: Morten Søborg. Editing: Pernille Bech Christensen, Mogens H. Christiansen. Production design: Gert Wibe. Players: Helena Bergström (Mona), Jonas Karlsson (David), Thomas Hanzon (Bosse), Björn Kjellman (Candy darling), Johan Ulveson (Producer), Regina Lund (Sabina), Lisa Olsen (Kikki) Produced by Thomas Heinesen, Ivar Köhn, Erik Crone, Rumle Hammerich, Johan Mardell, Peter Possne. 108 mins

2002
ELSKER DIG FOR EVIGT
(Open Hearts; Dogma # 28)

Script: Anders Thomas Jensen, Susanne Bier. Photography: Morten Søborg. Editing: Thomas Krag, Pernille Bech Christensen. Production design: William Knuttel. Players: Sonja Richter (Cæcile), Nikolaj Lie Kaas (Joachim), Mads Mikkelsen (Niels), Paprika Steen (Marie). Produced by Vibeke Windeløv, Sisse Graum Jørgensen, Jonas Frederiksen, Peter Aalbæk Jensen (Zentropa Entertainments). 103 mins

2004
BRØDRE (Brothers)
Script: Anders Thomas Jensen, based on idea by Susanne Bier. Photography: Morten Søborg. Editing: Pernille Bech Christensen. Production design: Viggo Bentzon. Players: Connie Nielsen (Sarah), Ulrich Thomsen (Michael), Nikolaj Lie Kaas (Jannik), Sarah Juel Werner (Natalie), Rebecca Løgstrup Soltau (Camilla), Bent Mejding (Henning), Solbjørg Højfeldt (Else), Niels Olsen (Allentoft), Niels Peter (Paw Henriksen). Produced by Sisse Graum Jørgensen, Peter Aalbæk Jensen, Peter Garde, Gillian Berrie, Anna Anthony, and Aagot Skjeldal (for Zentropa Entertainments, Sigma Films Ltd, Memfis Film International AB, and Fjellape Film AS). 116 mins

2006
EFTER BRYLLUPPET
(After the Wedding)
Script: Anders Thomas Jensen, based on idea by Susanne Bier and Anders Thomas Jensen. Photography: Morten Søborg. Editing: Pernille Bech Christensen. Production design: Søren Skjær. Players: Mads Mikkelsen (Jacob), Sidse Babett Knudsen (Helene), Rolf Lassgård (Jørgen), Stine Fischer Christensen (Anna), Christian (Christian Tafdrup), Neeral Mulchandani (Pramod), Meenal Patel (Mrs

Shaw). Produced by Sisse Graum Jørgensen, Peter Aalbæk Jensen, Gillian Berrie (for Zentropa Entertainments, Sigma Films Ltd). 122 mins

2007
THINGS WE LOST IN THE FIRE
Script: Allan Loeb. Photography: Tom Stern. Editing: Pernille Bech Christensen, Bruce Cannon. Production design: Richard Sherman. Players: Halle Berry (Audrey Burke), Benicio del Toro (Jerry Sunborne), David Duchovny (David Burke), Alison Lohman (Kelly), John Carroll Lynch (Howard Glassman), Paula Newsome (Diane), Robin Weigert (Brenda). Produced by Sam Mendes, Sam Mercer, Barbara Kelly. 119 mins

Guillermo del Toro by Jason Wood

A longside compatriots Alfonso Cuarón and Alejandro González Iñárritu, Guillermo del Toro is one of the most visible and distinctive artists in recent Mexican cinema. A leading figure in Mexican cinema, the universal acclaim generated by the multi-award-winning *Pan's Labyrinth* (*El Laberinto del fauno*, 2006), has elevated del Toro to the front rank of contemporary filmmakers. A superlative visual stylist closely associated with the horror and fantasy genres, del Toro's work frequently examines the nightmares of the past, employing history to speak of the often traumatic passage from childhood to maturity. As he has stated: 'Why is horror so popular? It's a part of morbid fascination that is part of human nature; we still secrete this fascination.'

The horrors of the world

Born in Guadalajara on 9 October 1964, del Toro cites his interest in horror as springing from staying up without permission to watch episodes of *The Outer Limits*. One episode in particular, 'The Mutant', fascinated him; Warren Oates' impressive make-up triggered an early interest in effects. Too afraid to even leave his bed in the dead of night, del Toro claims to have made a pact of friendship with the

monstrous visions tormenting him: 'Since this time I have had a very intimate relationship to creatures.' Already possessed of an extremely active imagination, del Toro also cites Mexico's gory religious imagery as a source of his fascination with the demonic and also with suffering and brutality.

It was whilst attending a Jesuit-run boys school that del Toro first began to nurture dreams of becoming a filmmaker, completing a number of Super-8 films at a very early age. His first serious forays into filmmaking were also shorts, with *Doña Lupe* (1985) and *Geometria* (1987) participating in numerous international film festivals. He became responsible for his own make-up and effects following a traumatic motorcycle accident that confined him to bed for severa weeks; he decided to learn the craft professionally, enrolling for a correspondence course with legendary SFX artist Dick Smith. For ten years del Toro was dedicated to this work through his company Necropia, supervising special effects make-up for several films, including *Bandidos* (1991), *Cabeza de vaca* (1991) and more than twenty episodes of the TV series *La hora marcada* (1986), three of which he also wrote and directed. It was through Necropia that del Toro met leading producer Bertha Navarro, with whom, alongside Laura Esquivel and Rosa Bosch, he later formed the Mexico City-based production company Tequila Gang.

Del Toro's first feature, *Cronos* (1993), came about partly by accident. Whilst studying scriptwriting under the acclaimed Mexican director Jaime Humberto Hermosillo, del Toro had written an early draft of what would become *The Devil's Backbone* (*El Espinazo del Diablo*, 2001). Stung by Hermosillo's criticisms of his presentation, he decided to 'write something else rather than go back

Cronos

and re-write the same script just because the margins weren't right'. A paragraph in a treatise about vampires, which stated that they first vampirise the family, inspired the fledgling director to embark on what would become *Cronos*. Described as a story of acceptance, the film was dedicated to his devoutly Catholic grandmother.

A bravura debut feature in which an elderly antiques dealer, played by Federico Luppi, discovers an artefact that once belonged to a sixteenth-century alchemist, unaware that the device – which resembles an ornate mechanical beetle and which was painstakingly designed by del Toro himself – houses a parasite that will grant eternal life to its host. The price for such a prize is an aversion to daylight and a thirst for human blood. The winner of the Cannes Critics' Week Award and the subsequent recipient of nine Mexican Academy Awards (and the Audience Jury Award at Fantasporto in 1994), *Cronos* combines a distinctive and surreal take on the vampire yarn with an intelligent allegory about US/Mexican relations (the film is set in 1997, in a post-North American Free Trade Area (NAFTA) Mexico). A turning point in Mexican cinema, the stylishly executed work also established the template for del Toro's subsequent career, not least in its use of symbolism and metaphor, and refusal to shy away from exposing children to the horrors of the world. Leading Mexican critic Leonardo García Tsao commented: 'I think that

Cronos really adds something to the vampire genre. I also think that with this film del Toro demonstrates that he has a unique vision and is also able to change the rules.'

Adventures in Hollywood

Having borrowed money from his father to extricate himself from the debts accrued whilst making *Cronos* and ostracised from the Mexican film industry infrastructure for his decision to work in a populist genre, del Toro found himself unable to raise the necessary finance and commitment to embark on another Mexican project. He endured numerous unsuccessful meetings with Universal Studios concerning both an adaptation of Christopher Fowler's *Spanky* and a period horror film. Unable to secure the funding or support to further develop a ghost story that would eventually become *The Devil's Backbone*, del Toro pitched a short film idea to Bob and Harvey Weinstein's Dimension Films. The brothers liked the concept and persuaded him to develop this project that would result in the 1997 feature *Mimic*.

The Devil's Backbone

A disease carried by the common cockroach is claiming the lives of Manhattan's young. Entomologist Dr Susan Tyler (Mira Sorvino) genetically engineers a mutant species of insect that can exterminate the roaches, before expiring itself. The project appears to be a success, with infant mortality rates in the city drastically reduced. A few years later, however, people begin disappearing and corpses turn up in and around the Manhattan subway. The mutant species has proved more durable and adaptable than she intended. Alongside her colleague and partner (British actor Jeremy Northam) and a reluctant New York subway cop (played by Charles S. Dutton), Susan sets out to destroy the mutant race she has unwittingly unleashed.

Mimic

Ostensibly a subterranean sci-fi thriller, *Mimic* is also a convincing parable about genetic manipulation and another expression of its creator's preoccupation with how the ghosts of the past come back to haunt us. Although proud of certain sequences, del Toro is not an admirer of the film, describing it as a painful experience: 'Back then it was the most expensive movie Dimension had ever made and it was also by far the most expensive movie I had ever done. I experienced many hardships with that movie. I sustain the belief that you learn through pain and I certainly learned a hell of a lot.'

Scarred by the process of trying to make a personal film with increased resources but in impossible circumstances, del Toro took comfort from the success of *Amores perros* (2000) (acting as Alejandro González Iñárritu advisor during the film's editing) and Alfonso Cuarón's homecoming movie *Y tu mamá también* (2001), and returned to Tequila Gang and Spanish-language productions. With Agustín and Pedro Almodóvar producing, del Toro began working on *The Devil's Backbone*. Set in 1938, with Franco's forces poised to rout the Republicans, the film concerns ten-year-old Carlos (Fernando Tielve), the son of

a fallen Republican who is sent to a remote orphanage run by sympathetic leftists Carmen (Marisa Paredes) and Casares (Federico Luppi). But there is much there to unnerve him: the attentions of bullies to an unexploded bomb in the courtyard; the ominous approach of Franco's troops to the orphanage's walls; teacher Conchita's (Irene Visedo) brooding boyfriend Jacinto (Eduardo Noriega); and the presence of the ghost of a boy called Santi who ominously predicts, 'Many of you will die'.

Originating from an early del Toro drawing of a man drowning in a pool of blood, the film, which also references Hitchcock and Buñuel, was at one time to have been set during the Mexican Revolution. Featuring superlative special effects and consummate performances, the film's use of a Fascist regime as the basis for a parable would become another abiding theme. Del Toro has stated: 'You have Fascism represented by Jacinto, and you have the people represented by the children, and you have the old Republicans represented by Carmen and Casares. It's a movie that doesn't say that everything ends up happily, it says that the bomb never exploded, the ghost never left the place and the only thing you have as a positive is that the children are going to march.' The film is imbued with a stylised and heightened representation of reality, thanks to the perfect partnership of del Toro and regular cinematographer Guillermo Navarro: 'I always try to take it a couple of notches above. The Spanish Civil War in *The Devil's Backbone* looks like a Sergio Leone western,

Blade II

except at night where it looks like a Mario Bava movie.' Once again critics and audiences were seduced by the director's vision.

Del Toro's next two assignments would take him back to Hollywood, with *Blade II* (2002) and *Hellboy* (2004). The first picture signalled the return to the screen of Marv Wolfman and Gene Golan's hugely popular comic-book vampire/warrior hybrid. Meshing stylishly executed set pieces with del Toro's eye for the macabre, this exhilarating and visceral blockbuster concerns the eponymous anti-hero's (played by Wesley Snipes) attempts to prevent a new super-race of indiscriminate blood-guzzlers from taking over the world. Del Toro speaks of the film fondly: 'It was a very joyful experience. It was the opposite to *Mimic* in that I didn't have any aspirations to making a personal film and just wanted to give a personal touch to a movie that was unequivocally commercial. I was in total agreement with the producers and the studio on the movie we were making.'

Hellboy

Del Toro's third collaboration with actor Ron Perlman, *Hellboy* was an even more thrilling experience and a project on which the director achieved the difficult synthesis of articulating a personal vision within a Hollywood structure: '*Hellboy* is ultimately what I think an atomic adventure-book movie could be and is very different from the other comic-book franchises. It has a huge heart and a lot of beauty in the horror. It's also a celebration of otherness and being different. It is a beauty and the beast story where at the end they kiss and they both turn to beasts.'

Guillermo del Toro directs Ron Perlman

During World War II, the Third Reich has joined forces with the evil Grigori Rasputin (Karel Roden) who has used his occult powers to summon up a young demon from the depths of Hell, to be used as the ultimate weapon. However, the demonic creature is captured by American forces, and put in the care of Professor Broom (John Hurt), the founder of a top-secret organisation called the Bureau for Paranormal Research and Defence. Under Broom's tutelage, the creature develops empathy and a desire to do good, while his physical powers and paranormal talents are honed into formidable weapons. Many years later, the demon, now known as Hellboy (Perlman), is part of an elite secret defence team, alongside Liz Sherman (Selma Blair), a woman who can create fire with her mind, and Abe Sapien (Doug Jones), an aquatic humanoid with the power of telepathy. Hellboy finds himself facing his greatest challenge when the powerful Rasputin returns, determined to bring the demon back to the forces of darkness so that evil may finally rule the world. Adapted from Mike Mignola's cult comic-book series, *Hellboy* achieves an intelligence not commonly associated with such fare. Del Toro has committed to a number of sequels, with the second instalment, *Hellboy 2: The Golden Army* (2008) nearing completion.

Inside the labyrinth

Screened in the main competition at the 2006 Cannes Film Festival, *Pan's Labyrinth* marks another fruitful return to Latin-American

Pan's Labyrinth

productions and is arguably the Mexican maestro's masterpiece.

Spain, 1944. Recently remarried Carmen (Ariadna Gil) moves with her daughter Ofelia (Ivana Baquero) into the house of her new husband, the coldly authoritarian Vidal (a superbly fearsome Sergi López), a captain in General Franco's army. Finding her new life hard to bear, young Ofelia seeks refuge in a mysterious labyrinth she discovers next to the sprawling family house. Pan, the guardian, a fantastical creature, reveals that she is none other than the long-lost princess of a magical kingdom. To discover the truth, Ofelia will have to accomplish three dangerous tasks.

A year's preparation, four months shooting and six months of post-production were necessary for del Toro to realise *Pan's Labyrinth*, the film of which the director claims to be most proud. Although inspired by the paintings of Francisco Goya, del Toro drew most heavily on the influence of illustrator Arthur Rackham, wanting to connect with the perversity and carnal content of the artist's work. His painting of Satan devouring his son was the principal inspiration for the Pale Man, one of the main characters in the Labyrinth.

The conception of the imaginary world, in which Ofelia seeks refuge and Pan roams, was entrusted to Carlos Gimenez for the sketches and then David Marti and his company Efectos Especiales, to give them form and bring them to life. Gimenez took care of designing the Labyrinth while Sergio Sandoval, who created

the mask for Kroenen, the Nazi assassin in *Hellboy*, concentrated on the creatures, in particular Pan. For this character, which del Toro wanted to be as organic as possible, it was decided that his lower body would be covered with foliage and branches, as if he was truly part of nature. To achieve this, the filmmakers used virtually no digital effects. Everything was done on the set with the help of animatronics, a first in the history of Spanish cinema.

Garlanded with acclaim and already one of the most commercially successful foreign-language films in recent memory (as well as the recipient of three American and British Academy Awards and nine Mexican Academy Awards, including the Golden Ariél for Best Direction), the film clearly echoes *The Devil's Backbone* in its Spanish Civil War setting and its dealing with repression and the very essence of Fascism: 'For me, Fascism represents the ultimate horror and for this reason is an ideal subject through which to tell a fairytale for adults, because Fascism is above all a form of perversion of innocence, and thus childhood. Thus the real "monster" of the film is Captain Vidal.' A fairytale, a political fable and a brilliant depiction of the intersecting worlds of fantasy and fiction, adulthood and innocence, Alfonso Cuarón, one of the film's producers, proudly describes *Pan's Labyrinth* as representing 'an explosion of the full potential of Guillermo's mind'.

As well as his own directorial projects, del Toro has shown his commitment to Mexican cinema, acting as producer on a number

Pan's Labyrinth

of diverse projects by both established filmmakers and newer talents. *Rudo y Cursi* (2008), the full-length debut feature of writer Carlos Cuarón, and *Cosas insignificantes* (2008) by Andrea Martínez are just two of the films to which the hardworking del Toro is attached: 'If you do not water your roots then you will go dry. The key of life is flow and if you don't make things flow they die. You have to make your experiences go beyond yourself and count for other people.'

JASON WOOD is a writer and film programmer. His books include *The Faber Book of Mexican Cinema* (2005), *Talking Movies: Contemporary World Filmmakers in Interview* (2006) and *100 Road Movies* (2006).

Guillermo del Toro filmography

[feature film directing credits only]

1993
CRONOS
Script: Guillermo del Toro. Photography: Guillermo Navarro. Production Design: Tolita Figuero. Editing: Raúl Dávalos. Players: Federico Luppi (Jesus Gris), Ron Perlman (Angel de la Guardia), Claudio Brook (De la Guardia), Margarita Isabel (Mercedes), Tamara Shanath (Aurora), Daniel Giménez Cacho (Tito), Mario Iván Martínez (Alchemist), Farnesio de Bernal (Manuelito), Juan Carlos Colombo (Funeral Director), Jorge Martínez de Hoyos (Narrator). Produced by Arthur Gorson, Bertha Navarro. 94 mins

1997
MIMIC
Script: Matthew Robbins, Guillermo del Toro, based on a short story by Donald A. Wollheim. Photography: Dan Laustsen. Production Design: Carol Spier. Editing: Peter Devaney Flanagan, Patrick Lussier. Players: Mira Sorvino (Dr Susan Tyler), Jeremy Northam (Dr Peter Mann), Alexander Goodwin (Chuy), Giancarlo Giannini (Manny), Charles S. Dutton (Leonard), Josh Brolin (Josh), Alix Koromzay (Remy), F. Murray Abraham (Dr

Gates). Produced by Stuart Cornfeld, Harvey Weinstein. 105 mins

2001
EL ESPINAZO DEL DIABLO
(The Devil's Backbone)
Script: Guillermo del Toro, Antonio Trashorras, David Muñoz. Photography: Guillermo Navarro. Editing: Luis de la Madrid. Players: Eduardo Noriega (Jacinto), Marisa Paredes (Carmen), Federico Luppi (Casares), Fernando Tielve (Carlos), Íñigo Garcés (Jaime), Irene Visedo (Conchita), José Manuel Lorenzo (Marcelo), Francisco Maestre (El Puerco), Junio Valverde (Santi), Berta Ojea (Alma), Adrián Lamana (Gálvez), Daniel Esparza (Marcos). Produced by Agustín Almodóvar, Pedro Almodóvar, Guillermo del Toro. 106 mins

2002
BLADE II
Script: David S. Goyer. Photography: Gabriel Beristain. Production Design: Carol Spier. Editing: Peter Amundson. Players: Wesley Snipes (Blade), Kris Kristofferson (Whistler), Ron Perlman (Reinhardt), Leonor Varela (Nyssa), Norman Reedus (Scud), Thomas Kretschmann (Damaskinos), Danny John-Jules (Asad). Produced by Avi Arad, Robert Bernacchi, Michael De Luca. 117 mins

2004
HELLBOY
Script: Guillermo del Toro, based on the comic books by Mike Mignola. Photography: Guillermo Navarro. Production Design: Stephen Scott. Editing: Peter Amundson. Players: Ron Perlman (Hellboy), John Hurt (Trevor 'Broom' Bruttenholm), Selma Blair (Liz Sherman), Rupert Evans (John Myers), Karel Roden (Grigori Rasputin), Jeffrey Tambor (Tom Manning), Doug Jones (Abe Sapien), Brian Steele (Sammael). Produced by Lawrence Gordon, Lloyd Levin, Mike Richardson. 122 mins

2006
EL LABERINTO DEL FAUNO
(Pan's Labyrinth)
Script: Guillermo del Toro. Photography: Guillermo Navarro. Production Design: Eugenio Caballero. Editing: Bernat Vilaplana. Players: Ivana Baquero (Ofelia), Sergi López (Capitán Vidal), Maribel Verdú (Mercedes), Doug Jones (Fauno / Pale Man) Ariadna Gil (Carmen Vidal). Produced by Alvaro Augustín, Alfonso Cuarón, Bertha Navarro, Guillermo del Toro and Frida Torresblanco. 119 mins

Paul Greengrass by Jason Wood

The third and most recent entry in the continuing adventures of CIA-trained assassin Jason Bourne, *The Bourne Ultimatum* (2007), offers another hugely satisfying continuation of director Paul Greengrass's ability to infuse Hollywood projects with his own distinctive aesthetic. Set in Madrid, Paris, Tangier, Turin, London and New York, the film finds Bourne, once again played with grim-faced conviction by Matt Damon, still on the run from his corrupt CIA superiors, here marshalled by the oily Noah Vosen (David Strathairn). But with the hunted becoming the hunter, Greengrass edges his seemingly invincible protagonist ever closer to discovering just how he became Jason Bourne.

Budgeted in the region of €62 million, *The Bourne Ultimatum*, like the director's *The Bourne Supremacy* (2004), is elevated above standard blockbuster fare by its intelligence and a firm grounding in both reality and politics (The *Guardian* described it as drawing many of its themes 'directly from the headlines and from our paranoid zeitgeist'). Its shooting style and fondness for hand-held camera also evokes its maker's background in low-budget documentary filmmaking and forays into the dramatisation of real-life events.

Career resurrection

Born 13 August 1955 in Cheam, Surrey and educated at Queen's College, Cambridge, Greengrass first worked as a director in the 1980s for the ITV current affairs programme *World in Action*. Previously responsible for forging the careers of Mike Hodges and Michael Apted, Greengrass arrived there in 1978, when the halcyon days of the current affairs show were considered long gone. However, the draconian politics of Margaret Thatcher had a galvanising effect. As he has stated: 'There was the great sense of being present at tumultuous events and being in a culture that prized the dispassionate eye rather than the involved ego, meaning that you sit back and record it and you don't put yourself in the process. In a sense it was the making of me. I was literally a college boy when I started and a man when I left.' He spent eight years at *World in Action* but with his aspirations to move into features meeting with resistance from his bosses, who were reluctant to see a talented employee break ranks. However, a change in career was precipitated when he co-wrote *Spycatcher*, the memoirs of Peter Wright, the notorious former Assistant Director of MI5. Containing highly sensitive information, the book was immediately blocked by the British Government who tried, unsuccessfully, to ban it, resulting in the book becoming a bestseller.

Weaned on the political filmmaking of Ken Loach (Greengrass cites *Kes* as a personal favourite), Peter Watkins and particularly Alan Clarke, whose observations on male violence and gritty aesthetic would influence him greatly, Greengrass finally moved into features with *Resurrected* (1989). Based on a true story that came to light during the Falklands War, the film tells the tale of a private (played by David Thewlis) who, after being listed as missing and presumed dead, wanders back into camp, a victim of amnesia. The Army, embarrassed at the situation and not fully believing his story, downplays the private's return and a hero's welcome is aborted amidst growing whispers that he was a deserter. With even his parents seemingly unwilling to believe the tale of amnesia, the disgraced private is forced to undergo a brutal and humiliating mock court-martial at the hands of his platoon members. In what would become a recurring facet of the director's work, *Resurrected* offers an uncompromising glimpse into institutionalised brutality, made all the more poignant by an outstanding performance by Thewlis. Tackling recreated events with a dispassionate documentary eye, Greengrass cites his intention as attempting to force a collision between the two, allowing for 'a bigger truth than by using just the one approach or the other'. *Resurrected* went on to win the Otto Dibelius Film Award and the OCIC Award at the Berlin Film Festival.

Greengrass then returned to the small screen, turning in episodes of *Cutting Edge*, *Kavanagh QC* and exceptional and politically controversial dramas such as *The Fix*, a fictional but nonetheless groundbreaking look into big-money corruption in football. Something of a companion piece to *Resurrected*, *The One that Got Away* (1996) intelligently dramatises the memoirs of Corporal Chris Ryan, a soldier sent on a mission to destroy SCUD missiles after Saddam Hussein threatened Israel. Ryan's team is attacked, leaving several dead and the rest captured. Detailing Ryan's arduous escape, Greengrass avoids the gung-ho sensibilities of similar fare, most notably Ryan's contemporary, Andy McNab, whose *Bravo Two Zero* was given a more sensationalist screen treatment. As Ryan, Paul McGann communicates palpable fear

The Theory of Flight

and confusion, whilst Greengrass punctuates the horror of warfare with some surprisingly surreal moments.

Greengrass's second feature, *The Theory of Flight* (1998), attempts to tackle the thorny issue of sexuality amongst people with physical disabilities. A low-budget production, it centres on a frustrated artist (played by Kenneth Branagh) whose eccentric behaviour sees him sentenced to community service and caring for Jane (Helena Bonham Carter), a strong-willed woman suffering from the neuromuscular disorder called ALS (otherwise known as Lou Gehrig's Disease). As the two come to learn to trust each other, Jane asks her newfound carer and confidante to rid her of her virginity. Though well-intentioned and performed with surprising integrity by Bonham Carter, then better known for period roles, the film, with its frequent allusion to literal and metaphorical flight, feels like something of an anomaly in the director's career.

Fact and fiction

The following year saw Greengrass back on more familiar terrain with *The Murder of Stephen Lawrence*. Again made for television, this potent and poignant docu-drama tells the story of the black London youth who was attacked and killed by a gang of racist thugs whilst waiting for a bus in South London. Stephen's parents, Neville and Doreen Lawrence (Hugh Quarshie and Marianne Jean-Baptiste), were understandably distraught by the death of their son, and were determined to see justice done. However, thanks to a faulty police investigation and the ineptitude of an overburdened court system, the charged men were allowed to go free, which sent Neville and Doreen on a long and difficult crusade to confront the system that failed them. Making a virtue of its frills-free approach and basis upon fact to offer a searing indictment of the British justice system and institutional racism in the police force, the film is one of the most important television events of its era. The winner of a BAFTA TV Award as Best Single Drama in 2000, *The Murder of Stephen Lawrence* also won the Special Jury Prize at the 2000 Banff Television Festival. Greengrass also gained the approval of Lawrence's parents and prominent members of the black community.

Bloody Sunday

Originally conceived for television, *Bloody Sunday* (2002) was granted a theatrical release after it met with unanimous praise at domestic and international festivals, going on to win the Golden Bear at the Berlin Film Festival

(shared with Hayao Miyazaki's *Spirited Away*) and the Sundance Audience Award. The film is a harrowing and provocative *vérité*-style account of the fateful events of Sunday, 30 January 1972, when 13 civilians were shot dead on the streets of Derry by British troops from the crack Paratroop Regiment. Set between the hours of dawn and dusk, and informed by eyewitness accounts, the film is a superlative synthesis of fact and fiction. The film was powered by two commanding, career-best performances: James Nesbitt as Ivan Cooper, the Protestant MP and idealistic civil rights leader who was an advocate of Martin Luther King's dream of peaceful change; and Tim Pigott-Smith as Major General Ford. Greengrass achieves the difficult task of imbuing his material with objectivity, sensitivity, compassion and outrage.

Omagh

Greengrass would return to the conflict in Ireland as the writer of *Omagh*. Directed by Pete Travis and aired in 2004 on British television, *Omagh* offers a topical examination of the aftermath of the 1998 'Real IRA' bombing that killed 29 people in Omagh, Northern Ireland. Avoiding didacticism, Greengrass's script again blends the personal and the political, analysing the events through the eyes of Michael Gallagher (Gerard McSorley), a soft-spoken mechanic forever changed by the loss of his 21-year-old son. Determined not to let the same grim fate befall his neighbours, Gallagher takes it upon himself to become the official spokesperson for the victims' families, challenging the government's official stand on terrorism and providing a voice

The Bourne Supremacy

for the grief-stricken families of the innocent victims killed in the blast.

American overtures

With the completion of these two projects, Greengrass sensed that he had reached the end of a chapter and felt the impulsive urge to try something new. He hooked up with an agent sympathetic to his talents and methodology. Hollywood, with its interest piqued by his obvious ability as a progressive action-movie director with an eye for the tragic and the political, soon came calling.

He accepted the invitation to direct the sequel to Doug Liman's *The Bourne Identity* (2002). A moderately well-received but efficiently executed adaptation of Robert Ludlum's page-turner about a covert government agent facing extinction after being deemed surplus to requirements by his CIA paymasters, naysayers feared for Greengrass's survival amidst the cut and thrust of Tinsel Town. They needn't have worried. Greengrass must also have secretly harboured some misgivings about his cutting-edge sensibility transferring intact: 'I remember being amazed at how people tried to help. When you make very low-budget films in Britain – or high-end television – you would be amazed how much of the time you feel like people are trying to fuck it up. And I remember the first day in Moscow, I thought: how the fuck am I going to get all these people to understand my aesthetic? Bear in mind, the whole thing about *Bourne* was that I wanted to take no one with me. I wanted to go on my own and have a crew and a cast and producers I didn't know. Then the first day I realised they've all looked at my films and they know what I like. I don't have to win a battle here.'

Smartly scripted by Tony Gilroy, writer and director of the commendable *Michael Clayton* (2007), *The Bourne Supremacy* re-enters the shadowy world of expert assassin Jason Bourne, who continues to find himself plagued by splintered nightmares from his former life. The stakes are even higher for the amnesiac agent who, flushed from hiding, coolly manoeuvres through the dangerous waters of international espionage. Replete with CIA plots, turncoat agents and ever-shifting covert alliances, he moves closer to finding the truth behind his haunted memories and fragmented past. Making compelling use of locations around the world (including Goa and Moscow) and employing a muscular cinematic edge, Greengrass maintains the aggressive style and fresh, non-traditional perspective established in the original *Bourne* outing. He equips himself well with marquee-value names, drawing particularly choice turns from Joan Allen and Brian Cox as machiavellian CIA bosses.

Paul Greengrass on location with Matt Damon and Julia Stiles

Incorporating thrills and spills aplenty, and featuring a memorable, white-knuckle car chase through the avenues and tunnels of Moscow, *The Bourne Supremacy* is an absorbing thriller drenched in tension. As he is pursued across continents without a soul to confide in (his girlfriend is murdered at the film's beginning), Greengrass's sometimes dizzying use of hand-held camera and frenetic jump-cuts hauls the spectator into Bourne's world with a jolt, giving a visceral, first-hand taste of the danger and chaos that surround him. His persistent and increasingly frenzied 'who was I?' line of enquiry becomes the film's motif, evoking Lee Marvin's quest to source the whereabouts of his money in John Boorman's seminal *Point Blank* (1967). Like Boorman, Greengrass proved wholly adept at bringing his own signature style to what, in other hands, could have been a relatively straightforward genre re-tread. In subsequent years, his influence on studio action pictures has been keenly felt.

The reward for *The Bourne Supremacy*'s success in terms of international box office gross (upwards of $288 million) was a very enviable creative *carte blanche*. Occupying a position similarly held by Steven Soderbergh, Greengrass was granted the freedom to oscillate between completing a third entry in the *Bourne* franchise and lower-budget, more personal work that more closely resembled the director's British docu-dramas. The first fruit of this arrangement, *United 93* (2006), served to bolster Greengrass's reputation.

The first feature film to deal directly with the events of 11 September 2001, *United 93* offers a sobering look at the final moments of the titular United Airlines flight that ended with a fatal struggle between hijackers and passengers. Daringly told in 'real time' (from the first plane crashing into the World Trade Center at 8:45am, to the fourth plane crashing into a field in Shanksville, Pennsylvania, at 10:03am) and using transcripts of mobile

United 93

phone calls and thirty minutes of cockpit voice recordings, the film is a chilling depiction of these tragic events. The cast of unknown actors, who each researched the backgrounds of their real-life characters, offer an ensemble performance of utter conviction. The tact of having many of the characters in the air traffic control scenes played by the actual participants themselves encapsulates both the respect with which the filmmakers approached the subject and compounds the sense of realism.

Paul Greengrass on the set of **United 93**

Offering a painstaking reconstruction of the hijacked plane that failed to reach its target (the Capitol dome in Washington, DC) owing to an uprising by its passengers, many of whom were aware of the attacks on the World Trade Center from frantic calls home on their cell phones, Greengrass shows ordinary, rather unremarkable people trapped in a situation utterly beyond their control. The filmmakers restrict access to the backgrounds and motivations of the hijackers, with the majority of the film taking place inside the doomed aircraft itself. Knowledge of events lends the earlier sequences – the pleasantries boarding the plane, the snatched goodbyes between loved ones at the beginning of what was for most just another routine journey – a terrible, sometimes sickening inevitability. Utterly respectful, the film refuses to substantiate the act of patriotic self-immolation implied by President George W. Bush in his memorial address. Unable to depict for certain what happened, Greengrass, a critic of Bush and Vice President Dick Cheney, both of whom are shown as being unreachable just when their leadership was needed most, imagines a final drive towards self-preservation with a plan to use a trained pilot onboard to wrest control and then land the plane safely.

Undoubtedly one of the most powerful and painful endeavours in modern cinema, *United 93* was not without controversy, especially when its production was initially announced. However, the sheer skill of its disciplined direction – and Barry Ackroyd's gut-wrenching cinematography – and its utter integrity ultimately leave even the most hardened viewer moved. Commended by the families of the United 93 passengers, the film, judged the best film of 2006 by UK critics at the *Evening Standard* British Film Awards, earned its director a BAFTA for Best Director and an Academy Award nomination in the same category.

The Bourne Ultimatum is allegedly the final outing in the increasingly pulsating Jason Bourne series. However, its impressive box office receipts have left both audiences and studio executives breathless for more. Once again using a frenzied and often subjective style, Greengrass stages one remarkable set-piece after another (a pursuit of Bourne and a *Guardian* journalist, the incomparable Paddy Considine, at Waterloo Station, is just one stand-out and, like many of the others, a wonder of logistics given the busy public space the action takes place in). Characteristically, the action is never purely for its own sake but rather employed as an accrual of telling character or narrative details.

Though the intelligence and integrity of the last two films have been credited to Greengrass's increasingly confident position behind the camera, it is also important to note the continuity and contributions of other key figures associated with the franchise: producers Frank Marshall, Patrick Crowley and Paul L. Sandberg; screenwriter Tony Gilroy (this time credited alongside Scott Z. Burns and George Nolfi); cinematographer Oliver Wood; editor Christopher Rouse; and composer John Powell. The role has of course also become Matt Damon's signature.

The Bourne Ultimatum

Keen to preserve his prolific work-rate and no doubt take advantage of his critical and commercial currency, Greengrass has already embarked on his next project, an adaptation of *Washington Post* reporter Rajiv Chandrasekaran's chastening exposé of Baghdad's Green Zone, *Imperial Life in the Emerald City*. Due on screens in 2009, Greengrass, who has again secured the talents of Matt Damon, is already wary of discussion of the film as a more overtly political proposition: 'I think one should always beware of polemics. The book isn't polemical at all. I think if you really want to understand what happened in Iraq you have to avoid condemnation and acquaint yourselves with an agenda of hope and engagement with the world. We must explore things with compassion, not polemicism.'

JASON WOOD is a writer and film programmer. His books include *The Faber Book of Mexican Cinema* (2005), *Talking Movies: Contemporary World Filmmakers in Interview* (2006) and *100 Road Movies* (2006).

Paul Greengrass filmography

[feature film directing credits only]

1989
RESURRECTED
*Script: Martin Allen. Photography:
Ivan Strasburg. Players: Tom Bell
(Mr Deakin), Rudi Davies (Julie),
David Thewlis (Kevin Deakin), Rita
Tushingham (Mrs Deakin), Michael
Pollitt (Gregory Deakin). Produced
by Adrian Hughes, Tara Prem.
96 mins*

1998
THE THEORY OF FLIGHT
*Script: Richard Hawkins.
Photography: Ivan Strasburg.
Production Design: Melanie Allen.
Editing: Mark Day. Players: Helena
Bonham Carter (Jane Hatchard),
Kenneth Branagh (Richard),
Gemma Jones (Anne), Holly Aird
(Julie), Ray Stevenson (Gigolo).
Produced by David M. Thompson.
101 mins*

2002
BLOODY SUNDAY
*Script: Paul Greengrass.
Photography: Ivan Strasburg.
Production Design: John Paul Kelly.
Editing: Clare Douglas. Players:
James Nesbitt (Ivan Cooper), Allan*

*Gildea (Kevin McCorry), Gerard
Crossan (Eamonn McCann),
Mary Moulds (Bernadette Devlin),
Carmel McCallion (Bridget Bond),
Tim Pigott-Smith (Major General
Ford), Nicholas Farrell (Brigadier
Maclellan), Christopher Villiers
(Major Steele). Produced by Jim
Sheridan, Rod Stoneman, Paul
Trijbits, Tristan Whalley.
107 mins*

2004
THE BOURNE SUPREMACY
*Script: Tony Gilroy, based
on the novel by Robert
Ludlum. Photography: Oliver
Wood. Production Design:
DominicWatkins. Editing: Richard
Pearson, Christopher Rouse. Players:
Matt Damon (Jason Bourne),
Franka Potente (Marie), Brian Cox
(Ward Abbott), Julia Stiles (Nicky),
Karl Urban (Kirill), Gabriel Mann
(Danny Zorn), Joan Allen (Pamela
Landy), Marton Csokas (Jarda).
Produced by Doug Liman, Henry
Morrison, Jeffrey M. Weiner.
108 mins*

2006
UNITED 93
*Script: Paul Greengrass.
Photography: Barry Ackroyd.
Production Design: Dominic
Watkins. Editing: Clare Douglas,
Richard Pearson, Cristopher Rouse.
Players: J. J. Johnson (Captain
Jason Dahl), Gary Commock
(First Officer LeRoy Homer), Polly
Adams (Deborah Welsh), Opal
Alladin (CeeCee Lyles), Starla
Benford (Wanda Anita Green),
Trish Gates (Sandra Bradshaw),
Nancy McDoniel (Lorraine G. Bay),
David Alan Basche (Todd Beamer),
Richard Bekins (William Joseph
Cashman), Susan Blommaert
(Jane Folger). Produced by Debra
Hayward. 111 mins*

2007
THE BOURNE ULTIMATUM
*Script: Tony Gilroy, Scott Z. Burns,
George Nolfi, based on the novel
by Robert Ludlum. Photography:
Oliver Wood. Production Design:
Peter Wenham. Editing: Christopher
Rouse. Players: Matt Damon
(Jason Bourne), Julia Stiles (Nicky
Parsons), David Strathairn (CIA
Deputy Director Noah Vosen),
Scott Glenn (CIA Director Ezra
Kramer), Paddy Considine (Simon
Ross), Edgar Ramirez (Paz), Albert
Finney (Dr Albert Hirsch), Joan
Allen (Pamela Landy). Produced by
Jeff Kirschenbaum, Donna Langley,
Doug Liman, Henry Morrison,
Jeffrey M. Weiner. 115 mins*

Jia Zhangke by Konrad Gar-Yeu Ng

Few other filmmakers have come to characterise China's alternative film culture or capture the dispiriting complexities of contemporary Chinese life as forcefully as Jia Zhangke. Jia's minimalist aesthetic, streak of independence and international acclaim distinguish him from other contemporary Chinese filmmakers. Although his film career consists of only five features, Jia has become one of the world's pre-eminent film directors. His recent film, *Still Life* (*Sanxia haoren*, 2006), won the Golden Lion at Venice, making him only the second director from China to win the award in the festival's 63 years. In 2007, he served as the Berlin Film Festival's first Prominent Patron of its Talent Campus, as well as President of the Cinéfondation and Short Films Jury at the Cannes Film Festival.

Jia's films feature long, lingering takes, shot on location, incorporating ambient sounds and the use of local dialects to compose a dystopian atmosphere. His stories feature despondent characters cognisant of the irony of their languid lives, but unable or unwilling to change. Instead, they tend to express themselves through videos, television, music, bars and karaoke. He works with the same small group of actors and crew to treat daily life in China as an aesthetic unto itself; it is a cinema of the vernacular, populated by modern-day zombies who are defined by popular culture and caught in parables without epiphany or closure.

Until recently, Jia's films were relatively unknown to mainstream filmgoers in China. His first three features, *Pickpocket* (*Xiao Wu*, 1997), *Platform* (*Zhantai*, 2000) and *Unknown Pleasures* (*Ren Xiao Yao*, 2002), were made 'unofficially', that is, without approval from China's Film Bureau and as such his films could not have public screenings in Chinese cinemas. To shoot and screen films in China, filmmakers must demonstrate support from an official state studio, submit scripts and a final cut of their film to the government for approval. Violators may have their filmmaking credentials revoked or face more serious sanctions, such as the confiscation of materials and/or imprisonment. The status of being 'unofficial', however, is not absolute. The Chinese government often displays ambivalence towards this film culture, seeing some worth in allowing its continued existence. Likewise, the country's open economy allows for forms of international financing that can circumvent the nation's studio system and screenings of unofficial films are assisted by DVDs, VCDs, film clubs and, of course, international film critics, programmers and festivals.

Since his first feature film, *Xiao Wu*, won the Wolfgang Staudte Forum prize at the Berlin Film Festival, Jia is considered to be the folk hero of this alternative film culture, often described as China's 'Sixth Generation', 'urban generation' or 'underground' filmmakers. If the Fifth Generation film directors are characterised by their lush epics about China's heartland and oblique critiques of government policies, Jia's generation are fugitives who offer an unpolished focus on urban displacement and the *minjian de jiyi* ('unofficial memories') of hardened people who exist in the shadow of their country's reforms. In 1999, Jia wrote an essay entitled 'The Age of Amateur Cinema Will Return'. In the piece, he called on Chinese filmmakers to engage in a cinema of directness and substance, and to resist the emphasis on what he believed to be cinematic excess: high production values and cultural insularity. He contends that amateur cinema offers a culture of accessibility and cinematic freshness that is crucial to salvaging Chinese film. Jia is not alone in making 'unofficial' films in China but his reputation and advocacy for alternative Chinese film culture has attracted attention in China and beyond.

Jia was born in 1970 in the town of Fenyang, a rural settlement in the province of Shanxi. Like many other small towns in China, Fenyang is a microcosm of the country's uneven journey towards social and economic reform. Jia's experiences in Fenyang have proven a strong influence throughout his films, with stories either being set in Fenyang and Shanxi or his characters coming from there. As a youth, Jia was interested in the arts, taking up performance, painting and writing. At 21, he published his first work of fiction, 'The Sun Hung on the Crotch'. After watching Chen Kaige's *Yellow Earth* (*Huang tu di*, 1984), Jia decided to pursue filmmaking at the Beijing Film Academy. For Jia, *Yellow Earth* was deeply affecting; Kaige's film offered a rare glimpse of Chinese life that Jia would later call 'a poetry of real life'. While at the Beijing Film Academy, Jia was drawn to realist and documentary films, two styles that have come to define his work. He also helped form the Academy's Youth Experimental Film Group. Before graduating in 1997, he directed three short films. *One Day in Beijing* (1994) is a short documentary about tourists from the countryside visiting Tiananmen Square. *Xiao Shan Goes Home* (*Xiaoshan huijia*, 1995) is about Xiao Shan's search through Beijing for

someone from his rural hometown to join him on a journey home. *Du Du* (1995) is an improvised portrait of a female college student faced with various opinions on what she should do with her life after graduation. *Xiao Shan Goes Home* and *Du Du* won prizes at the 1997 Hong Kong Independent Short Film and Video Awards. While in Hong Kong, Jia met his longtime cinematographer, Yu Likwai, and began preparations for his first feature film, *Pickpocket*.

Pickpocket

Pickpocket follows the life of Xiao Wu, its eponymous anti-hero, played by Wang Hongwei. A petty thief with a flexible code of honour, Xiao Wu exists in a world in flux with Maoist values twisted by free-market capitalism. His childhood friend, Xiao Yong (Hao Hongjian), is a successful entrepreneur, trafficking cigarettes and managing karaoke bars, activities that are seen as legitimate examples of 'free trade' and 'entertainment'. After Xiao Wu appears unexpectedly at Xiao Yong's wedding, the groom rejects Xiao Wu's wedding gift because it is 'dirty', having not come from 'legitimate' sources. Xiao Wu also meets a karaoke girl named Mei Mei (Zu Baitao) and the two share a fleeting relationship. Eventually, Mei Mei leaves Xiao Wu for a wealthier suitor and the pager that he bought to remain in touch with her becomes the device that leads to his very public disgrace.

Stylistically, *Pickpocket* follows the naturalism of the neo-realist film tradition, offering an astute commentary on post-socialist China. The film is a manifestation of China's social and economic reforms: demolition, construction, unfettered trade, clubs, bars and prostitution flourish, while legality gives way to an increasingly abstract and flexible sense of custom. The cinematography is edgy and the editing favours long takes, allowing the scenes to unfold from a voyeur's point of view. Jia cast non-professional actors to allow for harsh, sometimes indiscernible, local dialects that distinguish the rural from the urban. The film was made 'underground', with financing coming from Hong Kong.

Pickpocket impressed Takeshi Kitano's film company enough for them to help with the funding for Jia's next project, *Platform*. However, Jia was summoned to the Chinese Film Bureau following a government report that suggested *Pickpocket* was potentially harmful to China's international image. His credentials as a filmmaker were revoked, yet Jia's status as a renegade filmmaker only emboldened his commitment to telling true stories about Chinese life, independent from government intervention.

Unofficial memories

In 2001, Jia returned to Berlin to premiere *Platform*. The film was well received, prompting film critics such as J. Hoberman to declare it 'the strongest Chinese movie in a decade'. The film presents a pensive portrait of Chinese life during the 1980s, a transitional period when allegiances shifted from Mao Zedong to Deng Xiaoping's new China. *Platform* follows the lives of the Fenyang Peasant Culture Group, a travelling performance troupe of young people who start the decade in bellbottoms staging pro-Maoist cultural productions and end the decade as the West-inspired 'All Star Rock and Breakdance Electronic Band', a punk-rock electric act who turn the values of Maoist China upside down. Shot on 35mm, the cinematography and editing compose a deliberately slow pace with long takes. The narrative meanders, punctuated by changes in daily life such as the introduction of electricity, the emergence

Platform

of new social trends and reactions to social reforms such as China's 'one child' policy. Jia brilliantly traces the group's metamorphosis from steadfast belief in China to a growing sense of alienation. *Platform* takes its title from a popular song from the 1980s; the song's lyrics and mood embody the decade's odd mixture of anxiety and detachment.

King of popular culture

After *Platform*, Jia was commissioned to make a DV documentary short for the Korean Jeonju Film Festival. The resulting project, *In Public* (*Gong gong chang suo*, 2001), observes how China's free market has changed the nature of everyday public space and created new spaces of consumption in the mining town of Datong. The short also formed the basis for his next film, *Unknown Pleasures*, which Jia also shot on DV, preferring the medium's grainy aesthetic qualities and convenience.

Unknown Pleasures continued Jia's campaign for cinema as real life by bringing into focus the unease and melancholy of China's post-Deng era. A study of contemporary Chinese life through the lives of four disaffected urban youths living in Datong, *Unknown Pleasures* is more experimental than Jia's previous work and depicts an aimless world saturated with popular culture. The year is 2001, a time of quiet anticipation and general stagnation in China. Xiao Ji (Wu Qiong), a man without visible means, is obsessed with Qiao Qiao (Zhao Tao), a fierce but vulnerable young woman who makes her living promoting liquor

Unknown Pleasures

and is the mistress of a local thug. Bin Bin (Zhao Weiwei) and Yuan Yuan (Zhou Qingfeng) are stuck in a relationship of convenience, passing the time singing karaoke, watching *Monkey King* videos and doing their best to avoid thinking about the future. Bin Bin has recently been made redundant and shows no motivation in finding another job and Yuan Yuan is an uninspired student. Bin Bin and Xiao Ji find inspiration in Quentin Tarantino's *Pulp Fiction* (1994) and decide to rob a bank, only to fail miserably. Xiao Wu makes a brief appearance in the film to complain to Bin Bin that it is impossible to find important films like *Pickpocket*!

Unknown Pleasures uses crude dialects, improvised dialogue, natural sound and a detached cinematography consisting of lengthy takes, medium and long shots, and natural lighting. It was in competition at the 2002 Cannes Film Festival and was well received by the international film community. *Unknown Pleasures* was Jia's first film to perform well at the international box office, albeit modestly.

Second life

In late 2003 the Chinese Film Bureau issued an oblique invitation to Jia, asking him to become an 'official' filmmaker in China – which he accepted. His next project, the ambitious *The World* (*Shijie*, 2004), was his first film to have official public screenings in China. It also competed at the 60th Venice Film Festival. Critics once again praised the film, which won the 2005 Toronto Film Critics Association Award for Best Foreign-Language Film.

The World's critical exploration of the cultural and economic effects of China's integration into a capitalist global community showed that government approval had not restrained Jia's filmmaking. Rather, *The World* was further proof of his characteristically sharp and provocative eye. The one noticeable difference was in the film's quality. Shot on HD, its production values evinced Jia's access to better facilities.

The World

Often described as one of Jia's 'most accessible films', *The World* locates itself in a spectacle open to theoretical deconstruction. It follows the daily life of a group of young men and women who have come from China's rural communities to live and work at Beijing's real-life World Park, a bizarre Las Vegas/Disney simulacrum of iconographic cultural sites. Characters such as Tao (Zhao Tao), a World Park performer, and her boyfriend Taisheng (Chen Taisheng), a World Park security guard, come to the burgeoning Beijing tourist attraction in search of work or stardom, but find their story overshadowed by the lavish cross-cultural shows and scale models of the Leaning Tower of Pisa, the Taj Mahal, the Eiffel Tower, the Great Pyramid and the World Trade Center. *The World* uses the artificial terrain of World Park to highlight the interconnected, but ultimately alienated, ethos of contemporary Chinese life.

The World departs from Jia's typical use of Fenyang or Shanxi as the setting for his films. It also includes, for the first time, an evocative musical score (by Taiwanese rock musician, Lim Giong), a wider, vibrant colour palette and playful animated sequences. The large ensemble cast, the lack of a privileged point of view and the absence of a sustained arc for any of the characters all encourage disconnection. Characters appear and disappear from the film without any strong narrative trajectory of cause and effect. Jia continues to employ natural lighting, long takes, long shots, overlapping dialogue and an array of sounds to convey feelings of isolation, confusion and malaise. *The World* exposes the façade of China's new internationalism by highlighting the impoverished lives behind shows performed to a global audience.

What's up doc(s)?

In 2006, Jia debuted his first feature-length documentary, *Dong*. The film follows Chinese painter, Liu Xiaodong, and his large-scale portraits of people displaced by China's Three Gorges Dam project as well as a group of young Thai debutants in Bangkok. *Dong* is an interesting companion piece to *Still Life*, as scenes and characters appear in both films. The film is also interesting for the creative and critical resonance between Jia and Liu. Jia highlights Liu's tireless and passionate desire to render everyday life on large canvases, using the murals as testimonies of the present.

In 2007, Jia premiered his second feature-length documentary, *Useless* (*Wuyong*). The film is a loose sketch of China's contemporary garment industry and includes portraits of workers in a Guangdong garment factory, abstract-clothing designer Ma Ke and a tailor from Fenyang. *Useless* focuses on how human forms interact with textiles and how these movements form, as Ma Ke suggests, 'memories'. It remains to be seen if *Useless* will make its way into one of Jia's future feature film projects.

The Golden Lion at Venice

Still Life is a haunting portrait of human displacement caused by the Three Gorges

Dam project. It stars Jia regulars Zhao Tao and Han Sanming as Shen Hong and Sanming, who are searching for family members in Fengjie, a small town on the Zhangtze river that is being flooded as a result of the project. Sanming has not seen his ex-wife, Missy, for over 16 years. He is shocked by the demolition of Fengjie, lamenting on the town's enormous changes and loss of history. Shen Hong arrives in search of her husband, Guo Bin. She contacts Wang Dongming, a mutual friend, who is vague when she enquires about Guo Bin. The search by both characters presents different worlds through which to understand Chinese life in Fengjie. Sanming lives among labourers charged with the demolition; Shen Hong resides among white-collar workers involved in recording and developing Fengjie life after the cessation of the flooding.

Still Life

In *Still Life*, the scarred landscape of Fengjie and the stillness of the Zhangtze river express a spectral malaise with astounding resonance. Through Yu Likwai's HD cinematography and the gritty production design of Lin Xudong, Liang Jindong and Liu Qiang, *Still Life* treats Fengjie like a living mausoleum. Similar to Liu Xiaodong's murals of the people displaced by the Three Gorges Dam, *Still Life* shows a world in the process of disappearance. The film is populated by partially dressed male workers, tourists, heavily accented local dialects, grey weather, muddied water, green hills consumed by concrete buildings, slowly moving diesel-fueled boats, motorcycles and cars, unruly street sounds and evocative interludes by composer Lim Giong. *Still Life* is divided into loose chapters marked by titles that read, for example, 'Cigarettes', 'Liquor', 'Tea' and 'Toffee'. Similar to *The World*, the film features a brief animated sequence in which a building launches into the sky like a rocket ship.

And now...

In late 2007, Jia directed the short film, *Our Ten Years*. The film is a meditative piece starring Zhao Tao and chronicles the silent encounters between two women who have been riding on the same train for a decade. Jia has also committed to two additional film projects. *24 City* consists of two works, a short documentary and a feature film. The documentary is about the demolition of an old factory while the film will follow the lives of three women who have lost their jobs at an aeronautic plant. Jia hopes to have *24 City* finished in the summer of 2008.

A second project, *The Age of Tattoo* (*Ciqing shidai*), is a historical drama about a group of young gangsters in 1975. Unfortunately, the project appears trapped in government bureaucracy because of its content.

Jia Zhangke's body of work resists the visual ethnography of a singular China developing uniformly. His films suggest that contemporary Chinese life is characterised by estrangement, cacophony and highly-mediated popular culture. Now working on *The Age of Tattoo* (*Ciqing shidai*), an adaptation of Su Tong's novel, Jia is a world-class filmmaker whose future continues to look bright.

KONRAD GAR-YEU NG is Assistant Professor in the Academy for Creative Media at the University of Hawaii.

Jia Zhangke filmography

[feature film directing credits only]

1997
XIAO WU (Pickpocket)
Script: Jia Zhangke. Photography: Yu Likwai. Editing: Lin Xiao Ling. Players: Wang Hongwei (Xiao Wu), Hao Hongjian (Xiou Yong), Zu Baitao (Mei Mei). Produced by Li Kit-Ming, Jia Zhangke for Beijing Film Academy, Hu Tong Communication, Radiant Advertising Company.
107 mins

2000
ZHANTAI (Platform)
Script: Jia Zhangke. Photography: Yu Likwai. Editing: Khung Jinlei. Production Design: Qiu Sheng. Players: Wang Hongwei (Cui Mingliang), Liang Jingdong (Zhang Jun), Zhao Tao (Yin Ruijuan), Yang Tiangyi (Zhong Pin). Produced by Li Kit-Ming, Shozo Ichiyama, Masayuki Mori, Joel Farges, Elise Jallandeau for Hu Tong

Communication, T-Mark, Office Kitano, Bandai Visual Co.
150 mins

2002
REN XIAO YAO
(Unknown Pleasures)
Script: Jia Zhangke. Photography: Yu Likwai. Editing: Chow Kueng. Production Design: Liang Jindong. Players: Zhao Tao (Qiao Qiao), Zhao Weiwei (Bin Bin), Wu Qiong (Xiao Ji), Zhou Qingfeng (Yuan Yuan), Wang Hongwei (Xiao Wu), Bai Ru (Bin Bin's mother), Liu Xian (Xiao Ji's Father). Produced by Shozo Ichiyama, Li Kit-Ming, Masayuki Mori, Hengameh Panahi, Paul Yi, Yuji Sadai for Office Kitano, Lumen Films, E-Pictures, T-Mark, Hu Tong Communication, Bitters End.
113 mins

2004
SHIJIE (The World)
Script: Jia Zhangke. Photography: Yu Likwai. Editing: Khung Jinlei. Production Design: Wu Lizhong.

Players: Zhao Tao (Tao), Chen Taisheng (Taisheng), Jing Jue (Wei), Jiang Zhongwei (Niu), Huang Yiqun (Qun), Wang Hongwei (Sanlai), Liang Jingdong (Liang), Ji Shuai (Erxiao), Xiang Wan (Youyou), Alla Chtcherbakova (Anna). Produced by Takio Yoshida, Shozo Ichiyama, Ren Zhonglun for Office Kitano, Celluloid Dreams, Lumen Films, Shanghai Film Studio, Xstream Pictures.
139 mins

2006
SANXIA HAOREN (Still Life)
Script: Sun Jianmin, Guan Na, Jia Zhangke. Photography: Yu Likwai. Editing: Khung Linlei. Production Design: Liang Jindong, Liu Qiang. Players: Zhao Tao (Shen Hong), Han Sanming (Sanming). Produced by Xu Pengle, Wang Tianyun, Zhu Jiong, Chow Keung, Dan Bo, Ren Zhonglun for Xstream Pictures. 108 mins

In Memoriam

MICHELANGELO ANTONIONI
29 September 1912 – 30 July 2007

In 1985 Michelangelo Antonioni suffered a stroke which left him partially paralysed and unable to speak. 'There is no need to explain; life is like that,' the Italian director claimed, before he was deprived of the power of statement or explanation. The irony was as sour and potent as an Antonioni love story: this supremely visual director, who claimed he had 'things to show rather than things to say' and whom Martin Scorsese has called a 'truly great modern painter' was left with no conduit but the visual.

Michelangelo Antonioni was born in Ferrara in 1912; his interest in film came early, although its full expression did not. The war got in the way – he edited a fascist cinema publication but was fired for being too left-wing – although it provided good training: Antonioni worked on scripts, including *A Pilot Returns* (*Un Pilota ritorna*, 1942) for Roberto Rossellini, and went to France to help Marcel Carné make *The Devil's Envoys* (*Les Visiteurs du soir*, 1942) as the Italian element of that Franco-Italian co-production. He wrote film criticism and made documentaries and in 1950 brought a documentary-maker's cool forensic tact to his remarkably assured first feature, *Chronicle of a Love* (*Cronaca di un amore*), which begins one of the great cinematic careers with a close-up on a set of photographs and a private detective's comment that 'this is not the same old story'. Actually it *was* the same old story – beautiful woman persuades beefcake to bump off her rich husband; Billy Wilder had told it in *Double Indemnity* a mere six years before – but recounted in a

Michelangelo Antonioni

startlingly different way. It is the husband's desire to find out about his wife that propels the story, and neither the gorgeousness of Lucia Bosè nor the architectural loveliness of Michelangelo's mise-en-scène can distract us from that central irony. 'Isn't life awful?' whispers the director, even as he beguiles us with its beauty. Antonioni's entire oeuvre plays out this way – as bleakly ravishing as a mountain outcrop and as dry as the desert. Antonioni wrote or co-wrote all his films, and with the exception of *Il Grido* (1957), this self-proclaimed Marxist wrote them about the wealthy, dissolute middle class he came from. Perhaps this explains the unusual divisiveness of his body of work: it is rare to find a director everyone agrees is great while arguing interminably about how, and with which films, that greatness is manifest.

Antonioni plugged away through the 1950s, mainly on films like *The Girlfriends* (*Le Amiche*, 1955), about the disastrous love lives of the bourgeoisie. His style – the langorous takes, the watchful yet detached camera that obliges actors to squabble and work for its attention – did not evolve; it didn't need to. Antonioni's philosophy is that nothing can be done; as someone once wrote of F. Scott Fitzgerald (one of the director's favourite writers), his style sings of hope, his message is despair. Antonioni doesn't believe in evolution – although, as befits a good Marxist, revolution is fine by him. When colour came along, he adopted it with the fervour of the converted, saying he wished he could go back and colour in all his films. He promptly made the lurid and labyrinthine *The Red Desert* (*Il Deserto rosso*) in 1964, his fourth and penultimate film with muse Monica Vitti. In it, colour was sprayed everywhere (literally painting outdoor sets) in his attempt to show a neurotic woman's alienation from the modern landscape around her – and that landscape's paradoxical beauty.

By this time, Antonioni was internationally famous. *L'Avventura* had caused a furore at Cannes in 1960, with audiences divided as to whether the slow takes and vague narrative constituted greatness or monumental dullness. The heroine disappears early on; her boyfriend and friend spend the rest of the film half-heartedly searching for her, while falling lethargically in love. Made the same year as Fellini's *La Dolce Vita*, and about the same kind of pampered, disillusioned people, *L'Avventura* is a kind of mirror image of that vivacious film, as angular as the other is voluptuous: La Vita Amara (The Bitter Life), if you like.

L'Avventura was the first of a trio with Vitti (a quartet, if you count *The Red Desert*): *La Notte* (1961) in which she causes further problems in Marcello Mastroianni's faltering screen marriage to Jeanne Moreau, and *L'Eclisse* (1962), where she leaves one man and finds another, played by Alain Delon, who proves to be no improvement on his predecessor. These films have more in common than Vitti's luminousity; their passion for desolation reduces narrative to insignificance. They are magnificent – but as hard to love as they are easy to admire.

In the mid-1960s, Antonioni branched out, coming to London (parts of which he also covered in paint) to make *Blow-Up* (1966), his tale of a photographer (based, apparently, on David Bailey) who believes he has captured a murder on camera. Has he? Hasn't he? It doesn't matter. For Antonioni, form always takes precedence over content – look how many of his films end spectacularly, from the empty spaces where once were lovers in the finale of *L'Eclisse* to the joyous explosion at the end of the otherwise gruesome US hippie flick *Zabriskie Point* (1970) (he used the title *Blow-Up* on the wrong movie, commented Pauline Kael sourly). *The Passenger* (1975), Antonioni's last great film, has a simply breathtaking ending, with the camera watching people come and go through a window; as always, Antonioni's relief to have the characters and their tedious insistence on narrative out of the way is palpable. In *The Passenger*, Jack Nicholson plays a self-hating journalist who, instead of killing himself, steals a dead man's identity and picks up Maria Schneider. Life, Antonioni evidently believes, is just a form of slow suicide, but he never lets that stop him from trying to create beauty.

After his stroke, he made one last feature, *Beyond the Clouds* (*Al di là delle nuvole*, 1995) with the help of Wim Wenders. The film, culled from several of Antonioni's own short stories, is not good, but there's a bitter appropriateness to that: an oeuvre largely devoted to the impossibility of communicating effectively ends with a failure to communicate, made by an old man who can no longer talk. La Vita Amara indeed. In 1995, he was awarded an honorary Academy Award; he died on 30 July 2007, the same day as fellow icon Ingmar Bergman. – *Nina Caplan*

Ingmar Bergman

INGMAR BERGMAN
14 July 1918 – 30 July 2007

Long ago, when the Cold War was young, Ingmar Bergman jousted with Death and won. His immense body of work has assured him his immortality; popularity, on the other hand, involved a life-long chess game of great delicacy with his critics and audiences.

Sweden's great writer-director was born in Uppsala in 1918; his pastor father's combination of religion and repression guaranteed over five decades of material, but it was the method, not the madness, that made Bergman so special; plenty of sensitive little boys have puritanical papas and quite a few of them (from Alfred Hitchcock to Paul Schrader) wind up as film directors, but none has ever turned out quite like Bergman. His films are spiritual questions, usually unanswered. As the *New Yorker* film critic Penelope Gilliatt pointed out, there can seldom have been a Christian artist who held up less hope of an afterlife. Small wonder, then, that his films are steeped in pain, or in 'terrible mental disturbances, physical and psychological acts of violence' as his 1969 film *The Passion of Anna* (*En Passion*) terms it.

Bergman began with a child's puppet theatre, became a script doctor, graduated to screenplays and finally took control; he remained obsessed with manipulation (his, God's, mere mortals') yet proved a remarkably sensitive director, drawing extraordinary work

from a select troupe of regular collaborators that began with Harriet Andersson and Max Von Sydow, and went on to include Bibi Andersson, Liv Ullmann, Erland Josephson, Gunnar Björnstrand and, perhaps most importantly, cinematographer Sven Nykvist. It is probably the same directing (or should that be manipulating?) talent that enabled him to remain friends with most of the women on this list after enthusiastically blurring the professional boundaries; even Ullmann, with whom he lived for several years and had a child, remained on-side enough not just to continue starring in his films but to direct *Faithless* (*Trolösa*, 2000) from his screenplay. Sensitively crafted in Bergman's mould, it is tempting to include *Faithless* in the list of films directed by him. The miserable relationships, profound doubt in the goodness of humanity, the internal bleakness encased in fleshly beauty: they're all there, as is the quietly predatory story, wherein very little happens yet the aftertaste of calamity lingers. It's as if the tide came in while we paddled in dank pools, looking around only to discover that a city had drowned.

His first film job was as scriptwriter and assistant director on the great Alf Sjoberg's *Frenzy* (*Hets*) in 1944; he nipped behind the camera when a more upbeat ending was required and never emerged, learning his trade on a ragtag assortment of films until the breakthrough of *Summer With Monika* (*Sommaren med Monika*, 1953), a voluptuous study in adolescent passion. His body of work after that is simply breathtaking, even if you ignore the plays he directed concurrently for the Royal Dramatic Theatre in Stockholm. In the 1950s he gave us *The Seventh Seal* (*Det Sjunde inseglet*, 1957) with its much admired, much mocked chess game between Max Von Sydow's medieval Crusader and Death; the same year (the same year!) another masterpiece was released: *Wild Strawberries* (*Smultronstället*) in which Strindberg's heir cast Sweden's glory, the director Victor Sjöström, as an ageing, embittered professor journeying to an honorary degree ceremony down memory lane. What is most astonishing about these two studies of spiritual anguish and regret is that their writer-director had yet to hit forty, although he was already on his third wife.

The 1960s began with rape-revenge drama, *The Virgin Spring* (*Jungfrukällan*, 1960) the first of Bergman's collaborations with Nykvist; he continued to direct films at a rate of about one a year, including *Persona* (1966), if not the greatest study of identity ever filmed then certainly the most cinematic, *Shame* (*Skammen*, 1968) and the exhilarating yet utterly forlorn *The Passion of Anna*. Another decade brought another clutch of masterpieces including *Scenes from a Marriage* (*Scener ur ett äktenskap*, 1973), which would eventually birth a final film which, like his ongoing professional relationships with his actress-lovers, illustrates Bergman's belief in everlasting love, however dangerous or damaging. Liv Ullmann and Erland Josephson's disastrous marriage may have been long over by the time of *Saraband* in 2003 but their history forged a bond stronger than physical passion and their complicated feelings provided an elegant and appropriate full-stop to a career too full, in quality and quantity, to properly delineate here. *Fanny and Alexander* (*Fanny och Alexander*, 1982), the study of brutalised childhood that won him the Best Foreign Language Film Academy Award, is worth a special mention. He went quieter after that, although only by his workaholic standards; the little boy whose father had locked him in a cupboard as punishment could never resist luring us into small dark rooms and unspooling his psyche, in all its torment and beauty, before us. Gilliatt said of him that 'he has made, again and again, films that are about people's terror of being eaten alive spiritually and about their mesmerised longing to risk it'. In the same spirit of duality, of the eternal yoke of fear and desire, it is also possible to say that Bergman brought Death to the table early and ensured love lasted until the very end. Which may have been his greatest achievement of all. – *Nina Caplan*

FREDDIE FRANCIS
22 December 1917 – 17 March 2007

Freddie Francis was regarded as one of the world's finest cinematographers. His disparate career began at Elstree Studios in the 1930s. After shooting propaganda films during the war years, he became a camera operator at Denham Studios, working under Michael Powell; shortly after, he began a fruitful collaboration with John Huston. Becoming a fully-fledged cinematographer in 1956, he worked with Joseph Losey and helped model the look of the British kitchen-sink drama on *Room at the Top* (1959).

Freddie Francis

Francis was at the peak of his powers with *Saturday Night and Sunday Morning* (1960), *Sons and Lovers* (1960), for which he won his first Academy Award, and *The Innocents* (1961). Partly motivated by financial concerns, Francis turned his hand to directing in 1961, and despite his ambivalence towards the horror genre, he made several Gothic thrillers. He returned to cinematography at the request of David Lynch and together they shot the beautiful *The Elephant Man* (1980). High-profile productions such as *The French Lieutenant's Woman* (1981) and *Dune* (1984) followed. After two failed attempts to revive his directorial career, Francis concentrated on being directed, on *Glory* (1989), for which he received his second Academy Award, and Scorsese's *Cape Fear* (1991). In 1998, Francis was awarded an International Award by the American Society of Cinematographers, which he described as 'an absolute highlight in my career'. – *Eleanor McKeown*

LÁSZLÓ KOVÁCS
14 May 1933 – 21 July 2007

László Kovács was one of the great cinematographers who influenced the look of American cinema during the 1970s, shooting, most famously, *Easy Rider* (1969), *Five Easy Pieces* (1970), *The Last Movie* (1971), *The King of Marvin Gardens* (1972), *Paper Moon* (1973), *Slither* (1973) and *Shampoo* (1975). Born in Cece, Hungary, Kovács was attending film school in Budapest in 1956 during the failed uprising which he and a friend surreptitiously filmed with a camera concealed in a bag. They fled across the border into Austria with their footage hidden in sacks. Unmarketable at the time, the footage now forms much of the basis of *Torn from the Flag*, a documentary released in 2006. Kovács worked on almost seventy films all told, including *Ghostbusters* (1984), *Mask* (1985) and *Miss Congeniality* (2000). In 2002 the American Society of Cinematographers honoured him with a lifetime achievement award. – *Matthew Winston*

László Kovács

CARLO PONTI
11 December 1912 – 10 January 2007

Carlo Ponti was known throughout the film world for his work as a producer, and throughout the rest of the world for being married to Sophia Loren. Their Mexican marriage, following his divorce from his first wife, caused a scandal in Italy and the threat of criminal charges. Many of the films for

Carlo Ponti

which he is best remembered were vehicles for Loren, including *Woman of the River* (*La Donna del fiume*, 1955) and Vittorio De Sica's *Two Women* (*La Ciociara*, 1960), for which she earned an Academy Award, the first ever to be awarded to an actress for a performance in a foreign-language film. In addition to promoting Loren, Ponti worked with Dino De Laurentiis to produce, among others, Rossellini's *Europa '51* (1952) and Fellini's *La Strada* (1954). Throughout his long career he produced a wide range of films, from the art-house to the big-budget epic. He was fond of saying 'I don't make deals, I make pictures,' and the pictures he made included King Vidor's *War and Peace* (1956), David Lean's *Doctor Zhivago* (1965) and Antonioni's *Blow-Up* (1966). – *Matthew Winston*

OUSMANE SEMBÈNE
1 January 1923 – 9 June 2007

Ousmane Sembène was a celebrated novelist and one of the most important directors in African cinema. Expelled for insolence from a colonial school in what was to become Senegal, Sembène was largely self-taught. In 1944, as a French citizen, Sembène was drafted into the army, serving in France

Ousmane Sembène

and Niger. After the war, he worked on the Marseilles docks until Senegalese independence in 1960. During this time he became a Communist and dedicated union activist. His first novel was published in 1956, but it was his account of the 1947-48 strike on the Dakar/Niger railway, 'God's Bits of Wood', that is regarded as his most significant literary work, and perhaps the greatest strike novel ever written. In 1962 he won a scholarship to study film at the Gorky Studios in Moscow. He turned to the medium in order to reach a wider audience; he has stated that 'Africa is my audience; the West and the rest are markets'. His films were intended to promote discussion of issues of power and exploitation. In 1966, after two short films, Sembène made his first feature, *Black Girl* (*La Noire de...*, 1966), concerning a female domestic servant in Antibes. But it was his second feature, *The Money Order* (*Mandabi*, 1968), depicting post-colonial life, which attracted international acclaim, winning the Special Jury Prize at the Venice Film Festival.

Sembène's films, though never didactic, were political works; he attacked religious and 'traditional' bigotry and intolerance in *Ceddo* (1977) and *Guelwaar* (1992), and French colonial exploitation and repression in *Emitai* (1971) and *Camp de Thiaroye* (1987). Senegal's exploitation of the poor by the new post-colonial ruling class also concerned Sembène. *Xala*'s (1975) thinly veiled attack on Senegal's new independent government led to it being banned. *Moolaadé* (2004), was a scathing attack on the practice of female circumcision and represented a return to Sembène's concern with certain African traditions and the subjugation of women.

Sembène won various international prizes and served on the juries of both the Cannes and Venice film festivals. Widely regarded as the father of African cinema, he was the co-founder of both the Senegalese Association of Filmmakers and the Pan African Federation of Filmmakers. He tirelessly devoted his career, and life, to fighting suffering and injustice in African society. – *Matthew Winston*

JACK VALENTI
5 September 1921 – 26 April 2007

A decorated pilot in World War II and a key aide and confidante of President Lyndon Johnson, Jack Valenti served as head of the Motion Picture Association of America from 1966 until his retirement in 2004. Throughout his tenure, he was, to a degree, a proponent of free expression in American entertainment. He replaced the Hays Code with the system

Jack Valenti

of rating films according to content and was vocal in his opposition to the many attempts made to impose censorship on Hollywood's output. He campaigned to create and maintain international markets for American films, opposing domestic quotas and subsidies elsewhere in the world. In later years Valenti focused his energy on working to counter the threat of digital piracy. He was the author of four books, including a novel and a popular guide to public speaking. – *Matthew Winston*

EDWARD YANG
6 November 1947 – 29 June 2007

Edward Yang was one of the key figures of the Taiwanese New Wave of the 1980s. Chinese-born, Yang and his family moved to Taiwan when he was two years old as part of the evacuation of the Nationalist government and its supporters. He studied electrical engineering at the University of Florida and worked in computer design in Seattle before returning to Taiwan, motivated to become a filmmaker by the experience of having seen Werner Herzog's *Aguirre: Wrath of God* (*Aguirre, der Zorn Gottes*, 1972). Yang wrote the screenplay for the feature, *The Winter of 1905* (1981), and in 1982 directed a short for the anthology, *In Our Time* (*Guangyinde gushi*). This film was an important part of the birth of the Taiwanese New Wave, which represented a flowering of artistic endeavour in a largely martial, anti-artistic society which was still defined by the older generation's impossible dreams of triumphant return to the mainland. Yang's films, heavily influenced by Antonioni and defined by the use of medium- and long-shots and slow, deliberate pacing, focused time and again on the middle class of Taipei, and its place in Taiwanese society and history. In *That Day, On the Beach* (*Haitan de yitian*, 1983), a young woman's coming of age plays out against a Taiwanese society in a state of flux. Of the seven movies he directed, two stand out: *A Brighter Summer Day* (*Guling jie shaonian sha ren shijian*, 1991) and his final work, *Yi-yi: A One and a Two* (*Yi-yi*, 2000). In *A Brighter Summer Day*, Yang dealt with semi-

Edward Yang

autobiographical subject matter, examining the lives of adolescents in Taipei in the 1960s, taking a real-life murder case as a springboard. The 237-minute epic had more than a hundred speaking roles and was an important step as far as Yang's international reputation as a director was concerned. *Yi-yi: A One and a Two*, a subtle, multi-perspective examination of the intersecting lives surrounding one family, won him the Best Director prize at the Cannes Film Festival and secured his reputation once and for all throughout the world. – *Matthew Winston*

Amongst those who sadly passed away in 2006...

ROBERT ALTMAN (b. 20 Feb. 1925)
REMY BELVAUX (b. 10 Nov. 1966)
FABIÁN BIELINSKY (b. 3 Feb. 1959)
WALERIAN BOROWCZYK (b. 2 Sept. 1923)
BETTY COMDEN (b. 3 May 1917)
SOLVEIG DOMMARTIN (b. 16 May 1966)
RICHARD FLEISCHER (b. 8 Dec. 1916)
VAL GUEST (b. 11 Dec. 1911)
DANIELE HUILLET (b. 1 May 1936)
SHOHEI IMAMURA (b. 15 Sept. 1926)
NIGEL KNEALE (b. 28 Apr. 1922)
SVEN NYKVIST (b. 3 Dec. 1922)
GORDON PARKS (b. 30 Nov. 1912)
GILLO PONTECORVO (b. 19 Nov. 1919)
PEER RABAN (b. 2 July 1940)
SHIN SANG-OK (b. 11 Oct. 1926)
PETER VIERTEL (b. 16 Nov. 1920)

Country Focus: Germany

A new wave in German cinema?
by Shane Danielsen

Florian Henckel von Donnersmarck's victory at the 2007 Academy Awards, taking the Best Foreign Language Film prize for his debut feature *The Lives of Others* (*Des Leben der Anderen*), only confirmed for American cinemagoers what many in Europe had understood for some time – that after long years of stagnation and fatigue, Germany was once again in the midst of a filmmaking renaissance. Not quite as profound, perhaps, as the New German Cinema of the 1970s, the decade that introduced a small, bright constellation of unclassifiable talents (Werner Herzog, Rainer Werner Fassbinder, Wim Wenders, Volker Schlöndorff, *et al.*), but appreciable and refreshing nonetheless.

Which is not to diminish the significance of von Donnersmarck's achievement; the day after his win, the mood in Berlin was almost as jubilant as when the country had reached the 2006 World Cup final. The writer-director's face could be found, beaming with quiet patrician pride, on the front page of almost every newspaper, and members of the local film industry were quick to agree, in private as well as in public, that his win was, on the whole, a very good thing.

If it registered especially strongly in that city, it's simply because the nation's cinema is once again synonymous with its capital – now firmly established as the heart of the reunified Germany (rendering Bonn, the former first city, little more than a coach-stopover). Yet Berlin also represents an economic and social anomaly: the only major European capital permanently teetering on the brink of recession. Its high unemployment and low incomes also ensure that it's by far the cheapest in which to live. Accordingly, it has become a low-rent haven for artists and writers, musicians, filmmakers and DJs from all over Europe. *Berlin Is in Germany* ran the (faintly disapproving?) title of Hannes Stöhr's film from 2001; but from the city's *dolce vita* vibe, its packed street cafes and hedonistic club-culture – so different from the cloistered provincialism of Bavarian towns, or the post-industrial malaise of the Ruhr – one could easily be forgiven for thinking otherwise.

The late Ulrich Mühe in **The Lives of Others**

The city's arts scene manages to seem at once edgy and inviting, and local audiences are hungry for new work. Most Thursday evenings see a new German feature premiere in a dedicated weekly showcase at Berlin's venerable Babylon-Mitte Kino, and it is increasingly difficult to traverse the city without running across one film shoot or another; even my own, admittedly picturesque, street in Charlottenburg was twice closed to traffic this summer, while crews set up equipment and actors sunned themselves beside the catering vans. The cinemas are crowded; the weekly what's-on guides list endless mini-festivals and retrospectives – fourteen in July alone. Everywhere, it seems, there is a renewed sense of possibility and potential.

And why not? It was in Berlin, after all, at the Hotel Adlon in April 1997, that then-Federal President Roman Herzog made his provocative 'Berliner Rede' speech ('Durch Deutschland muss ein Ruck gehen!' he thundered – 'A shock must go through Germany!'), castigating the nation's ossified bureaucracies and urging its citizens to unite and create a new society, one in which complacency would be abolished and audacity rewarded. As wake-up calls go, it was hard to ignore. Yet his words were intended as much for filmmakers as for greengrocers or bankers. For a number of years – certainly more than a decade – German cinema had seemed curiously irrelevant, as if cowed by its own recent achievements.

This is not uncommon: French cinema, after the mid-1970s, struggled to regain the momentum of its *nouvelle vague* heyday; nor has the Italian industry ever again achieved the critical or commercial heights it scaled in the 1950s. Even now, in Taipei, auteurs such as Tsai Ming-liang are taking the refined aesthetics of the 1980s Taiwanese New Wave into ever more airless stylistic cul-de-sacs. These things are cyclical, after all. They ebb and flow. But Germany, for some reason, always seemed a special case, perhaps because there the stakes were so unusually high. As the crucible of the Cold War, the physical emblem of divided Europe, it inevitably came to represent something much larger than itself, a kind of cultural petri dish in which the warring aesthetics of Stalinism and post-Eisenhower democracy might be tested.

For a time, though, the contest seemed about as lively as a Soviet debating competition. West German cinema was stylistically moribund, capable of speaking only to itself,

while its East German equivalent went practically unseen west of the Wall. (Though, in this respect, it's worth noting that enterprising companies such as Icestorm Entertainment are at last packaging English-subtitled DVDs of DEFA productions, forgotten gems like Kurt Maetzig's *I am the Rabbit* (*Das Kaninchen bin ich*, 1965), thereby introducing non-German viewers, albeit belatedly, to a remarkably little-known strand of post-war cinema.)

The signing of the Oberhausen Manifesto, back in 1962, offered a typically Teutonic response to the problem: formalising youthful disillusion into a list of due-deliverables. ('We have concrete intellectual, formal and economic conceptions about the production of the new German film.') Out of this, admittedly, came the early films of Alexander Kluge and Edgar Reitz and, a few years later, the full flowering of the New German Cinema. For a time, then, all seemed well. But the premature death of Fassbinder in 1982, the departure of Wenders to the US (for the ill-fated *Hammett* (1982), and then, more happily, for *Paris, Texas* (1984)) and Kluge's shift away from filmmaking and into television, seemed to suck the air out of the movement. A void beckoned. Younger filmmakers seemed unable, for whatever reason, to seize the mantle and become the major figures the moment required.

Lamenting Fassbinder's demise at a conference in Boston in 2000, one academic seemed ready to cover himself in ashes: 'What treasures he would yet have given us!' he wailed. Well, yes, one wanted to reply, his early death was indeed a loss. But it was romantic at best, and absurd at worst, to imagine that, had he lived, he could have continued to produce features at the freakishly prolific rate he'd sustained through the 1970s. His stamina was not at issue; rather, it was that the world around him was changing. Funding, even in Germany, was becoming more cautious and conditional; and art-house audiences around the world were beginning the slow decline that continues, unabated, to this day.

Franka Potente in **Run Lola Run**

One could, I think, make a strong case that German cinema's present resurgence dates back to 1998, and Tom Tykwer's groundbreaking *Run Lola Run* (*Lola Rennt*), a watershed release in many senses. For non-German viewers, exhausted by years of grim fodder in the Neue Deutsche Kino sidebar of the Berlinale, that film's structural ingenuity (mimicking the multiple lives/outcomes of a video game) was rather less revelatory than its unabashed desire to delight its audience. Clearly aimed at an international market, it nonetheless managed to be as specific to its locale, as deeply anchored in the streets and neighbourhoods of Berlin, as its grungier, strictly-for-local-consumption contemporaries (Leander Haussmann's *Sun Alley* (*Sonnenallee*, 1999), for instance).

A cheerfully amoral study of love and chance, *Run Lola Run* was slick, concise (just 81 minutes long) and purely entertaining – and as a result, offered a high-voltage jolt to an industry in serious danger of flat-lining. As the film scholar Margit Sinka has noted, German critics were quick to recognise the difference it represented, and responded with eager relief 'at not having to comment on yet another specimen of the Cola Light, middle-class relationship comedies that had proliferated in recent years [and] amazement that a German film could be so incredibly fast-paced and such sheer fun to watch'.

More than anything, though, *Run Lola Run* arrived at an opportune historical moment.

However well crafted it might have been, a local hit like *Comedian Harmonists* (1997) was unlikely to convert international audiences to the cause of German cinema. So too Tykwer's previous film, *Wintersleepers* (*Winterschläfer*, 1997), an elegant, meditative critique of the contemporary German psyche, slumbering under the rule of longtime Chancellor, Helmut Kohl. But *Run Lola Run* more or less coincided with the 1998 elections that ended Kohl's 16-year tenure. Division and reunification, the ruptures that had transformed German society, were each receding into history; Roman Herzog's words hung in the air. The moment had arrived.

Tykwer's film also introduced two memorable faces, in the form of its stars Franka Potente and Moritz Bleibtreu. The former has since juggled local roles with occasional forays into Hollywood productions – notably, opposite Matt Damon in *The Bourne Identity* (2002) – while the latter has become the unofficial face of contemporary German cinema, starring in a host of high-profile releases, from *In July* (*Im Juli*, 2000) and *The Experiment* (*Das Experiment*, 2001) to recent would-be prestige productions like *Atomised* (*Elementarteilchen*, 2006). As such, they stand at the forefront of a new generation of talented, utterly distinctive performers, including Daniel Brühl, Julia Hummer, Nina Hoss and August Diehl.

The stars were in alignment. The talent was there. All that was missing was a bona-fide

Bruno Ganz in **Downfall**

international blockbuster; unmistakably German, yet universal in theme. Oliver Hirschbiegel's *Downfall* (*Der Untergang*, 2004) hastened to oblige. An unflinching study of the last days of Hitler and his inner circle, going slowly mad in their bunker as the Russians advanced, it boasted a *tour de force* performance from Bruno Ganz as a decaying, paranoid Führer. Nominated for an Academy Award, it gained a commercial release in more than forty territories around the world, an achievement rivalled only by Hermine Huntgeburth's *The White Massai* (*Die Weisse Massai*, 2005). The following year came another wartime drama, Marc Rothemund's *Sophie Scholl: The Final Days* (*Sophie Scholl – Die letzten Tage*, 2005). It, too, was rewarded with an Academy Award nomination.

Marc Rothemund's **Sophie Scholl: The Final Days**

Also on a historical theme, Edgar Reitz delivered the third instalment of his Heimat sequence: *Heimat 3 – Chronik einer Zeitenwende* (2004), this time charting the convulsions of German society from reunification in 1989 to the present day. Weighing in at a tidy 689 minutes (as opposed to 1,532 minutes for the preceding instalment), it brought this magnum opus, unprecedented in the annals of cinema, to a fitting, if exhausting, conclusion.

Tykwer, meanwhile, followed his international success with a puzzling though undoubtedly heartfelt epic, *The Princess and the Warrior* (*Der Krieger und die Kaiserin*, 2000), a severely underrated Kieslowski adaptation (*Heaven* (2000)) and, most recently, *Perfume: The Story of a Murderer* (*Das Parfüm – Die Geschichte eines Mörders*, 2006), a long-anticipated adaptation of Patrick Suskind's bestseller, and a Euro-pudding in the grand old style.

A chequered career, to be sure – but perhaps inevitable for any German filmmaker hoping to reach a major audience. Most of the country's commercial filmmaking seems intended solely and squarely for local consumption: dopey regional comedies, dusty police procedurals, weirdly passionless 'romances' – all of which travel about as well as sauerbraten. Among the exceptions was Chris Kraus's *Four Minutes* (*Vier Minuten*, 2006), the tale of a young female criminal who becomes a piano prodigy in prison, formulaic but charged with an admirable conviction. And Austrian director Stefan Ruzowitzky's *Anatomy* (*Anatomie*, 2000) proved a local hit, as did its sequel, though both paled beside the US slasher flicks they strove to emulate. Far better was Robert Schwentke's *Tattoo* (2002), an agreeably gruesome genre piece, redolent of 1970s grindhouse.

Robert Schwentke's **Tattoo**

Among the art-house set, meanwhile, this decade has seen the emergence of what has become known as the 'Berlin School', a style of filmmaking which, while grounded in the quotidian realities of contemporary life, nods in the direction of the metaphysical and allusive. They are serious films, though not pompous; self-absorbed, but not insular. Insofar as they can be categorised, they tend to favour meditative pacing, formalist compositions

Christian Petzold's **Yella**

and a refreshing faith in the viewer's ability to decode relationships and motivations from the comparatively limited information with which they're provided.

Christian Petzold is perhaps the leading example of this mini-movement, rivalled only by Fatih Akin as the most talented German filmmaker to emerge in his generation. (For a detailed study of the latter, refer to Eddie Cockrell's excellent essay earlier in this volume.) Following his international breakthrough with *The State I'm In* (*Die Innere Sicherheit*, 2000), Petzold has crafted a formidable body of work – knotty psychological dramas fuelled by his apparent fascination with intrusions of the irrational into the seemingly mundane, reminiscent at times of Hitchcock and Fritz Lang.

Andreas Dresen has, in films such as *Night Shapes* (*Nachtgestalten*, 1999), *Grill Point* (*Halbe Treppe*, 2002) and – most recently – *Summer in Berlin* (*Sommer vorm Balkon*, 2006), made a speciality of the multi-strand relationship movie, its tone teetering between satire and drama. His direction of actors is assured and even the pictorial flatness of his early work, bordering at times upon actual ugliness, has begun to improve, hinting at a growing visual sensibility.

Most careers, though, are still too nascent to sustain detailed assessment. Recent years have seen a huge number of accomplished debuts, whose makers have yet to capitalise on their initial breakthroughs. Oliver Rihs's

Black Sheep (*Schwarze Schafe*, 2006) was a scabrous comedy of bad manners, punk moviemaking at its most unapologetic, set in Berlin and prodding at the city's fractious relationship between its Eastern and Western inhabitants. In a similar vein was Jörn Hintzer and Jakob Hüfner's *Measures to Better the World* (*Weltverbesserungsmaßnahmen*, 2005), a collection of absurdist sketches, as deadpan as Roy Andersson, which mocked both the Germanic fetish for precision and the nation's supposed humourlessness.

Carsten Gerbhardt's *Weekdays* (*Wochentag*, 2005) offered seven linked vignettes, days in the life of an unidentified young woman. While the result failed to find the audience it deserved, it demonstrated considerable talent on the part of both the writer-director and his fearless young star, Zoé Naumann. *Hounds* (*Jagdhunde*, 2007), the graduation film by Ann-Kristin Reyels, walked a fine line between black comedy and coming-of-age drama, each equally involving, before ending with a coda so unnecessarily mean-spirited as to almost undo the good work that had preceded it.

Birgit Grosskopf's **Princess**

Birgit Grosskopf fulfilled the promise of her short films with an excellent first feature, *Princess* (*Prinzessin*, 2006), which favoured the unadorned socio-realism of Ken Loach and the Dardenne brothers. Ulrich Kohler followed the flawed *Bungalow* (2003) with *Windows On Monday* (*Montag Kommen die Fenster*, 2005), a compelling study of one woman's flight from the meagre consolations of domestic life. Bavarian-born Maria Speth's

Ulrich Kohler's **Windows On Monday**

debut, *The Days Between* (*In den Tag hinein*, 2001), operated in similar territory to equally impressive ends, although *Madonnas* (2007), her follow-up, seemed muddled and schematic by comparison.

Thomas Durchschlag's *Alone* (*Allein*, 2004) ploughed much the same furrow of female alienation. Its tone of unalloyed self-loathing and its equation of sexuality with disgust seemed to place it in the company of recent Austrian features, like Jessica Hausner's *Lovely Rita* (2001). Comparable in tone – though evincing a far lighter touch – was Maren Ade's *The Forest for the Trees* (*Der Wald vor lauter Bäumen*, 2003), a pitch-black comedy about an idealistic but socially maladroit teacher.

Jessica Hausner's **Lovely Rita**

The undisputed queen of bourgeois angst, however, remains Berlin's Angela Schanelec. After some interesting, if mannered, early features – notably, *Passing Summer* (*Mein langsames Leben*, 2001) and *Places in Cities* (*Plätze in Städten*, 1998) – Schanelec's films

have become increasingly hermetic and obtuse; her latest film, *Afternoon* (*Nachmittag*, 2007), is a maddeningly inscrutable Chekhov adaptation where she seems to have abandoned every trace of concession to, or interest in, her audience. With their long, static takes and banal exchanges, one can only assume these films are intended to instill the same sense of numbed despair among viewers as that being depicted with such meticulous care onscreen. If so, she succeeds, but it's far from an edifying experience.

Which brings us to Romuald Karmakar, who with *Nightsongs* (*Die Nacht Singt Ihre Lieder*, 2004) delivered one of the most unintentionally hilarious misfires of the decade: a theatrical adaptation so pretentiously heavy-handed it played like a parody of a European art movie, right down to the supposedly 'kinky' (though actually rather insipid) sex. Far better – perhaps because it contained some actual human content – was his semi-documentary, *Hamburg Lectures* (*Hamburger Lektionen*, 2006), a meticulous restaging of Mohammed Fazazi's January 2000 'lessons' while serving as Imam at the Al Quds mosque in Hamburg, which had been attended by three of the four 9/11 pilots.

Florian Hoffmeister had served as cinema-tographer on a drama on much the same subject: British director Antonia Bird's Channel 4 drama *Hamburg Cell* (2004). He subsequently made his own directorial debut with an intelligent, unashamedly modernist drama, *3 Degrees Colder* (*3° kälter*, 2005),

Florian Hoffmeister's **3 Degrees Colder**

FilmFernsehFonds Bayern

The Lives of Others

Academy Award „Best Foreign Language Film" 2007
Director: Florian Henckel von Donnersmarck
Director of Photography: Hagen Bogdanski
Production Design: Silke Buhr
Producers: Quirin Berg, Max Wiedemann
Production Company: Wiedemann & Berg Film/Munich, in co-production with
BR/Munich, ARTE/Strasbourg, Creado Film/Constance
Principal Cast: Martina Gedeck, Ulrich Muehe, Sebastian Koch, Ulrich Tukur

World Cinema Made in Bavaria
Supported by FilmFernsehFonds Bayern

Perfume – The Story of a Murderer

Director: Tom Tykwer
Director of Photography: Frank Griebe
Production Design: Uli Hanisch
Producer: Bernd Eichinger
Production Company: Constantin Film/Munich,
in co-production with Film & Entertainment VIP Medienfonds/Munich
Principal Cast: Ben Whishaw, Alan Rickman, Rachel Hurd-Wood,
Dustin Hoffman, Karoline Herfurth

Trade

Director: Marco Kreuzpaintner
Director of Photography: Daniel Gottschalk
Producer: Roland Emmerich, Roselyn Heller
Production Company: Claussen+Wöbke+Putz Filmproduktion/Munich,
Centropolis, Roland Emmerich/L.A. VIP Medienfonds/Munich
Principal Cast: Kevin Kline, Alicja Bachleda, Cesar Ramos

Munich and Bavaria – Germany's traditional film location

FilmFernsehFonds Bayern

FilmFernsehFonds Bayern GmbH
Sonnenstr. 21 | 80331 München
Tel. 089-544 602-0 | Fax 089-544 602 21
filmfoerderung@fff-bayern.de
www.film-commission-bayern.de | www.fff-bayern.de

which channelled the narrative ambiguities and pictorial elegance of mid-period Antonioni, yet emerged finally, unmistakably, as its own work. Likewise *Gun-Shy* (*Schussangst*, 2003), by Dito Tsintsadze, which followed the transit of a lonely, rather lovesick young man from misfit to killer.

In Hamburg, meanwhile, Michael Busch crafted the dreamlike *Seven Heavens* (*Sieben Himmel*, 2006), a genuinely unsettling vision of submission and degradation, whose semi-experimental approach seemed more suited to art spaces than cinemas. Similarly unclassifiable, though clearer in intention, was *Love in Thoughts* (*Was nützt die Liebe in Gedanken*, 2004) from Achim von Borries, which filtered the events of the 1927 Steglitz Student shooting through the swooning, homo-erotic aesthetic of an Abercrombie & Fitch ad. Dangerously deluded they may have been, but those boys certainly knew how to wear a partially buttoned linen blouson.

But what of the old guard? How fare the former *enfants terribles*, now older than the generation they once sought to usurp?

Wim Wenders' decline, sadly, ranks among the most precipitous in cinema history. His most recent film, the English-language *Don't Come Knocking* (2005), which re-teamed him with former *Paris, Texas* collaborator Sam Shepard, was almost comically inept in every respect. And given his indiscriminate weakness for rock stardom, few could have been cheered by the announcement of his latest project, *The Palermo Shooting* (2008), a film shot in his native Dusseldorf, starring Lou Reed, Patti Smith and the singer from antediluvian German punks, Die Toten Hosen.

By contrast his contemporary, Werner Herzog, has gone from strength to strength, producing a string of critically acclaimed, typically oddball documentaries, one of which – *Grizzly Man* (2005) – even managed to achieve a modest commercial success around the world. And with *Rescue Dawn* (2006), a fictionalised

re-telling of his famous documentary *Little Dieter Needs to Fly* from 1997, he delivered a perfectly creditable impersonation of a Hollywood action flick; one in which, admittedly, many distinctively Herzogian elements had been sublimated, even smothered, but a convincing demonstration of his technical prowess nevertheless.

Alexander Kluge continued to produce fiction. In 2003, he received Germany's most prestigious literary award, the Georg Büchner Prize, and it is likely that posterity will regard him primarily as a writer who worked occasionally in the cinema. Volker Schlöndorff co-wrote and directed one of the liveliest and most compelling German features in years, *The Legend of Rita* (*Die Stille nach dem Schuss*, 2000), a sneakily thrilling study of a female former terrorist in the Ulrike Meinhof mode. He followed it four years later with *The Ninth Day* (*Der Neunte Tag*, 2004), a sober World War II drama which travelled widely on the festival circuit. His most recent work – the German-Polish *Strike* (*Strajk*, 2006), a rather schematic look at the birth of the Solidarity movement, and the existential piece *Ulzhan* (2007) – has failed to reach the same heights, but you sense a filmmaker gaining his second wind with more interesting work to come. His former wife, Margarethe von Trotta, has continued her erratic career with the almost defiantly old-fashioned *Rosenstrasse* (2003), before making an ill-advised detour into genre filmmaking with a lurid, almost incomprehensible thriller, *I Am the Other Woman* (*Ich bin die Andere*, 2006).

Volker Schlöndorff's **The Ninth Day**

Milestones in German Cinema

1962 – Signing of the Oberhausen Manifesto by 26 young German filmmakers.

1965 – Foundation of the Young German Film Committee, under the auspices of the Federal Ministry of the Interior, to support new German films financially.

1972 – Werner Herzog makes *Aguirre: Wrath of God*; Rainer Werner Fassbinder makes *The Merchant of Four Seasons* (*Händler der vier Jahreszeiten*) and *The Bitter Tears of Petra von Kant* (*Die Bitteren Tränen der Petra von Kant*); Wim Wenders makes *The Goalkeeper's Fear of the Penalty* (*Die Angst des tor manns beim elfmeter*).

1974 – The 'Film and Television Accord' agreed between ARD and ZDF, the Federal Republic's main broadcasters, and the German Federal Film Board.

1977 – The 'German Autumn' sees an unprecedented level of domestic terrorism in West Germany, with a series of kidnappings, hijackings and murders. Andreas Baader, one of the leaders of the Red Army Faction, is found dead in his cell in Stammheim Prison in October.

1979 – Volker Schlöndorff's *The Tin Drum* wins the Palme d'Or at Cannes.

1982 – Wim Wenders wins the Golden Lion at the Venice Film Festival for *The State of Things*. Rainer Werner Fassbinder dies in Munich.

1984 – Edgar Reitz premieres the first instalment of his 11-episode TV drama *Heimat: A German Chronicle*.

1989 – Fall of the Berlin Wall; reunification of Germany begins.

1990 – Michael Verhoeven's *The Nasty Girl* (*Das Mädchen schreckliche*) opens, inspiring controversy with its treatment of German revisionism over World War II. It is nominated for an Academy Award.

1991 – Klaus Kinski dies in California.

1992 – Edgar Reitz premieres the second instalment of *Heimat: A German Chronicle*.

1994 – Producer Stefan Arndt unites with filmmakers Dani Levy, Wolfgang Becker and Tom Tykwer to launch the production company X-Filme.

1998 – The Export-Union of German Cinema devises the 'Next Generation' programme in conjunction with the Cannes Film Festival. Tom Tykwer's *Run Lola Run* becomes the most internationally successful German film in a decade.

2001 – Moritz de Hadeln is replaced as Director of the Berlin Film Festival by Dieter Kosslick.

2004 – Oliver Hirschbiegel's *Downfall* premieres, becoming a sensation – selling to more than forty international territories, and earning an Academy Award nomination.

2007 – *The Lives of Others* wins the Best Foreign Language Film Academy Award.

Key players

Shane Danielsen profiles twelve leading figures in German cinema

FATIH AKIN, writer, director, producer, actor

Akin was born in Hamburg in 1973, and it's telling that he continues to live and work in that city's Altona district which has provided the setting for several of his films. Arguably the face of second-generation German filmmaking, this son of Turkish immigrants began as an actor, playing small roles in movies for cinema and television until 1995 when he formed a production company (Wueste Film) and released his debut short film as writer-director. But it was his debut feature, *Short Sharp Shock* (*Kurz und schmerzlos*, 1998), which marked the beginning of his career: a tale of hapless young thugs, it became a commercial hit and earned several awards, including a Bronze Leopard at the Locarno Film Festival. Akin followed it two years later with *In July* (*Im Juli*, 2000) a charming international road movie shot in Germany, Hungary, Romania and Turkey, starring Moritz Bleibtreu, with whom he re-teamed in 2002 for *Solino*, which proved a liberal translation of his own story – as two brothers, the children of guest-workers, struggle to find their place in Germany. But *Head-On* (*Gegen die wand*, 2004) cemented his stature. A corrosive story of *amour fou*, it won Akin the Golden Bear at Berlin and a European Film Award for Best Feature, and swept that year's German Film Awards. His subsequent feature, *The Edge of Heaven* (*Auf der anderen Seite*, 2007) seemed a little overshadowed by comparison, but displayed a newfound wisdom and maturity. As good as he currently is, he is still growing.

MORITZ BLEIBTREU, actor

One could argue that Moritz Bleibtreu never had a choice: born in Munich, in 1971, to actor parents Hans Brenner and Monica Bleibtreu, he knew from an early age that his future also lay under the bright lights. After travelling widely as a youth, and taking drama classes in various cities (Rome, Paris, New York), he returned to Germany to work on the stage in Hamburg. Neither a matinee idol nor a character actor, Bleibtreu has instead cultivated an unassuming, everyman persona, which served him well in his early films – Rainer Kaufmann's comedy *Talk of the Town* (*Stadtgespräch*, 1995) and Thomas Jahn's *Knockin' on Heaven's Door* (1997) – before he made his international breakthrough alongside Franka Potente in Tom Tykwer's *Run Lola Run*. His prodigious work ethic has allowed him to form significant relationships – notably with writer-director Fatih Akin, with whom he has worked twice, on *In July* and *Solino*. He was commanding in Oliver Hirschbiegel's breakout thriller *The Experiment*, drew further international attention in 2001, co-starring opposite Harvey Keitel in István Szabó's *Taking Sides*, and if Oskar Roehler's adaptation of Michel Houellebecq's controversial bestseller *Atomised* proved a failure, Bleibtreu, in the lead, at least demonstrated his willingness to push the boundaries. He'll need it: next up, he plays Red Army Faction leader Andrea Baader for Uli Edel.

AUGUST DIEHL, actor

Rivalling Moritz Bleibtreu for visibility, the 32-year-old Diehl is, like Nina Hoss, a graduate of the Hochschule für Schauspielkunst Ernst Busch, arguably the most prestigious acting academy in Germany. He first came to attention as a hacker in Hans-Christian Schmid's *23* (*23 - Nichts ist so wie es scheint*, 1998). His technique is formidable and his range stunning – from genre pieces like Robert Schwentke's *Tattoo* and Stefan Ruzowitzky's *Anatomy 2* (*Anatomie 2*, 2003) to refined art-house fare like Achim von Borries' *Love in Thoughts* (*Was nützt die liebe in gedanken*, 2004). He was superb in Volker Schlöndorff's World War II religious drama *The Ninth Day*, bringing a passionate intensity to what might

AUGUST DIEHL in **The Counterfeiters**

easily have been a schematic parable of conflicted morality, and recently revisited this period – and re-teamed with Ruzowitzky – for *The Counterfeiters* (*Die Fälscher*, 2007). However, his finest performance to date has been as the rich, amoral Sebastian – torturing a succession of unfortunates with the bored detachment of a child killing insects – in Michael Glawogger's *Slumming* (2006). Diehl's undoubted good looks would seem to make him a natural leading man, and he's clearly not lacking in ambition: he's currently playing the doomed, privileged son Christian, alongside Armin Mueller-Stahl and Jessica Schwarz, in Heinrich Breloer's adaptation of Thomas Mann's 'Die Buddenbrooks', one of the canonical works of German literature.

BERND EICHINGER, producer

Arguably the most powerful producer in Germany today, Eichinger occupies a place in Germany analogous to that of Robert Lantos in Canada – overseeing a raft of 'quality' productions distinguished by lavish production values, esteemed pedigrees and middlebrow sensibilities. Beginning with Wim Wenders' *Wrong Move* (*Falsche bewegung*, 1975), an early flirtation with the art-house saw him produce Hans-Jürgen Syberberg's massive (442-minute) *Hitler: A Film from Germany* (*Hitler – Ein film aus Deutschland*, 1978). Uli Edel's *Christiane F.* (1981) achieved a cultish level of success but Eichinger's real watershed came three years later, with Wolfgang Petersen's adaptation of Michael Ende's bestseller, *The Never-Ending Story*

(*Die Unen dliche geschichte*, 1984), a breakout hit in English-language territories around the world. Then followed, in swift succession, a string of films good (*The Name of the Rose* (1986) and *Last Exit to Brooklyn* (1989)), bad (*Body of Evidence* (1993) and *Smilla's Sense of Snow* (1997)) and indifferent. With the *Resident Evil* franchise, he struck paydirt, but the real triumph was 2004's *Downfall*, an unflinching study of the last days of Adolf Hitler (shades of Syberberg!) which brought honours on director Oliver Hirschbiegel, lead actor Bruno Ganz and Eichinger himself, here serving as co-screenwriter as well as producer. Since then he's delivered two more *Resident Evil*s, begun a new franchise in collaboration with Marvel Comics – *The Fantastic Four* – and served up one of the more conspicuous Euro-puddings of recent years with *Perfume: The Story of a Murderer*, which he also co-scripted. He is prolific, erratic and seemingly unstoppable.

MARTINA GEDECK, actress

After graduating from Berlin's Hochschule der Kuenste in 1986, Gedeck first came to attention in two successive television films by director Dominik Graf: *Die Beute* (1988) and *Tiger, Loewe, Panther* (1989). For a time she seemed to concentrate on her small-screen career, building a reputation for compelling performances in high-end TV dramas while managing to perform at most of the country's

MARTINA GEDECK

leading theatres – Frankfurt's Theater am Turm, the Kammerspiele in Hamburg and the Deutsches Theater in Berlin. But it was her lead performance in Sandra Nettelbeck's theatrical feature *Mostly Martha* (*Bella Martha*, 2001) that catapulted her to international attention. In 2006 alone, she starred in two of the year's finest German features – *Sommer 04* by Stefan Krohmer, and Florian Henckel von Donnersmarck's Academy Award-winning *The Lives of Others* – while also delivering a scene-stealing supporting turn in Robert De Niro's underrated espionage drama *The Good Shepherd*, her first English-language picture. Her forthcoming projects – first starring as the wife of the composer Robert Schumann in Helma Sanders-Brahms' *Clara*, and then as terrorist Ulrike Meinhof – only attest to her formidable range, intelligence and fearlessness. At 46, an age at which most Hollywood actresses seem consigned to oblivion, Gedeck is at the height of her powers.

WERNER HERZOG, writer, director, producer, actor

Though residing these days in Los Angeles, Werner Herzog remains perhaps the most German of living filmmakers – his passionate, conspicuously un-cynical stance ('I do not understand irony,' he once declared) an enduring testament to his homeland and his

WERNER HERZOG on location

heritage. He's also the undisputed survivor of the New German Cinema: with Fassbinder dead, Kluge retired from the cinema and

OLIVER HIRSCHBIEGEL (right) directs

Wenders sliding into irrelevance, the 66-year-old Herzog's reputation is stronger than ever. Having for many years alternated feature filmmaking with a steady output of documentaries, it's telling that his recent non-fiction output has ranked among his finest to date – films like *The White Diamond* (2004), *Grizzly Man* (2005) and *The Wild Blue Yonder* (2005) possessing all the sense of wonder and pictorial elegance for which he's renowned. And while *Invincible*, his 2001 return to fiction, was a misfire, his latest feature, *Rescue Dawn* – a fictional re-telling of one of his most acclaimed docs, *Little Dieter Wants to Fly* (1997) – showed that he can even play by mainstream cinema's rules when it suits him: an action thriller with intelligence as well as sinew, it marks the culmination of the second act in this fascinating, avowedly singular career.

OLIVER HIRSCHBIEGEL, director

Or, a cautionary tale. Coming off the international hit that was 2004's *Downfall*, and with the 2001 local smash *The Experiment* also to his credit, one might reasonably have expected Hirschbiegel to become the pre-eminent German commercial filmmaker of his day. Instead he set his sights higher, and did what an entire generation of his compatriots would have sold their souls to do – he went to Hollywood. Before long he had a major tentpole release to his name: *The Invasion* (2007) – a frankly unnecessary third remake of *Invasion of the Body Snatchers* (1956), this time starring the decidedly A-list Nicole

NINA HOSS in **Epstein's Night**

Kidman and Daniel Craig. So far, so good – except that Hirschbiegel, whose previous films had proved more nuanced and thoughtful than their box office tallies might suggest, soon ran afoul of Warner Bros. and producer Joel Silver, who considered his cut too slow and cerebral for a summer blockbuster. Before long, his American debut was in ruins; he was replaced as director, the studio brought Andy and Larry Wachowski in for rewrites, and their *V For Vendetta* hired-gun James McTeigue to direct the new scenes. The result, unsurprisingly, was a loud, boorish flop – and Hirschbiegel should feel vindicated; one day, perhaps, his cut will surface on DVD and audiences will be able to judge for themselves. But if, right now, he's slinking back home to work, German cinema will be all the better for it.

NINA HOSS, actress

Nina Hoss's breakthrough came in 1996 with a TV remake, for Bernd Eichinger, of Rolf Thiele's 1958 classic *A Girl Called Rosemarie*; she followed this with a number of film roles – in , amongst others, Nina Grosse's *Fire Rider* (*Feuerreiter*, 1998) and Ottokar Runze's *The Volcano* (*Der Vulkan*, 1999). Her obvious intelligence, coupled with that grave, faintly aloof beauty, has drawn a number of admirers, including writer-director Christian Petzold – the Hitchcock to her Grace Kelly, perhaps? – who has now cast her in three films: *Something to Remind Me* (*Totermann*,

2002), *Wolfsburg* (2003) and *Yella* (2007), the latter of which earned her the Best Actress award at the Berlin Film Festival. Meanwhile, she has maintained a high-profile theatrical career, frequently starring at Berlin's Deutsches Theater (she was a member of the company between 1998 and 2000), and receiving the Gertrud Eysoldt Ring – one of the country's most respected acting prizes, for her interpretation of Euripides' 'Medea', under the direction of Barbara Frey. Her performance in Hermine Huntgebruth's *The White Massai*, in 2005, brought her yet another Best Actress trophy – this time from the Bavarian Film Awards – and marked her biggest commercial success to date; while Doris Dorre's *Naked* (*Nacht*, 2002) showed a very different side – more playful than one might have expected, though every bit as sexy. Her next role looks intriguing: playing 'Lenin' in *The Anarchist's Wife.*

DIETER KOSSLICK, film festival director

As director of the Berlin Film Festival, a position he has held since 2001, Kosslick is widely regarded as the international gatekeeper of German cinema. It is a

Berlinale Director DIETER KOSSLICK

somewhat surprising development in a wayward but intriguing career: born in Pforzheim in 1948, he initially took a degree in Communication, Politics & Education in Munich, then stayed on at the university after receiving his Masters degree to work as a research assistant, before moving to Hamburg in 1979 to work as a speechwriter for the city's then-mayor, Hans Ulrich Klose. There was a brief foray into journalism (for the magazine *Konkret*, once the home of reporter-turned-terrorist Ulrike Meinhof) before he moved into film funding – firstly at the Hamburg Film Office, later as co-founder of the European Film Distribution Office and then as executive director of Filmstiftung NRW. This administrative background has led to accusations of bloodlessness from certain critics. And indeed, Kosslick does occasionally seem more cultural bureaucrat than aesthete. His Competition selection has frequently come under fire – most recently for overlooking *The Lives of Others*, arguably the biggest German film in years (as, in fairness, did Cannes; the film eventually premiered at Locarno). But the Berlinale has generally prospered during his tenure, and his role as a tastemaker, and his eminence in contemporary German cinema, remains secure.

BERND NEUMANN, politician

A longtime cinema buff – he ran the film club at his high school in Bremen – Neumann's appointment in November 2005 as State Minister for Culture and the Media, under the current Chancellorship of Angela Merkel, has meant that the 66-year-old politician now finds himself at the nexus of German film funding, production and distribution – responsible for devising and implementing Federal policy regarding the country's cinema and television (he is also a member of the supervisory board of national public broadcaster ZDF). Inevitably, he's been both praised and castigated by the local industry – there are, after all, too many conflicting agendas at work to ensure any consensus of opinion – but there are also signs of his teenage passion: Neumann has stated

on a number of occasions that he considers the €30 million-plus in annual film support funds issuing from the Federal Government as a necessary investment in cultural development, not simply as an annual hand-out – and he has expressed interest in adopting and adapting other economic models (notably the French) to benefit the German industry. A career politician who manages to balance over four decades of public service with a keen sense of artistic mission, he's a key figure in German cinema's renaissance.

CHRISTIAN PETZOLD, writer, director

Other German filmmakers (notably, Fatih Akin and Oliver Hirschbiegel, and more recently Florian Henckel von Donnersmarck) have become more widely known, but there's a growing critical fraternity who believe that Berlin-based Christian Petzold might be producing the most consistent, singular and rewarding body of work of his generation. He initially came to international attention with *The State I'm In*, a tough, remarkably compelling study of a young girl (played by Julia Hummer) trying to enjoy a normal adolescence, despite the on-the-run status of her former-terrorist parents; the result successfully fused the political with the personal, the thriller with the art-house, and announced a talent at least equal to anything

CHRISTIAN PETZOLD

CHRISTOPH TERHECHTE, Programmer of the Berlinale's International Forum of New Cinema

coming out of France. (In fact it was his fifth feature, but his theatrical debut; his previous four films had been made for German TV.) From this point on, Petzold has continued to work steadily and extraordinarily well, crafting a succession of dramas characterised by their calm tone, elegant mise-en-scène, and intimations of the metaphysical. Films like *Something to Remind Me* and *Wolfsburg* betray a debt to the meticulous set-ups and delicious morbidity of tone of classic Hitchcock. But his latest feature, *Yella*, is something else again – a ghost story that manages somehow to reconcile the paranormal with the corporate (improbably enough, many scenes are set in business meetings). What he does next, and where he takes these obsessions, will be fascinating to see.

CHRISTOPH TERHECHTE, festival programmer

For over twenty years the International Forum of New Cinema, Berlin's equivalent to Cannes' Quinzaine des Realisateurs, was co-directed by husband-and-wife team Ulrich and Erika Gregor, and the selection – with its emphasis on 'young filmmakers and works that push the limits of the medium and perception itself' – proved a petri dish in which many of today's ranking auteurs (Bela Tarr, Alexandr Sokurov, Gus Van Sant, and so on) were weaned. Terhechte took over the selection in 2001, when the Gregors left to run the Arsenale kino, but he continues to work closely alongside them and to preserve the values his predecessors espoused, and as the quality of the Panorama has slipped, the Forum has been regarded as the standout section of recent Berlinales: the most challenging, the least complacent, delighting and frustrating audiences in more or less equal measures. For neophyte filmmakers – particularly those from 'disadvantaged' film cultures throughout Africa, Latin America and Asia – it remains a vital gateway to international recognition.

SHANE DANIELSEN was Artistic Director of the Edinburgh International Film Festival from 2002 to 2006; he now lives in Berlin.

Industry Focus: Documentary

Manufacturing Realities
by Hannah Patterson

Despite nervous predictions that the renewed interest in documentary may just be a flash in the pan, the genre, in all its myriad forms, has continued to flourish over the last few years. Away from its more traditional television platform, record numbers of films have been signed for theatrical release, with increased DVD sales and sorties into on-line and mobile phone distribution. Considerably more important now at the Academy Awards, the films that do best theatrically adopt the rise-and-fall narrative commonly associated with fiction, playing their educational intent down, instead entertaining, humouring, provoking or shocking.

The last two years alone have proffered an astonishing array of subject matters, more varied, and often engrossing, than fiction: fonts (*Helvetica*), suicide (*The Bridge*), dance (*Ballet Russes*), puzzles (*Wordplay*), faith (*Into Great Silence*), corruption (*Enron: The Smartest Guys in the Room*), censorship (*This Film is not Yet Rated*), Space (*In the Shadow of the Moon*), sport (*Once in a Lifetime: The Extraordinary Story of the New York Cosmos*), class and corruption (*Manda Bala*), cinema and memory (*Back to Normandy*), music (*Air Guitar Nation*), law (*Terror's Advocate*) and, of course, nature, with the extraordinary success of *March of the Penguins*, following in the wake of *Winged Migration*, winning the 2006 Academy Award and becoming the second-highest-grossing documentary of all time.

At a time when many people are mistrustful of what they hear in the news, documentaries are offering more in-depth, alternative or independent views of the world.

The two topics currently dominating the genre are the environment and the war in Iraq.

Environment

An Inconvenient Truth was the event documentary of 2006. Director Davis Guggenheim and former Vice President Al Gore took an environmental theme, specifically the issue of global warming, away from the Discovery and National Geographic channels and into the cinemas. A hit at Sundance at the beginning of 2006, winning the Academy Award in 2007 for Best Documentary, it defied expectations, grossing over $49 million worldwide. Essentially a film of Gore's travelling lecture on the dangers of global warming and the future of the planet, it proved what celebrity punch can do for an unsexy topic.

Al Gore and Robert de Niro attend the Opening Gala screening of **An Inconvenient Truth** *at the Tribeca Film Festival*

Other environmental documentaries have undoubtedly benefited from *An Inconvenient Truth*'s success and subject bolstering. Chris Paine's *Who Killed the Electric Car?* charts

Aaron Woolf's **King Corn**

the hopeful rise and unnecessary fall of the battery-operated electric vehicle, while the Leonardo DiCaprio-produced and narrated *The 11th Hour* focuses on the state of our natural environment and future of humanity. Aaron Woolf's *King Corn* hones in on our consumable lifestyle, à la *Super Size Me* (burgers) and *Black Gold* (coffee), to investigate America's reliance on corn. 2007 also saw the launch of Robert Redford's Sundance Green Channel, a platform for long-form environmental documentaries, and new film festivals devoted to the issue.

War

The war in Iraq has prompted an entire sub-genre all of its own: some well funded through broadcasters or foundations, others made on the hoof on shoestring budgets. James Longley's haunting *Iraq in Fragments* and Laura Poitras' *My Country, My Country* – focusing on Iraq's 2005 elections – were both nominated for Academy Awards, telling their

Deborah Scranton's **The War Tapes**

stories from Iraqi perspectives. As did Alex Gibney's important work on military torture, *Taxi to the Dark Side*. Charles Ferguson revealed the reasons for and consequences of the invasion of Iraq in *No End in Sight*, Eugene Jarecki looked at why America goes to war in *Why We Fight*, and Robert Greenwald highlighted how American corporations reap rewards from investing in the war in *Iraq for Sale*. Deborah Scranton put cameras into the hands of soldiers to tell their own version of events on the ground in *The War Tapes*. Vital documentaries have also emerged on the largely unreported war in Sudan with the chilling *The Devil Came on Horseback* and *Darfur Now*.

Michael Moore

Subject matter aside, the figure that still dominates documentary worldwide is Michael Moore. His films transcend topic, in thrall to his personality and author-led style, applauded by enthusiasts, derided by detractors, mimicked by documentary wannabes. *Bowling for Columbine*, *Fahrenheit 9/11* and *Sicko* are up there in the top-ten list of highest-grossing documentaries, with *Roger and Me* only marginally behind, at number twelve. Screening at Cannes in 2007, *Sicko* has performed extremely well for a film about healthcare, or lack thereof, in the US. Interestingly – though perhaps not surprisingly – it has proved more popular in theatres in its own country than other territories.

Yet one of the most important documentaries to be released in 2007, dividing critics, was *Manufacturing Dissent*, the investigation by Canadian filmmakers Rick Caine and Debbie Melnyk into Moore's filmmaking practices. Ostensibly setting out to make a film about their documentary hero, on further investigation they found that he was (allegedly) guilty of manipulating his footage to the point of inaccuracy. He didn't just walk into a bank and get a gun there, they contend, it had all been pre-arranged; and he *did* interview chairman of General Motors, Roger Smith.

Questions of whether Moore is actually a documentary maker or polemicist aside, this throws into new question the age-old debate of whether documentary itself is 'true'.

Crisis of reality

The issue of whether or not we can believe what we see in so-called factual filmmaking has become more and more pressing in recent years. In our current crisis of reality, how real is real? To what extent can audiences believe what they see? Are documentaries as biased or untrustworthy as the news can be? This reached crunch point in the UK with the revelations that callers were being encouraged to call premier lines that had already closed, their votes discounted in favour of better editorial outcomes, and that a trailer of Her Majesty the Queen had been edited out of sequence to make it look as if she'd stormed out of a photo session with Annie Leibowitz. If the BBC, that last bastion of non-bias, was cheating, then who could ever be trusted again?

Form

With this line between factual and fictional filmmaking significantly blurring, the number of drama documentaries, factual dramas or fictions based on reality – the labels morphing depending on who may be funding or distributing the product – has increased significantly in recent years. A new UK-based festival conference called 'Crossing the Line', dedicated to this very topic, took place in 2007 and began with the question: Why are so many documentary makers turning to drama, and fiction directors to fact?

Documentaries, after all, are cheaper to make than drama, which is good for producers and commissioners. Yet drama, particularly on television, has the potential to reach a much wider audience. While the crossover is not a new phenomenon after the theatrical success of *Touching the Void*, which mixed recreation so dextrously and suspensefully

Ai Qin Lin in Morecambe Bay in Nick Broomfield's **Ghosts**

with talking heads, leading documentary makers such as Nick Broomfield are going one step further in making fictional recreations of real events. His 2006 *Ghosts* re-enacted the events leading to the deaths of Chinese cockle-pickers in Morecambe Bay, using non-professional actors, who sometimes played themselves, in real locations. *Battle for Haditha* (2007) reconstructed the 2005 killing by American marines of Iraqi civilians in Haditha in retribution for the killing of one of their soldiers in a road-side bombing. Made under the auspices of the Channel 4 documentary department, for the purposes of the wider world it was distributed by FILM4.

Directors who have traditionally worked wholly in the realm of fiction are turning to documentary techniques to tell real-life stories within a fiction framework – stories that could have been impossible to make as documentaries due to problems with access. Unsurprisingly, these tend to be about events connected with the war in Iraq: Paul Greengrass's *United 93*, where some people, including air-traffic control staff, play themselves re-enacting the events of 9/11; Michael Winterbottom's recreation of the fate of four British-based Muslims accused of being terrorists in *The Road to Guantánamo*; and *A Mighty Heart*, about the abduction and murder of journalist Daniel Pearl, also directed by the prolific Winterbottom. Of the more controversial, *Redacted*, by Brian de Palma, shot in *vérité* style, sits on the fence between documentary and fiction, drawing from soldiers' home-made war videos, blogs and journals and footage posted on YouTube. It's a direct response, de Palma has said, to the mainstream media's silence, wearing its desire to inform and educate on its sleeve.

Festivals

In the wake of the genre's popularity, specialist documentary festivals have continued to spring up globally. In addition to well-established big-hitters such as Hot Docs, the major North American documentary event held in Toronto, IDFA in Amsterdam, the largest and most significant in the world, Thessaloniki Documentary Festival in Greece and Sunny Side of the Doc in France, there's the International Leipzig Festival for Documentary and Animated Film, cph:dox in Denmark, DocsBarcelona, Sheffield Doc/Fest in the UK, Yamagata International Documentary Festival in Japan, It's All True Documentary Festival in Brazil and Full Frame in North Carolina, amongst many others.

Sheffield Doc/Fest

More recent newcomers worthy of note include Britdoc, which has quickly established itself as an important boutique event in the calendar after only two years, with a pitching forum attended by representatives from throughout the documentary commissioning and broadcast sectors, a British and International Competition strand and myriad panel discussions. Maryland's Silverdocs, started in 2003, has also proved its credentials. The Big Sky Documentary Festival in Montana began in 2004, as did the True/False Festival,

in Columbia, Missouri – a favourite with filmmakers. ZagrebDox International Festival of Documentary Films started in 2005, and the new travelling documentary festival, Ambulante, set up by Gael García Bernal, Diego Luna and Pablo Cruz, aims to bring more documentaries to Mexicans. EcoVision Festival in Palermo – with 2008 its fourth year – is just one of the many new festivals dedicated to the environment.

Countless more generalised film festivals are giving greater prominence to documentaries. Sundance, of course, has long been the holy grail for filmmakers, increasingly so since *Roger and Me* screened and was sold there for $3 million in 1990, and in 2004 it significantly opened for the first time with a documentary – Stacy Peralta's entertaining look at surfing subculture, *Riding Giants*. Rotterdam has always supported documentary, so too Berlin, London and Cape Town, and SXSW in Austin is a great place to have a world premiere and gain crucial critical attention. Festivals such as the Edinburgh International Film Festival are now offering separate documentary prizes.

Funding

The opportunities for documentary funding haven't exponentially increased in line with the form's popularity. They are far cheaper to make than fiction, and as such can offer rich rewards if successful. But the runaway successes are few and far between, and only a handful make it into theatres. In America, foundations offer enormous support, the Ford and MacArthur foundations chief among many diverse and specialist funds. Sundance Documentary Fund is the first port of call for filmmakers around the world that want to make films about human-rights issues, freedom and social justice, and 2007 saw the Tribeca Film Institute and fashion designer Gucci announce the joint launch of the Gucci Tribeca Documentary Fund which plans to provide grants totalling $80,000 to a minimum of three filmmakers in 2008. Sundance's may be five times that amount but it all helps.

Mr Vig and Sister Ambrosija in Pernille Rose Grønkjær's extraordinary **The Monastery: Mr Vig and the Nun**

Funding in Europe still lies by and large in television broadcasting through one-off commissions or international co-production, though alternative funding foundations and documentary funds are opening up. Some countries offer support through their film councils and institutes – Denmark, for instance, the country that brought us Dogme 95, is particularly supportive of the genre and has seen recent critical successes with the excellent *The Monastery: Mr Vig and the Nun* and *Enemies of Happiness*. A significant addition in the UK – the home of the father of documentary, John Grierson – is the Channel 4 British Documentary Film Foundation, which has €500,000 to distribute to projects throughout the year. Foundations outside the United States are also coming to realise that they can take America's lead and dip their toes into the documentary reservoir, particularly NGOs who can team up with experienced directors to have films tailor-made to promote their particular cause.

Distribution

With such funding options, cheap digital technology for shooting and editing and filmmakers' collective determination to make films, the world is unlikely to run dry of product. Distribution, however, is as always an issue. The fear that the documentary bubble will burst still lurks, and the genre is high risk – aside from Michael Moore, a 'name' doesn't make much difference when it comes to marketing. Many more distributors are now acquiring documentaries – HBO, Zeitgeist, Magnolia, Typecast Releasing, IFC, Lionsgate, THINKfilm, Paramount Classics, Sony Classics, Soda Pictures to name just a few – but they don't make a great deal of money at the cinema and it's still a buyer's market.

DVD provides an alternative distribution, either for the documentaries that don't make it into the cinemas or for the majority that do still need to find their audiences. It's also a way of re-packaging older titles to bring them to a revitalised doc audience, either domestically or in the potentially lucrative educational market. Notable examples include the Criterion Collection's Maysles brothers' 1976 hit *Grey Gardens* packaged together with the 2006 follow-up *The Beales of Grey Gardens*, the documentaries of Louis Malle and Orson Welles' *F for Fake* (Masters of Cinema and Criterion, respectively). Zipporah Films are finally comprehensively bringing out the films of Frederick Wiseman and Tartan have started packaging by theme. Their 'Protest' DVD

Robert Greenwald's **Wal-Mart: The High Cost of Low Price**

features *The Yes Men*, *Wal-Mart: The High Cost of Low Price* and *Super Size Me*; their 'Music' DVD, *End of the Century: The Story of the Ramones*, *Mayor of Sunset Strip* and *The Devil and Daniel Johnston*. Docurama, a label devoted exclusively to releasing documentary, has partnered with POV PBS to release their films. And First Run/Icarus continues to go strong after 25 years solely in the business of documentary distribution.

Alex Gibney's **Taxi to the Dark Side**

Jeff Feuerzeig's **The Devil and Daniel Johnston**

Though the larger theatrical studio distributors may be able to plough money into marketing campaigns and grab audience attention, many documentaries' only option is cheaper, viral marketing. With on-line distribution, filmmakers can interface directly with audiences, who in turn help to market through word of mouth and social networking sites such as MySpace. Robert Greenwald famously used MoveOn.org to have his films such as *Wal-Mart: The High Cost of Low Price*, *Outfoxed*, *Uncovered* and most recently *Iraq for Sale* reach thousands. The potential of this scenario is that filmmakers can work independently of traditional gatekeepers: film festivals who must accept the film, critics who praise it, sales agents who might represent it, distributors who want to take it on, to the retailers who place it in their shops. It's now possible to mount such a campaign via the Internet, targeting key, specialist audiences, and Greenwald, for instance, keeps the rights to his films; as a campaigning documentary-maker his priority is getting the films seen by as many people as possible.

The future

It's an irony that as the documentary form becomes more popular, its traditional home – television – seems to be investing less, opting instead to plough more money into its bastardised son, reality TV. In Britain, for example, the threat looms of 60% cuts for one of the BBC's premier documentary strands, Storyville. This not only affects UK-based filmmakers but directors, producers and consumers around the world who often can only fund their documentary through co-productions. Recent documentary successes that have had theatrical releases and were funded in part by Storyville include *Taxi to the Dark Side*, *Why We Fight*, *Black Sun* and *Guerilla: The Taking of Patty Hearst*. But with more writing devoted to documentary films and business as evidenced in *indieWire*, The D-Word, *DOX* magazine, *Documentary Magazine*, *Reelworld*, *Film&Festivals* magazine and Shooting People, more books on documentary theory and practice aimed at a new generation of scholars, students and filmmakers (including the 'Nonfictions' series published by Wallflower Press), an unresolved issue of global warming, and a war with no end in sight, the form, for the forseeable future, looks to be going strong.

HANNAH PATTERSON is commissioning editor of *Kamera Books* and *Creative Essentials*, a freelance film critic and author, and documentary producer.

Special Focus: The DVD Market

From art-house to our house
by Brad Stevens

In the UK during the 1980s, television was the only source for any cinephile not living in London to see such standard works as *The Seventh Seal*, *Rashomon* or *8½*. Back then, one eagerly awaited screenings of these films on BBC2 or Channel 4, carefully recording the broadcasts on VHS tapes, assuming that the opportunity to add these classics to a permanent library would never again present itself. Cut to the present and even the most sparsely stocked high-street store displays DVD box sets dedicated to Fassbinder, Ozu and Bergman, alongside more recent foreign-language films and an eclectic selection of cult classics (Meyer, Bava, Jodorowsky).

Art-house cinema has experienced a long, if problematic, relationship with home video. The reluctance of Hollywood's major studios to make their films available in cassette form meant that the earliest video releases mostly consisted of low-budget horror, European exploitation and foreign classics. As far back as 1979, the catalogue of Intervision, among the first companies to release films on video in the UK, included Truffaut's *A Gorgeous Bird Like Me*, Shindo's *Onibaba*, Franju's *Eyes Without a Face*, Rohmer's *Claire's Knee*, Chabrol's *The Unfaithful Wife*, Bergman's *Cries and Whispers*, Malle's *Dearest Love* and Scola's *A Special Day* – all available for rental only, and all dubbed into English! Strangely enough, the only subtitled tape released by Intervision during this period was of Gunnar Hoglund's Swedish sexploitation film *As the Naked Wind From the Sea*.

Other labels that dabbled in subtitled films were Thorn EMI, who released Andrzej Wajda's war trilogy in 1982, and Warners, who, after issuing dubbed editions of *Day for Night*, *La Cage aux Folles* and *The Decameron*, decided to distribute subtitled transfers of *Fellini-Satyricon* and, rather oddly, Marco Vicario's now totally forgotten *Wifemistress*. This paved the way for Palace Video, who catered specifically to art-house audiences, offering certain titles in both dubbed and subtitled versions, occasionally on the same tape (their cassette of Godard's *Alphaville* contained both an uncut English-dubbed transfer and a heavily truncated subtitled print).

All these cassettes were priced for rental and none of them were easy to find; indeed, the nature of video distribution in the 1980s and 1990s – geared as it was towards the demands of the rental market – made it virtually impossible to profitably release foreign-language films (the Warner Bros. video of Kurosawa's *Dreams*, for example, shifted fewer units than any other film put out by that company). It wasn't until the growth of what was initially called the sell-through market during the late 1980s that the idea of releasing world cinema classics aimed at the serious collector began to take root. Unfortunately, companies such as Tartan, Redemption and Aikman Archive had, at least initially, a rather cynical view of exactly what serious collectors would put up with. Subtitles would be those burnt into theatrical prints (sometimes unreadable on a television screen), picture quality would often be abysmal, and footage would frequently be missing. Among the most notorious releases were Aikman's *Metropolis* (missing almost the whole 'Tower of Babel' sequence and projected at much too slow a speed), and Tartan's *Dr Mabuse*, a truncated edition of Lang's two-part film, which reduced the five-hour original to an 82-minute fragment.

All, or almost all, of this would change with the arrival of first laserdiscs, followed by DVD. The higher quality of these formats led to the emergence of a new breed of collector who refused to accept anything second-rate (a process reinforced by the simultaneous rise of the Internet, which allowed information about the flaws of any particular release to circulate much more quickly).

The US label Criterion was certainly the pioneer as far as art-house DVDs were concerned, quickly realising that their primary market consisted of informed consumers who would support a company that went out of its way to ensure that their discs were uncut, of the best quality, in the correct ratio and contained extensive extras. Criterion have engaged in ambitious restoration projects, the most impressive of which is arguably their

three-disc set of Orson Welles' *Mr Arkadin* which contains the longest American release version, the differently edited European version entitled *Confidential Report*, and a newly restored cut that combines material from the other two variants, with some footage never previously included in any print. This set includes documentaries, episodes of radio shows, interviews, commentaries by Welles scholars and a reproduction of the *Mr Arkadin* novel (including a preface that charts this book's curious history).

Teshigahara's **Woman of the Dunes**

At the opposite extreme is Image Entertainment, a label notorious for the poor quality of its discs: burnt-in subtitles, sparse extras, ragged prints, and several films – including Fellini's *Il Bidone*, Robert Hartford-Davis' *The Fiend*, Abel Ferrara's *Ms.45* and Teshigahara's *Woman of the Dunes* – released in heavily truncated editions. Thankfully, their recent three-disc special edition of Tinto Brass's *Caligula* – containing two different edits of the film, commentary tracks and a wealth of extras – suggests that Image are starting to become aware of the problem. Indeed, it seems increasingly unlikely that companies run by individuals who know less about their product than their customers do will survive for long in the increasingly competitive DVD market.

Between these two extremes are such labels as Other Cinema (a specialist in experimental works), Facets and Kino on Video. The latter label has a remarkably eclectic catalogue: lots of Lang, Chabrol, Gitai, Pagnol and Kieslowski,

Orson Welles is **Mr Akadin**

Poster for **Rogopag**

German mountain films, Miike's *Dead or Alive* trilogy, Albert Lewin's *Pandora and the Flying Dutchman*, Sirk's *La Habanera*, collections of Brakhage and Keaton, several American Film Theatre productions, the portmanteau *Rogopag* and a number of film noirs, notably Budd Boetticher's *Behind Locked Doors* which curiously anticipates the plot of Samuel Fuller's *Shock Corridor* (even some of the character names are the same), and may well have been ghostwritten by Fuller. Among the highlights of Kino's catalogue is their two-disc set of Joseph Losey's *Eve* (or *Eva*, as it says on the packaging), which includes both the short theatrical version and a longer print with Finnish subtitles (each variant containing scenes not in the other). Kino have had many problems with poor source materials and lacklustre transfers (*Eve* being a case in point), but one feels that this company is at least making an effort.

In the UK, the label that has the best claim to being 'the British Criterion' is Masters of Cinema whose adventurous catalogue includes definitive editions of Lang's *Metropolis*, Murnau's *Nosferatu*, De Sica's *Shoeshine* and Kobayashi's *Kwaidan* (an uncut version, restoring twenty minutes of footage missing even from Criterion's disc). But on the whole, Masters of Cinema prefers to avoid the more obvious titles, concentrating instead on lesser-known works by the great auteurs: Kurosawa's *The Idiot*, Dreyer's *Michael*, John Ford's *The Prisoner of Shark Island*, Rossellini's *Francesco Giullare di Dio*, Visconti's *Bellissima*,

Nicholas Ray's *The Savage Innocents* (another stunning restoration), Renoir's *Toni* and Welles' *F For Fake*. Their catalogue also includes box sets dedicated to Buster Keaton, Naruse Mikio and Lanzmann's *Shoah*, as well as films by such undeservedly little-known directors as Matsumoto Toshio (*Funeral Parade of Roses*) and Yamanaka Sadao (*Humanity and Paper Balloons*). The existence of such an adventurous operation testifies to the current maturity of the UK's DVD market.

Almost as impressive is the British Film Institute's BFI Video label. Though the BFI's initial venture into video distribution, in the form of Connoisseur Video, had a slapdash quality (dubbed versions of several Tati films, cut transfers of *The Gospel According to St Matthew* and *Weekend*), their DVD catalogue is extremely impressive, including lots of Kurosawa, a restored version of the original *Godzilla*, a collection of shorts by Evgenii Bauer and, at last, definitive editions of Tati's films. The BFI seem to have a particular skill at repairing the damage wreaked by Image Entertainment, issuing discs of *Il Bidone* and *Woman of the Dunes* that restore footage missing from the US discs. They even located an uncut print of *Salo* that includes a short sequence absent from Criterion's disc (which was, admittedly, an early release by that company). At the present time, extras on the BFI's discs tend to be a little on the sparse side – their single-disc edition of Visconti's *The Leopard* compares poorly with Criterion's

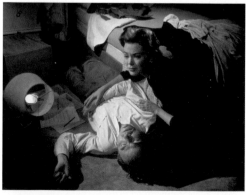

Nicholas Ray's **Bigger Than Life**

three-disc set. But the recent release of Nicholas Ray's *Bigger Than Life* includes several fascinating extras, which suggests that progress is being made on this front.

Tartan, another label dating back to the VHS era, have released an intriguing selection of documentaries, American independent films and world cinema, including impressive box sets of Edgar Reitz's *Heimat*, Ingmar Bergman (a remarkable thirty-disc collection), and Yasujiro Ozu (four volumes), as well as an extensive 'Asia Extreme' collection. Quality is generally high (though the first Ozu set contains some unattractive NTSC transfers) and extras often generous, though the label seems prone to easily avoidable errors, notably their initial releases of Wong Kar-wai's *As Tears Go By* and *Days of Being Wild*, both of which were cut and dubbed into Mandarin. Perhaps unable to forget their bad experiences releasing silent films in the days of VHS, Tartan have only recently entered silent waters again, with an Eisenstein box set (the first of three), Victor Sjöström's wonderful *The Phantom Carriage* and Benjamin Christensen's *Häxan: Witchcraft Through the Ages* (including the original score, two newly commissioned scores and the William Burroughs-narrated soundtrack).

Victor Sjöström's **The Phantom Carriage**

Artificial Eye have also made the leap from VHS to DVD, releasing a fine selection of mostly recent world cinema, alongside a handful of older titles, notably the complete works of Vigo and Tarkovsky. Highlights include

Kusturica's **Life is a Miracle**

Feuillade's *Fantomas* and a lavish two-disc edition of Kusturica's *Life is a Miracle*. Artificial Eye, like so many of the more enlightened UK DVD labels, tends to nurture relationships with individual filmmakers, releasing, for example, every film made by Turkish director Nuri Bilge Ceylan. They currently plan to release the entire oeuvre of Theo Angelopoulos, an ambitious project that testifies to this company's courage and taste.

Nuri Bilge Ceylan's **Climates**

Of those labels to have emerged in recent years, Second Run is among the most distinctive. Bravely ignoring commercial considerations, Second Run's catalogue is made up entirely of films which reflect the personal taste of its founder, Mehelli Modi: many titles from Czechoslovakia, Poland and Hungary (including several masterpieces by Miklós Jancsó), two classics of 1960s American independent cinema (Jim McBride's *David Holzman's Diary* and Shirley Clarke's *Portrait of Jason*), Avi Mograbi's *Avenge But One of My Two Eyes* (an acclaimed documentary on the Arab/Israeli conflict), Artur Aristakisyan's *Palms*, Apichatpong Weerasethakul's marvellous *Blissfully Yours* (which restores ten minutes of previously missing footage) and František Vláčil's 1967 film, *Marketa Lazarová*, which has been voted the greatest Czech film of all time. Most of these discs include intelligently assembled extras, often involving the participation of the films' directors, and, in the case of the Jancsós, a rarely seen series of shorts. Unfortunately, Second Run have suffered at the hands of the British Board of Film Classification, who removed several shots of horses falling over from Aleksander Ford's *Knights of the Teutonic Order*, a film which had not previously encountered censorship problems anywhere, even being shown uncut in Iran! Second Run's discs have a relatively low retail price and the healthy sales figures enjoyed by even their most obscure titles suggest that other companies would be well advised to adopt a more realistic approach to pricing.

František Vláčil's **Marketa Lazarová**

A case in point is the ICA. If Masters of Cinema can be seen as the British Criterion, ICA might be described as the UK equivalent of Image Entertainment. But whereas Image's catalogue consists largely of public-domain and exploitation product, the ICA's is filled with such typical art-house fare as Panahi's *Crimson Gold*, von Trier's *The Five Obstructions*, Khrzhanovsky's *4* and a documentary about

Jafar Panahi's **Crimson Gold**

Derrida. Common sense should tell us that there would be little to gain by treating the likely audience for these discs as idiots, but the ICA's releases are notable for their poor quality and lack of extras. The treatment of Hou Hsiao-hsien's masterpiece *Café Lumiere* is sadly typical. Wellspring's US DVD of this film contains an anamorphically enhanced transfer, high-quality optional English subtitles, an hour-long documentary, a trailer and interviews. The French and Japanese discs include all these extras, as well as a 30-minute deleted scene/alternate ending. By contrast, the ICA's disc contains no extras of any kind, a letterboxed transfer that is not anamorphically enhanced and burnt-in subtitles taken directly from the theatrical print, many of which are unreadable (the problem is particularly glaring during the opening scene). Some of the other ICA releases are admittedly a little better: their transfer of Kore-eda's *Nobody Knows* is attractive and anamorphically enhanced, with readable (though non-removable) subtitles. But on the whole, the ICA operated as if they were still living in the pre-DVD era, when VHS releases of this standard would have been considered quite acceptable. It was hardly surprising that the company decided to stop issuing DVDs in 2006, after discovering that their discs were consistently losing money (it seems unbelievable that the reason for this failure was not blatantly obvious to them). At the time of writing, the ICA have announced that they will shortly be resuming their DVD operation. One hopes they have learned from past mistakes.

Gus Van Sant's **Last Days**

Optimum have a wide-ranging catalogue that mixes Asian films, an interesting selection of world cinema (Godard's *À bout de souffle*, Erice's sublime *The Spirit of the Beehive*, a wonderful Jean Renoir box set), and several English-language titles, including a special edition of Bertolucci's *The Last Emperor* (containing two separate cuts of the film), Van Sant's *Last Days* and a series of films licensed from 20th Century Fox (Kazan's *Wild River*, Nicholas Ray's *The True Story of Jesse James*, the latter yet another victim of BBFC cuts). Picture quality, subtitles and extras are usually of a reasonably high quality, though the CinemaScope Fox titles are not anamorphically enhanced and Optimum have been criticised for not including optional English subtitles for the hearing impaired on their English-language releases (the single exception being *Fahrenheit 9/11*).

Then there are Anchor Bay, an exploitation specialist starting to feel its way into the art-house market, with box sets of Wenders and Herzog; Yume, whose catalogue includes Kurosawa's final film *Madadayo* (never before seen in the UK), several rare Buñuels and a selection of films by such cult Japanese directors as Seijun and Masamura; and Second Sight, who have released four Max Ophuls films with an intelligently assembled selection of extras and a fine box set of Fassbinder's acclaimed television series, *Berlin Alexanderplatz*.

The existence of so many small labels releasing art-house product allows the discerning viewer to free themselves from those shackles imposed by international film distribution: such masterpieces as Jia's *The World*, Hou's *Millennium Mambo* and Ferrara's *New Rose Hotel* have not had any UK exposure, but have been released on DVD in the US by, respectively, Zeitgeist Films, Palm Pictures and Sterling Home Entertainment, and can easily be ordered via the Internet. Korean director Hong Sang-soo may be virtually unknown in the UK, but four of his seven films are available on DVD in America on the Tai Seng, YA Entertainment and New Yorker Video labels, and English-subtitled discs of the remaining three can be obtained from Korea.

This is clearly a period of great uncertainty for the DVD market. There seems little doubt that there are a number of UK companies who will soon have to abandon their 'we couldn't care less' attitude and realise that the days when they might get away with releasing a markedly inferior product are over: who could reasonably be expected to pay for a truncated 158-minute, bare-bones, UK edition of Wim Wenders' *Until the End of the World* when a three-disc set of the complete five-hour version, released by the German label Arthaus, can be acquired for about the same price at the click of a mouse? But other questions are less easily answered: Will High Definition become the new standard? (Probably not, even if the format war is resolved.) Will electronic downloads eventually replace DVDs? (Quite possibly, though not in my lifetime.) Will the market for world cinema soon become saturated? (I suspect that precisely the opposite is true.) The only thing that can be said with any confidence is that it won't be too long before much of what has been written here will seem a thing of the very distant past.

BRAD STEVENS is a freelance film critic and the author of books on Abel Ferrara and Monte Helman.

DVD Round-Up by Ian Haydn Smith

In the wake of the Luis Buñuel retrospective at the British Film Institute early in 2007 (a similar retrospective has been programmed for the 2008 Berlin Film Festival), many of the great director's works are finally available on DVD.

The excellent **Luis Buñuel Collection** (Optimum, R2) covers the director's final years, displaying the work of a man unwilling to mellow with age. Beginning with *The Young One* (1960) and ending with his last film, the hilarious *That Obscure Object of Desire* (1977), this collection includes Buñuel's most popular work. Uncompromising in his disdain for religion, yet never quite able to free himself from the strictures of his Catholic upbringing, Buñuel was unafraid to explore the hypocrisy of his own double standards before turning that same mirror onto the world.

To leave Buñuel there would be a shame, as his earlier work is no less rewarding. Arrow have released **Exterminating Angel** (1961) and **Viridiana** (1962) (both R2), two of the director's finest works, the latter featuring one of Fernando Rey's most sublime

Au revoir les enfants

performances. Yume Pictures (R2) have released the Mexican comedies, **The Great Madcap** (1949) and **Ascent to Heaven** (1952), as well as the remarkable **Nazarin** (1959). Like Salvador Dalí, Buñuel was fascinated by dreams and *Ascent to Heaven* features one of his best dream sequences. Finally, Facets have unearthed two little-known dramas, **A Woman Without Love** (1952) and **The Brute** (1953) (both R1). They also plan to release other films from this period, including the wonderful *The River and Death* (1955).

The New Wave returns

Of the many movements in world cinema, few are as well represented as the *nouvelle vague*. The last year has seen numerous box sets released, offering highlights of these directors' work.

The **Claude Chabrol Collection** volume 1 & 2 (Arrow Films, R2) presents an eclectic mix, ranging from the late 1960s through to more recent work. Best are the earlier films, *Les Biches* (1968), *The Breach* (1970) and *Nada* (1974). *Le Boucher* (1970) might be Chabrol's most Hitchcockian work; few films capture such tension with so little action. Only the disappointing *Madame Bovary* (1991) seems out of place.

The two volumes of **Louis Malle** (Optimum, R2) feature one of the finest early works by these directors, *Lift to the Scaffold* (1958), as well as *Les Amants* (1958), *Au revoir les enfants* (1987) and the riveting *Lucien Lacombe* (1974), which saw the director become *persona non grata* in France for his assertion that not every one of his fellow countrymen was a member of the Resistance. Optimum have also released two **Jean-Luc Godard** collections (R2), which mostly cover the director's 'watchable' period in the 1960s, with two of the better films from the 1980s: *Passion* (1982) and *Détective* (1985). Though many of the films are available elsewhere, the selection for both box sets presents a solid introduction to a filmmaker who can be inspiring and infuriating, often within the same scene. Particularly welcome is *Made in USA* (1966), Godard's comedy thriller, which only hints at the political dogmatism that would come to dominate his films.

Eric Rohmer is somnambulant by comparison with Godard. His films are reflective, wry and beautifully observed. The **Eric Rohmer Collection** (Arrow Films, R2) includes the wonderful *Pauline at the Beach* (1983) and *The Green Ray* (1986), as well as some rare footage of the director in interview. Artificial Eye's releases bookend the Arrow collection. **The Early Works** (R2) includes Rohmer's debut, *The Sign of Leo* (1959), as well as two of his 'Moral Tales'. The later **Tales of Four Seasons** (R2) ranks alongside Rohmer's best work.

Jacques Rivette may be amongst the least widely appreciated directors of the New Wave but he is well served by two BFI releases, his first feature, **Paris Belongs to Us** (1960) and his most commercially successful film, **Céline and Julie Go Boating** (1974) (both R2). Alongside an astonishing array of extras, these films have been meticulously restored by the BFI, giving audiences the opportunity to watch two titles by arguably the finest director of his generation.

The BFI have also excelled with their release of Jean-Pierre Melville's wartime masterpiece, **Army of Shadows** (1969) (R2). One of the director's most personal films, with powerful performances by Jean-Pierre Cassel and Simone Signoret, it also ranks as one of the best films about the role of the Resistance during World War II. The insightful commentary

Jean-Pierre Melville's **Army of Shadows**

by Ginette Vincendeau contextualises the film in terms of French history and Melville's body of work. There is also a documentary on the Resistance narrated by Noel Coward. Criterion's version of **Les enfants terribles** (1950) (R1), Melville's adaptation of Cocteau, is also a delight. Restored with a meticulousness Criterion have long been praised for, the edition includes a superb essay by Gary Indiana (with drawings by Cocteau himself).

Finally, The **Henri-Georges Clouzot Collection** (Optimum, R2) features three films by the 'French Hitchcock'. Ranging from social realism (*Quai des Orfevres*, 1947) and unsettling drama (*Le Corbeau*, 1943) to one of the best white-knuckl thrillers ever made (*Wages of Fear*, 1953), the collection reaffirms Clouzot's position as one of French cinema's best writer-directors.

Japanese master

The work of Yasujiro Ozu, once almost impossible to see, is becoming more widely available through labels on both sides of the Atlantic. Although some collections overlap, there is now a fair selection from the mid- to late period of the director's career.

Tartan have done much to champion Ozu's work. Released over four volumes, **Ozu** (Tartan Video, R2) brings together some of his finest films. Sadly the quality of the first volume is quite poor (a particular disappointment as this contains 'The Noriko Trilogy'). However, it is to Tartan's credit that they still felt that the films were important enough to warrant their release and subsequent volumes show a marked improvement, culminating in volume four's pairing of *Late Autumn* (1960) with the tender *An Autumn Afternoon* (1962). Artificial Eye have released **Japanese Masters** (R2), which combines *The End of Summer* (1961) and *Floating Weeds* (1959) with Mizoguchi's *The Life of O-Haru* (1952) and *The Lady from Musashino* (1951). Although there is no clear reason why the films should be grouped together, they do offer a fine introduction to both directors' later works.

Late Autumn

New kid on the block

Criterion has launched a sister label, Eclipse, which brings together 'lost, forgotten, or overshadowed classics in simple, affordable editions'. Five volumes have been released so far and, like their more expansive sibling, have already proven their worth. **Late Ozu** (R1) features four of the films available in the collections above, with the very welcome addition of *Early Spring* (1956). One can only hope that an 'Early Ozu' collection is in the works, which will include *I Was Born, But...* (1932).

Eclipse have also released **The First Films of Samuel Fuller** (R1), which includes *I Shot Jesse James* (1949), *The Baron of Arizona* (1950) and Fuller's first great work, *The Steel Helmet* (1951). **Early Bergman** (R1) continues the Criterion connection with the Swedish master, offering a mixed bag, from the

The Steel Helmet

scripted-only *Crisis* (1946), to the impressive *Port of Call* (1948) and his first great film, *To Joy* (1950). All three box sets are packaged simply with no extras, which only emphasises Eclipse's remit: to offer quality films that, for the most part, were previously unavailable.

The trump card in Eclipse's deck so far is the excellent **The Documentaries of Louis Malle** (R1) which finally makes available his epic six-hour series, *Phantom India* (1969). If this weren't enough, there is Malle's companion piece, *Calcutta* (1969), two documentaries on America and three on France, including the hilarious *Vive le Tour* (1962), an affectionate short on the world's most arduous cycle race (also available as an extra on volume one of the Louis Malle collection).

To Joy

Documentary

The renaissance of documentary in cinemas is the tip of the iceberg when compared with their availability on DVD. Almost every label has realised the potential of what might once have been seen as a commercially unpalatable genre. With filmmakers like Martin Scorsese and Spike Lee (whose epic **When the Levees Broke** (HBO, R2) is essential viewing) venturing more and more into factual films, labels are becoming ever more daring in their releases.

Masters of Cinema (aka the British Criterion) have released two films by documentary pioneers, Albert and David Maysles. **Salesman** (1968) and **Grey Gardens** (1974) (both R0) are excellent examples of their work. If *Grey Gardens* is an intimate, eccentric portrait of two women leading a Haversham-like existence in a world that only exists in their memories, *Salesman* tears apart the fabric of the American Dream. Recently restored, both DVDs feature an interview with Albert Maysles and include fully illustrated booklets.

Masters of Cinema worked closely with Claude Lanzmann to produce the director-approved edition of **Shoah** (1985) (R0). Accompanied by a 184-page booklet, including an introduction by Stuart Liebman, this important film remains essential viewing and is a very welcome addition to the label's impressive list of UK releases. (The film has already been released in an equally impressive edition in the US by Criterion.)

Chris Marker has always skirted the boundary between fact and fiction. **La Jetée/Sans Soleil** (1962/83; Criterion, R1) combines his most famous and accessible works with a wealth of extra material to illuminate the career of one of cinema's most articulate essayists. A particular highlight is *Chris on Chris*, a video piece about Marker directed by critic and filmmaker, Chris Darke.

Gary Tarn was inspired by Marker in making **Black Sun** (2005; Second Run, R0), the remarkable story of Hugues de Montalembert, an artist who, living in New York in the late 1970s, was blinded in a mugging. Tarn expressionistically recreates de

Black Sun

Montalembert's life, from the days following the attack, as his sight diminished, through to his recovery and the solo journeys he has made around the world. Tarn achieves the seemingly impossible, enabling us to experience the world from the point of view of his subject.

Few films blur the line between fact and fiction as well as Mikhail Kalatozov's revolutionary tract, **I Am Cuba** (1964; Milestone, R1). Opening with the decadent opulence of Batista's regime, the film is divided into four parts, tracing the movement that rose up against the wealthy bourgeoisie. Both a fascinating historical document and a richly rewarding piece of filmmaking, the three-disc edition features a documentary about the director, an award-winning feature about the making of the film and a video interview with Martin Scorsese. All packaged in a replica Cuban cigar box!

Few directors have been as successful as Werner Herzog in crossing between fiction and documentary. The success of **Grizzly Man** (2005; Revolver Entertainment, R2) has seen the increasing availability of his more eclectic documentaries. **The Wild Blue Yonder** (2005), **Wheel of Time** (2003) and **Little Dieter Needs to Fly** (1997) (all Soda Pictures, R2) display Herzog's skill at balancing storytelling with more philosophical ruminations on the state of the world. *Little Dieter Needs to Fly* in particular (recently remade as the fiction-feature *Rescue Dawn*) displays Herzog's skill at conveying both horror and fascination at the human capacity for cruelty and endurance. There is also a six-disc box set, **Werner Herzog – Documentaries and Shorts** (Werner Herzog Film, R0), which features some of the director's finest films, including *The Flying Doctors of East Africa* (1969), *Wings of Hope* (2000) and *God's Angry Man* (1980). *Land of Silence and Darkness* (1971) shows Herzog at his most compassionate, relating the story of Fini Straubinger, a deaf and blind woman who has made it her mission to help others similarly afflicted. *Lessons of Darkness* (1992), like *The Wild Blue Yonder*,

Wheel of Time

could easily be mistaken for science fiction; however, Herzog's vision of a world on fire – the Kuwaiti oilfields that were set alight by a defeated Iraqi Army following the first Gulf War – lacks the optimism of the more recent film, presenting us with a landscape we barely recognise as our own. Through these works, we witness Herzog's dark view of the world, which is only occasionally alleviated by human kindness. One of the best releases of the year, it is only available via Werner Herzog's website (www.wernerherzog.com).

Hollywood

Not as well known as it should be, **Hellzapoppin'** (1941; Second Sight, R2) may be the most delirious film Hollywood has ever made. With more gags per minute than a Marx Brothers film, Ole Olsen and Chic Johnson transferred their manic stage act to the screen with aplomb. Employing every cinematic device to hand, they eschew a coherent narrative in favour of a series of set pieces that beggar belief.

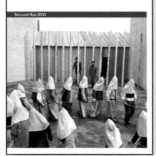

If *Hellzapoppin'* revels in the sheer delight of filmmaking, **Ace in the Hole** (1951; Criterion, R1), Billy Wilder's bleak satire, shines a light on the cynicism of the modern press. Pre-dating the media circuses that are now routine, Kirk Douglas excels as the amoral hack, willing to pay any price to get his story. Unavailable for a long time, Criterion's resplendent transfer is accompanied by a whole disc of extras, including a documentary on Wilder, an interview with Douglas, a video afterword by Spike Lee and new essays by critic Molly Haskell and filmmaker Guy Maddin.

Another 1950s classic, **Bigger Than Life** (1956; BFI, R2) is arguably Nicholas Ray's finest achievement and James Mason's most accomplished performance. A superb transfer, capturing the beauty of Joe MacDonald's Scope photography, the DVD also includes a discussion between critic Jonathan Rosenbaum and filmmaker Jim Jarmusch, who rightly deserve their own film programme.

Silent classics

The work of Louis Feuillade is finally available on DVD in two excellent collections. **Fantômas** (1913; Artificial Eye, R2) may be the best known of the director's films, featuring the mysterious master criminal who strikes fear into the heart of Paris. On the opposite side of the law, **Judex** (1916; Flicker Alley, R1) shows a progression in Feuillade's style and in the complexity of the central character. Increasingly dreamlike and sprightly in its pacing, it is the highlight in the catalogue of an excellent new label, Flicker Alley.

Masters of Cinema have released most of Murnau's major works in pristine editions. The pride of their silent collection, however, is G. W. Pabst's **Diary of a Lost Girl** (1929) (R0). Beautifully restored, Louise Brooks is radiant in one of her finest performances. As Henri Langlois once said of her, 'she embodies within herself all that the cinema rediscovered in its final silent years: a perfect naturalness, a complete simplicity'.

Cult and experimenta

Other Cinema is one of the most vital labels in promoting experimental films. Whether it's alternative documentaries about the Unabomber (*The Net*, 2004), the history of airline hijackings through the prism of Don DeLillo's writings (*Dial H-I-S-T-O-R-Y*, 1998) or an entire DVD of kitsch adverts and public information films (*The 70s Dimension*), the label is an essential barometer of American underground filmmaking. The best of their collection are the films of Craig Baldwin and in particular the astonishing **Tribulation 99: Alien Anomalies Under America** (1992) (R1). An expert at giving new meaning to found footage, Baldwin constructs an anarchic science-fiction film that satirises America's foreign policy in Latin America. Few filmmakers have expressed their disdain of their government as articulately or imaginatively as Baldwin does here.

The National Film Board of Canada calls its authoritative collection of Norman McLaren's films, **Norman McLaren: The Master's Edition** (available in the UK through Soda Pictures, R2), 'a jewel in the crown of film history'. And right they are. It is something of a misnomer to place McLaren's formidable body of work in this section, but it is a difficult proposition to figure out where one could rightly place it. No animator – and few filmmakers for that matter – have displayed the range that McLaren did for fifty years. The best of his work, *Neighbours* (1952), *A Phantasy* (1952) and *Pas de Deux* (1968) defy description. The box set of seven DVDs includes 58 films, 38 of which have been digitally restored, as well as unfinished films, a fascinating documentary and an accompanying booklet.

From the sublime to the utterly ridiculous, **The Russ Meyer Collection** (Arrow Films, R2) presents every film you ever wanted to watch by him, but were always afraid to rent from your local video store. This 18-film box set is a marathon of, well, epic proportions. Though

Meyer's skill as a filmmaker rarely registered as more than adequate, films such as *Finders Keepers, Lovers Weepers* (1968), *Supervixens* (1975) and *Faster, Pussycat... Kill! Kill!* (1965) do possess their own unique charm.

Homecoming

Joe Dante has always threatened to make a satirical masterpiece about the American condition. **Homecoming** (Anchor Bay, R1) might just be it. Part of the 'Masters of Horror' series, Dante has the dead soldiers of an unspecified, very unpopular war rise from their graves to vote against the hawkish President. Updating Romero's 'Dead' series to the current Iraq conflict, Dante attacks politicians, the media and a country's apathy, with a vengeance.

The best of Europe

Pier Paolo Pasolini Vol 1 & 2 (Tartan Video, R2) presents a comprehensive overview of the director's work during the 1960s. Along with the more popular titles *Accatone* (1961), *Hawks and Sparrows* (1966) and *Oedipus Rex* (1967) are the fascinating documentary *Love Meetings* (1965) and *Pigsty* (1969), Pasolini's most controversial film after *Salo*. The collections – arguably Tartan's finest release – include a novel and a memoir by the director.

Having long been unavailable on DVD, it is now possible to see two films by controversial Polish filmmaker, Andrzej Żuławski. **Third Part of the Night** (1971; Second Run, R0) is a hallucinatory account of one man's struggle to survive during World War II. **The Devils** (1972;

Facets, R1) is no less traumatic. Set during the Prussian Army's invasion of Poland in 1793, the 1972 film was banned in Poland until 1988. Rich in allegory and presenting a nightmarish vision of the world, the films may not be to everyone's taste, but they remain singular visions in contemporary European cinema.

Paul Verhoeven's **Black Book** (Tartan Video, R2) might be the most entertaining film ever made about the Nazi occupation of the Netherlands. Outdoing *Soldier of Orange* in every way, and ably supported by two charismatic performances from Carice van Houten and Sebastian Koch, Verhoeven has produced his most accomplished film since *The Fourth Man*. His politics remain deeply suspect, particularly his fascination with fascism, but there is no denying his ability to entertain.

Black Book

However, Verhoeven's film pales against the welcome release of **Overlord** (1975; Criterion, R1), Stuart Cooper's almost forgotten masterpiece about a 20-year-old's journey from basic training to the D-Day landings. Avoiding bombast, Cooper's intense drama is a moving account of the impact of war on one young man. Once again, Criterion have excelled with the transfer and an abundance of extras, collated with the participation of Cooper and the Imperial War Museum.

Personal best

Amongst the many impressive releases over the last year, a few still managed to stand out. Both Criterion and Masters of Cinema released Orson Welles' last great film, **F For**

Fake (1974). Like Chris Marker's work, Welles' film is almost impossible to categorise: part documentary, part cine-essay, part private joke. On the Masters of Cinema edition (R0), Jonathan Rosenbaum does his best to pin the film down, finally deciding that it's probably best to just watch the film over and over to revel in its director's delight at the process of making films.

Another film almost impossible to define, Artur Aristakisyan's **Palms** (1992; Second Run, R0) proves that it is still possible to be genuinely original. Ten love stories set amongst the homeless and destitute of Moldova's capital, the film is neither fiction nor documentary. Narrated by Aristakisyan as a letter to his unborn son, *Palms* is a magnificent achievement.

Kasaba

Nuri Bilge Ceylan's **The Early Works** (Artificial Eye, R2) offers the chance to see the first two films by one of contemporary cinema's finest directors. *Kasaba* (1997) already shows signs of Ceylan's mastery of framing. Told in four parts and from the perspective of two children, it records exchanges between extended family members in a small Turkish town. *Clouds of May* (1999) lies closer to *Uzak* (*Distant*) in its account of a filmmaker attempting to balance his art with his family life.

One of the most eagerly awaited releases, **Killer of Sheep** (1977; Milestone, R1) is Charles Burnett's portrait of black life in Watts, Los Angeles. Stan works in a local slaughterhouse. Numbed by his daily encounter with death, he tries to take pleasure in the minutiae of everyday life. Influenced by the work of the neo-realists and imbued with a lyricism that belies the drudgery of his characters' lives, Burnett's film is a genuinely beautiful and moving experience.

The Ken Loach Collection (Sixteen Films, R2) covers the director's career from the 1970s to the present day (absent is much of his 1980s work and the groundbreaking 1970s drama, *Days of Hope*). Divided into two box sets, the sixteen films show a filmmaker committed to tackling social and political issues, often attracting the opprobrium of those in power (it's no secret that Loach was an object of aversion within Margaret Thatcher's cabinet). The best of his films, such as *Raining Stones* (1993), *Land and Freedom* (1995) and *The Navigators* (2001), are impassioned calls for social change. Avoiding the epic, his work focuses on the individual as a symbol of greater problems within society. Rarely missing the mark and never irrelevant, Ken Loach is an essential voice in the filmmaking of the UK.

Finally, **Distant Voices, Still Lives** (1988; BFI, R2). Terrence Davies' stunning feature debut draws from his experiences as a young boy growing up in Liverpool during the 1940s and 1950s. Littered with music, yet not a musical, Davies' film refuses to paint a nostalgic portrait of post-war Britain, yet never revels in self-pity. The result is a moving, elegiac and visually sumptuous film from one of Britain's great directors.

Distant Voices, Still Lives

Key DVD labels

Ian Haydn Smith profiles the essential distributors of world cinema on DVD

Arrow Films

One of the most interesting UK labels with releases from across the spectrum of world cinema. Extras are mostly basic but the transfer quality is generally excellent.
www.arrowfilms.co.uk

Artificial Eye

A major UK label, whose catalogue reflects the best in contemporary and art-house cinema.
www.artificialeye.com

BFI

The British Film Institute's DVD label spans classic European and Hollywood cinema as well as more experimental fare. Recent releases have shown a marked increase in the quantity and quality of their extras.
www.filmstore.bfi.org.uk

Criterion

The benchmark of excellence amongst DVD labels, whose stunning back catalogue is matched by the plethora of extras that accompany each film.
www.criterion.com

Facets

A US distribution company whose own independent label features an eclectic and impressive selection of films, with a back catalogue hundreds long.
www.facets.org

Flicker Alley

A promising label whose small collection of films and documentaries offer a fine introduction to early cinema.
www.flickeralley.com

Kino International

One of the oldest US labels. Recent releases have seen Kino follow the approach of the best DVD labels with higher production values.
www.kino.com

Masters of Cinema

MoC match Criterion's quality with a growing list of films, featuring extensive extras and valuable booklet essays.
www.eurekavideo.co.uk/moc

Milestone

One of the most prominent boutique distributors in the US, Milestone now stands alongside Criterion as an essential label and a marker of quality DVD releases.
www.milestonefilms.com

Optimum World

Of the major UK labels, Optimum World features one of the most expansive array of films. Extras are basic but the transfer quality is generally high.
www.optimumreleasing.com

Other Cinema

Conspiracy theories abound amongst this wonderfully eccentric collection of underground and experimental films from this superb San Fransisco-based label.
www.othercinemadvd.com

Second Run DVD

A relatively new distributor, championing films by many directors who have dropped off the cinematic radar, making the label an essential port of call for discerning cineastes.
www.secondrundvd.com

Soda Pictures

A distinctive UK label releasing lesser-known titles from the world of contemporary cinema, including feature films and documentaries.
www.sodapictures.com

Tartan Video

In addition to their extensive range of Asian films, Tartan boasts an impressive back catalogue featuring giants of European film.
www.tartanvideo.com

World Survey

6 continents | 100 countries | 1,000s of films...

Afghanistan Sandra Schäfer

Film production in Afghanistan is undergoing a lengthy process of reconstruction. The only available funding bodies for film are international charities. In addition, most directors have second jobs; some are employed as teachers, members of the police force or even diplomats. A few filmmakers have followed the lead of Roya Sadat and Saba Sahar in setting up their own production companies, producing their films independently or in partnership with other organisations, both domestic and international. The state-owned film institute, Afghan-Film, is still responsible for funding many projects, as is state television and the more recently created private television channels.

There are currently only ten cinemas in operation in Afghanistan, seven of which are in Kabul. A visit to the cinema is still perceived by some as immoral, hence many Afghans prefer to watch films at home; this is the most viable solution for Afghan women in particular.

Educational films dominate cinema pro-grammes, along with action films and the odd documentary. Latif Ahmadi's humorous **Ruschany** is a case in point. In it, an illiterate

Latif Ahmadi's **Ruschany**

woman succeeds in convincing her husband that she should learn to read and write. An engineer by profession, Ahmadi produced the film with the help of UNESCO, a Japanese cooperation agency and a Christian charity. It was edited on the director's home computer.

Film producer Azim Najm made the short film, **Terror** (*Dashat*), as a reaction to a 2006 suicide attack on a school in Kabul. In order to help his family out of financial misery, a young boy agrees to become a suicide bomber for the Taliban, aware that, due to his involvement with the group, from the moment he puts on the jacket filled with explosives there is no future for him.

In the same year, the Goethe Institute in Kabul, in cooperation with the Centre Culturel Français, funded the documentary project 'Les Ateliers Varan'. Working with students from Kabul University the workshop produced ten short documentaries, each focusing on a specific problem in the capital. One of the highlights was Nazifa Zakizada's portrait of an all-girl Taekwondo team, **The Path to Follow** (*Edame Rah*). Between warming up and sparring, the girls discuss the problems they face, both at home and in the world at large. In **Issa the Wrestler** (*Yamak Pahlawan Issa*), Reza Hosseini records the anxiety and pain suffered by a family struggling to deal with their traumatised son, following his release from prison. Hosseini observes the family carrying on with their everyday activities while Issa lies on his mattress, seemingly unable to move. Only towards the end of the film does it become apparent that Issa's feet are actually shackled, preventing him from moving, perhaps out of concern that he may hurt himself or those around him.

Other films from the collective include those on attempts by labourers to find work, an electrician struggling to cope with the demands of his workload, and everyday life in a care home for women with mental illness.

Sayed Fahim Hashimy, who had previously worked as a cameraman on Roya Sadat's 2004 feature, *Three Dots*, directed the award-winning short, **The Way** (*Rah*). Told through a series of long shots Hashimy shows the transformation of a young boy into a thief. Redemption comes with the arrival of a young girl, who smiles at the boy and offers him an apple. He lowers his rifle to take the gift. Hashimy took part in the 2007 Talent Campus at the Berlin International Film Festival.

David Edwards, Gregory Whitmore and Maliha Zulfacar's **Kabul Transit**

A film that managed to break international boundaries is the documentary **Kabul Transit** directed by Maliha Zulfacar in collaboration with David Edwards and Gregory Whitmore. For this Afghan/US co-production, the filmmakers gained unprecedented access to many high-security areas – including the US embassy – as well as public places to record the problems faced by those living in the Afghan capital. Accompanying an employee of the Ministry of the Interior, a NATO commander, students at Kabul University and a former policeman who now works as a day labourer, the film is a fascinating account of life in an occupied country. One student in the film comments on the presence of the NATO soldiers: 'As an Afghan I accept that they are here for our safety, but they should not be so tense. They seem to think that we Afghans

Postcards from Tora Bora, *directed by Kelly Dolak and Wazmah Osman*

are wild animals.' The director Maliha Zulfacar is currently working as Afghan ambassador in Berlin.

The year's best films
Kabul Transit (David Edwards, Gregory Whitmore, Maliha Zulfacar)
Postcards from Tora Bora (Kelly Dolak and Wazmah Osman)
The Path to Follow (Nazifa Zakizada)
Ruschany (Ingenieur Latif Ahmadi)

Quote of the year
'I make films to educate men.'
SABA SAHAR, *Afghanistan's first female producer and actress to release a film*

Directory
All Tel/Fax numbers begin (+93)
Afghan-Film, Grand Masood Ave 2, Kabul. Tel: 20 210279.
Filmmakers Union, Kabul. Tel: 79 375530. cinemaf@hotmail.com.
Foundation for Culture and Civil Society, Salang Watt 869, PO Box 5965, Kabul. Tel: 70 278905. culture@afghanfccs.org.

SANDRA SCHÄFER is a filmmaker and curator. She co-curated the *Kabul/Teheran 1979* film festival in Berlin in 2003 and is co-editor of a book of the same title. With Elfe Brandenburger she made the documentary *Passing the Rainbow* about actresses and political methods

Algeria Roy Armes

Domestic filmmaking in Algeria has ground virtually to a halt in the new millennium, with few directors continuing to live and work in the country. Mohamed Chouikh is one of those who remained throughout the difficulties of the past decade, ably assisted by his sister and editor, Yamina Bakir-Chouikh, who also directed one of the more striking films of the period, *Rachida*. Mohamed Chouikh's new feature, **Hamlet of Women** (*Douar des femmes*), is an unexpected surprise: a comedy that plays with role-reversal, as the women of a village threatened by outsiders take up arms to protect themselves, while their men are away, working in a local factory.

Djamila Sahraoui's **Barakat!**

The immigrant community in France have been increasingly attracted to the prospect of filming in North Africa, which they either never knew (because they were born in France) or left when they were young. Djamila Sahraoui, a resident of France since 1975 and an acclaimed director of a series of Algerian-set documentaries, chose two characters' exploration of hitherto unknown Algerian realities as the format for her first fictional feature, **Bararkat!** Bourlem Gherdjou has chosen a more action-packed variant of the journey of exploration and discovery with **Zaina, Horsewoman of the Atlas** (*Zaïna, cavalière de l'Atlas*), the follow-up to his award-winning debut, *Living in Paradise*. Caught up in a savage family feud after the murder of her mother, Zaïna develops the relationship with her previously absent father, accompanying him on a horse trek through the magnificent scenery of the Atlas Mountains, to Marrakesh. Upon her arrival, despite her age and inexperience, she wins a prestigious tribal horse race.

Rabah Ameur-Zaimèche, who has lived in France since the age of two, directed the

Mohamed Chouikh's **Hamlet of Women**

feature-length docu-drama, **Bled Number One**. He also stars as Kamel, a man released from a French prison and into an Algeria he does not recognise. He eventually finds himself in a remote village inhabited by Ameur-Zaimèche's own distant relatives. As with his first, Paris-based feature, *Wesh wesh, qu'est-ce qui se passe?*, Ameur-Zaimèche rejects conventional narrative. Kamel's own motives – beyond a vague desire to be elsewhere – are unclear and he fails to make genuine contact with either the younger members of his extended family, who are drawn towards puritanical Islamism, or their elders, who set up roadblocks to control local traffic. His interest is mainly focused on his cousin Louisa, who wants to leave her husband and pursue a career as a singer.

Rabah Ameur-Zaimèche's **Bled Number One**

Nadir Moknèche is an enigma. Though raised in Algeria until the age of eighteen and the director of three features that deal with Algerian issues, his work nonetheless presents an outsider's view of the country. The way he prepares for each production goes some way in accounting for this. He recreated the Algiers of 1993 in Tangier in order to shoot his first feature, *Madame Osmane's Harem*. His subsequent productions – *Viva Algeria* and his most recent film, **A Paloma Sweet** (*Délice Paloma*) – have been filmed on location in Algeria with noteworthy Algerian actresses. However, he chooses to work with

French crews and use French dialogue. *A Paloma Sweet* presents a lively and surprising insight into a very different emerging Algeria, where fraud and corruption are commonplace. Structured as a series of flashbacks, it tells the life story of a woman released from prison after three years.

Mehdi Charef is more at ease depicting Algerian life. He left at the age of ten, experiencing life as an adolescent in Parisian suburbs, before emerging as a novelist and filmmaker in the mid-1980s. While his previous feature, *Keltoum's Daughter*, was a conventional tale of a young, half-Arab girl's 'return' to an unknown Algeria, **Gallic Cartridges** (*Cartouches gauloises*) is a more deeply felt reconstruction of Charef's own childhood. Taking place during the last months of French rule in Algeria, the film deals with an ethnically mixed group of ten-year-olds. The protagonist, Ali, is Algerian, while his best friend, Nico, is of French descent. But mainland France is as unknown to Nico, who is destined to return there with his parents, as it is to Ali. Ali's particular situation, as the son of a resistance fighter who has a job selling the local French-language newspaper, allows Charef to paint a vivid picture of the mixed loyalties and commitments of a society breaking apart under the pressure of increasing division and violence.

The most widely distributed film by a director with Algerian roots was Rachid Bouchareb's

Rachid Bouchareb's **Days of Glory**

Rachid Bouchareb's **Days of Glory**

Days of Glory (*Indigènes*), which opened the Journées Cinématographiques de Carthage, in Tunis in November 2006. Bouchareb belongs to the same immigrant generation as Mehdi Charef and, though he began his film career in the mid-1980s with a film about young migrants, he has constantly shown a desire to cover a wider range of subjects. Highlighting the involvement of soldiers from North Africa in the liberation of France in 1943, *Days of Glory* focuses on four very diverse individuals who all volunteered to help free the 'motherland' they have never seen from the Nazi occupation. The film traces their progress from Italy through France to Alsace, detailing their encounters along the way. A celebration of human commitment, *Days of Glory* is a welcome reminder of the efforts of African soldiers, whose role in history has been overlooked.

ROY ARMES is Emeritus Professor of Film at Middlesex University and author of many studies of cinema, most recently *Postcolonial Images: Studies in North African Film* (2005)

The year's best film
Days of Glory (Rachid Bouchareb)
Gallic Cartridges (Mehdi Charef)

Quote of the year
'The cinema must pay attention to the spectator, it must have a dimension which goes beyond the historical context, so as to plunge into the heart of what is human, closest to what touches us most, depite all our differences.' *Director* RACHID BOUCHAREB *on his film* Days of Glory

Directory
All Tel/Fax numbers begin (+213)
Cinémathèque Algérienne, 49 rue Larbi Ben M'Hidi, Algiers. Tel: (2) 737 548. Fax: (2) 738 246. www.cinematheque.art.dz

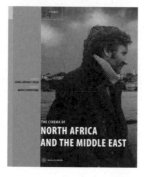

Argentina Alfredo Friedlander

There is a widespread feeling amongst the public and critics that the quality as well as the quantity of recently produced Argentine features has declined in the last couple of years. The number of Argentine films released (including co-productions) has levelled at around seventy per year, although that figure should have been closer to the hundred or so actually produced. Clearly, not all local films guarantee enough of an audience to justify their release.

The 22nd International Film Festival of Mar del Plata was overseen by director Miguel Pereira for the fifth and last time. Mario Monicelli was the guest of honour (2006 saw Susan Sarandon and Tim Robbins as guests), presenting his most recent movie **The Roses of the Desert** (*Le Rose del deserto*). The Jury, headed by American director Charles Burnett, awarded Cesc Gay's Spanish film **Fiction** (*Ficció*) the Golden Astor. The Ernesto Ché Guevara prize went to Argentine Nicolás Prividera's first film, **M**. A poignant documentary, it follows Prividera's quest to find out how and why his mother disappeared during the military dictatorship.

In 2008, the festival will return to its original November slot, distancing it from the Buenos Aires International Film Festival (BAFICI), which takes place in April. BAFICI's ninth year witnessed its largest roster to date – over 400 films were screened – with the Jury choosing So Yong Kim's Canadian immigration drama, **In Between Days**, as the best international film.

Argentina's strong presence at international film festivals continued. Two films were in competition at Cannes. Lucía Puenzo's debut, **XXY**, deservedly won the International

Inés Efrón in **XXY**

Critics' Week competition. It is also Argentina's foreign-language film choice for the Academy Awards. The story of a 15-year-old teenager who carries the heavy secret of being a hermaphrodite, it features an outstanding performance by Inés Efrón and sensitive direction by Puenzo. Ana Katz's **A Stray Girlfriend** (*Una novia errante*) was presented as part of the 'Un Certain Regard' competition. It tells the story of a young woman, impressively portrayed by Katz, who is abandoned by her boyfriend in a solitary resort with very peculiar inhabitants.

Ariel Rotter's **The Other**

Argentine films also performed well at Berlin. Ariel Rotter's **The Other** (*El otro*) won the Jury Grand Prix (Silver Bear), with Julio Chávez walking away with the Silver Bear for Best Actor. In 2006, Rodrigo Moreno's **The Minder** (*El custodio*), also featuring Chávez, won the Alfred-Bauer Prize. Curiously, though featuring outstanding performances by their lead, both films lacked action and performed poorly at the local box office.

When faced with the difficult task of choosing the best Argentine films of 2007, it is impossible to overlook the strength of some recent documentaries. Eduardo Walger's **Mothers** (*Madres*) is the account of sixteen Mothers of the Plaza de Mayo and their efforts to rescue the memory of their 'disappeared' children, a euphemism for their murder during the 1976–83 regime. **Next Past Times** (*Los próximos pasados*) presents a fascinating portrait of the Mexican painter David Alfaro Siqueiros who in 1933 painted, in the basement of an eccentric Argentine millionaire's mansion, a mural that is today locked in five containers and at the mercy of the weather. Finally, Fernando E. Solanas's **Latent Argentina** (*Argentina latente*) is the third of a series of four documentaries which looks optimistically at the potential resources Argentina has at its disposal in the field of science and technology. Although released in 2006, mention should also be made of José Luis García's **Cándido López** (*Cándido López, los campos de batalla*), the compelling story

Ricardo Darin and Martín Hodara's **The Signal**

of a painter and soldier who participated in the terrible war that saw Argentina, Uruguay and Brazil locked in a violent conflict against Paraguay, 150 years ago.

Two of Argentina's most established directors, Fabián Bielinsky and Eduardo Mignogna passed away during 2006. Both cast, in more than one film, Ricardo Darin, who has become the country's most popular actor. Darin, together with Martín Hodara (who had also worked with the two deceased filmmakers), has directed **The Signal** (*La señal*). Based on a book written by Mignogna, it is set in 1952 when a mediocre private detective (portrayed by Darin) is hired by a beautiful woman. The film is a thriller where nothing is what it seems, and one of the few Argentine productions with a solid performance at the box office.

Daniel Burman's **Family Law**

Carlos Sorin's **The Road to San Diego** (*El camino de San Diego*) proved to be something of a disappointment. Employing non-professional actors again, the road movie follows Tati (Ignacio Benítez) who is obsessed with Diego Maradona and is determined to offer him as a gift a tree with a silhouette that resembles the soccer player. Daniel Burman had more success with **Family Law** (*Derecho de familia*), the story of two lawyers, father and son, with very different approaches to life.

The Antenna (*La antena*), an experimental black and white film directed by Esteban Sapir,

Esteban Sapir's **The Antenna**

tells the story of a powerful businessman who, as the owner of the sole TV channel in a city, endeavours to convince or force consumers to buy goods produced by his own factories. The film displays the strong influence of German expressionist cinema.

2007 closes with an increase in the number of releases, close to 270 films; about half will be from the USA, taking an even higher share of the box office (about 75%). Domestic features will again represent slightly over 10% of the box office, but a much higher figure (25%) of the total number of releases. The only other significant country whose cinematic output features significantly is France (10%), with the notable absence of European territories such as Italy, Spain and, to a lesser degree, the United Kingdom.

Many new Argentine films (a fair number of them documentaries) will continue to be screened at one or two cinemas where they will presumably stay for only a few weeks. This picture will not change in the next few years, unless there is a radical change to the local subsidy system.

ALFREDO FRIEDLANDER is a member of the Asociación de Cronistas Cinematográficos de Argentina. He writes regularly for www. leedor.com, and regularly presents movies at the 51-year-old Cine Club Núcleo.

The year's best films
XXY (Lucía Puenzo)
Mothers (Eduardo Walger)
The Signal (Ricardo Darin, Martín Hodara)
Buenos Aires, 1977 (Adrián Caetano)
Family Law (Daniel Burman)

Quote of the year
'I really did not expect such a welcome in this country, it is too much. Today, more than ever, I think that here in Argentina cinema is a life force.' MARIO MONICELLI, *the International Film Festival of Mar del Plata's guest of honour*

Directory
All Tel/Fax numbers begin (+54)
Critics Association of Argentina, Maipu 621 Planta Baja, 1006 Buenos Aires. Tel/Fax: 4322 6625. cinecronistas@yahoo.com.
Directors Association of Argentina (DAC), Lavalle 1444, 7° Y, 1048 Buenos Aires. Tel/Fax: 4372 9822. dac1@infovia.com.ar. www.dacdirectoresdecine. com.ar.
Directors of Photography Association, San Lorenzo 3845, Olivos, 1636 Buenos Aires. Tel/Fax: 4790 2633. adf@ba.net. www.adfcine.com.ar.
Exhibitors Federation of Argentina, Ayacucho 457, 1° 13, Buenos Aires. Tel/Fax: 4953 1234. empcinemato@infovia.com.ar.
Film University, Pasaje Guifra 330, 1064 Buenos Aires. Tel: 4300 1413. Fax: 4300 1581. fuc@ucine. edu.ar. www.ucine.edu.ar.
General Producers Association, Lavalle 1860, 1051 Buenos Aires. Tel/Fax: 4371 3430. argentinasonofilm@impsat1.com.ar.
National Cinema Organisation (INCAA), Lima 319, 1073 Buenos Aires. Tel: 6779 0900. Fax: 4383 0029. info@incaa.gov.ar.
Pablo Hicken Museum and Library, Defensa 1220, 1143 Buenos Aires. Tel: 4300 5967. www.museudelcinedh@yahoo.com.ar.
Producers Guild of Argentina (FAPCA), Godoy Cruz 1540, 1414 Buenos Aires. Tel: 4777 7200. Fax: 4778 0046. recepcion@patagonik.com.ar.
Sindicato de la Industria Cinematográfia de Argentina (SICA), Juncal 2029, 1116 Buenos Aires. Tel: 4806 0208. Fax: 4806 7544. sica@sicacine. com.ar. www.sicacine.com.ar.

Armenia Susanna Harutyunyan

With the privatisation of the largest state-controlled film studio, Hayfilm (also known as Armenfilm), in August 2005, Armenian cinema entered the 'modern age'. According to the agreement, the new owner of Hayfilm Studio, investing in up-to-date technical equipment, is to complete all projects that are in pre-production, currently shooting or in post-production. However, this remains only a paper agreement for the moment, as no money has yet been invested in the current slate of films being produced. Nor has renovation begun on the studio, which is in a severe state of dilapidation.

Soon after the privatisation of Armenfilm, the Armenian National Film Centre was founded. A state-funded organisation, it will adhere to the strictures of government policy on film and is responsible for the allocation of state subsidies for film production, where most of the financing for films comes from. In 2008, the state subsidies for the national film industry will be approximately $1.5 million; 54% will be invested in feature-film production, 24% in animated films and 22% in the 'Hayk' State Documentary Studio. Interestingly, subsidies for documentary films have increased by 300% compared with previous years.

Narine Mkrtchyan & Arsen Azatyan's **The Return of the Prodigal Son**

In production...

Among projects completed in 2007 were the docu-drama **Nakhsho** by Harutyun Khachatryan, whose previous film, **Return of the Poet** (2006), was presented at over thirty international film festivals, and **The Return of the Prodigal Son** (*Anarak Vordu Veradardze*) by Narine Mkrtchyan and Arsen Azatyan.

The Return of the Prodigal Son is the story of a successful family and the single, wayward son. The father is rich and seemingly wise, the eldest son a successful businessman and the youngest not old enough to decide upon his role in life. By contrast, the middle son has drifted aimlessly through his life. Having run away from home in an attempt to find some purpose to his existence, he returns, defeated. Accepting that he has missed opportunities and lost his way, he wants to start over, only to discover that friends and neighbours are unwilling to give him a second chance.

Nakhsho takes us back to the the post-war period of the mid-1990s, when the extent of the destruction wreaked by the Armenian/Azeri conflict had only just begun to be realised. Khachatryan skillfully builds a portrait of real characters who have lived through a turbulent period of war and political conflict. Although the wounds inflicted have yet to heal, the film displays no aggression or hatred, with the director's documentary background seeking a form of 'pure cinema' through which to communicate the hardship suffered by a small Armenian village. Daily life in thevillage, including attempts by refugees to settle into their new home, is seen through the eyes of a wild buffalo caught near the border. We witness the joys and disappointments of daily life and how refugees try to attempt some semblance of normality amidst the disruption that conflict has brought to their lives.

Three other films currently in production are set in the 1990s, a difficult period for Armenia, following the collapse of the Soviet Union, and the subsequent economic, political and energy crises. Albert Mkrtchyan's **Dawn** (*Aygabats*), set in Gyumri during the conflict in Nagorno-Karabagh, is a portrait of family life and the effect war has upon it. Karo Boryan's **Idyll** (*Idillia*) focuses on an intellectual whose unhappiness with his life in Armenia affects his relationship with his wife and friends. And Ruben Kochar creates a very different conflict in **Metamorphose** (*Kerparanapokhutyun*), an Armenia-USA co-production, in which a man's wife becomes lost in her own, internalised world.

Armenia's image as a film centre for the region is due in no small part to the success of its film festival, the Golden Apricot. The fourth Golden Apricot Yerevan International Film Festival took place 9–14 July and hosted the first Regional Co-production Forum, during which twelve projects from seven countries – Armenia, Azerbaijan, Georgia, Turkey, Romania, Russia and Serbia – were presented. Two of the projects received development grants of €5,000 (from the Hubert Buls Fund) and $5,000 (from the Golden Apricot Fund). A number of the other projects also attracted interest from visiting producers. For the first time, an Armenian film, Mikayel Vatinyan's **Joan and the Voices** (produced by Armine Anda), was submitted and selected for the Pusan International Film Festival. Moreover, the film won the Pusan Project Award ($20,000) and has effectively opened the Asian film market to Armenia. Vardan Hovhannisyan's documentary, **A Story of People in War and Peace**, a favourite at the festival, won four awards. Soon after, it was nominated for the 2007 Asia Pacific Screen Awards.

Hovhannes Galstyan's Bonded Parallels

The year's best films
Return of the Poet (Harutyun Khachatryan)
A Story of People in War and Peace (Vardan Hovhannisyan)

Quote of the year
'From the moment I first visited Armenia in 1991, I knew that this country would have a profound influence on me. I had already been introduced to the soul of this astonishing culture through the great films of Paradjanov, Peleshian and Malian (amongst many others), but it was my physical contact with this land and its people which was to mark me so deeply.' **ATOM EGOYAN**, *President of the 2007 Golden Apricot Yerevan International Film Festival*

Directory
All Tel/Fax numbers begin (+374)
Armenian National Cinematheque, 25A Tbilisyan Highway, 375052 Yerevan. Tel: 285 406. filmadaran@yahoo.com.
Armenian Union of Filmmakers, 18 Vardanants, Yerevan. Tel: 540 528. Fax: 540 136.
Association of Film Critics & Cinema Journalists, 5 Byron Str, 374009 Yerevan. Tel/Fax: 564 484. aafccj@arminco.com. www.arm-cinema. am. www.arvest.am.

SUSANNA HARUTYUNYAN graduated in film criticism from Moscow's State Cinema Institute in 1987. She has been the film critic of the daily *Respublika Armenia* since 1991 and is president of Armenia's Association of Film Critics and Cinema Journalists.

Australia Peter Thompson

Baz Luhrmann's **Australia** is one of the most keenly anticipated films of the last few years. Shooting through much of 2007 and due for release some time in 2009, it boasts characteristic Luhrmann-esque extravagance. Financed by 20th Century Fox with a rumoured budget in the region of $120 million, it climaxes with the bombing of the northern town of Darwin by Japanese forces in 1942, just months after their attack on Pearl Harbor. Borrowing from Harry Watts's 1946 Outback epic, *The Overlanders* (not to mention *Gone With the Wind*), it has Nicole Kidman's recently widowed English aristocrat teaming up with Hugh Jackman's 'rough-hewn' stockman on a perilous cattle drive through the desert. It is hoped that *Australia* will fill a long-vacant gap. Arguably, not since *Crocodile Dundee* in 1986 has there been a film that celebrates, or

Nicole Kidman in rehersals for **Australia**

exploits, the romantic potential of Australia's wilderness on such a grand scale.

Luhrmann can be expected to make a popular, if multi-layered, film. But it will disguise, to some extent, the typical state of the Australian film industry. For years, runaway Hollywood movies have helped to prop up local production. However, they're hardly dependable, with investment dropping from around $195 million (seven titles) in 2003/4 to $17 million (four titles) in 2005/6. The Australian dollar is climbing in value while other countries, including China, with its mushrooming studio facilities, have become attractive competitors.

Since 2004, when local production hit the nadir of 15 features, with a dismal audience share of 1.3% (down from a 12-year average of 5.2%), domestic filmmaking has shown a marked improvement. There has been a reasonable diversity of films, mostly made on modest budgets, with the notable exception of George Miller's foreign-financed, Academy Award-winning *Happy Feet*. The daringly ambitious Miller continues to ride the cutting edge of technical innovation and he once again proved his ability to tap popular sentiment.

2006 will also be remembered for Rolf de Heer's precedent-setting **Ten Canoes**, the first Australian film made entirely in an indigenous language; the result of a notable collaboration with iconic Aboriginal actor David Gulpilil, Yolngu man and co-director Peter Djiggirr, and the people of Ramingining in Arnhem Land, Northern Territory. It's a unique landmark in Australian cultural history because it tells an Aboriginal story from a time when they didn't have a 'white' problem, that is, before the

Rolf de Heer & Peter Djigirr's **Ten Canoes**

European invasion. A cautionary, moral tale and a character study full of disarming good humour and luminous photography, it more than justified its Special Jury Prize in the 'Un Certain Regard' section at Cannes, as well as a stack of Australian Film Institute awards.

In a different vein, **Kenny** hid its compassionate nature under a brazen exterior. Kenny Smyth's job is sewage disposal; he installs huge toilet cubicles at public functions. It is an all-consuming job that plays havoc with his personal life. The Jacobson brothers conceived and executed their mockumentary with plenty of laughter and energy, with Shane playing the title role and Clayton directing. Word-of-mouth made it one of the most popular successes of 2006, spinning off into a television series, *Kenny, A World Tour of Toilets*.

If there is a trend emerging, it is the growing number of Australian actors (and, to a lesser extent, directors) with international profiles, coming home to bolster home-grown movies. There has always been a tendency for producers to enlist international stars; the difference today is that those stars are, more often than not, Australian. Radha Mitchell flew home to appear in the killer-croc pic **Rogue**, director Greg McLean's follow-up to the phenomenally successful *Wolf Creek*. She also features in the World War II drama **The Children of Huang Shi**, directed by Roger Spottiswoode. Guy Pearce buffed up (again) to play Harry Houdini in Gillian Armstrong's **Death Defying Acts** and Toni Collette lent her prestige to at least two forthcoming

productions, Cathy Randall's **Hey Hey It's Esther Blueburger** and Elissa Down's **The Black Balloon**.

Two more cosmopolitan names returned for **Romulus, My Father**. Eric Bana plays the title role with actor Richard Roxburgh making his directorial debut. Based on the memoir of internationally recognised philosopher Raimond Gaita, the project has been carefully nurtured over several years by the creative partnership of John Maynard and Robert Connolly (*The Boys* and *The Bank*), but it owes much to Bana. The star's box office clout greenlit the project and his own background has parallels with that of the central character. Bana's father is Croatian and his mother German and they migrated to Australia before he was born in 1968. Romulus Gaita was Romanian, his wife German, but they arrived in Australia in 1950, when life was considerably tougher for immigrants. In the film, the family cracks and breaks under the pressures of their new environment, but Raimond finds strength and courage in his father's stoicism, honesty and compassion. Roxburgh successfully brings to life a period few young people in today's more affluent Australian society will easily recognise, and from ten-year-old Kodi Smit-McPhee he draws out a remarkable performance as the young Raimond. Franka Potente's Christina Gaita is a fascinating but damaged woman, precociously sexual and deeply conflicted. It may not have a similar impact in Europe, where such characters are perhaps more routinely explored, but Christina is a rare bird in Australian cinema.

Franka Potente in **Romulus, My Father**

Like the US, Canada and many other former British colonies, Australia is a land of immigrants. Approximately half the population was born overseas or has parents who were, so there is a rich history of true immigrant stories. Most are uneventful – Australia is, for the most part, a very safe country. But, like Raimond Gaita, filmmaker Tony Ayres struggled as a child to come to terms with an emotionally unstable mother. In **The Home Song Stories**, his follow-up to *Walking On Water* (2002), he tells the story of Rose (Joan Chen), a Shanghai nightclub singer with a son and daughter who marries a well-meaning Australian sailor (played by Steve Vidler) and finds herself adrift in a somnolent suburb on the outskirts of Melbourne. There she rapidly unravels. With no Romulus to provide an anchor for little Tom (Joel Lok) and May (Irene Chen), the emotional storms each character endures leave them pulverised. For some critics, Ayres lacks the required detachment to fully exploit his material, but *The Home Song Stories* is visually resplendent and features a number of remarkable performances.

Joan Chen and Yuwu Qi in **The Home Song Stories**

The dark side of the heroic migrant saga is the world's exploding refugee crisis. One of the most controversial issues in Australia over the last decade has been the Howard Government's policy towards asylum seekers. Building impenetrable barriers to all but a small group of approved applicants probably has the support of the majority of Australians – Howard won two elections on the issue – but consequences in terms of human rights have been dire. A number of films have grappled with the issue. The virtue of **Lucky Miles** is that it skirts the political mudslinging to create

Michael James Rowland's **Lucky Miles**

a story of almost whimsical charm, giving names and faces to people often seen as no more than anonymous statistics. Indonesian people-smuggler Muluk (Sawung Jabo) dumps twelve Cambodian and Iraqi refugees on a remote stretch of coastline in northwestern Australia, lying to them that there is a bus to Perth over the next sand hill. Most of them are picked up and imprisoned but Youssif (Rodney Afif), an Iraqi engineer, and Arun (Kenneth Moraleda), a Cambodian with an Australian father, try to escape across the desert. With Muluk and his crew stranded as well, and three army reservists (played by Glen Shea, Sean Mununggurr and Don Hany) in pursuit, the stage is set. Superbly photographed by veteran Geoff Burton and well directed for the most part by first-timer Michael James Rowland, *Lucky Miles* deserved to make more of an impact with local audiences than it did.

The search for national identity is open-ended and movies inevitably reflect this, however distorted the picture might become. Australian actors working in the US and elsewhere have raised the global awareness of their native cinema, but there are some odd consequences. Scrambling up the ladder with their faultless American accents and operating just below the main celebrity radar, people like Frances O'Connor, Rose Byrne, Alex O'Loughlin, Miranda Otto and Simon Baker (to name just a few) can be indistinguishable from American or English actors. Combine this with the trend of Australian actors coming home to work in local films and you have a situation that is both dynamic and loaded with implications. Young Australians increasingly measure success by international yardsticks, seeing local films as little more than a passport overseas. They're encouraged by, for example, the praise heaped on *The Assassination of Jesse James by the Coward Robert Ford* and would willingly emulate its Australian writer-director Andrew Dominik, whose previous feature was the break-out hit *Chopper*.

Another popular trend is the attraction genre filmmaking has for this new crop of directors. Making a film that fits a convenient pigeonhole might give it an edge in the international market. In the halcyon days of the Australian film revival, Peter Weir, Bruce Beresford, Fred Schepisi and others were intent on creating their own genres or, at least, were trying to draw directly on Australian life as they perceived it. But a film like **Noise**, by first-time writer-director Matthew Saville, seems intent on exploring and, to a degree, expanding the

Matthew Saville's **Noise**

boundaries of a familiar genre, the cop thriller. The twist is that the anti-hero, McGahan, played by an impressive Brendan Cowell, has tinnitus and the film self-consciously manipulates the soundtrack, putting us inside his head. Many believed *Noise* to be the best film of the year.

The evolution of digital technology is having a profound impact on all levels of film culture in Australia, as it is elsewhere. More than half of the recent productions listed by the Australian Film Commission originated on digital formats. People are also talking seriously about watching movies on their mobile phones. The cost savings through all stages of production have seen a flush of first-time directors tackling feature-length projects. Significantly, few broach social or political issues, with the notable exception of **The Jammed**. Formerly the South African Duncan McLachlan, director Dee McLachlan now lives as a woman. Meticulously researched, her debut looks at three young women (played by Emma Lung, Sun Park and Saskia Burmeister) trapped in Melbourne's sex trade. As brutally honest as Lukas Moodysson's *Lilya 4-Ever*, McLachlan's film graphically details how globalised slavery operates. Positive critical response and strong word-of-mouth have rescued *The Jammed* from oblivion.

Not all the international names in Australian films are native-born. Susan Sarandon and Emily Blunt visited in 2006 to appear in Ann Turner's stalker drama **Irresistible** alongside Sam Neill, Bud Tingwell and a strong local cast. Daniel Radcliffe appeared in Rod Hardy's coming-of-age tale **December Boys**. **Clubland**, written by Keith Thompson and directed by Cherie Nowlan, was released in the US with the unfortunate alternative title, *Introducing the Dwights*. It showcases Brenda Blethyn in a role not unlike the one she performed in *Little Voice*. She plays Jean Dwight, brought to Australia years ago by singer husband John (Frankie J. Holden), but still longing for the bright lights of the British club circuit. Jean is in trouble because the fantasy she clings to depends on her symbiotic relationship with son Tim (Khan Chittenden) who has discovered girls and wants a life of his own. The standout performance is by Emma Booth as Tim's girlfriend. Booth is one to watch; she will soon be seen as Germaine Greer in Beeban Kidron's **Hippie Hippie Shake**, based on 1960s counterculture guru Richard Neville's memoir of Swinging London.

Feature-length documentaries were particularly strong in 2007. Sunny Abberton's **Bra Boys** vividly captures the life of his family, growing up on a housing estate in Sydney's Maroubra, near the beach where Sunny became a surfing champion while his brothers found themselves in trouble with the law. Alec Morgan's charming dramatised documentary **Hunt Angels**, featuring Ben Mendelsohn and Victoria Hill, recreates the life and times of notorious filmmaker Rupert Kathner, who relentlessly pursued financial backers for his wildly ambitious projects but typically squandered the money. Anna Broinowski's **Forbidden Lie$** tells the extraordinary story of Norma Khouri who became a best-selling author in 2003 with her stunning book about fellow Jordanian, Dalia, allegedly murdered by her family for an innocent love affair with a Christian soldier. But a year later Khouri was exposed as a fake. With Khouri's eager cooperation, Broinowski tries to untangle the mystery but her search spins deliciously out of control.

Taking *Lucky Miles* as a metaphor, the Australian film industry is lost in the desert without a compass. But it's not hopeless – there is help over the next hill. In November 2007, John Howard's Conservative Government suffered a crushing defeat at the hands of Kevin Rudd's Labour Party. Howard had belatedly promised financial reform of the film sector and Rudd many honour those promises. But he might go furhter and usher in more far-reaching changes. So, there's a renewed optimism amongst producers. We're certainly not short of people itching to have a go.

The year's best films
Romulus, My Father (Richard Roxburgh)
Lucky Miles (Michael James Rowland)
The Home Song Stories (Tony Ayres)
The Jammed (Dee McLachlan)
Forbidden Lie$ (Anna Broinowski)

Quote of the year
'It actually represents the most radical change to the Government's support for the film industry for about the last twenty years.'
RICHARD HARRIS, *former Director of the Australian Screen Directors Association speaking about the new tax rebate promised for 2008*

Directory
All Tel/Fax numbers begin (+61)
The National Screen and Sound Archive, GPO Box 2002, Canberra ACT 2601. Tel: (2) 6248 2000. Fax: (2) 6248 2222. enquiries@screensound.gov.au. Stock: 3,800 Western Australian titles.
Australian Entertainment Industry Association (AEIA), 8th Floor, West Tower, 608 St Kilda Road, Melbourne, VIC 3004. Tel: (3) 9521 1900. Fax: (3) 9521 2285. aeia@aeia.org.au.
Australian Film Commission (AFC), 150 William St, Woolloomooloo NSW 2011. Postal address: GPO Box 3984, NSW 2001. Tel: (2) 9321 6444. Fax: (2) 9357 3737. info@afc.gov.au. www.afc.gov.au.
Australian Film Finance Corporation (AFFC), 130 Elizabeth St, Sydney NSW 2000. Postal address: GPO Box 3886, Sydney NSW 2001. Tel: (2) 9268 2555. Fax: (2) 9264 8551. www.ffc.gov.au.
Australian Screen Directors Association (ASDA), Postal address: PO Box 211, Rozelle NSW 2039. Tel: (2) 9555 7045. Fax: (2) 9555 7086. www.asdafilm.org.au.
Film Australia, 101 Eton Rd, Lindfield NSW 2070. Tel: (2) 9413 8777. Fax: (2) 9416 9401. www.filmaust.com.au.
Screen Producers Association of Australia (SPAA), Level 7, 235 Pyrmont St, Pyrmont NSW 2009. Tel: (2) 9518 6366. Fax: (2) 9518 6311. www.spaa.org.au.

PETER THOMPSON is a filmmaker and writer. He has also been reviewing and presenting movies on Australian television for 25 years.

Austria Gunnar Landsgesell

An Austrian film critic once commented that, for a small film-producing nation, Austria has one potential asset in a globalised film world: the development of an auteur cinema to increase its visibility; 2006 saw this potential realised with a number of striking films (and reflected in the 600 invitations Austrian films received from festivals around the world during 2006).

Falling (*Fallen*), Barbara Albert's sensitive drama, was invited to compete at the Venice Film Festival. The film reunites five women at the funeral of their former teacher and explores the sense of alienation they feel in their lives. A crucial figure in New Austrian Cinema, Albert also produced and co-wrote **Esma's Secret** (*Grbavica*), directed by Bosnian Jasmila Zbanic. An emotionally fierce post-war drama set in Sarajevo, it won the Golden Bear at the Berlinale. Filmed with a stark immediacy, it deals with the frictions between a mother and her teenage daughter, the former a Bosnian single mother who gave birth to a daughter after being imprisoned and repeatedly raped during the war.

Barbara Albert's **Falling**

Amongst the many distinctive films made during 2006, there was also one bona fide box office success. Erwin Wagenhofer's **We Feed the World** focused on the impact of globalisation and industrialisation on food production. Though lacking any specific visual style, the documentary scored with its ambitious, consumer-orientated approach. With its audience exceeding 200,000, it became Austria's most successful documentary.

Andreas Prochaska's **Dead in Three Days**

Genre film

There has been an increasing trend towards genre filmmaking. Andreas Prochaska's **Dead in Three Days** (*In 3 Tagen bist du tot*) profits from the popularity of horror and has been promoted as the first 'national' horror movie. Set in a village on the banks of the Traunsee lake in Upper Austria, a group of young people are being slaughtered one by one. Their only clue is an SMS, sent to each victim, telling them they will be 'dead in three days'. For a film featuring an unknown cast, it attracted a significant amount of hype, ensuring its success at the box office. It succeeds through its blend of modern technology and symbols of national folklore, and is directed with a ruthless efficiency.

Pepe Danquart's **To the Limit**

Documentaries

Austrian documentaries are steadily attracting larger audiences. Pepe Danquart's **To the Limit** (*Am Limit*) follows two extreme mountain climbers, brothers Thomas and Alexander Huber, on their speedy, record-breaking climb up the spectacular rock face of El Capitan in Yosemite National Park. A suspenseful and vertigo-inducing experience for its audience, the film dominated the Austrian box office for a number of weeks. Udo Maurer's **About Water** (*Über Wasser: Menschen und gelbe Kanister*) looks at the global impact of water shortage and excess, from seasonal flooding in Bangladesh to deprivation in one of Africa's most overpopulated areas, Kibera, in Nairobi. Favouring a mosaic-like narrative trajectory over linearity, the film details how the world deals with water issues. The film's success shows that there is an audience for socially conscious cinema in Austria.

Auteur cinema

Guilt appears to play a significant role in many of the serious Austrian productions, no more so than in the circumstances faced by the central character of Versatile Austrian director Stefan Ruzowitzky's **The Counterfeiters** (*Die Fälscher*). A prisoner in a concentration camp, master forger Salomon Sorowitsch (Karl Marcovics) becomes a pivotal figure in the Nazis' counterfeiting operation. In trying to stay alive while questioning his role as a saboteur, he finds himself in a moral quandary that places at risk more than his own life. Ruzowitzky was acclaimed for the strong impact of his film, but also criticised for the way he emphasised thriller elements at the expense of historical accuracy.

It took Ulrich Seidl five years to produce his follow-up to *Dog Days*. The Venice Film Festival's Grand Special Jury Prize placed a great deal of pressure on Seidl, but **Import/Export** was deemed worthy of the main competition at Cannes. Again, Seidl deals with the quest for happiness in a world of sorrow and despair. A Ukrainian nurse (played by Ekaterina Rak), who moonlights as a stripper for a Ukrainian/local webcam site, emigrates to Austria. There, on the outskirts of Vienna, Seidl refuses her a better existence, instead detailing the hardship of immigrant life. Worse still is the fate of a young Austrian man (the impressive Paul Hoffmann) who finds himself lost on the snowy streets of a Ukrainian city. Seidl is aided in no small part by Ed Lachman's

Ulrich Seidl's **Import/Export**

Hans Weingartner's **Free Rainer**

remarkable cinematography, capturing every moment of drama on poorly lit streets. *Import/ Export* sees Siedl achieve great subtlety in the portrayal of these outsiders.

Michael Haneke recently completed the remake of his own thriller, **Funny Games**, in the USA. In 1997, he shocked audiences by challenging their capacity to stomach violence, simultaneously questioning contemporary society's consumption of violence as entertainment. In the remake, the terrorised parents are played by Naomi Watts and Tim Roth, with Michael Pitt as one of the malevolent youths.

Haneke's long-time producer Veit Heiduschka has just finished his collaboration with one of the most promising talents of Austrian cinema, Arash T. Riahi. **For a Moment Freedom** (*Für einen Augenblick, Freiheit*), a relatively expensive Austrian film (€4 million), traces the journey of refugees from Iran to Austria. The Tehran-born filmmaker skilfully combines dramatic events with a sense of irony. The film will be screened in its original language – a precedent in Austria for such a high-profile production.

With a growing number of highly distinctive and challenging filmmakers emerging on to the world cinema stage, 2008 looks set to continue the rise of Austrian cinema.

GUNNAR LANDSGESELL is a freelance writer for *Blickpunkt:Film*.

The year's best films
Exile Family Movie (Arash T. Riahi)
Zorros Bar Mizwa (Ruth Beckermann)
Free Rainer (Hans Weingartner)
Unser täglich Brot (Nikolaus Geyerhalter)
Calling Hedy Lamarr (Georg Misch)

Quote of the year
'When Sweden's Olof Palme was shot coming out of a cinema I thought, this cannot happen to Austrian politicians.' *A producer quoting late Austrian filmmaker Axel Corti*

Directory
All Tel/Fax numbers begin (+43)
Austrian Film Museum, Augustinerstr 1, A-1010 Vienna, Tel: (1) 533 7054-0. Fax: (1) 533 7054-25. office@filmmuseum.at. www.filmmuseum.at.
Filmarchiv Austria, Obere Augartenstr 1, A-1020 Vienna. Tel: (1) 216 1300. Fax: (1) 216 1300-100. augarten@filmarchiv.at. www.filmarchiv.at.
Association of Austrian Film Directors, c/o checkpointmedia Multimediaproduktionen AG, Seilerstätte 30, A-1010 Vienna. Tel/Fax: (1) 513 0000-0. Fax: (1) 513 0000-11. www.austrian-directors.com.
Association of Austrian Film Producers, Speisingerstrasse 121, A-1230 Vienna. Tel/Fax: (1) 888 9622. aafp@austrian-film.com. www.austrian-film.com.
Association of the Audiovisual & Film Industry, Wiedner Hauptstrasse 53, PO Box 327, A-1045 Vienna. Tel: (1) 5010 53010. Fax: (1) 5010 5276. film@fafo.at. www.fafo.at.
Austrian Film Commission, Stiftgasse 6, A-1070 Vienna. Tel: (1) 526 33 23-0. Fax: (1) 526 6801. office@afc.at. www.afc.at.
Austrian Film Institute (OFI), Spittelberggasse 3, A-1070 Vienna. Tel: (1) 526 9730-400. Fax: (1) 526 9730-440. office@filminstitut.at. www.filminstitut.at.
Location Austria, Opernring 3, A-1010 Vienna. Tel: (1) 588 5836. Fax: (1) 586 8659. office@location-austria.at. www.location-austria.at.
Vienna Film Fund, Stiftgasse 6, A-1070 Vienna. Tel: 526 5088. Fax: 526 5020. office@filmfonds-wien.at. www.filmfonds-wien.at.

Bangladesh Ahmed Muztaba Zamal

The political situation in Bangladesh has changed significantly in recent years. The clampdown on corruption has seen an increased number of convictions, including those of politicians, bureaucrats and businessmen. The military-backed interim government plans to hold a free election at the end of 2008.

Cinema, like every other arena of Bangladeshi life, is set to go through a number of changes. With reform on the increase, it is hoped that there may be a change to the ban on importing foreign films. Bangladeshi cinema can be seen in some markets around the world, but the local population have long been deprived of foreign fare.

Not surprisingly, the film industry was greatly affected by the political turmoil that raged through 2006. In the latter part of the year, it was even impossible to screen local films in cinemas because of the deadlock between political parties.

One of the films that did get a release that year was **Made in Bangladesh**, directed by Mostafa Sarwar Farooki. A slapstick comedy based on a true story, the film was a success in the few cinemas in Dhaka where it was screened. **Queen of Nichol** (*Nacholer Rani*) was another independent production that found success in local cinemas. Directed by Whaiduzzaman Diamond, it was another true story, this time of an ordinary housewife who becomes a revolutionary.

Inner Journey (*Ontorjatra*) was the latest feature by *Clay Bird* director, Tareque Masud. It tells the story of a young boy who travels with his mother to their ancestral home. Tauquir

Ahmed's second film, **A Fairy Tale** (*Rupkothar Golpo*), was produced by Impress Telefilms. It depicts the life of an average man and the struggles in his life.

Golam Rabbani Biplob walked away with an award at the 2007 Shanghai International Film Festival for **On the Wings of Dreams** (*Swopnodanay*), his account of the real-life struggle of the Bangladeshi people. **Forever Flows** (*Nirontor*), directed by Abu Sayeed, follows the travails of a family in Dhaka. While the father's blindness prevents him from working, his unemployed son refuses to work. It is left to the beautiful daughter, Tithi, to save the family by becoming a prostitute. A non-judgemental look at the predicament faced by these characters, it won two awards at film festivals in India. Both films were produced by Impress Telefilms.

A number of notable documentaries were produced over the last year. **Iron Eaters**, directed by Shaheen Dill-Riaz, explores the struggles of the people employed at the shipyard in Chittagong. Dill-Riaz's second film, it has yet to be released in Bangladesh. **Garment Girls** and **Tajuddin Ahmed** were both directed by Tanvir Mokammel. The former documents the lives of women who work in garment factories; the latter is a portrait of Bangladesh's first prime minister. Impress Telefilms also produced two documentaries: **Truth and Beyond** (*Sattyer Gahiney*), directed by Ahmed Muztaba Zamal, and Sabnam Ferdousi's **And We Crossed the Road**.

At a time when both the independent and mainstream cinema circuits are faced with many challenges, Impress Telefilms continues to promote the production of better films for

Ahmed Muztaba Zamal's **Truth and Beyond**

both the local audience and the global market. Most of the films mentioned in this article were produced by them (surprisingly, they did not produce Tauquir Ahmed's **An Island Called Daruchini** (*Daruchinni*), another of the biggest domestic successes of 2007). Undoubtedly, their ownership of Channel-I, the world's first Bengali digital satellite television channel, is a major benefit.

Away from the mainstream, filmmakers like Tareque Masud and Tanvir Mokammel carry the torch of independent cinema in Bangladesh, successfully drawing attention to their country's cinema on the world stage.

However, with cinema prices sometimes reaching DBT200 ($3) a ticket, a great deal of money for the average audience member and at a time when the cost of living is rising, cinema in Bangladesh may, sadly, become the entertainment of choice for only the wealthier middle class.

AHMED MUZTABA ZAMAL is Secretary General of Rainbow Film Society and Director of the Dhaka International Film Festival.

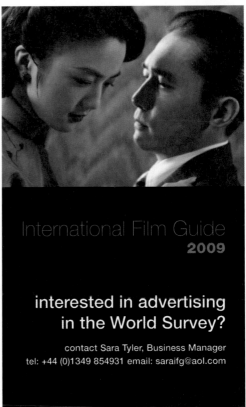

Belarus Andrei Rasinski

The main theme of Belarusian cinema in 2007 has been World War II. Ala Krynitsina's **Motherland or Death** (*Rodina ili smiert'*), a Russian co-production, is the story of a woman who recruits Belarusian children into the Soviet secret police (NKVD). **Chaklun and Rumba** (*Chaklun i Rumba*), the first film by Andrei Golubeu, is a variation on the buddy-buddy theme, about a sapper and his dog. In both cases, characters and plot are secondary to the action. Another co-production, Maria Mazhar's **Enemies** (*Vragi*), about occupying troops and locals co-existing in Belarus, is an interesting attempt to break new ground with a war film due to

Maria Mazhar's **Enemies**

its representation of the relationship between occupier and occupied.

Victor Asliuk's feature debut was an adaptation of Mihas' Zaretski's **Mysterious Land** (*Nyabachany krai*). Asliuk's documentary, **Maria**, presented at the Leipzig Film Festival, is a portrait of a heroine who now has only her memories to live with.

Three documentaries were shot in Polesye, a unique region possessing its own distinctive traditions. **As Is Their Wont** (*Zavyadzionka*), by Galina Adamovich, won a number of international awards for its account of a large family whose matriarch applies her religious beliefs to daily activities around the house. Another documentary by Adamovich, **Man's Realm** (*Muzhchynskaja sprava*), focuses on the last few traditional folk musicians in the region. Siargei Rybakou's **I Will Be Lit by the Sun** (*Sontsam asvyachusya*), centring on the history of songs and music from Polesye, was presented at the New York Film Festival.

Animation turned to literature for inspiration. **Gold Horseshoes** (*Zolotye podkovy*) by Irina Kadzyukova is adapted from Hans Christian Andersen's fairytales; Uladzimir Piatkevich's **The Travelling Frog** (*Lyagushka-puteshestvennitsa*) animates a tale by V. M.Garshyn; and **Grandfather's Proverbs** (*Dzedavy prymauki*), by Mikhail Tumelya, illustrates a series of Belarusian proverbs. **Jet Pig 8** (*Reaktivnyi porosienok 8*) is Alexander Lenkin's sequel to *Jet Pig 7*.

Eleven cartoons, 13 documentaries and eight features were presented at the sixth biennale of Belarusian films. Of the international festivals, Magnificat (43 Christian

Gold Horseshoes *directed by Irina Kadzyukova*

documentaries from 14 countries) and Listapad (42 participating countries) were held in June and November respectively. Uladzimir Zamiatalin, appointed as Head of the National Film Company, has cemented his reputation as a propagandist with a significant organisational restructure. His aim is to have an annual output of twelve films by 2009. The new projects under his tenure are Dzianis Skvartsou's **The Free Heaven** (*Svobodnoe nebo*), an action film about Western spies in Belarus, and another film detailing the collapse of the USSR, which has been announced for 2008.

Exiled director Jury Hashchavatski has completed **Kalinovski Square** (*Ploshcha*), a documentary about those who fought against authoritarian rule. 'Navinki', an underground anarchist group, has made the political 'videocomic', **Good-bye, Father!** (*Good-bye, Batc'ka!*). Belarusian scriptwriter Andrei Kureichyk's **Love-carrots** was filmed in Russia (attracting box office receipts of $11,640,308). Andrei Kudzinenka is finishing a remake of **The Practical Joke** (*Rozygrysh*) in Moscow. Theatrical director Valer Mazynski has adapted Yanka Kupala's **The Locals** (*Tuteishyja*) for the screen. A historical tragicomedy about conformism and colonial occupation, Mazynski intends to film it in Poland.

ANDREI RASINSKI is a cinema and cultural critic and regular contributor to *Nasha Niva* newspaper, and director of two documentaries.

The Year's Best Film
Maria (Victor Asliuk)
As Is Their Wont (Galina Adamovich)
Man's Realm (Galina Adamovich)
Gold Horseshoes (Irina Kadzyukova)
Jet Pig 8 (Alexander Lenkin)

Quote of the year
'We were inspired by our social-psychiatric reality.' PAULYUK KANAVAL'CHYK, *Group 'Navinki', at the premiere of* **Good-bye Father!**

Directory
All Tel/Fax numbers begin (+375)
Belarusfilm, Scaryna Prospect 98, 220023 Minsk. Tel: 233 8820.
Ministry of Culture, Film & Video Department, Masherov Avenue 11, 220004 Minsk. Tel: 223 7114. Fax: 223 9045.

Belgium Erik Martens

The Belgian federal elections of June 2007 created an uncomfortable situation in the country's complicated political life. A large number of Dutch-speaking Belgians (the Flemish community) voted for parties with separatist tendencies in their programme. Since the French-speaking community did not share the same views on living apart together, negotiations for the new federal government became extremely difficult. Outside the political arena, Belgians experience little problem with their national identity; some consider it a surrealist invention, while for most it is simply not an issue, unless national sports are at stake.

It is true that the two communities know one another less and less. Even their cinemas have grown apart over the years. The cliché has it that the Flemish make popular films, televisual in style and for local use only. The Walloons (including French-speaking filmmakers in the Brussels region) make art-house cinema. They are the children of Luc and Jean-Pierre Dardenne, who produce harsh, documentary-inspired social drama, or the more intellectual kind of auteur film. While abroad they represent the best of Belgian cinema, with no less than two Palme d'Ors to their name, at home, particularly in Wallonia, their following is limited.

As with most clichés, there is some truth in these crass statements. On the whole, Flemish cinema does have a more populist output. In 2006, the local share for Flemish films came to 6.75%, matching 2003's figures, when Eric Van Looy's noir thriller, The Alzheimer Case, attracted an audience of 750,000. Last year, MMG, the company behind Van Looy's film, attempted to recreate that

Hans Herbots' **Stormforce**

success with an adaptation of their popular TV series, **Stormforce** (*Windkracht 10: Koksijde Rescue*). With a budget of €4.5 million, it became Flemish cinema's most expensive production. The story of a rescue team who risk their lives on the open sea, it attracted little more than a third of *The Alzheimer Case*'s audience.

Dominique Deruddere's comedy **A Chicken is no Dog** (*Firmin*) was also aimed at a large audience, with the central character, Firmin, played by popular TV comic, Chris Van den Durpel. Attempting to replicate the previously successful formula of turning local comics into box office stars, the film failed to repeat popular comic Urbanus's success in the early 1990s. However, over 200,000 admissions was a respectable number. Like most films in this genre, *A Chicken is no Dog* is predictable and politically correct. An old boxer gives way to a new generation and, thanks to Firmin, Moroccan boxer Mohammed becomes the Belgian champion, teaching his racist opponent a lesson along the way.

Television remains a major influence on Flemish cinema, with veteran filmmakers such as Guido Henderickx joining the fray. Derived from a television series, **The King of the World** (*Koning van de wereld*) concerns a young boxer's downfall at the hands of cynical businessmen. The film's lack of originality was reflected in its poor performance at the box office. Two children's films – Matthias Temmerman's **Plop in the City** (*Plop in de stad*) and Bart Van Leemputten's **Pete the Pirate and the Flying Ship** (*Piet Piraat en het vliegende schip*) – were also adapted from TV programmes, highlighting the tendency to make films with a ready-made audience.

Geoffrey Enthoven's **The Only One** (*Vidange perdue*) featured popular theatre actor Nand Buyl as a grumpy old man struggling with the social and physical pain of ageing. Jan Decleir plays a similar role in Miel Van Hoogenbemt's **A Perfect Match** (*Man zkt vrouw*), as a schoolmaster who falls in love with his young housekeeper, played by the fresh-faced Maria Popistasu. Both films enjoyed a theatrical release, though neither looked particularly cinematic. *The Only One* was part of a series of tele-films ('Faits Divers') produced by the commercial station VTM and co-financed by the Flemish Film Fund.

Three young filmmakers offered a more personal cinematic style, each of their works dealing with young adults struggling with existential concerns. Stylistically, each film is raw, using dark comedy to tell the story. Though none could be called a masterpiece, each had its moment in the limelight.

Koen Mortier's **Ex Drummer**

Koen Mortier's **Ex Drummer** is the grotesque story of a writer who becomes the drummer of a lousy rockband. **With Friends Like These** (*Dagen zonder life*), the second film by Felix van Groeningen, takes place in the provincial town of Sint-Niklaas. Van Groeningen once again creates a distinctly personal world, with the action – or lack of it – revealing the emptiness in the lives of his young protagonists. **The Last Summer** (*De laatste zomer*) follows a group of teenagers attempting to relieve the boredom of the summer break. Newcomer Joost Wijnant displays a skill for creating an atmospheric environment with a distinctive visual style and convincing dialogue.

Peter Brosens & Jessica Woodworth's **Khadak**

Only two Flemish productions were successful internationally. Nic Balthasar's **Ben X** won three awards at the Montreal World Film Festival. Borrowing narrative and stylistic elements from on-line gaming, it tells the story of a boy afflicted with Asperger's Syndrome, who takes revenge on the 'friends' who have made his life a misery. Peter Brosens and Jessica Woodworth's **Khadak** was the winner of the Luigi De Laurentiis Award at the 2006 Venice Film Festival. Drawing on their experience as documentary filmmakers, Brosens and Woodworth convincingly detail the world of rural Mongolia, which is gradually being destroyed by the country's aggressive mining policies. Visually sumptuous, the film is a truly international endeavour: Brosens is Flemish, Woodworth is American, they both live in Wallonia and the dialect used in the film is Mongolian.

French-language Belgian cinema displays a similar desire to explore new territories. Marion Hänsel's latest feature, **Sounds of Sand** (*Si le vent soulève les sables*), rails against the political, economic and ecological situation in many African countries. Adapted from Marc Durin-Valois' novel, the film witnesses a family's descent into hell as they struggle across the vast desert in search of water. The sumptuous imagery is a marked contrast to the desperate plight of the family.

Marion Hänsel's **Sounds of Sand**

Thierry Michel's documentary, **Congo River** (*Congo river, au-delà des ténèbres*), investigates life at the border of the river that was once the thriving artery of the country, but whose trade and economy has since dried up. The film was released theatrically and was well received, both critically and commercially.

The interest of Belgian filmmakers in their country's former colony is hardly new. An English-language, French-directed Belgian film, however, is a little more rare. Sam Garbarski's second film, **Irina Palm**, features Marianne Faithful as Maggy, an ageing widow who jokingly refers to herself as 'the wanking widow' as she masturbates clients in order to earn enough money to pay for her grandson's operation. The film was nominated for the Golden Bear at the Berlin Film Festival and was met with enthusiasm by audiences.

Marianne Faithful in **Irina Palm**

Chantal Akerman's latest feature, **Là-bas**, continues her exploration of the boundaries of the audiovisual arts. Staying in an apartment in Tel Aviv, she records her every experience and the world immediately around her. Rarely venturing outside, the audience mostly hears vague noises in the distance and Akerman's own voice, reading from a diary. The film's implications remain ambiguous, with subtleties far beyond the reach of the average cinema audience.

Relative newcomer Joachim Lafosse's latest film, **Private Property** (*Nue Propriété*), is his most accomplished. A talented and intelligent writer-director, Lafosse casts Isabelle Huppert as a woman who decides to sell her house and live with her lover, much to the consternation of her two sons (played by Jérémie and Yannick Renier). The tension this uneasy situation creates makes for extremely compelling and uncomfortable viewing.

Joachim Lafosse's **Private Property**

Martine Doyen's **Komma** features Belgian rock star Arno. Comprised of a series of carefully composed images, Arno plays a man traumatised by past experiences who meets a similarly troubled woman (played by Valérie Lemaître). Throughout, Doyen conveys meaning visually rather than through dialogue.

Olivier Masset-Depasse's **Cages** employs a similar approach to tell the story of a woman who, after losing her voice in an accident, tries to find ways to prevent her husband from leaving her. Like *Komma*, the film creates a delicate atmosphere that would be difficult to capture with a traditional narrative.

Alain Berliner's **Gone for a Dance** (*J'aurais voulu être un danseur*) proved to be one of the year's most disappointing films. The story of a video-shop owner who is passionate about musicals and leaves everything to become a full-time tap-dancer, the film failed to realise its comic potential and did not repeat the success of the director's earlier hit, *Ma vie en rose*.

Olivier Van Hoofstadt's **Dikkenek**, Belgian-Flemish slang for 'arrogant prick', refers to main character Greg, played by Jérémie Renier, who, like all his self-centred and arrogant friends, is the unattractive face of Belgian society. Von Hoofstadt's debut is a chaotic mix of spontaneity and absurdist humour, offering an alternative to the tourist-guide image of Belgium.

Although the country experienced constitutional uncertainty in 2007, Belgian cinema is in a healthy state. No Palme d'Or for the Dardenne brothers this year, but on both sides of the linguistic border there is a notable vitality. Thanks to tax-shelter measures, more money is being invested in the traditionally under-financed Belgian film industry, ensuring the domestic cinema runs smoothly.

ERIK MARTENS is a film critic and editor-in-chief of DVD releases at the Royal Belgian Film Archive.

Thierry Michel's **Congo River**

The year's best films
Private Property (Joachim Lafosse)
Khadak (Peter Brosens and Jessica Hope Woodworth)
Congo River (Thierry Michel)
Komma (Martine Doyen)
Dikkenek (Olivier Van Hoofstadt)

Quote of the year
'I see a scenario of growth for the coming three years [in which] the total budget for fiction film will be doubled by 2010. This budgetary space must make it possible to double the number of subsidised Flemish films from six to twelve a year.' *Flemish Minister of Culture* BERT ANCIAUX *speaking on the occasion of the Film Fund's presentation of their annual report*

Directory
All Tel/Fax numbers begin (+32)
Royal Film Archive, 23 Rue Ravenstein, B-1000 Brussels. Tel: (2) 507 8370. Fax: (2) 513 1272. cinematheque@ledoux.be. www.ledoux.be.
Communauté Française de Belgique Centre du Cinéma et de l'audiovisuel, Boulevard Léoplod II, 44, 1080 Brussels. Tel: (2) 413 25 19. Fax: (2) 413 24 15.
Flanders Image, Handelskaai 18/3, 1000 Brussels. Tel: (2) 226 06 30. flandersimage@vaf.be.
Flemish Audiovisual Fund (VAF), Handelskaai 18/3, B-1000 Brussels. Tel: (2) 226 0630. Fax: (2) 219 1936. info@vaf.be. www.vaf.be.
Wallonie Bruxelles Images (WBI), Place Flagey 18, 1050 Brussels. Tel: (2) 223 23 04. wbimages@skynet.be. www.cfwb.be.

Bolivia José Sánchez-H.

2006 saw the Smithsonian Institute award its prestigious James Smithson Bicentennial Medal to Bolivian pioneer filmmaker Jorge Ruíz for his contribution to visual anthropology. Ruíz's work includes *Alaska Mine*, the first Latin American film restored by the Academy Film Archive of the Academy of Motion Picture Arts and Sciences. His gift for capturing the indigenous cultures in his homeland influenced such notable Bolivian filmmakers as Jorge Sanjinés.

Five digital productions were produced in 2006, three of which were transferred to 35mm for exhibition. Martín Boulocq's **The Most Beautiful of My Very Best Years** (*Lo mas bonito y mis mejores años*) is a drama about friendship set in present-day urban Cochabamba. Boulocq wisely teamed up with US independent executive producer Chris Hanley in an effort to secure wider distribution. First-time director Anche Kalashnikova's **I Am Bolivia** (*Soy Bolivia*), an allegorical drama set in current times, deals with the kidnapping of an indigenous girl by four young men from well-to-do families in Santa Cruz. The film topped the box office for three weeks. Rodrigo Bellot's **Who Killed the Little White Llama?** (*Quién mató a la llamita Blanca?*) is the first production to come out of Cochabamba's Factory International Film School. It was the year's biggest commercial success. A comedy set in present-day Bolivia, indigenous people playing the film's main protagonists.

Battling piracy

The Bolivian government declared 21 March 2007 Bolivian Cinema Day, commemorating the 1980 assassination of filmmaker and critic Father Luis Espinal. Plagued by economic frustrations, Bolivian filmmakers wrote a manifesto railing against piracy, which was presented to the National Film Council's director, Armando de Urioste. Economic impoverishment, which makes piracy appealing, has created a situation in which filmmakers cannot recoup costs in order to make further films.

Claudia Ortiz in **The Andes Don't Believe in God**

The most anticipated film of 2007 was Antonio Eguino's **The Andes Don't Believe in God** (*Los Andes no creen en Dios*), an adaptation of the Adolfo Costa du Reis novel, set in the mining town of Uyuni, on Bolivia's high plateau, during the 1920s. It was the only Bolivian production to be shot on celluloid in 2007 (Super-16 blown up to 35mm). The film opened to a warm public reception.

Digital technology has enabled more filmmakers to make documentaries. **Evo Pueblo**, about the life of Bolivian president Evo Morales, was directed by Tonchy Antezana. The election of Bolivia's first indigenous president generated many other documentaries, including **This Land is Ours** (*Abya Yala* in Aymara) by French-born Bolivian resident, Patrick Vanier. His film took the

Alejandro Landes' **Cocalero**

Aymara perspective towards current events in Bolivia and the election to the presidency of the former union leader. The phenomenon of indigenous empowerment in Bolivia was also captured by Brazilian-born director, Alejandro Landes in **Cocalero**. A personal portrait of Evo Morales, the film is listed as an Argentine/Bolivian production, although Landes received no Bolivian funding. Marcos Loayza's fourth film, **The State of Things** (*El estado de las cosas*), looks at the political and economic climate in Bolivia. Class and regional divisions within the country are questioned in a film that examines the aspirations of the people in relation to the state and the universal rights of every individual. **The Abandoned Ones** (*Los abandonados*) by German-born Frank Weber, a resident in Bolivia since 1985, tells the story of six homeless young men who manage to travel to Germany and stage a theatre production.

A task befitting Quixote

Despite both financial and distribution difficulties, as well as widespread piracy, Bolivian filmmakers continue to pursue the Quixote-like task of making films. Mela Márquez's **Don't Breathe a word...** (*No le digas...*), about the life and work of leading Bolivian writer Jaime Sáenz (1921–86), is in post-production and expected to be released in 2008. Rodrigo Bellot's **Perfidy** (*Perfídia*), shot in the US, is a peculiar love story which uses only three minutes of dialogue and one actor for the duration of its 90-minute running time. Juan Carlos Valdivia is in pre-production on **Kandire**, a film about the indigenous Guarani culture. Marcos Loayza is also preparing his

next feature project, **Serpent** (*Arcano Katari* in Aymara), about a boy named Tupah who enters the mythic world of the Andean night.

Mela Márquez's **Don't Breath a Word**

The year's best films
The Andes Don't Believe in God
(Antonio Eguino)
This Land is Ours (Patrick Vanier)
Cocalero (Alejandro Landes)
The State of Things (Marcos Loayza)
The Most Beautiful of My Very Best Years
(Martín Boulocq)

Quote of the year
'Today is the day that my baby is born.'
Director **ANTONIO EGUINO** *talking at the premiere of* The Andes Don't Believe in God

Directory
All Tel/Fax numbers begin (+591)
Cinemateca Boliviana, Calle Oscar Soria, Prolongación Federico Zuazo s/n, Casilla 9933, La Paz. Tel: (2) 244 4090. info@cinematecaboliviana. org. www,cinemateca.siesis.com.
Consejo Nacional de Cine (CONACINE), Calle Montevideo, Edificio Requimia, Piso 8, La Paz. Tel: (2) 244 4759. contacto@conancine.net. www.conacine.net.
Fundación Jorge Ruíz, Casilla 4336, Cochabamba. Tel: (4) 445 0756. siempremarina@yahoo.es.

JOSÉ SÁNCHEZ-H. is a filmmaker and author of *The Art and Politics of Bolivian Cinema* (1999). He teaches in the department of Film and Electronic Art at California State University, Long Beach.

Bosnia & Herzegovina Rada Sesić

Film audiences in Bosnia and Herzegovina are remarkably supportive and enthusiastic towards domestic films. No wonder, then, that Jasmila Zbanić's debut, **Esma's Secret** (*Grbavica*) made the whole country proud, winning the Golden Bear at the Berlin Film Festival, becoming a box office hit at home and performing well internationally. Esma is a Bosnian single mother who gave birth to a daughter, Sara, after being imprisoned and repeatedly raped during the war. She attempts to hide the truth from Sara, who believes her father died a war hero (*shehid*, or martyr). It is only when she is required to show her father's death certificate in order to go on a free school trip that the truth begins to surface. Popular Serbian actress Mirjana Karanović and newcomer Luna Mijović impress as the mother and daughter, while the sober photography of Christine A. Meier and an eclectic soundtrack, from lyrical religious *Ilahijas* to loud, pounding, turbo folk, create an imposing atmosphere. The film stirred up heated debates in the press, particularly after its screening at FEST in Belgrade. It was refused a release in the Republic of Srpska, a political entity within Bosnia and Herzegovina. Jasmila Zbanić and

members of the crew began campaigning for women raped during the war to be officially recognised as war victims.

Srdjan Vuletić's popular second feature **It's Hard to be Nice** (*Tesko je biti fin*) opened the 2007 Sarajevo Film Festival. A tragi-comedy set amongst taxi drivers for whom 'business as usual' means small-scale smuggling, theft and cheating, the film features a strong script and fine performances, particularly by Sasa Petrović as Rafko and Emir Hadzihafizbegović as Sejo. In order to save his marriage, a taxi driver decides to go straight, but opposition from his colleagues and the temptation of making easy money breaks down his resolve. Guaranteed a significant run at festivals, Vuletić should also see his film do well on general release across the region.

Srdjan Vuletić's **It's Hard to be Nice**

Recently completed, Aida Begić's debut, **Snow** (*Snijeg*), awaits a release date. It is a post-war drama set in the isolated village of Slavno, which is populated by twelve widows who lost their families during the war and have to fight for the survival of their community.

Interesting films of 2006 include the intriguing experimental feature by film critic and writer,

Mirjana Karanovic in **Grbavica**

Faruk Loncarević. **Mum 'n' Dad** (*Mama i Tata*) witnesses an old couple's relationship turn sour after fifty years of marriage, descending into a series of grotesque fights. Mocking the reality-show 'genre', the film explores the boundaries of film language in search of a fresh style. Jasmin Duraković, another former film critic and currently the director of the largest Bosnian public broadcaster, FTV, directed **Nafaka**. A satire about an Afro-American woman trapped in wartime Sarajevo, Duraković's debut is a balanced combination of typical Bosnian humour and poetry. Nenad Djurić debuted with the comedy **Skies Above the Landscape** (*Nebo iznad krajolika*). Starring the impressive Haris Burina, it is set in a rough mountain area in post-war Bosnia and is a funny love story about the culture clash between a French paraglider and a shepherd into whose lap she unexpectedly falls from the sky.

The relatively small documentary scene in Bosnia and Herzegovina is becoming more organised. The last two years have seen a handful of impressive productions. Alen Drljević, in collaboration with journalist Seki Radoncić, directed **Carnival** (*Karneval*), about the disappearance in Monte Negro of a hundred Muslim war refugees from Bosnia and Herzegovina, and **Esma**, in which a single mother is searching for the remains of her husband, an officer who disappeared in the war. *Carnival* was selected for IDFA in 2006, an honour also bestowed on Namik Kabil in 2007 for his film **Interrogation** (*Informativni razgovori*). This winner of the last Sarajevo festival investigates the meaning of the war for different individuals through interviews – or rather 'questionings' – which are set in an abandoned factory. In **Statement 710399** (*Izjava 710399*), Refik Hodzić follows a father's search for his missing sons, eleven years after the genocide in Srebrenica. **Dream Job** (*Posao snova*), directed by the young Danijela Majstorović, one of the few filmmakers from the Republic of Srpska, brings to the surface all the oddities and risks involved when girls become turbo folk stars. **Ambassadors Learn**

Namik Kabil's **Interrogation**

the Languages (*Ambasadori uce jezike*) is the third documentary by Semsudin Gegić, dealing with the fate of children taken from the orphanage during the war and sent to Italy. **Fantasy** (*Fantazija*) by newcomer Aldin Arnautović explores the issue of Post-Traumatic Stress Disorder among former Bosnian soldiers and the attitude of society towards this problem.

The feature production company Refresh moved into documentary production. They released **It's Still Me** (*Jos uvijek ja*) by Amra Mehić and Elvir Muminović, an engaging and mature film about the uncertain position of disabled people in Bosnian society.

A new feature at the 2007 Sarajevo Film Festival was the Talent Campus, organised in collaboration with the Berlinale Campus and gathered around eighty young film professionals from the region. 2007 will also see the completion of Sarajevo's first cinema multiplex. Art-house movies will also find a new home in the city: the non-profit art-house cinema *Kriterion* in Amsterdam, entirely run by students, will establish a counterpart in Saravevo.

RADA SESIĆ is a filmmaker and film critic based in the Netherlands where she collaborates on the programme of IDFA and IFF Rotterdam. She is also head of the documentary competition at the Sarajevo Film Festival as well as the main selector of the Bucharest Film Festival.

The year's best films
Grbavica (Jasmila Zbanic)
It's Hard to be Nice (Srdjan Vuletic)
Mum 'n' Dad (Faruk Loncarevic)
Interrogation (Namik Kabil)
Carnival/Esma (Alen Drljevic)

Quote of the year
'It's a big European shame that wartime
Bosnian Serb leaders, Radovan Karadzic and
Ratko Mladic, responsible for rapes, murder
and persecution, still have not been arrested.'
JASMILA ZBANIC, *director of* **Esma's Secret**, *as she
received the Golden Bear at the Berlin Film Festival*

Directory
All Tel/Fax numbers begin (+387)
Academy for Performing Arts, Obala, Sarajevo.
Tel/Fax: 665 304.
Association of Filmmakers, Strosmajerova 1,
Sarajevo. Tel: 667 452.
Cinemateque of Bosnia & Herzegovina, Alipasina
19, Sarajevo. Tel/Fax: 668 678. kinoteka@bih.net.ba.

Brazil Nelson Hoineff & Leonardo Luiz Ferreira

Piracy reached a critical level in 2007 when over three million unauthorised DVD copies of José Padilha's **Elite Squad** (*Tropa de Elite*) were sold months before the film was released. A cop thriller about corruption and drug trafficking, set in a violent neighbourhood of Rio de Janeiro, the film nevertheless became the year's top-grossing domestic feature, with 2.1 million viewers in the first month. It was also a talking point amongst the country's intellectuals who debated its positive representation of police action against drug dealers.

Wagner Moura, left, in **Elite Squad**

Despite the controversy surrounding Padilha's film, Cao Hamburger's emotionally engaging **The Year My Parents Went on Vacation** (*O Ano em que Meus Pais Saíram de Férias*) was chosen as the official entry for the 2008 Academy Awards. Michael Joelsas plays young Mauro, stranded in a Jewish neighbourhood on the outskirts of São Paulo, where he befriends Shlomo, the neighbour of his recently deceased grandfather; together they watch Brazil win the 1970 World Cup and the country fall under the yoke of military rule.

Besides *Elite Squad*, only one local title attracted more than two million viewers,

Maurício Farias' adaptation of the popular TV sitcom, **The Big Family: The Movie** (*A Grande Família: O Filme*). A number of independent features scored modest successes with audiences. The best example is Heitor Dhalia's **Drained** (*O Cheiro do Ralo*), a black comedy about the owner of a pawn shop who takes advantage of people in desperate situations. A success at the Sundance Film Festival, it received little publicity but still managed to draw an audience of 170,000.

Cinema attendance throughout most of the year dropped off by around 5%, but there was an increase of 4.3% in the average price of a cinema ticket. However, attendance for Brazilian films showed a slight increase of 1%.

Brazilian documentaries went from strength to strength, led by two important features: veteran fimmaker Eduardo Coutinho's **Mise-en-scene** (*Jogo de Cena*), and **Santiago**, by João Moreira Salles, Walter's brother and one of the main driving forces behind the thriving documentary scene.

Santiago, *directed by João Moreira Salles*

Mise-en-scene assembles a group of performers and members of the public whose testimonies form Coutinho's investigation

Eduardo Coulinho and Marina D'elia in **Mise-en-scene**

into the thin line that separates fiction and documentary. *Santiago*, which João started shooting 13 years ago, was originally intended to be a documentary about his family's butler, but, upon returning to the project, he saw it transform into a reflection on the lies, truth and ethics involved in making a documentary.

2008 sees the return to cinemas of Fernando Meirelles, directing Julianne Moore and Mark Ruffalo in **Blindness** (*Cegueira*), an international co-production; it is the story of the inhabitants of a city who suddenly lose their sight. Director and renowned cinematographer Walter Carvalho will follow up his successful 2004 biopic of the life of singer Cazuza with an adaptation of Chico Buarque's 'Budapeste'.

NELSON HOINEFF is a film critic, vice president of the Association of Film Critics of Rio de Janeiro and president of the Institute of Television Studies.

LEONARDO LUIZ FERREIRA is the film editor of the website Almanaque Virtual, film critic of the magazine *Revista Paisà* and member of the Association of Film Critics of Rio de Janeiro.

The year's best films
Santiago (João Moreira Salles)
Mise-en-scene (Eduardo Coutinho)
Suely in the Sky (Karim Aïnouz)
The Year My Parents Went on Vacation
(Cao Hamburger)
The Milky Way (Lina Chamie)

Quote of the year
'Before the premiere, researches indicates that 11.5 million viewers had already seen an illegal copy of the movie. That's a frightening number.' JOSÉ PADILHA, *talking about his film* Elite Squad

Directory
All Tel/Fax numbers begin (+55)
ANCINE (National Agency for Cinema), Praça Pio X, 54, 10th Floor, 22091-040 Rio de Janeiro. Tel: (21) 3849 1339. www.ancine.gov.br.
Brazilian Cinema Congress (CBC), (Federation of Cinema Unions/Associations), Rua Cerro Cora 550, Sala 19, 05061-100 São Paulo. Tel/Fax: (11) 3021 8505. congressocinema@hotmail.com. www.congressocinema.com.br.
Cinemateca Brasileira, Largo Senador Raul Cardoso, Vila Clementino 207, 04021-070 São Paulo. Tel: (11) 5084 2318. Fax: (11) 5575 9264. info@cinemateca.com.br. www.cinemateca.com.br.
Grupo Novo de Cinema, (Distributor), Rua Capitao Salomao 42, 22271-040 Rio de Janeiro. Tel: (21) 2539 1538. braziliancinema@braziliancinema.com. www.gnctv.com.br.
Ministry of Culture, Films & Festivals Dept, Esplanada dos Ministerios, Bloco B, 3rd Floor, 70068-900 Brasilia. www.cultura.gov.br.

Karim Aïnouz's **Suely in the Sky**

Bulgaria Pavlina Jeleva

2007 turned out to be the most important year for Bulgaria since the fall of the Berlin Wall in 1989. After a long period of united effort and collective expectation, the country became a member of the European Union. Looking back on recent Bulgarian history, 2006 will be remembered as the last year of uncertainty and 2007 as the first year of real hope.

Bulgarian cinema experienced some change during this period. The film community continues to gain in confidence and enjoys the creative environment it has built up over the years. Through the Film Law, public support has increased to €3.5 million, enabling the National Film Centre to contribute more successfully to film production. The funding has also encouraged Bulgarian National Television to participate more actively in some projects.

Bonka Ilieva in **Monkeys in Winter**

The biggest surprise of 2006 came from the younger generation of filmmakers. **Monkeys in Winter** (*Maimuni prez zimata*) is the feature debut of Milena Andonova. With Nevena Andonova producing, the two daughters of cult Bulgarian director Metody Andonov (*The Goat's Horn*) teamed up with writer Maria Stankova, to present a triptych of personal – and quite rude – stories of three young women. Starring Diana Dobreva, Bonka Ilieva and Angelina Slavova, *Monkeys in Winter* won the East of West Award at the 2006 Karlovy Vary Film Festival and six awards at the Varna Film Festival. It was also the Bulgarian entry for Best Foreign Language Film at the Academy Awards.

As for the 2007 Academy Awards, Ilyan Simeonov's **Warden of the Dead** (*Pazachat na martvite*) was selected. The story of a boy who lives and works in a cemetery starring Nikolay Urumov, Valentin Tanev, Diana Dobreva and father and son Itzhak and Samuel Fintzi, it features a remarkable performance by 13-year-old Vladimir Georgiev. The film is beautifully shot by Dimitar Gotchev.

Writer-directors Ivan Cherkelov and Vassil Zhivkov's **Christmas Tree Upside Down** (*Obarnata elha*) tells six individual stories, linked by the journey of a Christmas tree from the mountains to Sofia. Strangely ornamental, the film observes fragments of contemporary life in Bulgaria, ranging from a melancholic dream (The Angel) to a story of destructive passions (The Boar). The film won the Special Prize of the Jury at Karlovy Vary in 2006, much to the joy of the film's producer, Rossitza Valkanova. **Investigation** (*Razsledvane*), Iglika Trifonova's second film after *Letter to America*, was also produced by Valkanova, who succeeded in attracting German and Dutch financing. Winner of the 2007 Cottbus Grand Prix, with Rali Ralchev conjuring up a dark mood with his cinematography, the film follows a female investigator (played by

Svetlana Yancheva) as she attempts to break down the psyche of a murder suspect (played by Krassimit Dokov).

Aleksandra Surchadzhieva, Violeta Markovska and Elen Koleva are the three impressive discoveries in the new film by *Emily's Friends* director, Liudmil Todorov. **Dressmakers** (*Shivachki*) tells the realistic stories of three young women trying to escape unemployment. A popular success, the film charmed audiences and reaffirmed Todorov as a filmmaker to watch.

Andrei Paounov's The Mosquito Problem & Other Stories

Of the recent documentaries, Andrei Paounov's Danube-set **The Mosquito Problem & Other Stories** (shown at the 2007 Cannes Critics' Week) and Adela Peeva's latest Balkan saga **Divorce Albanian Style** (which secured a nomination for Best European Documentary, 2007) are the most impressive. Paounov's film chronicles the life of a town that, at various stages, has been a concentration camp and a subjected to a pompous, never-ending project for a power plant.

Currently in production is **Prima Primavera**, a Hungarian-Bulgarian-UK-Dutch co-production, directed by Janos Edelenyi. It features Berlinale Shooting Star Vessela Kazakova alongside Andor Kovács and Antonie Kamerling in the story of a Gypsy prostitute who befriends a mentally disabled man whose mother has only recently died.

The year's best films
Christmas Tree Upside Down
(Ivan Cherkelov, Vassil Zhivkov)
Dressmakers (Liudmil Todorov)
Investigation (Iglika Trifonova)
The Mosquito Problem & Other Stories
(Andrei Paounov, documentary)
Monkeys in Winter (Milena Andonova)

Quote of the year
'After having studied four years to become an actress I definitely do not want to work as a waitress.' *Actress* **ELEN KOLEVA**, *commenting on unemployment in the Bulgarian artistic circle*

Directory
All Tel/Fax numbers begin (+359)
Bulgarian National Film Library, 36 Gurko St, 1000 Sofia. Tel: (2) 987 0296. Fax: (2) 987 6004. bmateeva@bnf.bg.
Bulgarian Film Producers Association, 19 Skobelev Blvd, 1000 Sofia. Tel: (2) 8860 5350. Fax: (2) 963 0661. geopoly@mail.techno-link.com.
Bulgarian National Television, 29 San Stefano St, 1000 Sofia. Tel: (2) 985 591. Fax: (2) 987 1871. www.bnt.bg.
Ministry of Culture, 17 Stamboliiski St, 1000 Sofia. Tel: (2) 980 6191. Fax: (2) 981 8559. www.culture. government.bg/.
National Film Centre, 2A Dondukov Blvd, 1000 Sofia. Tel: (2) 987 4096. Fax: (2) 987 3626. nfc@mail.bol.bg.
Union of Bulgarian Film Makers, 67 Dondukov Blvd, 1504 Sofia. Tel: (2) 946 1068. Fax: (2) 946 1069. sbfd@bitex.com.

PAVLINA JELEVA is a film critic and journalist, regularly contributing to many Bulgarian newspapers and magazines. Having been national representative on the boards of Eurimages and FIPRESCI, she is now artistic and foreign-relations director of her own film company.

Canada Tom McSorley

In 2006, Canada's two dominant linguistic communities (or 'solitudes', as they are known in Canadian cultural parlance), French and English, were ingeniously combined in the enormously successful bi-lingual buddy movie, **Bon Cop, Bad Cop**. Two detectives, one from each side of the linguistic divide, are assigned to work together on a murder investigation involving Canada's national passion, ice hockey. Erik Canuel's clever comedic *policier* became the most successful Canadian film in domestic box office history. Proving that the 'solitudes' do still exist, over 80% of the box office revenues were earned in Quebec alone. The Canadian film industry's search for commercial success and critical respectability appeared to have been achieved with Canuel's film, but sadly, almost exclusively in Canada's French-speaking province.

Robert Favreau's **A Sunday in Kigali**

Elsewhere, Canadian feature films embraced, in terms of production and theme, a kind of internationalism, exploring the Canadian position in global contexts and in foreign territories. Robert Favreau's **A Sunday in Kigali** (*Un dimanche a Kigali*) tells the story of a Canadian journalist in Rwanda at the time of the genocide (a theme revisited in the 2007 drama by Roger Spottiswoode, **Shake Hands With the Devil**, which was based on Canadian General Romeo Dallaire's experiences as a commander of the UN peacekeeping force). Accomplished actress Sarah Polley directed an international cast (British screen legend Julie Christie as well as Americans Olympia Dukakis and Michael Murphy) in **Away From Her**, a subtle and elegantly rendered love story about a elderly man coping with his wife's descent into Alzheimer dementia. Zacharias Kunuk and Norman Cohn's **The Journals of Knud Rasmussen** dramatised the encounter with and demolition of Inuit society and cosmology by Danish explorers. While Philippe Falardeau's drama, **Congorama**, revolves around a Belgian inventor who learns that he was actually born in Quebec and decides to visit his 'homeland'.

The traditional strengths of Canadian documentary were also much in evidence in 2006, with such impressive features as Gary Burns's wry exploration of suburbia, **Radiant City**; Allan King's *cinéma vérité* examination of racial politics and teenagers at risk in Toronto's suburbs, **EMPz 4 Life**; Jennifer Baichwal's multi-award-winning **Manufactured Landscapes**, a portrait of Canadian photographer and environmental activist Edward Burtynsky; and veteran aboriginal

Jennifer Baichwal's **Manufactured Landscapes**

filmmaker Alanis Obomsawin's exploration of her family and tribal history, **Waban-aki: People of the Rising Sun**.

Rounding out a solid year were Guy Maddin's daring 'silent film', **Brand Upon the Brain!**, an oneiric melodrama about a man and his mother; Reginald Harkema's low-budget marvel about love, politics, marijuana and the generational divide, **Monkey Warfare**; and Andrew Currie's **Fido**, a zombie comedy set in an impossibly perfect American town in the 1950s and starring Scottish comedy legend Billy Connolly.

Whether from the demands of the narratives themselves, or the perceived advantages for production financing and marketability, the Canadian cinema has definitely gone global, both inside and outside the frame. Its cinematic 'internationalism' continued well into 2007. Jeremy Podeswa's handsome but over-written Holocaust drama of memory and identity, **Fugitive Pieces**, is based on Canadian writer Anne Michaels' novel and is a co-production with Greece. It features a cast that includes British performers Stephen Dillane and Rosamund Pike, as well as Croatian actor Rade Serbedzija. Working in the UK, Canadian auteur David Cronenberg delivered **Eastern Promises**, a tale of the Russian mob in London starring Viggo Mortensen, Naomi Watts and Armin Mueller-Stahl. Arguably the most international of them all, however, is Paolo Barzman's **Emotional Arithmetic**, a tale of a Holocaust survivor living in Canada whose world is shaken with the arrival of

David Cronenberg and Viggo Mortensen at Sitges Film Festival

the Polish dissident who saved her life in the camps. Based on the novel by Canadian Matt Cohen, the cast is an international who's who with Max von Sydow, Susan Sarandon, Gabriel Byrne, and even a Canadian, Christopher Plummer. There is also Clement Virgo's impressive boxing drama, **Poor Boy's Game**, about race and identity set in Halifax, Nova Scotia, starring Danny Glover.

Guy Maddin's **My Winnipeg**

The year also witnessed a return of many veteran directors. In addition to Cronenberg, Podeswa and Virgo, new films arrived by such established filmmakers as Denys Arcand (**Days of Darkness**), Bruce McDonald (**The Tracey Fragments**), Bruce Sweeney (**American Venus**), and Guy Maddin (**My Winnipeg**).

Denys Arcand's *Days of Darkness* (*L'Age des tenebres*) was the closing film at the 2007 Cannes Film Festival and the third instalment of the trilogy that included *The Decline of the American Empire* and *The Barbarian Invasions*. A satirical tale, it follows the exploits of a government employee who escapes his drab reality by dreaming of a glamorous life.

Bruce McDonald's inventive visual split-screen design in *The Tracey Fragments* explores the inchoate thoughts and emotions of distraught teenager Tracey (Ellen Page) as she travels from her small town to big city Winnipeg in search of her younger brother who has mysteriously disappeared.

Bruce McDonald's **The Tracey Fragments**

In *American Venus*, Rebecca De Mornay plays a ruthless American mother determined to mould her daughter, Jenna, into an Olympic figure-skating champion but is thwarted when she flees across the border to Canada.

Maddin's diaristic paean to his home town is as visually poetic as all his remarkable fiction films; here, the often arresting imagery is perfectly integrated into his dreamy, perceptive voice-over narration about growing up in Winnipeg.

Conspicuously absent from the 2007 list is Atom Egoyan. Having had an unpleasant experience in the world of big-budget international co-productions with 2005's critical and commercial disappointment, *Where the Truth Lies*, Egoyan is now in post-production in Toronto on his latest, decidedly less expensive feature. An intimate drama about identity, obsession and the Internet, the tentatively entitled **Adoration** will likely premiere at Cannes in 2008.

State funder Telefilm Canada has rightly reconfigured its earlier insistence on funding mostly 'commercial', 'audience-friendly' Canadian production; however, given the Canadian context of almost total box office domination by Hollywood interests (domestic films hold a lower than 5% share of Canadian screens), this insistence seems misguided as the search for domestic audiences continues, particularly in English-speaking territories. (In Quebec that mix appears to have been perfected by films like *Bon Cop, Bad Cop*.)

Perhaps the internationalist tendency in current Canadian cinema will address that. However, it does appear that the traditional ace of Canadian cinema – the auteur-driven art-house film – is making a sustained comeback. Indeed, there are signs of a gradual re-emergence of the Canadian auteur film in 2007 in both Quebec and English-speaking Canada.

The return of McDonald and Maddin to their auteurist and, in Maddin's case, personal roots is an important indicator. Documentary is also experiencing a similar drift. One example is the startling **Here Is What Is**, co-directed by Adam Vollick, Daniel Lanois and Adam Samuels. It uses digital image technology not to aggrandise the subject of the film – internationally renowned musician Daniel Lanois – but rather to explore and articulate the paradoxical processes of creation through the use of technology, be that musical or cinematic. Inventive and experimental, *Here Is What Is* is an eccentric and collective auteurist film about a musical artist who also happens to work with various musical collectives.

Here Is What Is, *co-directed by Adam Vollick, Daniel Lanois and Adam Samuels*

Meanwhile, in Quebec, the year yielded several exciting examples of the auteurist tendency in feature drama. Bernard Emond's **Summit Circle** (*Contre toute esperance*) is an austere account of a woman whose life falls apart when her employer downsizes his company and how she plots her revenge. With its Zola-esque fatalism, Emond's critique of the human consequences of corporate greed is potent art-house filmmaking.

Bernard Emond's **Summit Circle**

François Delisle's **You** (*Toi*) is a dark, tautly constructed melodrama about one woman's search for self-fulfillment at the expense of her family. And in the most promising feature debut in years, Stephane Lafleur's deadpan marvel, **Continental, A Film Without Guns** (*Continental, un film sans fusil*), presents an elliptical, episodic narrative concerning the disappearance of a businessman and the encounters this triggers between his angry, seemingly abandoned wife, a lonely travelling insurance salesman and a hotel receptionist. Part Aki Kaurismäki, Roy Andersson and Jean Pierre Lefebvre, Lafleur's work is utterly engaging and distinctly uncommercial. It is uncompromisingly auteurist and announces a significant new talent on the Canadian cinematic landscape.

TOM McSORLEY is Executive Director of the Canadian Film Institute in Ottawa, a Sessional Lecturer in Film Studies at Carleton University, film critic for CBC Radio One, and a Contributing Editor to POV Magazine.

Stephane Lafleur's **Continental, A Film Without Guns**

The year's best films
Continental, a Film Without Guns
(Stephane Lafleur)
My Winnipeg (Guy Maddin)
Summit Circle (Bernard Emond)
The Tracey Fragments (Bruce McDonald)
Here Is What Is (Adam Vollick, Daniel Lanois, Adam Samuels)

Quote of the year
'I guess I'll have to finally tell my grandmother the title.' MARTIN GERO, *director, on the premiere of his film,* **Young People Fucking**

Directory
All Tel/Fax numbers begin with (+1)
Academy of Canadian Cinema & Television, 172 King St E, Toronto, Ontario, M5A 1J3. Tel: (416) 366 2227. Fax: (416) 366 8454. www.academy.ca.
Canadian Motion Picture Distributors Association (CMPDA), 22 St Clair Ave E, Suite 1603, Toronto, Ontario, M4T 2S4. Tel: (416) 961 1888. Fax: (416) 968 1016.
Canadian Film & Television Production Association, 151 Slater Street, Suite 605, Ottawa, Ontario, K1P 5H3. Tel: (613) 233 1444. Fax: (613) 233 0073. ottawa@cftpa.ca.
La Cinémathèque Québécoise, 335 Blvd de Maisonneuve E, Montreal, Quebec, H2X 1K1. Tel: (514) 842 9763. Fax: (514) 842 1816. info@ cinematheque.qc.ca. www.cinematheque.qc.ca.
Directors Guild of Canada, 1 Eglinton Ave E, Suite 604, Toronto, Ontario, M4P 3A1. Tel: (416) 482 6640. Fax: (416) 486 6639. www.dgc.ca.
Motion Picture Theatre Associations of Canada, 146 Bloor Street W, 2nd Floor, Toronto, Ontario, M5S 1P3. Tel: (416) 969 7057. Fax: (416) 969 9852. www.mptac.ca.
National Archives of Canada, Visual & Sound Archives, 344 Wellington St, Ottawa, Ontario, K1A 0N3. Tel: (613) 995 5138. Fax: (613) 995 6274. www.archive.ca.
National Film Board of Canada, PO Box 6100, Station Centre-Ville, Montreal, Quebec, H3C 3H5. Tel: (514) 283 9246. Fax: (514) 283 8971. www.nfb.ca.
Telefilm Canada, 360 St Jacques Street W, Suite 700, Montreal, Quebec, H2Y 4A9. Tel: (514) 283 6363. Fax: (514) 283 8212. www.telefilm.gc.ca.

Chile Andrea Osorio Klenner

No Chilean films released in the last two years have succeeded in lighting up the box office the way Boris Quercia and Andrés Wood did with *Sex With Love* in 2003 and *Machuca* the following year. Although the 2006 box office top ten included Quercia's second feature, **The King of Idiots** (*El Rey de los Huevones*), and 2007 saw Roberto Artiagoitía's debut, **Heart Radio Station** (*Radio Corazón*), perform well, neither could attract a large enough audience to compete with films like *The Da Vinci Code* or *The Chronicles of Narnia*.

Ten features and two documentaries were released by Chilean filmmakers in 2006. In 2007, only half that number reached cinemas. The popularity of foreign, particularly mainstream American, films has squeezed domestic fare out of many cinemas, leaving them with no places to show. In turn, cinemas would rather not programme Chilean films which will never make as much money.

First-time directors

Our Father (*Padre Nuestro*), by Rodrigo Sepúlveda, was inspired by the director's family life, particularly his relationship with his father. Caco, an elderly man who has long abandoned his family, returns home with the news that he is seriously ill, in the hope that he can spend his final days with them. Sepulveda's finely tuned comedy-drama features an excellent central performance from Jaime Vadell and strong support from Argentine actress Cecilia Roth.

Sebastián Lelio's (previously known as Sebastián Campos) **The Sacred Family** (*La Sagrada familia*) relied on the strength of his

cast's improvisational skills. With little technical support, a ten-page, dialogue-free script and just three days within which to shoot, Lelio pulled together a terse family drama, featuring an egocentric father, a confused mother and a dominated son who descend upon their beach house for the Easter holidays. Thrown into the mix is the son's first 'real' girlfriend, whose rebellious spirit is unlikely to pacify the atmosphere. Lelio spent a year editing, resulting in a coherent and well-received film which was officially selected for several film festivals, including San Sebastián, Montreal and Rotterdam, just to name a few.

Heart Radio Station, *directed by Roberto Artiagoitía*

Heart Radio Station was originally meant to have been the official sequel to the remarkable 1999 box office success, *The Sentimental Teaser*. However, because of a dispute between that film's director, Cristián Galaz, and its producer, Roberto Artiagoitía, 'The Sentimental Teaser 2' was renamed and reorganised, with Artiagoitía in the director's chair. *Heart Radio Station* is the biggest domestic success this year. Both films were based on Artiagoitía's radio show, where people call in to unburden themselves of their personal problems, love affairs or something more playful. Despite the schematic formula of a collection of short stories linked by the ubiquitous voice on the radio, Artiagoitía's film won over audiences with the empathy it displayed in attempting to understand problems and concerns affecting everyday Chileans. It is also supported in no small part by a strong line-up of actresses, including Manuela Martelli, Claudia di Girolamo, Tamara Acosta and Amparo Noguera.

Cristóbal Valderrama's first feature, **Malta With Egg** (*Malta con Huevo*), is a black comedy that tells the story of two buddies who decide to share accommodation but realise very soon that their decision could have been a mistake. Although starting out strong, the film weakens, partly because of a disappointing plot twist. Though interesting, Valderrama doesn't yet possess the skill to convince.

Diego Muñoz and Nicolás Saavedra in **Malta With Egg**

Matías Bize has expressed the desire that each of his films possess the freshness of his first. His third feature certainly achieves that. Shot in Barcelona City over eleven nights, **About Crying** (*Lo Bueno de Llorar*) documents the end of a relationship, taking place over one long night in which Vera and Alejandro explore the lies and truths that not only they, but couples generally, tell each other.

About Crying received a special mention at the 14th Valdivia International Film Festival where it also won the Critics' Award. With his innovative style and convincing characterisation, Matías Bize is one of the hopes for the future of Chilean cinema.

Vicenta N'Dongo and Alex Brendemühl in **About Crying**

The year's best films
The Sacred Family (Sebastián Lelio)
About Crying (Matías Bize)
Our Father (Rodrigo Sepúlveda)
Heart Radio Station (Roberto Artiagoitía)
Malta With Egg (Cristóbal Valderrama)

Quote of the year
'Not having much practice about awards, it's impressive anyway. It's like passing exams, and me, someone who always refuse passing exams I'm passing now…being over 60 years old.' RAÚL RUIZ *on the Master of Cinema award presented to him by Filmcritica Magazine, during the opening of the Second Roma Film Festival*

Directory
All Tel/Fax numbers begin (+56)
Consejo Nacional de la Cultura y las Artes, Fondo de Fomento Audiovisual, Plaza Sotomayor 233, Valparaíso. Tel: (32) 232 66 12. claudia. gutierrez@consejodelacultura.cl. www.consejodelacultura.cl
Corporación de Fomento de la Producción (CORFO), Moneda 921, Santiago. Tel: (2) 631 85 97. Fax: (2) 671 77 35. lordonez@corfo.cl. www.corfo.cl.
Ministerio de Relaciones Exteriores, Dirección de Asuntos Culturales, Teatinos 180, Santiago. Tel: (2) 679 44 07. Fax: (2) 699 07 83. acillero@ minrel.gov.cl. www.minrel.cl

ANDREA OSORIO KLENNER is a journalist, Director of the Cine Club of the Universidad Austral de Chile and Head of Programming of the Valdivia International Film Festival.

China Sen-lun Yu

Like China's dynamic economy, the Chinese film industry has grown rapidly over the last four years. Since 2003, the industry has seen a continuous rise in box office figures and films in production. Since 2004 the annual box office figure has increased more than 30% every year and is expected to grow at the same rate over the next few years. Annual production reached 330 films in 2006, the highest of any East Asian country. As a result of this success, filmmakers and film companies have become increasingly market-oriented. More big-budget films were made between 2006 and 2007 than ever before. The largest so far is $50 million, although that record will soon be broken.

Genre films, particularly comedies, are on the rise. Varying in budget and quality, they reflect the attempts of producers to cater to the demands of China's diverse audience. The flip-side of this sees more problems for art-house films. Traditionally winning international recognition for China and seen as a window through which the Western world could view and understand contemporary Chinese society, many of these more specialised films now face greater challenges domestically than. Although Chinese films won at both the Berlin and Venice Film Festivals in the last two years, Chinese audiences were less than enthusiastic about seeing them. In a year when China's film industry has been striding towards a more open market economy, the so-called Sixth Generation filmmakers were largely ignored.

By the end of 2006, a category of Chinese-language blockbuster, or 'Da Pian' (literally, 'big film'), began to take shape. These are films budgeted between $20 million and $50 million,

Chen Kaige's **The Promise**

recruiting pan-Asian stars and featuring martial arts, fantasy or epic elements. Chen Kaige's **The Promise** (*Wu Ji*), a period drama about loyalty, ambition, love and destiny, set the precedent, becoming the box office champion of 2005, with $24 million.

Following the success of *The Promise*, two other heavyweight filmmakers, Feng Xiaogang and Zhang Yimou, presented two period dramas at the end of 2006. **The Banquet** (*Ye Yan*) was Feng's take on Shakespeare's *Hamlet*, with a prince seeking vengeance on his uncle who he believed had murdered his father. Starring Zhang Ziyi, Daniel Wu, Ge You and Zhou Xun, the film earned over $17 million.

Feng Xiaogang's **The Banquet**

Gong Li in **The Curse of the Golden Flower**

Two months later, Zhang Yimou's period drama **The Curse of the Golden Flower** (*Man Cheng Jin Dai Huang Jin Jia*) experienced even greater success. Set in the Tang Dynasty and loosely based on the play 'Thunderstorm' by contemporary writer Cao Yu, the film tells of a vicious power struggle within the royal family, ending in a failed coup inside the palace walls. Chow Yun-fat plays the cruel emperor, with Gong Li as the unfaithful empress slowly being poisoned by her husband. Despite criticism by local reviewers, the film has become the most successful Chinese-language film in Chinese cinema history, taking in over $37 million.

The 'Da Pian' trend has continued into 2007. Hong Kong director Peter Ho-sun Chan has cast Jet Li, Andy Lau and Takeshi Kaneshiro in his Ching dynasty epic, **Warlords** (*Tou Ming Zhuang*). The story of three bandits and blood brothers joining a battle to suppress the Taiping rebellion, it combines psychological drama and fierce war scenes. The $40 million film will be released at the end of 2007, with the American premiere following in autumn 2008.

If the 2006 local blockbuster trend featured costume dramas set in opulent ancient Chinese palaces, in 2007 it was war and ancient battles. In addition to *Warlords*, John Woo began shooting his long-anticipated **Red Cliff** (*Chi Bi*) in mid-2007. The most expensive Chinese film to date (with a budget of $50 million), it takes place during one of the most famous and decisive battles in Chinese history

over 1,700 years ago. It is expected to be released in 2008.

The low-budget comedy wave continues to attract audiences. Ning Hao's black comedy, **The Crazy Stone** (*Feng Kuang De Shi Tou*), was an overnight hit in late 2006, thrusting its young director, who previously had only two art-house films to his name, into the limelight. Set in Chongqing, a city in southwest China, a group of bumbling thieves, a powerful gangster boss and a pair of loyal security workers all chase after a precious stone. With its dark, gritty humour, the film has been compared to Guy Ritchie's *Snatch*. Ning Hao makes the most of the script's earthy dialogue and the unique setting of Chongqing's chaotic and lively streets. The film was made for $400,000 but earned over $3.1 million. As a result, filmgoers have been subjected to numerous films attempting to cash in on or emulate *The Crazy Stone*'s success.

Ning Hao's **The Crazy Stone**

Big Movie (*Da Dian Ying*), a parody of a series of well-known martial arts epics from director Agan, performed well at the beginning of 2007. Within a month, Zhang Jianyas' **Call for Love** (*Ai Qing Hu Jiao Zhuan Yi*), a comedy fantasy about a man encountering twelve different women during his marriage crisis, also performed well.

Some comedies felt no need to follow *The Crazy Stone*'s template. Chen Daming's **One Foot Off the Ground** (*Ji Quan Bu Ning*)

Zhang Yang's **Getting Home**

is set in Henan Province and concerns an unsuccessful theatre troupe who decide to enter the chicken-fighting business. In Zhang Yang's **Getting Home** (*Luo Ye Gui Gen*), a migrant worker travels thousands of miles to carry his colleague's dead body home. Cao Baoping's **Trouble Makers** (*Guangrong De Fen Nu*) is a story about a group of reckless villagers intent on 'overthrowing' the corrupt village head and his bullying brothers.

As previously mentioned, art-house fare has suffered over the last two years. Wang Quanan was awarded China's first Golden Bear at the 2007 Berlin Film Festival for **Tuya's Marriage** (*Tuya De Hun Shi*), a realistic drama about a strong-willed Mongolian woman struggling to survive and find happiness in her life. Despite actress Yu Nan's impressive performance, the film did not win the hearts of Chinese audiences. Jia Zhangke won the Golden Lion at Venice the previous year, but **Still Life** (*San Xia Hao Ren*), about two couples

facing gigantic changes in their lives after the completion of the Three Gorges Dam project, only attracted a meagre $266,000.

Maverick director Jiang Wen tells four inter-related stories in **The Sun Also Rises** (*Tai Yang Zhao Chang Sheng Qi*). 'Madness', 'Love', 'Gun' and 'Dream' deal with fate and the absurdity of life, set against the exotic landscapes of Yunnan and the Xinjiang desert. Because of Jiang Wen's popularity as an actor in China, the film was one of the few auteur films to perform acceptably at the box office.

Jiang Wen's **The Sun Also Rises**

Other films, though praised overseas, struggled to find a domestic audience, or a cinema that would programme them. Renowned Fifth Generation filmmaker Tian Zhuangzhuang's **The Go Master** (*Wu Qingyuan*) is a meditative bio-pic about the ordinary life of extraordinary Go master, Wu Qingyuan, over the last sixty years. Li Yu's **Lost in Beijing** (*Ping Guo*) focuses on a migrant worker couple who arrive in Beijing hoping for a better life, but become lost in the glamour and chaotic values of the capital city. They soon find themselves entangled in a relationship with a wealthier Beijing couple. The film barely passed Chinese censors, who removed 15 minutes of the film, including a minor sub-plot. It is still waiting to be released amid the competition from local and foreign blockbusters.

For those who advocate a film rating system in China, 2007 was another disappointing year.

Wang Quanan's **Tuya's Marriage**

Tian Zhuangzhuang's The Go Master

Although the heads of China's Film Bureau announced in 2005 that a Film Promotional Law, featuring a rating system, would be implemented within a year, the law is still pending review in China's National Congress, for which no date has yet been set.

The total gross of 2006 reached $349 million, while industry players suggest the 2007 figure could pass $400 million. One of the main reasons for such a steady growth is the proliferation of cinemas in the last three years. Around a hundred new cinemas and more than 700 screens – or two new screens a day – opened in China in 2007 alone.

Another reason for the box office growth is the audience favouring both foreign and local blockbusters. The number of admissions has increased by approximately 33% in 2007. 'There are more and more people who like to watch movies,' is a common saying among cinema business analysts this year. But with cinema attendance on the rise, the question of a rating system allowing a wider and more diverse range of films, as well as effective marketing campaigns alerting audiences to the diversity available to them, is a priority for those working in the film industry.

The year's best films
The Go Master (Tian Zhuangzhuang)
The Sun Also Rises (Jiang Wen)
The Crazy Stone (Ning Hao)
Trouble Makers (Cao Baoping)
Tuya's Marriage (Wang Quanan)

Quote of the year
'We need films of all different budgets: big, medium and small. It's like a city that cannot just have five-star hotels. People need snack bars and street vendors too!' NING HAO, *director of* The Crazy Stone.

Directory
All Tel/Fax numbers begin (+86)
Beijing Film Academy, 4 Xitucheng Rd, Haidian District, Beijing 100088. Tel: (10) 8204 8899. http:www.bfa.edu.cn.
Beijing Film Studio, 77 Beisanhuan Central Rd, Haidan District, Beijing 100088. Tel: (10) 6200 3191. Fax: (10) 6201 2059.
China Film Archive, 3 Wenhuiyuan Rd., Xiao Xiao Xitian, Haidian District, Beijing 100088. Tel: (10) 6225 4422. chinafilm@cbn.com.cn.
China National Film Museum, 9, Nanying Rd., Beijing 100015. Tel: (10) 64319548. cnfm2007@yahoo.com.cn

SEN-LUN YU is a Beijing-based journalist who contributes to *Screen International* and Beijing-based *City Weekend* magazine.

Colombia Jaime E. Manrique & Pedro Adrián Zuluaga

Colombian cinema is currently engaged in a love affair with its audience. The eight national titles released in 2006 were viewed by 2.8 million spectators – 14% of the total market. The most successful of the eight, **Dreaming Has No Price** (*Soñar no cuesta nada*) by Rodrigo Triana, tells the story of a real-life incident concerning a group of soldiers who found a buried stash of money belonging to the FARC (Revolutionary Armed Forces of Colombia). Because it was based on a very recent and well-publicised event, the story attracted significant media attention. Felipe Aljure's **The Colombian Dream** (*El Colombian Dream*) was a riskier venture, presenting an innovative and formal rendering of a story about the allure of easy money. And Juan-Felipe Orozco's **At the End of the Spectra** (*Al final del espectro*) was a respectable attempt to make a horror movie that could hold its own against international competition.

During the first months of 2007, three Colombian films attracted approximately 1.5 million spectators. By the end of the year, a total of ten or twelve local films will have opened on the commercial circuit, proving the existence of a viable Colombian film culture. The 'Ley del Cine' (law of film), which was passed in 2003, is now regularly used by producers, who can receive benefits as well as tax-deductible donations by private investors. It is perhaps because of this that critics and audience are now demanding more from their cinema.

If the 2006 releases were reticent in taking risks (except for *The Colombian Dream*), 2007 shows more promise. Felipe Martínez's **Bluff** and Andi Baiz's **Satan** (*Satanás*) are two

Damián Alcázar in **Satan**

outstanding debuts. Martínez's black comedy is an impressive entertainment, whereas *Satan* tries for something a little more sophisticated, a drama that peels away the layers of 'evil' of which each of us is capable. Veteran filmmaker and playwright Jorge Alí Triana's **This Smells Fishy** (*Esto huele mal*) regressed into a series of clichés to present a confusing episode set against the backdrop of an actual terrorist attack on a swanky nightclub in Bogotá. Actor and director Juan Fisher's second feature, **Searching for Miguel** (*Buscando a Miguel*), is a naïve morality play about a politician who suffers a bout of amnesia. Javier Mejía's **Apocalypse** (*Apocalípsur*), which took seven years to complete, plays with structure and narrative in presenting a visceral and sincere account of a group of young friends living in Medellin during the late 1980s, when drug-related terrorism was rife.

In March 2007, the Festival Internacional de Cine de Cartagena played host to 13 new Colombian films, reinforcing the dynamic climate of the filmmaking scene. In May, Colombia was invited to the 'Tous les cinémas du monde' section of the Cannes Film Festival. **PVC-1**, directed by Spiros Stathoulopoulos, and Andi Baiz's short film **Bonfire** (*Hoguera*) participated in the Quinzaine des Réalisateurs.

Ramón Marulanda and Andrés Echavarrío in **Apocalypse**

However, Colombian cinema has some way to go before it makes an impact outside its domestic market.

Some films yet to be released possess specific regional characteristics and as a result may be less commercially viable than many productions from the last two years. Luis Fernando Bottía's **Juana Had Golden Hair** (*Juana tenía el pelo de oro*) and Alessandro Basile's **Heaven** (*El cielo*) were produced in the Colombian Caribbean, while **Paradise Dream** (*El sueño del paraíso*), by Carlos Palau, was shot and set in the southwestern region of Valle del Cauca. During the 1980s, a significant number of films were produced, but projects considered more artistic than commercial were produced outside the capital so as to display the diversity of the country. By contrast, contemporary Colombian cinema appears more homogenous and less compromised in its role of speaking about the times we live in.

The relationship between Colombian film and its audience is not without its thorns; it is too early to offer more than hope for the future. The whole film industry, including its audience, is being tested; we must wait and see what the new year brings.

The year's best films
Apocalypse (Javier Mejía)
Satan (Andi Baiz)
A Tiger of Paper (Luis Ospina)
The Dragon of Comodo [short] (José Luis Rugeles)
City of Chronic Features [short] (Klych López)

Quote of the year
'Nowadays most Colombian films are merely short versions of soap operas.' OSCAR CAMPO, *documentary filmmaker discussing scripts and scriptwriters in Colombian cinema*

Directory
All Tel/Fax numbers begin (+57)
Association of Film & Video Producers & Directors, Calle 97, No 10-28, Bogotá. Tel: (1) 218 2455. Fax: (1) 610 8524. gustavo@centauro.com.
Colombian Association of Documentary Film Directors, Calle 35, No 4-89, Bogotá. Tel: (1) 245 9961. aladoscolombia@netscape.net. www.enmente.com/alados.
Colombian Association of Film Directors, Carrera 6, No 55-10, Apartado 202, Bogotá. Tel: (1) 235 9798. Fax: (1) 212 2586. lisandro@inter.net.co.
Colombian Film Archives, Carrera 13, No 13-24, Piso 9, Bogotá. Tel: (1) 281 5241. Fax: (1) 342 1485. patfilm@colnodo.apc.org. www.patrimoniofilmico.org.co.
Film Promotion Fund, Calle 35, No 4-89, Bogotá. Tel: (1) 287 0103. Fax: (1) 288 4828. claudiatriana@proimagenescolombia.com. www.proimagenescolombia.com.
Ministry of Culture, Film Division, Calle 35, No 4-89, Bogotá. Tel: (1) 288 2995. Fax: (1) 285 5690. cine@mincultura.gov.co. www.mincultura.gov.co.
National Film Council, Calle 35, No 4-89, Bogotá. Tel: (1) 288 4712. Fax: (1) 285 5690. cine@mincultura.gov.co. www.mincultura.gov.co.

JAIME E. MANRIQUE is a journalist and editor of *Pantella Columbia* newsletter, and is director of the Association of New Film Directors. **PEDRO ADRIÁN ZULUAGA** is a journalist and editor of *Kinetoscopio* magazine.

Croatia Tomislav Kurelec

2006 saw the release of the Croatian film industry's greatest commercial success of the past decade, Hrvoje Hribar's comedy **What's a Man Without a Moustache** (*Što je muškarac bez brkova*). It attracted an audience of 160,000, beating most American blockbusters at the box office. Hribar's hit notwithstanding, the last two years have seen little change in box office returns, even though a slew of awards from international film festivals, not to mention positive reviews from film critics, point to an increase in the quality of Croatian films. 2007 saw a drop in the number of films produced to just six features; however, it has been announced that the country's film production will increase by at least 50% in 2008.

Rajko Grlić's **The Border Post** (*Karaula*) managed to make more of a splash than most domestic releases, attracting an audience of over 40,000. It focuses on the interaction between soldiers of different nationalities at an isolated observation point on the Yugoslav/Albanian border in 1987. How the relationships develop foreshadows the root of the conflict that will later result in the war between the states of former Yugoslavia. Antonio Nuić's debut, **All for Free** (*Sve džaba*), attracted a far smaller audience, although it won the Grand Prix at the 2006 Pula Film Festival. Set in Bosnia and influenced by the films of Aki Kaurismäki, albeit with a broader sense of humour, it is a bizarre tale of a lost generation that grew up during the break-up of former Yugoslavia.

A number of films received significant accolades in 2006. Branko Schmidt's **The Melon Route** (*Put Lubenica*) is a powerful story of human trafficking along the Croatian-Bosnian border; its authenticity, both in characterisation and environment, contributes to the film's convincing representation of the hardships facing the world today. Dalibor Matanić's **I Love You** (*Volim te*) is a well-directed and touching film about a young man infected with the AIDS virus after a blood transfusion and how this changes his world, his relationships with friends and business partners as he reveals to them his predicament.

Ognjen Sviličić's **Armin**

Ognjen Sviličić, one of Croatia's most promising young filmmakers, was the recipient of several international awards, among them the East of West Award presented at the Karlovy Vary Film Festival, for his film **Armin**. A middle-aged man takes his teenage son to Zagreb in order to audition for a part in a German film shooting on location in Bosnia. Through the pauses in their fragmented conversations, Armin Omerovic and Emir Hadzihafisbegovic (who won prizes at the Pula and Durban film festivals) draw out the differences in mindset and tradition between the two characters, subtly playing out the complex parent/child relationship.

Three other noteworthy films from 2007 include Kristijan Milić's **The Living and the Dead** (*Živi i mrtvi*), winner of eight Golden Arena awards at Pula. Arguably one of the finest Croatian war films ever produced, it focuses on two groups of Croatian soldiers, located in the same place, some fifty years apart: in World War II and the more recent war in former Yugoslavia. The film details their struggle to survive under extreme conditions, their existential crises, suffering and death. The enemy here is not physical, but an omnipresent sense of impending threat and danger. Reasons for the latter conflict, the ideological debates surrounding it, issues of nationality and what constitutes ethical and justified action, are never discussed. Visually impressive, with convincing characterisation and a control of rhythm and pace, *The Living and the Dead* is more suggestive than graphic in its presentation of the horrors of war.

Goran Kulenović's **Play Me a Love Song** (*Pjevajte nešto ljubavno*) received the audience award at Pula. It is an entertaining film about four young rock musicians trying to earn enough money to produce their first album, who reach a point of debasing themselves by performing at weddings. Kulenović highlights how easily reality can undermine the ideals and aspirations of today's younger generation.

For his second film as a director, renowned actor Dejan Ačimović recounts a nostalgic story set in 1970 in the Herzegovinian town of Mostar, showing how events and environment influence and shape the life of a nine-year-old boy. By focusing on him, **I Have to Sleep, My Angel** (*Moram spavat', anđele*) succeeds in presenting a complex, though certainly idealised, notion of the co-existence of various nationalities, religions and ideologies. The boy's perspective highlights disparities, both cultural and political, for the audience, but they are of no consequence to the nine-year-old, nor to those around him who could not possibly anticipate the catastrophe that was to ensue some twenty years later.

Good Morning (*Dobro jutro*) was veteran director Ante Babaja's return to filmmaking after 15 years. It might also be the best gauge of the success of the Croatian film industry in 2007. Babaja, living in a home for the elderly, uses a DV camera to record his everyday life. Creativity, which Babaja believes to be essential in giving meaning to life, is utilised to instil the daily routine at the home with a deeper sense of significance. Recording through his bedroom window, filming his friends as they meet for coffee, or even crossing the street (an exercise shot as though fraught with danger), Babaja observes infirmity, old age and death. But rather than approach his situation with a sense of gloom or despair, he celebrates the human spirit in standing up to physical disability and the onset of old age.

The year's best films
Good Morning (Ante Babaja)
The Border Post (Rajko Grlić)
Armin (Ognjen Sviličić)
The Living and the Dead (Kristijan Milić)
All for Free (Antonio Nuić)

Quote of the year
'This film was not made to be liked. It's about the cruelty of war, the apocalypse of war.'
KRISTIJAN MILIĆ *on his film* The Living and the Dead

Directory
All Tel/Fax numbers begin with (+385+
Croatia Film, Katanciceva 3, 10000 Zagreb. Tel: (1) 481 3711. Fax: (1) 492 2568.
Croatian Film Directors Guild, Britanski Trg 12, 10000 Zagreb. Tel: (1) 484 7026. info@dhfr.hr. www.dhfr.hr.
Croatian Film Club's Association, Dalmatinska 12, 10000 Zagreb. Tel: (1) 484 8764. vera@hfs.hr. www.hfs.hr.

TOMISLAV KURELEC is a film critic, mostly for radio and television. He has directed five short films and many television items.

Cuba Jorge Yglesias

The last two years have seen impressive advances in digital filmmaking, enabling young directors to make films that frequently feature pointed critiques of contemporary Cuban society.

Manuel Pérez's **Pages From the Diary of Mauricio** (*Páginas del diario de Mauricio*) and Esteban García Insausti's **Exist** (*Existen*) were two contrasting films from 2006. Pérez, who trained at the legendary Cuban Institute of Art and Cinema Industry (ICAIC) during the 1960s, employs an opaque, almost televisual style, focusing on the last twelve years of a man's life, and producing a fascinating account of one person's mortality. In contrast, Insausti's documentary suggests a postmodern aesthetic, in the tradition of the great Nicolás Guillén Landrián, one of the idols of the new generation of filmmakers. An effective collage of opinions about the current situation of the island, with contributions from some of the most 'famous crazy people' on the streets of Havana whose reflections confer a carnivalesque significance on the archival material used, this documentary uses a provocative tone of irreverence typical of the new generation.

Narrated in a quiet, evocative tone, Pavel Giroud's **The Age of the Peseta** (*La edad de la peseta*) is set at the end of the 1950s, on the threshold of great social change. The title is a popular Cuban expression referring to the period just prior to adolescence. **El Benny**, perhaps the most anticipated film in Cuban cinema in the last few years, is loosely based on the life of the most famous popular Cuban musician, Benny Moré. Its director, Jorge Luis Sánchez, avoids a typical hagiographic account of a national legend, opting instead for a sincere attempt to uncover the man hidden by myth and popular imagery. For the musical numbers, Sánchez had to use a Moré impersonator, as he could not afford the expensive rights charged by RCA Victor.

Jorge Luis Sánchez's **El Benny**

If there is one Cuban film that deserves to be called an independent production, it is Alejandro Moya's **Mañana**, whose narrative structure bewildered critics. A portrait of daily life on the point of disintegration, Moya's debut is an unusual experiment in the landscape of Cuban cinema, disturbing the majority of spectators more used to the conventions of television. 2007 also featured Daniel Diaz Torres's **Road to Eden** (*Camino

Pavel Giroud's **The Age of the Peseta**

al Edén) featuring love and betrayal in Cuba at the end of the nineteenth century. Arturo Sotto directed **The Night of the Innocents** (*La noche de los inocentes*), an unsuccessful combination of genres that exposes one of the recurring themes in current Cuban cinema: the choice between spiritual and material happiness.

Fernando Pérez's **Madrigal**

Madrigal, the best film of 2007, may also be the finest achievement of its director, Fernando Pérez. It is divided into two parts, one telling the 'real' story within a conventional narrative, the other employing strong visuals accompanied by ambiguous dialogue to communicate with its audience. With its minimalist soundtrack, the film establishes a nexus between a reality that is consciously theatrical and the idea of 'pure' experience. The Havana from other films by Fernando Pérez is transformed here into a highly illusory city, populated by smoke and darkness, not dissimilar to science fiction. In it, the sense of reality becomes vague. Filmed in high definition, the most sophisticated ever used in a Cuban film, it is a homage to René Clair's love story based on lies, *Les Grandes manoeuvres*.

The documentary scene in Cuba is thriving, with many filmmakers focusing on social conditions within the country. In **Degeneration** (*Degeneración*), Aram Vidal Alejandro looks at people who grew up during the 1990s economic crisis, canvassing their opinion on their current situation and what their future holds for them. It won the Best Documentary

prize at the Sixth National Sample of Young Producers. In **Searching for You Havana** (*Buscándote Habana*), Alina Rodríguez Abreu explores life in the marginal neighbourhoods of the capital, where improvised homes have been built by immigrants from the east of the country, a phenomenon ignored by state media. Sandra Gómez Jiménez's **The Lonely Beds** (*Las camas solas*) focuses on the inhabitants of a dilapidated building in the heart of Havana, as the city prepares itself for the arrival of a hurricane. In **Model Town**, Laimir Fano shows the deplorable state of a town built around a sugar-processing plant.

Some of these filmmakers produce their films from competition prize money, while others have the support of foreign companies. A small number finance their films themselves. What remains important for them all is that they capture a Cuban reality that has been largely absent from the screen until now.

The year's best films
The Age of the Peseta (Pavel Giroud)
Exist (Esteban García Insausti)
Madrigal (Fernando Pérez)

Quote of the year
'We are trying to make the films we wanted to see when we were only spectators.' PAVEL GIROUD *on the* The Age of the Peseta

Directory
All Tel/Fax numbers begin (+53)
Cuban Institute of Art and Cinema Industry (ICAIC), Calle 23, No 1155, Entre 8 & 10, Vedado, Havana. Tel: (7) 552 859. Fax: 833 3281. internacional@icaic.cu. www.cubacine.cu.
Escuela Internacional de Cine y TV, Carretera Vereda Nueva, KM 4.5, San Antonio de Los Baños, Havana. Tel: (650) 383 152. Fax: (650) 382 366. eictv@eictv.org.cu. www.eictv.org.

JORGE YGLESIAS is a poet and movie critic, and Professor of Film History and Chair of Humanites at the International School of Film and Television.

Czech Republic Eva Zaoralovà

Although the film industry in the Czech Republic is in the hands of private production companies and can rely only on limited support from public funding, the number of feature films increased to 29 titles in 2006. A further 23 full-length films, largely features, were in production in 2007.

At the beginning of 2007, the amendment to the law on cinematography finally came into effect. The State Fund of the Czech Republic for the Support and Development of Czech Cinematography, which had relied hitherto solely on funds supplied by distributors and acquired through the sale of older films, received a further CZK100 million (€3.4 million) out of the state budget. In February 2007, the fund divided CZK220 million (€7.5 million) among more than sixty projects at various stages of production.

Jiří Vejdělek's **Holiday Makers**

Czech films have performed quite well domestically. In 2006, two Czech films held the top position at the box office: Jiří Vejdělek's **Holiday Makers** (*Účastníci zájezdu*) and Karel Janák's **The Rafters** (*Raftáci*). Another two were placed fourth and eighth. The audience figures for *Holiday Makers* reached almost 800,000 (a little less than 10% of the total

Jiří Menzel's **I Served the King of England**

population). Czech films have also performed well at international festivals in recent years, though less so in distribution. **I Served the King of England** (*Obsluhoval jsem anglického krále*) is an exception, having been sold to a number of countries, following its huge success at home. With Jiří Menzel directing, and based on the novel by *Closely Observed Trains* author Bohumil Hrabal, the film played at the 2007 Berlin Film Festival, where it won the FIPRESCI Award. The story of a waiter who longs to become a millionaire and whose destiny takes an unexpected turn when his dream comes true, it is set against a backdrop of modern Czechoslovak history, from the 1930s, through World War II and Nazi occupation, to the 1960s when the unscrupulous, but now wiser, hero is released from a Communist-run prison after almost 15 years. Menzel's film won the top of them Czech Lion awards and was nominated by the Czech Film and Television Academy to represent the Czech Republic at the Academy Awards.

Holiday Makers also performed well on the festival circuit, following a successful screening at the Tribeca Film Festival. The feature debut of Vejdělek and an adaptation of the highly successful novel by best-selling Czech author Michal Viewegh, the film captures the comic antics of a group of typical Czech tourists as they make their way to Italy. Vejdělek followed this success with another road-trip comedy, **Roming**, about a man's journey to meet his gipsy bride. Of the films which competed for the 2006 Czech Lion awards, special mention should be made of **Beauty in Trouble** (*Kráska v nesnázích*) by the prolific and successful director Jan Hřebejk. Featuring excellent performances, Hřebejk's tragi-comedy deals with the complexity of human relationships. Though not as successful as his previous film, *Up and Down*, Hřebejk re-teamed with regular writer, Petr Jarchovsky, for **Teddy Bear** (*Medvídek*), again dissecting personal relationships within contemporary society.

Jan Hřebejk's **Beauty in Trouble**

David Ondříček's fourth feature, **Grandhotel**, about the relationship between four young people and featuring a futuristic mountaintop hotel in northern Bohemia, did not win over either critics or audiences in the same way his earlier *Loners* had done. Conversely, a member of the older generation of Czech filmmakers and one of the leading figures of the New Wave of Czechoslovak film during the 1960s, Věra Chytilová, enjoyed considerable acclaim for **Pleasant Moments** (*Hezké chvilky bez záruky*), a morality piece about the disintegration of strong inter-personal bonds.

Věra Chytilová's **Pleasant Moments**

2006 saw the appearance of three accomplished debut films. **The Indian and the Nurse** (*Indián a sestřička*), portraying a clash between the representatives of minority groups and established societal conventions, was directed by Dan Wlodarczyk. Experienced documentary filmmaker Robert Sedláček's **Rules of Lying** (*Pravidla lži*) was a psychological drama set in a drug rehabilitation centre. And Marta Nováková saw the release of **Marta,** her graduation film from FAMU (the Prague Film School), a drama about three characters situated outside time and space.

Marta Nováková's FAMU graduation film, **Marta**

2006 also saw the release of the animated feature **Fimfárum 2** (*Fimfárum 1* was made in 2002), with filmmakers Jan Balej, Aurel Klimt, Břetislav Pojar and Vlasta Pospíšilová returning to the fairytales of Jan Werich, and Karel Vachek's film essay **Záviš, the Prince of Pornofilm under the Influence of Griffith's Intolerance and Tati's Monsieur Hulot's Holiday, or the Foundation and the Doom of Czechoslovakia (1918 – 1992)** (*Záviš, kníže pornofilmu pod vlivem Griffithovy Intolerance a*

Tatiho Prázdnin pana Hulota, aneb vznik a zánik Československa (1918 – 1992)), in which the director expounds his idiosyncratic reflections on society and the state, with his own special kind of humour.

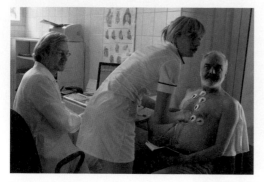

Empties, *directed by Jan Svěrák*

Of the films produced in 2007, Jan Svěrák's comedy **Empties** (*Vratné lahve*), co-produced with the UK, attracted an audience of over one million. The Academy Award-winning director based his film on a screenplay written by his father, Zdeněk Svěrák, who plays a man refusing to grow old gracefully. The third film by the talented Alice Nellis, **Little Girl Blue** (*Tajnosti*), is an intimate portrait of a woman who, during a single day, discovers that her seemingly happy life is in tatters. It was hailed by critics as Nellis's most successful work to date. Writer and director Petr Nikolaev approached Jan Pelc's cult work **...It's Gonna Get Worse** (*...a bude hůř*) in a quasi-documentary style. The film describes the colourful destinies of a group of young people following the suppression of the Prague Spring in 1968. The lead-up to November 1989, and the years that followed, are captured in **Marcela**, a hard-hitting documentary by Helena Třeštíková. The director spent several years following the eponymous character whose life is shattered by the mysterious death of her daughter.

The successful debut by Karin Babinská, **Dolls** (*Pusinky*), was filmed in a documentary style. The story of three girls travelling together during the summer holidays, it sensitively

introduced the theme of lesbian love for the first time in Czech film history . The romantic relationships are more conventional in Irena Pavlásková's **The Bitch's Diary** (*Bestiář*), which opts for an appealing story set against the backdrop of tourist destinations. The experienced but always experimental Tomáš Vorel combined traditional teen comedy with the 'aerosol art' graffiti phenomenon for his adolescent drama, **High School** (*Gympl*). After several controversial films, Vorel succeeded in creating a work that delighted both critics and audiences.

A few recent productions have yet to be released. Jiří Vejdělek's third film in as many years, **Václav**, sees him adopt a more serious tone, with the study of a mentally disabled man. Vladimír Michálek reflects upon the relationships formed between two generations in **Parents and Children** (*O rodičích a dětech*). Petr Zelenka's **Karamazovs** (*Bratři Karamazovi*) brings together preparations for the staging of the well-known novel by Dostoyevsky with the real lives of the performers.

Helena Třeštíková's **Marcela**

Acclaimed cinematographer, František A. Brabec, returns to directing with an adaptation of **May** (*Máj*), the epic poem by Romantic author Karel Hynek Mácha, while Václav Marhoul chose a decisive battle from World War II for his psychological drama about courage and cowardice, **Tobruk**.

Bathory is the new film by one of the leading directors of the Czechoslovak New Wave, Juraj Jakubisko. Based on a seventeenth-century legend in which a noblewoman is supposed to have found eternal youth by bathing in the blood of virgins, Jakubisko sees his central character as an uncharacteristically emancipated and energetic woman who unsettled those around her and thus became the victim of slander. The film's significant budget has seen several production companies invest in the director's highly ambitious project.

43rd**KARLOVY VARY**
INTERNATIONAL FILM FESTIVAL

JULY 4–12, 2008
Call for Entries – Deadline April 18, 2008

CONTACT ADDRESS
Film Servis Festival Karlovy Vary
Panská 1, 110 00 Prague 1, Czech Republic
Tel: + 420 221 411 011, Fax: + 420 221 411 033
E-mail: program@kviff.com, www.kviff.com

The year's best films
I Served the King of England (Jiří Menzel)
Empties (Jan Svěrák)
Rules of Lying (Robert Sedláček)
Little Girl Blue (Alice Nellis)
The Indian and the Nurse (Dan Wlodarczyk)
Grandhotel (David Ondříček)

Quote of the year
'Even without a formalised financial incentive, Prague's infrastructure, locations and professionalism remain appealing, especially to A-list projects. Walden Media's *The Chronicles of Narnia: Prince Caspian* and Universal Pictures' *Wanted* are both shooting in the Czech capital. However Prague is no longer the bargain it once was.' THEODORE SCHWINKE *in Screen International*

Directory
All Tel/Fax numbers begin (+420)
Association of Czech Filmmakers (FITES), Pod Nuselskymi Schody 3, 120 00 Prague 2. Tel: (2) 691 0310. Fax: (2) 691 1375.
Association of Producers, Národní 28, 110 00 Prague 1. Tel: (2) 2110 5321. Fax: (2) 2110 5303. www.apa.iol.cz.
Czech Film & Television Academy, Na Îertvách 40, 180 00 Prague 8. Tel: (2) 8482 1356. Fax: (2) 8482 1341.
Czech Film Centre, Národní 28, 110 00 Prague 1. Tel: (2) 2110 5302. Fax: (2) 2110 5303. www.filmcenter.cz.
FAMU, Film & Television Faculty, Academy of Performing Arts, Smetanovo 2, 116 65 Prague 1. Tel: (2) 2422 9176. Fax: (2) 2423 0285. kamera@f.amu.cz. Dean: Karel Kochman.
Ministry of Culture, Audiovisual Dept, Milady Horákové 139, 160 00 Prague 6. Tel: (2) 5708 5310. Fax: (2) 2431 8155.
National Film Archive, Malesická 12, 130 00 Prague 3. Tel: (2) 7177 0509. Fax: (2) 7177 0501. nfa@nfa.cz. www.nfa.cz.

EVA ZAORALOVÀ is Artistic Director of the Karlovy Vary International Film Festival, editor of *Film a doba* magazine and author of books on Czech, French and Italian cinema.

Denmark Jacob Neiiendam

The hype surrounding Danish films at festivals and markets around the world has cooled down in recent years. Acclaimed Danish filmmakers appear to be struggling to connect with their domestic audiences. Even though solid government funding and a healthy local market share continue, the much-envied drive and success of recent years has seemingly evaporated. 'Is it really that bad?' one might ask. No one is quite as good at announcing a crisis (both commercially and artistically) as the Danish film industry and press. This time, however, everyone appears to be convinced by the pessimists. That, in turn, has profoundly affected the morale of Danish cinema over the last year.

In need of a new Dogme?

One of the most impressive achievements of the Dogme movement was that it bridged the gap between art-house and mainstream cinema. Films like Thomas Vinterberg's *Festen*, Lone Scherfig's *Italian for Beginners* and Susanne Bier's *Open Hearts* managed to be successful with critics and audiences. But in recent years, 'relationship' dramas have lost their appeal and the market has returned to 'normal', split between popular commercial fare and struggling art-house releases. Many see this as a sign of crisis. However, the market share of local films is still healthy, with 25% in 2006, only a fraction less than the 1999–2006 average of 26%.

The 2007 market share owes a great deal to a seemingly unending series of family films, the most recent of which were Claus Bjerre's **Father of Four – Living Large** (*Far til fire – i stor stil*) and Niels Nørløv Hansen's **Anja &**

Erik Clausen's **Temporary Release**

Viktor – Flaming Love (*Anja og Viktor – brændende kærlighed*). Though unpopular with critics, they each attracted an audience of over 300,000, as did the latest comedy drama from the folksy Erik Clausen. In **Temporary Release** (*Ledsaget udgang*) Clausen once again stars as a habitual criminal, this time on day release from prison in order to attend his son's wedding.

Former Dogme acolytes, Lars von Trier, Lone Scherfig and Thomas Vinterberg returned to Danish shores in a more cheerful mood, following their bigger-budget, English-language films. Maverick von Trier expressed his eagerness to leave his USA trilogy unfinished

Lars von Trier's **The Boss of it All**

for the moment in order to revitalise with an office-based black comedy, **The Boss of it All** (*Direktøren for det hele*). Featuring local actors, Jens Albinus Peter Ganzler and Iben Hjejle, it tells the story of an actor hired to pose as a big-shot company manager in a film that features the director's characteristically cynical and razor-sharp wit. However, local critics failed to understand that von Trier wasn't striving for the moral complexity of *Manderlay* or the visual reinvention of *Breaking the Waves* and unjustly panned the film, which failed to find an audience.

Scherfig and Vinterberg also failed to win over audiences and critics, although the lack of interest in their films was more justified. Scherfig's attempt to recapture *Italian for Beginners'* loose, improvised charm in **Just Like Home** (*Hjemve*) was undermined by an underwritten script following a group of lonely people in a small town turned upside down by the rumour of a naked man running through the streets. Vinterberg's **A Man Comes Home** (*En Mand kommer hjem*) also echoed his Dogme past, albeit with a lighter, less engaging tone. Thomas Bo Larsen plays an opera star who returns to his childhood home in the countryside, his presence affecting those around him, not least a young, stammering apprentice cook.

Hollywood visuals in local settings

While some Dogme directors returned to their roots, other filmmakers distanced themselves from the austere rules of that manifesto. Nikolaj Arcel, whose successful debut *King's Game* was inspired by *All the President's Men*, dared to be even more ambitious with his new project, **The Island of Lost Souls** (*De fortabte sjæles ø*). The big-budget fantasy film, inspired by Steven Spielberg and the *Harry Potter* movies, was an impressive technical achievement and solid family entertainment. But in its eagerness to match the Hollywood blockbuster it lacked any genuine identity, performing less well than expected at the box office.

Nikolaj Arcel's **The Island of Lost Souls**

With regular writing partner, Rasmus Heisterberg, the prolific Arcel also found time to script the horror film **Cecilie** for director Hans Fabian Wullenweber. An excellent genre film, falling somewhere between *Rosemary's Baby* and the recent glut of Japanese horror films, it nevertheless failed to strike a note with local audiences, underlining the problems faced by all domestic genre films which lose out to similar US fare at the box office.

Ole Bornedal, another filmmaker long committed to proving that Denmark isn't too small for genre films, released two films in 2007. **The Substitute** (*Vikaren*) is nothing short of a science-fiction horror film for children, featuring the excellent Paprika Steen as an alien posing as a substitute teacher. **Just Another Love Story** (*Kærlighed på film*) is closer to Bornedal's breakthrough debut *Nightwatch*. Anders W. Berthelsen's role is that of a likeable family man involved in a car crash and then falls in love with the victim who a result of the accident is in a coma; he is then mistaken for being her boyfriend. Although the visuals impress, the thriller's many twists result in an overly convoluted plot.

Ole Bornedal's **The Substitute**

Without stars there's room for more...

What the Danes may have missed in 2007 was their two most popular filmmakers, Susanne Bier and Per Fly. In 2006 Bier's powerful drama, **After the Wedding** (*Efter brylluppet*), about a man suddenly faced with a grown-up daughter he never knew existed, was the highest-grossing domestic release, by now a familiar story for each of Bier's films since her international breakthrough, *Open Hearts*. It was also the first Danish film to be nominated for an Academy Award since 1989. Her Hollywood debut, the Sam Mendes-produced **Things We Lost in the Fire**, stars Halle Barry and Benicio Del Toro. Following his commercially successful and award-winning trilogy (*The Bench*, *The Inheritance*, *Manslaughter*), Fly was convinced by national broadcaster DR to direct a mini-series. **Performances** (*Forestillinger*), focusing on Dejan Cukić's stage director, attracted critical acclaim, but few viewers tuned in to his Bergmanesque television drama.

Pernille Fischer Christensen's **A Soap**

In the absence of Bier and Fly, other interesting new talents emerged. Pernille Fischer Christensen's **A Soap** (*En Soap*) focused on the relationship between the owner of a beauty clinic and a transexual, while Anders Morgenthaler's partly animated feature **Princess** involves a dead porn star, her grieving missionary brother, his five-year-old niece and a mission to ensure that no traces remain of the porn star's career.
In documentary, Asger Leth attracted controversy and acclaim in equal measure

Asger Leth's **Ghosts of Cité Soleil**

with his account of the last days of President Aristide's regime, **Ghosts of Cité Soleil**. Eva Mulvad recorded the election of Afghanistan's first member of Parliament in **Enemies of Happiness** (*Vores lykkes fjender*). And in **The Monastary: Mr Vig and the Nun**, Pernille Rose Grønkjær tells the story of an 82-year-old man who bought a castle with the intention of transforming it into a place of worship. With the arrival of Russian orthodox nuns, his dream may have come true, but his problems are only just beginning.

Peter Schønau Fog's assured debut, **The Art of Crying** (*Kunsten at græde i kor*), became a festival darling after its 2006 premiere at San Sebastián. A surprise box office hit, it is based on the popular autobiographical novel by Erling Jepsen. Life within a deeply dysfunctional family during the 1970s is seen through the eyes of an 11-year-old boy, whose willingness to do anything to keep his manic-depressive father happy includes covering up the sexual abuse of his sister.
The most thought-provoking, if not commercially successful, film of the year came

Peter Schønau Fog's **The Art of Crying**

from Morten Hartz Kaplers. A provocative and entertaining mockumentary, **AFR** uses real and fake interviews, as well as newsflashes, to spin a fascinating lie about a love affair between the Danish Prime Minister and a young rebel.

Anders Morgenthaler's Echo

Things to come

So is there a crisis? The answer of course depends on the films to come. Looking back over the last two years, only a few films stood out, but that does not mean the remainder were poor. With a few exceptions they were all well made, and more diverse in style and genre than in previous years. No doubt producers and distributors are pressed financially, not least those making films outside the mainstream. But they will regain their footing and find the best new projects and filmmakers to back. For now the future looks bright, and a number of up-coming films look highly promising: Anders Morgenthaler's **Echo** (*Ekko*), Pernille Fischer Christensen's **Dancers** (*Dansen*), Ole Christian Madsen's **Flame & Citron** (*Flammen & Citronen*) and Søren Kragh Jacobsen's **What No One Knows** (*Det som ingen ved*), are all slated for release in 2008.

JACOB NEIIENDAM is the Head of Programming at Copenhagen International Film Festival, but also a film critic and journalist contributing to national and inter-national publications, including being the Nordic correspondent for *Screen International* 1999–2005.

The year's best films

Princess (Anders Morgenthaler)
AFR (Morten Hartz Kaplers)
A Soap (Pernille Fischer Christensen)
The Art of Crying (Peter Schønau Fog)
The Boss of it All (Lars von Trier)

Quote of the year

'One of the advantages of being a small country is that we always feel threatened and for that reason try to forestall the next crisis instead of resting on our laurels.' NIKOLAJ SCHERFIG, *former film consultant at the Danish Film Institute*

Directory

All Tel/Fax numbers begin (+45)
Danish Actors' Association (DSF), Sankt Knuds Vej 26, DK-1903 Frederiksberg C. Tel: 3324 2200. Fax: 3324 8159. dsf@skuespillerforbundet.dk. www.skuespillerforbundet.dk.
Danish Film Directors (DF), Vermundsgade 19, 2nd Floor, DK-2100 Copenhagen Ø. Tel: 3583 8005. Fax: 3583 8006. mail@filmdir.dk. www.filmdir.dk.
Danish Film Distributors' Association (FAFID), Sundkrogsgade 9, DK-2100 Copenhagen Ø. Tel: 3363 9684. Fax: 3363 9660. www.fafid.dk.
Danish Film Institute/Archive & Cinemateque (DFI), Gothersgade 55, DK-1123 Copenhagen K. Tel: 3374 3400. Fax: 3374 3401. dfi@dfi.dk. www.dfi.dk.
Danish Film Studios, Blomstervaenget 52, DK-2800 Lyngby. Tel: 4587 2700. Fax: 4587 2705. ddf@filmstudie.dk. www.filmstudie.dk.
Danish Producers' Association, Bernhard Bangs Allé 25, DK-2000 Frederiksberg. Tel: 3386 2880. Fax: 3386 2888. info@pro-f.dk. www.producent-foreningen.dk.
National Film School of Denmark, Theodor Christensen's Plads 1, DK-1437 Copenhagen K. Tel: 3268 6400. Fax: 3268 6410. info@filmskolen.dk. www.filmskolen.dk.

Ecuador Gabriela Alemán

Late 2006 saw the approval of the first Ecuadorian Film Law which permitted the creation of the first state-funded film body, the CNC (National Film Council). The much-vaunted $1 million offered to the audiovisual sector did not materialise until October 2007 when 140 projects were sent to a panel of ten jurors, two of whom were from Ecuador. Of these, 16 projects, at various stages of production (script development, production, post-production and distribution of shorts, documentaries and fiction films), will be funded.

Almost a year after the film law was passed, Ecuador also became member of the IBERMEDIA programme, whose main objective is to foster the development of Latin American and Spanish cinema. In the ten years of its existence, it has funded 972 projects in 17 countries.

There was also the 'discovery' of an untapped sector: an audience for Ecuadorian films. Seen for the most part only in festivals, and mostly unknown outside the country's frontiers, the breakthrough success of Tania Hermida's road movie, **How Much Further?** (*Qué tan lejos?*), in both Ecuador and Spain brought

Yanara Guayasamín's **Cuba, The Value of Utopia**

hope for the development of a national film industry. The film, seen in a handful of Spanish cities, was a phenomenon. It premiered in art-house theatres completely unprepared for the thousands of Ecuadorian migrants who turned up with their families to 'see' Ecuador. According to official statistics there are more then two million Ecuadorians living abroad.

Documentary proof

The past two years have seen a growing interest in documentary, an interest that continues to develop around the Cine Memoria Corporation and its annual EDOC Festival, now in its sixth year. This festival has not only found an audience for documentary film, but has had repercussions in the wider film community, with distributors now carrying non-fiction films in their catalogues. This has also had an impact on television stations. The 2006 festival screened seven national productions. Among the more interesting were **George Febres: The Fabulous Story of the Cousin of a Saint and His Crocodile Shoes** (*George Febres: la fabulosa historia del primo de un santo y sus zapatos de cocodrilo*) by Ivo Huahua, about an unknown figure in the Ecuadorian art scene; **Untitled** (*Sin título*), Cristina Mancero's short film on how sexual and national identities are viewed; and **Velasco: Portrait of an Andean Monarch** (*Velasco: retrato de un monarca andino*) by Andrés Barriga, which explores the many faces of the most elected, and overthrown, president of Ecuador. María José Martínez, from Loja, won the Best Cultural Video award at the Muestra Iberoamericana de TV y Video Educativo, Científico y Cultural de México in 2006, showing that Quito and Guayaquil are no longer the only sites of film production in the country.

The 2007 EDOC Festival screened seven documentaries: **Cuba, the Value of Utopia** (*Cuba, el valor de una utopía*) by Yanara Guayasamín; Felipe Terán's look at racism in Ecuadorian society, and its relationship to soccer and Ulises de la Cruz, one of Ecuador's top players, **Score a Goal, Win!** (*Mete Gol Gana!*); **Taromenani: the Extermination of the Occult People** (*Taromenani: el exterminio de los pueblos ocultos*) by Carlos Andrés Vera; **Alfaro Vive Carajo! From Dreams to Chaos** (*Alfaro Vive Carajo!, del sueño al caos*) by Isabel Dávalos; Gabriela Batallas's short about the value of photography and identity, **Uncle Arturo's Car** (*El carro del tío Arturo*); the first short ever made about gay and lesbian communities in Ecuador, Pablo Mogrovejo's **On the Front Page** (*En Primera Plana*); and **Free Style** (*Estilo Libre*) a short film about hip-hop culture in Quito, by Victor Carrera.

Guayasamín's film was not only the first Ecuadorian production to be accepted for the Joris Ivens competition at the 2007 International Documentary Film Festival Amsterdam, it was also selected, along with 19 other productions, to be part of the collection celebrating twenty years of the IDFA. The three other feature documentaries screening at EDOC this year were shown at prime time on national television.

Alvaro Muriel's **Women** (*Ellas*), about women prisoners in Quito jails, and Rodolfo Muñoz's **Red Card** (*Tarjeta Roja*), about another important figure of the national soccer scene, 'Tin' Delgado, were also screened in 2007.

New audiences, old mores

The Cero Latitud Film Festival has become the Quito Film Festival. Due to its pre-selection process, it opts for mainstream fare. The result of this is that Ecuadorian audiences see only a small percentage of films actually made. Nevertheless, the festival is now in its fifth year and is the main showcase for Ecuadorian and Latin American fiction films. A major draw for filmmakers is the 'Work-In-Progress' category for Andean cinema, with a $10,000 prize. Highlights of the festival included **Anytime Soon** (*Estas no son penas*) by Anahí Hoeneisen and Daniel Andrade, which had already been screened at festivals in Toulouse, Guadalajara and Mar del Plata and **In the Edge of Love** (*Filo de Amor*), José Rafael Zambrano's uneven movie about the flip-side of the machista myth, which provoked strong reactions from the film community, although it proved popular with audiences.

Finally, **When Will it Be My Turn** (*Cuando me tocará a mí*), the second feature by Victor Arregui (whose debut, *Offsides*, won the 2002 'Cine en Construcción' category at the San Sebastián Film Festival), will premiere in Ecuador in January 2008 after its leading actor, Manuel Calisto, won the Best Actor award at the Festival of Biarritz.

The year's best films
Cuba, the Value of Utopia (Yanara Guayasamín)
Score a Goal, Win! (Felipe Terán)
Alfaro Vive Carajo! From Dreams to Chaos (Isabel Dávalos)
Untitled (Cristina Mancero)

Quote of the year
'Cinema is finally it its rightful place. In everybody's house: the Presidency'. CNC *Director* **JORGE LUIS SERRANO** at the first film awards ceremony in the Presidential Palace

Directory
All Tel/Fax numbers begin (+593)
INCINE, Vizcaya E13-39 & Valladolid, Tel. 2904724, info@incine.edu.ec, www.incine.edu.ec
Cine Memoria Corporation, Veintimilla E8-125, Quito, Tel. 2902250, info@cinememoria.org, www.cinememoria.org
Consejo Nacional de Cine (CNC), www.cncinec-uador.blogspot.com

---

GABRIELA ALEMÁN is a writer and journalist with a PhD from Tulane University, where she specialised in Latin American film. She is affiliated to Andina University in Ecuador.

Egypt Fawzi Soliman

Forty new domestic films were screened in 2006, eleven more than 2005. For the first time, five new Egyptian features were premiered at the Cairo International Film Festival, three in competition, one of which featured in the digital films section.

A crop of new production companies have appeared on the scene in the last two years, increasing the competition, both in terms of cinema exhibition and the over-populated world of satellite television broadcasting, which is a significant source of financing for features. These include El Alamia, Hussein el Qalla, Hany Guirguis Fawzi Co. and El Adl group. The big trio, El Nasr, El Masa and Oscar, formed a new holding company, backed by ART and Rotana, to produce TV films for the two channels. A new company, Good News, produced two big-budget films, **The Yacoubian Building** (*Omaret yakobean*) and **Halim**, and was involved in the development of **Bibby Doll**.

Marwan Hamed's **The Yacoubian Building**

Critics in Egypt have been scathing about the commercial success of farcical comedies, particularly those starring Mohamed Saad,

which have achieved the biggest box office returns in the history of Egyptian cinema. In films such as *Limby*, *Awkal*, *Karker* and, most recently, Ahmed Awad's **Katkout**, Saad relies on physical comedy, never developing his one-dimensional characters.

The directorial debut of Marwan Hamed, *The Yacoubian Building* was a big success for Good News, who had gathered a strong cast for acclaimed writer Waheed Hamed's adaptation of Alaa El Aswani's equally famous novel. Though successful, the film met with opposition from across the political spectrum. Members of parliament accused it of violating moral values and demanded that it be either cut or banned. Ali Abu Shady, the head of the censorship board, refused to do either, allowing the film to be shown uncut for adults.

The Yacoubian Building is a microcosm of Egyptian society, with its rich inhabitants living in luxurious apartments and the poor on the roof. Various stories interweave throughout the film: the businessman who bribes his way to power; the rich son of a playboy who only appears interested in prostitutes; the relationship between a homosexual journalist and the porter's son, who becomes a terrorist after having been rejected by the police academy.

Hussein Qalla, who produced some of the country's most important films of the 1980s and 1990s, returned with **Leisure Time** (*Awqat Faragh*), the directorial debut of Mohammed Moustapha. In exploring the spiritual and emotional emptiness of the younger generation, who have no contact with or understanding of their elders, *Leisure Time* raises the question of who is to blame:

parents, the education system or society as a whole? The film's success has encouraged Qalla to use the same actors for a new project, **Magic**. He has also teamed up with Hani Guirguis Fawzi to co-produce the film. Ihab Lamei's **Special Relations** (*Elakat Khasa*) also dealt with the disparity between generations, this time representing youths from many different classes, all of whom are revolting against old traditions. The film's tone condemned the schizophrenia of the Arab personality.

Mohamed Khan – one of the most important figures of the 1980s new realism movement – returned with his **In the Heliopolis Flat** (*Fi shaket Masr El- Gedida*), written by his wife Wissam Soliman, who also wrote *Down Town Girls*. A man rents an apartment in Cairo's suburbs only to find the spirit of someone who once lived there still present. With the arrival of a rural girl, the man decides to find out what happened to the former tenant. At the same time, his relationship with the girl blossoms. It was shot by Nancy Abdel Fattah, Egypt's first female cinematographer.

Female directors

Four female directors have had their films distributed in the last two years. Hala Khalil also wrote her second film, **Cut and Paste** (*Kas wa lazk*). A cynical portrait of contemporary Egyptian society, Hanan Turk plays a woman who hopes to emigrate to New Zealand. In order to do so, she must be married, so she sells everything she has and proposes to a young man she scarcely knows. Kamla Abu Zikri followed *Head and Tail* with **Of Love and Infatuation** (*Al Ishq wal Hawa*), written by Tamer Habib. Egyptian actor Ahmed El Saqqa, better known for performing in action films, starred in this tear-jerking melodrama. Inas El Deghedi adapted **Let's Dance** (*Matigi Norkos*) from *Shall We Dance?* Always provocative in her defence of women's rights, El Deghedi's film justifies the entitlement of a hard-working woman, played by Youssra, to relax by dancing. Director Sandra Nashaat

Tahani Rashed's **These Girls**

followed the success of *Alexandria Private* with another action-packed espionage thriller, **The Hostage** (*El Raheena*), once again featuring Ahmed Ezz.

Other films released included Khaled Al-Hagar's sophisticated revival of the musical **None But That** (*Mafish Gheir Keda*), based on Brecht's *The Seven Deadly Sins* and starring Nabila Ebeid. **El Banate Dol** (*These Girls*), by Tahani Rashed, takes us into the perilous existence of adolescent girls living on the streets of Cairo. Avoiding police shakedowns and robbery by fellow street-dwellers, the girls stand by each other, always living in the present and ready to enjoy any moment of levity that comes their way. An account of police corruption, **Heya Fawda!** (*Chaos*) by octogenarian Youssef Chahine and Khaled Youssef – his assistant on previous films – was premiered at the 2007 Venice Film Festival. There was also Aiteen Amin's **Her Man**, Rami Abdel Gabbar's **House of Flesh**, Mahmoud Soliman's **Red and Blue** and Tamer El Bostany's **Stray Cats**.

Youssef Chahine and Khaled Youssef's **Heya Fawda!**

Independent film production flourished in 2006 and 2007, with a host of young directors courageously ignoring taboos, censorship and commercial demands to express their ideas, producing their own films on video and digital, and being rewarded for their efforts at national and international film festivals.

FAWZI SOLIMAN is a journalist and critic who has contributed to magazines and newspapers in Egypt and the Arab world. He has served on the FIPRESCI jury of many film festivals.

The year's best films
The Yacoubian Building (Marwan Hamed)
In the Heliopolis Flat (Mohamed Khan)
Cut and Paste (Hala Khalil)
Passtime (Mohammed Moustapha)
These Girls (Tahani Rashed)

Quote of the year
'The film rings the bells of danger, and uncovers the real roots of corruption in our society.' *Director and film critic* HASHAM EL NAHAS *commenting on* **The Yacoubian Building**

Directory
All Tel/Fax numbers begin (+20)
Chamber of Film Industry, 1195 Kornish El Nil, Industries Union Bldg, Cairo. Tel: 578 5111. Fax: 575 1583.
Egyptian Radio & TV Union, Kornish El Nil, Maspero St, Cairo. Tel: 576 0014. Fax: 579 9316.
National Egyptian Film Archive, c/o Egyptian Film Centre, City of Arts, Al Ahram Rd, Guiza. Tel: 585 4801. Fax: 585 4701. President: Dr Mohamed Kamel El Kalyobi.
National Film Centre, Al-Ahram Ave, Giza. Tel: 585 4801. Fax: 585 4701.

Estonia Jaan Ruus

2007 was yet another positive year for the emerging Estonian cinema. At the end of 2006, celebrated theatre director Elmo Nüganen's comedy, **Mindless** (*Meeletu*), proved popular with audiences. In it, a millionaire decides to give up his fortune in order to settle for a simple life in the country. Audiences were drawn to the film's emphasis on a society polarised by haves and have-nots. Also in 2006, the first feature-length Estonian animated film, **Lotte from Gadgetville** (*Leiutajateküla Lotte*), was released. Directed by Heiki Ernits and Janno Põldma and adapted from a popular TV series, the film followed the adventures of girl dog Lotte in a whimsical and family-orientated entertainment.

Heiki Ernits and Janno Põldma's **Lotte from Gadgetville**

2007 opened with novelist Kadri Kõusaar's debut, **Magnus**, which premiered in the 'Un Certain Regard' section at the Cannes Film Festival. With shades of black humour throughout, Kõusaar's philosophically minded drama focuses on suicide and parental neglect. It features an excellent performance by pop star Kristjan Kasearu. An analysis of schoolyard violence earned Ilmar Raag's **Class** (*Klass*) two awards – an 'East of West' special mention and Label Europa Cinemas prize – at the Karlovy Vary Film Festval. The brutal climactic massacre may not be new to those who have seen Gus Van Sant's *Elephant*,

Kadri Kõusaar's **Magnus**

but the film's emotional power guaranteed its nomination as Estonia's official selection for Best Foreign Language Film at the Academy Awards. Veiko Õunpuu's melancholic comedy of relationships, **Autumn Ball** (*Sügisball*), was awarded the Horizons Award at the 2007 Venice Film Festival. One can see the influence of Antonioni and Cassavetes in the detailed episodes depicting chaotic and disjointed human relations in a metropolitan suburb.

Awards from esteemed festivals are an important recognition for a small film-producing nation, whose annual output has never exceeded eight features. No less important are commercially successful films. The blackly comic road movie, **186 Kilometres** (*Jan Uuspõld läheb Tartusse*), directed by Andres Maimik and Rain Tolk, was a runaway domestic success. Jan Uuspõld parodies himself as an actor forced to hitchhike across Estonia in order to star in a reputable theatre company's new play, encountering an assortment of misfits along the way. **Georg**, directed by Peeter Simm, recently opened in cinemas. Culled from research and interviews with his second wife, the film tells the life story of Georg Ots, one of the most beloved opera singers of the last century, whose baritone voice made him a household name in Estonia, Russia and Finland.

Ilmar Raag's **Class**

Audiences welcomed two feature-length documentaries: **Singing Revolution** (*Laulev revolutsioon*) by US directors James and Maureen Castle Tusty, which analysed Estonia's bloodless breakaway from the Soviet Union in the 1980s through a wealth of archive material; and Toivo Aare's **Estonians in Kremlin** (*Eestlased Kremlis*), which documents the Estonian delegation's days at the Congress of Deputies in Moscow, when the Soviet Union was dissolved at a parliamentary level. **The Art of Selling** (*Müümise kunst*), directed by Jaak Kilmi and Andres Maimik, presents a merciless satire focusing on a manipulative character from commercial advertising, while the bitter confessions of a society's lower classes have been captured in **Jonathan from Australia** (*Jonathan Austraaliast*), directed by Sulev Keedus.

Tallinn Black Nights Film Festival, which each December presents more than a hundred new features from around the world, celebrated its tenth anniversary in 2006. And the Pärnu Documentary and Anthropology Film Festival, held each summer, is now joined by the Tartu Festival of Visual Culture in spring and Matsalu International Nature Film Festival in autumn.

Within the framework of project Eesti Film100, several classic films have been restored, and the Estonian Film Museum has opened its doors. Animation studio Nukufilm, which has sustained high artistic levels throughout the most fickle of times, celebrated its fiftieth anniversary.

In addition, Tallinn University Baltic Film and Media School, which was founded in 2005, now offers students a masters programme in English.

There is little doubt that robust economic growth has been a motivating force behind the renewed enthusiasm in the film industry. State support for film has been growing steadily, reaching over $7 million in 2007, up 23% from 2006.

Per capita cinema attendance was 1.2 million in 2006, up 40% year-on-year; and 161 feature films premiered in Estonian cinemas in 2007. Short films have also found their way to the Internet. Rasmus Merivoo's **Alien** (*Tulnukas*), which ridicules bullies, has reached a near-cult status, boasting over 600,000 visitors over one year.

By the end of 2007, Estonian films made up 13% of all cinema admissions. Hardi Volmer and Ain Mäeots's tragi-comedy **Taarka** will be the first Estonian film of 2008, scheduled to premiere in the spring. It portrays the life of a tiny nation (similar to the Sami of Finland, Sweden and Norway) living in southeastern Estonia, not far from the Russian border. It will be followed by Andrus Tuisk's **Bankrobbery** (*Pangarööv*), Hannu Salonen's **Kid Killer** and **I Was Here** (*Mina olin siin*) directed by René Vilbre. All the films are co-productions, mostly with Finnish producers.

JAAN RUUS works as a film critic for the biggest Estonian weekly, *Eesti Ekspress*, and is the president of the Estonian FIPRESCI.

186 Kilometres, directed by Andres Maimik and Rain Tolk

The year's best films
Autumn Ball (Veiko Õunpuu)
Magnus (Kadri Kõusaar)
Mindless (Elmo Nüganen)
Lotte from Gadgetville
(Heiki Ernits and Janno Põldma)
Jonathan from Australia
(Sulev Keedus)

Quote of the year
'A new profession emerges – that of a Euro project writer. He, like Mr Wolf in *Pulp Fiction*, enters the scene at the last minute. And in a jiffy he clothes the film project in a silky dress of sexy marketing phrases.' ANDRES MAIMIK, *screenwriter and cultural critic*

Directory
All Tel/Fax numbers begin (+372)
Estonian Association of Film Journalists, Narva Mnt 11E, 10151 Tallinn. Tel: (6) 533 894. Fax: (6) 698 154. jaan@ekspress.ee.
Estonian Film Foundation, Vana-Viru 3, 10111 Tallinn. Tel: (6) 276 060. Fax: (6) 276 061. film@ efsa. ee. www.efsa.ee.
Estonian Film Producers Association, Rävala pst 11-12, 10143 Tallinn. Tel: (6) 67 8 270. Fax: (6) 67 8 721. produtsendid@rudolf.ee.
Estonian Filmmakers Union, Uus 3, 10111 Tallinn. Tel/Fax: (6) 464 068. kinoliit@online.ee.
Estonian National Archive, Ristiku 84, 10318 Tallinn. Tel: (6) 938 613. Fax: 938 611. filmiarhiiv@ra.ee. www.filmi.arhiiv.ee.
Union of Estonian Cameramen, Faehlmanni 12, 15029 Tallinn. Tel: (6) 662 3069. Fax: (6) 568 401. bogavideo@infonet.ee.

Finland Antti Selkokari

The films that dominated the local scene for most of 2006 were polar opposites in style and content: Aleksi Mäkelä's **Matti – Hell is for Heroes** (*Matti*) and **Lights in the Dusk** (*Laitakaupungin valot*) by Aki Kaurismäki.

Mäkelä's biopic of ski-jumper Matti Nykänen was the biggest domestic box office success of the year, boosted in no small way by producer Markus Selin's aggressive marketing campaign, part of his ongoing desire to dominate the home market with highly publicised productions. Beginning with the announcement that shooting had commenced on the film, Selin employed his innate talent for courting and manipulating the media to achieve maximum coverage. *Matti* proved to be a bigger crowd-pleaser than expected, attracting a total audience of 461,665. Naturally the film plays to expectations. The storyline is plucked from the tabloid headlines of Nykänen's scandal-filled life, detailing his lapses into binge drinking and attempts at pop stardom and professional stripping following his retirement from competitive sports. Though impressively portrayed by Jasper Pääkkönen, the film teeters on the verge of exploitation, leaving audiences mixed in their emotional responses. Selin's production company, Solar Films, will return to celebrity filmmaking in 2008 with **Dark Floors** (*Punainen liitu*), a horror film starring Eurovision song contest winners, Lordi.

Kaurismäki's *Lights in the Dusk*, the story of a night watchman enduring impossible hardships in Helsinki, became Finland's Cannes participant *de rigueur*. It is a tragi-comedy with strong noirish elements, featuring Helsinki as an emotionally and physically cold place, with human kindness in short supply. Despite the

Aki Kaurismäki's **Lights in the Dusk**

relatively new face of Janne Hyytiäinen in the lead, the film is a coda to Kaurismäki's past themes and imagery. It was not surprising to learn that the director had expressed his wish to retire from filmmaking. This was emphasised when he announced to the jury who selected the Finnish Academy Award entry that he wanted the film withdrawn from competition, leaving Finland with no entry for the awards. *Lights in the Dusk*'s box office takings were less than 10% of *Matti*'s.

Still darker, colder visions

Aku Louhimies finally saw his bleak vision of Helsinki, first unveiled to audiences in the mini-series, *Irtiottoja*, transfer to cinemas in two separate films. 2005's *Frozen Land* featured life on a broad canvas, whereas **Frozen City** explored in more detail one strand from the TV series, which focused on a dysfunctional couple. As the taxi driver whose estranged wife exploits his emotional fragility, Janne Virtanen is heartbreakingly direct. He is helped in no small part by Louhimies's talent as a gifted storyteller and cinematographer Rauno Ronkainen's roaming Steadicam.

The influence of television's reality shows could be seen in **The Dudesons Movie** (*Duudsonit elokuva*), featuring a Jackass-style stunt show, where a group of adolescents dare each other to submit to cruel pranks, which include becoming a human dartboard and being subjected to a wake-up call with a baseball bat. Watching the cumulative stupidity is hardly a cathartic experience. The grainy picture quality only further proves the amateurishness of this sort of comedy.

Fresh views for film foundation

When the managing director of the Finnish Film Foundation, Jouni Mykkänen, retired after ten years at the end of June 2006 it marked the end of a transitional period in the Foundation's history. Mykkänen was a great moderator who saw his duty as creating stability, putting an end to the many intrigues and bickering between filmmakers and cultural figureheads. His successor, Irina Krohn, sees her duty as continuing the positive advancement of the Finnish filmmaking community and securing more funds for film production. Previously a member of Parliament, her network of contacts finds her well positioned to continue the progress made by Mykkänen.

Krohn has been lobbying for an increase in the funds for production. Her efforts doubled in September 2007, when producers began a strike to protest against the diminishment of state subsidies, which lag behind other Nordic countries. The strike was aimed directly at the actions of the cultural minister, Stefan Wallin, whom the producers accuse of breaking his promise to increase subsidies. The strike may cause some Finnish cinemas to close their doors for good, as they are dependent on a constant influx of local films.

Despite the political unease, one local film is likely to come out close to the top of the 2007 box office figures. **Ganes** is a biopic of the singer/drummer of Finland's most famous 1970s rock group, directed by Jukka-Pekka Siili. The conventionally told story of Remu Aaltonen, whose sheer willpower drove his band to success, features a charismatic performance by Eero Milonoff in the lead role.

The best crop

New filmmakers constantly appear on the horizon. Petri Kotwica, whose 2005 debut, *Homesick*, conveyed the inner turmoil of an institutionalised teenager, returns with **Black Ice** (*Musta jää*), which charts the breakdown of a marriage. Kotwica's strength lies in creating a narrative that involves the audience in her characters' lives. Martti Suosalo, Outi Mäenpää and Ria Kataja play the three individuals caught up in a web of deceit. Mäenpää in particular is outstanding as Saara. The film also represents a welcome change of pace in Finnish filmmaking which has, for the best part of the last decade, been dominated by generic fare catering mostly to the youth market. *Black Ice* is therefore refreshingly grown-up.

Aleksi Salmenperä's second film, **A Man's Job** (*Miehen työ*), ranks as one of the best of 2007. The story of a laid-off worker, Juha, who, out of the need to provide for his family, resorts to a career as a male prostitute for single, lonely or older women, Salmenperä invests his drama with an impressive degree of maturity. Tommi Korpela plays Juha, a man whose shame increases in direct proportion to his family's prosperity. With this film Salmenperä explores the nature of Finnish masculinity. Perhaps falling short of an exhaustive analysis of the

Petri Kotwica's **Black Ice**

Aleksi Salmenperä's **A Man's Job**

alpha male in Finnish society, *A Man's Job* is nonetheless a good study of one family's predicament.

Of the recent documentaries, Jouko Aaltonen's **Revolution** (*Kenen joukoissa seisot*) and Taru Mäkelä's **Catch** (*Saalis*) impressed the most. Made in 2006, Aaltonen's film looked at the intense period of radicalism amongst young leftists in the 1960s and how their lives have progressed since. Some have maintained the ideals of their youth, while others have been happy to pursue a career in business. Aaltonen's astute observations resulted in a fascinating film.

Mäkelä's more recent *Catch* turned the filmmaker's gaze upon her own family, famous cinema owners and founders of Kinosto, the largest distribution and exhibition company of its time. Kinosto later became Finnkino, the ruling exhibitor. Both a study of the Finnish bourgeoisie and an intimate piece of filmmaking, Mäkelä turns her slightly amused gaze on herself, analysing her role in her family.

A sad note

2007 ended on a sad note. One of the major artists of Finnish filmmaking, Rauni Mollberg, died on 11 October, aged 78. Mollberg will be remembered for his stunning debut in 1973, *The Earth is a Sinful Song*, and a groundbreaking version of a Finnish classic, *The Unknown Soldier*. Mollberg was an original, who possessed a remarkable gift for storytelling.

The year's best films
Lights in the Dusk (Aki Kaurismäki)
Frozen City (Aku Louhimies)
A Man's Job (Aleksi Salmenperä)
Catch (Taru Mäkelä)
Black Ice (Petri Kotwica)

Quote of the year
'My job is not to act as the supreme judge on taste. I consider every Finnish film produced worth watching.' *The recently appointed head of the Finnish film foundation,* MS IRINA KROHN

Directory
All Tel/Fax numbers begin (+358)
Finnish Film Foundation, Kanavakatu 12, FIN-00160. Tel: (9) 622 0300. Fax: (9) 622 0305. ses@ses.fi. www.ses.fi

ANTTI SELKOKARI is a freelance film critic and regular contributor to the newspaper *Aamulehti* and cultural magazine *Parnasso*.

France Michel Ciment

'The professionals of the profession', as they were called by Jean-Luc Godard, had never been so optimistic. In 2006, French cinema conquered 44.7% of the market share, superseding American cinema for the first time in the last two decades. The public attendance had increased by 7.6%, reaching 188,670,000 spectators, the second-best performance in 22 years; 84,290,000 tickets were purchased in order to see local films, a jump of 31.4% in one year.

But the films which were seen by two to three million people were neither very exciting nor particularly original, and none of them could be compared to Hollywood successes like *Charlie and the Chocolate Factory*, *War of the Worlds* or *Million Dollar Baby*.

Marina Hands in Pascale Ferran's **Lady Chatterley**

On the night of the Césars (the French equivalent to the Academy Awards), at which Pascale Ferran won the Best Film award for **Lady Chatterley**, Marina Hands, who gave an admirable performance as the titular heroine, made a sobering point to the distinguished guests stating that 'the industry produces, on the one hand, films that are more and more expensive and on the other films with a smaller and smaller budget'. According

to her, the films in the middle – those of Renoir, Truffaut, Becker, Resnais, and so on – used to represent the best of the French cinematographic art. And it is this kind of film that is vanishing, due mostly to the policies of the TV channels.

However, French cinema was still in a healthier state than most of its neighbours, the result of various systems of funding regulated by the CNC (the National Centre for Cinematography); during the same period, cinema attendance fell by almost 5% in both Spain and the UK, and hardly progressed in Italy (+1.7%), with only Germany showing an increase. The most worrying factor was the plethora of film releases – 247 French films out of a total of 589 (averaging a dozen new titles per week), an intimidating number for audiences and critics alike.

There were nevertheless some reasons to rejoice. 2006 registered two remarkable films on the country's colonial past, a subject rarely dealt with on the screen: **Paths of Glory** (*Indigènes*) by Rachid Bouchareb, about the predicament of Algerian soldiers enlisted in the French army to fight against the Nazis,

Bruno Dumont's **Flanders**

and **The Betrayal** (*La Trahison*) by Philippe Faucon, focusing on a French officer in the Algerian War and his relationship with his native subordinates who might be secretly working for the rebels. **Flanders** (*Flandres*) by Bruno Dumont was another strong war movie, featuring the director's typically bleak view of humanity and his powerful visual sense. Robert Guédiguian went back to his roots for the first time with **Armenia** (*Voyage en Arménie*), a dialectical view of post-communism in the Caucasus. The sleeper hit of the year was **Je vais bien ne t'en fais pas** by Philippe Lioret, a classical movie displaying shrewd psychological insight about a family disrupted by the disappearance of a son. And among so many vulgar, uninspired comedies three stood out: Otar Iosseliani's **Gardens in Autumn** (*Jardins en automne*), where the Georgian exile once more extols old lifestyles, poetic encounters and idle characters; **Quatre Étoiles** by Christian Vincent, a Lubitsch-like triangular love story set on the French Riviera; and **Change of Address** (*Changement d'adresse*) by Emmanuel Mouret, a fledgling director inspired by Rohmer's moral tales. Besides these (relatively) new talents, the year was marked by Claude Chabrol's **A Comedy of Power** (*L'Ivresse du pouvoir*), in which a dogmatic, incorruptible judge (authoritatively played by Isabelle Huppert) fights the political and business establishment while being devoured by ambition herself. It was, however, Alain Resnais' Silver Lion winner, **Private Fears in Public Places** (*Coeurs*), which mesmerised critics and audiences with its supreme formal elegance, its portrayal of urban solitude and the audacity of its 84-year-old director.

Emmanuel Mouret and Frédérique Bel in **Change of Address**

2007 was brightened by a number of worthwhile films, even if the list of the ten best failed to match those listed as box office successes. It is depressing that fewer and fewer interesting films are seen by large audiences. The figures increased marginally; 34.8 million people went to the cinema at least once a year – 1,620,000 more than in 2005. The share of senior citizens (50+) increased (28.8% against 25.3% in 2005) while people under 34 (maybe because of the Internet and DVDs) saw fewer French films. There were 203 domestic films produced (of which 76 were co-productions), with an increase at the top and bottom end of the budgetary scale. Even if there were fewer debuts, those 56 films represented one quarter of the releases for the year. The atomisation of production was as conspicuous as usual, with 142 organisations actively producing; Gaumont led the field with only seven films produced during the year, followed by Fidelity, Pan European and Pathé, with five films each. There was also a worrying decline in French exports to Spain (-38.6%), Italy (-40.4%) and the UK (-38.5%), with only the US and Germany (+47.5%) showing an increased interest in Gallic fare.

One of the striking features of the French cinema scene remains the persistent activity of directors like Claude Chabrol, Alain Resnais, Jacques Rivette, Eric Rohmer, Agnès Varda and Chris Marker, the youngest being 77 and the oldest 87, who still create original and stimulating films worthy of their prestigious careers. With **The Romance of Astree and Celadon** (*Les Amours d'Astrée et de Céladon*) Rohmer adapted the obscure seventeenth-

Sabine Azéma and Pierre Aditi in **Private Fears in Public Places**

century classic 'L'Astrée', transforming this love story among fourth-century shepherds into a modern moral tale. Directing unknown young actors as usual, Rohmer blends spontaneity and sophistication, a sense of nature and an eroticism all the more troubling for its being allusive.

While Rohmer reveals himself as the heir of Shakespeare and Marivaux's festive comedies, Rivette resumes his long relationship with Balzac, adapting 'La Duchesse de Langeais' as **Don't Touch the Axe** (*Ne touchez pas la hache*). Once more, the theme of conspiracy is at the centre of his narrative, which posits a coquettish aristocrat against an artillery general, remarkably interpreted by Jeanne Balibar and Guillaume Depardieu, respectively. Less eclectic than his elders, Claude Chabrol is nevertheless on top form with **The Girl Cut in Two** (*La Fille coupée en deux*), one of those scenes of provincial life that constitutes his best work. Freely inspired by the story of the New York architect Stanford White, who was murdered by the husband of his former mistress, Chabrol sets up a triangular relationship between a sex-obsessed writer (played by François Berléand), a schizophrenic young heir (the magnetic Benoît Maginel) and a young and ambitious TV announcer (the always versatile Ludivine Sagnier) in contemporary Lyon. All are observed with a detached gaze.

If Agnès Varda seems to have stayed away from filmmaking for some time, she has devoted herself to fascinating installations with

Claude Chabrol's **The Girl Cut in Two**

multiple screens for the Fondation Cartier and to a visual tribute to the 'Justes' (those French people who saved the Jews from the Nazi persecutions during the Occupation) inside the Pantheon. The freedom that these elder statesmen exemplify was to be found again in the latest work by Manoel de Oliveira (100 years old in 2008), *Belle toujours*, an update of Buñuel's *Belle de jour*. It is an affectionate and ironic homage to the great Spanish artist, and a tribute to Paris. Michel Piccoli is in search of Séverine (Bulle Ogier, substituting for Catherine Deneuve) in order to discover some secret that she won't reveal. As a sprightly and humorous *divertimento*, *Belle toujours* proves once more Oliveira's capacity to surprise.

Vernon Dobtcheff and Audrey Tautou in **Priceless**

Comedy remains France's leading popular genre. This year, six out of the ten top-grossing films belonged to this lucrative trend. But contrary to Italy or the USA, where a number of film directors have shown a certain level of talent, French cinema has rarely produced comedies of quality. In the last few years, several cineaste directors, inspired by classical comedies (Guitry, Becker, Tati), their modern inheritors (De Broca, Deville, Rappeneau) and foreign masters (from Lubitsch to Risi, and Wilder to Monicelli), have avoided the vulgarity of so many commercial successes. In **Priceless** (*Hors de prix*) by Pierre Salvadori, a credulous man (played by Gad Elmaleh), a waiter in a Riviera palace, falls into the arms of a young woman looking for a sugar daddy (the well-cast Audrey Tautou). A true sense of pace and superb performances give a refined

Daniel Boon and Daniel Auteuil **My Best Friend**

elegance to this game of false identities. Patrice Leconte, prolific as always (**Friends Forever** (*Les Bronzés 3: amis pour la vie*), with its audience of ten million, was released a few months before), directed one of his better films, **My Best Friend** (*Mon meilleur ami*); a romantic comedy in which a workaholic antiquarian (the versatile Daniel Auteuil), accused by his associate (played by Julie Gayet) of self-centredness, bets her that he will introduce her within ten days to his best friend. He meets a taxi driver (rising star Dany Boon), and once more Leconte deals with one of his favourite themes: the confrontation between two opposite characters.

Another excellent filmmaker, Pierre Jolivet, also entered the romantic-comedy fray, with Vincent Lindon and Sandrine Bonnaire in **Could This Be Love?** (*Je crois que je l'aime*), a classic boy-meets-girl story. This time, a rich and divorced entrepreneur falls in love with the woman who decorates his office. Male chauvinist and suspicious, he will of course be seduced by the charms of Elsa, despite the blundering private detective he has hired

Noémie Lvovsky's **Faut qu'ça danse!**

to investigate her. Finally, in **Faut qu'ça danse!**, Noémie Lvovsky mixes screwball comedy with the portrayal of a man (played by the extraordinary Jean-Pierre Marielle) who refuses to grow old gracefully and instead reminisces about his family, who perished in the Holocaust. Noémie Lvovsky and her actors (Sabine Azema, Bulle Ogier and Valeria Bruni-Tedeschi) achieve a delicate balance between outrageous situations and dramatic moments.

The *enfants terribles* of French cinema didn't go unnoticed either. Jean-Claude Brisseau attempted the impossible in **The Exterminating Angels** (*Les Anges exterminateurs*): how can a man find out how women are sexually satisfied? The central character pays heavily for his transgressive curiosity. Catherine Breillat, directing her first costume drama, **The Last Mistress** (*Une vieille maîtresse*), from a nineteenth-century novel by Barbey d'Aurevilly, is nevertheless faithful to her favourite theme – the war of the sexes. An incandescent relationship links an aristocrat to a Spanish gipsy whom he cannot abandon even after he is married. Period dramas appear to be popular at the moment, with François Ozon directing **The Real Life of Angel Deverell** (*Angel*), based on the novel by Elizabeth Taylor. Mixing irony with lyricism Ozon, puzzled his audience while remaining totally himself.

Stylistic experiments were present in **Among Adults** (*Entre adultes*) by Stéphane Brizé, shot in a few days with unknown stage actors in a narrative structure reminiscent of Arthur Schnitzler's 'La Ronde', each scene featuring no more than two characters. Julian Schnabel rightly deserved the Best Direction prize at Cannes for **The Diving Bell and the Butterfly** (*Le Scaphandre et le Papillon*), a bold adaptation of Jean-Dominique Bauby's autobiographical work. Left completely paralysed after suffering a stroke, the protagonist communicates with the outside world through the blinking of his left eye-lid. Schnabel, without ever being sentimental,

Mathieu Amalric and Anne Consigny in **The Diving Bell and the Butterfly**

manages to create a daring narrative with impressive emotional tension.

Older directors like André Téchiné and Claude Miller offered new films worthy of their talent. In **The Witnesses** (*Les Témoins*), the eruption of the AIDS epidemic in the early 1980s provides the background for a portrayal of a group of friends and the repercussions of the illness on their relationships. Without any mawkishness, Téchiné orchestrates his choral narrative at the centre of which stands out Sami Bouajila, a married man and father of a child, who leaves his wife (played by Emmanuelle Béart) for a young man who is dying of AIDS. In **Un secret**, Claude Miller organises a complex narrative to tell the story of a Jewish family between the 1930s and the present day. Escaping Nazi persecution, they find refuge in the countryside. Miller, a gifted director at expressing hidden tensions, works marvels with a great cast (including Cecile de France, Julie Depardieu, Ludivine Sagnier).

Alain Chabat and Cecile de France in Claude Miller's **Un secret**

The rewarding aspect of the French production system is the presence each year of new talent. Even if there is a surplus of first and second features (50% of the total output), this fresh blood cannot be considered a negative factor. There were worthy revelations such as **Just About Love?** (*Et toi t'es sur qui?*) in which Lola Doillon, in the footsteps of her father Jacques Doillon, reveals a talent for depicting teenagers and their first amorous feelings. Céline Sciamma in **Water Lillies** (*Naissance des pieuvres*) is a sensitive observer of the budding desires in (again) a trio of young girls. Distinguishing himself from so many of his colleagues who prefer to portray young boys and girls of their own generation, Gabriel Lebomin in **Antonin's Stories** (*Les Fragments d'Antonin*) tells the story of a soldier in World War I who has been traumatised by his wounds and becomes mute. Mixing a voiceover, clinical observations by a medical officer and an intimate diary, Lebomin proposes a fragmented narrative that reflects the mental chaos of his protagonist.

Marion Cotillard in **La Vie en rose**

Among the best performances of the year one should mention Marion Cotillard, who with infinite energy and pathos embodies Edith Piaf in Oliver Dahan's kaleidoscopic **La Vie en rose**; Isabelle Carré, who is astounding as a woman obsessed by her doctor and becoming insane in **Anna M**; and Julie Delpy in her own **Two Days in Paris**, a Woody Allen-esque comedy about the confrontation between a French woman and her American lover during a weekend in Paris.

Animation and documentary films also had their champions. **Persépolis** (winner of the

Julie Delpy's **Two Days in Paris**

Jury Prize at Cannes) brings to the screen the four autobiographical volumes drawn by Marjane Satrapi who, with the collaboration of screenwriter-director Vincent Paronnaud, has been able to convey through movement her satirical view of Iranian and Western societies. Barbet Schroeder's **Terror's Advocate** (*L'Avocat de la terreur*) is an absorbing study of a famous lawyer, Jacques Vergès, whose anti-Western passion has led him to defend controversial defendants such as Klaus Barbie, Carlos the Jackal and leaders of the Khmer Rouge. Finally, the most formally innovative documentary of the year might well be **Beyond Hatred** (*Au-delà de la haine*) where Olivier Meyroux traces the events that led to the murder of a young homosexual by three skinheads in 2001. Following the victim's family between his death and the trial of his assassins the film questions man's capacity to overcome grief and to preserve his dignity.

Marjane Satrapi's **Persépolis**

The year's best films
The Romance of Astree and Celadon
(Eric Rohmer)
Private Fears in Public Places (Alain Resnais)
Un Secret (Claude Miller)
Lady Chatterley (Pascale Ferran)
La Graine et le Mulet (Abdellatif Kechiche)

Directory
All Tel/Fax numbers begin (+33)
Archives du Film, 7 bis rue Alexandre Turpault, 78395 Bois d'Arcy. Tel: (1) 3014 8000. Fax: 3460 5225.
Cahiers du Cinema, 9 passage de la Boule Blanche, 75012 Paris. Tel: (1) 5344 7575. Fax: (1) 4343 9504. cducinema@lemonde.fr.
Centre National de la Cinématographie, 12 rue de Lubeck, Paris 75016. Tel: (1) 4434 3440. Fax: (1) 4755 0491. webmaster@cnc.fr. www.cnc.fr.
Cinémathèque de Toulouse, BP 824, 31080 Toulouse Cedex 6. Tel: (5) 6230 3010. Fax: (5) 6230 3012. contact@lacinemathequedetoulouse.com. www.lacinemathequedetoulouse.com.
Cinémathèque Française, 4 rue de Longchamp, 75116 Paris. Tel: (1) 5365 7474. Fax: (1) 5365 7465. contact@cinemathequefrancaise.com. www.cinemathequefrancaise.com.
Ile de France Film Commission, 11, rue du Colisée, Paris 75008. Tel: (1) 5688 1280. Fax: (1) 5688 1219. idf-film@idf-film.com. www.iledefrance-film.com.
Institut Lumière, 25 rue du Premier-Film, BP 8051, 69352 Lyon Cedex 8. Tel: (4) 7878 1895. Fax: (4) 7878 3656. contact@institut-lumiere.org. www.institut-lumiere.org.
Positif, 3 rue Lhomond, 75005 Paris. Tel: (1) 4432 0590. Fax: (1) 4432 0591. www.johnmichelleplace.com.
Unifrance, 4 Villa Bosquet, Paris 75007. Tel: (1) 4753 9580. Fax: (1) 4705 9655. info@unifrance.org. www.unifrance.org.

MICHEL CIMENT is Honorary President of FIPRESCI, a member of the editorial board of *Positif*, a radio producer and author of fifteen books on cinema.

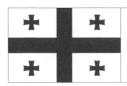

Georgia Nino Ekvtimishvili

The emergence in 2006 of Georgia's first cinema magazine, *Kino*, suggested that the difficult times the country's cinema experienced following the collapse of the Soviet Union might be over. Which is not to suggest that the industry is free from all problems. Distribution has yet to take hold in the country, leaving it in the hands of the Russian distribution network.

Reverse, *directed by Dito Tsintsadze*

Dito Tsintsadze's **Reverse** was the most controversial film of 2006. Four men playing poker in a Tbilisi flat share erotic fantasies about their ideal woman. Tsintsadze deconstructs the cinematic stereotype of the Georgian woman as eternal victim, devoid of eroticism, instead presenting a modern, defiant woman, who materialises to take swift revenge on the men. Aleko Tsabadze's **The Russian Triangle** (*Rusuli samkudhedi*) was the first Georgian film in some time to be distributed in Russia and is Georgia's official entry for the Academy Awards. The main characters of the film are victims of the Chechen War who are lost in a Russian city as a series of murders are being committed there.

Aleko Tsabadze's **The Russian Triangle**

Archil Kavtaradze's **Subordination** tackles the problem of drug addiction in Georgia's capital, Tbilisi, highlighting the lack of opportunities for the young in the city, leaving them with nowhere left to turn. Soso and Badri Jachvlianis's drama **The Svan** is set in Svaneti, a mountainous region of Georgia, where an old Christian community still follows an ancient tradition of vendetta. A similar region, Racha, inspired Aleqsandre Rekhviashvili's documentary, **The Lasts**, about two small Georgian villages seemingly trapped in the Middle Ages with no adequate facilities to allow contact with the outside world. Whereas young people in search of a better future have left, elderly people continue to live there, existing through hard work and prayer.

At the 2007 Festival of Documentary of Mexico City, Salome Jashi was awarded the prize for Best Short Documentary Film, for **Their Helicopter**. It is the story of a Chechen military helicopter that crashed in Upper Khevsureti, Georgia, ten years ago. Abandoned on the ground, a ruined vestige of civilisation, the helicopter has become a shelter for cows and a children's private playground.

Vano Burduli's short, **Graffiti**, won a Grand Prix Award at the 29th Montpellier International

Salome Jashi directed the documentary short, **Their Helicopter**

Film Festival. Loosely based on a short story by Julio Cortasar, the film, set in a fictional country, depicts a peculiar love story between a photographer and a writer. The couple use wall graffiti as a way of expressing their passion for freedom in a fearful time of governmental suppression and terror.

Georgian cinema was represented at a foreign film market for the first time at the 2007 Berlin Film Festival. It will next be represented at the 2008 Cannes Film Festival, Georgia having its own pavilion there, again a new event.

The year's best films
Reverse (Dito Tsintsadze)
Graffiti (Vano Burduli)
The Russian Triangle (Aleko Tsabadze)
Their Helicopter (Salome Jashi)
The Lasts (Aleqsandre Rekhviashvili)

Quote of the year
'We should speak freely, if we do so, we are healthy. I'll always shoot the risky films, and films which irritate.' *Director* DITO TSINTSADZE *on his film,* **Reverse**

Directory
All Tel/Fax numbers begin (+995)
Ministry of Culture, Sport and Monument Protection, 4 Marjvena Sanapiro St., 0105 Tbilisi, Tel: (32) 98 74 30. info@mc.gov.ge.
Georgian National Film Center, Agmashenebeli Avenue 164, 0112 Tbilisi, Tel/Fax: (+995 32) 342 975, Tel/Fax: (32) 342 897. office@filmcenter.ge. www.filmcenter.ge.

Film Studio – Remka, 36 Kostava st., 0179 Tbilisi, Tel: (32) 990 542. Fax: (32) 933 871. remka@remkafilm.ge. www.remkafilm.ge.
Taia Group ltd., 74, Chavchavadze Ave., 0162 Tbilisi. Tel: (32) 912 945. Fax: (32) 253 072.
Studio 99, 10 Sharashidze St., 0162 Tbilisi. Tel: (32) 220 79064. Fax: (32) 230 412. Berlin office: Greifenhagener Str. 26, D-10437 Berlin, Germany, Tel: (+49 30) 44031861. Fax: (+49 30) 44031860.
Sanguko Films, 7 Tamarashvili St., 0162 Tbilisi. Tel: (32) 22 40 61. info@sanguko.ge. www.sanguko.ge.
Sakdoc Film – 2007, 121 Zemo Vedzisi St., 0160 Tbilisi. Tel: (93) 24 32 72/(93) 32 39 29. info@sakdoc.ge. www.sakdoc.ge.

NINO EKVTIMISHVILI is reporter for the TV company Mze and a freelance film critic.

THE CINEMA OF WIM WENDERS
The Celluloid Highway

Alexander Graf

'Graf has done an excellent job of contextualising and explaining Wenders' views on filmmaking in a way that leads to productive textual analysis of his films. This book is a must for Wenders fans.' – Julia Knight, University of Luton

pbk £16.99 / $26.00
978-1-903364-29-1

THE CINEMA OF WERNER HERZOG
Aesthetic Ecstasy and Truth

Brad Prager

'Herzog remains one of the most important and controversial filmmakers of the last thirty years. This incisive and articulate study provides an exceptionally balanced, thorough and intelligent account of the filmmaker and his films.' – Timothy Corrigan, University of Pennsylvania

pbk £16.99 / $26.00
978-1-905674-17-6

www.wallflowerpress.co.uk

Germany Andrea Dittgen

There has rarely been such worldwide acclaim and accolades for a German film as there has for **The Lives of Others** (*Das Leben der Anderen*), the debut of 33-year-old director Florian Henckel von Donnersmarck (seven German Film Awards, four awards from the German Film Critics Association, three European Film Awards, the Best Foreign Language Film Academy Award, more than twenty festival prizes). With this impressively made drama about the East German Secret Police (Stasi) listening to everyone's private lives, featuring an extraordinary performance by Ulrich Mühe, who sadly passed away in 2007, Germany made a huge step forward in dealing with a subject that was neglected for too long (and one that doesn't deal with the Third Reich). Of course *The Lives of Others* was unlikely to outperform Tom Tykwer's adaptation of Patrick Suskind's novel, **Perfume: The Story of a Murderer** (*Das Parfüm – Die Geschichte eines Mörders*), which cost €48 million – the biggest budget ever for a German movie – and attracted an audience of 5.5 million. Well, at least not domestically.

The third film that made 2006 an extraordinary year in German film history, with a market share for local films edging past 25% – the first time since 1974 – was Sönke Wortmann's

Andreas Dresen's **Summer in Berlin**

Germany – A Summer's Tale (*Deutschland. Ein Sommermärchen*), a documentary about the 2006 Football World Cup in Germany. It captured the unique mood of the fans and national football team (who were knocked out

Marcus H. Rosenmüller's **Grave Decisions**

in the semi-finals) and was another big surprise with an audience of four million. Andreas Dresen's tragi-comedy, **Summer in Berlin** (*Sommer vorm Balkon*), about two women and their daily struggle for love and survival set in Berlin played well to art-house audiences, as did Marcus H. Rosenmüller's debut, **Grave Decisions** (*Wer früher stirbt, ist länger tot*). The film, shot entirely in the Bavarian dialect, tells the darkly funny tale of a young boy who thinks he's responsible for his mother's death.

Into 2007...

With no large productions looming into view, the auteur and art-house directors tried to concentrate on their own country and history. As a result, the market share for local films was reduced to 19.5% for the first six months. However, a fresh wind blew in from the US and improved German/American relations, albeit only in cinematic terms. Three films made in Hollywood by young directors German-born were released: the mystery thriller **Premonition** by Mennan Yapo, the horror remake **The Invasion** by Oliver Hirschbiegel, and the tale of human trafficking, **Trade**, by Marco Kreuzpaintner. Although none of the films was very successful, the fact that Hollywood is looking for talent in Germany is an indication of the progress made in Germany's film culture. Moreover, for the first time, Hollywood was interested in a part of German history that is quite unknown abroad: the failed assassination of Adolf Hitler by German officer Graf Stauffenberg in 1944. **Valkyrie**, the movie Tom Cruise shot in Berlin

with director Bryan Singer, caused a strong intellectual debate in Germany involving the Stauffenberg family, the film industry and the ministry of defence: could a 'suspicious' American film star, member of the Scientology Church, be allowed to play the hero of the German resistance, and in the actual locations where the events took place? He could and now everyone's eager to see the film when it is released in 2008.

Dani Levy's **Mein Führer – The Truly Truest Truth about Adolph Hitler**

There was also brief excitement about Jewish (Swiss) director Dani Levy, releasing his comedy **Mein Führer – The Truly Truest Truth about Adolf Hitler** (*Mein Führer – Die wirklich wahrste Wahrheit über Adolf Hitler*). It showed a new version of Hitler as a man who at the end of the war knew that everything was lost and fell into depression until one of his followers had the idea of freeing a Jewish actor (played by Ulrich Mühe) from a concentration camp. With a cabaret-like setting and directing to match, the film has a few funny moments, but is not the artistic achievement everyone had hoped for. A more

Robert Thalheim's **And Along Come Tourists**

serious attempt to deal with the Third Reich was seen in Robert Thalheim's drama, **And Along Come Tourists** (*Am Ende kommen Touristen*). Meeting the last survivor of the Auschwitz concentration camp, a young German comes to understand the degree of post-Holocaust resentment still present in the nearby Polish town and felt by his Polish girlfriend.

Michael Herbig's **Lissi and the Wild Emperor**

In terms of commercial success, but almost entirely lacking in ambition, sequels such as **The Wild Soccer Bunch 4** (*Die wilden Kerle 4*) performed well. The children's film series started in 2003, with two rival groups of kids playing football. Now teenagers, there's very little football and more falling in and out of love. The female variation, **Wild Chicks in Love** (*Die wilden Hühner und die Liebe*), returns to two groups of schoolgirls. The best children's movie, at least from an artistic point of view, was the animated film **The Three Robbers** (*Die drei Räuber*) by Hayo Freitag. A fairytale about a little girl hiding with robbers to avoid the orphanage, it resembled the sensitive drawings in the book by Tomi Ungerer, upon which it was based. Germany's major box office hit was also an animated film: **Lissi and the Wild Emperor** (*Lissi und der wilde Kaiser*). Popular comedian Michael Herbig's first foray into this genre, it is astonishingly well crafted, featuring historical figures like Empress Sissy of Austria and employing elements from well-known fairytales – including more recent discoveries like the yeti – with deft humour.

Although hailed at international festivals, Chris Kraus's **Four Minutes** (*Vier Minuten*), starring upcoming actress Hannah Herzsprung as a

Hannah Herzsprung in **Four Minutes**

young convict being trained by an elderly piano teacher at a women's penitentiary, was not a success at the box office. Director Marcus H. Rosenmüller tried another *Heimat*-style film in Bavarian dialect with **Heavyweights** (*Schwere Jungs*), the true story of two rival German bobsledders at the 1952 Winter Olympics, but couldn't recapture the cosy atmosphere of his previous film. Nevertheless, he returned with **Best Times** (*Beste Zeit*), about a teenager in love with a girl and America, and has already finished **Beste Gegend**, which will be released in 2008. Born in 1973, Rosenmüller is already a unique figure in the landscape of German film.

Martin Gypkens' **Nothing but Ghosts**

The Berlin School, dealing with the everyday lives of young single people or small families, mixing fiction and documentary in a dry style, showed both continuity and development. Angela Schanelec surprised with the emotionally powerful **Afternoon** (*Nachmittag*), about an actress, her lover and her teenage son, who is in love with his mother, during the holidays; while Christian Petzold moved tentatively towards mainstream aesthetics

Ann-Kristin Reyels' **Hounds**

without neglecting the inner struggle of his characters in **Yella**, set between East and West Germany, an elusive thriller about a woman attempting to escape her past, eking out an existence in the hinterlands of modern business parks. **Nothing but Ghosts** (*Nichts als Gespenster*) by Martin Gypkens beautifully switches between eight Germans on holiday in different countries. And for the first time it was possible to laugh in a Berlin School film, thanks to director Ann-Kristin Reyels, who created a wonderfully ironic tone, almost British in its humour, with **Hounds** (*Jagdhunde*). A boy meets a girl in the lonely landscape of the Uckermark in wintertime, while the parents, both divorced and with new partners, try to create a new, patchwork family, leading to bizarre situations.

Exactly this kind of lightness was missing in Fatih Akin's art-house thriller **The Edge of Heaven** (*Auf der anderen Seite*). Akin intertwines the lives of six people: a Turkish widower and his son, the older man's prostitute lover, her daughter, the daughter's

Hanna Schygulla and Baki Davrak in **The Edge of Heaven**

German friend, and her mother. The story seems a bit confusing but Akin manages to keep the balance between the cultures – a rare talent that he surprisingly shares with veteran Volker Schlöndorff, whose road movie, **Ulzhan**, is about a French teacher journeying determindly to what he believes will ultimately be his death, through the deserts of Kazakhstan and into the mountains of China. It is a truly universal movie, representing a new tendency, not only in Germany's attempt to deal with different cultures, but also in its worldview.

Volker Schlöndorff's **Ulzhan**

There will be new dimensions in tackling history in 2008. While Academy Award-winner Florian Gallengerg's **John Rabe** tells the true story of a Nazi who saved more than 200,000 Chinese during the Nanjing massacre in the 1930s, Uli Edel's **The Baader Meinhof Complex** remembers Germany's most wanted terrorist group of the 1970s, based on a bestselling work of nonfiction. Besides Bryan Singer's Tom Cruise vehicle **Valkyrie**, Tom Twyker's new thriller, **The International**, also a Hollywood production shot in Berlin, is anxiously awaited. And of course there is **The Red Baron** about the notorious World War I pilot Manfred von Richthofen.

ANDREA DITTGEN is a film critic and editor of the daily newspaper *Die Rheinpfalz*, contributor to the magazine *Filmdienst* and member of the board of the German Film Critics Association.

The year's best films

Ulzhan (Volker Schlöndorff)
And Along Come Tourists (Robert Thalheim)
Nothing but Ghosts (Martin Gypkens)
The Edge of Heaven (Fatih Akin)
Hounds (Ann-Kristin Reyels)

Quote of the year

'Germany's hope has a name: Tom Cruise.
He will be able to do more for Germany's
reputation than ten World Cups could
do.' *Director* **FLORIAN HENCKEL VON
DONNERSMARCK,** *referring to whether the
American and Scientology Church-member Tom
Cruise should play Count Stauffenberg in* **Valkyrie**

Directory

All Tel/Fax numbers begin (+49)

Deutsches Filminstitut-DIF, Schaumainkai 41,
60596 Frankfurt am Main. Tel: (69) 961 2200.
Fax: (69) 620 060. info@deutsches-filminstitut.de.
www. deutsches-filminstitut.de.

Deutsches Filmmuseum Frankfurt am Main,
Schaumainkai 41, 60596 Frankfurt am Main. Tel:

(69) 2123 8830. Fax: (69) 2123 7881.
info@deutsches-filmmuseum.de. www.deutsches-
filmmuseum.de.

Federal Film Board (FFA), Grosse Praesidentenstr
9, 10178 Berlin. Tel: (30) 275 770. Fax: (30) 2757
7111. www.ffa.de.

Filmmuseum Berlin-Deutsche Kinemathek,
Potsdamer Str 2, 10785 Berlin. Tel: (49 30) 300
9030. Fax: 3009 0313. info@filmmuseum-berlin.de.
www.filmmuseum-berlin.de.

Kino Arsenal/Home of Independent Cinema,
Potsdamer Str 2, 10785 Berlin. Tel: (30) 2695 5100.
Fax: (30) 2695 5111. fdk@fdk-berlin.de. www.fdk-
berlin.de.

Münchner Stadtmuseum/Filmmuseum, St Jako-
bsplatz 1, 80331 Munich. Tel: (89) 2332 2348.
Fax: (89) 2332 3931. filmmuseum@muenchen.de.
www.stadtmuseum-online.de/filmmu.htm.

New German Film Producers Association,
Agnesstr 14, 80798 Munich. Tel: (89) 271 7430.
Fax: (89) 271 9728. ag-spielfilm@t-online.de.

Umbrella Organisation of the Film Industry,
Kreuzberger Ring 56, 65205 Wiesbaden. Tel: (611)
778 9114. Fax: (611) 778 9169. statistik@spio-fsk.de.

Greece Ninos-Fenek Mikelidis

The number of multiplexes continued to increase in Greece over the last year. However, there was no increase in cinema attendance. One of the main reasons, besides the influence of TV and DVDs, is the way films have been distributed over the last few years. Distributors now release between six and eight films per week, even during the summer period (something unheard of a few years ago), resulting in the disappearance of most films after their opening week, thus making it difficult for audiences to see them. Many of these films are intended for DVD, their theatrical release little more than a marketing ploy. However, some films, even high-profile releases like Sofia Coppola's *Marie Antoinette*, are given no chance of theatrical distribution. Of course, the films harmed by such a policy, when the majority of theatres are controlled by big distributors, are usually the artistic, non-American films.

2007 saw the decline, both in quality and quantity, of Greek films. Only three of them have managed to attract an audience of over 200,000: Yiannis Smaragdis's **El Greco**, Olga Malea's **Godfather for the First Time** (*Proti fora nonos*), and Nicos Perakis's latest film, **Loafing & Camouflage: Sirens in the Aegian** (*Loufa kai parallagi: Sirines sto Egeo*), whose audience topped 400,000.

Dimitra Matsuka and Nick Ashton in **El Greco**

The sum spent on film production by the Greek Film Centre, the main financing source for Greek films (except for Malea's film, which was co-produced by one of the big distributors), was reduced this year, resulting in fewer films being made. Consequently, 2007 ended with a meagre 14 features and three documentaries having been made. The most talked about film was *El Greco* due to its large – by Greek standards – budget of €7 million, part of which came from the Minister of Culture's own 'special' budget. The film follows the Cretan painter, Dominicos Theotokopoulos, or El Greco, from his early years in Crete and his sojourn in the royal courts of Venice, through to his arrival in Toledo, Spain. There, he painted his masterpieces and clashed with the priest and, later, Holy Inquisitor, Nino de Guevara. Though overly reverential in its earlier stages, the film becomes more interesting once the action moves to Spain and the uncompromising artist fights against the tyranny of Guevara and the Inquisition. With its clear, linear narrative, impressive crowd scenes and an evocative score by Vangelis and fine performances from the two leads, Juan Diego Boto (Guevara) and Nick Ashton (El Greco), Smaragdis's film is a solid, entertaining bio-pic.

Artistically, the most important Greek film of the year was Yiannis Economidis's **Soul Kicking** (*I Psyhi sto stoma*), presented in the Critics' Week at Cannes. An original, uncomfortably claustrophobic film, it deals with the psychological tension and personal problems experienced by an ordinary, lower-class man, attempting to survive under the continuous pressures and demands of family and work. Economidis balances realism – particularly with his emphasis

Shooting in Greece
www.shootingingreece.com

CL Productions
www.clproductions.gr
The Leading Production Services Company in Greece

on the everydayness of his character's life – with suggestive dialogue, underpinned by subterranean, corrosive humour, faintly reminiscent of Beckett and Pinter, to depict the characters and their psychology.

With his musical film **Dying in Athens** (*Pethainontas stin Athina*), Nicos Panayiotopoulos managed to talk about death with humour, panache and subtlety. The fluid camera movements were more a homage to Jacques Demy than the Hollywood musical. Katerina Evangelakou's **False Alarm** (*Ores koinis isixias*) is a mosaic of human passions and hopes, set over one evening in an apartment block. Notwithstanding the influence of ensemble films such as *Crash*, as well as the danger of presenting stereotypical characters in predictable situations, Evangelakou successfully interweaves the intersecting narratives of her characters' often-fraught lives, drawing strong performances from the cast. In **Eduart**, which is based on a true story, Angeliki Antoniou relates, in

Eduart, *directed by Angeliki Antoniou*

brief, direct images, the odyssey of a young Albanian murderer from the execution of his crime to the moment of his punishment when he returns to Greece to give himself up. An intense film, Antoniou directs with sureness and sincerity. **Roz**, an independent, low-budget film, dealing a young musician's memories of his childhood and his present-day platonic affair with a little girl (perhaps his alter ego?), is the second feature by young director Alexandros Voulgaris, after *Crying?* (*Klais?*) from 2004. Presented in diary form, with Voulgaris as

the main protagonist, *Roz* is an imaginative, humourous film. Dreams, thoughts, elements of psychoanalysis and the young hero's letters to his mother are loosely linked, with an array of images and in-jokes, making for a charming and original film from a talented director. During their Easter holidays in a small village, two Athenian couples are forced to face the secrets and lies of their complacent lives in Sotiris Goritsas's interesting, if uneven, film, **Pals** (*Parees*). Through a series of dramatic situations, the director draws out the doubts and issues facing his characters. At the same time, he presents two other sub-plots, concerning the villagers and an escaped convict, offsetting the drama with comedy.

Of the three documentaries produced in 2007, the most impressive was Spyros N. Taraviras's **Buzz**, a gripping portrait of the famous Greek scriptwriter and pulp-fiction writer, A. I. 'Buzz' Bezzerides, who was responsible for *They Drive By Night*, *Thieves' Highway*, *On Dangerous Ground* and *Kiss Me Deadly*. Stefan Haupt's Greek-Austrian documentary, **A Song for Argyris**, is a portrait of Argyris Sfountouris, who, at the age of four, witnessed the massacre of the inhabitants of his village, Distomo, by German troops; included with the dead were his parents and relatives. Besides archive footage of the massacre, the director follows Argyris in his exile and subsequent studies in Switzerland, as well as his political and judicial fight to make the massacre accepted as a war crime and force Germany to pay the compensation due to Greece and the victims' families.

Yiannis Economidis' **Soul Kicking**

The year's best films
Soul Kicking (Yiannis Economidis)
Roz (Alexandros Voulgaris)
El Greco (Yiannis Smaragdis)
Buzz (Spyros N. Taraviras)
Pals (Sotiris Goritsas)

Quotes of the year
'I do not care about cinema that reminds you of life. I prefer the cinema that speaks about life.' *Director* **YIANNIS ECONOMIDIS** *on his film* **Soul Kicking**

'The kind of politician who functions through marriage, kinship or any other kind of exchange has not disappeared. On the contrary, he prevails.' *Director* **OLGA MALEA** *speaking about her film* **Godfather for the First Time**

Directory
All Tel/Fax numbers begin (+30)
Association of Independent Producers of Audiovisual Works (SAPOE), 30 Aegialias, 151 25 Maroussi. Tel: (210) 683 3212. Fax: (210) 683 3606. sapoe-gr@otenet.gr.
Greek Film Centre, President & Managing Director: Diagoras Chronopoulos, 10 Panepistimiou, 106 71 Athens. Tel: (210) 367 8500. Fax: (210) 364 8269. info@gfc.gr. www.gfc.gr.
Greek Film, Theatre & Television Directors Guild, 11 Tossitsa, 106 83 Athens. Tel: (210) 822 8936. Fax: (210) 821 1390. ees@ath.forthnet.gr.
Hellenic Ministry of Culture, 20 Bouboulinas, 106 82 Athens. Tel: (210) 820 1100. w3admin@culture.gr. http://culture.gr.
Union of Greek Film Directors and Producers, 33 Methonis, 106 83 Athens. Tel: (210) 825 3065. Fax: (210) 825 3065.
Union of Greek Film, TV & Audiovisual Sector Technicians (ETEKT-OT), 25 Valtetsiou, 106 80 Athens. Tel: (210) 360 2379/361 5675. Fax: (210) 361 6442. etekt-ot@ath.forthnet.gr.

NINOS-FENEK MIKELIDIS is a film critic and curator of the Panorama of European Cinema film festival in Athens.

when shooting ends

graal

begins

Digital Intermediate
Film Restoration
HD & SD Definition
Editing
Compositing / VFX
DVD Authoring
Graphic Design
Sound Studio

10, Panepistimiou Str., Athens 10671, Greece, tel.: +30 210 33 90 481-4
fax: +30 210 36 36 216 info@graal.gr
www.graal.gr

Hong Kong Tim Youngs

It has been ten years since Hong Kong reverted back to Chinese control. In 2007, it took a collective look back over a decade of changing fortunes. For the city's film industry, the picture has been one of turbulent times, with a marked decline in output and box office takings since the mid-1990s. But 2006 saw it regain a firm foothold; 51 local films were released, a fraction of early 1990s figures, yet down only slightly from the previous year, while total box office receipts and local films' audience share were largely unchanged. The box office takings per film remained weak in 2006, with just two local films in the city's top ten, and several cinemas downsized or closed, including a drive-in.

Many of the problems that have hurt the industry in recent years continue. Strong competition from Hollywood and a lacklustre slate of domestic releases have dented interest in local fare. Despite increased efforts to raise quality, cinemagoers' tastes remain hard to gauge. Piracy remains a serious problem, as do concerns about the limited talent pool and opportunities for aspiring young actors.

Recent years have been marked by filmmakers increasingly looking to China for investors and audiences, aided by the Closer Economic Partnership Arrangement (CEPA), first introduced in 2003. Lavish period epics, like mainlander Zhang Yimou's imperial family saga, **Curse of the Golden Flower** (*Man cheng jin dai huang jin jia*), still hold the highest profile among Hong Kong/China co-productions. However, these links go further, from Chinese director Jiang Wen's Cultural Revolution-set drama **The Sun Also Rises** (*Tai yang zhao chang sheng qi*) to contemporary, Hong Kong-set thrillers and comedies.

While the partnership benefits Hong Kong as a production and film-development centre, it remains a challenge to meet a distinct set of audience expectations and the strictures of state censorship. And while top-tier co-productions are bringing great opportunities for Hong Kong's leading men, like Chow Yun-fat, Tony Leung Chiu Wai and Andy Lau, filmmakers often prefer to draw on the mainland's most talented actresses as co-stars. Questions have also been raised about how co-productions can continue to present a clear local identity, and indeed what may merit the 'Hong Kong movie' label today.

Responding to industry woes, the government announced a $38.5 million lifeline in early 2007, forming the Film Development Council to handle it. In October, the body called for applications for financing of up to 30% for small-to-medium-sized productions geared toward mass audiences. The spring's annual Entertainment Expo has meanwhile become a stronger film-industry bash, bundling established events, including the Hong Kong International Film Festival and the Hong Kong International Film & TV Market (Filmart), together with new ones like the glitzy Asian Film Awards. Another positive development is

Anthony Wong in Johnny To's **Exiled**

the growth of autumn's Hong Kong Asian Film Festival, premiering local commercial and indie highlights to packed multiplex houses.

Quality draws

2006's local box office charts were topped by Ronny Yu's blockbuster **Fearless** (*Huo Yuan Jia*), a period martial-arts extravaganza starring Jet Li and released during the Chinese New Year. Though *Fearless*'s haul was hard to match, local directors still delivered strong films throughout the year and into 2007. Johnnie To's work remains a particular draw, both locally and abroad. His **Exiled** (*Fong juk*) in late 2006 saw the return of players from his cult hit *The Mission* for a Macau-set tale of camaraderie among rogues, leavened with elaborate gunfights and playful throwbacks to westerns. In 2007, he partnered with Ringo Lam and Tsui Hark to piece together the contemporary crime thriller **Triangle** (*Tai saam gok*) – with each director shooting one of the three 30-minute segments – before teaming up with writer-director Wai Ka-fai to shoot **Mad Detective** (*Sun taam*), an off-kilter story with a supernatural element, about a missing gun and an unorthodox investigator.

Patrick Tam and Pang Ho-cheung also attracted critical attention and audiences at home and internationally. Tam, part of Hong Kong's late-1970s new wave movement, returned to directing after a 17-year hiatus with **After This Our Exile** (*Fu ji*). His meticulous Malaysia-set family drama, a big winner at 2007's Hong Kong Film Awards, featured impressive performances as it covered the painful relationship between a young boy and his abusive father. Pang, meanwhile, continued to steer his work away from his early black comedies towards increasingly polished drama in **Exodus** (*Cheut ai kup gei*). The story of a cop investigating a conspiracy involving an organisation of women secretly plotting the elimination of the male species, Pang's film effectively downplayed action in favour of compelling personal drama, and featured superb cinematography by Charlie Lam.

Charlie Yeung and Aaron Kwak in Patrick Tam's **After This Our Exile**

While holiday-season fare has been gradually reshaped as a result of closer mainland links – not least with an increased focus on the October National Day holidays – Christmas 2006 nonetheless peaked with the high-budget gumshoe adventure **Confession of Pain** (*Seung sing*), from co-directors Andrew Lau and Alan Mak. Featuring an A-list cast, the film drew crowds despite lacking the tension of the pair's earlier hit, *Infernal Affairs*. The following Chinese New Year took an unusual detour from traditionally festive fare: **Protégé** (*Moon to*), a polished narcotics-trade drama

Simon Yam in Pang Ho-cheung's **Exodus**

from director Derek Yee, delivered violent action and explicit scenes of drug-taking.

The handover anniversary added an extra season of celebration for 2007. The highlights of a slew of nostalgic films marking the occasion were Samson Chiu's **Mr Cinema** (*Lo kong ching chuen*) and Law Wing-cheong's **Hooked on You** (*Mui dong bin wan si*). Chiu's often fascinating and touching *Mr Cinema* focused on a pro-Beijing family's past three decades in Hong Kong, successfully tracing the territory's social and economic development from a unique angle. Law's *Hooked on You*, his second solo film after the breast cancer-themed romantic comedy **2 Become 1** (*Tin sun yat deui*) from 2006, proved timely by highlighting Hong Kongers' increased civic activity and concern for local heritage, and incorporating them into an affecting, bittersweet love story.

Genre staples

Action and thriller buffs continue to find their fill in a variety of features. Benny Chan's **Rob-B-Hood** (*Bo bui gai wak*), a Jackie Chan action-comedy about thieves who have their hands full with a hostage baby, staged inventive high-stakes set pieces and good-natured cheer in late 2006. Jacob Cheung's ambitious period piece, **A Battle of Wits** (*Muk gong*), cloaked a tense desert-siege story with an intelligent, pacifist message.

2007 also delivered in the action department. Benny Chan's summer picture **Invisible**

Benny Chan's **Rob-B-Hood**

Target (*Nam yi bun sik*) opted for maximum firepower, with three young cops meting out lessons in the law amid a series of impressive pyrotechnic set-ups. Wilson Yip's modern martial-arts flick **Flash Point** (*Dou fo sin*) allowed screen fighter and action choreographer Donnie Yen to strut his stuff, successfully following up Yip and Yen's 2005 fan favourite, *SPL*. And at the close of summer Oxide Pang's Bangkok-shot **The Detective** (*C+ jing taam*) melded a murder mystery and ghost-movie cues with quirky, offbeat humour.

Comedies, too, remain a hometown staple. In late 2006, Lawrence Lau's **My Name is Fame** (*Ngor yiu sing ming*) presented a star-is-born tale of an aspiring Chinese starlet who moved to Hong Kong and was mentored by a jaded local actor. As the tutor renews his enthusiasm for acting, Lau's film trumpets perseverance, making for an upbeat and charming entertainment. In a similar vein, Patrick Leung and Chan Hing-ka's **Simply Actors** (*Hei wong ji wong*) drew on the mass appeal of stage actor Jim Chim, casting him as the teacher of a porn-film actress. A surprise hit for 2007 came in the form of Patrick Kong's **Love is Not All Around** (*Sup fun oi*), with its idol-strewn romantic comedy striking a chord among young viewers, despite a haphazard script and performances that had cineastes reeling in shock.

Whereas the first post-CEPA years saw local filmmakers leaning toward safer, China-friendly efforts, late 2006 and early 2007 delivered tougher fare. Soi Cheang's **Dog Bite Dog** (*Gau nga gau*) featured a brutal scenario, with a tough Hong Kong cop pursuing an animal-like Cambodian hit man, while Herman Yau's thriller, **On the Edge** (*Hak bak do*), used the popular undercover-cop theme to signify identity crises within the post-colonial administration. Always prolific, Yau followed it with the critically acclaimed, low-budget prostitution drama, **Whispers and Moans** (*Sing kung chok tse sup yut tam*), and the black-magic-themed horror flick, **Gong Tau**.

New blood

The slower film output hasn't kept promising young directors from new projects. Late in 2006 Lee Kung-lok's solo debut **My Mother Is a Belly Dancer** (*See lai ng yi cho*) sparkled, with its take on everyday housewives dancing away the daily grind in a housing estate delivering vibrant flights of fancy onscreen. Noted music-video director Susie Au delivered the hyperactive drama-thriller **Ming Ming**. Though laudable for its extravagance, Au's film ultimately suffered as flashy, avant-garde technique overwhelmed the plot.

Adam Wong was more successful on the creative front. His energetic, low-budget **Magic Boy** (*Mo shuet nam*) conjured up extravagant mixed-media flourishes that neatly complemented a love-triangle plot. Taking a calmer, art-house-friendly route, editor Stanley Tam's directorial debut, **A Breeze of July** (*Chut yuet ho fung*), is an ambitious, HD-shot drama exploring the complexities of family relations. Among the new directors, Yau Nai-hoi was the most successful domestically with his slick police-surveillance actioner **Eye in the Sky** (*Gun chung*), aided by fine performances and a zippy plot. It premiered at the Berlin Film Festival, opened the Hong Kong Film Festival, and went on to earn respectable summer returns.

At the close of summer, Hong Kong moviegoers gave a strong reception to Ang Lee's Hong Kong-linked, World War II-set, adults-only spy thriller **Lust, Caution** (*Se, jie*). Both **Triangle** and **Mad Detective** await release, along with the likes of Derek Chiu's colonial-era gangland saga **Brothers** (*Hing dai*) and Kenneth Bi's genre-blending and Zen-inspired **The Drummer** (*Jin, gwu*). Christmas, however, promises a spectacle unmatched by anything else in 2007, with the release of Peter Chan's expensive period battlefield epic **Warlords** (*Tou ming zhuang*). Its marquee megastars include hometown favourites Andy Lau, Jet Li and Takeshi Kaneshiro. With such a heavy-hitter slotted into the high-season line-up, Hong Kong's movie buffs were guaranteed some top-notch attractions, and gave the local film industry the chance to usher in 2008 on a positive note.

The year's best films
Exodus (Pang Ho-cheung)
After This Our Exile (Patrick Tam)
Exiled (Johnnie To)
Mr Cinema (Samson Chiu)
Hooked on You (Law Wing-cheong)

Quote of the year
'The film industry has been in such a dive in the last ten years. I think that if we had given up, the film industry would have been long dead already.' *Director* LAWRENCE LAU, *on local filmmakers' continued perseverance*

Directory
All Tel/Fax numbers begin (+852)
Hong Kong Film Archive, 50 Lei King Rd, Sai Wan Ho. Tel: 2739 2139. Fax: 2311 5229. www.filmarchive.gov.hk.
Film Services Office, 40/F, Revenue Tower, 5 Gloucester Road, Wan Chai. Tel: 2594 5745. Fax: 2824 0595. www.fso-tela.gov.hk.
Federation of Hong Kong Filmmakers, 2/F, 35 Ho Man Tin St, Ho Man Tin, Kowloon. Tel: 2194 6955. Fax: 2194 6255. www.hkfilmmakers.com.
Hong Kong Film Directors' Guild, 2/F, 35 Ho Man Tin St, Ho Man Tin, Kowloon. Tel: 2760 0331. Fax: 2713 2373. www.hkfdg.com.
Hong Kong, Kowloon and New Territories Motion Picture Industry Association (MPIA), Unit 1201, New Kowloon Plaza, 38 Tai Kok Tsui Rd, Kowloon. Tel: 2311 2692. Fax: 2311 1178. www.mpia.org.hk.
Hong Kong Film Awards Association, Room 1601–1602, Austin Tower, 22–26 Austin Ave, Tsim Sha Tsui, Kowloon. Tel: 2367 7892. Fax: 2723 9597. www.hkfaa.com.

TIM YOUNGS is a Hong Kong-based writer and a consultant on Hong Kong cinema for the Udine Far East Film Festival and the Venice Film Festival.

Hungary Eddie Cockrell

'Hungary for Success' trumpeted one trade headline in early 2007, and if the pun can be overlooked the phrase serves neatly as the Magyar film industry motto at present. Can the t-shirt or coffee mug be far behind?

In 2003, the government passed legislation through which visiting producers can recover a 20% rebate on all production costs. By late 2006, trade paper *Variety* was speculating that it may be 'the most cinema-friendly incentive package in the world'.

As popular as the tax law has been, both at home and abroad, few envisioned how quickly, and thoroughly, the local business would be transformed. In early 2006, Culture Minister Andras Bozoki pledged to increase film subsidies to the domestic industry some $386,000 over the $31 million already set aside for filmmakers. 'I believe films and Hungarian films are profitable investments,' he proclaimed. 'Culture shouldn't be the last area of investment [in an economy]. It is the first step in competitive positioning.' How refreshing to see a government supporting the arts, particularly with such apparent sincerity and enthusiasm.

With all this domestic and foreign production, there needs to be somewhere to shoot it all. Enter not one, but two brand new studio complexes. In December 2006, the Stern Film Studio and Media Center opened its first phase in Pomaz, north of Budapest. Andrei Konchalovsky shot his new **Nutcracker: The Untold Story** there in late 2007. 'The more movies that are attracted to Hungary,' said one honcho, 'means more movies and business for everyone.'

Be careful what you wish for, honcho: in June 2007 the $124 million Korda Film Studio opened on the site of an abandoned missile base not far from the capital. Four soundstages were operational at that time, with two more – including a mammoth floodable water tank – expected to be online by the end of the year. Accelerated construction meant that Guillermo del Toro's *Hellboy* sequel, **Hellboy II: The Golden Army**, was able to move from Prague to the new facility. The Hungarian Film Office estimated seven or eight major shoots at these state-of-the-art facilities during 2007, pumping some $172 million into state coffers.

And this largesse has trickled down to local production too, resulting in a breathtaking increase in the physical number and dramatic scope of Hungarian films. In a crowded field, the three most resonant films of 2006 were first-timer Ágnes Kocsis's Kaurismäkian deadpan tragi-comedy, **Fresh Air** (*Friss levegö*), Academy Award-winning veteran István Szabó's old-guard political corruption fable **Relatives** (*Rokonok*) and Szabolcs Hajdu's

Ágnes Kocsis' **Fresh Air**

Szabolcs Hajdu's **White Palms**

muscular, quasi-autobiographical sports drama **White Palms** (*Fehér tenyér*), which became the official Academy Award submission for Best Foreign Language Film in 2006.

Certainly the most well-travelled of these was *Fresh Air*, a retro-kitsch meditation on mother/daughter relations that parlayed its First Film prize at the Hungarian Film Week to a place at the Cannes Critics' Week and the *Variety* Critics' Choice sidebar of the Karlovy Vary Film Festival, not to mention a nomination by the European Film Academy for the First Feature award.

György Pálfi's **Taxidermia**

The late 2006 release with the most notoriety was unquestionably **Taxidermia**, the body-horror endurance test that marks director György Pálfi's follow-up to the acclaimed *Hukkle*. Moving from an explicit exercise in Central European miserabilism to grotesque comedy to David Cronenberg's worst nightmare, each segment tracing three generations of men in a single family mixes

shock value with macabre, faintly sentimental mystery. Winner of numerous Hungarian Film Week awards, including best picture, art direction and the coveted critics' kudos, *Taxidermia* also snared the audience award at Portugal's Oporto fantasy festival and the Transylvania Film Festival's best director prize.

How busy is domestic production? So prolific that for the first time in its nearly four decades as a cosy confab at which to view all the new films, in 2007 the Hungarian Film Week was forced to curate the event. From this perspective, the three films that emerged with the most light and heat were Gabor Rohonyi's canny senior-citizen crime-spree tragi-comedy **Konyec**, János Szász's unflinching asylum-set period drama **Opium: Diary of a Madwoman**, and Tamás Sas's frothy romantic comedy **S.O.S. Love!** (*S.O.S. szerelem!*).

János Szász' **Opium: Diary of a Madwoman**

Konyec is the most fully formed of these, grafting western genre elements to Central European social concerns in its story of a pair of senior citizens, survivors of the volatile mid-1950s, who go on a half-hearted robbery spree

Gabor Rohonyi's **Konyec**

when they find their meagre state subsidy doesn't even provide enough money to keep the lights turned on. Dubbed the 'Blood Money Pensioners', they're pursued by a couple of desperate cops grappling with their own volatile relationship. Though it did modest local business, this is precisely the balance of new and old that Hungarian cinema is working hard to project to the world.

Another home-grown title with significant remake potential is *S.O.S. Love!*, in which the heads of two high-tech matchmaking firms engineer an eventual romantic, er, merger. Again, this release, a huge local success, points to the Hungarian public's newly developed love of genre films. With the addition of Krisztina Goda's fairly self-explanatory 2006 comedy, **Just Sex and Nothing Else** (*Csak szex és más semmi*), Péter Rudolf's lowest-common-denominator rural laffer **Glass Tiger 2** (*Üvegtigris 2*) and Goda's *Sex* follow-up, **Children of Glory** (which transforms the quelled 1956 uprising against Soviet-led Communist rule into an action picture), market share for local product rose some 16% in the first half of 2007.

Krisztina Goda's **Just Sex and Nothing Else**

A handful of films premiered outside the Hungarian Film Week, each to varying degrees of approbation. These included Béla Tarr's long-delayed black-and-white existential thriller, **The Man from London**, and Benedict Fliegauf's long-take meditation on ambience and chance, **Milky Way** (*Tejút*). While Tarr is

Béla Tarr's latest opus, **The Man from London**

to be applauded for stubbornly flying the flag of inscrutable art-house cinema, the daunting combination of a troubled production history and narrative claustrophobia places the new film a few rungs below his transcendental one-two punch of *Sátántangó* and *Werckmeister Harmonies*. Significantly, *The Man from London* was the first Hungarian film in 19 years to be invited to compete at the Cannes Film Festival; equally significantly, it walked away empty handed.

Somewhat more involving but no less inscrutable is *Milky Way*, the latest effort from the director of *Forest* and *Dealer*. It comprises a series of nine fixed-camera tableaux in which various people interact with nature and each other, what the director describes as an 'ambient movie' along the lines of a Brian Eno composition (and Fliegauf did his own, clearly Eno-inspired score). It could be argued that the film should more appropriately be labelled a gallery installation, as *Variety* critic Alissa Simon pointed out upon its Locarno Film Festival premiere, where it won the experimentally oriented 'Filmmakers of the Present' competition.

In light of Tarr's patchwork quilt of funding from Hungary, France and Germany, it's worth mentioning that not only is co-production action on the rise, but more and more of the major sales companies are taking Hungarian films on board for international business.

Which raises the pertinent question: when is a Hungarian film not a Hungarian film? No matter the answer, it may now be truly and proudly said that the country's film industry has emerged as a major player not only in the region, but in the world.

In fact, the Hungarian Film Office now works actively with almost 300 film festivals worldwide, presenting some 150 new shorts and features by more than a hundred directors internationally. In 2006, that aggressive coverage, which culminated in no less than five features being selected for various sections of the 2007 Berlin Film Festival, resulted in over a hundred official festival awards.

With all this production activity, and exciting diversity, what's next? Writing of India's recent backpedalling from the entrenched 'Bollywood' tag, *Variety*'s Shalini Dore suggests a new appellation for the Magyar industry. 'Mollywood', of course. Open with a pun, close with one too: but the success of the Hungarian film industry is no laughing matter.

The year's best films
Fresh Air (Ágnes Kocsis)
Konets (Gabor Rohonyi)
Opium: Diary of a Madwoman (János Szász)
Relatives (István Szabó)
S.O.S. Love! (Tamás Sas)
White Palms (Szabolcs Hajdu)

Quote of the year
'We're very busy.' EVA VEZER, *Hungarian Film Union General Manager, stating the obvious*

Directory
Association of Hungarian Filmmakers, Városligeti fasor 38. Budapest, Hungary-1068. filmszov@t-online.hu.
Association of Hungarian Producers, Eszter utca 7/B. Budapest, Hungary-1022, mail@mpsz.org.hu. www.mpsz.org.hu.
Hungarian Directors Guild, Ráday utca 31/K., Budapest, Hungary-1092. mrc@filmjus.hu. www.mmrc.hu.
Hungarian Independent Producers Associations, Róna utca 174. Budapest, Hungary-1145. eurofilm@t-online.hu.
Hungarian National Film Archive, Budakeszi út 51/E. Budapest, Hungary-1021. www.filmintezet.hu.
Hungarian Society of Cinematographers (H.S.C.), Róna utca 174. Budapest, Hungary-1145. hsc@hscmot.hu. www.hscmot.hu.
MEDIA Desk Hungary, Városligeti fasor 38. Budapest, Hungary-1068. info@mediadesk.hu. www.mediadesk.hu.
Motion Picture Public Foundation of Hungary Városligeti fasor 38. Budapest, Hungary-1068. mmka@mmka.hu. www.mmka.hu.
National Film Office, Wesselényi utca 16. Budapest, Hungary-1075. info@filmoffice.hu. www.nationalfilmoffice.hu.

EDDIE COCKRELL is a *Variety* film critic and freelance programming consultant who, when not reviewing from festivals in Europe and Canada, splits his time between Maryland and Sydney.

Iceland Freyr Gigja Gunnarsson

Hopes were high for 2007 after the success of **Jar City** (*Mýrin*), which broke box office records the year before. Baltasar Kormákur's thriller, based on Arnaldur Indridason's bestseller, won the Krystal Globe at the Karlovy Vary Film Festival and some were convinced of its chances at the Academy Awards. Shortly after, Ragnar Bragason's **Children** (*Börn*), a dramatic account of life in a troubled area of Reykjavik, featuring the theatrical group, Vesturport, was awarded the Golden Swan at the Copenhagen Film Festival.

However, 2007 was not quite so successful. The year began with Björn Björnsson's thriller, **Cold Trail** (*Köld Slóð*), which received mixed reviews and failed to light up the box office the way *Jar City* did. Anita Briem, the film's star, went on to perform in *Journey 3-D* alongside Brendan Fraser and was cast in the critically acclaimed television series *The Tudors*. Similarly high expectations surrounded the release of **Parents** (*Foreldrar*), Bragason and Vesturport's sequel to *Children*. Focusing on life in the suburbs of Reykjavik, critics were impressed, but audiences failed to attend.

The surprise of the year was **Astropia**, the debut film of Gunnar Björn Guðmundsson.

An adventurous tale based on role-playing games and featuring TV star, Ragnhildur Steinunn Jonsdóttir, the film attracted a large audience, although not everyone was convinced of its merit. Gudny Halldorsdóttir directed **Vedramót**, which was loosely based on a news story concerning abuse at a juvenile institution in Vestfirðir during the mid-1960s. It was hailed as one of the best Icelandic films ever made, but people were not interested in the subject, to the disappointment of both the director and producers. **Dugguholufólkið**, directed by Ari Kristinsson, the former cinematographer for Fridrik Thor Fridriksson and Hrafn Gunnlaugsson, directed the first children's film for almost five years, receiving positive reviews and prepared to take on the might of the Hollywood Christmas blockbusters.

Gudny Halldorsdóttir's **Vedramót**

Dugguholufólkið, *directed by Ari Kristinsson*

2007 also saw some significant Icelandic co-productions: **The Boss of it All** (*Direktøren for det hele*) by Lars von Trier, **The Bothersome Man** (*Den brysomme mannen*) by Jens Lien and Larry Fessenden's **Last Winter** (*Síðasti Veturinn*) starring Ron Perlman. And there was **Beowulf & Grendel**, based on an ancient tale. The media were negative in their response to the latter film. Director Sturla Gunnarsson, a Canadian-raised Icelander, was surprised by the bad reviews but was confident that Stellan Skarsgaard and *300* star Gerard Butler would attract audiences. However, few turned out to see the film.

Of the documentaries, Dean DeBlois' **Heima**, featuring Icelandic rock band Sigur Rós travelling around their homeland, and **Syndir Feðranna**, which focused on the same case as *Vedramót*, both received positive reviews but were unsuccessful. **Wrath of Gods**, Jon Einarsson Gustafsson's account of the making of *Beowulf & Grendel*, was shown at numerous festivals.

The highlight of the Icelandic film and TV industry year is Eddan, an awards ceremony broadcast live on national television. Ragnar Bragason's *Parents* was awarded Best Picture and Best Director, which was something of a shock to the team behind *Vedramót*, which had been nominated in eleven categories.

2008 will see the directorial debut of Valdis Oskarsdóttir, the BAFTA-winning editor of *Eternal Sunshine of the Spotless Mind*. She will team up with Vesturport on **Sveitabrúðkaup**. There are also high expectations for **Reykjavik-Rotterdam**,

a thriller by Óskar Jónasson, starring Baltasar Kormákur. There is also a great deal of talk about **Higher Force**, featuring *Sopranos* star Michael Imperioli, alongside one of Iceland's funniest comedians, Petur Johann Sigfusson. And Dagur Kári will begin shooting his first film in English early next year.

The year's best films
Parents (Ragnar Bragason)
Astropía (Gunnar Björn Guðmundsson)
Syndir feðranna (Bergsteinn Bjorgulfsson and Ari Alexander Ergis)

Quote of the year
'The Icelandic television and movie industry is very fragile. But with more money in place we should try to focus on making more documentaries.' *Journalist* ASGRIMUR SVERRISSON

Directory
All Tel/Fax numbers begin (+354)
Association of Icelandic Film Directors, Leifsgata 25, 101 Reykjavík. Tel: 588 6003/898 0209. ho@ismennt.is.
Association of Icelandic Film Distributors, SAM-Bíoin, Álfabakka 8, 109 Reykjavík. Tel: 575 8900. Fax: 587 8910. thorvaldur@sambio.is.
Association of Icelandic Film Producers, Túngötu 14, PO Box 5367, 125 Reykjavík. Tel: 863 3057. Fax: 555 3065. sik@producers.is. www.producers.is.
Icelandic Film Centre, Túngötu 14, 101 Reykjavík. Tel: 562 3580. Fax: 562 7171. info@icelandicfilm-centre.is. www.icelandicfilmcentre.is.
Icelandic Film Makers Association, PO Box 5162, 128 Reykjavík. Tel: 562 6660. Fax: 562 6665. bjorn@spark.is.
Icelandic Film & Television Academy/EDDA Awards, Túngötu 14, 101 Reykjavík. Tel: 562 3580. Fax: 562 7171. bjorn@ spark.is.
National Film Archive, Hvaleyrarbraut 13, 220 Hafnarfjordur. Tel: 565 5993. Fax: 565 5994. kvikmyndasafn@kvikmyndasafn.is. www.kvikmyndasafn.is.

FREYR GIGJA GUNNARSSON writes on film for *Frettabladid*, Iceland's largest-circulation newspaper.

India Uma Da Cunha

For the Indian film industry, 2006 will be a hard act to follow. It was one of the most financially rewarding in the country's 110 years of filmmaking. Profits totalled some $135 million. Burgeoning multiplex audiences, lucrative markets abroad, increasing Internet content, options on satellite rights, pay-per-view and video-on-demand added to the soaring revenues.

Business increased by 25% over 2005. The international market earned an astonishing $25.8 billion. Actors and directors were wooed with contracts from multinational media giants, aware of their bankability overseas. And it wasn't just the big-budget films that succeeded. Small films, like Dibakar Banerjee's **Khosla's Nest** (*Khosla ka Ghosla*) – an ironic interplay on land grabbing by real estate sharks – and Saket Chaudhary's **Side Effects** (*Pyar ke*) – a take on the proverbial bachelor being tamed into marriage – performed well at the box office.

Rakeysh Om Prakash Mehra's **Rang de Basanti**

Of the successes, there was Rakeysh Om Prakash Mehra's story about patriotic but disillusioned youth, **Rang de Basanti**, which was produced by UTV. A further five films proved incredibly popular with audiences,

Rakesh Roshan's **Krrish**

covering a variety of genres: crime in Anurag Basu's **Gangster**; romance in Kunal Kohli's **Fanaa** and Neeraj Vora's **Phir Hera Pheri** (*Hera Pheri 2*); Rakesh Roshan's Chinese martial arts-inspired fantasy adventure, **Krrish**, with Hrithik Roshan flying through the air; and Rajkumar Hirani's feelgood **Munnabhai Meets Mahatma Gandhi** (*Lage Raho Munnabhai*), the story of a small-time rogue who is lucky enough to have Mahatma Gandhi as a spiritual advisor.

The dubbed import of Sam Raimi's **Spider-Man 3** dominated the box office over the 2007 New Year. At the same time local blockbusters fared poorly; even big names failed to attract audiences. Neither Vidhu Vinod Chopra's **Eklavya: The Royal Guard** (*Eklavya*), a fable-like parable on family skeletons leading to palace killings, Ram Gopal Verma's sexy **Nishabd** nor Nikhil Advani's **Salaam-e-Ishq** (six love stories strung together) managed to light up the box office. Only Mani Ratnam's **Guru**, starring real-life couple Abhishek Bachchan and Aishwaria Rai, in a drama about the pitfalls of big business, actually did any real business. The downturn was reversed as summer approached. Actor-producer Shah Rukh Khan's **Forward, India!** (*Chak de! India*) was as much of a success at the box office as his on-screen character, the coach of a women's hockey team. Following this, the domestic market began to reach the heights of the previous year.

Overseas markets have provided both the profits and inspiration for a better cinema. The departure from overworked plots and stereotypes has had a dramatic effect domestically and prompted the desire to see higher-quality releases. However, the stakes are high in the world's largest cinema market. The big-budget successes can easily mask the fate of the vast majority of releases.

Diwali (the Festival of Lights) marks the start of the Hindu New Year and the season of big-budget films. In November, two major releases squared-off against each other: Shah Rukh Khan was directed by former choreographer Farah Khan in **Om Shanti Om**, a reincarnation tale shifting from the film studios of the 1970s to the present day; and visionary director

Shah Rukh Khan's rippling six-pack in **Om Shanti Om**

Sanjay Leela Bhansali conceived the magical tale, **Saawariya**, about two ill-fated lovers. There was an unprecedented marketing drive for both films and other releases were put on hold – both big- and small-budget – until the clamour had died down.

Om Shanti Om's success, with its in-jokes about Mumbai's film world, proved that a film featuring a major star will always win. But *Saawariya* did show that the right surname can launch new stars. Ranbir Kapoor, the youngest in the star-laden Raj Kapoor clan, and Sonam Kapoor, daughter of Anil Kapoor, now have their careers laid out for them, with leading roles in forthcoming major studio releases. This continues the tradition of a well-known name being passed down from older stars – Abhishek Bachchan, Hrithik Roshan, Sunny Deol, Bobby Deol, Kareena Kapoor, Konkana Sen Sharma, Raima Sen … the list is endless.

The astonishing production rate of films – over a thousand annually – has resulted in the release of more than one big-budget film every single week, a situation once unheard of. Producers are spending more on marketing to ensure maximum returns in that vital first week. Competing blockbusters in the pre-Christmas season are Aamir Khan's directorial debut **Taare Zameen Par** about a dyslexic boy who sees the world differently, Feroz Nadiadwala's **Welcome** starring Akshay Kumar and Anil Kapoor, and Raj Kumar Santoshi's **Halla Bol** starring Ajay Devgan and Vidya Balan.

Indian cinema has never been more star-driven, with 'King Khan' – Shah Rukh – as its leading light. Other top rankers are Salman Khan, Hrithik Roshan and Abhishek Bachchan, each of whom eye their rivals with hawk-like concern. In early 2007, Rajnikanth, superstar of southern India, hit the screens with his magnum opus **Sivaji**. The end of the year saw the return of Madhuri Dixit, whose physical prowess and dazzling smile lit the screen for two decades before she settled into marriage and motherhood. Her new film, **Aaja Nachle**,

Madhuri Dixit in **Aaja Nachle**

was released late November and featured a US-based dancer who returns to her roots to rescue the school where she first learned to dance.

A new development in 2007 has been the more left-field Indian film finding distribution in the US. Emerging Pictures in New York led the way with **Vanaja**, directed by Rajnesh Domalpalli, about a village girl's poignant and spirited attempt to better her life, and **Amu**, by Los Angeles-based Shonali Bose, based on the 1984 anti-Sikh riots and killings that shook Delhi.

Scriptwriters are becoming more adventurous in an attempt to attract more people to the cinema. The calculated risk of Shimit Amin's runaway hit, *Forward, India!* set the standard for other writers to break new ground. Shah Rukh Khan took on the very different role of a cynical manager given the job of training an all-girl hockey team who eventually go on to win the Gold Cup in Australia. Expensively mounted, with no song nor dance, the film broke all existing records. Sports films appear to be in vogue, the next being a thriller starring John Abraham as a coach leading an Indian football team in the UK.

Period and 'flashback' films are still popular, but feature a different approach, as was the case with *Om Shanti Om*. Comedy, a staple of Indian cinema, is ever more popular. Sagar Bellary's modest debut, **Bheja Fry**, outgrossed bigger films thanks to clever marketing by far-sighted producer Sunil Doshi. It is a remake of Francis Verber's 1998 French hit *Le Dîner de cons*, in which a manipulative city slicker uses the ungainly and the gullible to allay his boredom, and featured a strong script and top actors.

The presence of female directors within Indian cinema is increasing. Actress Nandita Das is directing her first feature, **Such Times**, on the controversial social upheavals in Ahmedabad. Based on her own story, it features Naseeruddin Shah, Paresh Rawal, Jimmy Shergill and Tisca Arora. Another actress, Deepti Naval, is set to make her first feature, based on an original script. And in the state of Manipur, six women have produced **Yenning Amadi Likia**, a drama about a child abused by his alcoholic father, directed by Makhonmani Mongsaba.

Indian cinema's increasing presence in the US and UK box office charts has resulted in Western financing of conventional Indian films. *Saawariya* was backed by Sony Pictures. Warner Bros. is said to be backing Nikhil Advani's Hindi film, **Made in China**. Los Angeles-based Ashok Amritraj looked for Indian actors for his mainstream American production, **The Other End of the Line**, a collaboration with MGM Studios and India's Ad Labs. And Aishwaria Rai, after featuring in Doug Lefler's **The Last Legion**, will be in Columbia Pictures' **Pink Panther II**.

Behind all the hoopla around the popular Hindi film is the reality that sound corporate financing and marketing is replacing individual funding. The big companies, which can absorb losses between infrequent hits, include UTV, Ad Labs, Yashraj Films, The Factory and Sahara. Locations are also becoming more daring.

The tourist spots of London and Paris are now passé. Aamir Khan's **Gajini** (a remake of a Tamil-language superhit) settled for the deserts of Namibia. Anurag Kashyap's **No Smoking** chose a snow-capped mountain in Uzbekistan for some eye-catching scenery. For his **Mission Istanbul**, Apoorva Lakhia found his modern city with an ethnic look in Turkey, while producer Vipul Shah has selected Australia's Gold Coast for Annes Bazmee's **Singh is King**.

For the US, India has become the promised land for filming. Wes Anderson arrived in Rajasthan to shoot his cathartic escapade, **The Darjeeling Limited**. Angelina Jolie kept Mumbai enthralled – with partner Brad Pitt in tow – when filming Michael Winterbottom's **A Mighty Heart**. And in Goa, Chris Smith shot his small film **The Pool**, a study linking lifestyles of the rich and poor using local untrained actors with just one known Indian name, Nana Patekar. The film, astonishingly, was made in Hindi, a language not known to the director. It went on to win a Special Jury Prize at Sundance in January.

Manish Acharya's **Loins of Punjab Presents**

The low-budget film manages to remain afloat. In September, two different genre films by first-time directors were released. They were Navdeep Singh's **Manorama Six Feet Under**, a noirish tale of an amateur sleuth in a small town who finds himself trapped in a web of lies, deceit and murder; and Manish Acharya's **Loins of Punjab Presents**, an English-language comedy about a singing contest among Indians living in New Jersey. Both films performed surprisingly well, finding supportive distributors in Shemaroo (leaders in the video

Deepa Mehta's **Water**

market) and the established PVR theatre chain. Boosting art-house cinema were Deepa Mehta's controversial **Water** and Mira Nair's **The Namesake**. The latter was co-produced by UTV and was relatively popular in India.

Regional-language cinema is growing, despite the lack of funding and distribution outlets. Veteran Adoor Gopalakrishnan's **Four Women** links four stories on the plight of women in India's male-dominated society. It premiered at the Toronto Film Festival 2007 in the 'Masters' Section' and performed well at the Kerala Film Festival. Another festival film, **Frozen**, the debut of Shivajee Chandrabhushan, has been lauded for its stark depiction of life in an isolated mountain village, disrupted by the arrival of the army. India's three main film

Adoor Gopalakrishnan's **Four Women**

Shivajee Chandrabhushan's **Frozen**

festivals, held over the winter months and showcasing the best that new Indian cinema can offer, never lack for choices.

Films to look forward to in 2008 include Ashutosh Gowarikar's long-delayed period film **Jodha Akbar**; Shyam Benegal's comedy, **Mahadev**; Jahnu Barua's venture into the big time, **Har Pal**, starring Preity Zinta and Shiney Ahuja; Jayabrato Chatterjee's **Love Songs**; Rituparno Ghosh's **Sunglass**; and Vishal Bhardwaj's as-yet-untitled bio-pic of actress Mary Evans, the famous 'Fearless Nadia' of the 1930s. From across the seas, Mira Nair is ready to join forces with Johnny Depp to film **Shantaram** in Mumbai. Deepa Mehta is poised to make her next film, titled **Luna** and set in San Francisco, as well as **Heaven on Earth**, about a Punjabi housewife living in Canada. M. Night Shyamalan is said to be headed to India to make a film co-produced by Fox and UTV. All of which bodes well for the coming year.

The year's best films
Frozen (Shivajee Chandrabhushan)
Four Women (Adoor Gopalakrishnan)
Dharm (Bhavna Talwar)
Loins of Punjab Presents (Manish Acharya)
Vanaja (Rajnesh Domalpalli)

Quotes of the year
'The way I see it, if an actor doesn't do well, 10,000 families are affected. It's a massive food chain of producer, director, writer, distributor, people who supply popcorn at cinema halls and also the audience. The entire network originates from a star who sells.'
Superstar, SALMAN KHAN

'I'm too materialistic, too selfish, too capitalistic. Besides, I'm too good looking.'
Mega-star SHAH RUKH KHAN *on ruling out his move to politics*

'In Bollywood it is hard to find proper accounting for Bollywood releases. We haven't been able to develop a single, foolproof, standardised method of measuring a film's box office success.' NAMRATA JOSHI *in Outlook magazine, 26 November 2007*

Directory
All Tel/Fax numbers begin (+91)
Film & Television Institute of India, Law College Rd, Pune 411 004. Tel: (20) 543 1817/3016/0017. www.ftiindia.com.
Film India Worldwide, Confederation of Indian Industry, 105 Kakad Chambers, 132 Dr Annie Besant Rd, Worli, Mumbai 400 018. Tel: (22) 2493 1790. Fax: (22) 2493 9463. www.ciionline.org. www.ciiwest.org.
Film Federation of India, B/3 Everest Bldg, Tardeo, Bombay 400 034. Tel/Fax: (22) 2351 5531. Fax: 2352 2062. supransen22@hotmail.com.
Film Producers Guild of India, G-1, Morya House, Veera Industrial Estate, OShiwara Link Road, Andheri (W), Mumbai 400 053. Tel: (22) 5691 0662/2673 3065. Fax: (22) 5691 0661. tfpgoli1@vsnl.net. www.filmguildindia.com.
National Film Archive of India, Law College Rd, Pune 411 004. Tel: (20) 565 8049. Fax: (20) 567 0027. nfai@vsnl.net.
National Film Development Corporation Ltd, Discovery of India Bldg, Nehru Centre, Dr Annie Besant Rd, Worli, Bombay 400 018. Tel: (22) 2492 6410. www.nfdcindia.com.

UMA DA CUNHA is based in Mumbai, where she works as a casting director, researcher and freelance journalist and edits the quarterly, *India Film Worldwide*. She is also a programmer for international film festivals, specialising in new Indian cinema, and organises film industry PR events.

Indonesia Lisabona Rahman

2007 saw a turning point in Indonesian cinema, with young filmmakers protesting against their government's role in film production and a run of horror films ending the craze in teen movies.

The big protest

In January 2007, around 300 filmmakers returned more than thirty Citra Awards to the Minister of Culture and Tourism. This was prompted by events at the 2006 Citra Awards, the Indonesian government's annual prizegiving for achievement in film, when Nayato Fio Nuala won for his film, **Ekskul**. A thriller about a bullied teen seeking revenge by taking his friends hostage at their school, the film allegedly made illegal use of scores

Susan Budiarjo in **Chants of Lotus**

from other films. The protest was aimed at the government's inability to regulate the local film industry.

The protesting filmmakers founded the Indonesian Film Society to press for the abolishment of the existing Law on Film which was passed in 1992, six years before the fall of the military regime. They demanded less state control over the film industry, with filmmakers determining the level of government support needed. They also wanted assessment of the present censorship system, advocating a film classification system instead.

The government's response to the protest has been limited. In June 2007, the newly elected Film Council overruled the Citra Award decision, but other demands remain poorly addressed.

The end of the teen flick

The teen movie, one of the dominant genres in popular Indonesian cinema since the 1990s, finally ran its course in 2007. The last of a long line of films was Upi Avianto's sophomore effort, **Reality, Love and Rock 'n' Roll** (*Realita, Cinta dan Rock 'n' Roll*), the story of two young boys finding love in Jakarta. Its use of slang made it the first film to successfully break the norms of standardised Indonesian screen language.

Upi Avianto is one of several female directors to find success in 2006. Nia diNata's polygamy comedy, **Love for Share** (*Berbagi Suami*), and Lola Amaria's **Betina**, the story of a girl falling in love with a religious leader in her village, were both critically acclaimed. *Love for Share* also won the Halekulani Golden Orchid Award for Best Feature Film at the 2006 Louis Vuitton Hawaii International Film Festival.

At the end of 2006, the Jakarta International Film Festival launched its first award for Indonesian film, judged by an international jury. The festival's best film was John de Rantau's **Denias: Song Above the Clouds** (*Denias: Senandung di Atas Awan*), a children's film about a Papuan boy who struggles to continue his schooling. It has been selected as Indonesia's entry for the Best Foreign Language Film category at the 2008 Academy Awards.

Scary movies taking their toll

Horror films became the ruling genre in the second half of 2006. One out of three films produced were horror, following the success of Rudy Soedjarwo's **Pocong** and **Pocong 2**. Both are urban ghost tales based around the 1998 riot in Jakarta, which cost the lives of many Indonesians, mostly of Chinese descent. The first film was banned from theatrical release by the Board of Censorship, which argued that its theme could create social unrest. Following the sequel's popularity, many producers nudged their way into the blossoming market, releasing low-budget, low-quality horror features every month.

A number of critically acclaimed directors returned in 2007. Joko Anwar released the critically-acclaimed **Dead Time: Kala** (*Kala*), Indonesia's first noir thriller about a hopeless community in search of its saviour. There was a similar response to Riri Riza's **3 Days to Forever** (*3 Hari untuk Selamanya*) and Nan T. Achnas's **The Photograph**. The much-anticipated work by Garin Nugroho, **Opera Jawa**, was released domestically and internationally, where it has scored at festivals and as a small art-house release.

What's next?

Edwin, a young director who has been quite successful at international festivals with his short films, among them *A Very Boring Conversation* and *A Very Slow Breakfast*, will release his feature-length debut in early 2008. **The Blind Pig Who Wants to Fly** (*Babi Buta yang Ingin Terbang*) is a tale of friendship between two Indonesian Chinese who have to cope with racism.

Kalyana Shira Films will open two films in 2008. Dimas Djayadiningrat's comedy, **Quickie Express**, is about a group of male prostitutes disguised as pizza delivery boys. **Chants of Lotus**, a portmanteau film, will be directed by Upi Avianto, Nia Di Nata, Lasja Fauzia and Fatimah Tobing Rony.

The year's best films
Love for Share (Nia diNata)
3 Days to Forever (Riri Riza)
Dead Time: Kala (Joko Anwar)
Denias: Song Above the Clouds (John de Rantau)
Reality, Love and Rock'n' Roll (Upi Avianto)

Quote of the year
'If I show you my script you'd probably laugh and think it's stupid.' *Director* **UPI AVIANTO**, *on writing dialogue for* **Reality, Love and Rock 'n' Roll**.

Directory
All Tel/Fax numbers begin (+62)
Ministry of Information for Film & Video, Departement Penerangan RI, Jalan Merdeka Barat 9, Gedung Belakang, Jakarta Pusat. Tel: 384 1260. Fax: 386 0830.
Ministry of Tourism, Art and Culture, Jalan Medan Merdeka Barat 17, Jakarta 10110. Tel: 383 8000/381 0123. Fax: 386 0210. http://gateway.deparsenibud.go.id.

LISABONA RAHMAN is a Jakarta-based freelance writer on film. She is a film critic for the *Sunday Jakarta Post* and programming manager of community cinema, *Kineforum*.

Iran Jamal Omid

Iranian cinema continues to be characterised by factors that have dominated the country's film scene for two decades. This includes the preponderance of mediocre, commercial productions over serious and artistically oriented films, filmmakers' perennial quest for finance, distribution and theatrical screenings, and other obstacles such as official supervision and piracy.

The election of president Mahmoud Ahmadinejad prompted some to expect fundamental changes in most artistic fields, particularly cinema, which would inevitably solidify the position of the group of filmmakers in the hard-line front. But Ahmadinejad emphasised that he had no intention of restricting the diversification of ideas and tastes, with filmmaking pretty much continuing as it had in the preceding years. However, Javad Shamaghdari, a film director who functions as presidential advisor in film affairs, continued to criticise those filmmakers who create experimental art films with a view to promoting their works at international festivals and thus, in his opinion, neglecting prevalent social issues and conditions at home.

A review of the film production statistics issued in September 2007 shows a healthy industry at work. A total of 105 films were in various stages of pre-production (41), shooting (16), post-production (32) and pre-release (16). These figures do not include films produced by IRIB (national television), or various organisations or young filmmakers working outside the mainstream on independently-funded projects, who will present their work at the Fajr International Film Festival in February 2008. Then there are the filmmakers who have created some one hundred films for the five local television channels and roughly the same number of channels who broadcast internationally.

In order to cope with the number of features being produced, measures have been taken to reconstruct old theatres, transforming them into cinema complexes. These policies have been fairly successful in drawing people back into the cinema, following the assault on the medium by the proliferation of TV channels and the abundance of pirated DVDs.

The flood of pirated DVDs reached an all-time high in May 2007. Concern increased, not only because of the ability to produce higher-quality pirated copies, but because the distribution network for these DVDs has spread beyond the capital and provincial centres to rural areas and even abroad. Producers' attempts to fight piracy proved ineffective. Yet a meeting between filmmakers from various film trade unions with the official authorities was one of the rare occasions when all sides forgot their differences and agreed on tougher measures to put an end to piracy. From the time the first complaints regarding film piracy had been lodged, police began comprehensive investigations. They did not want to limit their actions merely to the arrest of the street distributors, preferring to wait until those in charge of the operation were revealed. However, after the meeting between filmmakers and the authorities, it was felt that the time had arrived for more decisive action. They began widespread arrests and broke up a number of groups, seizing millions of DVDs. By September, three months after the police raids, the illegal distribution of CDs and DVDs seemed to have been largely curbed. Nevertheless, producers are still apprehensive about the possibility of its resumption, although they have now regained enough assurance on the piracy front to return to the perennial internal differences and group conflicts that have plagued Iranian cinema since its early days.

This year saw the formation of the Iranian Society of Filmmakers. This aroused objections from two previously formed organisations (the Iranian Union of Film Producers and Distributors and the Iranian Film Producers Centre). The Society of Filmmakers pointed out that the monopolistic advantages enjoyed by the Union of Film Producers and Distributors created obstacles for the emergence of a viable national cinema, but this of course was not meant as a serious opposition to members of the Union or members of the Film Producers Centre. The Union issued a statement, opposing the formation of the new organisation, reasoning that it was not clear whether it's members were directors or producers. This, they said, could create a precedent for the creation of a society of Actors-Producers, or any other variation. At the same time, producers who have split from the Union to form the Film Producers Centre and are mostly supported by government organisations exhibited milder reactions, but argued that the creation of new entities would always create new problems.

In an attempt to stop further divisions among film producers, the Ministry of Culture and Islamic Guidance formed a committee of experts to look at legal and practical measures that would guarantee the interests of Iranian cinema. But the central council of the Union issued a statement denouncing measures that could weaken its position. Finally, the Deputy Minister for Cinematographic Affairs, Mohammad Reza Jafari-Jelveh, approved the establishment of the High Council of Iranian Film Producers and Distributors. The Council will comprise members of all three groups and will attempt to settle any differences, thus guaranteeing the overall interest of Iranian cinema.

There are also debates over who should control exhibition, with the Union of Film Producers and Distributors insisting they organise all screenings, to ensure the maximum commercial potential of each film; a position supported by the Union members and cinema owners.

Irrespective of these conflicts, film production continues. Tahmineh Milani's **Ceasefire** (*Atash bas*), with box office receipts totalling over $2 million, emerged as the most successful title of 2006. Sayeh, intending to get a divorce from her husband Yusef, accidentally finds herself in a psychiatrist's office. He advises the couple to separate in order to reflect upon what they need out of life. They follow the psychiatrist's instructions but after a brief period apart are reconciled. After a decade of dealing with social issues, Milani's comedy, though heavy handed, played well to audiences. However, its success would have been greater had the film not been so widely available on pirate DVDs.

Milani's success was soon eclipsed by Masud Dehnamaki's first feature after his documentaries, *Which Independence?, Which Victory?* and *Poverty and Prostitution*. **The Outcasts**, screened in early 2007, broke all previous box office records. From the age of 16 to 20, Dehnamaki, an outspoken critic and writer, experienced war at close hand, serving on various battle fronts. *The Outcasts* uses popular jokes and anecdotes previously considered taboo in cinema to tell the story of various characters whose humour belies the bitter tragedy of conflict.

Often compared with Mohsen Makhmalbaf because of their similar world views, Dehnamaki has remarked: 'Makhmalbaf started with *Nasooh's Repentance* and ended with *Sex and Philosophy*. I wonder how I will end considering that I started with *Poverty and Prostitution*.'

M for Mother (*Mim mesle madar*) by Rasul Mollaqolipur, who died earlier this year, was also popular with audiences and became Iran's entry for the 2007 Academy Awards. Indirectly related to the war he fought in and which has more or less shaped all of his previous films, it tells the story of two young combatants who fall in love and marry when the war is over.

PROMOTING
IRANIAN CINEMA

F A R A B I
CINEMA FOUNDATION

PRODUCTION, CO-PRODUCTION, ACQUISITIONS, SALES, DISTRIBUTION

International Affairs:
#19, Delbar st., Toos St., Valiye Asr Ave.,
Tehran 19617, Iran.
Tel: +98(21) 22741252-4, 22734939
Fax: +98(21) 22734953
E-mail: fcf1@dpi.net.ir/intl@fcf.ir

Central Office:
75, Sie Tir Ave., Tehran 11358, Iran
Tel: +98(21) 66708545, 66705454
Fax:+98 (21) 66720750
E-mail: info@fcf.ir
www.fcf.ir

When the wife becomes pregnant they discover that the chemical weapon she was exposed to during the war has affected the unborn baby. The man leaves his wife after she refuses to have an abortion. The baby is born and years later the mother, a violinist before the war, teaches her son to play. He eventually performs at a concert for the handicapped as she is receiving treatment for the illness caused by the chemical weapons. *M for Mother* is a bitter and often violent film, despite its melodramatic plot line. It became a success largely due to its popularity amongst female audiences.

Crossroads (*Taghato*) by another outspoken writer, Abolhassan Davudi, delivered a powerful drama that earned praise from critics. A terrible car accident intertwines the destinies of a number of people, affecting their lives on a personal, financial and moral level. The narrative moves from character to character, with each individual ending their story by coming into contact with the person whose story is about to begin. A similarly experimental structure is employed in Saman Moqaddam's **Café Star** (*Cafe Setareh*). The story revolves around the lives of several families living near a café run by a woman, Fariba, whose idle husband is murdered. The reactions of the families to the incident intertwines their fates. It is based on 'Meduk Alley', a story by Najib Mahfouz and is the best film of Moqaddam's career so far.

The most interesting film of the year is **Mainline** (*Khoon bazi*) by Rakhshan Bani-Etemad. A mother tries to save her daughter from the oblivion of drug addiction and prepare her for her wedding to a fiancé who will soon be arriving from abroad. Bani-Etemad, a distinguished documentary filmmaker before she started feature filmmaking, has teamed up once again with another documentary fimmaker, Mohsen Abdolvahab, for what is their best film so far. Boasting superb black-and-white photography by Mahmoud Kalari (colour is only used to highlight blood in certain scenes) and fine performances by Bita Farrahi and Baran Kowsari as the mother and daughter, *Mainline* dominated the award ceremony at the Fajr Film Festival.

Mainline, directed by Rakhshan Bani-Etemad

The year's best films
Mainline (Rakhshan Bani-Etemad)
Santouri, the Musician (Dariush Mehrjui)
The Night Bus (Kiumars Pourahmad)

Quote of the year
'My relationship with my country is similar to my ties with a mother, who remains to be my mother, in spite of all her shortcomings. In my view, the problem in our country does not derive from its government. It has more to do with the artificially halted cultural development and it could be overcome through a hard process of cultural progress.'
Filmmaker **ABBAS KIAROSTAMI**

Directory
All Tel/Fax numbers begin (+98)
Institute for Intellectual Development of Children & Young Adults. Tel: 871 0661. Fax: 872 9290. info@kanoonparvaresh.com.
National Film Archive of Iran, Baharestan Sq, Tehran 11365. Tel: 3851 2583. Fax: 3851 2710. crb@kanoon.net.
Sahra Film Cultural Institute, 39 Corner of 6th Alley, Eshqyar St, Khorramshahr Ave, Tehran. Tel: 876 5392/6110. Fax: 876 0488. modarresi@dpir.com.
Tamasha Cultural Institute, 124 Khorramshahr Ave, Tehran 15537. Tel: 873 3844/876 9146. Fax: 873 3844/9146. info@tamasha.net.

JAMAL OMID is a prolific screenwriter and author, whose works include the three-volume *History of the Iranian Cinema*. He is a member of the organising committees of the Tehran, Fajr and Isfahan international film festivals, and has produced for television.

Ireland Michael Dwyer

After a period of uncertainty, the last two years have seen a more positive outlook within the Irish film industry. The crucial Section 481 tax-incentive scheme, which was under threat, has been extended to the end of 2008, with the government raising the cap on total investment in any one film from €10.5 million to €15 million. Government funding for the Irish Film Board was increased and now stands at an annual total of €20 million. And the board established the Irish Film Commission, with permanent offices in Dublin and Los Angeles, to ensure that the country continues as a film-friendly location for international film and television production.

However, the industry faces strong competition from other countries adopting similar attractive tax incentives. Eastern Europe also offers reasonable locations and much lower wages. And attracting US productions has become more difficult as the Euro continues to rise in value against the dollar. The end result has been that most features made in Ireland in recent years have been at the lower end of the budgetary scale.

The industry saw more revenue coming from high-end television series. US channel Showtime chose Ireland as the location for the ten-part drama, *The Tudors*, starring Irish actor Jonathan Rhys Meyers as the young King Henry VIII, providing employment for large numbers of Irish actors and crew over the six-month shoot. Following the success of the first series, a second went into production in Ireland over the summer of 2007.

The most successful feature made in Ireland over the past two years was Ken Loach's **The Wind That Shakes the Barley**, which featured an all-Irish cast and was made by a predominantly Irish crew, entirely on locations in the south of the country. Loach's thoughtful, powerful, political drama explores turbulent events in early-1920s Ireland, during the War of Independence and the subsequent Civil War. The dramatic prism is the changing relationship between two brothers, played with terrific conviction by Cillian Murphy and Padraic Delaney. The film earned Loach the Palme d'Or at Cannes in May 2006. Released in Ireland a month later, it drew audiences in such numbers that it came very close to topping the year's box office chart, finishing a close third.

Ken Loach's Palme d'Or winner, **The Wind That Shakes the Barley**

Cinema exhibition in Ireland continues to thrive as more sites open across the country. Box office figures soared in the summer of 2007 as a succession of hit franchises opened to benefit from the worst summer weather in years.

The only Irish film to score at the Irish box office in 2006 was Neil Jordan's **Breakfast on Pluto**, taking just under €1 million. Jordan's second collaboration with author Patrick McCabe after *The Butcher Boy*, it once again features Ireland's most adventurous actor,

Neil Jordan's **Breakfast on Pluto**

Cillian Murphy, in a remarkable performance as the transvestite, Patrick 'Kitten' Braden. In the tradition of Candide, Kitten is an eternal optimist whose good nature is rewarded in the unexpectedly beautiful resolution of a film that is as uproariously funny as it is dramatically jolting.

Several movies addressed the societal changes in the new Ireland at the height of its economic boom. John Boorman, a resident in the country since the early 1970s, takes a caustic view in **The Tiger's Tail**, an unsubtle satire that targets the malaise of the 'Celtic Tiger': corruption, gridlock, conspicuous consumption and overcrowded hospitals. This is filtered through the awkward narrative of a successful businessman (played by Brendan Gleeson) who is alarmed to discover he has a doppelgänger. The Irish audience failed to respond in any significant numbers.

Writer-director David Gleeson followed his engaging debut *Cowboys & Angels* with **The Front Line**, which deals with Ireland's substantial immigrant population. A tightly knit thriller, it features Eriq Ebouaney as a Congolese asylum seeker whose dreams of a new and better life in Dublin are shattered when criminals take his family hostage, coercing him into playing a part in a heist at the bank where he is employed as a security guard.

Director Brian Kirk made an assured feature debut with **Middletown**, a dark, brooding drama set in late-1950s Northern Ireland with

Matthew Macfadyen convincingly scary as a fundamentalist clergyman spouting fire and brimstone. Through him, the film anticipates the intolerance that will preoccupy the region for years to come.

Selected for the Directors Fortnight at Cannes in 2007, **Garage** reunites director Lenny Abrahamson and screenwriter Mark O'Halloran, whose low-budget *Adam & Paul* became a surprise Irish box office hit in 2004. A haunting, quietly powerful rural drama, *Garage* features Ireland's most popular comedian, Pat Shortt, turning serious in a revelatory performance as a lonely, good-natured social misfit who unwittingly triggers a crisis in his life.

Set in another rural Irish area, Niall Heery's first feature, **Small Engine Repair**, is an affecting picture of friendship, betrayal and guilt. Iain Glen plays a middle-aged country singer hanging on to a slender hope for recognition. Heery allows the intimate atmosphere to breathe and build as he leads us into the broken lives of his empathetically drawn characters.

Writer-director Tom Collins treats his protagonists with equal concern in **Kings**, charting the experiences of six Irishmen who moved to London in 1977 and are reunited thirty years later when one dies. Led by Colm Meaney, the actors are flawless in this melancholy picture of failed ambitions and wrecked lives. With dialogue mostly in

Matthew Macfadyen in **Middletown**

Colm Meaney in Tom Collins' **Kings**

Gaelic, *Kings* was released in Ireland with English subtitles in October 2007 and was Ireland's first foreign-language film entry at the Academy Awards.

Another possible Irish contender at the 2008 Academy Awards, most likely for the Best Original Song award, is John Carney's disarmingly charming musical **Once**, which observes the tender relationship that forms between a Dublin busker (played by Glen Hansard) and a Czech pianist (the excellent Marketa Irglova). Their instinctive chemistry is beautifully expressed when they write music together in an irresistibly appealing movie that is full of heart and packs a fair emotional punch. The micro-budget production won the audience award at the 2007 Sundance festival, prompting a bidding battle won by Fox Searchlight. It went on to take the audience award at the Dublin International Film Festival. And Steven Spielberg told *USA Today*: 'A little movie called *Once* gave me enough inspiration to last the rest of the year.'

Despite all this acclaim, *Once* did only average business at Irish cinemas, whereas it has taken over $9 million at the US box office. Perhaps if *Once* wins an Academy Award, it could benefit from a re-release in Ireland, as happened in 1990 when *My Left Foot* received five Academy Award nominations and won two. Sometimes it seems that Irish talent – in film and other art forms – requires the validation of international success if it is to be accepted at home.

The year's best films
Breakfast on Pluto (Neil Jordan)
Garage (Lenny Abrahamson)
Once (John Carney)
Small Engine Repair (Niall Heery)
Kings (Tom Collins)

Quotes of the year
'This is extraordinary. I hope Ireland feels it's their film. It is their film.' *Director* KEN LOACH, *after accepting the Palme d'Or at Cannes for* The Wind That Shakes the Barley

'I wanted to be feminine and flirtatious as much as possible. I spent a lot of time observing women as I went around London, on the streets and on the Tube. I went out at night with some transvestites, and I was dressed as Kitten.' *Irish actor* CILLIAN MURPHY, *on preparing to play tranvestite Kitten in* Breakfast on Pluto

Directory
All Tel/Fax numbers begin (+353)
Film Censor's Office, 16 Harcourt Terrace, Dublin 2. Tel: (1) 799 6100. Fax: (1) 676 1898. info@ifco.gov.ie.
Film Institute of Ireland, 6 Eustace St, Dublin 2. Tel: (1) 679 5744. Fax: (1) 679 9657. www.fii.ie.
Irish Film Board, Rockfort House, St Augustine St, Galway, Co Galway. Tel: (91) 561 398. Fax: (91) 561 405. www.filmboard.ie.
Screen Directors Guild of Ireland, 18 Eustace St, Temple Bar, Dublin 2. Tel: (1) 633 7433. Fax: (1) 478 4807. info@sdgi.ie.
Screen Producers Ireland, The Studio Bldg, Meeting House Sq, Temple Bar, Dublin 2. Tel: (1) 671 3525. Fax: (1) 671 4292. www.screen-producersireland.com.

MICHAEL DWYER has been Film Correspondent of the *Irish Times* since 1989. He is chairman and co-founder of Dublin International Film Festival. He was appointed as a Chevalier des Arts et des Lettres by the French government in 2006.

Israel Dan Fainaru

Two years ago, I defined 2005 as a transitional year for Israeli cinema, with bigger things to come. The following year, both the industry and the critics agreed something was beginning to happen. **Aviva My Love** (*Aviva Ahuvati*), Shemi Zarhin's tale of a harassed housewife who dreams of becoming a writer despite all the obstacles she encounters, was a major hit. As was **Sweet Mud** (*Adama Meshuga'at*), Dror Shaul's portrait of the kibbutz society crushing any individual who doesn't conform to its rules.

And they were not the exception to the rule. Eytan Fox's **The Bubble** (*Ha-Buah*), showing how youthful exuberance is ground down by nationalist rhetoric and religious fanaticism, Dina Zvi-Riklis' **Three Mothers** (*Shalosh Ima'ot*), the family saga of three sisters born in Alexandria and living in Israel, and Oded Davidoff's **Someone to Run With** (*Mishehu Larutz Ito*), a coming-of-age story taking place in Jerusalem, may have been less popular with critics, but audiences were evidently enthusiastic, judging by their respective performances.

In 2007, the industry is just anxious to keep the momentum going. Indeed, there is cause

Shemi Zarhin's **Aviva My Love**

for celebration at the current state – and status – of Israeli cinema. The year began with *Sweet Mud* winning a Grand Jury prize at the Sundance Film Festival, followed by Josef Cedar's Silver Bear in Berlin for **Beaufort**. David Volach's **My Father My Lord** (*Hofshat Kaits*) won Best Film in Tribeca, while Etgar Keret and Shira Geffen were awarded the Camera d'Or for their portrait of dysfunctional modern Israeli families, **Jellyfish** (*Meduzot*), and Eran Kolirin was awarded an International Film Critics' Award for **The Band's Visit** (*Bikur Ha-Tizmoret*) at the Cannes Film Festival. Who would have ever dared dream, only a few years ago, of such success?

But it's not just the honours. The 2007 box office reflected the success of the acclaimed

Shira Geffen and Etgar Keret's **Jellyfish**

The Secrets, *directed by Avi Nesher*

Beaufort and *The Band's Visit*, as well as **The Secrets** (*Ha-Sodot*), Avi Nesher's kabbalistic tale of two girls in an ultra-orthodox boarding school in search of spiritual redemption for a stranger (played by Fanny Ardant), and Ayeleth Menahemi's **Noodle**, a bittersweet melodrama about a Chinese boy abandoned by his mother in Israel who finds his way back to Beijing thanks to an El Al stewardess.

On an international level, some 40% of all the investments in recent Israeli productions came from foreign sources. France's National Centre for Cinematography confirmed that, since 2001, French companies have been involved in no less than 28 co-productions with Israel. In the past, their main beneficiary was Amos Gitai. This year, all three Israeli films selected for Cannes had French money attached to them. Germany is close behind and even Japan has been known to invest (with a share in *Sweet Mud*). This is a dream come true for a small country whose home audience is far too limited to cover the cost of anything but minuscule productions.

These changes reflect a shift in attitudes, which makes Israeli cinema more accessible, both at home and abroad. Politics, once a prevailing theme with ambitious local filmmakers, has receded as a prominent theme, with a far more personal, less stentorian approach being adopted. One way or another, the films may still be political (after all what isn't?), but a more subtle language is being employed.

The Band's Visit is a perfect example; a whimsical comedy about an Egyptian police band landing in Israel for a concert – a pretty impossible concept at the present time – and their meeting with the inhabitants of a tiny desert town. It soon turns out there is much in common between the two sides, and a language barrier and different cultural backgrounds disappear after the first few awkward moments. With Sasson Gabbai, Ronit Elkabetz and Salah Bakri intentionally underplaying their roles and Kolirin's deadpan eye allowing the irony of certain situations to develop naturally, the picture was awarded eight of the Israeli Film Academy's 14 awards. No one thought to complain that the film didn't once mention political tensions or national animosities.

Beaufort also carefully avoided grand political statements. Josef Cedar's spectacular (certainly for the modest means of Israeli film production) and riveting war film about the last stand of the Israeli forces before their final retreat from Lebanon in 2000, is a profoundly affecting, tensely directed and powerfully claustrophobic drama. Focusing on the handful of soldiers inside a fortified bunker as they wait for the final order to withdraw, the film never discusses the reasons for the war, only the way it is waged. If there is anything political in it, it is about the pressures that determine disastrous military decisions, just to please public opinion.

Even Amos Gitai, whose didactic tendencies are not universally appreciated, found it necessary to devote attention to a slightly irresponsible and generally apolitical member of the affluent French bourgeoisie (played by Juliette Binoche), before throwing her into the turmoil of the Israeli withdrawal from the Gaza Strip colonies. In **Disengagement** the Israeli settlers, who under normal circumstances would hardly qualify for Gitai's sympathies, deservedly benefit from his compassion, as scapegoats of a system that first told them to establish their homes in the Gaza strip only to drive them away as it is claimed they stand in the way of a peace agreement that has yet to be negotiated.

The major surprise of the year is *My Father My Lord*. Shot in eight days (with two more to tie up some loose ends), this modern version of Abraham's sacrifice of Isaac, which in the Bible has a happy ending, takes place in a Jerusalem *yeshiva*. But in Volach's version, no one produces a ram at the last moment to replace the designated victim. Subtly told in whispers, this heartbreaking film (and brief – only 72 minutes long) is not just a personal tragedy that progresses relentlessly to its ineluctable ending, but a cruel reminder to fanatics of all creeds of how destructive blind faith can be. The confident direction is all the more astonishing since Volach, who was born in an ultra-orthodox family, the eighth of twenty children, had never made a film before.

Israeli documentaries are doing at least as well as the feature films, not only in their award victories but also in international investment. Tali Shemesh's soulful **Cemetery Club** (*Moadon beit hakvarot*), in which philosophy and the future of the world are discussed under the shade of the Mount Herzl National Cemetery; Shahar Cohen's nostalgic **Souvenirs**, following a son who takes his father to Europe to rekindle memories of the past; Ido Haar's bitter **Nine Star Hotel** (*Malon 9 Kochavim*), portraying the inhuman conditions of illegal Palestinians working in Israel; or David Offek's **The Hebrew Lesson**, showing immigrants adapting to an Israeli reality they previously ignored: these are only a few of the films that travelled extensively around the world. **The Champagne Spy** (*Meragel Ha-Shampaniya*), in which Nadav Schirman evokes the exploits of an Israeli spy who reached the highest levels of Egyptian society in the 1960s, before being discovered, was fascinating enough to warrant its acquisition for release in German cinemas. Finally, Ran Tal's **Children of the Sun**, a compilation of archive footage on childhood and youth in a kibbutz, with a live commentary by those who have lived through it, traces the dream of an ideal society that never materialised.

Is all this just a temporary fluke – here today and gone tomorrow? Veteran producer, Marek Rozenbaum, always a realist, believes there's more to it: 'We are in the early stages of a mounting wave, the kind that usually takes some ten years before it expires.' He has no doubt that there is still plenty of talent left untapped: 'Commercial television pays far more than the cinema; no wonder many young people prefer to make more there in a month than they would in films for a whole year.' But the prestige of working in cinema is still powerful enough to attract them.

The year's best films
My Father My Lord (David Volach)
The Band's Visit (Eran Kolirin)
Beaufort (Josef Cedar)
Jellyfish (Etgar Keret and Shira Geffen)
Aviva My Love (Shemi Zarhin)

Quote of the year
'Right now we are riding a wave going on our way up, getting a lot of credit and generating a lot of sympathy. This type of wave usually peters out after ten years or so, and then, it's everyone for himself.'
Veteran producer, MAREK ROZENBAUM

Directory
All Tel/Fax numbers begin (+972)
Israel Film Archive, Jerusalem Film Centre, Derech Hebron, PO Box 8561, Jerusalem 91083. Tel: (2) 565 4333. Fax: (2) 565 4335. jer-cin@jer-cin.org.il. www.jer-cin.org.il.
Israel Film Fund, 12 Yehudith Blvd, Tel Aviv 67016. Tel: (2) 562 8180. Fax: (2) 562 5992. info@filmfund.org.il. www.filmfund.org.il.
Israeli Film Council, 14 Hamasger St, PO Box 57577, Tel Aviv 61575. Tel: (3) 636 7288. Fax: (3) 639 0098. etic@most.gov.il.

DAN FAINARU is co-editor of Israel's only film magazine, *Cinematheque*, and a former director of the Israeli Film Institute. He reviews regularly for *Screen International*.

Italy Lorenzo Codelli

Did Nanni Moretti's anti-Berlusconi satire, **The Caiman** (*Il caimano*), released just before the elections in May 2006, convince any of those 3,000 voters – a narrow margin – who determined the fall of Silvio Berlusconi's right-wing government and the victory of Romano Prodi's centre-left coalition? *The Caiman*'s success was so fierce that even Berlusconi-owned cinema chains wanted to screen it, but Moretti replied, 'No, thanks.' His film humorously describes both the impossibility of portraying such an almighty manipulator, and how a whole country has deteriorated under his leadership. Federico Fellini would have been very proud of Moretti, having landed the first blow in 1986 with *Ginger and Fred*.

Angelo Orlando in Nanni Moretti's **The Caiman**

Authors in revolt

Several film directors – both young and old – feature in *The Caiman*, side by side with its director, as a sign of solidarity. One hundred of them founded, at a Trastevere bookstore in Rome, a movement baptised 'CentoAutori' ('100 Authors'). Through frequent public meetings and propaganda shorts, they are urging the Prodi government to reform film and television law, and to extensively support the film industry. Bernardo Bertolucci, one of the group's leaders, wrote a passionate open letter to *La Repubblica* lamenting how Italian national heritage itself is in danger. Culture Minister Francesco Rutelli reacted by promising increased financial resources, tax shelters and other remedies. Too late and not enough, responded angry filmmakers, to revive production and distribution on as large a scale as is needed.

Italy's annual output of approximately eighty films remains scandalously divided into two echelons: at one end, a dozen guaranteed blockbusters, widely released for Christmas, Easter, or the early November holidays; at the other, all the remaining films, parsimoniously screened for elite audiences, or through festivals, late-night TV and DVD releases.

It is mainly the festivals, from the Alps to Sicily, that feature most of the non-commercial films screened in Italian cinemas. The battle between Mostra del Cinema of Venice and its agressive new rival, the fledgling – though certainly very healthy – Festa del Cinema of Rome (its €15 million budget is mayor Walter Veltroni's proud accomplishment), concerns grand international cuisine as opposed to small home-cooked delicacies. Nanni Moretti, freshly appointed head of the Turin Film Festival, the nation's third major event, might make a difference because of his longstanding plea for challenging Italian talents.

Regional film commissions are investing more money in local companies and filmmakers, building state-of-the-art facilities, labs and specialised schools. Cinecittà studios in Rome are also trying to keep up with stronger European competition. American directors such as Abel Ferrara (**Go Go Tales**) and Spike Lee (**Miracle of St Anna**, announced for 2008) are wisely capitalising on these novel opportunities springing up around the peninsula.

Junk vs diamonds

Tycoon Aurelio De Laurentiis replicated his own farcical Filmauro potpourris, producing both Carlo Verdone's formulaic farce, **My Best Enemy** (*Il mio miglior nemico*) and Giovanni Veronesi's dull portmanteau, **Love Manual 2** (*Manuale d'amore 2*). Riccardo Tozzi's somewhat more sophisticated Cattleya company inaugurated another popular sub-genre: Riccardo Scamarcio romances, adapted from Federico Moccia's mega-selling pulp novels. But not every single one of Scamarcio's vehicles means sheer teen-trash, as shown by **My Brother is an Only Child** (*Mio fratello è figlio unico*), which was well received at Cannes. Guided by expert director Daniele Luchetti and following a muscular script by *Best of Youth*'s screenwriters, Sandro Petraglia and Stefano Rulli, Scamarcio convincingly portrays a communist student duelling with his fascist brother (played by Elio Germano) during the 1970s.

Ricardo Scamarcio's **My Brother is an Only Child**

Nicolas Vaporidis, another romantic icon, starred in two high-school romps, **Night Before Finals** (*La notte prima degli esami*), and **Night Before Finals – Today** (*La notte prima degli esami – Oggi*), both concocted by writer-director Fausto Brizzi and produced by Fulvio Lucisano. The celebrated increase in box office

Fausto Brizzi's **Night Before Finals**

figures is mainly due to this adolescent vogue; a trend naturally snubbed by adults and more discriminating audiences.

Carlo Vanzina's **2061 An Exceptional Year** (*2061 Un anno eccezionale*), a droll prophecy of a new Middle Ages, promotes Diego Abatantuono's clownish verve, while ex-buffoon Lando Buzzanca shines in a dramatic role in Roberto Faenza's pageant **The Viceroys** (*I viceré*).

The auteurs in particular are having a rough time, forced to pick easier stories and cheaper sets. A few exceptions still survive, mostly supported by the state-backed Rai Cinema's. Gianni Amelio travelled to the Chinese provinces in order to shoot his ambitious **The Missing Star** (*La stella che non c'è*). Acclaimed at Venice in 2006, this odyssey of a stubbornly earnest Italian technician – Sergio Castellitto, on top form – looking for a blast furnace sold off to China without some crucial gearing, dissects the psychological

Tai Ling in Gianni Amelio's **The Missing Star**

Marco Bellocchio's **The Wedding Director**

and philosophical gap between the decaying West and booming Asia. With **The Wedding Director** (*Il regista di matrimoni*, 2007) Marco Bellocchio creates his own *8½*, a brilliant and ambiguous self-portrait. A doubtful filmmaker – again played by actor-chameleon Sergio Castellitto, made up exactly as he was in Bellocchio's masterful *My Mother's Smile* (2002) – pursues love, glory and his super-ego along a surreal Sicilian riviera invaded by bizarre movie ghosts. Truths and lies about contemporary cine-martyrdom, distilled by a Lubitsch-like Bellocchio. Similar material, but in an impromptu, *cinéma vérité* vein, was offered by Mimmo Calopresti's **The Blow-Out** (*L'abbuffata*), where a pair of wannabe filmmakers attempt their first movie.

Raz Degan in Ermanno Olmi's **One Hundred Nails**

Ermanno Olmi announced that **One Hundred Nails** (*Centochiodi*) would be his last film. Should we believe him? He is unique for his profound vision as well as for his one hundred and more disciples, who learned their craft at Olmi's school 'Ipotesi Cinema', once based at Bassano del Grappa, but now located

in Bologna. His 'final' parable is scathingly anti-evangelical: a barbarian scholar literally crucifies ancient bibles inside a monastery, then escapes civilisation and lives like a hermit. A hymn to inner, natural religious instincts, as opposed to formal, repressive, Vatican rules, it sheds new light on Olmi's fruitful career.

Horrors – fake & real ones

Dario Argento, the pope of terror, completed his 'Three Mothers' triptych, which began with his classic *Suspiria* and *Inferno*, and ends with the deliriously baroque **Mother of Tears** (*La terza madre*) starring his daughter, Asia, as a damsel lost in hell. Pupi Avati directed a personal blood-feast, **The Hideout** (*Il nascondiglio*), starring Laura Morante as a would-be restaurant manager tormented by nun-witches. Also from Avati's unstoppable film factory – he is able to write, finance and direct a couple of highly original movies per year – is **The Get-Together Dinner** (*La cena per farli conoscere*), a comedy lampooning degenerate TV networks. Despite schematising the Armenian genocide in Turkey, **The Lark Farm** (*La masseria delle allodole*) reaffirmed Paolo and Vittorio Taviani's pictorial flamboyance. Saverio Costanzo's **In Memory of Myself** (*In memoria di me*), the follow-up to his award-winning *Private*, relates a seminarist's theological anxieties through a monotonous *kammerspiel* annihilated by its overblown self-importance. For **Saturn in Opposition** (*Saturno Contro*) Ferzan Özpetek reunited a large cast of actors to attempt a grotesque fresco on friendship and mortality.

André Dussollier in Paolo and Vittorio Taviani's **The Lark Farm**

Only ex-TV starlet Ambra Angiolini's witty charm rescues this lifeless soap opera from total bathos.

Gianni Zanasi's hilarious **Don't Think About It** (*Non pensarci*) reawakened the lost traditions of *Comedy – Italian Style*. A family of sympathetic fools are held together by the black-sheep son, an awful rock singer, played by Valerio Mastandrea. 92-year-old director Mario Monicelli, a supreme exponent of this previously dormant genre, directed **The Desert Roses** (*Le rose del deserto*), a World War II saga featuring a bunch of Italian soldiers stranded on Libya's dunes. Monicelli mirrors the different ages through his characters, lamenting the missed opportunities of his long life. Francesca Archibugi took a couple of brainless Italian brats to India for **Flying Lessons** (*Lezioni di volo*). Her unpredictable and unpretentious travelogue offers some funny morals along the way.

Valerio Mastandrea in Gianni Zanasi's **Don't Think About It**

Established filmmakers such as Neapolitans Paolo Sorrentino and Vincenzo Marra experienced a bumpy ride with their new features. Sorrentino's **The Family Friend** (*L'amico di famiglia*), about a libidinous usurer (Giacomo Rizzo) enslaving a voluptuous blonde (Laura Chiatti) before suffering at the hands of those who have waited years for revenge, evokes Marco Ferreri's ruthless comedies with its dark atmosphere, but suffers from a tricksiness in style. Moreover, Rizzo's villain needed a little more of the outrageousness displayed by Ugo Tognazzi at his reptilian best. Austere realism, a self-imposed code

Giacomo Rizzo in Paolo Sorrentino's **The Family Friend**

for Vincenzo Marra, who has frequently been compared to Roberto Rossellini, based the events in **Rush Hour** (*L'ora di punta*) on real events. An attempt to expose corruption within financial practices and the haute bourgeoisie, paper-thin characters, lousy acting and a convoluted plot contributed to Marra's first aesthetic misfire. In stark contrast, his feature documentary, **The Session is Open** (*L'udienza è aperta*, 2006), was a remarkably detailed account of Italy's chaotic judiciary system, and much scarier than Argento's horrors.

Welcome newcomers

A few debutants worthy of mention and not (yet) handicapped by predominant TV mannerisms have appeared on the scene. Andrea Molaioli, previously an assistant of Nanni Moretti, expertly handles **The Girl by the Lake** (*La ragazza del lago*), adapted by Sandro Petraglia from a novel by Norwegian writer Karin Fossum. An old-fashioned detective story à la Maigret and set in an Alpine village, Toni Servillo plays an inspector who tracks down a girl's killer through a series of tough interrogations during which he uncovers an avalanche of secrets. Unlike most debuts, the film was popular with audiences. Giorgio Diritti, one of Olmi's pupils, also set his film, **The Wind Blows Round** (*Il vento fa il suo giro*), in the Alps. However, the film's involved, multi-layered account of a small town, seen through the eyes of a French peasant immigrant ignored by the locals, failed to attract audiences. Immigration troubles are

Toni Servillo and Valeria Golino in **The Girl by the Lake**

also at the core of Marina Spada's **Like a Shadow** (*Come l'ombra*). A Russian girl in Milan suddenly disappears, but the mystery is never solved by this inspired storyteller who lyrically mixes Antonioni and Hitchcock. Alessandro Angelini's **Salty Air** (*L'aria salata*) analyses a conflict between a stern father and his son, but ultimately proves to be too uneven a drama.

The event of the year, sorry, millennium, was the publication of Federico Fellini's *The Book of Dreams*; a massive encyclopedia reproducing

in extenso the private albums in which the Jungian-influenced director had scrupulously drawn, in glowing colours, night after night, his obsessive reveries and nightmares with unashamed psycho-sexual sincerity. Michelangelo Antonioni, months before saying farewell to this world, exhibited in a Rome gallery his latest paintings, under the title 'The Silence in Colours', scores of small and large abstract pictures, under the spell of Klee and Mondrian, as amazing and revealing as Fellini's phantoms. Finally, the late Mario Bava, who had collaborated both with Antonioni and Fellini, was resurrected – strangely not in his beloved country but in Cincinnati, Ohio, thanks to Tim Lucas' titanic tome *Mario Bava – All the Colours of the Dark*.

Finally, a note on three films we should be looking forward to in 2008: Marco Tullio Giordana's **Crazy Blood** (*Sanguepazzo*), Matteo Garrone's **Gomorrah** (*Gomorra*) and Paolo Sorrentino's **The Divo** (*Il divo*).

The year's best films
The Caiman (Nanni Moretti)
The Girl by the Lake (Andrea Molaioli)
The Missing Star (Gianni Amelio)
The Wedding Director (Marco Bellocchio)

Quote of the year
'TV is superior to cinema – you always know where the WC is.' DINO RISI, *director*

Directory
All Tel/Fax numbers begin (+39)
Audiovisual Industry Promotion-Filmitalia, Via Aureliana 63, 00187 Rome. Tel: (6) 4201 2539. Fax: (6) 4200 3530. www.aip-filmitalia.com.
Cineteca del Comune, Via Riva di Reno, 40122 Bologna. Tel: (51) 204 820. www.cinetecadibologna.it.
Cineteca del Friuli, Via Bini 50, Palazzo Gurisatti, 33013 Gemona del Friuli, Udine. Tel: (4) 3298 0458. Fax: (4) 3297 0542. cdf@cinetecadelfriuli.org. www.cinetecadelfriuli.org.
Cineteca Nazionale, Via Tuscolana 1524, 00173 Rome. Tel: (6) 722 941. www.snc.it.
Fondazione Cineteca Italiana, Villa Reale, Via Palestro 16, 20121 Milan. Tel: (2) 799 224. Fax: (2) 798 289. info@cinetecamilano.it. www.cinetecamilano.it.
Fondazione Federico Fellini, Via Oberdan 1, 47900 Rimini. Tel (541) 50085. Fax: (541) 57378. fondazione@federicofellini.it. www.federicofellini.it.
Museo Nazionale del Cinema, Via Montebello 15, 10124 Turin. Tel: (11) 812 2814. www.museonazionaledelcinema.org.

Vincenzo Marra's **Rush Hour**

LORENZO CODELLI is on the board of Cineteca del Friuli, a Cannes Film Festival adviser and a regular contributor to *Positif* and other cinema-related publications.

Japan Tomomi Katsuta

2006 was a memorable year for Japanese cinema. For the first time in 21 years, the share for domestic films exceeded foreign imports, rising to 53.2%; 417 films were distributed, the largest number since 1971. This is partly because of a decline in the quality of foreign films, which dropped by 18% at the box office, but also because local product, co-produced by the major TV networks, was significantly stronger. The networks provide ideas for the cinema, backed by ample funds and publicity, and using TV writers and directors who understand mass-audience taste. In the 2006 box office top-ten list, not one film was made independently of the TV networks.

Test of Trust Umizaru 2 (*Limit of Love Umizaru*) by Hazumi Eiichiro, a sequel about marine coast guards, and made with Fuji TV, grossed $61 million, while a CGI disaster film, **Sinking Japan** (*Nihon Chinbotsu*) by Higuchi Shinji, co-produced by TBS, grossed $46 million. Two **Death Note** sequels, both by Kaneko Shusuke, occult thrillers adapted from bestselling manga, co-produced by NTV, grossed $69 million in total. Both were distributed by Warner Bros. Japan which, following this success, has announced that it will make more local films. **Saiyuki** (*Monkey Magic*) by Sawada Kensaku was an adventure fantasy about a mighty monkey, based on a classic Chinese novel. Following a successful TV drama series, Fuji TV transferred the story to film, and both starred Katori Shingo, a member of a popular 'idol' group SMAP, which boosted the box office, grossing almost $38 million. **Hero**, by Suzuki Masayuki, was another spin-off of a Fuji TV drama series about an unconventional District Attorney. Featuring Kimura Takuya, a colleague of Katori in SMAP,

it had already grossed $69 million by the end of 2007. These films, placed somewhere between big TV dramas and scaled-down Hollywood blockbusters, energised the box office. However, there are signs that audiences already seemed to be growing bored with such lowest-common-denominator offerings. The fact that the domestic box office fell by about 7% in the first half of 2007 might ring alarm bells for the film industry.

Hara Keiichi's **Summer Days with Coo**

Anime appears to have become a Japanese national treasure, picked as one of the government's 'products' to export along with games and mangas. A new generation of talent has emerged who were raised on franchised anime such as Pokemon and Doraemon, and the works of Miyazaki Hayao and Studio Ghibli, awa well as Otomo Katsuhiro. The latest Ghibli anime was **Tales of Earthsea** (*Gedo Senki*), an adaptation of the Ursula K. Leguin fantasies by Miyazaki Goro, Hayao's son. It topped the 2006 box office chart of domestic films with a gross of nearly $66 million, despite many critics who disparaged its lack of originality, a sure sign that the family name and Ghibli brand are review-proof. Kon Satoshi's **Paprika**, shown in Venice in 2006 in competition, was a sci-fi action fantasy in which a young woman therapist tries to stop the turmoil caused by a stolen therapy machine that allows a person to enter the patients' dreams. The dazzling images of the dreams flowing into reality, expressed with minute drawings, proved that anime could go far beyond live action. Hara Keiichi's **Summer Days with Coo** (*Kappa no Coo to Natsuyasumi*) was essentially targeted at children, although parents who accompany their kids might enjoy it more. The heart-warming buddy movie about a boy and a Kappa, a Japanese mythological creature, became a bitter criticism of the media scrum that ensues when the snooping media starts targeting Kappa. **Tekkonkinkreet** is an ambitious debut feature from the American visual-effects artist, Michael Arias. Based on a Japanese manga, it's about a pair of delinquent orphan kids and their fight against the town gangs. Adapting the characters of the original manga, Arias exploded his imagination, adapting computer technology to his avant-garde art style.

The film that attracted the most media attention in the first half of 2007 was the Cannes Grand Prix winner **The Mourning Forest** (*Mogari no Mori*) by Kawase Naomi, who had won the Camera d'Or in 1997 at Cannes with *Suzaku*. A caregiver at a home for the aged and one of her patients get lost in a deep forest and stay over night. Through the exhausting journey, both suffered the loss of their dearest ones, finally finding solace. Shot in a *vérité* style and with improvised acting, this tale of healing and recuperation benefits from the verdant backdrop of Nara Kawase's

The Mourning Forest, *directed by Kawase Naomi*

hometown. Though profound and undeniably beautiful, this quiet, slow, self-absorbed tale couldn't find a general audience.

Female directors also returned to the scene after a long silence. Nishikawa Miwa, who used to work for Koreeda Hirokazu, dominated the domestic film awards in 2006 with her second feature **Sway** (*Yureru*). A static but tense thriller about two brothers, it attracted both critics and moviegoers, enjoying a long run in art-houses. Ogigami Naoko impressed with **Kamome Diner** (*Kamome Shokudo*), about a small Japanese restaurant in Finland. In 2007 she released **Spectacles** (*Megane*), applying the same approach, but in a more sophisticated manner, featuring the easy-going inhabitants of a small beach-side café, who attempt to ease the everyday worries of passers by.

Kurosawa Kiyoshi's **Retribution**

A number of internationally recognised directors impressed with releases over the last two years. Aoyama Shinji made **Sad Vacation**, in which he focused on the power of motherhood. Kurosawa Kiyoshi's **Retribution** (*Sakebi*) is a terrifying ghost horror that takes place in modern society. Old master Yamada Yoji brought out **Love and Honour** (*Bushi no Ichibun*), the final part of a samurai trilogy, which follows a blind samurai fighting to save his honour and love, against a sly superior who is plotting to steal his wife. Thanks to box office star Kimura Takuya, the film grossed $34.5 million, the highest gross for any of Yamada's films. Suo Masayuki made a brilliant comeback following *Shall We Dance?* with **I**

Matsuoka Joji's **Tokyo Tower: Mom & Me, and Sometimes Dad**

Just Didn't Do It (*Soredemo Bokuwa Yattenai*). Tackling unfamiliar material – the Japanese judicial system – he told the story of a man's struggle for freedom after he's falsely accused of molesting someone on a train. Suo's questioning of the system was serious, but his suspenseful and well-researched narrative kept the audience entertained. Matsuoka Joji's **Tokyo Tower: Mom & Me, and Sometimes Dad** (*Tokyo Tower Okan to Boku to Tokidoki Oton*), based on a bestselling autobiography, follows the relationship between a loving mother and her negligent son over thirty years, until the mother's death. Its finely nuanced sentiment proved popular with audiences. Lee Sang-il's **Hula Girls** was a variation on *The Full Monty*, set in a small, declining mining town, where working-class girls struggle to become Hawaiian dancers in a recently opened resort. Fuelled by vivid depictions of the girls trying to achieve their dreams and become famous, and featuring a marvellous lead performance by Aoi Yu, the film exceeded box office expectations.

Lee Sang-il's **Hula Girls**

No film could be compared with Miike Takashi's **Sukiyaki Western Django**. A bizarre blend of Japanese sword action and spaghetti westerns, performed in English with Japanese accents, and featuring a cameo by Quentin Tarantino, it looks set to become a cult hit.

Quentin Tarantino in Miike Takashi's **Sukiyaki Western Django**

Comedy remains a profitable genre, following the watershed success of Mitani Koki's 1997 debut, *Welcome Back Mr McDonald*. Mitani made **The Wow-choten Hotel** (*Uchôten hoteru*) in 2006, which takes place over one night in a large hotel, with a group of guests facing their final moment on earth. Mi Zuta Nobuo's **Maiko Haaaan!!!** presented a hilarious sequence of gags. With an amazing script by Furusawa Ryota, Sato Yuichi's **Kisaragi** enjoyed an enthusiastic reaction from critics and audience. In one room, five men gather to mourn the first anniversary of their idol's suicide. With its funny characters and conversations revolving around the men's memories of their beloved deceased, the film cleverly reveals the truth behind her death.

Internationally acclaimed Kitano Takeshi revisited his past with the slapstick self-parody, **Glory to the Filmmakers!** (*Kantoku Banzai!*). Initially daring, it eventually tested the audience's patience a little too far. Another famous TV comedian, Matsumoto Hitoshi, made a controversial debut with the mockumentary **Big Man Japan** (*Dai-Nipponjin*), which follows the waning superhero, Daisato. Unlike more conservative Japanese filmmakers, Matsumoto didn't

Kitano Takeshi's **Glory to the Filmmakers!**

hesitate to use the story of a superhero fighting against the external enemy as a political metaphor. *Dainipponjin* surprised the industry when it made $8.6 million.

Also worthy of mention are the outstanding performances of Japanese actors and actresses in foreign films. Ken Watanabe, who was nominated for an Academy Award for his performance in *The Last Samurai*, starred in Clint Eastwood's **Letters from Iwo Jima**, while Sanada Hiroyuki, who also appeared in *The Last Samurai*, demonstrated tremendous skill in James Ivory's **The White Countess** and Danny Boyle's **Sunshine**. Kikuchi Rinko became the first Japanese Academy Award-nominated actress in 49 years for her performance in Alejandro González Iñárritu's **Babel**. In addition, the Japanese government started to support co-productions with other Asian countries, such as China and Korea, looking for more funding and a broader market. Various projects are now in progress.

Ken Watanabe in Clint Eastwood's **Letters From Iwo Jima**

Documentaries have also been fruitful in recent years. **The Virgin Wild Sides** (*Dotei wo purodusu*) by Matsue Tetsuaki, is about two virgin men in their mid-twenties. The director gave them a video camera to record their daily lives. The resulting film, also edited by Matsue, displays a fine sense of humour, offering a convincing portrait of the lives of disaffected youth in modern Japan. Shibata Shohei's **Himeyuri** took thirteen years to complete. He recorded the statements of survivors from the World War II conflict on the island of Okinawa where many thousands died, either in battle with US troops arriving near the end of the war or as victims of Japanese Army injunctions to commit suicide in the face of the enemy.

The year's best films
I Just Didn't Do It (Suo Masayuki)
Hula Girls (Lee Sang-il's)
Sway (Nishikawa Miwa)
Tekkonkinkreet (Michael Arias)
Kisaragi (Sato Yuichi)

Quote of the year
'Isn't Japanese-accented English cool? The Japanese actors and actresses will become hotshots after this film.' MIIKE TAKASHI, *talking about the reason for using English in* **Sukiyaki Western Django**

Directory
All Tel/Fax numbers begin (+81)
Kawakita Memorial Film Institute, Kawakita Memorial Bldg, 18 Ichiban-cho, Chiyoda-ku, Tokyo 102-0082. Tel: 3265 3281. Fax: 3265 3276. info@ kawakita-film.or.jp. www.kawakita-film.or.jp.
Motion Picture Producers Association of Japan, Tokyu Ginza Bldg 3F, 2-15-2 Ginza, Chuo-ku, Tokyo 104-0061. Tel: 3547 1800. Fax: 3547 0909. eiren@mc.neweb.ne.jp.
National Film Center, 3-7-6 Kyobashi, Chuo-ku, Tokyo 104-0031. Tel: 5777 8600. www.momat.go.jp.

KATSUTA TOMOMI writes on film for *Mainichi Shimbun*, one of Japan's major newspapers.

Kazakhstan Gulnara Gabikeyev

One of the most significant changes to affect Kazakh film production over the last two years was the freedom of filmmakers to work outside the auspices of the government, immediately impacting on the number of films produced. In 2005, there were only five full-length feature films, all produced by 'Kazakhfilm', the national film studio. In 2006, nine films were produced, three of which came from private studios. In 2007, the Kazakh filmmaking landscape has shown significant change. Of the twenty films completed or in production, only one third were made with the financial support of 'Kazakhfilm'. The quality of the films produced has also increased.

The biggest film of the year is Sergei Bodrov's historical epic, **Mongol**. With a budget of $12 million, 40% of the funding came from Russia and Germany. The film tells the story of the ten 'missing' years in Genghis Khan's life, when he is believed to have been imprisoned, only to be rescued by his wife, Borte. In the prison, he drew up the plans by which he would later rule his empire. It is Kazakhstan's entry at the 2008 Academy Awards.

Rustem Abdrashev's **Kurak Korpe**

Volker Schlöndorff's **Ulzhan**

Rustem Abdrashev's **Kurak Korpe**, is seen as the 'Kazakh answer' to *Borat*. On the one hand, the film is a comedy, on the other an attempt to redress *Borat*'s portrait of contemporary Kazakhstan. One part takes place in the city with its skyscrapers and highways, while the other is set in the suburbs, focusing on Kenzhe, a young boy who has moved out of the city to live with his grandparents. Contemporary Kazakhstan is seen as a melting pot for various identities.

Darezhan Omirbaev's **Shuga** is loosely based on Tolstoy's *Anna Karenina*, updated to a contemporary setting but accurately transposing the love triangle of a man, his wife and the 'New Kazakh' (businessman) she falls in love with and for whom she leaves her family.

Kazakhstan is increasingly attracting internationally renowned filmmakers. Volker Schlöndorff has just completed **Ulzhan**, the story of a determined Frenchman who, following the death of his wife, decides to travel east on a death wish. Arriving in Kazakhstan, he meets a beautiful woman, Ulzhan, who shows him how to live again.

The future of cinema in Kazakhstan looks safe for the moment, with the appearance of the so-called 'Kazakh New Wave'. Leading the vanguard are Abai Kulbai and Akhan Sataev. Kulbai's **Strizh** tells the story of a teenage girl whose problems are ignored by her parents, their only concern being her school grades. Sataev's **Rakiteer** is a crime drama that looks back to the business enterprise boom of the early 1990s.

Future productions include Rustem Abdrashev's **Present for Stalin**, Ardak Amirkulov's **Goodbye, Gulsary!**, Sergey Dvortsevoi's **Tulip** and **Mustafa**, by Satybaldy Narymbetov.

The year's best films
Strizh (Abai Kulbai)
Kurak Korpe (Rustem Abdrashev)
Rakiteer (Akhan Sataev)
Ulzhan (Volker Schlöndorff)
Mongol (Sergei Bodrov)

GULNARA ABIKEYEVA is a Director of the Centre of Central Asian Cinematography, Almaty, and Artistic Director of International Film Festival 'Eurasia'. She has written three books on Kazakh and Central Asian Cinema.

Kenya Ogova Ondego

The Kenya Film Commission created by Presidential Decree in January 2005 has yet to impact the filmmaking community. It is viewed by some as too closely linked to special interests to successfully improve filmmaking practices in the country.

The only films produced in the last two years have been a handful of low-budget, straight-to-video releases. Catherine Muigai's **Clean Hands** takes place in Nairobi and offers a cautionary tale about the dangers of AIDS, taking an ethical and traditionally religious stance on sexual practice. Mary Migui's **Backlash** also dealt with AIDS in a drama about a wealthy family whose son has contracted the virus. Migui also directed **Benta**, about a 16-year-old girl who is forced to work as a domestic worker to fend for her siblings following the death of her parents in a motor accident. Robert Bresson's **Help!** illustrated the predicament Africa faces in terms of foreign aid. Wanuri Kahiu directed a 26-minute feature, **Ras Star**, set in Nairobi's settlements, about an aspiring young music star on South Africa's pay TV channel, M-Net. And Bob Nyanja's **Malooned** finds a man and woman trapped in a toilet on the fifteenth floor of a Nairobi office-block over the Easter weekend. A critical success, winning awards at film festivals in Kenya and Zanzibar, it has become one of the few local success stories.

Kenya now has eleven cinemas (up from eight) with 27 screens (previously 15), courtesy of South Africa's Nu-Metro Cinemas. The average ticket price is over $4. Nu-Metro's share of the market is 65%, with Fox Theatres and Nyali Cinemax taking 35%. The share of local films to Hollywood productions is a mere 0.01%.

Cinema owners say they is very little audience for local productions.

Lola Kenya Screen, eastern Africa's first and only audiovisual media festival, production workshop and market exclusively targeted at children and the youth of the region, returned it 2007. It won the the Africa Grand Prix and increased attendance by over 300% from its first event in 2005.

It enabled eleven children to make their own films, equipped 15 youths to make television programmes aimed at their peers, allowed six children to work as arts and culture journalists, and six others to judge film productions. Other children worked as programme presenters (MCs) during the six days of the festival. The annual Lola Kenya Screen has added 21 child filmmakers, eight journalists, nine film judges, four MCs and 15 youth television producers to Kenya's creative spectrum, while another ten young women and men studied film and cultural events management. 250 films from 46 nations were screened. In August 2008, Lola Kenya Screen will award an All Africa prize to films made by children in Africa.

A Pan-African short film competition titled, 'Killing Africa – Healing Africa', targeting filmmakers in eastern and central Africa, and organised by the Women Filmmakers of Zimbabwe and the Goethe Institute, with support from the Art in Africa Foundation, ran in Kenya in 2007. The chosen films will premiere at the 2009 Berlin Film Festival.

OGOVA ONDEGO writes on socio-cultural and audiovisual media matters in eastern and southern Africa.

Latvia Andris Rozenbergs

One needs to look no further than the National Film Festival of Latvia and its award, the 'Lielais Kristaps' (named after the legend that 'Great Cristoph' took a little boy across a torrential flow on his shoulders) to know that a new generation of Latvian filmmakers has emerged.

Vogelfrei, which was awarded the Best Film prize in the 2007 National Film Festival, is the joint project of four young filmmakers: Janis Kalejs, Janis Putnins, Gatis Smits and Anna Viduleja. Each directed a section devoted to a specific period in the life of one man – 'Childhood', 'Adolescence', 'Youth' and 'Old Age'; the overriding theme being the importance of human values. The last two sections are particularly impressive. The main character in 'Youth', directed by Smits, is a successful manager who, after a series of mishaps, discovers that life exists outside the world of office buildings and sales talk. In Viduleja's 'Old Age', Lithuanian actor Ljubomiras Laucavichus, with a screen presence not dissimilar to Jean Gabin, deals with two city dwellers who want him to provide them with a falcon for hunting. His expressive silences contrast with the nervous impatience of the two men who look so out of place in the natural surroundings.

After several successful documentaries, Juris Poskus moved into features with his debut, **Monotony**. Bored by the dullness of provincial life and spurred by a newspaper ad, Ilze goes to Riga hoping to participate in a film as an extra. Her boyfriend Ojars follows, intending to bring her home. Both mingle with the frenzied, though no less humdrum city life: dirty suburbs, inhospitable dwellings, people who feel like immigrants in their own country.

Iveta Pole in **Monotony**

The film succeeds thanks to the spontaneous performances, particularly by newcomer Iveta Pole, who won Best Actress at the National Film Festival.

Latvian documentary filmmakers are increasingly concerned about the impact of global events on their lives. In the early 1990s, when bloody conflicts expanded across the former Soviet Union, the world

Yelena Bonner in **My Husband Andrei Sakharov**

Atis Lejins in **Debt to Afghanistan**

listened to the father of the Soviet H-bomb, Andrei Sakharov, and his wife, human-rights activist Yelena Bonner, when they defended Russia's democratic development. Now, with Russia reasserting its power, concerns have been raised about how the country will act – democratically or imperially? In her award-winning film, **My Husband Andrei Sakharov**, Inara Kolmane highlights the need to be vigilant.

Latvian soldiers have frequently been compelled to fight under foreign flags. The last time was in 1979 when Soviet troops invaded Afghanistan. Askolds Saulitis returns to this topic in **Debt to Afghanistan**. Some twenty or so years ago, a young idealist, Atis Lejins, went from Sweden to Afghanistan with the intention of explaining to the mujahedeens that amongst the Soviet troops there were Latvians and other nationals from the Baltic states fighting against their will and that this should be taken into account if they were captured. Upon his arrival the Soviets assaulted the village he was staying in. An Afghan peasant and mujahedeen commander hid Lejins, saving his life. Now an acclaimed political scientist and director of the Latvian Institute of Foreign Affairs, Lejins and a group of Latvian volunteers set out on a risky trip to Afghanistan in order to meet the same mujahedeen commander and thank him for the debt he is owed.

Amidst the films dedicated to Latvian history, **Little Bird's Diary**, an animated documentary about an 80-year-old woman who kept a diary of pictures instead of writing, is particularly poignant. By depicting her own life she unwittingly documents the last century, sometimes with a smile, sometimes with bitter irony, but always intimately. Producer Bruno Ascuks and his team – director Edmunds Jansons and writer Nora Ikstena – succeeded in tackling the difficult genre of documentary animation.

Latvia's film festival has repeatedly proved that the country's filmmakers have vigour and talent. *Nocturnal*, Anna Viduleja's graduation film from the National Film and Television School in Britain in 2000, won an award at Cannes. Gatis Smits was praised as best director at the previous Great Cristoph awards for his graduation project, *Agent Madly in Love*, in 2004. After several years, these newcomers have confirmed their potential. But financing is far from easy. In order to raise the profile of the new generation and not constrain the creativity of the middle and older generations, Latvia has to produce at least six fiction films per year, as well as documentaries and animation. Given the high rates of inflation, continuing this trend is the toughest challenge for Latvia's National Film Centre. Unless they succeed, the little boy on Cristoph's shoulder will never grow up.

The year's best films
Monotony (Juris Poskus)
My Husband Andrei Sakharov
(Inara Kolmane)
But the Hour Is Near (Juris Poskus)
The Anatomy of National Holiday
(Askolds Saulitis)

Quote of the year
'One leg of my camera's tripod is always in Latvia, the other two are set in the world around Latvia. *Documentary filmmaker,* ASKOLDS SAULITIS

ANDRIS ROZENBERGS is Head of the Film Registry at Latvia's National Film Centre, and has directed seven fiction films and a dozen documentaries.

Mexico Carlos Bonfil

Much has been written on the recent blossoming of Mexican cinema. Most of this praise is related to the undeniable success of a number of remarkable Mexican filmmakers, including Alfonso Cuarón, Alejandro González Iñárritu and Guillermo del Toro. Renowned international film festivals and high-profile media circuses, such as Hollywood's annual Academy Award ceremony, have contributed to the illusion that Mexican cinema is experiencing a second Golden Age. Although there has been a remarkable development of talented individuals, both in the fields of film direction and cinematography, the truth is that the Mexican film industry is only gradually recovering from a long-standing crisis that had all but crippled it. This crisis provoked, among other calamities, the exodus to Hollywood or Europe of those very talents who are now being hailed as the symbols of Mexican cinema's boom.

The last two years have seen an impressive variety of subjects and styles being adopted by independent Mexican filmmakers. Their films have been produced in often difficult conditions and far too many still remain unknown to Mexican audiences. Sadly, these films have something in common: they are poorly distributed and when they finally reach the screen they are lucky to remain in the programme for two weeks, after which they are relegated to art-house circuits as products for limited cultural consumption.

The best Mexican cinema today is not produced abroad, although co-productions remain the best financial incentive for its development; it is clearly a domestic phenomenon that local audiences manage to discover with scarcely any publicity.

To most Mexican viewers, this 'miracle boom' in their domestic cinema comes as both a big surprise and something of a paradox. Local productions are constantly struggling for visibility, publicity, distribution and fair exhibition quotas. Additionally, they require a stronger commitment and investment from the government, private enterprises and television networks. Although some gains have been registered, the prevailing feeling is that the support the government claims to give to the film industry is continuously hindered by the bureaucratic machinations of the Department of the Treasury. It appears more interested in implementing economic reforms to ensure tax incentives for those enterprises that are investing, or might be willing to invest, in Mexican films.

Mario Garibaldi in Francisco Vargas's **The Violin**

The current diversity of Mexican cinema is overwhelming, both in fiction and documentary. It includes remarkable films such as Francisco Vargas's **The Violin** (*El violin*), which tells the story of don Plutarco, an old violinist trapped between the Mexican Army and the guerrilleros. Along with his son Genaro, who plays the guitar, and his grandson Zacarias, he travels through small towns in the tropical sierra, playing his instrument to

Juan Pablo Castañeda in Gerardo Naranjo's **Drama/Mex**

support himself, while in the country social turmoil and government repression prevail. As the army invades don Plutarco's hometown and his son hides in the mountains with the guerrillas, the old man manages to enchant an officer with his music. An odd relationship of complicity and mutual mistrust grows between these characters which the director conveys convincingly through a solid narrative.

Ruben Imaz's **La Familia Tortuga** is a sensitive portrayal of a dysfunctional family, conveying with an impressive degree of originality and lack of sentimentality the painful process of mourning experienced by four people since the death of their family's matriarch. This elegantly paced film slowly presents an intimate chronicle of these people's lives as they unveil their fears and desires before the camera, with little dialogue, long takes and an intriguing narrative that privileges psychological observation over plot in order to enhance the dramatic power of separations and reunions, recovery and readjustment. Furthermore, Imaz's cinematic style successfully blends social realism with the fantasy world of Uncle

Manuel, an old man taking refuge in child-like behaviour as a strategy for avoiding the grief around him.

In **Drama/Mex**, young filmmaker Gerardo Naranjo overlaps three tales of romance and disenchantment to present a sensitive, albeit ironic, portrayal of contemporary middle-class Mexican youth. From a rich house in Mexico City, where two young characters express their mixed feelings for each other with passionate sex and coarse language, to the beaches of Acapulco, where a middle-aged man about to commit suicide is both rescued and seduced by a teenage girl, Naranjo chronicles the hardships of young people striving for moral fulfilment in a world of grown-ups who, at best, choose to ignore them.

After two remarkable international successes, *Japón* and *Battle in Heaven*, Carlos Reygadas once again moved in another radical direction. **Silent Light** (*Luz silenciosa*), set amongst a Menonite community in the northern region of Chihuahua, is a profound allegory of moral redemption. A man cheats on his wife and confesses his fault, ignoring the potentially fatal consequences of his actions. His inner struggle is rendered through a series of long takes, recording minute changes of light and sound. Resembling no other film in contemporary Mexican cinema, suggesting a new route through which stories can be told, *Silent Light* cements Reygadas's reputation as arguably the most talented filmmaker of his generation.

Silent Light, *directed by Carlos Reygadas*

Everardo González also pushes the boundaries of film. **Old Thieves and the Legends of a trade** (*Los Ladrones viejos. Las leyendas del artegio*) chronicles the lives of pickpockets and robbers from the 1950s and 1960s who looted the mansions of rich Mexicans, including those of two Presidents, ending up in the jail from where they narrate their experiences with a touch of humour. Explaining their codes of honour and behaviour at the time, the film uses archive images of Mexico City in a remarkable and extremely entertaining film.

Everardo González' **Old Thieves and the Legends of a Trade**

Other documentaries tended to concentrate on social and political realities following the 2006 presidential election, when Felipe Calderón, the conservative leader, narrowly beat his rival, leftist Andrés Manuel López Obrador, in a victory that some believe was fixed. Luis Mandoki's **Fraude, México 2006** is a harsh indictment of political corruption. Lucia Gajá's **Mi vida dentro** is a dramatic chronicle of a Mexican woman imprisoned in the United States after being unjustly accused of an American child's death under her care, when he swallowed a piece of paper and choked. Her direct testimony from jail, where she is sentenced to 99 years, is one of the most harrowing accounts of immigration, social injustice and racial prejudice. Alejandra Isla's **Los demonios del Edén**, Eva Aridjis's **La santa muerte** and Juan Sepúlveda's **La frontera infinita** deal, respectively, with the subjects of the unpunished sexual abuse of children, the popular cult of Death (as incarnated in a grim female saint carrying a scythe) and the struggle for survival of people who try to cross the American border in search of a better life.

Enrique Arreola and Cecilia Suárez in Ernesto Contreras' **Blue Eyelids**

Short feature films also explored social realities. Elisa Miller's **Watching it Rain** (*Ver llover*) was awarded the Palme d'Or for the best short fiction film at Cannes. A teenage boy is infatuated with an older girl, who dreams of leaving her hometown to try her luck in the big city. The boy faces the moral dilemma of choosing between staying with his widowed mother or following the girl.

Looking back on the Mexican features of the last year, the best have either focused on the inner conflicts of their characters or presented a form of social realism increasingly removed from the generic conventions of melodrama. Films such as Enrique Begne's **Two Embraces** (*Dos abrazos*), Ernesto Contreras's **Blue Eyelids** (*Párpados azules*), Simón Bross's **Bad Habits** (*Malos hábitos*) or Nicolás Pereda's **Dónde están sus historias?** are some examples of how independent filmmaking can detach itself from the bulk of commercial fare (which reached around fifty titles this year), by committing itself to a combination of low budgets and strong talent. The Mexican film industry urgently needs a legal framework

Helena de Haro in Simón Bross's **Bad Habits**

that protects its films from the hegemony of American blockbusters and a more vigorous contribution of private and public financing to encourage film production before anyone can proclaim that Mexican cinema is indeed experiencing a second Golden Age.

The Mexican film industry urgently needs a legal framework that protects its films from the hegemony of American blockbusters. During the 2007 summer season, the Motion Pictures Association of America (MPAA) distributed six titles in Mexico, which occupied 88% of the screens; this prevented the release of a number of important Mexican films which had to wait until less economically favourable times of the year for their screenings. Last October, during the Morelia International Film Festival, President Felipe Calderón promised to officially encourage the production and distribution of Mexican cinema.

However, barely two months later Congress announced that the 2008 funds for IMCINE, the national film institute, would be subject to a budgetary reduction of $2.7 million, instead of the expected increase of a similar amount. Furthermore, private investors who had previously agreed to contribute tax-deductible funds for the production of new films now conditioned such support to a strict control of content, in which sex, violence and social criticism were to be banned, and family entertainment to be encouraged.

The year's best films
Silent Light (Carlos Reygadas)
The Violin (Francisco Vargas)
Old Thieves (Everardo González)
Drama/Mex (Gerardo Naranjo)
Turtle Family (Ruben Imaz)

Quote of the year
'Mexico is a prey of ignorance, of a double ignorance: firstly, for not seeing the business that cinema represents; secondly, for the willingness to turn the whole country into a big enterprise for the profit of international corporations.' *Director* **ALFONSO CUARÓN**

Directory
All Tel/Fax numbers begin (+52)
Cineteca Nacional, Avenida México-Coyoacán 389, Col Xoco, México DF. Tel: 1253 9314. www.cinetecanacional.net.
Association of Mexican Film Producers & Distributors, Avenida División del Norte 2462, Piso 8, Colonia Portales, México DF. Tel: 5688 0705. Fax: 5688 7251.
Cinema Production Workers Syndicate (STPC), Plateros 109 Col San José Insurgentes, México DF. Tel: 5680 6292. cctpc@terra.com.mx.
Dirección General de Radio, Televisión y Cine-matografía (RTC), Roma 41, Col Juárez, México DF. Tel: 5140 8010. ecardenas@segob.gob.mx.
Instituto Mexicano de Cinematografía (IMCINE), Insurgentes Sur 674 Col del Valle, CP 03100, México DF. Tel: 5448 5300. mercaint@institutomexicanodecinematografía.gob.mx.

CARLOS BONFIL is a film critic, contributing a weekly article on cinema to *La Jornada*, a leading Mexican newspaper. He is the author of *Through the Mirror: Mexican Cinema and its Audience* (1994).

Morocco Roy Armes

Morocco continues to offer strong support to its filmmakers. The result of this is that output has continued to rise to around a dozen films in each of the last two years. However, such strong support allows the state a huge say in what gets made. Indeed, it has become virtually impossible for a film to obtain production funding or stand a chance of being distributed in Morocco without 'aid fund' support. But the system does enable Moroccan films to compete against imported films; in 2006, the top four places at the box office were occupied by Moroccan films. The scheme also permits Moroccan filmmakers the rare opportunity of building a career through regular production. The previous model is exemplified by Latif Lahlou who made his first film in 1969, his second in 1986 and went into production with his new film in 2007. By contrast, Hassan Benjelloun, whose career began in 1990, released his eighth feature, **The Red Moon** (*La Lune rouge*) in 2006 and already had his ninth selected for the Festival National du Film (FNF) in October 2007.

The greatest strength of the current Moroccan system is its eclectic nature – it even backed the French thriller **I Saw Ben Barka Get Killed** (*J'ai vu tuer Ben Barka*), directed by *Cahiers du Cinéma* editor, Serge Le Péron, in collaboration with a Moroccan journalist, Saïd Smihi. There was also backing for filmmakers who had made hit films in the past. Saïd Naciri, whose 2004 hit, *The Crooks*, was one of the most popular Moroccan films of all time, completed **Abdou With the Almohades** (*Abdou chez les Almohades*), a comedy about a petty crook caught up in a time-travel experiment and propelled back into the past. Hakim Noury made a sequel to his 2000 hit mother-in-law

comedy and gave it an even longer title: **She is Diabetic and Hypertensive and Still She Refuses to Die** (*Elle est diabétique et hypertendue et elle refuse toujours de crever*). But the top box office success of 2006 in terms of receipts was Laïla Marrakchi's **Marock**, a forceful study of idle rich youth in Casablanca. It was shown throughout Europe in 2005 but its problems with the censor, which delayed its release in Morocco, seem to have helped rather than hindered its progress. Two other female directors released new features, albeit with less box office success. Farida Benlyazid premiered her third film, **Juanita from Tangier** (*Juanita de Tanger*), a Moroccan-Spanish co-production adapted from a popular Spanish novel, while Narjiss Nejja returned with her second, **Wake Up Morocco**, about the dreams of an old footballer looking after his grand-daughter. We are also promised the welcome return of Farida Bourquia, whose previous feature, *Embers*, was made back in 1982.

Three filmmakers from the 1970s with very different styles also returned to the cinema. Nabyl Lahlou's **Tabite or not Tabite** is a typically convoluted tale of a man writing a

Saïd Naciri's **Abdou With the Almohades**

script about a police investigation, whereas Moumen Smihi's **The Boy From Tangier** (*Le Gosse de Tanger*) is a sensitive and realistic study of urban life. Ahmed El Maânouni – after a break of 25 years – returned with **Broken Hearts** (*Cœurs brûlés*), which is, appropriately, the tale of a man who returns to Fez to confront images of his past.

Hakim Belabbes's **Why the Sea?**

Four filmmakers who made their debut in the 2000s returned with second features. Driss Chouika's **The Game of Love** (*Le Jeu de l'amour*) is the story of a life-long relationship told at three key points. Hakim Belabbes's **Why the Sea?** (*Pourquoi la mer?*) is a mix of fairytale and real events, based on the legend of a beautiful woman who lures sailors to their deaths. Two films by members of this group occupied third and fourth positions at the Moroccan box office: Kamal Kamal's **Moroccan Symphony** (*Symphonie marocaine*), a hymn to peace inspired by the war in Lebanon, and Abdelmajid Rchich's **Broken Wings** (*Les Aîles brisées*), the story of a three-year-old child who is kidnapped only to be retured to his parents ten years later. Disappointingly, one of Morocco's brightest talents, Faouzi Bensaidi, internationally acclaimed for his short films and meticulous debut feature *A Thousand Months*, came up short with his second feature, **What a Wonderful World**, an uneven comedy-thriller about an inept professional assassin.

As always there were opportunities for newcomers. Badr Abdellilah made the

first Berber-language comedy, **Bouksasse Boutfounaste**, while Mohamed Zineddaine told the story of a young writer struggling to tell the story of his generation in **The Awakening** (*Le Réveil*). Hamid Faridi made **The Bike** (*Le Vélo*), in which a dying father leaves his two daughters to face the injustice of Morocco's inheritance laws. In Mohamed Ali El Mejoub's **The White Wave** (*La Vague blanche*), a drug trafficker released from prison returns to his old ways. Mohamed Mernich's **Tilila** is a tale of family passions aroused when a girl is seduced and abandoned. Nabil Ayouch's brother, Hichem Ayouch, debuted with **Edges of the Heart** (*Les Arêtes du cœur*), in which the discovery of a severed arm on a beach makes villagers confront the reality of their lives. Finally, real generational shift was signalled by the appearance of **Heaven's Doors** (*Les Portes du paradis*), the story of a young workman led astray by greed, which was co-directed by veteran filmmaker Hakim Noury's two sons, Sohael and Imad.

The prospects for Moroccan cinema look good. It has conquered its domestic audience and is gaining increasing recognition at film festivals, though it has so far failed to achieve the level of international recognition acquired by Algeria in the 1970s or by Tunisia in the early 1990s.

Quote of the year
'It's important for Morocco to preserve and indeed improve its situation as a location for important productions from around the world. It's necessary on financial as well as employment grounds of course, but equally for professional and artistic purposes: we have much to learn from these collaborations.'
NOUR-EDDINE SAÏL, *Director of the Centre Cinématographique Marocain*

ROY ARMES is Emeritus Professor of Film at Middlesex University and author of many studies of cinema, most recently *Postcolonial Images: Studies in North African Film* (2005).

Netherlands Leo Bankersen

They could hardly be more different. Veteran Paul Verhoeven's dark, cynical and sometimes vulgar World War II drama **Black Book** (*Zwartboek*), about the shady sides of collaboration and resistance, and Joram Lürsen's third feature **Love is All** (*Alles is liefde*), a lightweight romantic comedy with 'Sinterklaas' – not to be confused with his imitator, Santa Claus – as one of the main characters. Yet they have one important thing in common. Both films brought Dutch audiences back into the cinema. Actually, there's a second common feature: versatile actress Carice van Houten, now embarking on an international career.

Carice van Houten in Paul Verhoeven's **Black Book**

Even before its Venice premiere, the much-talked about *Black Book* was already the Dutch cinema event of 2006. When it opened on 14 September, filmgoers were undeterred by mixed reviews, responding enthusiastically to Verhoeven's film. Attendance passed the one million mark by January 2007, a figure seldom reached by Dutch features.

Love is All opened on 11 October 2007, and surpassed *Black Book*'s success. How did they do it? Is it the casting of a large number of well-known actors and television personalities? Is it Lürsen's confident, fast-paced way of combining romantic farce (a real prince and a white horse) with more serious themes? Is it the inventive script by screenwriter Kim van Kooten, loosely modelled on *Love Actually*? Amazingly, *Love is All* effortlessly rises above its rather corny theme – 'love is like Sinterklaas, you have to believe in it' – and the secret to its success lies in the blanket media coverage it managed to generate.

Compare this success with the fate of another appealing comedy, **HannaHannaH**, the first feature by director Annemarie van de Mond. Starring the relatively unknown actress Maria Kraakman, who plays a fickle young woman who takes a one-night-stand to a family party, an unenthusiastic release in too few cinemas resulted in low returns at the box office.

The Dutch market share in 2006 was a healthy 11%, not unsatisfying compared to previous years. However, *Black Book* alone accounted for almost 5%. Without a Verhoeven film in the wings, the Dutch domestic share for the first three quarters of 2007 plummeted to 4.9%. A lot now depends on *Love is All*, together with new family films like Steven de Jong's **Bontekoe's Young Sailors** (*De scheepsjongens van Bontekoe*), which recreates the adventurous journey of a seventeenth-century merchant ship bound for the East Indies.

One of the artistic highlights of recent Dutch cinema was writer-director Mijke de Jong's **Stages** (*Tussenstand*). Developed in close collaboration with the actors, this slightly experimental film juxtaposes fierce verbal fights between a separated couple unable to let go of each other with the silent world their

Elsie de Brauw and Stijn Koomen in Mijke de Jong's **Stages**

17-year-old son has withdrawn into. Deeply moving, and not without hilarity, this dissection of emotional turmoil is an impressive piece of filmmaking. It was awarded the Golden Calf for best direction, best actress and best sound at the Netherlands Film Festival.

Other examples from a new generation of Dutch filmmakers are Nanouk Leopold's observations of loneliness, **Wolfsbergen**, and Erik de Bruyn's second feature **Nadine**, about the crises of a childless single woman, played by three different actresses. These impressive and powerful psychological dramas were better recognised abroad than at home. *Wolfsbergen* premiered at the Berlin Film Festival, while *Nadine* was chosen to open the Mannheim-Heidelberg festival.

A few recent Dutch films dealt directly with contemporary issues. Dana Nechushtan found inspiration for her thriller **Nightrun** (*Nachtrit*) in the troubles experienced by a taxi driver caught up in a scam when he borrows money to buy into a taxi company,

Karina Smulders and Fedja van Huêt in Nanouk Leopold's **Wolfsbergen**

unaware that his dreams will be undermined by new legislation allowing anyone to own a taxi. Hardly highbrow, but Nechushtan has a feel for the settings and the character of the naïve driver trapped in a violent subculture. After his surprise hit *Hush Hush Baby* (2004), Albert ter Heerdt approached racial conflict in the Netherlands more seriously in **Kicks**, a tableau of life in a multicultural society, which displayed the talents of newcomer Mimoun Oaïssa.

Old-school Dutch filmmaking, imbued with poetic imagery and a vein of absurdism, was represented by two well-known directors: Alex van Warmerdam and Jos Stelling. Van Warmerdam opened the 2006 Utrecht Film Festival with his wry comedy **Waiter** (*Ober*), which focuses on the internal struggle between an unhappy waiter (played by van Warmerdam) and the screenwriter who is creativing his life. The film won the Golden Calf for its screenplay and production design. After a long absence, Stelling opened Utrecht in 2007 with **Duska**, a charming – though overlong – fantasy about a film critic, a girl who works at the local cinema and an uninvited guest from Russia. *Duska* was chosen as the Dutch entry for the 2008 Academy Awards.

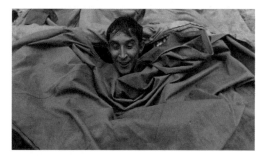

Jiska Rickels' **4 Elements**

Documentaries, still a Dutch stronghold despite pressure on budgets caused by the restructuring of public broadcasting, remained strong over the last two years. Jiska Rickels impressed with her ambitious debut, **4 Elements**. Shooting deep underground in a German coal mine, among fire-fighters in Siberian woods, in rough seas on a fishing boat near Alaska and in a Russian training camp for cosmonauts, Rickels stubbornly eschews eco-critical trends, instead composing a lyrical masterpiece.

In **Forever**, acclaimed filmmaker Heddy Honigmann filmed visitors to the Père-Lachaise graveyard in Paris. Recording their response to the surroundings the film becomes a moving meditation on life.

Students at Amsterdam's Film Academy continue to display the impact of the Dutch documentary tradition. The 2007 Pathé Tuschinski Award for best graduation work went, for the third consecutive year, to a documentary. Marijn Frank's **Daddy's Gone and Left Me Puzzled** (*Papa is weg... en ik wilde nog wat vragen*) records her brave and sensitive search for answers her deceased father – never a great talker – can no longer give her.

Family films and films for children continue to reign solidly, some even without the aid of the Dutch Filmfund. Steven de Jong signed a contract with producer Bridge Entertainment/FMG to direct five features. Johan Nijenhuis directed the sequels **Zoo Rangers in India** (*Zoop in India*) and **Zoo Rangers in South America** (*Zoop in Zuid-Amerika*), following the unpretentious and rather cartoonish adventures of animal-loving teenagers, based on a popular television series. Maria Peters brought the popular teenage novels by Carry Slee to the big screen. Dealing with first loves and teenage strife, **XTC Just Don't Do It** (*Afblijven*) and **Timboektoe** connected well with their target audience.

Critics were, in most cases, not terribly enthusiastic about these films. However, there were some films aimed at younger viewers that managed to impress. Mischa Kamp's charming **Where is Winky's Horse?** (*Waar is het paard van Sinterklaas?*), the follow-up to *Winky's Horse*, about a Chinese immigrant girl in a Dutch village, was a tailor-made delight for young children. As was the ambitious English-language production aimed at older children **Crusade in Jeans** (*Kruistocht in spijkerbroek*), by Ben Sombogaart. Featuring time-travel to the Middle Ages and starring Emily Watson, it won the 2007 Golden Calf for best film.

Looking forward to early 2008, Threes Anna's metaphorical drama **The Bird Can't Fly** is to be released, featuring American actress Barbara Hershey as a woman journeying to the village she grew up in, now almost buried in the sands of the South African desert.

In terms of the domestic film industry, June 2007 saw the end of a period of insecurity about film funding, during which many producers postponed future projects. Earlier tax incentives have been replaced by a new matching fund with approximately €12 million at its disposal to help producers who have secured 65% of their budget from other sources.

Digitalisation is slowly making progress. As of the end of 2007, 21 Dutch cinemas are equipped with 2k digital projectors; eleven have upgraded their equipment to accommodate 3D. CinemaNet Nederland is developing a network with digital servers and (at present) has 26 smaller art-house cinemas with 1.4k digital projectors. Until now, most of the titles screened by this network have been documentaries. CinemaNet's ambition is to upgrade these cinemas to 2k and to incorporate mainstream films into their programme.

Joe Flynn (centre) in Ben Sombogaart's **Crusade in Jeans**

The year's best films
4 Elements (Jiska Rickels)
Stages (Mijke de Jong)
Forever (Heddy Honigmann)
Love is All (Joram Lürsen)
Daddy's Gone and Left Me Puzzled
(Marijn Frank)

Quote of the year
'Do you know the line "God punishes who wants to be a rocker in Holland" from the song by Jan Rot? The same goes for filmmakers.'
ERIK DE BRUYN, *on having his new script* Odessa Star *rejected by the Filmfund*

Directory
All Tel/Fax numbers begin (+31)
Circle of Dutch Film Critics (KNF), PO Box 10650, 1011 ER Amsterdam. Tel: (6) 2550 0668. Fax: (6) 627 5923. knfilm@xs4all.nl.
Cobo Fund, PO Box 26444, Postvak M54, 1202 JJ Hilversum. Tel: (35) 677 5348. Fax: (35) 677 1995. cobo@nos.nl. Contact: Jeanine Hage.
Dutch Film Fund, Jan Luykenstraat 2, 1071 CM Amsterdam. Tel: (20) 570 7676. Fax: (31) 570 7689. info@filmfund.nl. Contact: Toine Berbers.
Filmmuseum, Rien Hagen, Vondelpark 3, PO Box 74782, 1070 BT Amsterdam. Tel: (20) 589 1400. Fax: (20) 683 3401. info@filmmuseum.nl. www.filmmuseum.nl.
Holland Film, Jan Luykenstraat 2, 1071 CM Amsterdam. Tel: (20) 570 4700. Fax: (20) 570 7570, hf@hollandfilm.nl. www.hollandfilm.nl.
Netherlands Cinematographic Federation (NFC), Jan Luykenstraat 2, PO Box 75048, 1070 AA Amsterdam. Tel: (20) 679 9261. Fax: (20) 675 0398. info@nfc.org. Contact: Wilco Wolfers.
Netherlands Film & Television Academy (NFTA), Markenplein 1, 1011 MV Amsterdam. Tel: (20) 527 7333. Fax: (20) 527 7344. info@nfta.ahk.nl. www.nfta.ahk.nl.
Netherlands Institute for Animation Film, PO Box 9358, 5000 HJ Tilburg. Tel: (13) 535 4555. Fax: (13) 580 0057. niaf@niaf.nl.
Netherlands Instituut voor Beeld en Geluid, PO Box 1060, 1200 BB Hilversum. Tel: (35) 677 2672/7. Fax: (35) 677 2835. klantenservice@naa.nl. www.naa.nl.
Rotterdam Film Fund, Rochussenstraat 3C, 3015

EA Rotterdam. Tel: (10) 436 0747. Fax: (10) 436 0553. info@rff.rotterdam.nl.

Alex van Warmerdam's **Waiter**

LEO BANKERSEN is a freelance film critic who writes regularly for the Netherlands Press Association. He also contributes to the monthly film magazine *de Filmkrant*.

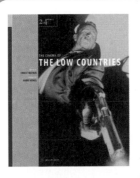

New Zealand Peter Calder

New Zealand commentators use the term 'cultural cringe' to describe the national tendency to regard imported culture as superior to home-grown product. It's a habit Kiwis have slowly begun to break in recent years – most notably in relation to chart music – but local films have always been a tough sell to domestic audiences. However, there were signs at the beginning of 2006 that this attitude was changing. Even discounting the major studio films with a strong New Zealand input (Peter Jackson's *King Kong*, entirely made here, and the first *Chronicles of Narnia* film, directed by New Zealand filmmaker and was partly shot here), New Zealand films have begun to show some traction at home, scoring an unheard-of 5% of the domestic box office.

Much of that popularity could be attributed to an eccentric Southlander who liked building motorcycles in his backyard. *The World's Fastest Indian*, directed by Roger Donaldson and starring Anthony Hopkins as the can-do Bonneville-conquering speed legend Burt Munro, became the most successful local film in New Zealand history, taking more than $5 million, passing the record held by *Once Were Warriors*. More than a few were moved to remark that it was cheering that our most popular film depicted the world-beating 'Kiwi ingenuity' on which we pride ourselves, rather than family violence in a grim urban ghetto.

Much of *The World's Fastest Indian*'s revenue was collected in 2005 – it was released in September – but it injected a feel-good factor into the local business that doubtless rubbed off on later films. The happiest film of 2006, Chris Graham's **Sione's Wedding**, took $3 million at local cinemas, taking it to third place

Ruby Dee in **No. 2**

on the all-time local money list. A cheerful and breezy comedy about a bunch of benign troublemakers, it was the work of a talented Samoan comedy group whose TV series, *bro'Town* – a title inexplicable to outsiders – is a strong sign of the growing presence of Polynesians in the local film industry. *Sione's Wedding* would have taken more had pirated DVDs, apparently made by someone who worked on the film's post-production, not sold briskly in the largely Maori and Pacific Island neighbourhoods of the film's target demographic.

Less successful was Toa Fraser's **No. 2**, a screen version of a successful local play about a Fijian-Kiwi matriarch (US import Ruby Dee) calling a gathering of the clan in order to name her successor. A warm, fuzzy sort of film, distinguished by a great theme song from local popster, Don McGlashan, it amounted to less than the sum of its parts.

If those films showcased New Zealanders' ability to laugh at themselves, the other big 2006 release, Robert Sarkies' **Out of the Blue** told a darker, true story of the Aramoana Massacre that took place in 1990. Featuring actor Karl Urban, the film was commendably restrained and unsensational in telling a story that remains a raw wound in the nation's psyche. Perhaps as a result of its reticence, the film lacked focus and it remains difficult to see it having much impact abroad.

Vincent Ward, one of the country's most acclaimed filmmakers, fared badly with his last feature, *River Queen* (2005), with both critics and audiences disappointed by its incoherent storyline. He is currently hard at work on **The Rain of the Children**, an extended remake of one of his short films, which will be a mixture of drama and documentary, playing once again on a Maori theme.

If 2007 is unlikely to generate the same level of box office buzz as the preceding year, there are still signs of hope. Jonathan King's **Black Sheep** is a bold attempt to manufacture a cult film about man-eating sheep running amok, playing heavily on the imbalance between the country's ovine and human populations (traditionally twenty to one, though more like ten to one these days). Zombie and splatter films are a Kiwi staple – they are the genres on which Peter Jackson cut his cinematic teeth

Taika Waititi's **Eagle vs Shark**

– and the film tapped into the public unease about genetic modification. Sadly, the comedy was forced and predictable, with little thought going into the woefully stereotyped characters.

Peter Burger's **The Tattooist** is a New Zealand-Singapore co-production with a largely local cast, led by horror film regular Jason Behr as an itinerant American tattooist who finds himself in a spot of bother when he encounters the Samoan traditional art of *tatau*. The film, executive produced by the queen of New Zealand's reality TV, Julie Christie, featured impressive production values but was disappointingly predictable and not particularly scary.

Much more impressive – and certain to be the local release of the year – was **Eagle vs Shark**, the feature debut of Taika Waititi, whose wonderful short, *Two Cars, One Night*, was an Academy Award nominee in 2005. An 'odd couple' love story, it successfully blended deadpan humour with geeky, offbeat Kiwi charm. Its appeal – and its commercial prospects – are boosted by the presence of lead actor Jemaine Clement, half of the musical comedy duo Flight of the Conchords, who have a well-regarded US television series on HBO.

Jonathan King's **Black Sheep**

Another impressive feature debut was writer-director Jonothan Cullinane's **We're Here to Help**, a black comedy based on the true, stranger-than-fiction story of a man hounded to the edge of ruin by officious bureaucrats in the tax department.

Dougray Scott in **Perfect Creature**

Other new releases include Chris Stapp's **The Devil Dared Me To**, a delightfully crude high-octane comedy about dumb stuntmen building a rocket-powered car. It was welcomed by the *New Zealand Herald* as 'one gleefully gruesome gag of motorised mayhem after another'. Glenn Standring's **Perfect Creature** is a time-confused vampire flick which, despite some visual stylishness and the appearance of UK stars Saffron Burrows and Dougray Scott, never transcends its muddled storyline and lack of dramatic tension.

In industry news, the Australian owners of Hoyts Cinemas, who opened a new 12-screen multiplex in suburban Auckland, including the largest screen in the world (30.6m x 13m), in September sold its business to Pacific Equity Partners. The other major cinema chain, SkyCity Cinemas, is also selling up, independent of its sale of the parent company's casino business.

Finally, the state-of-the-art $5 million sound studio in Waitakere City, west of Auckland (dubbed Westywood), is seeking to wrest away some of the business that has gone to Wellington (aka Wellywood) facilities bankrolled by Peter Jackson.

PETER CALDER is a journalist and writer who has been a film critic for the country's major daily newspaper, the *New Zealand Herald*, for 22 years.

The year's best films
Eagle vs Shark (Taika Waititi)
Sione's Wedding (Chris Graham)
Out of the Blue (Robert Sarkies)
Squeegee Bandit (Sandor Lau)
We're Here to Help (Jonothan Cullinane)

Quote of the year
'We have a film industry of NZ$2.6 billion and we need to protect it.' TONY EATON *of the New Zealand Federation Against Copyright Theft (NZFACT) on the successful prosecution of a man who made and sold pirated DVDs of the hit film* **Sione's Wedding**

Directory
All Tel/Fax numbers begin (+64)
Film New Zealand, PO Box 24142, Wellington. Tel: (4) 385 0766. Fax: (4) 384 5840. info@filmnz.org.nz. www.filmnz.com.
New Zealand Film Archive, PO Box 11449, Wellington. Tel: (4) 384 7647. Fax: (4) 382 9595. nzfa@actrix.gen.nz. www.filmarchive.org.nz.
New Zealand Film Commission, PO Box 11546, Wellington. Tel: (4) 382 7680. Fax: (4) 384 9719. marketing@nzfilm.co.nz.
Ministry of Economic Development, 33 Bowen St, PO Box 1473, Wellington. Tel: (4) 472 0030. Fax: (4) 473 4638. www.med.govt.nz.
Office of Film & Literature Classification, PO Box 1999, Wellington. Tel: (64) 471 6770. Fax: (4) 471 6781. information@censorship.govt.nz.
Screen Production & Development Association (SPADA), PO Box 9567, Wellington. Tel: (4) 939 6934. Fax: (4) 939 6935. info@spada.co.nz.

Chris Stapp's **The Devil Dared Me To**

Nigeria Steve Ayorinde

In the Nigerian film industry, which is propelled by digital video, prolificacy is measured by the numbers of feature films shot on micro budgets on video and sold to audiences on DVDs, VCDs and video cassettes.

In the first half of 2007, more than a thousand films were produced, surpassing all previous records, according to the National Film and Video Censors Board. Even for the most able film reviewer, it would be impossible to view all the output of 'Nollywood' with a critical eye.

Confronted by a shrinking audience, a few outstanding directors have adopted various formulas to create new markets and attract more people to their films. Among the outstanding releases at the end of 2006 were movies such as Tunde Kelani's **The Narrow Path**, a traditional drama set in rural Lagos during the 1960s. It was screened at the Pan African Film and Television Festival of Ouagadougou (FESPACO) and a number of festivals in Europe. Also popular was Ifeanyi Onyeabor's **New Jerusalem**, an off-beat 'Tarantino-esque' genre thriller that takes place in Lagos during the 1990s.

Of the major productions soon to be released, there is Faruk Lasaki's **Changing Faces**, a romantic thriller set in Ibadan which concerns the transference of spirits through sexual intercourse. Tarila Thompson's **Olulu**, a big-budget (by Nollywood standards, about $200,000) adventure, is set in eastern Nigeria during the last century. It was substantially funded by the African Movie Academy Awards (AMAA), organisers of the annual film awards in Nigeria.

Nollywood in the theatres

Nollywood is not dominated by a single popular genre. Instead, themes are affected by regional cultures as much as they are by tastes, occasionally influenced by ideas that a few notable producers believe could win over the mainstream.

The only 35mm film of 2006, Jeta Amata's **The Amazing Grace**, set in Calabar during the height of the slave trade, was screened at the Cannes market. It was subsequently distributed in Nigeria and South Africa through Nu-Metro cinemas, who have shown a renewed interest in screening films at cinemas before they are released on DVD.

Another new format that has allowed films to receive theatrical distribution was used for Tunde Kelani's **Abeni**, a romantic drama set in Nigeria and Benin Republic during the identity scams of the late 1990s. Returning from the Toronto Film Festival in 2006, it was screened to local audiences through an ingenious Mobile Cinema project.

Jointly directed by Kunle Afolayan and Biodun Aleja, **Irapada**, a broad multilingual drama, is

Kunle Afolayan in **Irapada**

currently riding the wave of success. It began the year by winning an award at AMAA, then screened at the Pan African Film Festival in Los Angeles in February before receiving a theatrical release at the new Lagos multiplex, Silverbird Galleria. Shot on HD, *Irapada* ended the year with a screening at the London Film Festival.

Many directors are embracing the opportunities offered by local festivals, such as Amaka Igwe's BOBTV Festival and Market, where in March 2007 the screen adaptation of Elechi Amadi's **The Concubine**, a pre-colonial drama directed by Andy Amenechi, received its world premiere.

Significantly, Nollywood is also courting the African Diaspora, particularly in the United Kingdom, with an eye to theatrical release. To many producers, distributing 35mm or high-end digital productions to cinemas abroad will hopefully cut out piracy and dishonest distributors who have, for 15 years, denied producers revenue from DVD sales in African and Caribbean communities in the UK. Niyi Towolawi's **Twisted**, a romantic thriller about a London returnee struggling with multiple relationships, was the first film to win a distribution deal with the Odeon cinema chain. Similarly, two other movies, on HD, Teco Benson's action thriller, **Mission to Nowhere** and Okey Zubelu Okoh's nineteenth-century Africa-set epic, **Mirror of Beauty**, were screened at seven Odeon and Cineworld cinemas in London.

New possibilities

Nollywood appears to have reached saturation point, with too many films struggling to shine in a shrinking local market, the result of fewer cinemas, a low average disposable income and DVD piracy. Consequently, a new policy by the National Film and Video Censors Board, the Distribution Framework, is being introduced to help expand and regulate the market. At present, there is ferocious debate between producers over the government's increasing

control of an industry that they themselves – arguably – single-handedly created.

However, where individual filmmakers have failed, four directors, Chico Ejiro, Fidelis Duker, Charles Novia and Fred Amata, jointly formed 'Project Nollywood' in mid-2007. With assistance from banks, they plan to produce and distribute movies using the banks' branches across Nigeria as sales outlets.

Of the recent films released, actress Stephanie Okereke, who survived a ghastly motor accident in 2005, returned to cinemas as the writer and director of **Through the Glass**, a romantic drama set amongst the immigrant communities of Los Angeles. The gifted Tunde Kelani continued his collaboration with Laha Productions of Benin with **Why Me?** (*Pourquios Moi?*), a cross-border romantic thriller set in Cotonou. With hopes that it will be the big film of 2008, the HD production is being transferred by Swiss Effects into 35mm. Finally, Peace Fiberesima's epic, **Isaac Boro**, a bio-pic about the hero of the struggle for self-determination in the oil-rich Niger Delta region.

The year's best films
30 Days (Mildred Okwo)
Maroko (Femi Odugbemi)
New Jerusalem (Ifeanyi Onyeabor)
Irapada (Biodun Aleja/Kunle Afolayan)
Mama Put (Seke Somolu)

Quote of the year
'If Nollywood dies, it will be because of the diaspora, where our movies are popular. Mortgages are paid off by people selling our DVDs in southeast London, but we get to see none of the money.' TUNDE KELANI, *talking about the piracy of Nollywood movies in the UK*

STEVE AYORINDE is a columnist and film critic with *Punch*, Nigeria's largest-circulation national daily. He is a member of FIPRESCI and covers major film festivals across the world, as well as being a regular contributor on Africine (www.africine.org).

Norway Trond Olav Svendsen

The last two years showed significant progress and an air of optimism within the Norwegian film industry. The Department of Culture's target of 25 features per year (including documentaries) has been successfully reached and will hopefully continue. Norwegian film producers proved that there are enough ideas and talent to sustain such a prolific rate. The directors are mostly quite young and recruited from a lively short-film scene, which gained attention when Bobbie Peers won the Palme d'Or at Cannes 2006 for **Sniffer** and Torill Kove won an Academy Award for his animated short, **The Danish Poet**.

Twenty films were released in 2006 and, while no single film proved really outstanding, at least half a dozen were impressively original. Jens Lien's **The Bothersome Man** (*Den brysomme mannen*) was a fable about a man (played by Trond Fausa Aurvaag) who finds himself in a strange city with no memory of how he got there. He meets people without ambition and finds himself a work place where no discussion is permitted. Only the sound of music from a crack in the wall hints at human emotion. Lien is a confident director, who leans more towards the strong mise-en-scene of the Coen brothers than the self-conscious hand-held style of Lars von Trier.

Joachim Trier's **Reprise**

In **Reprise**, director Joachim Trier tells the story of two young men who aspire to be celebrated authors, with one harnessing his talent and the other spiralling towards a mental breakdown. Cutting between past and present, Trier does not make it easy for his audience to follow his plot, going against the grain of the average Norwegian film, whose battle cry has long been 'connect with your audience'.

Christopher Nielsen's **Free Jimmy**

Social democracy, with its cradle-to-grave services based on an almost incredibly affluent oil-driven economy, is the target of several Norwegian filmmakers. Even the fate of a drug-addicted and paranoid circus elephant comes to symbolise the plight of man in a society full of restrictions, as seen in

Jens Lien's **The Bothersome Man**

Christopher Nielsen's rowdy animated feature **Free Jimmy** (*Slipp Jimmy fri*). Nielsen's film was in production for years, which resulted in the largest budget ever approved for a Norwegian film. The result was strikingly original, though perhaps let down by the lack of appealing characters.

Cold Prey (*Fritt vilt*), made by debutant Roar Uthaug, is an impressive piece of genre filmmaking. Shot as an American slasher movie and set in a Norwegian landscape where a killer lurks in an abandoned mountain resort, the film's well-timed moments of horror reveal Uthaug to be a craftsman of the first order.

Roar Uthaug's **Cold Prey**

Erik Richter Strand directed **Sons** (*Sønner*). A middle-aged man stalks young boys near a public swimming pool and one of the lifeguards who works there makes it his mission to stop him. Neither sensationalist nor provocative, Strand skilfully manages to face the subject head on. Utilising an impressive cast, he plays out the narrative like a piece of crime fiction, but set within an all-too-real context.

The aptly titled **Winterland** (*Vinterland*), directed by the talented Hisham Zaman, opened as nights were drawing in. At less than an hour long, the film succeeded in getting a theatrical release. It tells the story of a Kurdish man trying to build a new existence in Norway. Zaman portrays the northern Norwegian landscape as a challenge to humanity, but also a thing of wonder, something not to be feared. Raouf Saraj, a Kurdish asylum seeker, was

awarded the Amanda for best actor – while awaiting extradition.

A similar theme was picked up by the talented Marius Holst. **Mirush** (*Blodsbånd*) told the story of a 15-year-old boy from Kosovo (the impressive Nazif Muarremi) who comes to Oslo to find his father, whom he idolises and has missed. The father (played by the well-known Italian actor Enrico Lo Verso) has a restaurant, but becomes entangled with gangsters to whom he owes a considerable sum of money. Holst builds strong characters within the story, directing in a clear, simple style.

Ulrik Imtiaz Rolfsen's **Bitter Flowers** (*Varg Veum – Bitre blomster*) is an adaptation of a novel by Gunnar Staalesen. Staalesen, a writer in the Sjöwall & Walöö mould, with a Bergen-based shabby private eye as his hero, presents Norwegian society as drab and depressing, with characters whose lives are littered with desperate crimes and sad histories. Trond Espen Seim is credible as the hero, but the film runs out of steam before its climax.

Raouf Saraj and Shler Rahnoma in Hisham Zaman's **Winterland**

Gone With the Woman, 2007

Kampf um Norwegen, 1940

Reprise, 2006

The Bridal Party in Hardanger, 1926

The Danish Poet, 2006

Mars and Venus, 2007

Screening Norway Worldwide

*The Norwegian Film Institute supports and promotes
Nowegian films around the world*

NORWEGIAN FILM INSTITUTE www.nfi.no
FILMENS HUS | DRONNINGENS GATE 16 | BOKS 482 SENTRUM | N-0105 OSLO | TLF: +47 22 47 45 00 | nfi@nfi.no

Enrico Lo Verso and Nazif Muarremi in **Mirush**

Petter Næss impressed once again with **Gone With the Woman** (*Tatt av kvinnen*). Based on a popular novel by Erlend Loe, it is a mad satire on love, sex and marriage, told from a young husband's (Fausa Aurvaag again) point of view. The woman in the relationship (the excellent Mariann Saastad Otttesen) is as superficial as she is manipulative, and the man fights a constant battle with her self-serving rants and desperate search for profound experiences. Næss successfully keeps the satire fresh for most of the film. When he fails, Fausa Aurvaag's screen presence carries the film. Peter Stormare's supporting role as the hero's swimming-pool companion is enjoyable, but his funny mix of Swedish and Norwegian will of course be lost on non-Scandinavians.

Early 2008 sees an important reorganisation of the government's film institutions with a definitive separation of the archive from the institutions connected to the production and marketing of films. On 1 January 2008 the archivists of the Norwegian Film Institute moved to the National Library, the main Norwegian institution for the preservation of text in all forms. The rest of the Film Institute, along with Norwegian Film Development, joins the Norwegian Film Fund to create a cetralised and powerful institution for the development of projects, the funding of films and production companies, and the presentation of Norwegian films at international film festivals.

TROND OLAV SVENDSEN is a film critic and historian, and has published a Theatre and Film Encyclopedia.

The year's best films
The Bothersome Man (Jens Lien)
Gone with the Woman (Petter Næss)
Winterland (Hisham Zaman)
Mirush (Marius Holst)
Sons (Erik Richter Strand)

Quote of the year
'Somewhere we got a little lost in the Dogme style, an impoverished look that does not carry meaning. I have grown tired of camera shots that do not have any value of their own.'
Mirush *director,* MARIUS HOLST

Directory
All Tel/Fax numbers begin (+47)
Henie-Onstad Art Centre, Sonja Henie vei 31, 1311 Høvikodden. Tel: 6780 4880. post@hok.no
Norwegian Film Fund, PO Box 752 Sentrum, 0106 Oslo. Tel: 2247 8040. Fax: 2247 8041. www.filmfondet.no.
Norwegian Film Institute, PO Box 482 Sentrum, 0105 Oslo, Tel: 2247 4500. Fax: 2247 4599. post@nfi.no. www.nfi.no.
Norwegian Film Development, PO Box 904 Sentrum, 0104 Oslo. Tel: 2282 2400. Fax: 2282 2422. mail@nfu.no.
Norwegian Film and TV Producers Association, Dronningens gt. 16, 0152 Oslo. Tel: 2311 9311. Fax: 2311 9316. pf@produsentforeningen.no.
Norwegian Film Workers Association, Dronningens gt. 16, 0152 Oslo. Tel: 2247 4640. Fax: 2247 4689. post@filmforbundet.no.
Norwegian Media Authority, Nygata 4, 1607 Fredrikstad. Tel: 6930 1200. Fax: 6930 1201. post@medietilsynet.no.

Trond Fausa Aurvaag and Mariann Saastad Ottesen in **Gone With the Woman**

Pakistan Aijaz Gul

Annual feature-film production in Pakistan has continued to face the problem of pirate cable TV and an extensive video and DVD smuggling operation, a situation the government appears indifferent to. Film production, which peaked in 1977 with 111 features, has now been reduced to 48 in 2005 and 43 in 2006. Only 24 Urdu and Punjabi films had been released up to November 2007 (this excludes Pashto films, whose data is currently unavailable).

A film conference was held at Islamabad in February 2007, whose conclusions were presented by the conference delegates to the Prime Minister: that there be governmental funding of film production as well as the establishment of a film academy, film awards and film festivals; that cable piracy and illicitly distributing videos and DVDs be outlawed; that film equipment and raw film be exempt from import duty and taxes; and that there be a more substantial co-production with India.

Writer-director Syed Noor's **Moody** (*Majajan*) played, against all odds, for months at local cinemas throughout 2006. In it, a married man who becomes infatuated with a low-caste singer. Noor returned in 2007 with the Urdu drama **Décor** (*Johmar*) which deals with the controversial subject matter of a woman who is not accepted by her in-laws because she cannot conceive, but is later raped and becomes pregnant. Although it received positive reviews, it did not perform as well as *Moody* at the box office, despite strong support from female audiences. Both *Moody* and *Décor* are well-made films with powerful scripts. The latter also features an impressive performance by actor-producer, Saima.

The biggest success of 2007 was Shoab Mansoor's **In the Name of God** (*Khuda Key Leye*) which responded well to an impressive publicity and promotional campaign by the Jang Group. They also marketed director Shahzad Rafiq's Punjabi romance, **True Love** (*Mohabatan Sachian*), which opened to moderate box office. Mansoor's film revolves around two brothers, caught up in the events that followed 9/11. The message conveyed by this impressively shot and engaging film is that Islam is a tolerant religion.

Dancer-actress Nargis made her debut as producer with the smash hit **Wedding Dress** (*Soha Jora*). In it, she plays the leading role as a young woman entering into a marriage to an aged landlord of a village.

With the success of *In the Name of God* and *Moody*, there has been some cinema construction. A state-of-the-art cinema opened in Lahore, and in Rawalpindi a five-screen multiplex opened in October 2007. A chain of similar multiplexes is hoped for nationwide.

The Kara Film Festival, now in its seventh year, has gained enormous popularity. Intended to celebrate excellence in filmmaking, its success is attributed to the hard work and imagination of Festival Director, Hasan Zaidi.

AIJAZ GUL writes on films for Pakistani and foreign publications and reviews new releases for Pakistani television. He has published three books on films, including a book on actress-singer Noorjehan. He is a member of FIPRESCI and NETPAC (Network for the Promotion of Asian Cinema).

Peru Isaac Léon Frías

The last two years have seen a decrease in the number of productions in Peru. In 2006, seven films were released commercially, a bonanza compared to three in 2007, the lowest number for several of years. The lack of a financial and legal infrastructure, which has increased production in other countries in the region such as Colombia, as well as the marginality of the local market, are the main obstacles preventing the development of a national film industry.

Nevertheless, there are an increasing number of young filmmakers shooting short films on video, as their first step to feature filmmaking. The last competition organised by the National Council of Cinematography (CONACINE), which award grants for feature projects, received a considerable number of scripts. Although the sum of money awarded is small, it allows filmmakers to begin production. From there, they can progress to other funding bodies, such as the Hubert Bals Foundation.

Gianfranco Quattrini's **Fuck Your Mother** (*Chicha tu madre*) is a comedy about a man who divides his time between his wife and a woman who lives in a marginal district of the city of Lima. Coco Castillo's **Ballplayers** (*Peloteros*) follows the sexual adventures of a group of teenagers. Eduardo Schuldt's **Dragons: Fire Destiny** (*Dragones: destino de fuego*) is Peru's second animation film, combining the legend of dragons with condors that live in the Andes. **Black Butterfly** (*Mariposa Negra*) is Francisco Lombardi's most recent film. The most prolific Peruvian filmmaker, Lombardi's latest film tells of the revenge of a young girl whose fiancé, a judge, has been murdered by the people who worked for Peruvian president Alberto Fujimori's

Gianfranco Quattrini's **Fuck Your Mother**

government, at the end of the 1990s. Judith Vélez's **The Proof** (*La Prueba*) tells the story of a young woman's voyage from Lima to a remote town in the Andes, in search of her father and her own past. **Goodbye Pachacútek**, from director Federico Gabriel García, is a tragi-comedy about two orphans who survive in hostile circumstances.

The most outstanding release of the year was **Madeinusa** by Claudia Llosa. It takes place in an Andean community, where a local girl takes advantage of a boy from the city in order to run away from her own town. The film received

Claudia Llosa's **Madeinusa**

Claudia Llosa's **Madeinusa**

several mentions at Latin American and European film festivals.

The first film of 2007 was Jorge Carmona's **The Big Blood** (*La gran sangre*), an urban adventure featuring Carlos Alcántara, Pietro Sibile and Aldo Miyashiro as three local avengers who fight a band of drug dealers. Augusto Tamayo San Román's **A Shadow in Front** (*Una sombra al frente*) is the story of an engineer who, at the beginning of the last century, helped set up the country's communications infrastructure. It was inspired by a biographical novel written by the director's father, Augusto Tamayo Vargas. Finally, Augusto Cabada's **I Die for Muriel** (*Muero por Muriel*) is a noir-inspired thriller about a ruthless femme fatale.

Conditions look unlikely to improve within the Peruvian filmmaking community for some time. This means that, for the moment, Peru will lag behind the advances of Colombia, Venezuela and Chile.

Directory

All Tel/Fax numbers begin (+51)
Consejo Nacional de Cinematografia (CONACINE), Museo de la Nación, Avenida Javier Prado 2465, Lima. Tel/Fax: 225 6479.

ISAAC LÉON FRÍAS is a film critic and Professor of Language and Film History at the University of Lima. From 1965 to 1985 he was director of *Hablemos de Cine* magazine and from 1986 to 2001 ran Filmoteca de Lima.

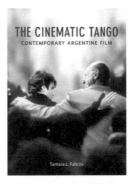

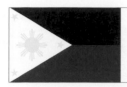

Philippines Tessa Jazmines

The Filipino movie industry experienced a boom in 2006 and 2007, if not in terms of box office success then certainly in the creativity and activity of an expanding cinematic environment.

The 'indie' wave reached a crescendo in 2007. Digital cinema has opened up a whole new horizon for local filmmakers and the old complaint about Filipino producers only managing to release thirty to forty films a year is no longer valid. A new breed of directors – young, bold, raw talent – are enhancing the scene with fresh new perspectives. Established actors and actresses have also joined the fray, lending their support to more experimental and non-commercial vehicles.

Digital film festivals are thriving, offering many first-time directors opportunities hitherto unavailable to them. Even veteran film directors are joining the technological revolution.

Cinemas have acknowledged the trend and include experimental films in their programmes. One cineplex – Robinson's Galleria – dedicated one screen solely to 'indie' films. Called Indie

The cast of Pablo Biglang-awa and Veronica Velasco's **Mother Nanny**

Sine, it is managed by the Independent Filmmakers Cooperative of the Philippines (IFCP).

Notable films for 2006 were Star Cinema's **To Marry, to Join, to Share** (*Kasal, Kasali, Kasalo*), the biggest success of the year. A charming tale of young romantic love suddenly facing the reality of marriage, in-law problems and occasional bouts of jealousy, the film touched a nerve with audiences.

Regal Film's **Blue Moon** (*Nasaan ka nang kailangan kita*) was directed by Joel Lamangan. A story of undying love, set against World War II and rekindled in the present, it won numerous accolades at the Film Academy of the Philippines, Golden Screen and Metro Manila Film Festival Awards.

Pablo Biglang-awa and Veronica Velasco's **Mother Nanny** (*Inang Yaya*), produced by Unitel Pictures, is a subtle but effective tearjerker. Pirouetting on the theme of motherhood and how a well-loved nanny tries to balance her time, love and loyalty between her real daughter and her young ward, it earned praise from critics and was avidly supported by civic groups that advocated for the fair treatment of domestic helpers.

Brilliante Mendoza's **Summer Heat** (*Kaleldo*) echoed Shakespeare's *King Lear* with its story of a father's despondency when his three daughters choose to pursue their own bold excursions into selfhood against his will. It received good reviews from critics at film festivals in Rome, Vienna, Hawaii and Cairo.

Blackout, another Unitel-supported film, directed by Ato Bautista, was invited to seven international film festivals before it

Robin Padilla in **Blackout**

was premiered domestically in mid-2007. A psychological thriller starring local action-hero Robin Padilla, Bautista's dark, fearsome film is a journey into the life of an alcoholic whose frequent blackouts from overdrinking and emotional stress cause him to teeter between reality and a nightmarish world.

Brillante Mendoza returned with three features: **Pantasya**, **Foster Child** and **Slingshot** (*Tirador*). The most impressive of these was *Foster Child*, produced by Seiko Films. The story of Thelma, a foster-parent-for-hire in the slums of Manila, the film was invited to screen at the Cannes, Montreal and Pusan film festivals.

Jeffrey Jeturian's **The Bet Collector** (*Kubrador*), which chronicles three days in the life of a *jueteng* (numbers game) collector, won numerous international prizes including the FIPRESCI Prize at the 2006 Moscow Film Festival and was accepted at 16 other international film festivals. It will open the 2008 Global Lens series in January at the Museum of Modern Art in New York City.

Lav Diaz's epic, nine-hour **Death in the Land of Encantos** (*Kagadanan sa banwaan ning mga Engkato*) is another international achiever. One of 13 films that competed for the Artistic Innovation Award at the Toronto Film Festival in September 2007, it received the Golden Lion Special Mention award in the 'Horizons' documentary section of the Venice Film Festival and was the closing night film in the sidebar section of the world's oldest film festival. This mixture of documentary and fiction tells the story of a fictional Filipino poet who returns to his hometown in the aftermath of a devastating typhoon.

Donsol, a digital film by Adolfo Alix Jr, is the love story of two lonely people, set against the backdrop of the whale season in the small coastal town of Donsol. It was the winner of various local and international awards (Cinemalaya, Cairo, Asian Marine Film Festival) and has been invited to the Fort Lauderdale and Dominican Republic film festivals. It is the Philippines' official entry to the Academy Awards in 2008.

Of the mainstream films, **Seance** (*Ouija*), by young director Topel Lee, was both a critical and commercial success. Lee quickly followed it with a family-oriented romantic comedy, **My Big Brother's Wedding** (*My Kuya's Wedding*), which grossed $82,000 when it opened in theatres nationwide in August.

The year's best films
Mother Nanny (Pablo Biglang-awa and Veronica Velasco)
Seance (Topel Lee)
The Bet Collector (Jeffrey Jeturian)
Blackout (Ato Bautista)
Foster Child (Brillante Mendoza)

Quote of the year
'That's the revolution that I want – a revolution of ideas. It feels great that a Filipino film is being noticed abroad because of its story and how well made it is.' *Filipino movie icon* ROBIN PADILLA *on* **Blackout** *and its scheduled showings in international film festivals*

Directory
Film Development Council, Unit 1001-02, 33 San Miguel Ave., Ortigas Center, Pasig City. Tel: (63 2) 633 2204. fdcp@filmdevcouncil.com.

TESSA JASMINES is Associate Professor of Journalism at the College of Mass Communication, University of the Philippines and a correspondent for *Variety* and *Asia Image*.

Poland Barbara Hollender

The last two years have been very important for Polish cinema. The Polish Film Institute has now been operating for some thirty months, while the impact of the 2005 Cinematography Act began to be felt in early 2006, when a new system for financing filmmaking was introduced.

Aside from state subsidies and revenue from the national lottery, the Institute receives 1.5% of its income from a variety of sources: cinema owners (ticket sales), VHS and DVD distributors (all sales), television broadcasters (advertising revenue, tele-shopping and sponsored programmes), digital platform operators (subscription fees) and cable TV operators (re-transmission revenue). Overall, the annual budget of the Polski Instytut Filmowy is some €25 million, of which approximately 70% is earmarked for filmmaking.

One can already feel the upswing in Polish film. In 2004, only twelve new Polish films were screened; in the last two years there have been 49 productions. Some succeed in making their way into the top ten grossing films of the year. The majority of the box office receipts for domestic releases are earned by comedies. 'Fem-prose' is a relatively new trend, based upon a series of popular novels, yet however much they appealed to audiences (attracting between 800,000 and 1.5 million viewers), Denis Delic's **I'll Show You!** (*Ja wam pokażę!*) or Ryszard Zatorski's **Never Ever!** (*Nigdy w życiu!*), as well as stories written for the screen, such as Zatorski's **Just Love Me** (*Tylko mnie kochaj*) and **Why not!** (*Dlaczego nie!*), were mercilessly savaged by critics.

Several important films were made over the past two years. The excellent **Saviour's**

Krzysztof Krauze and Joanna Kos-Krauze's **Saviour's Square**

Square (*Plac Zbawiciela*), by Krzysztof Krauze and Joanna Kos-Krauze, is a painful story about a tragedy in a 'normal' family, in which there is no alcohol abuse or physical violence but where pain is caused by the things people say. A gripping portrait of people too weak to face the changes affecting the country as well as their own unfulfilled ambitions.

Marek Koterski has always dealt with stories of the Polish 'intelligentsia', making deeply personal films that can be too hermetic for consumption and comprehension by foreign viewers, yet are deeply important for the Polish viewer. **We Are All Christs** (*Wszyscy jesteśmy Chrystusami*) is just as dramatic as his previous work, spinning a tale of an educated person suffering from alcoholism.

Another noteworthy title of 2006 was the promising debut of Sławomir Fabicki (previously an Academy Award nominee for the short, *A Man's Thing*). His film, **Retrieval** (*Z odzysku*), was awarded the ecumenical prize at Cannes. It is the tale of a boy from a small town who, in an attempt to make some money, goes to work for the local gangster. Fabicki articulately explores the difficult moral choices the boy faces and the importance

AWARD WINNING DIRECTOR
ANDRZEJ WAJDA

KATYŃ

POLAND'S OFFICIAL ENTRY FOR THE 80TH ANNUAL ACADEMY AWARDS
AND 65TH ANNUAL GOLDEN GLOBES

THE UNTOLD STORY OF THE CRIME STALIN COULD NOT HIDE

AKSON STUDIO, TELEWIZJA POLSKA S.A., TELEKOMUNIKACJA POLSKA S.A. PRESENT

AN ANDRZEJ WAJDA FILM KATYŃ CO-FOUNDED BY POLISH FILM INSTITUTE BASED ON ANDRZEJ MULARCZYK'S NOVEL "POST MORTEM"

SCREENPLAY ANDRZEJ WAJDA WŁADYSŁAW PASIKOWSKI PRZEMYSŁAW NOWAKOWSKI

CAST ANDRZEJ CHYRA MAJA OSTASZEWSKA ARTUR ŻMIJEWSKI DANUTA STENKA JAN ENGLERT MAGDALENA CIELECKA

SOUND JACEK HAMELA LESZEK FREUND MAREK WRONKO COSTUME DESIGNER MAGDALENA BIEDRZYCKA

ART DIRECTOR MAGDALENA DIPONT PSM RAFAŁ LISTOPAD PSM PRODUCTION MANAGER KAMIL PRZEŁĘCKI EXECUTIVE PRODUCER KATARZYNA FUKACZ-CEBULA

PRODUCER MICHAŁ KWIECIŃSKI COMPOSER KRZYSZTOF PENDERECKI DIRECTOR OF PHOTOGRAPHY PAWEŁ EDELMAN P.S.C. DIRECTOR ANDRZEJ WAJDA

World sales:
Telewizja Polska SA
17 Woronicza Street, 00-999 Warsaw, Poland,
tel. +48 22 547 6139, sales@tvp.pl,
festivals@tvp.pl,
www.international.tvp.pl

Sławomir Fabicki's **Retrieval**

of basic values. Another promising director is Xawery Żuławski, with his debut, **Chaos**, charting the attepts of three brothers to make their way in contemporary Polish society.

2007 brought the long-awaited **Katyń** by Andrzej Wajda, an important film, openly addressing, for the first time, the human-rights abuses committed by the Soviets during Stalin's reign. Following Hitler's pact with Stalin in 1939, over 20,000 Polish officers were rounded up. At first incarcerating them at camps in Kozielsk and Ostaszkov, the Soviets then murdered them and buried their bodies in mass graves in the Katyń forest. Wajda also repudiates the 'Big Lie' perpetuated by the communist regime until 1989: that the mass murder of POWs had been carried out by the Nazis. Artistically, the movie might lack the power of Wajda's best work, but it enjoyed large audiences in Poland, helped in no small part by trips to the cinema organised by schools and army units.

Maja Ostaszewska and Artur Zmijewski in **Katyn**

There remains a lack of films dealing with Poland's very recent history; the period of totalitarianism, or the need to reveal the contents of Secret Police archives. Yet there is no shortage of directors interested in looking at Poland. Łukasz Barczyk, Iwona Siekierzyńska, Marek Lechki, Jan Komasa, Maciej Migas and Anna Kazejak-Dawid have all made films about the lack of prospects for the new generations; about unemployment, over-populated estates, small towns from which it is impossible to escape and the possibilities of working abroad. This cinema has already earned the nickname – adapted from Russian cinematography – 'czarnuch' ('a darker shade of black', or very pessimistic and sad).

Evidently drawing inspiration from British social cinema and the Czech New Wave, the most interesting films of 2007 focused on provincial Poland, showing a country longing for authentic values, kindness and law and order. These movies have happy endings, though they are often bittersweet. The filmmakers focus on people, offering portraits full of drama and empathy.

Tomasz Wiszniewski's **All Will Be Well**

The main character in Tomasz Wiszniewski's **All Will Be Well** (*Wszystko będzie dobrze*), is a boy, Pawełek (Adam Werstak), who runs half-way across Poland to the pilgrims' site at Częstochowa to plead to God for his mother's health. God does not listen, but a man appears whose life is also in a precarious state. Pawełek and his retarded brother perceive this lonely, alcoholic PE teacher to be their salvation from a life in an orphanage. The man sobers up, admitting, 'This idea sucks. I suck too. So we go together nicely'.

Andrzej Jakimowski's **Tricks**

Another child, in Andrzej Jakimowski's **Tricks** (*Sztuczki*), tries various methods to attract his neglectful father's attention. Jakimowski's intimate drama was the winner of this year's Polish Film Festival in Gdynia.

In **Strawberry Wine** (*Wino truskawkowe*), an interesting adaptation of Andrzej Stasiuk's novel *Opowieści galicyjskie* ('Tales from Galicia') by Dariusz Jabłonski, a man running from his past takes refuge in a small village in the Beskidy Mountains. There he enters a world of barely concealed emotions. In Łukasz Palkowski's debut, **Preserve** (*Rezerwat*), a young photographer is transformed through his contact with the inhabitants of a traditional Warsaw neighbourhood. Once again, despite the urban setting, natural law, solidarity and an unwritten moral code are in force.

In **Time to Die** (*Pora umierać*), directed by Dorota Kędzierzawska, 93-year-old Danuta Szaflarska stars as an old woman whose only companion in her last years has been her dog. She decides to battle her neglectful son and selfish neighbours who underestimate the old lady's wily nature when they attempt to wrestle away control of the property she has lived in for most of her life. Wisely focusing on the remarkable Szaflarska, Kędzierzawska has created an emotionally rich feature anchored by a charming and award-deserving central performance.

A final film worth mentioning is **Louise's Garden** (*Ogród Luizy*) by Maciej Wojtyszko,

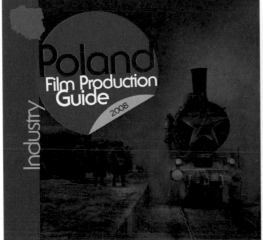
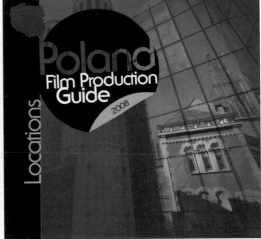

a fine counterweight to the many stupid romantic comedies out there.

Co-productions

Polish producers have been turning up en masse at major film festivals where they are keen to negotiate co-production deals. Assisted by the Polish Film Institute, a co-production is nowadays eligible for a grant of up to €2 million.

Poland is also popular as a location for international productions. Volker Schlöndorff made **Strike** (*Strajk*) in Gdańsk. David Lynch shot parts of **Inland Empire** in Lódz in co-operation with Marek Zydowicz from Camerimage Film Festival. Most of Peter Greenaway's **Nightwatching** was shot in Wróclaw (with more then €1 million Polish input). Ken Loach spent a few days filming for **It's a Free World...** in Katowice and Israeli director Uri Barbash shot some of **Spring 1941** in Poland.

A modern 'cinema city', which is to resemble the Czech Barrandov, is being built some 80km south of Warsaw. The plans are to build ten production halls, the largest of which is to be 7,000 square metres in size. It will also include a scenery construction shop, stables, a greenhouse, a centre for small animals, storage space for costumes, weapons, vehicles, props, and a series of casting studios. Two more centres are also being built: the World Art Centre in Lódz, co-founded by David Lynch, and Multimedia City, linked to the Higher Business School in Nowy Sącz.

BARBARA HOLLENDER is a Warsaw-based journalist and film critic for the daily *Rzeczpospolita*. She covers the Berlin, Cannes, Venice and Karlovy Vary film festivals, and has written, amongst other works, a study of Studio Tor (2000).

The year's best films
Saviour's Square (Krzysztof Krauze and Joanna Kos-Krauze)
Time to Die (Dorota Kędzierzawska)
Tricks (Andrzej Jakimowski)
Saviour's Square (Krzysztof Krauze and Joanna Kos-Krauze)
All Will be Well (Adam Werstak)
We Are All Christs (Marek Koterski)

Quote of the year
'I don't want to attract the viewer's attention by showing aggression and violence. I think that action is not the only force of cinema.'
ANDRZEJ JAKIMOWSKI, *director of* Tricks

Directory
All Tel/Fax numbers begin (+48)
Muzeum Kinematografi, Pl Zwyciestwa 1, 90 312 Lódz. Tel: (42) 674 0957. Fax: (42) 674 90006.
National Film Library, Ul Pulawska 61, 00 975 Warsaw. Tel: (22) 845 5074. filmoteka@filmoteka.pl. www.fn.org.pl
Association of Polish Filmmakers, Ul Pulawska 61, 02 595 Warsaw. Tel: (22) 845 5132. Fax: (22) 845 3908. biuro@sfp.org.pl. www.sfp.org.pl
Film Polski, Ul Mazowiecki 6/8, 00 048 Warsaw. Tel: (22) 826 0849. Fax: (22) 826 8455. info@filmpolski.com.pl. www.filmpolski.com.pl
Film Production Agency, Ul Pulawska 61, 02 595 Warsaw. Tel: (22) 845 5324. info@pakietyfilmowe.waw.pl. www.pakietyfilmowe.waw.pl
National Board of Radio and Television (KRRIT), Skwerks Wyszynskiego 9, 01 015 Warsaw. Tel: (22) 635 9925. Fax: (22) 838 3501. krrit@krrit.gov.pl. www.krrit.gov.pl
National Chamber of Audiovisual Producers, Ul Pulawska 61, 02 595 Warsaw. Tel: (22) 845 6570. Fax: (22) 845 5001. kipa@org.pl
Polish TV Film Agency (TVP), Ul JP Woronicza 17, 00 999 Warsaw. Tel: (22) 547 9167. Fax: (22) 547 4225. www.tvp.pl
WFDIF Film Studio, Ul Chelmska 21, 00 724 Warsaw. Tel: (22) 841 1210-19. Fax: (22) 841 5891. wfdif@wfdif.com.pl. www.wfdif.com.pl

Portugal Martin Dale

ortuguese cinema has carved an
important niche in the festival circuit
on the basis of its austere, auteur-led
films which generally possess a strong poetic
resonance, combining haunting imagery, non-
linear narratives, slow pacing and a brooding
sensibility.

Teresa Villaverde's **Trance**

Teresa Villaverde's hypnotic **Trance** (*Transe*),
selected for Cannes' 'Directors Fortnight',
lives up to its name, as it follows a Russian
girl's descent into the hell of white slavery.
Ana Moreira's anguished portrayal of Sonia is
disturbing, but unfathomable, as we follow her
harrowing journey from Russia to Portugal.

In **Colossal Youth** (*Juventude em Marcha*),
Pedro Costa returns to the real-life characters
Ventura and Vanda, previously portrayed in
Bones and *In Vanda's Room*. Costa spent 15
months making the film, sometimes reaching
Kubrickian heights of perfectionism, with
ninety takes per shot and up to one month
on a single scene. His focus on poverty,
bleakness and loneliness is riveting for some,
but numbing for others.

Sérgio Tréfaut's feature-length documentary
Lisboners (*Lisboetas*) reveals a fascinating,
personal insight into Lisbon's lifestyles,

working experiences, religion and identities, as
seen through the eyes of immigrants (Africans,
Brazilians, Russians, Ukrainians and Chinese).

The doyen of Portuguese auteurs, 99-year-old
Manoel de Oliveira, has been stepping up his
impressive output. **Belle Toujours**, starring
Michel Piccoli and Bulle Ogier (as Severine),
offers a sequel to Buñuel's classic, *Belle du
jour*. Although abstaining from the dark sado-
masochism of the original, the film offers a
beautifully shot view of Paris and a moving
exploration of the essence of growing old, a
theme powerfully explored in Oliveira's 2000
film, *I'm Going Home*.

In the 2007 Venice Film Festival, Oliveira
premiered his latest film, **Christopher
Columbus – the Enigma** (*Cristóvão Colombo:
O Enigma*) based on the theory that Columbus
was born in a small town in Portugal's
hinterland, called Cuba, in whose honour he
named the Caribbean island.

The biggest box office hit this season, with an
audience of 279,000, was José Sacramento's
irreverently titled **Filme da Treta** (literally,
'Bullshit Film') featuring a series of comic
sketches between Toni (António Feio) and Zezé

Bulle Ogier, Manoel de Oliveira and Michel Husson in **Belle Toujours**

(José Pedro Gomes). It is based on 'Conversa de Treta', one of Portugal's biggest theatre hits in the late 1990s, which also spawned a popular TV comedy series. It reflects a very different tradition to the seriousness of Portugal's auteur cinema, employing parody, swearing, bawdiness, nonsensical comedy, poking fun at religion and the glorification of down-to-earth Portuguese identity.

The second-biggest hit, with an audience of 30,000, was Portugal's 'first horror film', **Wicked Thing** (*Coisa Ruim*), by Tiago Guedes and Frederico Serra. It competed in Europe's leading fantasy film festivals, Sitges and Fantasporto. Strong on atmosphere, but with few chills, this 'haunted house' tale explores demonic possession and superstitious belief in a remote Portuguese village.

Miguel Borges in Tiago Guedes and Frederico Serra's **Wicked Thing**

A village in the Portuguese interior was also the setting for Luís Galvão Teles's tongue-in-cheek comedy **Dot.com**, wherein the villagers of the picturesque Aguas Altas defend their newly created local website against the fury of a Spanish multinational drinks company that has patented the name. The local priest goes so far as to claim that if Jesus were alive he'd have his own Internet site.

Jorge Queiroga's feelgood debut, **Behind the Clouds** (*Atrás das Nuvens*), also makes a trip to the countryside, where troubled six-year-old Paulo (Ruben Leonardo) goes to stay with his grandfather (played by Nicolas Breyner) and discovers that he has a magical 1960s Citroën

DS that can fly through the clouds and help heal family wounds.

A sleek BMW convertible is the car chosen by veteran director Fernando Lopes for his stylishly filmed road movie **98 Octanes** that exudes a definite 1950s flavour, including car sequences with back projection, sultry sex and plenty of whiskey and tobacco smoke. Sadly, the film suffers from its monotonous dialogue.

Jorge Paixão da Costa follows a very different road in his period piece, **Mystery of the Sintra Road** (*Mistério da Estrada de Sintra*). The narrative is not always convincing but the film has excellent production values, a powerful soundtrack and a magnetic performance by young Portuguese actor Ivo Canelas in the role of novelist Eça de Queiroz.

José Fonseca e Costa's **Viúva Riuca Solteira Não Fica**, is a comedy of manners set in the late nineteenth century. Ana Catarina (Bianca Byington) returns to Portugal from Brazil and works her way through four husbands, while remaining true to her peasant lover, Adriano (Ricardo Pereira).

Once the darling of Portuguese audiences, Joaquim Leitão launched a subtle trilogy of films on the colonial war in 1999. In 2006 he released the second in the series, **20,13 – Purgatory** (*20, 13 Purgatório*). Unfortunately, it only managed to attract a meagre audience of 10,600. The claustrophobic exploration of 48 hours in a border camp in Mozambique is atmospheric but lacks powerful characters or narrative elements to draw us into the story.

New Film Fund

The Portuguese Film Institute, recently renamed ICA, has been subject to considerable criticism in recent years, due to its poor track record in selecting films that strike a popular chord with audiences.

Since 2004, the country's four biggest box office hits – *Filme da Treta*, *The Crimes of*

Father Amaro, Rotten Luck and Bullets & Biscuits – have all been produced without direct support from the ICA, and were seen by over 800,000 people. In the same period, the majority of state-funded films have attracted an average audience of 3,000, with the total number for all forty films released reaching little over 400,000.

Private broadcaster SIC has a stronger track record, having backed virtually all of the country's recent box office successes, including Filme da Treta.

Since the late 1990s, ICA has promised the creation of a Film Fund to complement the Institute's activity, aimed at generating a stronger domestic film and TV industry. By late 2007, this commitment appeared likely to happen.

For the first time, the country's main telecommunications and pay TV operator, Portugal Telecom (PT), is to provide funding for the sector, to the tune of €25 million over five years. The shareholders of the new €83 million fund will be the State (40%), PT (30%) and the broadcasters SIC, TVI and RTP (30%). The Fund's Executive Director has yet to be named.

The core objective underlying this initiative – fostering a more structured support for films with box office appeal – has aroused considerable opposition. It led, in 2004, to the creation of a manifesto claiming that the new fund would 'entangle cultural funds in the mire of shady business dealings'. It was signed by leading auteurs such as Teresa Villaverde, Pedro Costa, Sérgio Tréfaut, João Mário Grilo, João Botelho and Fernando Lopes.

The structural impact of the new Film Fund will only be felt in a couple of years. In the meantime, forthcoming titles include João Canijo's revenge thriller, **Ill-Born** (Mal Nascida), João Botelho's football scandal film, **Corruption** (Corrupção) and the Paulo Branco-produced **Inner Life of Martin Frost**, by acclaimed novelist, Paul Auster.

Ventura in Pedro Costa's **Colossal Youth**

The year's best films
Belle Toujours (Manoel de Oliveira)
Trance (Teresa Vilaverde)
Colossal Youth (Pedro Costa)
Wicked Thing (Tiago Guedes and Frederico Serra)
Filme da Treta (José Sacramento)

Quote of the year
'We want to be known for our creativity and competance, for believing in projects and for managing to produce films without the need to wait for financial backing or complex schemes. We have the necessary resources to make all our "utopias" come true.'
ALEXANDRE VALENTE *of Utopia Films, producer of several of Portugal's recent biggest hits including* The Crime of Father Amaro *and* Corruption

Directory
All Tel/Fax numbers begin (+351)
Cinemateca Portuguesa, Rua Barata Salgueiro 63, 1269-059 Lisbon. Tel: (21) 359 6200. Fax: (21) 352 3180. www.cinemateca.pt.
Institute of Cinema, Audiovisual & Multimedia (ICAM), Rua de S Pedro de Alcântara 45, 1°, 1250 Lisbon. Tel: (21) 323 0800. Fax: (21) 343 1952. mail@icam.pt. www.icam.pt.

MARTIN DALE has lived in Lisbon since 1994 and works as an independent media consultant. He has written several books on the film industry, including The Movie Game (1997).

Romania Christina Corciovescu

For the last few years, the Romanian film industry has experienced a state of grace unprecedented in its long history. The reason lies in the appearance of several young, talented directors, including Cristian Mungiu, Cristi Puiu, Corneliu Porumboiu, Catalin Mitulescu and Radu Muntean. Constantin Popescu, Radu Jude, Adrian Sitaru, and Andrei Gruzsnicki are also making their mark, embarking on their feature debuts, after establishing themselves with short films.

Festivals award them, international critics applaud them, the Romanian public looks at them with curiosity, and Romanian critics are trying to hang a pithy epithet on them: 'the young film industry directors', 'the new wave', 'the new generation', or something a little more poetic – 'the expected generation'.

In 2006, there were three films about the Romanian 'revolution' that took place in December 1989. Corneliu Porumboiu, in his bitter comedy, **12:08 East of Bucharest** (*A fost sau n-a fost?*), looks back at it from the standpoint of a TV talk show, broadcast live by an insignificant provincial radio station, in which two alleged witnesses of the events of that time are participating. The film was awarded the Camera d'Or at Cannes and the Golden Swan at Copenhagen.

Corneliu Porumboiu's **12:08 East of Bucharest**

In **The Paper Will Be Blue** (*Hartia va fi albastra*), Radu Muntean reconstructs one of the many dramas that took place on the night of 22 December, when a group of young people were the victims of both general confusion and their revolutionary enthusiasm. Muntean received the Special Prize at Cottbus, the Jury Special Prize at Namur and the Golden Orange at Antalya.

Catalin Mitulescu's **The Way I Spent the End of the World**

Catalin Mitulescu's **The Way I Spent the End of the World** (*Cum mi-am petrecut sfarsitul lumii*) portrays the lead-up to the revolution from the standpoint of a child brought up in one of Bucharest's slums where dissidence, after years of paranoia and suspicion, is beginning to simmer. Doroteea Petre was the recipient of the Best Actress award in the 'Un Certain Regard' section at Cannes in 2006.

Then, in 2007, Romania was granted the much-coveted Palme d'Or at Cannes for Cristian Mungiu and his powerful abortion drama, **4 Months, 3 Weeks & 2 Days** (*4 luni, 3 saptamani si 2 zile*). The film takes place in a provincial town at the end of the 1980s, when Ceausescu's demographic policy made victims of women who had no access to contraception or the right to have an abortion.

Anamaria Marinca in the Palme d'Or winner, **4 Months, 3 Weeks & 2 Days**

Mungiu creates a sober and deep drama about friendship, sacrifice and fate's whimsical turns. The strongest character is, ironically, the one who suffers, while the apparently helpless character finds hope. The film's toughness comes as a surprise for a director whose previous work was lighter in tone.

The year's other Cannes success, **California Dreamin'** (*Nesfarsit*), was directed by Cristian Nemescu, who died in a car accident during post-production. The 'dream' is that of millions of Romanians who, for decades, were waiting for the Americans to rescue them from communism. The presence of a group of NATO soldiers, accompanying a train with military equipment on its way to Kosovo, is yet another disillusionment, and an opportunity to confront the social and human confusion that has taken root in Romania since 1989.

The spectacular revival of the Romanian film industry is primarily happening at a creative level. It is less prominent in production, and is almost entirely absent amongst the general public. Funding remains a problem. The National Centre of Cinematography awards grants through competitions, which can cover from 50% to 80% of a film's estimated budget. However, not all winning projects manage to find the remaining budget to start filming. Others develop over a series of stages, with the finished film sometimes years away.

Audacious initiatives to encourage low-budget filmmaking, with financing exclusively obtained from private funds, nevertheless exist. *12:08 East of Bucharest* is a good example. As is Adrian Sitaru's debut, **Angling** (*Pescuit sportiv*). An interesting drama with three characters, boldly filmed from subjective points of view, it is reminiscent of Polanski's debut, *Knife in the Water*, in terms of style and atmosphere.

With a market share of under 5%, the Romanian public is still steering clear of local films when they go to the cinema, preferring American alternatives. A local film is unable to raise people's interest unless it has made a splash at international festivals; the national premiere of a local film can sometimes take place long after it has screened internationally.

The poor condition of the screening facilities, whose number decreases year by year, is yet another problem. Cristian Mungiu organised a 'cinema caravan' to tour *4 Months, 3 Weeks & 2 Days* throughout the country, to towns where there is no cinema and audiences jostled to watch the Cannes winner.

Film festivals, which increase in number from one season to the next, provide a further opportunity to watch Romanian films. Seven festivals already exist, allowing the exhibition of the – approximately – 14 features and dozen or so shorts that are produced annually. The Transylvania International Film Festival, which takes place every June in Cluj, remains the most serious and professional amongst them.

The year's best films
4 Months, 3 Weeks & 2 Days
(Cristian Mungiu)
12:08 East of Bucharest (Corneliu Porumboiu)
Angling (Adrian Sitaru)
The Paper Will Be Blue (Radu Muntean)
The Way I Spent the End of the World
(Catalin Mitulescu)

Directory
Romania Film, Str Henri Coanda 27, Bucharest. Tel: (40 1) 310 4499. coresfilm@hotmail.com.

CRISTINA CORCIOVESCU is a film critic and historian, and the author of several specialised dictionaries.

Russia Kirill Razlogov

Film production and distribution in Russia has increased significantly in the last seven years. In 2000 the box office for local films was $1.5 million; by 2006 it was $106 million. The total box office in the country grew from $34.5 million to $412 million during the same period. But this is not to say that the industry has cured itself of the problems of state support, as well as strife between film producers and distributors.

Nikolai Lebedev's **Volkodav**

With a 25% share of the Russian and CIS box office, the slew of local blockbusters remain highly competitive, even if Hollywood imports such as **Pirates of the Caribbean: At World's End** present strong competition. Recent domestic successes include the fantasy blockbuster **Volkodav** (*Volkodav iz roda serykh psov*) by Nikolai Lebedev and the comedies **Heat** (*Zhara*) by Rezo Gigineishvili and **Love-Carrot** (*Lubov-Morkov*) by Alexander Strizhenov, which were targeted at a younger demographic. Combined, these films earned over $45 million.

The number of multiplex cinemas grows steadily by 25% each year: 1,397 screens in 622 cinemas in mid-2007, against 1,115 and 562 the year before. The first digital cinemas opened at the end of 2006, with 19 fully operational at the end of 2007.

A new law concerning cinema is currently under discussion between the Federal Agency for Culture and Cinematography, the Ministry for Culture and Mass Media of the Russian Federation and the Culture Committee of the State Duma. There has been talk of the reorganisation of the state apparatus after the presidential election, with a separate body governing cinema (some kind of Goskino (the recently dismembered state committee for cinematography).

Kinotavr Festival between film and TV

In 2006 the National Russian Film Festival Kinotavr in Sochi opened with the biggest sensation of the year: Pavel Lungin's mystical drama **The Island** (*Ostrov*). Although it received a less-than-ecstatic fanfare at the opening, it has subsequently received numerous awards and attained recognition thanks to the second (state) TV channel.

The festival showed a preference for films clearly influenced by theatre. The main award

Dimirti Dyuzhev in Pavel Lungin's **The Island**

went to Kirill Serebrennikov for **Playing the Victim** (*Izobrazhaya Zhertvu*), a film version of his own stage interpretation of the Presnyakov brothers' shocking tragi-comedy. Another theatre director, Ivan Vyrypaev, presented his stylish love triangle, **Euphoria** (*Eyforiya*), which was subsequently screened at the Venice Film Festival. Kinotavr's film programme showed the variety of directions in which STS, the television company that organises it, is currently working. Alexander Rodnianskii, the director of STS and, as a film producer, the head of Kinotavr, envisions a film process that is built on the logic of Hollywood, with its large conglomerates trying to control every link in the chain of a film's existence – from cinemas to video and television to the Internet. Film is merely one of the component parts of what is a huge media culture.

Sergei Puskepalis in Aleksei Popogrebskii's **Simple Things**

The festival's programme, by contrast, did not adapt to any kind of global norm. Sitora Alieva, Kinotavr's Programme Director, selected films that belonged to different registers and trends, in order to show the film industry's full diversity. Thanks to the jury's verdict, which gave its full support to one film – Aleksei Popogrebskii's **Simple Things** (*Prostye veshchi*) – there was discussion over what Russian cinema should be: life-affirming and consoling, or stimulating and provocative. Unlike many directors and festival selection committees, the jury unequivocally opted for the feel-good factor.

Simple Things features an unambiguously happy ending: two pregnant women are about

Agniya Kuznetsova and Alexei Poluyan in Aleksei Balabanov's **Cargo 200**

to give birth for the benefit of humanity. None of the film's heroes die; the one that should have is simply forgotten by the end. In contrast to the superficiality of *Simple Things*, Aleksei Balabanov's **Cargo 200** (*Gruz 200*), set in 1984, is a story of rape and murder. Unsurprisingly for Balabanov, its picture of life in the Soviet Union during this period is both harsh and horrific.

Feminine touch

Between these two extremes, paradoxically, are films that reveal a feminine perception of conflict. The international jury at the Moscow Film Festival praised Vera Storozheva's traditional psychological drama, **Travelling with pets** (*Puteshestvie s domashnimi zhivotnymi*). Russian critics preferred Larisa Sadilova's **Nothing Personal** (*Nichego lichnogo*), in which love affairs and personal conflicts are given an Hitchcockian treatment.

Kseniya Kutepova in Vera Storozheva's **Travelling with Pets**

In Sochi, there were a number of amusing films representing different generations.

Though initially appearing marginal, they actually represented major cultural trends. Marina Razbezhkina's **The Hollow** (*Iar*) was an interpretation of Sergei Esenin's bucolic story, while Valeriia Gai-Germanika's **Infant's Birthday** (*Den' rozhdeniia Infanty*) featured a series of sado-masochistic games. Arguably the most important Russian actress working today, Viktoriia Tolstoganova, played the lead role in Tatiana Voronetskaia's utterly original **The Model** (*Naturshchitsa*). Voronetskaia attempted to reconstruct the primitive Georgian lives of the beginning of the twentieth century against the background of imaginary poetic conflicts. Although the film was impressively stylised, critics were scathing in their reviews, complaining that the film was too slow.

Aleksei Mizgirev's **Hard-Hearted** (*Kremen'*), which received a jury award, represented the

Galina Vishnevskaya in Aleksandr Sokurov's **Alexandra**

grim reality of a man who travels from the countryside to a seemingly depraved capital, where he struggles to survive. Aleksandr Mindadze's **Soar** (*Otryv*) demonstrated that even a good script needs a director and editor. Had the film's plot been clearer, the film would not only have been more accessible, but also more successful. Interestingly, it became a talking point at the Venice Film Festival Critics' Week for exactly this reason.

These films will eventually find their audience, either via DVD or television, but numbers will always be small as the subject matter is likely to have limited appeal. Even *Hard-Hearted* has little chance of any great success at the box office. Iaroslav Chevazhevskii's sentimental children's melodrama **Kuka** may stand more of a chance, particularly with TV commissioners, because it is more accessible than *Hard-Hearted* and *Cargo 200*.

Films not in competition varied, nowhere more so than with the new works by Andrei Konchalovskii and Aleksandr Sokurov. Konchalovskii's **Gloss** (*Glianets*), a caustic satire about the fashion industry, shows the director revelling in the business of selling beauty, while simultaneously highlighting the ugliness of the people involved. The film featured excellent performances by Aleksei Serebriakov, Iuliia Vysotskaia and Efim Shifrin. Sokurov's **Alexandra** could not have been more different. Galina Vishnevskaia plays the titular old woman who moves with difficulty, carrying the whole weight of her life. Imbued with the philosophical asides one has come to expect of the director, *Alexandra* is stately, measured and intimate.

Khuat Akhmetov's debut **Wind Man** (*Chelovek-Veter*) is a relatively low-budget comedy-drama set in Central Asia and inspired by Gabriel García Marquez. The film was screened at Sochi, then in the 'Window to Europe' section at the national film festival in Vyborg, where it received two awards. It also screened at the World Film Festival in Montreal and the Telluride Film Festival in Colorado.

Other highlights from Vyborg included **The Players** (*Igroki*) by Pavel Chukhrai (a new version of Nikolai Gogol's classic play), Stanislav Govorukhin's joyous comedy, **The Actress** (*Artistka*), and Aleksei Fedorchenko's deceiving parable (following the success of *First on the Moon* in 2005), **The Railway** (*Zheleznaya doroga*). Sergei Bodrov opened the 'Window to Europe' section with his transnational production (with funds from Russia, Mongolia, Kazakhstan and Germany), **Mongol**, a spectacular account of Ghengis Khan's formative years.

Nikita Mikhalkov's **12**

Cannes and Venice hosted two long-awaited features by world-famous directors. Andrei Zvyagintsev followed his Venice Golden Lion-winner, *The Return*, with **The Banishment** (*Izgnanie*), a dark Bergmanesque story of deception and lies featuring Scandinavian actress Maria Bonnevie and Konstantin Lavronenko. Nikita Mikhalkov returned after almost a decade and received a Special Lion at Venice for **12**, a brilliant remake of Sidney Lumet's classic *Twelve Angry Men*, set in Chechnia. He is currently working on **Burnt by the Sun 2** (*Utomlennye Solntsem 2*).

KIRILL RAZLOGOV is Director of the Russian Institute for Cultural Research and former Programme Director of the Moscow International Film Festival. He has written 14 books on cinema and culture and hosts Kultura's weekly TV show, *Movie Cult*.

Konstantin Lavronenko and Maria Bonnevie in **The Banishment**

The year's best films
Cargo 200 (Aleksei Balabanov)
12 (Nikita Mikhalkov)
Alexandra (Alexandr Sokurov)
The Banishment (Andrei Zvyagintsev)
Wind Man (Khuat Akhmetov)

Quote of the year
'You came here looking for our money and don't pretend otherwise.' ALEXANDER RODNYANSKY, *President of the STS TV Company and head of Kinotavr Film Festival, at a meeting with European producers in Sochi*

Directory
All Tel/Fax numbers begin (+7)
Alliance of Independent Distribution Companies. Tel: 243 4741. Fax: 243 5582. felix_rosental@yahoo.com.
Federal Agency of Culture & Cinema of the Russian Federation, Film Service, 7 Maly Gnezdnikovsky Lane, Moscow 103877. Tel: 923 8677/229 7055. Fax: 299 9666.
Ministry of Culture & Mass Communication of the Russian Federation, 7 Kitaisky Proezd, Moscow. Tel: 975 2420. Fax: 975 2420/928 1791.
National Academy of Cinema Arts & Sciences, 13 Vassilyevskaya St, Moscow 123825. Tel: 200 4284. Fax: 251 5370. unikino@aha.ru.
Russian Guild of Film Directors, 13 Vassilyevskaya St, Moscow 123825. Tel: 251 5889. Fax: 254 2100. stalkerfest@mtu-net.ru.
Russian Guild of Producers, 1 Mosfilmovskaya St, Moscow 119858. Tel: 745 5635/ 143 9028. plechev@mtu-net/ru.
Union of Filmmakers of Russia, 13 Vassilyevskaya St, Moscow 123825. Tel: 250 4114. Fax: 250 5370. unikino@aha.ru.

Serbia & Montenegro Goran Gocić

In 2006, the teenage 'pink wave' comedy returned, with **We Are Not Angels 3: Rock and Roll Strike Back** (*Mi nismo andjeli 3: Rock & roll uzvraca udarac*), in which an ageing folk star and a young rock musician find themselves in each other's body. Directed by Petar Pasić, the film was financed by Serbian channel Pink, with series mastermind Srdjan Dragojević writing and producing.

Goran Paskaljević is also dragging his down-and-out-in-Serbia sentiment towards a trilogy with **The Optimists** (*Optimisti*), five unrelated episodes on the brutality and stupidity of his compatriots. It starred Lazar Ristovski (who also produced), yet tested the patience of domestic viewers. It was nevertheless appreciated at festivals abroad, receiving the Golden Spike in Valladolid. Zdravko Sotra's period comedy of manners, **Ivko's Fete** (*Ivkova slava*) was the box office hit of 2006.

Debuts

The most pleasant surprises of 2006 were the few newcomers. **The Devil's Warrior** (*Sejtanov ratnik*), directed by Stevan Filipović, was an accomplished teenage slasher movie with no stars. Exceeding 30,000 admissions, it secured a place in the top 20.

The Shutka Book of Records (*Sutka – grad sampiona*) was the crowning achievement of the lively documentary scene. It's director, Aleksander Manić, spent two years in Shutka, Macedonia, filming it. Shutka is not only the largest Gypsy settlement in the world but one built and governed by the Gypsies who like to compete in crazy feats, from finding the DJ with the strongest *duende* to the sexiest

Milos Timotijevic in **Seven and a Half**

resident. It was a festival hit wherever it screened.

Screenwriter Miroslav Momcilović (whose *When I Grow up I'll be a Kangaroo* was a major draw) directed **Seven and a Half** (*Sedam i po*). A fairly dark comedy that locates the seven deadly sins in Belgrade, it was the most insightful film of the season, lacking the misanthropy shared by its colleagues. In addition to this impressive directorial debut, Momcilović also found time to co-script *Ivko's Fete*.

An uncommonly productive season

An impressive proportion of the federal budget was allocated to Serbian cinema, as it is considered a mark of the country's prestige. The result was uncommon prolificacy: 16 features were released in 2007, the highest since the break-up of Yugoslavia. And after some decades spent in isolation, Serbian films were produced in a mix of genres and languages.

The period drama, **Belle Époque**, set between 1910 and 1914, was retrieved from Bosnia (where it was trapped during the wars), completed and finally premiered at the newly established Serbian National Film Festival in Novi Sad where it won the 2007 Grand Prix. It was a good season for the Bosnian Serb director, Nikola Stojanović, whose extensive study on Akira Kurosawa was published in late 2006.

Cast Out (*Odbacen*, but could have easily been called 'Serbian zombies') is yet another introspective drama on despair, written and directed by experienced filmmaker, Milos 'Misa' Radivojević. It starred his favourite actor and producer, Svetozar Cvetković, and was partly shot in Montenegro, which became an independent state in 2005, but has yet to produce any features.

Cast Out is unlikely to play well with audiences, following the fate of *The Optimist* or Emir Kusturica's latest, **The Vow** (*Zavet*), a story about a peasant love affair, and his first flop. It was premiered at Cannes in 2007 and shown at the Serbian Film Festival, after which the director decided to withdraw to Mecavnik, his 'Wild West' retreat in the Serbian countryside, which is the only place he only allows *The Vow* to be shown.

Aleksandra Jankovic in **Cast Out**

Gypsies ride again

Kusturica might have given up Gypsies, but others were happy to take his place. The regional co-production, **Gucha – Distant Trumpet** (*Guca!*), was the story of an unlikely love affair between a Serbian peasant girl and a dark-skinned Roma youth, set against the milieu of a traditional Serbian brass-band folk festival in Guca.

More interestingly, a variation on Shakespeare's monumental play, **Hamlet** (*Hamlet, ciganski princ*) by newcomer Aleksandar Rajković was set in a Gypsy garbage-recycling community. The producers eventually re-cut the final version of the film against Rajković's wishes.

Zelimir Zilnik followed the presentable and charismatic Gypsy, Kennedy Hasani, on his road to riches, as he desperately tries to emigrate from Serbia, in **Kennedy Gets Married** (*Kenedi se zeni*). This striking film, whose cast switches easily from German to Serbian and from Romany to Turkish, is probably the best from 2007, skilfully balancing hilarious comedy and bitter social drama.

Gasterbeiters and co-productions

Ethnic Hungarian Sabols Tolnai's **Sand Glass** (*Pescanik*), a Serbian-Hungarian-Slovenian co-production, was an arty dramatisation of the life and writings of famous Serbian author, Danilo Kis, shot in stylish black and white. Croatian filmmaker Rajko Grlić's **The Border Post** (*Karaula*), a tense drama set in army barracks before the Yugoslav break-up, was partially financed by Serbian state funds, featured a mixed cast, and played well in local cinemas.

In Ivan Živković's **Huddersfield**, a Serbian version of *The Big Chill*, three schoolmates in their twenties, one of whom is an emigrant in the UK, reunite for a night of honest discussion. An admirable adaptation of Ugljesa Sejtinac's play, it was warmly received at home and the Edinburgh and Chicago film festivals.

Emigrants are the subject of a family drama about Serbian guest workers in Sweden, **Made in YU**, written and directed by Miko Lazić. A Swedish feature from 2005, with a mixed crew and Serbian locations, it was released here in 2007. Vladan Nikolić's introspective film noir, **Love**, a US-Serbian co-production, won the Golden Reel for direction, in Tiburon, USA.

Worst box office in years

Back home, Srdan Golubović's **The Trap** (*Klopka*), a thriller in which a man becomes a contract killer in order to collect money for his child's operation, was partially financed by German and Hungarian money, and played well at home and on the festival circuit, winning the Grand Prix in Sofia. Srdjan Koljević's script is currently being discussed as a possible Hollywood remake. Golubović's peer, Dejan Zecević, also directed a thriller. The hero of his **The Fourth Man** (*Cetvrti covek*) is an army major in the intelligence branch, who has lost his memory, recalling the *Bourne* franchise.

Stefan Lazarevic in **Aggie and Emma**

Two films for children – a genre popular in communist times and neglected for two decades – **Agie and Emma** (*Agi i Ema*) by Milutin Petrović and **Paper Prince** (*Princ od papira*) by Marko Kostić – were also released in 2007. Like other genre films, they could be seen as a desperate attempt to attract audiences back to the cinema; admissions in 2006 were the lowest for a decade.

The low figures may also be due in part to the demise of the country's major cinema chain Beograd *film* and the steady rise of

ticket prices (from just over $1 in 2001 to $4 in Belgrade in 2006). The rise of home entertainment is also a contributing factor, accounting for more than half of the lost revenues.

The situation might improve, at least in Belgrade, with two multiplexes hosting 16 screens due to open by early 2008. With its 46 screens, the capital took over 55% of the market share in 2006. Most Serbian cities have no more than two screens and account for less than 2% of the total admissions.

The year's best films
The Trap (Srdan Golubović)
Belle Époque (Nikola Stojanović)
Seven and a Half (Miroslav Momcilović)
The Shutka Book of Records (Aleksander Manić)

Quote of the year
'People's Office of the President of Serbia will buy 40,000 tickets for the film *Huddersfield* and give them free of charge to pupils and students in sixty cinemas all over the country.'
News published in biggest Serbian daily Novosti

Directory
All Tel/Fax numbers begin (+381)
Association of Film Producers, Kneza Viseslava 88, 11000 Belgrade. Tel: 323 1943. Fax: 324 6413. info@afp.yu. www.afp.co.yu.
Yugoslav Film Archive, Knez Mihailova 19, 11000 Belgrade. Tel/Fax: 622 555. kinoteka@eunet.yu. www.kinoteka.org.yu.
Yugoslav Film Institute, Cika Ljubina 15/II, 11000 Belgrade. Tel: 625 131. Fax: 634 253. ifulm@eunet.yu.

GORAN GOCIĆ is a broadcast and print journalist whose works have been published by over thirty media outlets in eight languages. He has contributed to many on the mass media, edited several magazines, authored studies on Warhol, Kusturica and pornography and directed two feature-length documentaries.

Singapore Yvonne Ng

Singapore's feature-film production has been on the rise since the beginning of the new millennium – its average annual output of six features almost doubling by 2007. This increase has been aided by the government's resolve to make the country a communications and media hub, by creating incentives and subsidies to co-productions and HD projects, as well as wooing established studios and prestigious universities to come to Singapore.

Colin Goh and Woo Yen Yen's **Singapore Dreaming**

However, there was little improvement in the artistic quality of the films themselves. One of the better efforts was **Singapore Dreaming** (*Mei man ren sheng*), the second feature of husband-and-wife team Colin Goh and Woo Yen Yen. This low-budget independent production is a subtle, bittersweet exploration of the hopes and aspirations of a working-class family. Released in September 2006, it failed to attract a large audience – a reminder that subtlety is not what the average Singaporean viewer appreciates.

Indeed, the most profitable homegrown feature of 2006 was Jack Neo's comedy **I Not Stupid Too** (*Xiaohai bu ben 2*), a sequel to his 2002 hit, *I Not Stupid*, produced for $1 million by MediaCorp Raintree Pictures and Scorpio East Pictures. The film satirises the deficiencies of Singapore's education system and targets parents who view childrearing almost entirely in materialistic terms. Though overly didactic, the film reaped almost $3 million, becoming the second top-grossing domestic feature.

Though not a feature, a film that deserves mention is Eric Khoo's 39-minute **No Day Off**, part of **Talk to Her: Digital Shorts by Three Filmmakers**, commissioned by the Jeonju International Film Festival. Khoo deftly chronicles the fictitious but realistic account of an Indonesian maid's life over four years. Restrained and revealing, *No Day Off* highlights the problem of the exploitation and abuse of Singapore's foreign maids. It also confirms the observation that the best achievements in Singaporean cinema are its short films. Anthony Chen's other recent short, **Ah Ma**, based on his memories of his grandmother's death, received a Special Mention at the 2007 Cannes Film Festival.

Former television journalist Grace Phan made a noteworthy directorial debut with **A Hero's Journey**, an 81-minute documentary on East Timor. Beautifully shot and narrated by the country's charismatic first president, José Alexandre ('Xanana') Gusmão, the film won the Amnesty International award at the 2006 Jakarta International Film Festival. Another praiseworthy Singaporean documentary on East Timor, **Passabe** by Lynn Lee and James Leong, was banned by the Indonesian authorities.

The first domestic release of 2007 was an international co-production by MediaCorp Raintree Pictures, the MDA and China-based

Ming Productions. Directed by Max Makowski, **One Last Dance** is a gangster drama set in Singapore, starring Hong Kong's Francis Ng and Taiwanese actress Vivian Hsu. Sadly, too much attention was paid to the style of the film with little time spent giving it any depth. Raintree continued its global drive by breaking its traditional Chinese New Year collaboration with Jack Neo and partnering instead Hong Kong filmmaker Derek Yee to make the anti-drug thriller, **Protégé** (*Moon to*). The film ran head-to-head with Neo's **Just Follow Law**, (*Wo zai zheng fu bu men de ri zi*) a comedy that satirises office politics and bureaucratic red tape. Starring popular media personalities Fann Wong and Gurmit Singh in cross-dressing roles, Neo's film took in almost $2 million. Though *Protégé* did less well at home, with $1.2 million, its strong commercial appeal elsewhere will no doubt spell lucrative returns.

Raintree also scored a critical success with the first Australia-Singapore co-production, **Home Song Stories**, released in Singapore in September 2007. This semi-autobiographical tale about Chinese immigrants in Australia stars Joan Chen and Singaporean Qi Yuwu, and was written and directed by Tony Ayres. Late November saw another Raintree co-production, this time with New Zealand, on Peter Burger's supernatural **The Tattooist**.

As the island's *de facto* film studio, most of Raintree's international co-productions are commercial ventures that may contribute to developing a nascent film industry, but ultimately have little to do with the country's life and identity. This is left to small, independent productions such as Tan Pin Pin's **Invisible City**, a companion piece to her earlier *Singapore GaGa*. The sixty-minute DV documentary is a journey of discovery into Singapore's lost history, through interviews with people involved in preserving the country's recent past.

Another fine effort was Wee Li Lin's debut feature **Gone Shopping**, a well-acted, sensitive portrait of the empty lives of a

Wee Li Lin's **Gone Shopping**

handful of characters who pass their time in the city's shopping centres: a rich but lonely housewife, a young Tamil girl abandoned in a 24-hour mall and a bored young man who falls for a Cosplay-obsessed girl.

The most popular domestic film of 2007 was **881**, a musical by Royston Tan. It was produced by Eric Khoo's Zhao Wei Films in association with Raintree and the MDA. A departure from his usual art-house fare, Tan's musical revolves around the world of *getai*, a boisterous form of entertainment that takes place during the Chinese 'Month of the Hungry Ghosts'. The story centres on how two young women rise to *getai* stardom. *881* floods the screen with campy fun, with a dazzling display of song, dance and extravagant costumes, before descending into mawkish sentimentality. Made for $700,000, it was one of a handful of Singapore films to cross the $2 million mark at the box office.

According to Man Shu Sum, the MDA director of broadcast and film development, and director of the Singapore Film Commission, Singapore is aiming for a sustainable annual production slate of 10–15 films within three to five years. If the film production growth in 2006–07 is anything to go by, and if the films increase their international appeal, this goal may well be within reach.

YVONNE NG is on the editorial board of *KINEMA*. She is co-author of *Latent Images: Film in Singapore* (2000) and *Latent Images: Film in Singapore CD-ROM* (2003).

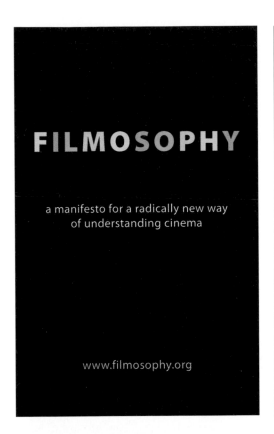

The year's best films
Invisible City (Tan Pin Pin)
Gone Shopping (Wee Li Lin)
881 (Royston Tan)
Singapore Dreaming (Colin Goh and
Woo Yen Yen)
No Day Off (Eric Khoo)

Quote of the year
'The current crop of directors is very well
educated film-wise. But being too educated
may prevent you from doing stuff that comes
from your heart.' *Local filmmaker,* SUN KOH

Directory
All Tel/Fax numbers begin (+65)
Cinematograph Film Exhibitors Association,
13th & 14th Storey, Shaw Centre, 1 Scotts Rd,
Singapore 228208. Tel: 6235 2077. Fax: 6235 2860.
Singapore Film Commission, 140 Hill St, Mita
Bldg #04-01, Singapore 179369. Tel: 6837 9943.
Fax: 6336 1170. www.sfc.org.sg.
Singapore Film Society, 5A Raffles Ave, #03-01
Marina Leisureplex, Singapore 039801. Fax: 6250
6167. ktan@sfs.org.sg. www.sfs.org.sg.

Slovakia Miro Ulman

Winter 2006 saw the inauguration of the Slovakian National Film Awards. Around the same time, it was announced that the country had seen the highest cinema attendance figures for eight years. Cultural event passes issued by the Slovak Ministry of Culture (one million passes worth $9 each were distributed to students and teachers in elementary and secondary schools, allowing them admission to cinemas, theatres, galleries, museums and libraries) contributed to the 55% increase. With an absence of passes and major blockbusters, the number of moviegoers dropped by 23% in the first half of 2007.

Marko Škop's **Other Worlds**

The Slovak cinematic landscape of the last two years has faced a paradox. The AudioVision grant programme of the Slovak Ministry of Culture distributed over $7 million in 2006, exceeding the previous year by nearly 70%. And yet not a single fiction feature was produced with major Slovak participation for the first time in the last sixty years. Marko Škop's double win (the Jury and Audience Awards) at the Karlovy Vary Film Festival for his documentary **Other Worlds** (*Iné svety*), about the impact of globalisation on individual lives in the Šariš region of eastern Slovakia, was both a celebration of his

achievement and recognition that it was the only a documentary in competition. Another Czech-Slovak co-production that garnered praise was Jiří Menzel's **I Served the King of England** (*Obsluhoval jsem anglického krále*), an adaptation of Bohumil Hrabal's novel, which won a FIPRESCI Award at the Berlin Film Festival in 2007. Hossein Martin Fazeli's short **T-shirt** (*Tričko*) walked away with over thirty awards from different international festivals, with its story of an American, travelling in Slovakia, who is offended by the design on the T-shirt worn by a man he encounters. Meanwhile, Doug Lefler's **The Last Legion** (*Posledná légia*), a big-budget project set during the fall of the Roman Empire, was the second large co-production shot in Slovakia.

2007 was marked by increased support from the state. Ten films were made, seven of which were produced with major Slovak participation – the highest number since the declaration of independent Slovakia in 1993. Four of the new films were by new directors. Patrik Lančarič's **Facing the Enemy** (*Rozhovor s nepriateľom*) is a World War II drama based on a story by Slovak author Leopold Lahola. Martin Repka's **Return of the Storks** (*Návrate bocianov*) tells

Tana Pauhofova in **Half-life**

an intimate story of a young German flight attendant visiting her grandmother in Slovakia. The film ponders issues of identity and the possibility of cross-cultural dialogue. After several years, Róbert Šveda finished what was originally his thesis, **Demons** (*Démoni*), consisting of three stories about three women looking for love during the Christmas holidays. Vlado Fischer's black comedy, **Half-life** (*Polčas rozpadu*), focuses on career-driven men in their forties who, trapped in the trivial flow of everyday life, perpetrate little frauds, lies and infidelities. *Half-life* was the first Slovak film in three years to be screened in competition at the Bratislava Film Festival.

Martin Šulík's Martin Slivka – The Man Who Planted Trees

Martin Šulík's documentary **Martin Slivka – The Man Who Planted Trees** (*Martin Slivka – muž, ktorý sadil stromy*) not only celebrates the work – as director, screenwriter, dramaturge, film scholar, professor and ethnographer – of one of the most significant figures of Slovak cinema and culture, but also attempts to explore his life. **Tepuy** (*Tepuy: Cesta do hlbín zeme*), a documentary about a Slovak expedition to the Chimanta table mountain in Venezuela, is the first 35mm film made by Pavol Barabáš, winner of a number of foreign awards and author of a wide range of mountain and adventure films as well as films about people living in extreme conditions.

The year saw the release of three low-budget co-productions. Jiří Vejdělek's **Roming** is a combination of a bitter comedy and a road movie about the life of the Roma minority in the modern world. Alice Nellis's third picture, **Little Girl Blue** (*Tajnosti*), is an intimate account of a woman in her early forties who has 24 hours to decide how to carry on with her life, while Dariusz Jabloński's **Strawberry Wine** (*Jahodové víno*) plays like a folk tale from a forgotten corner of Central Europe.

The approval of an amendment to the Audiovisual Act comes into effect on 1 January 2008. It is hoped that a new system will be introduced for grant applications to the Ministry of Culture's AudioVision programme.

Fourteen new films have been announced for release next year. They include Juraj Nvota's **Music** (*Muzika*), a sociological portrait of Slovak society during the so-called normalisation of the 1970s, focusing on the unfolding career of a band from a small village. 2008 should also see the much-awaited premiere of **Bathory**, which cost €10 million, making it the most expensive project in the history of Central European cinema. Director Juraj Jakubisko's aim is to restore the reputation of the 'bloody' countess Elisabeth Bathory, to be played by English actress, Anna Friel.

The year's best films
Other Worlds (Marko Škop)
Martin Slivka – The Man Who Planted Trees
(Martin Šulík)
Little Girl Blue (Alice Nellis)

Quote of the year
'Alcohol is strictly forbidden. They will have to hand in their civilian clothing and mobile phones when entering the programme. VÁCLAV MARHOUL, *producer and director of Tobruk, speaking before the actors started their training*

MIRO ULMAN is a freelance journalist. He works for the Slovak Film Institute and is a programmer for the Bratislava International Film Festival.

Slovenia Ziva Emersic

Slovenian film has witnessed crucial changes in the last two years. Firstly, the industry has faced a general decline in the domestic box office. Local audiences are less inclined to pay to see films that aren't crowd-pleasing, populist fare. Certainly, there is little demand for anything approaching film art. As a result, the situation is extremely tough for local filmmakers with any ambition. The share of domestic films is a grim 0.88%, with the majority of the box office dominated by Hollywood and a few European films.

The second change relates to substantial amendments to audiovisual legislation. The Slovenian Film Fund is the central body responsible for financing films. Earlier this year, the Ministry of Culture called into question the money used on making films. Due to this fruitless intervention, only two features went into production this year: Vinko Moederndorfer's **Landscape No.2** and **Personal Luggage** by Janez Lapajne, who last year won at the Slovenian National Film Festival in Portoroz for *Short Cuts*. All other films screened at the national film festival (seven features) were from previous years. New legislation, which will merge the Film Fund (financing) and Studio Viba (production) will be passed next spring. There are reservations about this move, mainly from the Association of Slovenian Filmmakers who fear they will lose their independence from the state.

Of the 18 films screened at the Portoroz Festival of Slovene Film, one of them, **Rooster's Breakfast**, by New York film school graduate Marko Nabersnik, smashed the box office record previously set by Branko Djurić's

Jam and Cheese. Adapted from the novel of popular writer Feri Lainscek, the story is set in Slovenia's northeast. Gajas and Djuro are two car mechanics who share their fantasies as they work. Gajas, played with some verve by Vlado Novak, dreams of Sevrina, the Croatian pop singer. Young Djuro's heart is closer to home with Bronja, the wife of the local bully and drug dealer, with whom he is having an affair. While the older man lives to see his dreams shatter, Djuro ends up with Bronja, who shares a rooster's breakfast – a local euphemism for sex in the morning – with him. Nabersnik's film attracted an audience of over 70,000 in the month it screened at cinemas in and around Ljubljana. Not to be outdone, Branko Djurić returned with **Tractor, Love & Rock'n'Roll**, also adapted from a novel by Feri Lainscek, about a Beatles-obsessed farmer in the early 1960s, who sets out to win the heart of a local beauty. Even Sevrina makes a brief, but welcome, appearance.

Silva Cusin received the best actress award at the Portoroz and Valencia film festivals for her portrayal of a famous violinist's widow who takes a talented young Bosnian boy under her wing in **Estrellita**. Directed by respected filmmaker Metod Pevec, the film attempts to show how music can help build bridges between cultures. A. W. Slak followed up his debut, *Blind Spot*, with the wonderful children's feature **Teah**, about a boy who enlists the help of some magical friends to save a local woods. Prague Film School (FAMU) graduate Janja Glogovać took some time to complete her debut, which offers an insight into her own student and artistic life.

Set in Prague, **L...Like Love** follows a group of people who arrive from different areas of

Miran Zupanič's **Children from Petricek Hill**

former Yugoslavia with the aim of becoming a part of the film industry. Embarking on their first film, the classmates gradually realise that the process of making a film is not as easy as they had imagined. When everything seems to be falling apart, romance enters. Love, or more specifically romance, is unlikely to be found in Maja Weiss's second feature **Installation of Love**, which deals with a fortysomething woman experiencing an identity crisis. Weiss expertly unveils the emptiness and desperation of modern urban life. Unfortunately she attempts to grapple with issues around modern art, through the artist the woman embarks on an affair with. An uneven pace and long-winded speeches are unlikely to attract audiences.

Finally, Miran Zupanič's **Children from Petricek Hill** avoided politics and ideology to explore the history of the one hundred children orphaned when their parents, returned from Austria by the British Army at the end of World War II, were massacred by partisan troops. Skilfully avoiding any judgement on actions committed in the past, Zupanič instead presents a moving portrait of these survivors, recording their feelings of loss, frustration and anger.

ZIVA EMERSIC is a journalist and film critic, former director of the Slovenian National Film Festival in Portoroz, currently head of documentary programming at TV Slovenija.

The year's best films
Rooster's Breakfast (Marko Nabersnik)
Children From Petricek Hill (Miran Zupanič)

Quote of the year
'We are at the starting point again, although it seemed we have reached the goal.' MARKO NABERSNIK, *the director of a record breaking movie* **Rooster's Breakfast** *at the opening of National Film Festival in Portoroz*

Directory
All Tel/Fax numbers begin (+386)
Association of Slovenian Film Makers, Miklošičeva 26, Ljubljana. e-mail. dsfu@guest.arnes.si.
Association of Slovenian Film Producers, Brodišče 23, Trzin, 1234 Mengeš. dunja.klemenc@guest.arnes.si
Slovenian Cinematheque, Miklošičeva 38, Ljubljana. Tel: 434 2520. silvan.furlan@kinoteka.si.
Slovenian Film Fund, Miklošičeva 38, 1000 Ljubljana. Tel: 431 3175. info@film-sklad.si.

South Africa Martin P. Botha

I n 2006, **Tsotsi** won the Academy Award for Best Foreign Language Film. Gavin Hood's acclaimed drama about a township gangster was the pinnacle of the South African New Wave that began in 2004 and to date has resulted in more than forty international awards for local features, documentaries and shorts. Sadly, the non-renewal of a special feature-film fund by the Department of Arts and Culture has stifled the movement and, as a result, feature-film production has significantly declined. The South African National Film and Video Foundation (NFVF), an essential institution within the country's film community, currently needs about $48 million per year in order to operate effectively. Unfortunately its annual allocation is a mere $3.5 million, with which it has to cover its administrative expenditure, as well as funding obligations.

As a result of this limited government funding, many filmmakers, both old and new, have to find private funding for their projects. **Faith's Corner**, the winner of Best South African Feature at the 2006 Apollo Film Festival, was made with no NFVF backing. The film tells the story of Faith, a homeless single mother of two young sons, who lives in an abandoned

Khalo Matabane's **Conversations on a Sunday Afternoon**

Mark Dornford-May's **Son of Man**

car in an alleyway in central Johannesburg and spends her days begging for money from disinterested commuters. Darrell Roodt's film is remarkable. Shot in the style of silent cinema, complete with inter-titles, Roodt attempts to grapple with poverty and unemployment in South Africa. The result is a vivid combination of social concern and formal experimentation. By adopting such an old style of filmmaking, the film implies that social conditions for the poor have changed little over the decades.

Several other award-winning features also received no NFVF funding: Khalo Matabane innovatively blends documentary and fiction in **Conversations on a Sunday Afternoon**, which deals with refugees and xenophobia. Gustav Kuhn's **Auntie's Clever Child** (*Ouma se Slim Kind*) examines relationships during the 1940s and how the dominant Afrikaner culture of the time destroyed any hope of racial tolerance. Winner of the Best Feature award at the 2007 Apollo Film Festival, Mark Dornford-May's **Son of Man** is a refreshing retelling of the Gospels within the setting of a South African township. Zulfah Otto-Sallies explores conflict in a Muslim family in the neo-realist **Don't Touch**. Veteran film director Regardt van den Bergh's **Faith Like Potatoes** focuses on the true story of Angus Buchan, a Zambian farmer of Scottish heritage, who left his farm in the midst of political unrest to seek a better life in South Africa. The film deals with issues such as cultural identity, racial reconciliation, faith and perseverance against the odds. Darrell Roodt's **Girl** (*Meisie*) takes place in a rural community, where a young girl is prevented from attending school by her father, who believes that she should spend her days tending goats. Shot in a neo-realist style, the film features wonderful natural performances by non-professional actors from the remote community of Riemvasmaak, on the edge of the Kalahari.

The funding crisis even affects South Africa's most acclaimed directors. Ross Devenish, who received international awards for *The Guest* and *Marigolds in August*, has struggled to find funding for new projects since his return to South Africa in 2002. His script for **Ways of Dying**, based on a novel by Zakes Mda, has been rejected twice by the NFVF. Devenish's

Aubrey Poo & Quinne Brown in **Auntie's Clever Child**

second project, **Nothing but the Truth**, based on actor John Kani's play, suffered from more complex problems. The film deals with the relationship between those black South Africans who stayed behind during the apartheid struggle and those who went into exile. Donor funding from the Ford Foundation, Kellogs and the C. S. Mott Foundation has been secured. The film was shot over four weeks in December 2006; after the shoot, the money paid by the US funders to the Film Resource Unit (FRU) for editing was not available because of problems with a short-term loan negotiated by the film's producer, Richard Green. Contentiously, the other half is still outstanding. Due to FRU's financial problems Devenish is unable to complete the film.

Co-productions, always a strong component of the film industry, continued. Recent films include Bille August's **Goodbye Bafana**, starring Joseph Fiennes and Diane Krüger. The film deals with the relationship between Nelson Mandela and his white prison guard on Robben Island. It received a lukewarm reception at the 2007 Berlin Film Festival. Phillip Noyce's **Catch a Fire** managed to avoid a didactic and issue-driven approach to South African history, instead concentrating on the human elements that drive the story about Patrick Chamusso (played by Derek Luke) who was apolitical until he was wrongfully jailed during the apartheid years.

The most outstanding productions of the past year have been a documentary and three short films. Francois Verster's **The Mothers' House** is profound and intimate, with moments that both overwhelm and shock. It is a record of four years in the life of Miché, a charming and precocious teenager growing up in post-apartheid South Africa. Living in a 'coloured' township outside Cape Town, she has to face not only life in a community beset by gangsterism and drug abuse but also what it means to break the cycle of violence imprisoning her female-only family. Miché's mother, Valencia, is an ex-Struggle activist, now unemployed, HIV positive and about to give birth to a third child. Dominated by unresolved conflict with her own mother, Amy, she projects her own frustrations onto her daughter. The film gives the viewer a powerful insight into three generations of women striving to free themselves of the ties that bind and to find peace and love amongst all the hurt and anger within their community and themselves.

The multi-award-winning **Bitter Water** was independently produced, written, directed and photographed by Garth Meyer, one of the most exciting young local filmmakers. Shot on a low budget, it is a powerful depiction of the effects of witchcraft on rural communities and why practices like mob justice still exist. Winner of the Best South African Short (Newcomer) award at the 2006 Apollo Film Festival, **Considerately Killing Me** is a tragic tale of love and loss. Willem Grobler's short takes an introspective look at the life of John, a young South African filmmaker who has to deal with concerns common to young adults: the unstable political climate of Southern Africa, not to mention the rest of the world. He struggles to break into the local film industry, but at the same time tries to escape from the harsh realities of this world by leading a hedonistic lifestyle.

Teboho Mahlatsi's **Meokgo and the Stickfighter** (*Sekalli Le Meokgo*) won both Best Short Film and Best South African Short Film awards at the 28th Durban International Film Festival. Visually ravishing, this innovative short tells the story of Kgotso, a reclusive, concertina-playing stickfighter, who encounters the spirit of a beguiling woman, Meokgo, and rescues her from an evil horseman.

Sadly, two giants of South African cinema passed away during 2007: Bill Flynn, one of our greatest actors, who appeared in landmark films such as **Saturday Night at the Palace** and **A Private Life**; and William Pretorius, probably our greatest film critic who died on 26 June 2007. Director Kenneth Kaplan said of

him: 'William was always a great supporter of local movies and filmmakers and seemed to have a word of inspiration and encouragement at the time it was most needed. He was more than a critic or reviewer. He was a true cineaste who took immense pleasure in seeing our own stories flicker across the big screen.'

The year's best films
The Mothers' House (Francois Verster)
Bitter Water [short] (Garth Meyer)
Faith's Corner (Darrell Roodt)
Meokgo and the Stickfighter [short] (Teboho Mahlatsi)
Considerately Killing Me [short] (Willem Grobler)

Quote of the year
'*Tsotsi* is the end of the wave. I think South African film is finished now. It will sleep for the next ten years.' *Director* DARRELL ROODT, *on the current state of South African cinema*

Directory
All Tel/Fax numbers begin (+27)
Cape Film Commission, 6th Floor, NBS Waldorf Bldg, 80 St George's Mall, Cape Town 8001. Tel: (21) 483 9070. Fax: (21) 483 9071. www.capefilmcommission.co.za.
Independent Producers Organisation, PO Box 2631, Saxonwold 2132. Tel: (11) 726 1189. Fax: (11) 482 4621. info@ipo.org.za. www.ipo.org.za.
National Film & Video Foundation, 87 Central St, Houghton, Private Bag x04, Northlands 2116. Tel: (11) 483 0880. Fax: (11) 483 0881. info@nfvf.co.za. www.nvfv.co.za.
South African Broadcasting Co (SABC), Private Bag 1, Auckland Park, Johannesburg 2006. Tel: (11) 714 9797. Fax: (11) 714 3106. www.sabc.co.za.

MARTIN P. BOTHA has published five books on South African cinema, including an anthology on post-apartheid cinema entitled *Marginal Lives and Painful Pasts: South African Cinema After Apartheid*. He is a professor of film studies in the Centre for Film and Media Studies at the University of Cape Town.

South Korea Nikki J. Y. Lee

I f annual statistics can be taken at face value, then 2006 was another record-breaking year for the thriving Korean film industry. A total of 108 domestic were released theatrically and Korean films dominated the domestic market with a 64% market share. The statistics for the first half of 2007 indicate that it also appears to be another outstanding year, with 72 Korean films released during the period and a market share of 80% during August. Yet despite such impressive figures, the local press and film industry still frequently talk about 'the crisis' and express concern about an uncertain future. Why?

Karm Woo-sung in Lee Jun-ik's **King and the Clown**

The list of top-ten box office hits for 2006 includes seven Korean features with Bong Jun-ho's **The Host** (*Goemul*), a genre-bending hybrid of monster movie and political satire, coming out on top with 13 million admissions nationwide. The year opened with the unexpected and sweeping success of Lee Jun-ik's **King and the Clown** (*Wang-ui Namja*) about the entangled relationships between a mad tyrant and two clowns, set in the Chosun period. It became the first Korean film to draw an audience of more than ten million, and then, with a total admission figure of twelve

million nationwide, the second biggest hit of the year.

Howovor, Hollywood dominated the Korean market during the first half of 2006, and no other domestic title could continue the success of *King and the Clown* until the summer release of two big domestic titles, *The Host* and **Hanbando**. *Hanbando*, another nationalist blockbuster by Kang Woo-suk (after 2004's *Silmido*), came in fifth at the domestic box office, with an audience of four million. Prior to these films, only a few releases were successful, albeit modestly. Released in February, Kim Dae-woo's **Forbidden Quest** (*Eumran Seosaeng*) demonstrated the ongoing popularity of films that re-draw the social customs of the Chosun period through exotic and erotic imagination, attracting an audience of 2.6 million. Two months later, Son Jae-gon's **My Scary Girl** (*Dalkom Salbeolhan Yeonin*), a low-budget comedy about a man who falls in love for the first time only to find out that the woman in question is a serial killer, won both critical and commercial success and was ranked tenth among domestic films, with a total of 2.3 million admissions.

The Host's remarkable success signalled an upturn for Korean movies, which continued through the major holiday in autumn. The golden season brought success for Choi Dong-hun's **War of Flower** (*Tazza*), an interesting and cleverly plotted film based upon a Korean manga, which came in third overall at the box office with 6.8 million admissions. Continuing the formula of popular comic gangster films, Jeong Yong-gi's **Marrying the Mafia 3** (*Gamun-ui Buhwal – Gamun-ui Yeonggwang 3*) was a commercial success drawing 3.5 million viewers and ranking eighth among domestic films. Song Hae-sung's **Maundy Thursday** (*Urideul-ui Haengbokhan Sigan*) is a sad story of two lost souls, one of whom is a prisoner awaiting execution. It demonstrated that the gangster comedy was not the only genre capable of performing well, attracting an audience of over three million. After opening in mid-December 2006, Kim Yong-hwa's **200 Pounds Beauty** (*Minyeoneun Georowo*), a touching comedy adapted from a Japanese manga about a young female singer's dramatic transformation into a stunning beauty through plastic surgery, continued to prove popular throughout 2007, with admission figures of 3.6 million.

Kim Ji-hoon's **May 18**

In contrast to 2006, the list of the overall top-ten box office hits for the first half of 2007 was heavily overshadowed by Hollywood releases, with only three Korean films featured. Hollywood's domination was most apparent in the months leading up to the release in July of Kim Ji-hoon's **May 18** (*Hwaryeohan Hyuga*), an epic film concerning the 1980 Gwangju Massacre, and the August release of **D-War** (*Di-Wol*), another big monster film, but this time set in southern California. Before these large-scale films recaptured the domestic audience, the market share for Korean movies had dropped to just 19.4%.

Of course, the South Korean government's decision in July 2006 to cut by half (from 146 to 73) the number of days allocated for the screening of domestic films had some effect. However, overheated competition among domestic production companies resulted in

Shim Hyung-rae's **D-War**

the release of too many similar films, which the distribution and exhibition sectors were unable to cope with. Indeed, only 20% of the 108 films produced in 2006 turned a profit. No wonder marketing costs have gone through the roof. In the face of a superfluous film supply, the competition to secure enough screens for a wide release has become fiercer than ever. The Korean film industry's Achilles Heel – that it has to recoup more than 80% of its revenue from domestic theatrical exhibition – is again under attack at the very time when international exports decreased by 68% in 2006 and the illegal Internet downloading of movies is ruining opportunities for profits in ancillary markets. It is to be hoped that investment from big communications conglomerates, such as KT and SKT, as well as various ongoing efforts to break into the North American and Chinese markets, may resolve some of the problems, but the uncertainty remains.

Following the summer 2006 example of *The Host*, monster film *D-War* took first place at the box office upon its release. While *The Host* depicts a medium-sized monster playing around in Seoul's Han River, *D-War* brings a legendary Korean monster, Imugi, to Los Angeles. As director Shim Hyung-rae, an ex-comedian and director of a previous monster film (*Yonggari* – a Korean version of *Godzilla*) emphasises, the film's main attractions are its enhanced levels of CGI technology and its size; at a reputed cost of over $30 million, it is the most expensive movie in Korean film history. If some were sceptical about the victory of Imugi, the success of *May 18* had been predicted far in advance. Following the formula of other recent 'Korean blockbusters', such as *Brotherhood*, *May 18* deploys a simple but touching narrative, this time recalling the tragic memories associated with the civilians killed by Special Army troops while demonstrating in Gwangju in May 1980.

Based on a kidnapping that occurred in 1991, Park Jin-pyo's **Voice of a Murderer** (*Geunom Moksori*) also illustrates contemporary South Korean cinema's interest in historical events. On the other hand, the thriller **Paradise Murdered** (*Geungrakdo Salinsageon*), directed by Kim Han-min, is not so much based on as inspired by a real-life incident from 1986 when the entire population of a small island vanished without a trace. The film, which sets its serial murder case on a remote island where only 17 residents live, has the whole population driven to madness through fear.

Amongst the overpopulated comedy genre, a few coming-of-age films stood out. Kim Hyun-su and Kim Sang-chan's **Highway Star** (*Bongmyeon Dalho*) concerns a young rocker who turns into a star of *trot* (a long-standing genre of Korean popular music developed from Japanese *enka*), while Lee Hae-jun and Lee Hae-yeong's **Like a Virgin** (*Cheonha Jangsa Madonna*) is a warm-hearted tale of a young boy who idolises the singer Madonna and wants to live his life as a woman.

Ryu Deok-hwan in Lee Hae-jun and Lee Hae-yeong's **Like a Virgin**

Horror remains one of the most prolific and popular genres of the summer season. **Black

House** (*Geomeun Jip*), directed by Shin Tae-ra, an adaptation of a Japanese novel, drew the interest of horror fans for its story of an insurance company employee trapped by a psychopath. Set in a hospital in 1942 in Gyeongseong (the name of Seoul during the Japanese colonial period), Jeong Sik and Jeong Beom-sik's **Epitaph** (*Gidam*) is distinguished by a melancholic, unsettling atmosphere and the subtle weaving of three stories.

Jeong Sik and Jeong Beom-sik's **Epitaph**

2007 also saw the release of a number of strong family films. Lee Hwan-kyung's **Lump of Sugar** (*Gakseoltang*) and Park Eun-hyung and Oh Dal-gyun's **Hearty Paws** (*Maeum-i*) both deal with love between lonely children and their animal friends. **Herb** (*Heobeu*), directed by Huh In-moo, is a coming-of-age story featuring a mentally handicapped teenager, while Kim Hee-jung's **The Wonder Years** (*Yeol se sal su-a*) and Jang Jin's **My Son** (*A-deul*) both address how children and parents come to terms with one another. Documentaries such as **Our School** (*Uri Hakgyo*) from Kim Myeong-jun and **No Regrets** (*Huhoehaji Ana*) by Leesong Hee-il deal with socially marginal (and taboo) subjects – Korean students at the Chosun school in Hokkaido, Japan, and gay relationships – managing to achieve a degree of success.

Lee Chang-dong's **Secret Sunshine** (*Milyang*) attracted a great deal of attention after Jeon Do-yeon, won the Best Actress award at the Cannes Film Festival for her portrayal of a desperate woman who loses her husband and son, finds solace in religious faith, and then

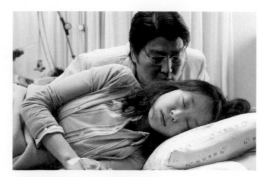

Song Kang-ho and Jeon Do-yeon in **Secret Sunshine**

descends into madness after believing God has deserted her.

2007 ended almost exclusively with comedies and melodramas. **The Mafia, the Salesman** (*Sangsabu Ilche*), directed by Shim Seung-bo, is another sequel to a well-established gangster comedy series while the romantic comedy **Two Faces of My Girlfriend** (*Du Eolgul-ui Yeochin*) from lee Seok-hoon is a variation of *My Sassy Girl*. Conversely, **A Love** (*Sarang*) is a large-scale action-melodrama by Gwak Gyeong-taek, and Hur Jin-ho's **Happiness** (*Haengbok*), a sad love story about a hard-drinking Seoul nightclub owner who enters a sanatorium and meets a women suffering from lung disease.

In 2008, Jung Ji-woo's **Modern Boy** (*Modeon Boi*) will explore Seoul under Japanese colonial rule in the 1930s and 1940s. Meanwhile, the popular trend of adapting manga for the big screen will continue to thrive: Jeon Yun-su's **Le Grand Chef** (*Sikgaek*) focuses on chefs competing for the title of Best Cook, and **26 Years** (*Isipyuk-nyeon*) by Lee Hae-yeong concerns a plot to assassinate the military dictator behind the Gwangju Massacre.

NIKKI J.Y. LEE is a film researcher based in Seoul and London. She contributed to *Cine21*, a weekly Korean film magazine, from 2001 to 2005 and has written articles on Korean directors Park Chan-wook and Im Kwon-taek. She currently teaches at Korean National University of Arts in Seoul.

The year's best films
No Regrets (Leesong Hee-il)
Like a Virgin (Lee Hae-jun and Lee Hae-yeong)
Highway Star (Kim Sang-chan and Kim Hyeon-su)
Epitaph (Jeong Sik and Jeong Beom-sik)
Our School (Kim Myeong-jun)

Quote of the year
'*D-War* is not a movie but rather like a fake American toaster that was made in the Korean black market back in the 1970s.' *Director* **LEESONG HEE-IL** *commenting upon the fervent support of fans upon the release of* **D-War**

Directory
All Tel/Fax numbers begin (+82)
Korean Film Archive, 700 Seocho-dong, Seocho-gu, Seoul 137-718. Tel: (2) 521 3147. Fax: (2) 582 6213. www.koreafilm.or.kr.
Korean Film Council (KOFIC), 206-46, Cheongnyangni-dong, Tongdaemun-gu, Seoul 130-010. Tel/Fax: (2) 958 7582. www.kofic.or.kr.

Spain Jonathan Holland

As far as foreign audiences are concerned, Spanish cinema in 2007 boils down to the two names on its Academy Award-winning A-team: Pedro Almodóvar, adored abroad but often merely admired at home, and Alejandro Amenábar, the country's top Hollywood director. Discounting Mexican Guillermo del Toro, whom sections of the industry gratefully consider an honorary Spaniard, given his cinematic concern with the Civil War, the A-men have won both critical and commercial success of which others can, and do, only dream of.

A cynic might suggest that the entire industry is being kept alive by these directors, along with a shifting, low-quality handful of others, with Spanish producers showing a startling lack of insight when predicting what will and will not guarantee domestic box office returns. The fact that the most successful Spanish-born director of the last twelve months, if only in commercial terms, has been Juan Carlos Fresnadillo, with **28 Weeks Later**, amounts to something of a warning.

The Spanish film industry seems to be permanently on the brink of a crisis that never quite seems to materialise – but the situation at the end of 2007 was, as many analysts agree, particularly worrying. Through the first part of the year, box office grosses were down 2.4% in 2006 and admissions down 6.7% to 45 million, contrasting unfavourably with other European territories such as the UK and Italy, where admissions rose. More troubling is the fact that during the same period the market share for Spanish films was down nearly 50% on 2006, from 15.5% to 7.9%. Of the top 25 films at the box office during the first part of the year, not one was Spanish; Spanish films' market share at home was not only lagging behind US product but the UK as well.

On-line file sharing has been a particular problem: in 2006, Spain's telecommunications giant Telefónica reported that 90% of usage on its broadband lines was for the Internet, of which a huge 71% was P2P traffic; an estimated 43% of Spaniards download films illegally. Despite 2006 legislation banning P2P file-sharing, the Spanish authorities are notoriously slow and inefficient at enforcing regulations. In September 2007, the country's second-largest exhibition chain folded, again citing piracy as the reason; in October, Sogecine, Spain's most successful film producer over the last decade, responsible for films such as Amenábar's *The Others*, announced that it was calling a halt to film production.

Agustin Díaz-Yanes's **Alatriste**

That there is a crisis is beyond dispute. But another issue – one over which the industry has more control – is that there is a widening gap between the interests of Spanish filmmakers – too often harking back to a more auteur-dominated era – and the young audiences on whom they depend. The 2006 figures relied heavily on three titles: Agustin Díaz-Yanes's seventeenth-century swashbuckler **Alatriste**, the most expensive Spanish-language film ever made; Almodóvar's **Volver**, which represented a return to his roots for the internationally acclaimed auteur; and del Toro's global box office hit **Pan's Labyrinth** (*El Laberinto del fauno*), which combined politics and fantasy in a way that seems destined to earn it the status of a classic.

Penélope Cruz stars in Pedro Almodóvar's **Volver**

But through July 2007, most of the films were clearly aimed at a wider audience. Inés Paris's English-language **Miguel and William**, about the invented friendship between Cervantes and Shakespeare, and Ray Loriga's **Teresa, the Body of Christ** (*Teresa, el cuerpo de Cristo*), dealing with the passions – religious

and otherwise – of Saint Teresa of Avila, fell far short of their studio's ambitions, leaving the way open, to the surprise of just about everyone, for the low-grade twentysomething comedy, *Love Expresso*, directed by Álvaro Díaz Lorenzo, to top the box office listings for live-action features.

Typically, the big industry debate through early 2007 did not deal with these key questions but with film financing as it related to the controversial new 'Cinema Law'. In its draft form, the law obliged Spanish broadcasters to assign 0.9% of annual revenue to the pre-purchase or co-production of films from independent producers. However, when the law was finally passed in June 2007, it failed to deal with this fundamental issue, though it does confirm that the tax breaks for investors will be maintained at 18% until 2011 – a no-change situation which is unlikely to improve the ever-strained relationships between investors and the industry.

So where is the hope? There is a growing international focus on Spain, as high-profile directors – among them Woody Allen, Milos Forman and Steven Soderbergh – have recently chosen to shoot there. As well as Fresnadillo, there is also much traffic in the other direction, with leading Spanish directors shooting abroad and carrying with them the sense that there is true cinematic talent in Spain, beyond the A-team. Among them are Isabel Coixet, making **Elegy**, with Ben Kingsley and Penélope Cruz, for Lakeshore, and Alex de la Iglesia, whose **The Oxford Murders** stars Elijah Wood and John Hurt and is based on the bestselling thriller.

There is still a place for the carefully crafted, personal projects that come as a pleasant surprise to the production companies when they perform well at the box office. But the kind of small-scale art-house film at which Spanish cinema has always excelled is becoming an increasingly hard sell. That said, two recent debuts buck this trend: Daniel Sánchez Arévalo's **DarkBlueAlmostBlack**

Carmelo Gómez in **The Night of the Sunflowers**

(*Azuloscurocasinegro*) and Jorge Sánchez-Cabezudo's beautifully plotted thriller, **The Night of the Sunflowers** (*La Noche de los girasoles*), both of which did decent box office at home and have sold healthily internationally. A cunning, idiosyncratic take on life in a working-class Madrid barrio, *DarkBlueAlmostBlack* marks out Sánchez Arévalo as perhaps the most interesting new director of recent years, while *The Night of the Sunflowers*, a narratively inventive, accomplished study of an accidental death in the Spanish badlands, topped any other Spanish thrillers produced in 2006 for quality. But, for their thrills, Spaniards still invariably turn to US product – *Sunflowers* was the only local thriller in the Top 25 Box Office.

Belén Rueda in **The Orphanage**

The best debut in 2007 was Juan Antonio Bayona's **The Orphanage** (*El Orfanato*), a stunning ghost story about a woman who sets up a home for disabled children, but whose own son then goes missing. Just as *The Sixth Sense* relied for much of its impact on the paternalistic relationship between Bruce

Willis and Haley Joel Osment, so the thrills of *The Orphanage* are carefully rooted in the psychology of mother/child relationships. One of the main accusations launched against contemporary Spanish cinema by its many critics is the lack of good scripts, or indeed of any script-dedicated culture at all. *The Orphanage*, Spain's nomination for the 2008 Academy Awards, shows that there are interesting scripts out there.

Juan José Ballesta in Jaime Marques' **Thieves**

Three other directors impressed with their new films: Mallorcan Rafael Cortés, whose daring **Yo**, about a German worker in Mallorca, was well received at a variety of festivals; Jaime Marques' **Thieves** (*Ladrones*), featuring Spanish cinema's most popular young film actor Juan José Ballesta, in a good-looking, lyrical homage to teen alienation; and Felix Viscarret's understated **Under the Stars** (*Bajo las estrellas*), about the troubled homecoming of a washed-up jazz musician, featuring a terrific central performance from Alberto San Juan. All combine an awareness of traditional filmmaking whilst attempting to deliver their stories in a new register.

Alberto San Juan & Julian Villagrán in **Under the Stars**

Funding can still be found for high-quality experimental cinema of the uncompromising variety. Two recent examples, both beautiful, stately studies of female isolation which have played well at festivals, are Jaime Rosales' **Solitude** (*La Soledad*) and Jose Maria de Orbe's **The Straight Line** (*La línea recta*). Add to those Jose Luis Guerin's stunning, radical **In Sylvia's City** (*En la ciudad de Sylvia*), an almost dialogue-free film about a young man hopelessly pursuing lost love through the Strasbourg streets, and you have the makings of a movement. At the bigger-budget end of the art-house market, Julio Médem's visually attractive **Chaotic Ana** (*Caótica Ana*), about a young woman who is found to be living the lives of other women who died in tragic circumstances, showed the country's best-known maverick auteur after Almodóvar remaining steadfast to his art-house principles, albeit with uneven results.

Sonia Almarcha in Jaime Rosales' **Solitude**

One new tendency sees directors mining the country's recent history for inspiration, generally with greater artistic distinction than those films set in more distant times (such as *Alatriste*, a box office success and critical failure, and the wasted opportunity that was Milos Forman's **Goya's Ghosts**, which, albeit chaotically, dealt with the life of the great painter). Standouts here include Manuel Huerga's urgent **Salvador Puig Antich**, starring Daniel Brühl as the eponymous Catalan anarchist executed by the Franco regime; Carlos Iglesias's dewy-eyed, winsome **One Franco, 14 Pesetas**, about Spanish emigration during the 1960s; and the punchy corruption thriller **GAL**, which showed Miguel Courtois maintaining the thriller credentials he successfully showed in *El Lobo*, in a film about the government's 'dirty war' against terrorism during the 1980s. The Spanish Civil War, a cinematic subject many Spaniards have tired of (*Pan's Labyrinth* notwithstanding), was the subject of Emilio Martínez-Lázaro's uneven **The Thirteen Roses** (*Las 13 Rosas*), about the execution of thirteen young girls shortly after the war had finished (although the film was a superb showcase for upcoming Spanish acting talent).

Contemporary Spain, meanwhile, seems to be a subject of scant interest to audiences. Of the top 25 features of 2006, the only edgy, supposedly streetwise item to deal decisively with the current state of the nation was **I am Juani** (*Yo soy la Juani*), made by the 60-year-old Bigas Luna. Troublingly, it is to documentaries such as **Septembers** (*Septiembres*), Carlos Bosch's affecting, searching study of love in prison, that Spaniards now have to turn to in order to find the most faithful reflections of who they currently are. But the figures would suggest, even though an increasing number of documentaries are receiving theatrical distribution, that Spain is not a country particularly interested in seeing itself on the big screen.

Other Spanish documentaries that have made their mark on the international festival circuit have included Fernando de France's lively, entertaining **If Only a Lament** (*Ar Meno un quejío*), about the trials and travels of an Andalucian 'flamenco-billy' group; Chema Rodríguez's **The Railroad All-Stars** (*Estrellas de La Línea*), which looks at a group of Guatemalan prostitutes who formed a soccer team to champion women's rights; and Ricardo Macían's **Ariana's Eyes**, about the attempts by some brave Afghan citizens to save their national film archive under the threat of the Taliban.

The biggest Spanish box office hit of 2007 was the Argentina-Spain co-produced animation, Juan Pablo Buscarini's **The Hairy Tooth Fairy** (*El Ratón Pérez*), which mixes live-action with 3D in a story about a mouse that leaves money under children's pillows. Spanish animation is experiencing a mini-boom: Filmax, responsible for the animated sections of *The Hairy Tooth Fairy*, will shortly deliver Jose Pozo's **Donkey Xote**, a children's take on Cervantes' classic, while Ilion Animation Studios will release **Planet One**, directed by Jorge Blanco, a comedy about a planet populated by little green people who live in fear of invasion. With a budget of around $54 million, it will be the most expensive Spanish film to date.

Women are as sadly underrepresented in Spanish cinema as they have always been. The 2007 San Sebastián Film Festival's attempt to rectify this by including the only two Spanish titles directed by women in its 'Official' section is unlikely to change things. They were Iciar Bollaín's **Mataharis**, a superbly acted drama dealing with a female-run detective agency, which played some interesting games against stereotype, and Gracia Querejeta's more traditional **Seven Billiards Tables** (*Siete mesas de billar francés*), a classically structured skeletons-in-the-closet drama featuring a stunning performance from perhaps the finest of the recent crop of Spanish character actors, Blanca Portillo.

The fact that a higher percentage of films made by women – as against those made by

Marta Etura and Quim Gutiérrez in **DarkBlueAlmostBlack**

men – are actually any good, should be another lesson to the industry. But as in so many other areas, it's a lesson to which Spain has yet to pay any attention.

The year's best films
DarkBlueAlmostBlack (Daniel Sánchez Arévalo)
Ficción (Cesc Gay)
The Night of the Sunflowers (Jorge Sánchez-Cabezudo)
Solitude (Jaime Rosales)
Volver (Pedro Almodóvar)

Quote of the year
'I'd like to work more in Spanish, but there aren't many interesting scripts in Spanish, so I've had to learn English.'*Actor,* JAVIER BARDEM

Directory
All Tel/Fax numbers begin (+34)
Escuela de Cinematografía y de la Audiovisual de la Comunidad de Madrdid (ECAM), Centra de Madrid a Boadilla, Km 2200, 28223 Madrid. Tel: (91) 411 0497. www.ecam.es.
Federation of Associations of Spanish Audiovisual Producers (FAPAE), Calle Luis Bunuel 2-2º Izquierda, Ciudad de la Imagen, Pozuelo de Alarcón, 28223 Madrid. Tel: (91) 512 1660. Fax: (91) 512 0148. web@fapae.es. www.fapae.es.
Federation of Cinema Distributors (FEDICINE), Orense 33, 3ºB, 28020 Madrid. Tel: (91) 556 9755. Fax: (91) 555 6697. www.fedicine.com.
Filmoteca de la Generalitat de Catalunya, Carrer del Portal de Santa Madrona 6-8, Barcelona 08001. Tel: (93) 316 2780. Fax: (93) 316 2783. filmoteca. cultura@gencat.net.
Filmoteca Espanola, Calle Magdalena 10, 28012 Madrid. Tel: (91) 467 2600. Fax: (91) 467 2611. www.cultura.mecd.es/cine/film/filmoteca.isp.
Filmoteca Vasca, Avenida Sancho el Sabio, 17 Trasera, Donostia, 20010 San Sebastián. Tel: (943) 468 484. Fax: (943) 469 998. andaluciafilmcom@fundacionava.org. www.filmotecavasca.com.

JONATHAN HOLLAND is *Variety*'s film reviewer in Spain.

Sweden Gunnar Rehlin

The death of Ingmar Bergman and the collapse of Triangelfilm and Astoria Cinemas were the biggest stories in Swedish cinema during 2007.

Both Bergman and Triangelfilm/Astoria were mourned by the media and Swedish populace. Bergman leaves a great legacy for generations to come. The collapse of Sweden's most prolific art-house distributor, however, sent shockwaves through the industry. The negative repercussions for smaller art-house films hoping to get Swedish distribution will be felt for a long time.

Astoria Cinemas was founded in 2005, when the cinemas owned by Sandrew Metronome were for sale. Fearing that Svensk, who already owned the majority of Swedish cinemas, was going to buy them, thus creating a monopoly, Triangelfilm and Atlantic Film, together with production company S/S Fladen, created a company of their own and bought the cinemas, renaming the chain Astoria.

The company had great plans to renovate the old cinemas and build new ones, but problems ensued and, in the summer of 2006, it emerged that Astoria was in financial trouble. Later, its owners claimed it was a result of major American studios withholding their summer blockbusters.

During the autumn and winter of 2006, the problems worsened. As it collapsed, Astoria dragged Triangelfilm, the most well-known and respected art-house distributor in Sweden, down with it. The company had introduced directors such as Ken Loach, Ang Lee, Hal Hartley, Emir Kusturica, Wong Kar-wai, Michael Haneke and Krzysztof Kieslowski to Swedish

audiences. In May, Triangelfilm filed for bankruptcy. Astoria followed suit in July. Some of the old Astoria cinemas are now owned by Svensk.

Film-wise, 2006 saw many – perhaps too many – films produced, with several failing to register with audiences. Lukas Moodysson's experimental **Container** was something of a shock, while the surprise festival hit was Jesper Ganslandt´s **Farewell Falkenberg** (*Farväl Falkenberg*), an ode to the town the director grew up in. The best film of the year was Johan Brisinger's **Suddenly** (*Underbara älskade*), a tragedy about a man trying to come to terms with his wife's death. The most popular Swedish film was Pelle Seth's **Gota Kanal 2** (*Göta kanal 2 – kanalkampen*), the sequel to an old comedy and evidence that it is not always quality that attracts the crowds.

Jesper Ganslandt's **Farewell Falkenberg**

At the Golden Bugs Awards in Stockholm in January 2007, Catti Edfeldt and Ylva Gustavsson's youth pic, **Kidz in Da Hood** (*Förortsungar*), a musical about young Swedes and immigrants, performed well, winning five awards. It went on to the Kinderfest at the Berlin Film Festival, where actor Gustaf Skarsgard was nominated as one of the Shooting Stars. Continuing in their father Stellan's footsteps, his two eldest sons are gradually making a name for themselves. Alexander Skarsgard spent much of 2007 playing the lead in the HBO series, *Generation Kill*.

The Gothenburg Film Festival in February saw the successful launch of the low-budget film **Darling**, directed by Johan Kling. Depicting the merciless world of cliques in Stockholm, it had been refused money from the Swedish Film Institute. The film was made through private investment and was rewarded with the festival's main prize; it was also popular at other international festivals. In a surprise move, the Film Institute consultant who had turned the film down issued a public apology.

Klaus Härö's **The New Man**

The Gothenburg festival showcased several of the year's best films. Finnish director Klaus Härö touched on a sensitive subject with **The New Man** (*Den Nya människan*), which dealt with the forced sterilisation of hundreds of young Swedish girls in the 1940s and 1950s. Popular actress Helena Bergström

made an assured debut as director with **Mind the Gap!** (*Se upp för dårarna*), an energetic comedy about two young women who meet at the Stockholm police school. And Danish director Hella Joof made her Swedish debut with **BitterSweetHeart** (*Linas kvällsbok*), a sensitive film about a young girl's first encounter with sex. The film made quite a stir with its frank sex scenes, as did Mani Maserrat Agah's **Ciao Bella**, another film about teenage sex, that was released in the summer.

At Cannes in 2007, Roy Andersson premiered **You the Living** (*Du levande*), the Swedish entry to the Academy Awards, and the sequel to his award-winning *Songs from the Second Floor*. It was greeted with positive reviews, although some people felt there was little progress from the previous film.

On 14 July 2007 Ingmar Bergman died, aged 89. People knew that he wasn't well, but his death still shocked Sweden and the world. Actors and directors, such as Ang Lee and Woody Allen, expressed their admiration for the legendary filmmaker. Swedish TV showed many of his features and documentaries and, in October, the Film Institute arranged a weekend, under the title 'Long Live Bergman!', which celebrated his legacy.

Autumn started well with the Swedish premiere of Andersson's *You the Living*, Åke Sandgren's hard-hitting domestic drama **To Love Someone** (*Den man älskar*), and an adaptation of Johan Hassen Khemiri's bestselling novel, **A Red Eye**, directed by Daniel Wallentin. Closer to Christmas came Josef Fares'

The 19th Stockholm International Film Festival November 20-30 2008

"Without question the most important film festival north of the 50th parallel – not to be missed."

"The most handsome film festival in the universe"

FILM Stockholm FESTIVAL

new film, the low-budget thriller **Leo**, and Leif Lindblom's **Sun Storm** (*Solstorm*), the first in a series of thrillers about a lawyer in the north of Sweden, starring one-time Bond girl Izabella Scorupco, who now lives in Los Angeles.

On Christmas Day, Peter Flinth's **Arn: The Knight Templar** (*Arn – Tempelriddaren*), the most expensive film ever made in Scandinavia, opened. Based on Jan Guillou´s bestsellers about a young Swedish knight during the Crusades, a further film and a television series are planned. There was a great deal of attention when co-financier Swedish Television pulled out of the project because they felt the rushes lacked quality. Commercial TV channel TV4 immediately stepped in. They plan to show the television series in 2008. The whole project has cost $30 million, a staggering sum for a Scandinavian film project. The second feature, **Arn** (*Arn – Riket vid vägens slut*), will open in Autumn 2008. Only then can the project be deemed a success or failure.

Joakim Nätterqvist in **Arn: The Knight Templar**

2008 looks set to be a good year for Swedish films, at least on paper. In March, Tomas Alfredson will premiere his vampire film **Let the Right One Come In** (*Låt den rätte komma in*), based on the critically acclaimed novel. The Cannes hopeful is Jan Troell's **Maria Larsson´s Everlasting Moment** (*Maria Larssons eviga ögonblick*), about one of Sweden´s first photographers. And in August, Lukas Moodysson will present **Mammoth**, his first film in English, starring Gael García Bernal as a man who makes life-changing decisions while on vacation in Thailand.

Roy Andersson's **You the Living**

The year's best films
You the Living (Roy Andersson)
Darling (Johan Kling)
To Love Someone (Åke Sandgren)
The New Man (Klaus Härö)
Mind the Gap! (Helena Bergström)

Quote of the year
'He always treated me as he treated his own children: with total negligence.' LARS VON TRIER *on the death of Ingmar Bergman*

Directory
All Tel/Fax numbers begin (+46)
Cinemateket, Swedish Film Institute, Box 27126, SE-102 52 Stockholm. Tel: (8) 665 1100. Fax: (8) 666 3698. info@sfi.se. www.sfi.se.
Swedish Film Distributors Association, Box 23021, SE-10435 Stockholm. Tel: (8) 441 5570. Fax: (8) 343 810.
Swedish Film Institute, Box 27126, SE-10252 Stockholm. Tel: (8) 665 1100. Fax: (8) 666 3698. info@sfi.se.
Swedish Film Producers Association, Box 27298, SE-102 53 Stockholm. Tel: (8) 665 1255. Fax: (8) 666 3748. info@frf.net.
Swedish National Archive for Recorded Sound & Moving Images, Box 24124, SE-10451 Stockholm. Tel: (8) 783 3700. Fax: (8) 663 1811. info@ljudochbildarkivet.se.

GUNNAR REHLIN is a Swedish film critic and journalist, working for different media in Sweden, Norway and Finland.

Switzerland Marcy Goldberg

2006 was quite a good year for Swiss cinema, both at home and abroad. The domestic market share for Swiss films, which had hovered around 2% for most of the past ten years, rose to 9.5%, second only to American films and ahead of releases from the UK, France and Germany. Internationally, the visibility of Swiss cinema was enhanced by increased sales and presence at significant festivals. For 2007 the domestic market share is expected to rank somewhat lower, although sales and festival presence continue to grow, and Switzerland's renewed participation in the MEDIA programme should bring more Swiss films to European screens.

The question remains, however, to what extent success at home can be linked with success outside the country. Needless to say, the local comedies favoured by Swiss audiences tend not to travel well, while art-house dramas may garner prizes around the world but fail to attract local moviegoers.

In 2006–07, for example, two films directed by Michael Steiner did very well within Switzerland, but disappointingly abroad. **Grounding: The Last Days of Swissair** (*Grounding – Die letzten Tage der Swissair*), a dramatisation of the events leading to the

Michael Steiner's **My Name is Eugen**

collapse of the airline once dubbed 'the flying bank', was successful in both the German- and French-speaking regions (an unusual feat for a film in Swiss-German dialect), but attracted little interest outside Switzerland. **My Name is Eugen** (*Mein Name ist Eugen*), an adaptation of the beloved Swiss children's book, became the third-highest-grossing film in Swiss history in 2007. The adventures of four boys from Berne, set in a nostalgic-looking but historically non-specific past, did reasonably well at international festivals for children's film, but fell short of expectations when it was released in neighbouring Germany.

Thomas Imbach's **Lenz**, a brilliant and idiosyncratic reworking of Georg Büchner's classic novella, was hailed by critics at home and abroad, but failed to attract viewers. Stina

Thomas Imbach's **Lenz**

Werenfels' **Going Private** (*Nachbeben*), a tense drama set in Zurich's high-finance milieu, and Andrea Štaka's **Das Fräulein**, a moving encounter between three women of different generations who left former Yugoslavia to work in Zurich, were two of the most accomplished and artistically ambitious features by young Swiss directors. Both earned critical acclaim and a number of awards, but performed disappointingly at the box office. Similar ex- amples from French-speaking Switzerland are Jean-Stéphane Bron's dramatic comedy **My Brother's Wedding** (*Mon frère se marie*) and Lionel Baier's 'autobiographical fiction', **Stealth** (*Comme des voleurs*), a road movie quest from Lausanne to Warsaw. All these filmmakers remain names to watch in future.

Andrea Štaka's **Das Fräulein**

Exceptions and rules

Two films succeeded in garnering both praise and healthy box office. Fredi M. Murer's **Vitus**, a modern-day fairytale about a musical boy wonder who also happens to be a genius at playing the stock market, made it into the top twenty box office figures, while winning prizes

and being sold to territories around the world. And Bettina Oberli's **Late Bloomers** (*Die Herbstzeitlosen*) exceeded all expectations, becoming the second-highest-grossing Swiss feature of all time (after Rolf Lyssy's classic 1978 satire, *The Swissmakers*). Oberli's light but intelligent comedy, about four elderly women who cause a scandal in their village by opening a lingerie boutique, achieved an unprecedented rating figure of 58% when it was broadcast on television in the autumn.

Switzerland has also seen an increase in the way films are marketed to and targeted at audiences. A survey commissioned by the Federal Office of Culture's film department found that two-thirds of Swiss viewers think the country's filmmakers should focus mainly on comedies, and on documentaries about aspects of Swiss life. Not surprisingly, these two genres have traditionally been most popular with local audiences. However, tailoring films to target audiences has proven to be a less predictable undertaking, with a number of attempts to generate popular films via this route failing badly. Recent examples were the hip-hop drama **Breakout** (an attempt at a Swiss version of *8 Mile*) and **Tell**, a ribald comedy about legendary Swiss hero William Tell; both fell far below expectations at the box office. These two films were directed by Mike Eschmann and produced by Zodiac Films.

Overall, attempts – mainly by young producers – to generate commercial successes seem to be working and the impressive increase in market share over the past few years can certainly be linked to a new attitude. Whether this level of success is sustainable and what means are required to support it are questions which have caused controversy within the film sector, particularly since the arrival of Nicolas Bideau, who was appointed head of the Federal Office of Culture's film department in October 2005. Bideau, who commissioned the survey on audience taste mentioned above, earned media exposure and to some extent notoriety within the film community with his slogan 'popularity and quality'. Under his direction, the federal film department has attempted to shift funding for production and distribution toward a select number of big-budget features, as opposed to the previous 'watering can' approach, which gave smaller amounts to a larger number of independent and often innovative filmmakers.

Documentary diversity

Whether this new strategy can bridge the gap between box office success and art-house prestige remains to be seen. But one obvious drawback so far has been the drop in funding for documentaries, previously a mainstay of Swiss cinema. Swiss documentaries have continued to be visible on the international scene, but the Swiss Filmmakers Association recently issued an open letter warning of the long-term consequences of under-funding in this sector.

For now, Swiss documentary continues to distinguish itself through a broad range of topics, many with a Swiss inflection. Marcel Schüpbach's **La Liste de Carla** looked at the International Criminal Tribunal's investigation of war crimes that took place during the recent conflict in former Yugoslavia, under chief prosecutor Carla Del Ponte, a former Swiss Attorney General. In **The Giant Buddhas**, Christian Frei retraced the history of the Bamiyan Buddha statues destroyed by the Taliban in 2001, touching on possible strategies for reconstruction that are being developed at the Swiss Federal Polytechnic. In **Building the Gherkin** Mirjam von Arx chronicled the construction of the distinctive Swiss Re

Building the Gherkin, *dircted by Mirjam von Arx*

tower in London, designed by internationally acclaimed architect Sir Norman Foster. A Swiss pharmaceutical company's responsibility for an industrial chemical disaster in Seveso, Italy in 1976 was uncompromisingly investigated by Sabine Gisiger in **Gambit**. In **Bruno Manser – Laki Penan** Christoph Kühn paid homage to the Swiss environmental activist who disappeared in the jungles of Borneo while protesting against the destruction of rainforests.

Some outstanding documentaries dealt explicitly with more traditional aspects of life in Switzerland. Among the most notable was Erich Langjahr's **Alpine Saga** (*Das Erbe der Bergler*), a fascinating observation of ancient haying practices still carried out on the steepest slopes by a few intrepid farmers. Stefan Schwietert's **Echoes of Home** (*Heimatklänge*) looked at how yodelling is being revived by a new generation of innovative vocal artists with links to world music and jazz.

Two other promising documentaries that found success at international festivals were

Pierre-Yves Borgeaud's **Return to Goree**

Pierre-Yves Borgeaud's **Return to Goree** (*Retour à Gorée*), a masterful portrait of Senegalese musician, Youssou N'Dour, which also examines the link between slavery and the spread of African music, and Peter Entell's **Shake the Devil Off**, about an impoverished New Orleans church community's struggle with the Catholic hierarchy in the aftermath of Hurricane Katrina. A personal favourite remains Thomas Haemmerli's **Seven Dumpsters and a Corpse** (*Sieben Mulden und eine Leiche*), an irreverent and sometimes scathing portrait of the filmmaker's recently deceased mother who suffered from 'Messie' Syndrome which rendered her unable to organise herself or keep her house in order.

Thomas Haemmerli's **Seven Dumpsters and a Corpse**

A look ahead

Among the new releases anticipated for 2008 are portraits of the famed Swiss author Max Frisch (**Mein Name sei Frisch** by Matthias von Gunten) and the murdered Russian journalist Anna Politkovskaya (**Anna P.** by Erich Bergkraut). On the non-documentary front, expectations are running high for Ursula Meier's feature, **Home**, starring Isabelle Huppert, and the animated feature, **Max & Co**, by Frédéric and Samuel Guillaume, which, alongside its distinction as the most expensive Swiss film ever produced, serves as a reminder that animation is another strong Swiss creative tradition.

Max & Co, *directed by Frédéric and Samuel Guillaume*

The year's best films
Fraulein (Andrea Štaka)
Gambit (Sabine Gisiger)
Lenz (Thomas Imbach)
Going Private (Stina Werenfels)
Seven Dumpsters and a Corpse (Thomas Haemmerli)

Quote of the year
'I think it's dangerous to drum into young creators' heads the notion that commercial success is indespensible. The creative process should focus on our cultural heritage, on Switzerland's in the world, and not simply attept to target audiences. I don't make films to sell tickets. I try to convey what bothers me, and what pleases me, in our society today.'
CLAUDE GORETTA *in Ciné-Bulletin*

Directory
All Tel/Fax numbers begin (+41)
Swiss Films Association, Neugasse 6, CH-8031 Zurich. Tel: (43) 211 40 50. Fax: (43) 211 40 60. info@swissfilms.ch/geneva@swissfilms.ch. www.swissfilms.ch.

MARCY GOLDBERG is a film historian and independent media consultant based in Zurich.

Taiwan David Frazier

The untimely death of Edward Yang on 29 June 2007 underscored the gradual passing of the realism of the Taiwanese New Wave cinema and possibly also the age of the auteur, of which Yang was at the vanguard, along with Taiwan's three other festival-celebrated giants, Hou Hsiao-hsien, Ang Lee and Tsai Ming-liang. Taiwan's industry is largely moving away from the art-house dramas that made its cinema famous and, understandably, following the Korean model with its emphasis on genre films and pop icons. Realism is now the staple of documentary only.

Taiwanese cinema had an unusually good year in 2007, thanks to two smash hits among a total of 19 releases: Ang Lee's erotic psycho-drama, **Lust, Caution** (*Se Jie*), and pop music idol Jay Chou's high-school romance, **Secret** (*Bu Neng Shuo de Mimi*), in which he also starred. In terms of box office receipts, Taiwan's top film of 2006 was ranked 33 overall, whereas *Lust, Caution* holds fourth place, with $4 million, although it continued to play to audiences into the new year. *Secret* managed a total of $824,000 in ticket sales and was at the bottom end of the top twenty. Interestingly, both were the only Taiwanese films to receive a major release in their home market, where distributors are generally locked up by Hollywood.

Lust, Caution was also Ang Lee's second consecutive film to win a Golden Lion award at the Venice Film Festival, an unprecedented feat. Pan-Chinese or pan-Asian casts are becoming the norm for productions of this scale and his cast included Hong Kong veteran Tony Leung, Taiwanese pop singer Leehom Wang and Chinese actress Tang Wei, whose cinematic debut, after rave reviews, is very

Ang Lee's **Lust, Caution**

likely to propel her to greater success. The script was adapted from a novel by Eileen Chang, a mid-twentieth-century Hong Kong novelist now enjoying a great renaissance, with adaptations by directors Hou Hsiao-hsien, Stanley Kwan and Tsai Ming-liang (a theatre production) all appearing in the last decade. But *Lust, Caution*'s box office draw was likely buoyed by its hefty erotic content, an element the media did not fail to emphasise.

In addition to his success with *Secret*, Chou was the number two pop star for both 2006 and 2007, and also appeared in Zhang Yimou's Chinese epic, **Curse of the Golden Flower** (*Man cheng jin dai huang jin jia*). He is now working on the basketball melodrama **Slam Dunk**, based on a Japanese comic book.

Other films attempted to cash in on pop stars, with significantly less success. These included Yun Chan Lee's romantic comedy, **My DNA Says I Love You** (*Jiyin jueding wo ai ni*) director Wu Mi-sen's drama of displacement, **Amour-Legende** (*Songshu Zisha Shijian*), which stars Japanese pop idol Yowusuke Kubozuka, and Fen Fen Cheng's **Keeping Watch** (*Shen Shui de Qing Chun*), which was essentially a teen romance, albeit with mental illness factored in.

Alexi Tan's period gangster film **Blood Brothers**, set in 1930s Shanghai and starring Taiwan's cinematic temptress Shu Qi, was a competent and rare attempt at the genre – Taiwan generally lacks expertise or history when it comes to action films, with only three or four individuals on the island able to provide special effects for gun shots, for example – but as a whole it lacked the atmosphere and complexity of Hong Kong gangster fare, even though its producer, Hong Kong's John Woo, is legendary for cinematic gun play. The film's domestic box office was respectable, at just over $114,000.

Alexi Tan's **Blood Brothers**

Gender and gay love continued to be major trends, but only those that ignited the box office caused controversy in the media. Such was the case with the voyage of personal discovery portrayed in **I Saw a Beast** (*Wo Kanjian Shou*) by Liu I-hung, which saw a lesbian renounce homosexuality through a Christian conversion. Meanwhile, Zero Chou's urban youth-oriented **Spider Lilies** (*Ci Qing*) turned a tidy profit with a story of underplayed female/female romance. Yu Jong-jong's

Zero Chou's **Spider Lilies**

rambunctious gay comedy **Go Go G-Boys** more purposefully tried to hit the niche in 2006.

Science fiction was attempted by poet-turned-director Hung Hung in **The Wall-Passer** (*Chuan Qiang Ren*), but low-budget and arty presentation limited its appeal. Hou Hsiao-hsien's long-time cinematographer En Chen meanwhile presented an endearing road movie, **Island Etude** (*Lianxi Qu*), which seemed to hover somewhere between drama and documentary.

Tsai Ming-liang continued to push beyond New Wave realism and into his own extreme aesthetic of speechless characters and long takes. His latest study in urban isolation, **I Don't Want to Sleep Alone** (*Hei Yan Quan*), was a flop at home. Tsai's first film set in his home Malaysia and costing just under $1 million, the Taipei premiere was accompanied by Tsai's increasingly common brand of off-screen drama. Originally slated as the opening film of the 2006 Golden Horse Awards, Taiwan's largest film festival and awards ceremony, Tsai pulled the film after a member of the festival's selection panel criticised it as 'too individualistic and indulging in personal style, so that it fails to move the general public'. It did attract a host of awards at European festivals, where he remains popular amongst art-house audiences.

Tsai also continues to dabble in the more permissive world of contemporary art. His short, **It's a Dream**, debuted in June at Taiwan's pavilion in one of the world's top contemporary exhibitions, the 2007 Venice Bienniale. A study in absolute stillness, it presented little more than people sitting inside a giant movie theatre for its entire 20-minute length.

Lee Kang-sheng, the leading actor in all of Tsai's films, directed his second feature, **Help Me Eros** (*Bangbang Wo Aishen*). It will be released in early 2008 and, if early reviews are correct, the static presentation of a man in a tail slide of marijuana, sex and seclusion will push the already stressed envelope of how much erotic content local audiences will tolerate.

If there is any common middle ground to be found between genre films and New Wave realism, it may be in the work of auteur Lin Jing-jie, who won the Critics' Week Award in Venice for his third feature, a searching drama entitled **The Most Distant Course** (*Zui Yaoyuan de Juli*). The film moved fluidly from despair to humour, with detailed characterisation and some truly bizarre moments. But it never seemed staged, overly symbolic or dense. Last year, Lin also produced a remarkable 21-minute vignette of a cop arresting a prostitute, **Street Survivor** (*Mai Xiang Hai*). Though out of vogue, Lin carries with him the torch of hope for the future of the now older New Wave cinema.

Lin Jing-jie's **The Most Distant Course**

2008 releases include veteran director Tsang Tso-chi's **Butterfly** (*Hudie*), a gritty poetic and fractured story of two small-time gangsters in a Taiwanese harbour town. The Berlin Film Festival has selected young female director Singing Chen's art-house drama **Gut Man Dog** (*Liulang Shengou Ren*); it was produced by Ocean Deep Films, one of the country's most active production houses, who are also due to release two features starring Eric Tsang, the light drama **Tea Fight** (*Dou Cha*) and the coming-of-age story **Winds of September** (*Jiujiangfeng*).

Lee Kang-sheng's **Help Me Eros**

The year's best films
Lust, Caution (Ang Lee)
The Most Distant Course (Lin Jing-jie)
Island Etude (En Chen)
Spider Lilies (Zero Cheou)
Secret (Jay Chou)

Quote of the year
'The 1980s and 1990s saw a fine oeuvre of film realism, but now Taiwanese cinema is limited. We will come to a dead end if things keep going the same direction.' *First-time director* , HUNG HUNG

Directory
All Tel/Fax numbers begin (+886)
Chinese Taipei Film Archive, 4F, 7 Chingtao East Rd, Taipei. Tel: 2392 4243. Fax: 2392 6359. www.ctfa.org.tw.
Government Information Office, Department of Motion Picture Affairs, 2 Tientsin St Taipei 100. Tel: 3356 7870. Fax: 2341 0360. www.gio.gov.tw.
Motion Picture Association of Taipei, 5F, 196 Chunghwa Rd, Sec 1, Taipei. Tel: 2331 4672. Fax: 2381 4341.

DAVID FRAZIER has written on Taiwanese art, film and music for the *International Herald Tribune*, *Art in America*, *Art AsiaPacific*, the *South China Morning Post* and other publications. He currently runs Taiwan's only underground film festival, the Urban Nomad Film Fest, and is managing editor at the culture magazine *Fountain*.

Thailand Anchalee Chaiworaporn

How complex the Thai film industry is can be gleaned by tracing its development in recent years. On the surface, the industry's growth is in line with the increase of film production and box office earnings. In 2007, the number of domestic releases rose to 50 titles, compared to 45 in 2006. The first two instalments of an epic historical trilogy, **King Naresuan I: Hostage of Hongsawadee** (*Tamnan Naresuan Maharaj: Phak Prathomwai*) and **King Naresuan II: Reclamation of Sovereignty** (*Tamnan Naresuan Maharaj: Phak Prakasisaraphab*), were a huge success. Made by the veteran 1970s new-waver Prince Chatreechalerm Yukol, they detail the true life of the King who liberated the Siamese from the control of Burma during the sixteenth century. Funded by the Royal Thai government, the epics were prescient in the timing of their release, following demonstrations and military rebellion that resulted in Prime Minister Thaksin Shinawatra being removed from power.

The Prince is now making the third installment of the trilogy, which was originally planned for release on the King's birthday on 5 December. The film is expected to be more geared towards an international audience, with a cast including Tony Jaa from *Ong bak* and veteran actress Jintara Sukphat, who played Robin Williams' Vietnamese heartthrob in *Good Morning Vietnam*.

A number of big-budget projects were shelved by studios, fearing a downturn in audience attendance for local films. Instead, more money and energy were invested in such dependable staples as comedy, horror and action. Comedy and horror were popular with local audiences, whereas horror and action were the most profitable exports. Both new and experienced directors took on horror, while a trend for comedians directing their own films increased. Some comedians even took on the filmmaker's genre, directing comedy-horror hybrids with varying degrees of success. Even the two most prestigious studios, GTH and Five Star Production, produced at least one slapstick film, despite their reputation for quality filmmaking and support of internationally renowned directors like Pen-Ek Ratanaruang and Wisit Sasanatieng, perhaps because the directors' films were rarely successful with local audiences.

Pen-Ek returned to his local crew for his sixth film, **Ploy**, after teaming up with Christopher Doyle and Asano Tadanobu for *Last Life in the Universe* and *Invisible Wave*. *Ploy* is a psychological drama about a couple's relationship falling apart following the man's befriending a young girl, who is invited to live with them. It opened in the 'Directors Fortnight' at Cannes 2007.

Lalita Panyopas in Pen-Ek Ratanaruang's **Ploy**

Wisit collaborated with Andy Lau on **Armful**, the remake of a Chinese film featuring an armless knight. It was preceded by a ghost story about a woman who is unaware of her own death, in **The Unseeable** (*Pen choo kab pee*). He has just announced his new project, **The Red Eagle**, a remake of the story of the legendary action hero, Mitr Chaibancha. Known as Thailand's James Dean, he died when he fell out of a helicopter during the making of a film. The film also starred popular Australian-Thai actor Ananda Everingham who was selected to join the 2007 Star Summit at the Pusan Film Festival. He is currently the busiest Thai star working today, featuring in seven separate film projects.

Nonzee Nimibutr, the vanguard of the new wave of filmmakers during the 1990s, returns with his fifth project, **Queen of Lungsaka**. An expensive epic about three princesses protecting their land against a wave of intruders in the south of Thailand, it is expected to play well both locally and internationally, hence the casting of Ananda Everingham and Jetsadaporn Pholdee, and Tony Jaa's protégé, Dan Choopong. *Ong Bak* director, Prachya Pinklaew, aims to make a woman his next action star in **Chocolate**, about a young girl who becomes involved with a gangster in order to retrieve money owed to her mother by debtors. And Tony Jaa has a plan to make his own directorial debut with his trainer-cum-director Panna Ritthikrai.

Indie power and Syndrome sffect

As most studios are very limited in their outlook, several filmmakers have chosen to become independent. This activity has significantly increased in the last two years. Apichatpong Weerasethakul remains at the forefront of this independent scene. His fifth feature, **Syndromes and a Century** (*Sang sattawat*), became the first Thai film to feature in competition at Venice. *Syndromes and a Century* is the final episode of a loose trilogy featuring elements of the director's own life: *Blissfully Yours* on his hometown in the northeastern part of Thailand; the Cannes Jury Prize winner *Tropical Malady* which is somewhat autobiographical; and *Syndromes*

Apichatpong Weerasethakul's **Syndromes and a Century**

and a Century on the lives of his parents, who were the doctors in Khon Kaen.

Unfortunately, just prior to its domestic opening, the Censor Board objected to four scenes – a monk strumming a guitar, another monk playing with a flying saucer toy, a group of doctors drinking alcohol, and a doctor getting an erection when he kisses his girlfriend. The director decided to cancel the screenings, but the uncut print remained with the authorities.

Censorship was a major point of conflict between the industry and the Culture Ministry throughout 2007. The present law dates back to 1931, at a time of absolute monarchy. *Syndromes and a Century* only highlighted what most people already know to be anachronistic. However, those in favour of progress rarely agree on what should be done, leaving the Culture Ministry in a strong position to reinforce the status quo. The Culture Ministry has passed the new ratings system law, despite protests from several renowned directors such as Apichatpong Weerasethakul, Pen-Ek Ratanaruang and Wisit Sasanatieng. The law still allows a rating board to ban films.

Ekachai Eukrongtham made his second film, **Pleasure Factory** (*Kuaile gongchang*) independently. Shot on HD in Singapore, it shows life in Singapore's red-light district, in Geylang. The film was premiered in Cannes'

Ekachai Eukrongtham's **Pleasure Factory**

'Un Certain Regard' section. Another former studio director, Pimpaka Tohveera, completed her second work, **The Truth Be Told**, a documentary about the female activist Supinya Klanarong, who was prosecuted by ex-premier Thaksin Shinawatra's company as a result of a critical article she wrote.

Aditya Assarat's directorial debut, **Wonderful Years**, won the Best Film award at the Pusan Film Festival. Made entirely from the fund both inside and outside Thailand, it tells the tragedy of two lovers in a small town in Phuket after it was hit by the Tsunami.

Aditya Assarat's **Wonderful Years**

The year's best films

Syndromes and a Century (Apichatpong Weerasethakul)
Ploy (Pen-Ek Ratanaruang)
The Unseeable (Wisit Sasanatieng)
Body (Paween Punjitpanya)
13 Beloved (Chookiat Sakveerakul)

Quotes of the year

'I, as a filmmaker, treat my works as I do my own sons or daughters. I don't care if people are fond of them or despise them, as long as I created them with my best intentions and efforts. If these offspring of mine cannot live in their own country for whatever reason, let them be free. There is no reason to mutilate them in fear of the system. Otherwise there is no reason for one to continue making art.' APICHATPONG WEERASETHAKUL, *on hearing that the Censor Board would delete four scenes in his* **Syndromes and a Century**

'Nobody goes to see films by Apichatpong. Thai people want to see comedy. We like a laugh.' LADDA TANGSUPACHAI, *head of the Cultural Surveillance Department at the Ministry of Culture*

Directory

All Tel/Fax numbers begin (+66)
Cinemasia, 73/5 Ladprao 23, Ladyao, Jatujak, Bangkok 10900. Tel: (2) 939 0693-4. office@cinemasia.co.th.
Film Board Secretariat, 7th Floor, Public Relations Dept, Soi Aree Samphan, Rama VI Rd, Bangkok 10400. Fax: (2) 618 2364/72. thaifilmboard@hotmail.com.
National Film Archive, 93 Moo 3, Phutthamonton 5 Rd, Salaya, Nakorn Prathom 73170. Tel: (2) 441 0263/4 ext 116.

ANCHALEE CHAIWORAPORN contributes to both local and international journals, and won 2000's Thai Best Film Critic award. She is now running a bilingual website on Thai cinema www.thaicinema.org.

Tunisia Roy Armes

Nacer Khemir's **Bab Aziz: The Prince Who Contemplated His Soul**

Because of the paucity of cinemas in Tunisia, the country's film production tends to be focused on the biennial film festival, the Journées Cinématographiques de Carthage in Tunis, where local films can anticipate being shown. Thus, there were eight features shown in 2004 and seven in 2006, but only two in 2005. But both of these were major works, shown to a wider public at the 2006 festival. Selma Baccar, the first woman to make a Tunisian feature, back in 1978, finally managed to complete a third feature, **Flower of Oblivion** (*La Fleur de l'oubli*), set in the 1940s. Her subject is a middle-class woman's recovery from drug addiction, triggered by a painful birth experience and the discovery that her husband is gay.

Selma Baccar's **Flower of Oblivion**

Also making his third feature was Nacer Khemir who, with **Bab Aziz: The Prince Who Contemplated His Soul** (*Bab Aziz, le prince qui contemplaît son âme*), completed a loose trilogy of films devoted to positive aspects of Muslim heritage. Whereas the first two films looked back to the glories of Andalusia and the role of the word – especially in its written form as calligraphy – within the Arabo-Islamic tradition, *Bab Aziz* looks towards Iran and is concerned with mystical Islam: the dances, songs and teachings of Sufism. The desert is central to Khemir's vision and the narrative follows an old man's journey across it, accompanied by his granddaughter. In true Sufi fashion, he carries nothing and travels in no direction. Linked to this narrative are a welter of stories and encounters, real and imaginary, spreading from a mythical past to the present, with its cars, aeroplanes and motorbikes. The film, initially inspired by a twelfth-century Iranian tale of a contemplative prince, was shot in Iran and Tunis, locations that fuse to form a timeless landscape without boundaries. As always with Khemir, the individual stories appear, grow and then vanish, as if consumed by the eternal desert.

A third major film shown at the festival was Nouri Bouzid's **Making Of**. Bouzid, as both writer-director of six features and scriptwriter for half-a-dozen more, is the major figure in Maghrebi cinema. Just as his first feature boldly tackled the problem of male rape, in *Making Of* he confronts the problem of what turns a thwarted young dancer into a potential suicide bomber. The story of this young man, Bahta, is interwoven with stories of a troubled director making a film about him and the actor

Nouri Bouzid's **Making Of**

playing him in the film. Set in 2003, against the background of the invasion of Iraq, *Making Of* is directed with Bouzid's customary flair and forcefulness and was deservedly awarded the top prize, the Tanit d'Or, at Carthage.

Among the half-a-dozen other Tunisian films shown at Carthage, three were second features. Jilani Saadi's **Wolf's Kindness** (*Tendresse de Loup*) is a tale of violence, revenge and thwarted love set in a bleak Tunis landscape. Moncef Dhouib's **The TV Comes** (*La Télé arrive*) is the comic tale of a village in southern Tunisia that gives its image a makeover when faced with the arrival of a German television crew. The second female director to have a feature in the festival, Kalthoum Bornaz, screened **The Other Half** (*L'Autre moitié*), the tale of twins who take divergent paths after the death of their father, who blamed them for their mother's death in childbirth and denied them all knowledge about her – even her name and resting place.

Madness (*Démences*) is Fadhel Jaïbi's first solo feature as director, after three remarkable collaborative films. In many ways it is reminiscent in its atmosphere of *The Wedding*, his first collaborative film, made back in 1977. Adapted from a controversial play recently staged in Paris, it is a dark tale of madness, dealing with the relationship between an illiterate youth from a wretched background and the psychoanalyst at the hospital to which he is sent. There were also two debut films.

Khaled W. Barsaoui's **Beyond the Rivers** (*Par-delà les rivières*) is the classic tale of a bride who runs away with the man she loves on her wedding day, here enlivened by a complex narrative structure and a plethora of filmic allusions. Néjib Belkadhi's **VHS-Kahloucha**, by contrast, is a documentary study of an amateur filmmaker, Moncef Kahloucha, shooting his version of 'Tarzan of the Arabs', starring himself and using the locals from the district of Sousse where he lives. Despite the economic problems caused by its virtually non-existent domestic market, Tunisian cinema continues in its diversity.

Néjib Belkadhi's **VHS-Kahloucha**

The year's best films
Flower of Oblivion (Selma Baccar)
Making Of (Nouri Bouzid's)
Madness (Fadhel Jaïbi)
VHS-Kahloucha (Néjib Belkadhi)
Beyond the Rivers (Khaled W. Barsaoui)

Quote of the year
'Fundamentalism, as well as radicalism, is a distorting mirror of Islam. This movie is a modest effort to give Islam its real image back. No other mission seemed as urgent to me as this one.' NACER KHEMIR, *Director of* **Baz Aziz**

ROY ARMES is Emeritus Professor of Film at Middlesex University and author of many studies of cinema, most recently *Postcolonial Images: Studies in North African Film* (2005)

Turkey Atilla Dorsay

The Turkish cinema boom continues: 34 films were released in 2006, twelve more than 2005. More importantly, the market share for local films climbed to 55%. The success came from purely commercial and big-budget films, or the plethora of youth-orientated comedies: Serdar Akar's **Iraq: Valley of the Wolves** (*Kurtlar Vadisi: Irak*), Ferdi Egilmez's **New Adventures of the Lazy Class** (*Hababam Sınıfı Üc Buçuk*), **The Magician** (*Hokkabaz*) by the very popular comedian Cem Yilmaz, **Keloglan Against the Black Prince** (*Keloglan Kara Prense Karsi*) by Tayfun Güneyer and Ömer Faruk Sorak's **The Exam** (*Sinav*). Almost all films were successful domestically and in Germany and Holland, countries with a large Turkish population. However, the films proved difficult to sell internationally.

Even films of a higher quality were successful at the box office. Acclaimed TV director Cagan Irmak's **My Father, My Son** (*Babam ve Oglum*) depicted a family's struggle to keep its integrity in the aftermath of the 1980 military coup. **Coming Home** (*Eve Dönüs*), by Ömer Ugur, offered a more political stance on the same troubled period. And Ezel Akay's **How Hacivat and Karagöz were Murdered?** (*Karagöz-Hacivat Nasil Öldürüldü?*) told the wonderful tale of heroes from the fourteenth century whose actions became the stuff of legend.

Nuri Bilge Ceylan's **Climates**

Reha Erdem's **Times and Winds**

Among more personal films, the leading auteur of the modern Turkish cinema, Nuri Bilge Ceylan, astonished with the maturity – visual and cinematic – of his latest opus, **Climates** (*Iklimler*), winning a host of international prizes. Zeki Demirkubuz's **Destiny** (*Kader*) was also acclaimed internationally, including being part of a major retrospective of the director's career in New York. Dervis Zaim, whose previous films, *Somersault in a Coffin* and *Elephants and Grass*, were popular with festival audiences, directed **Waiting for Heaven** (*Cenneti Beklerken*), a dazzling tale about an artist during the Ottoman Empire. And Reha Erdem made a tremendous comeback with two films, **Mother I'm Scared** (*Korkuyorum Anne*) and **Times and Winds** (*Bes Vakit*), a poetic and dream-like depiction of life in a small Aegean village, with the tempo of passing time dictated by the five calls to prayer.

The Turkish Academy Award entries

Ice Cream, You Scream (*Dondurmam Gaymak*) by newcomer Yüksel Aksu was the Turkish entry for the 2007 Academy Awards. A unique example of 'rural filmmaking', it was shot in a remote Mediterranean town with a non-professional cast. Its warmth, reminiscent of the Italian comedies once popular in Turkish

Özer Kızıltan's **Takva – A Man's Fear of God**

cinemas, guaranteed its success with audiences. Özer Kızıltan's debut **Takva – A Man's Fear of God** (*Takva*), co-produced by Fatih Akin, is the entry for the 2008 Academy Awards. It tells the story of a devoutly religious man led astray by materialism and selfish desires. It has won numerous awards and hopes are high for its chances at Hollywood's most glittering night.

2007: new films and surprises

2007 began less impressively. Only 14 local films were released in the first ten months, although a number of significant films were planned for release towards the end of the year. Among those, there were the usual local blockbusters, some of which followed a recent trend for historical films such as **The Last Ottoman** (*Yandim Ali – Son Osmanli*) by Mustafa Sevki Dogan, a tale from the early 1920s when the Turks were fighting for their freedom, **Zincirbozan** by Atil İnac, again about the aftermath of the military

Mustafa Sevki Dogan's **The Last Ottoman**

coup of 1980, but this time drawing together real historical figures from the period, and **The Masked Five/Iraq** (*Maskeli Besler/ Irak*) by Murat Aslan, a pure action film about the Iraqi situation. Comedies remained popular, particularly Zeki Alasya's **A President Lost in Deep Turkey** (*Öteki Türkiye'de Bir Cumhurbaskani*), about a president eloping with his wife to a small town on the Black Sea for an unplanned holiday and at a time when Ankara is expecting the American president, and **The Crazy Class** (*Cilgin Dersane*) by Faruk Aksoy, whose title speaks for itself. Of the action films, the highlight was Osman Sinav's **Operation Cherry** (*Pars: Kiraz Operasyonu*), which effectively traces the drug trade from Afghanistan, via Turkey, to New York.

Among the more interesting films were Onur Ünlü's debut, **The Police** (*Polis*), a stylish noir, and Serdar Akar's violent but impressively made crime film, **Barda**. Turgut Yasalar's second feature, **Fog and the Night** (*Sis ve Gece*), was also a contemporary noir, adapted from a novel by Turkish crime writer, Ahmet Ümit.

More intimate projects

Of the more personal films, writer-director Baris Pirhasan's **Adam and the Devil** (*Ademin Trenleri*) dealt with the unusual story of an Imam who marries an abandoned woman and becomes responsible for her child, only for the real father to show up a few years later. Biket Ilhan's **Blue Eyed Giant** (*Mavi Gözlü Dev*) was the first successful film to look at the period in the early 1950s when the great Turkish poet Nazim Hikmet was imprisoned on the charge of being a communist. **International** (*Beynelmilel*), by the newcomers Sirri Süreyya Önder and Muharrem Gürses, was another attempt to look back to the early 1980s, but this time through the prism of comedy.

The Little Apocalypse (*Küçük Kiyamet*), by Yagmur and Durul Taylan, is an interesting attempt to combine the atmosphere of a horror movie with the national fear of an earthquake.

Özgü Namal in **Bliss**

And finally, **Bliss** (*Mutluluk*), the second film by Abdullah Oguz, is a visually striking and emotionally breathtaking adaptation of the well-known writer and musician Zülfü Livaneli's bestseller, a complex study of three characters based on 'the honour murders', an old feudal ritual.

What lies ahead?

What to expect in the near future? With multiplexes opening around the country, the film industry is looking healthy, a reflection of the visible, albeit brittle, economic boom. Imported films continue to increase (at around 200 per year), but local production is likely to keep its share of over 50% of the box office. The new government is promising to encourage co-productions and take advantage of the stunning Turkish landscape and climate to attract foreign productions. The 'Turks abroad' such as Fatih Akin and Ferzan Özpetek are also performing well.

The Istanbul International Film Festival will be 27 years old in April 2008. 2007 saw Jeanne Moreau, Gerard Dépardieu, Catherine Deneuve, Paul Schrader and Abbas Kiarostami in attendance. There is also the Antalya festival, which changed its emphasis from international to Eurasian cinema in 2005. With the continuing support from the government and EURIMAGES there is good reason to be optimistic about the future.

The year's best films
Times and Winds (Reha Erdem)
Bliss (Abdullah Oguz)
Takva – A Man's Fear of God (Özer Kiziltan)
Waiting for Heaven (Dervis Zaim)
Climates (Nuri Bilge Ceylan)

Quote of the year
'The Miramax company told me I could work with stars such as Al Pacino, Robert de Niro or Harvey Keitel if I wanted to. But I would prefer to work with Turkish actor Ugur Yücel. How could I possibly talk to a legend like Pacino and tell him "Mr Pacino, please move to the other side!"' FATIH AKIN, *talking to Vanity Fair*

Directory
All Tel/Fax numbers begin (+90)
Association of Actors (CASOD), Istiklal Caddesi, Atlas Sinemasi, Pasaj- C Blok 53/3, Beyoglu, Istanbul. Tel: 251 9775. Fax: 251 9779. casod@casod.org.
Association of Directors (FILM-YON), Ayhan Isik Sokak 28/1, Beyoglu, Istanbul. Tel: 293 9001.
Association of Film Critics (SIYAD), Hakki Sehithan Sokak-Barlas Apt 33/13, Ulus, Istanbul. Tel: 279 5998. Fax: 269 8284. al.dorsay@superonline.com. Contact: Atilla Dorsay.
Istanbul Culture & Arts Foundation (IKSV), Istiklal Caddesi, Louvre Apt 146, 800070 Beyoglu, Istanbul. Tel: 334 0700. Fax: 334 0702. film.fest@istfest-tr.org.
Turkish Cinema & Audiovisual Culture Foundation (TÜRSAK), Gazeteci Erol Dernek Sokak, 11/ 2 Hanif Han, Beyoglu, Istanbul. Tel: 244 5251. Fax: 251 6770. tursak@superonline.com.
Turkish Film & Television Institute, 80700 Kislaönü-Besiktas, Istanbul. Tel: 266 1096. Fax: 211 6599. sinematv@msu.edu.tr.

ATILLA DORSAY has been a film critic since 1966 and has published over thirty books, including biographies of Yilmaz Güney and Türkan Soray. Founder and honorary president of SIYAD-Association of the Turkish critics, he is also one of the founders and consultants of the Istanbul film festival.

Ukraine Volodymyr Voytenko

There was a marked increase in the theatrical distribution of locally produced films in the Ukraine during 2006 and 2007. However, the domestic cinema is unable to compete with films from the US and Russia, which take up over 90% of the market. The box office in 2006 amounted to $50 million; the forecast for 2007 sees an increase of 50%, due to the improvement in the economy and the construction of more multiplexes. The Multiplex-Holding Company has a monopoly in this market and will soon open the largest screening complex in the country, a twelve-screen megaplex, in spring 2008.

Distributors are becoming increasingly independent of their Russian counterparts and since 2006 there has been an increase in the number of films dubbed into Ukrainian. With the desire for such independence increasing, a series of initiatives have led to the formation of the Film Commission, created to encourage the industry to use Ukrainian locations and services, and the Ukrainian Film Foundation for the promotion and advancement of a national cinema, both locally and internationally. On the eve of the 2007 Parliamentary election, President Victor Yushchenko issued an order to introduce a bill to Parliament, 'On the national programme of national film industry development in 2008–2012.' If adopted, it will bring sweeping reforms to the industry.

Kira Muratova, who hails from Odessa, directed **Two in One** (*Dva v odnom*) which blends drama, farce and black comedy in telling two stories about murder and love at a theatre. Featuring the excellent Bohdan Stupka, the two stories intertwine, using the same actors to play characters in each. Stupka shines in the latter, as a man dissatisfied

with his life. A success at various festivals, the film was produced by Oleg Kokhan and his company, Sota Cinema Group. Sota are presently producing **The Chosen One** (*Izbrannik*) by Roman Balayan, another important Ukrainian director, and the new Muratova film, **Melody for a Barrel Organ** (*Melodiya dlya sharmanki*), which is planned for release in 2008. They are also co-producing a project with Poland, Krzysztof Zanussi's **Heart on a Palm** (*Sertse na doloni*), and plan to produce a further five feature debuts in the near future.

Nina Ruslanova and Marina Politseymako in **At the River**

Another inhabitant of Odessa, debut director Eva Neymann, who trained in Germany and worked with Kira Muratova on *The Tuner*, directed **At the River** (*U reki*), based on the stories of Ukrainian Fridrikh Gorenshtein (who scripted Tarkovsky's *Solaris*). An elegiac account of a journey of discovery and understanding taken by a 90-year-old woman and her 60-year-old daughter, the film premiered at the Rotterdam Film Festival, before travelling on to the Moscow Film Festival.

Three directorial debuts, inspired by the events leading up to the peaceful Orange Revolution of 2004 were released during the last year. The most successful was Sasha Kyrienko's **Orange Sky** (*Pomarancheve nebo*), a love story between a boy and girl from either side of the political divide. Alan Badoyev's **Orangelove** is a tragic story of two lovers in Kiev who are faced with the HIV virus. Ivan Kravchyshyn's **Stop Revolution!** (*Prorvemos*) is an unsuccessful attempt to merge fantasy and adventure in a story about a local gangster searching for the 'formula of eternity'.

Oksana Bayrak's latest film, **Aurora** (*Avrora*), is a banal melodrama that nevertheless became hugely popular, grossing $296,000. The story of a girl who suffers from radiation sickness after the Chernobyl disaster, and is helped by a former Soviet ballet dancer living in the US, the film is the Ukraine's selection for the Best Foreign Language Film Academy Award.

Oleksandr Shapiro's latest film, **Happy People** (*Kheppi pipl*), features two characters who wander through the Ukrainian capital playing out an intellectual game. Though supported by

Volodymyr Abazopulo in **Bohdran-Zinoviy Khmel'Nytskiy**

his faithful admirers, Shapiro's film has little appeal to a larger audience.

Three veteran directors, who made their names during the days of the USSR, returned with state-produced films. Of those, the most fascinating was Mykola Mashchenko, who shot the historical drama **Bohdran-Zinoviy Khmel'Nytskiy** in an archaic style, narrating the story of the famous Ukrainian Cossack commander-in-chief who, in the seventeenth century, went into battle against Poland.

Serhiy Bukovskiy, arguably the most interesting Ukrainian documentary filmmaker, directed **Spell Your Name** (*Nazvy svoye imya*). Based on testimonies about the Holocaust, it's a Ukrainian-American co-production, co-produced by Steven Spielberg.

The year's best films
Two in One (Kira Muratova)
At the River (Eva Neymann)
Liza (Taras Tomenko)
Zlydni (Stepan Koval)
Spell Your Name (Serhiy Bukovskiy)

Quote of the year
'In fact, female directors are not at all weak; I understood that at the festival of female films: it was an accumulation of tough films without any implication of sentimentalism.'
KIRA MURATOVA *on being a female filmmaker.*

Directory
All Tel/Fax numbers begin (+380)
Central State Archives of Film, Photo & Sound Documents, 24 Solomyanska St, Kiev 252601. Tel: 277 3777. Fax: 277 3655.
Ministry of Culture & Art, 19 Franka St, Kiev 252030. Tel: 226 2645. Fax: 225 3257.
Ukrainian Filmmakers Union, 6 Saksaganskogo St, Kiev 252033. Tel: 227 7557. Fax: 227 3130.

VOLODYMYR VOYTENKO is a film critic, editor-in-chief of the analytical quarterly *KINO-KOLO* and presenter of the weekly programme about art cinema on national TV.

United Kingdom Philip Kemp

It is a widely accepted tenet among the British film community that, whenever the industry manages to get up off its knees and stagger a few steps unaided, the government strolls up and whisks the rug out from under it. This view isn't entirely paranoid. Over the last couple of years, the intricate series of hurdles imposed by HM Treasury on would-be filmmakers have been shifted, raised, lowered, re-angled and re-shuffled, until only the most competent amongst them can feel confident of completing the course unscathed.

The Treasury's first major initiative in 2006 had been openly anticipated for some months. There had long been official grumbling about the gaping loopholes in the tax-credit systems known as Sections 42 and 48, through which – so it was alleged – certain 'middlemen' were making off with stacks of publicly funded cash. New rates of tax relief were planned, allowing 16% of the budgets of larger-budget and 20% of smaller-budget productions to be eligible for relief. With some exceptions, the changes were generally welcomed within the industry.

The switchover was supposed to happen in April 2006, at the start of the new tax year. However, not until a week before this date did the government issue 'initial clarifications' of the new system; it was August before the bill received Royal Assent; the Inland Revenue's 'final guidance' on how it would work eventually emerged in October; and the credits themselves weren't legal until January 2007. And by then yet another hurdle had arisen, courtesy of the European Union. The EU ruled that from April 2008, in order to qualify for tax incentives, a film must be 'culturally specific' to the country it was made in. The implications

of this aroused dismay. As observed by Mike Downey, MD of production company Film & Music Entertainment, it was 'a bit like the Earl of Southampton telling Shakespeare he's withdrawing his patronage because *Romeo and Juliet* is about Italians and set in Verona'. It also seemed, some felt, an anomalous move at a time when, in Europe at least, national boundaries were becoming steadily less relevant.

Several producers voiced concerns that the new regulations would deter foreign production companies from shooting in the UK, at a time when co-production figures have been dropping dramatically. 'The new tax system is a narrow doorway through which films have to pass,' complained Iain Smith of Paramount. 'It will naturally therefore inhibit the number of films that are going to come into Britain.' This nervousness was exacerbated in March 2007, when the government suddenly closed another loophole, the so-called GAAP funds (the acronym stands for Generally Accepted Accountancy Principles, a device allowing investors to use films as a tax write-off). Though this move could have been predicted, the abruptness of the Treasury's action sent spasms of alarm through the industry. 'A lot of films that were going to shoot over the next few weeks are going to fall apart,' noted Paul Brett of Prescience Film Finance. Furthermore, the fear of seeing the tax rules changed at a moment's notice could act as a further disincentive to visiting producers.

Still, some took a more optimistic view. With an upbeat inclination, Andrew Eaton of Revolution Films and producer of Michael Winterbottom's films found the new system

Investing in film across the UK

Regional and national film agencies across the UK work with the UK Film Council and other partners, investing in local filmmakers, providing film finance and offering a range of services to incoming productions. Their film activities also include audience and archive development, training and education

Scottish Screen
249 West George Street
Glasgow G2 4QE
Tel +44 (0) 141 302 1700
Email info@scottishscreen.com
www.scottishscreen.com

Northern Film & Media
Central Square, Forth Street
Newcastle-upon-Tyne NE1 3PJ
Tel +44 (0) 191 269 9200
Email info@northernmedia.org
www.northernmedia.org

Northern Ireland Screen
3rd Floor Alfred House,
21 Alfred Street, Belfast BT2 8ED
Tel +44 (0) 28 9023 2444
Email info@northernirelandscreen.co.uk
www.northernirelandscreen.co.uk

Screen Yorkshire
Studio 22, 46 The Calls
Leeds LS2 7EY
Tel +44 (0) 113 294 4410
Email info@screenyorkshire.co.uk
www.screenyorkshire.co.uk

North West Vision and Media
Ground Floor, BBC New Broadcasting House
Oxford Road, Manchester M60 1SJ
Tel +44 (0) 870 609 4481
Email info@northwestvision.co.uk
www.northwestvision.co.uk

EM Media
35-37 St Mary's Gate
Nottingham NG1 1PU
Tel +44 (0) 115 934 9090
Email info@em-media.org.uk
www.em-media.org.uk

Screen WM
9 Regent Place
Birmingham B1 3NJ
Tel + 44 (0) 121 265 7120
Email info@screenwm.co.uk
www.screenwm.co.uk

Screen East
1st Floor, 2 Millennium Plain
Norwich NR2 1TF
Tel +44 (0) 1603 776920
Email info@screeneast.co.uk
www.screeneast.co.uk

Film London
Suite 6.10, The Tea Building
56 Shoreditch High Street, London E1 6JJ
Tel +44 (0) 20 7613 7676
Email info@filmlondon.org.uk
www.filmlondon.org.uk

Film Agency for Wales
Suite 7, 33-35 West Bute Street
Cardiff CF10 5LH
Tel +44 (0) 29 2046 7480
Email enquiries@filmagencywales.com
www.filmagencywales.com

South West Screen
St Bartholomews Court
Lewins Mead
Bristol BS1 5BT
Tel +44 (0) 117 952 9977
Email info@swscreen.co.uk
www.swscreen.co.uk

Screen South
The Wedge, 75-81 Tontine Street
Folkestone, Kent CT20 1JR
Tel +44 (0) 1303 259777
Email info@screensouth.org
www.screensouth.org

To find out more about the UK Film Council visit
www.ukfilmcouncil.org.uk Tel: +44 (0) 20 7861 7861

UK FILM | COUNCIL
LOTTERY FUNDED

user-friendly. 'Touch wood, it's so far so good. It's much simpler for everyone to see how the credit works in a finance plan'. Whether Winterbottom's latest project **Genova**, a ghost story set in Italy, would pass the forthcoming EU test of 'cultural specificity' has yet to be determined. As *Screen International* rather cynically commented, 'the new system seems almost as full of loopholes as its predecessor'.

In any case, tax regulations seemed less of a threat to the industry's prosperity than currency exchange rates. The continuing weakness of the dollar against the pound has made the lower costs and overheads of Eastern Europe and the southern hemisphere increasingly attractive and the effects have been felt in British studios and London's post-production houses. However, damage has been partly offset by the industry's reputation for professionalism and expertise. Tim Burton's **Sweeney Todd** was shot at Pinewood (where the studio's 70th anniversary celebrations were only partly marred by the fire that swept through the James Bond stage); **The Golden Compass**, the first in the projected Philip Pullman trilogy, came to Shepperton; the box office gold *Harry Potter* series continued at Leavesden; and Ealing harked back to its glory years of black-tinged comedy with **St Trinian's**. Meanwhile, Zhang Yimou's martial-arts spectacular, **The Curse of the Golden Flower**, became the first Chinese film to use London's post-production facilities.

Even in the midst of the apprehensions and uncertainties of 2006, hope came from Cannes where, for the first time in ten years, a British film won the Palme d'Or. Ken Loach's **The Wind That Shakes the Barley** is set in Ireland during the fraught period immediately following World War I, when the nascent independence movement came up against the brutalities of the Black and Tans paramilitary units recruited by the British government. Loach's film traces events through the story of two brothers, at first comrades fighting against the Black and Tans but later divided when the elder accepts the compromise deal

offered by Westminster while the younger furiously opposes it. As always with Loach, the powerful political message does not preclude moments of humour and lyrical tenderness. The Cannes award did little to appease certain sections of the British press who expressed pre-determined indignation over the film's allegedly 'anti-British' bias.

Cillian Murphy in Ken Loach's **The Wind That Shakes the Barley**

To get Loach's film off the ground, his producer, Rebecca O'Brien, had to pull together 21 different sources of finance. Commentators on the British film industry often point to two major structural weaknesses: distribution and financing. Compared to the all-powerful Hollywood-based combines, independent British distributors can exert relatively little weight; and if a British distribution company does manage to acquire some sort of power, it is always liable to find itself taken over by a more powerful overseas rival, as were Redbus by Lionsgate and Optimum by StudioCanal. And as far as finance goes, there are only three sources of any continuing significance: the government-funded UK Film Council, Film4 and BBC Films.

With a back catalogue that includes *Dirty Pretty Things*, *Ratcatcher*, *Mrs Brown*, *Billy Elliot* and **Notes on a Scandal**, the BBC's filmmaking branch exerts far more influence than its modest $20 million annual budget might suggest. 'We are a tadpole in the film industry in terms of what we invest,' observed David Thompson, the unit's widely respected head honcho, 'but a tadpole with a big punch.' So there was considerable disquiet when, in what seemed ominously like an echo of the fate of Film Four in 2002, it was announced that BBC Films would be quitting their Soho offices to move back into BBC TV headquarters in West London – and that Thompson would be stepping down to be replaced by a four-person production board.

Inevitably, it was speculated that this move was connected to the BBC's current cost-cutting exercise, following its failure to secure the hoped-for increase in licence fee from the government. Equally inevitably the BBC denied any such motivation, insisting that the move simply indicated the intention to keep BBC Films 'at the centre of things', and pointing to a forthcoming production slate that included film versions of two fondly remembered TV series, **Brideshead Revisited** and **Edge of Darkness**, costume dramas **The Duchess** (starring Keira Knightley) and **The Other Boleyn Girl** (with Scarlett Johansson, Natalie Portman and Eric Bana), Sam Mendes' **Revolutionary Road** and a live-action version of Kipling's 'Jungle Book'. Still, it seems unlikely that the unit's projected budget of $600 million over the next ten years, promised earlier in 2007, will now materialise.

Of BBC Films' 2007 offerings, Richard Linklater's **Fast Food Nation** and Kenneth Branagh's **As You Like It** (set in nineteenth-century Japan) were both found disappointing and the insipid **Miss Potter** suggested that the public's appetite for tastefully costumed pseudo-biographies (as with **Becoming Jane**, in which Miss Austen finds – and loses – love) might be on the wane. *Notes on a Scandal*,

Cate Blanchett and Judi Dench in Richard Eyre's **Notes on a Scandal**

adapted from Zoë Heller's bestselling novel and directed by Richard Eyre, exerted more bite, giving British acting legend Dame Judi Dench the chance to play embittered and malicious as an ageing secondary-school teacher.

Notes on a Scandal (both novel and film) relies on that currently fashionable device, the unreliable narrator – as does the year's most eagerly awaited adaptation, **Atonement**. Taken from Ian McEwan's novel and directed by Joe Wright (fresh from his feature-debut success with *Pride and Prejudice*), it is set before and during World War II, rounded off with a present-day coda that calls into question much of what we've already seen.

Keira Knightley and James McAvoy in Joe Wright's **Atonement**

The opening scenes, on a day in and around an English country house in 1935, are bathed in idyllic sunlight, but with intimations of darker undercurrents. Much of the action is observed through the cool, censorious eyes of 13-year-old Briony (an astonishingly controlled performance from Saoirse Ronan), as she watches the growing attraction between her older sister Cecilia (played by Keira Knightley) and the housekeeper's son Robbie (rising star James McAvoy) – and fatally misinterprets what she witnesses.

The disastrous consequences of her subsequent actions echo down the years that follow, through the war and long after and the story ends with Briony as an old woman (played by Vanessa Redgrave), still futilely trying to atone for what she did.

Wright does justice to McEwan's limpid prose and ingenious narrative structure, though occasionally there's the feel of a film that's just a touch too impeccably crafted to be as moving as it should be. The intricate five-minute tracking shot through the chaos of the beach at Dunkirk is a stunning piece of virtuoso, if slightly flamboyant, filmmaking.

Jamie Bell in David Mackenzie's **Hallam Foe**

Both *Notes on a Scandal* and *Atonement*, though by no means conventional, adhere to the mainstream of British literary adaptation; they intrigue, sometimes even surprise, but there's nothing quirky or subversive about them. **Hallam Foe** proudly proclaims its bizarreness and tone of manic obsession right from the start, as the eponymous hero, adorned in homemade war paint and a badger mask, abseils down from his tree-house with a Tarzan-like whoop to land on top of a startled pair of rutting teenagers. At 17, Hallam is a teenager himself, but anything as vanilla as straight sex could scarcely interest him. Given to wearing his dead mother's clothes and crawling over rooftops to spy on the object of his affections as she is having sex with another man, he seems perfectly content with his erotic fetishism.

It's a notable achievement of director David Mackenzie and his lead actor Jamie Bell (finally laying the ghost of *Billy Elliott* to rest) that they make a necrophiliac voyeur appealing and even romantic. Mackenzie also puts the craggy Edinburgh skyline to a strikingly memorable use. Adapted from the novel by Peter Jinks, and following on from *Young Adam* and

Asylum, *Hallam Foe* consolidates Mackenzie's reputation as one of the most idiosyncratic and left-field of younger British directors.

Other directors who had carved out distinctive niches for themselves with a previous film did not have an equally successful follow-up. After the runaway worldwide success of *Shaun of the Dead*, co-written by Edgar Wright and Simon Pegg, with Wright directing and Pegg in the lead, expectations were running high for the team's follow-up. **Hot Fuzz**, a black comedy with Pegg as a hotshot Metropolitan police officer exiled to a seemingly sleepy West Country village, seemed to rely too much on references to American cop movies. In a different vein, Neil Hunter and Tom Hunsinger's **Sparkle** proved an enjoyable melancholy-tinged comedy of mismatched pairings, but missed the fascinating time-lapsed structure of their *Lawless Heart*.

Simon Pegg and his task force in **Hot Fuzz**

Ever since his groundbreaking early career (*Shallow Grave*, *Trainspotting*) took a wrong turn with *A Life Less Ordinary* and *The Beach*, Danny Boyle seems to have been casting around to find his niche. After his zombie movie *28 Days Later* and the family comedy *Millions*, 2007 found him in a science-fiction mode with **Sunshine**, in which a multi-national team of astronauts is sent, fifty years hence, to re-ignite the dying sun. Despite the implausible premise, the film starts promisingly, but descends well before the end into a sententious mishmash. Meanwhile, Boyle and his screenwriter Alex Garland stepped back from the *28 Days Later* sequel,

Danny Boyle's **Sunshine**

28 Weeks Later, acting as executive producers and handing direction to Spanish director Juan Carlos Fresnadillo (*Intacto*). Despite some interesting ideas and symbolic references to terror and the Iraq war, the film suffered from slapdash plotting and missed the tension of the original.

Shane Meadows has never shown the least doubt about where he belongs. All his films have remained firmly based in his native East Midlands, and his ear for local idiom and the wry, laconic humour of the region have stood him in good stead, even when – as in his disappointing *Once Upon a Time in the Midlands* – the plot fell short of its potential. *Dead Man's Shoes* marked a caustic return to form, with Paddy Considine at his edgy best as an avenging angel; and, with **This Is England**, Meadows draws on his own childhood experiences to telling effect.

The date is 1983, heyday of Thatcherism and the skinhead cult. Twelve-year-old Shaun, whose father was killed in the Falklands

Shane Meadows' **This Is England**

War, falls in with a local skinhead gang led by the easygoing Woody. Desperate to belong, young Shaun (a performance of breathtaking truthfulness from Thomas Turgoose in his screen debut) eagerly adopts the clothes, haircut and habits of his new friends as a rite of passage, and is affectionately adopted as something of a mascot. At this stage there's no racism involved; the gang even includes black members. But then Combo, a Liverpudlian hard-case fresh out of jail, shows up and takes over the gang, ousting Woody and showing a sinisterly paternal interest in Shaun. Before long the lad finds himself attacking 'Pakis' and attending National Front meetings.

There are echoes here of Oliver Stone's *Platoon*, with Woody and Combo representing the 'good father/bad father' figures played in Stone's movie by Willem Dafoe and Tom Berenger. But Meadows' film absorbs all its influences and turns them into something wholly personal and indigenous. In its fidelity to his regional roots his work recalls the early years of the British New Wave and such films as *Saturday Night and Sunday Morning* or *A Kind of Loving*. But those films were made by metropolitan outsiders and could not easily escape a veiled hint of condescension. Meadows is utterly at home on his own turf, and shows no inclination to be tempted away from it.

Two British documentary directors moved into feature films in 2007, with startlingly different but equally powerful results. Kevin Macdonald (*One Day in September*, *Touching the Void*) directed **The Last King of Scotland**, co-adapted from Giles Foden's novel by Peter Morgan (who also scripted the Academy Award-winning **The Queen**). The *tour de force* performance by Forest Whitaker as the ruthless, charismatic Ugandan dictator, Idi Amin, did not overshadow the increasingly impressive James McAvoy as Amin's young Scottish doctor and sometime adviser, gradually realising the lethal Faustian pact he's entered into.

Forest Whitaker and James McAvoy in **The Last King of Scotland**

Far more downbeat was Nick Broomfield's **Ghosts**, a sober and sobering – and only lightly fictionalised – study of the condition of Chinese illegal immigrants in the UK. Something of a companion piece to Michael Winterbottom's *In This World*, Broomfield's film was inspired by the tragic death of 23 Chinese cockle-pickers in Morecambe Bay in February 2004. Filmed entirely without scripted dialogue and focusing on the heartbreaking performance by Zhe Wei (in her screen debut) as a young Chinese woman forced to travel from her homeland in order to support her little daughter, *Ghosts* comes as a far cry from Broomfield's aggressive, self-led documentary style. His compassion even extends to the Chinese gang-master who houses the immigrants in bleak squalor and rents out their services to the highest bidder. Initially seen as a brutal, callous figure, he's gradually revealed to us as yet another victim of harsh economic forces.

Zhe Wei in Nick Broomfield's **Ghosts**

Winterbottom himself, protean as ever, moved closer than usual to Hollywood with **A Mighty Heart**, an account of the killing of American journalist Daniel Pearl by Islamic extremists in Pakistan in 2002. As Pearl's wife Mariane, Angelina Jolie gives a dedicated, unglamorous performance – but by casting her and basing the script on Mariane's book, the film inevitably ends up slightly skewed to one angle. On the straight documentary front, brothers Marc and Nick Francis, with no previous track record, produced **Black Gold**, a hard-hitting, cogently argued study of the global trade in coffee. Shrewdly moving from the particular to the general, the brothers enquire why the international Big Four who control the coffee market can clear massive profits while Ethiopian farmers, who pride themselves on growing the world's finest beans, can barely keep their families from starvation. The film gained enough international exposure to produce pained denials from Starbucks.

Angelina Jolie in Michael Winterbottom's **A Mighty Heart**

One proud British cinematic tradition suffered a hiatus in 2007. For the first time in sixty years, there was no Royal Command Performance. The chosen film – **Brick Lane**, directed by Sarah Gavron from Monica Ali's bestselling novel of life in East London's Bangladeshi district – aroused protests from the community; as it turned out, on entirely erroneous grounds. Even so, HRH Prince Charles felt it better to absent himself from the proposed screening.

In conclusion, despite the best efforts of the government and the pressures of the international exchange rate, the British film industry continues to produce a heartening

Tannishtha Chatterjee in Sarah Gavron's Brick Lane

range and quality of work. Barring further unheralded bombshells from the Treasury, the tax system seems likely to remain unchanged for the foreseeable future, which should leave a breathing space to work out how – among other issues – international co-productions can once again be enticed back to the UK. It is a sign of confidence that London's first Production Finance Market ran for two days in October during the London Film Festival, and was accounted a promising success – and that Pinewood Studios have applied for planning permission to add an extra 105 acres of land, on which they hope to construct standing sets to include an amphitheatre, a castle, a Venetian canal, and Italian lakeside, and street scenes from London, New York, Paris and Los Angeles.

The year's best films
Hallam Foe (David Mackenzie)
The Last King of Scotland (Kevin Macdonald)
Venus (Roger Michell)
Ghosts (Nick Broomfield)
This Is England (Shane Meadows)

Quotes of the year
'We've got a rich cinematic history here and some fantastic directors; we just enjoy moaning about how crap we are.' *Filmmaker* ANAND TUCKER

'You talk to American buyers about British cinema and they think it's all about kids on council estates sniffing glue.' SHANE DANIELSEN, *former artistic director of the Edinburgh International Film Festival*

'Nothing looks more foolish than a British actor with a gun.' *Filmmaker* TERRENCE DAVIES

Directory
All Tel/Fax numbers begin (+44)
British Academy of Film & Television Arts (BAFTA), 195 Piccadilly, London, W1J 9LN. Tel: (20) 7734 0022. Fax: (20) 7734 1792. www.bafta.org.
British Actors Equity Association, Guild House, Upper St Martins Lane, London, WC2H 9EG. Tel: (20) 7379 6000. Fax: (20) 7379 7001. info@equity.org.uk. www.equity.org.uk.
British Film Institute, 21 Stephen St, London, W1T 1LN. Tel: (20) 7255 1444. Fax: (20) 7436 7950. sales.films@bfi.org.uk. www.bfi.org.uk.
Directors Guild of Great Britain (DGGB), Acorn House, 314-320 Grays Inn Rd, London, WC1X 8DP. Tel: (20) 7278 4343. Fax: (20) 7278 4742. guild@dggb.org. www.dggb.org.
National Film & Television Archive, British Film Institute, 21 Stephen St, London W1P 1LN. Tel: (20) 7255 1444. Fax: (20) 7436 0439.
Scottish Screen, 249 West George St, 2nd Floor, Glasgow, G2 4QE. Tel: (141) 302 1700. Fax: (20) 302 1711. info@scottishscreen.com. www.scottishscreen.com.
UK Film Council, 10 Little Portland St, London, W1W 7JG. Tel: (20) 7861 7861. Fax: (20) 7861 7862. info@ukfilmcouncil.org.uk. www.ukfilmcouncil.org.uk.
UK Film Council International, 10 Little Portland St, London, W1W 7JG. Tel: (20) 7861 7860. Fax: (20) 7861 7864. internationalinfo@ukfilmcouncil.org.uk. www.ukfilmcouncil.org.uk.

```
    1996 Modem Festival

http://www.acrobat-services.com/
         modfest.html

      to be continued
```

PHILIP KEMP is a freelance writer and film historian, and a regular contributor to *Sight & Sound*, *Total Film* and *DVD Review*.

United States Eddie Cockrell

As 2007 drew to a close, the Writers Guild of America and the Alliance of Motion Picture and Television Producers broke off negotiations some two months into an acrimonious strike that is affecting all levels of an industry already roiled by uncertainty – even as it continues to fine-tune global profit margins on tent-pole pictures in the face of imminent change.

Thankfully, this strike had no impact on a 2007 that, by year's end, was shaping up to be weak at the box office but strong on important, resonant films. A bright symptom of this well-being is the fact that there have been no clear front-runners for that holy grail of Hollywood approbation, the Academy Award. And with no *Million Dollar Baby* or *Crash* left in the wings to do a stealth eleventh-hour release-and-conquer, the next generation of Academy Award winners is anyone's guess.

Principally at issue in the industry clash is revenue for writers over DVD sales and profits from so-called 'new media'; that is, residuals from content delivered via such ancillary and still nascent methods as the Internet. The writers, still smarting from the poor deal they negotiated for the now-dead videocassette format in the late 1980s, do not want a repeat of that fiasco. For their part, the producers are unwilling to commit to specific profit participation for revenue streams they claim to be still unproven, and therefore risky.

Though the strike hit the American television networks quickest and hardest, the film industry has already felt troubling ripples that could grow into rough seas for the new year and the short term beyond that. Barely a fortnight into the strike, productions that

Russell Crowe in James Mangold's 3:10 to Yuma

had been outright delayed or postponed included Ron Howard's *The Da Vinci Code* sequel, **Angels and Demons**, Oliver Stone's **Pinkville**, the film version of the hit Broadway show **Nine** and **Shantaram**, starring Johnny Depp. Frustrated that he wasn't able to effect script changes prior to the strike, Brad Pitt abandoned the film adaptation of the BBC miniseries *State of Play* at the last minute; he was replaced only days later by Russell Crowe, whose own career heated up in 2007 with **3:10 to Yuma** and **American Gangster**.

Simultaneously and with no small amount of ironic coincidence, a new report suggests the sell-through DVD market is cooling off. According to the *New York Post*, for the first time in a decade, studios and retailers are bracing for a decline in DVD sales. For the late 2007 holidays, hopes were pinned on big sales figures for summer franchises of **Pirates of the Caribbean: At World's End**, **The Bourne Ultimatum** and **The Simpsons Movie**. Should they perform as disappointingly as DVD sales for **Spider-Man 3** and **Shrek the Third**, a format recession will have begun.

For years, at least since the advent of television (the original 1950s 'movie-killer'), the conventional wisdom, beyond the panic, has been that new media does not threaten the profit pie so much as dramatically expand it. Yet some months into the confusing format war between the next-generation DVD formats, HD DVD and Blu-ray, and coupled with the increasing technical sophistication and affordability of home-theatre equipment, moviegoers are finding more and more reasons to, well, stay home.

Yet if DVD numbers are not just levelling out but dropping, this suggests that 'new media' is indeed distracting rank-and-file filmgoers. The overall entertainment pie may be getting bigger, but there's no longer any doubt cinema's slice is slowly but surely being consumed. A new poll reveals that up to half the television audience with high-speed broadband connections may resort to the Internet to take up the entertainment slack during a strike; once those surfers get a taste of downloaded movies both legitimate and illegal, what percentage can be expected to return to traditional television viewing or film attendance? Add to this what some are calling 'the ongoing disintegration of the physical moviegoing experience' and the rise of such alternate venue technologies as IMAX and digital projection and the future is volatile indeed. To paraphrase 1960s hippie paragon Country Joe and the Fish, 'Well, it's one two three, what are we fightin' for?/Don't ask me, I don't give a damn/I'll just rig up my webcam.'

Jonathan Dayton and Valerie Faris's **Little Miss Sunshine**

Meanwhile, at the US's multiplexes, box office revenue reflected this pervasive uncertainty. A brief recap of 2006 reveals US box office receipts up 5.5% to $9.5 billion. Gross ticket sales rose slightly more than 3% to $1.45 billion (reversing a three-year downward dip), with the average ticket price taking a 2.2% rise to $6.55. The number of films released rose 11%, from 2005's tally of 549, to 607.

The two most interesting statistics posted by the Motion Picture Association of America were the 11% increase in worldwide box office, to $25.8 billion, and the fact that a full 85% of Hollywood films were rated either PG or PG-13. These two figures point to the continued mainstreaming of the product, with the year's most monetarily successful films bearing this out: no fewer than six films broke the $200 million mark, including **Pirates of the Caribbean: Dead Man's Chest** ($423 million), **Night at the Museum** ($250 million), **Cars** ($244 million), **X-Men: The Last Stand** ($234 million), **The Da Vinci Code** ($217 million) and **Superman Returns** ($200 million).

An additional 13 films finished above $100 million domestic gross, though it should be noted that the gulf between *Pirates of the Caribbean*'s $423 million and **Dreamgirls**' $103 million is tellingly significant. Though Hollywood continues to refine the franchise concept, their global marketing machines can handle both populist entertainment and breakout titles.

The films of 2006 were a mixed bag. The year began with *Crash* upsetting *Brokeback Mountain* for the Best Picture Academy Award and ended at the 2007 Awards with Martin Scorsese's **The Departed** limping to the win in a wide-open field that included Alejandro González Iñárritu's cross-cultural **Babel**, Clint Eastwood's World War II meditation **Letters from Iwo Jima**, the grassroots dysfunctional family comedy **Little Miss Sunshine** and the highly regarded Stephen Frears' biopic, **The Queen**.

The fact that few of these films figured on the year's best-films lists is neither surprising nor particularly important. There were plenty of solid titles to go around: Paul Greengrass's urgent and absorbing **United 93** forced brave moviegoers to confront a version of what happened to the doomed passenger flight on 9/11, while Alfonso Cuarón's harrowing **Children of Men** imagined a dystopian future not too far out of the realm of possibility. Amongst the year's most successful comedies was Larry Charles' **Borat: Cultural Learnings of America for Make Benefit Glorious Nation of Kazakhstan**, in which comedian Sasha Baron Cohen holds a mirror up to US cultural prejudices with laceratingly funny results.

Sidney Lumet's **Before the Devil Knows You're Dead**

Two wily veterans scored big as well. Sidney Lumet skipped back to the spotlight with the breezy mob comedy **Find Me Guilty**, while Robert Altman brought his ensemble magic to Garrison's Keillor's esteemed middle-American radio programme, **A Prairie Home Companion**. While Lumet's film can now be seen as a warm-up to his acclaimed 2007 drama, **Before the Devil Knows You're Dead**, *A Prairie Home Companion* proved the mellow swan song for Altman, who sadly died on 6 November 2006.

2007 began with promise, both artistically and financially. The year's first memorable film was David Fincher's **Zodiac**. A deliberate and disarmingly straightforward account of the never-caught serial killer who terrorised the

Robert Downey Jr and Jake Gyllenhaal in David Fincher's **Zodiac**

San Francisco Bay area in the late 1960s and early 1970s, the film is at once the ultimate police procedural and a respectful account of one man's obsession with finding a shadowy killer.

Satisfyingly, Fincher takes his time laying out the story's major players: newspaper cartoonist Robert Graysmith (played by Jake Gyllenhaal), on whose two memoirs the script is based, fellow journalist Paul Avery (the charismatic Robert Downey Jr), and cops Toschi and Armstrong (portrayed by Mark Ruffalo and Anthony Edwards, respectively). Magnificently performed by a shrewdly chosen ensemble cast, the film is a riveting experience that retains its power through multiple viewings.

Interestingly enough, the decision to release *Zodiac* so early in the year may have contributed to its tepid box office performance. The film so impressed international critics, however – it was screened at the Cannes Film Festival to much acclaim – that it appeared consistently on end-of-year best lists. One wonders if the film would have performed better and, indeed, been held in higher esteem domestically were it to have followed the subsequent release pattern of the Coen Brothers' **No Country for Old Men**, which had its world premiere at Cannes and was held back from commercial release until shortly after Telluride and Toronto festival screenings.

US screen comedy continued its post-Farrelly romance with R-rated material, the principle exponent of which was *The 40-Year-Old Virgin's* writer/director, Judd Apatow. In the late May release **Knocked Up**, Seth Rogen, Apatow's burly onscreen alter-ego, played a befuddled slacker facing fatherhood, while the actor's long-cherished screenplay for **Superbad**, which Apatow produced, revealed itself a profanely funny treatise on high-school angst. The success of the latter was hailed by its studio, Sony, as being almost single-handedly responsible for a 5% rise in profits during the second quarter.

Greg Mottola's **Superbad**

Another genre trend, though one that may have crested, is the much-debated 'torture porn'; a phrase first trotted out to describe the sadistic, sexually suggestive violence of Eli Roth's 2005 horror film *Hostel*, it also embraces the *Saw* franchise which actually began a year earlier. One prominent American critic flatly refused to see any film of this ilk, while horror mainstay Stephen King defended it by saying that 'good art should make you uncomfortable'.

Roth stumbled badly with the underperforming **Hostel II** in 2007 and the wildly indulgent **Grindhouse** double-feature project proved a

Quentin Tarantino's **Death Proof**

step backwards for directors Robert Rodriguez and Quentin Tarantino, each of whom directed pseudo-film trailers screened at the beginning of both films. A strong pre-Halloween weekend performance by **Saw IV** may prove to be the last hope of a genre that, like its predecessor the splatter film, has yet to bring anything new or original to the horror table.

By the traditional end-of-summer Labor Day weekend in early September, the US box office was 7% ahead of 2006 tallies, with a 3% rise in filmgoers' admissions. By early December, 23 films had already passed the $100 million mark, with eight pulling in more than $200 million: *Spider-Man 3* ($336 million), *Shrek the Third* ($321 million), **Transformers** ($319 million), *Pirates of the Caribbean: At World's End* ($309 million), **Harry Potter and the Order of the Phoenix** ($291 million), *The Bourne Ultimatum* ($227 million), **300** ($210 million) and **Ratatouille** ($206 million).

Matt Damon in **The Bourne Ultimatum**

The most satisfying of these box office smashes was Paul Greengrass's *The Bourne Ultimatum*, a high-adrenalin thrill-ride that continues the saga of mysterious super-agent Jason Bourne (played by Matt Damon) and his single-minded quest to find the shadowy US officials who made him the unstoppable machine he is. Greengrass's hyperkinetic style, developed in *Bloody Sunday* and *United 93*, perfectly matches the breakneck pace of Bourne's quest, and he remains one of the few filmmakers who understands how to use edgy, hand-held camera work for the story, and not vice versa.

Yet for all the summer's successes, disaster lurked just around the corner. Between Labor Day and Christmas, the US box office not only squandered those profits and attendance figures but managed to fall 6% behind 2006 to-date grosses – and lose an astonishing 10% of the previous year's audiences.

What caused this precipitous slide? The answer to this question contains both good and bad news. The bad news is that a product glut, composed in large part of dramatic films about the US involvement in Iraq and the Middle East, failed to attract the interest of those same moviegoers who surged to see the summer slate. One by one they opened, and one by one they were ignored in droves: Paul Haggis's **In the Valley of Elah**, Gavin Hood's **Rendition**, Peter Berg's **The Kingdom**, Brian de Palma's **Redacted**. However, there has been some interest in Mike Nichols' comedy **Charlie Wilson's War** and Marc Forster's **The Kite Runner**, which is not strictly considered a war film but tackles issues of Taliban-controlled Afghanistan.

Perhaps the most interesting, if fatally strident, of the films that grappled with the Iraq conflict was Robert Redford's **Lions for Lambs**, a star-studded lecture on responsibility and commitment. As a smooth senator (a subtle Tom Cruise) and a veteran journalist (played by Meryl Streep) debate the philosophy of war in a Washington office, on a California university campus an idealistic professor (director/ star Robert Redford) debates commitment with a recalcitrant student (a breakthrough performance by Andrew Garfield). Meanwhile, in Iraq, two of the professor's former students, now soldiers, are trapped behind enemy lines during a doomed mission. Although made with a clear passion and a consummate craft, the subject matter and structure render the message unavoidably preachy; as the maiden project of Tom Cruise's regime at the newly resuscitated United Artists, the film's critical savaging and minuscule box office success did not bode well for the esteemed producer's future under new management.

John Cusack in James C. Strouse's **Grace is Gone**

Much more affecting is **Grace is Gone**, the directorial debut of *Lonesome Jim*'s screenwriter, James C. Strouse. Winner of the audience prize and the Waldo Salt screenwriting award at the 2007 Sundance festival, Strouse's film walks a fine line between the maudlin and the profound in its sad tale of an average, patriotic Minnesotan, Stanley Philipps (John Cusack), whose soldier wife is killed in action. Shy by nature, Stanley is unable to give his young daughters the news, and so travels with them to a Florida theme park to work up the nerve. The film is remarkable primarily for Cusack's clenched, restrained turn as Stanley; the fact that the actor does not share his character's political views towards the war gives the film an added layer of tension. In 2007 Cusack also appeared in the vaguely similar but far more commercial **The Martian Child**, as well as the terrific B-movie **1408**, a fine adaptation of a Stephen King short story.

The good news about the autumn box office fragmentation is that many of the more challenging films released during the year came out in these later months. Chief among them is *No Country for Old Men*, Joel and Ethan Coen's boldly faithful adaptation of a Cormac McCarthy book seemingly written to the filmmakers' sensibilities. When average guy Llewelyn Moss (played by Josh Brolin) steals a bag of money from a botched drug deal in the desert, he is pursued by monstrous killer Anton Chigurh (a frightening Javier

Bardem). Their tense and bloody game of cat-and-mouse is observed and commented on by smalltown sheriff Ed Tom Bell (the revered Tommy Lee Jones), who waxes ruminatively on the sorry state of affairs amongst contemporary mankind.

Joel and Ethan Coen's **No Country for Old Men**

Perhaps too visually violent and narratively risky (particularly in the last third) to become a crossover hit, the film is nevertheless a career-best achievement for the Coen brothers. They have cannily combined many of the best elements of their greatest films – *Fargo*, *Raising Arizona*, *Barton Fink* – yet created something fresh and new. It is not a stretch to see the film's unchecked greed and barbarism as a metaphor for current geopolitical messes, but as a good, old-fashioned down-and-dirty thriller it also delivers the genre goods.

The film most often evoked to summarise the visual splendour and brooding earthiness of Andrew Dominik's **The Assassination of Jesse James by the Coward Robert Ford** is Terrence Malick's landmark film, *Days of Heaven*. The linkage is an apt one, though Dominik's film comes naturally closer to traditional western genre tropes than does Malick's. And in his complete inhabitation of the unbalanced acolyte Ford, Casey Affleck gives one of the year's supremely calculated and inspired performances; this profoundly creepy young man, the progenitor of the modern fanboy/stalker, gets under one's skin and stays there a good while. For his part, lead actor and co-producer Brad Pitt brings a less-is-more intensity to his scruffy outlaw;

his performance is an interesting companion piece to the more self-conscious but no less impassioned turn of his partner, Angelina Jolie, as real-life widow Mariane Pearl in the early-year drama **A Mighty Heart**, directed by Michael Winterbottom.

Unfortunately, the exhilarating *Assassination of Jesse James* was virtually orphaned by its US distributor Warner Bros., who employed a stutter-stop release strategy and in some cases refused to show it to local critics at all (this industry-wide disdain for reviewers peaked during the year and pointed to a democratisation of the form both sad and inevitable). Yet by year's end at least one such group, the San Francisco Critics Circle, had bestowed both best picture and best supporting actor (for Affleck) kudos on the film. A further award groundswell is a long shot, but the film rewards its supporters.

Casey Affleck and Brad Pitt in Andrew Dominik's **The Assassination of Jesse James by the Coward Robert Ford**

A pattern begins to emerge amongst these powerful films: raw dramas of almost punishing length and/or structure, in which white men in turmoil grapple with their demons in the at once familiar and threatening USA. The most deranged of these, perhaps appropriately held back until the year's end, is Paul Thomas Anderson's much-anticipated **There Will Be Blood**. It is a loose adaptation of Sinclair Lewis's novel *Oil!*, which charts the tragic and obsessive adulthood of a black-gold speculator over and beyond the turn of the last century; the film is a strong showcase for Daniel Day-Lewis as the determined Texas

Paul Thomas Anderson's **There Will Be Blood**

prospector Daniel Plainview. Channelling *Chinatown*-era John Huston, Day-Lewis strides through an American frontier that calls to mind the dirty wilderness of Robert Altman's *McCabe and Mrs Miller*, without the snow or human comfort of any kind. Anderson, who acted as shadow director to Altman's *A Prairie Home Companion* for insurance reasons, dedicated *There Will Be Blood* to Altman's memory and the influence of the late director is obvious in the film.

As fiercely unique as these films are, can American audiences reasonably be expected to approach and embrace them as entertainment? In a year of such distance between box office success and artistic merit, the question resonates as never before.

Other films from late in the year stick in the mind: Sean Penn's **Into the Wild** is a gratingly naïve, yet ingratiatingly persuasive realisation of Jon Krakauer's book about an idealistic young man who marches into the Alaskan wilderness as if it were his own private Walden. Ridley Scott's **American Gangster**, one of the few commercially successful early autumn releases, is the muscular saga of a 1970s drug kingpin (an imposing Denzel Washington) and the eccentric cop chasing him (played by Russell Crowe); the film owes as much to Lumet's great *Prince of the City* as it does to the modern action film convention.

Michael Clayton, directed by Tony Gilroy, is a no-nonsense legal thriller that has begun

to garner George Clooney some of his best reviews ever, while James Mangold's assured western remake *3:10 to Yuma* pits an idealist rancher (played by Christian Bale) against a notorious outlaw (again Russell Crowe).

Non-fiction filmmaking continues to be strong and varied. The extensive 2007 crop yielded a number of surprises, chief among them the relatively indifferent reception by US moviegoers to Michael Moore's **Sicko**; the documentary exposes the country's profoundly broken health-care system and manages to be both dignified in its restraint and biting in its fury. Could this be why it underperformed at the box office? Or could it be the existence of a pristine digital on-line copy prior to release, seen by some as a trendy marketing ploy gone awry?

Of the many documentaries made about the conflict in Iraq, the most level-headed and illuminating one seems to be Charles Ferguson's **No End in Sight**. A step-by-step analysis of the US's march towards a military presence there, Ferguson reveals with methodical precision the numerous mistakes made in the planning stages of the war and implicates by cold hard fact some of the principal players in the current administration. A consistent winner in early critics' polls, the film is also amongst the 15 finalists announced thus far to be considered for the Best Documentary Academy Award.

George Clooney in **Michael Clayton**

Though not possessing quite the status of these and other high-profile works, the quirky little documentary **The King of Kong** secured a good deal of critical attention. Fairfield, Iowa is 'ground zero' for competitive retro gaming and self-appointed 'World's Video Game Referee' Walter Day runs an outfit called Twin Galaxies; gamers who continue to sharpen their skills a quarter century after the introduction of the most famous arcade games can either submit tapes of their high scores or compete in person, preferably at the universally respected Fun Spot arcade in Lake Winnipesaukee, New Hampshire. Every bit as absorbing as it sounds, *The King of Kong* is about the unorthodox showdown between acknowledged 'Donkey Kong king' Billy Mitchell and challenger Steve Wiebe (Wee-bee, please), an aw-shucks family man who takes on the champ. 'It's not about Donkey Kong anymore,' Wiebe says near the end of this complex, edge-of-the-seat documentary thriller, and he is right: *The King of Kong* can perhaps best be described as Wordplay with a joystick.

In the end, 2007 saw a good number of important, resonant films come to the marketplace. That the year's box office tally threatens to fall short of 2006, which was a far weaker year overall, suggests it may be awhile before so many quirky, distinctive films are greenlit at the same time.

As for that strike, in the big picture it's yet another step on the road to the realisation that Hollywood – and worldwide filmmaking as a whole – is changing in ways that promise a revolution in the creation and the delivery of visual stories.

The year's best films

No Country for Old Men (Joel and Ethan Coen)
There Will be Blood (Paul Thomas Anderson)
Zodiac (David Fincher)
The Assassination of Jesse James by the Coward Robert Ford (Andrew Dominik)
The Bourne Ultimatum (Paul Greengrass)

Quotes of the year

'Many years ago, it would have been vulgar to print box office grosses in the paper. Now the *New York Times* does it, and it's the big story for people interested in arts and entertainment on Monday. Which is why emphasis has shifted away from filmmakers and fallen on movie stars and business people.' WILLEM DAFOE *on the vulgarity of box office reporting, venting to The Onion AV Club, 26 September 2007*

'I applaud filmmakers for dealing with real issues in the real world. At the same time, the feel-bad genre … is becoming downright oppressive. Filmgoers have a right to ask: when do we get some comic relief?' *Variety* editor PETER BART *on 2007's march of movie misery, 12 October 2007*

Directory

All Tel/Fax numbers begin (+1)
Academy of Motion Picture Arts & Sciences, Pickford Center, 1313 North Vine St, Los Angeles, CA 90028. Tel: (310) 247 3000. Fax: 657 5431. mpogo@oscars.org. www.oscars.org.
American Film Institute/National Center for Film & Video Preservation, 2021 North Western Ave, Los Angeles, CA 90027. Tel: (1 323) 856 7600. Fax: 467 4578. info@afi.com. www.afi.com.
Directors Guild of America, 7920 Sunset Blvd, Los Angeles, CA 90046. Tel: (1 310) 289 2000. Fax: 289 2029. www.dga.org.
Independent Feature Project, 104 W 29th St, 12th Floor, New York, NY 10001. Tel: (1 212) 465 8200. Fax: 465 8525. ifpny@ifp.org. www.ifp.org.
International Documentary Association, 1201 W 5th St, Suite M320, Los Angeles, CA 90017-1461. Tel: (1 213) 534 3600. Fax: 534 3610. info@documentary.org. www.documentary.org.
Motion Picture Association of America, 15503 Ventura Blvd, Encino, CA 91436. Tel: (1 818) 995 6600. Fax: 382 1784. www.mpaa.org.

EDDIE COCKRELL is a *Variety* film critic and freelance programming consultant who, when not reviewing from festivals in Europe and Canada, splits his time between Maryland and Sydney.

Uruguay Jorge Jellinek

The last two years have been marked by significant developments in Uruguayan cinema. Three new features screened in different sections of the San Sebastián Film Festival, one of which, **Kill Them All** (*Matar a todos*), a political thriller directed by Esteban Schroeder, was included in the official competition. This is unusual for a country whose annual output over the last decade has rarely exceeded five films, and reveals the quality of recent Uruguayan work and its growing international reputation.

The success, confirmed by numerous prizes at various film festivals, is a novelty for an industry that has such a small local market and virtually no official production support. At least five new films are now in post-production and more than ten at different stages of development. Uruguayan locations and facilities have also attracted international productions such as **Blindness** (*Ceguera*), directed by Brazilian Fernando Meirelles, inspired by *Essay on Blindess* by Nobel Prize-winner José Saramago, with a cast that includes Hollywood stars Julianne Moore, Danny Glover and Mark Ruffalo. Mickey Rourke has also been seen on the streets of Montevideo filming **The Informers**, directed by Gregor Jordan, an adaptation of a novel by Bret Easton Ellis.

Such renewed activity is surprising given the economic crisis that almost stopped all production four years ago. And then there was the sudden death of Juan Pablo Rebella, the young co-director (with Pablo Stoll) of *Whisky*, a dark and melancholic comedy that put Uruguayan films on the international map. His suicide at age 32, in July 2006, was a shock and a big blow for the local cinema community and put an end to one of the most brilliant and promising careers of that new generation.

Still, Control Z, the production company that Rebella founded with his friends and collaborators, Pablo Stoll and Fernando Epstein, has continued to work. A few weeks before his death, they released **Dog Pound** (*La perrera*), by Manuel Nieto, another dark and witty comedy, which received a Tiger Award at Rotterdam Film Festival. Not as successful as *Whisky*, its unconventional humour and documentary style nonetheless reflected the younger generation's unease and lack of perspective. The main character, David, is a failed student. After losing his scholarship, he's living at the family house in the isolated sea resort of La Pedrera. Pressed by his authoritarian and absent father, he must construct his own home on a piece of land given to him. Without resources, this hopeless but charming character spends the winter in the lonely and depressing town, with only abandoned dogs for company and a supply of drugs and alcohol. With its slow pace and episodic structure, the film does not cater for all tastes, but expresses with remarkable eloquence the pangs and disorientation of this late adolescent.

Pablo Riera & Sergio Gorfain in **Dog Pound**

The difficulties of coming of age are also explored through drugs and alcohol in **Acne**, by newcomer Federico Veiroj and once again produced by Control Z. This light-hearted comedy, which will be released in 2008, shows the problems of Rafael Bregman, a Jewish boy who at 13 has already lost his virginity, without having ever kissed a girl. To conquer the heart of the classmate he likes, he must struggle with his clumsiness, overcome his shyness and clear his acne rash. The film received an important prize in the 'Cine en Construcción' section at the San Sebastián Film Festival, to assist in its post-production.

Hope and glory

The most interesting Uruguayan film of 2007, and one of the more successful at the box office, was **The Pope's Toilet** (*El baño del Papa*), a co-production with Brazil, directed by scriptwriter Enrique Fernández and cinematographer César Charlone, well known for his work with Brazilian director Fernando Meirelles on *City of God* and *The Constant Gardener*, for which he received BAFTA and Academy Award nominations. Employing low-key humour, this minimalist story about hope and popular religion describes a real situation that occurred in Melo, a small city near the border with Brazil, which received a brief visit from Pope John Paul II in 1988. It brought hope to the poor local people who expected thousands of visitors. Neo-realist in style, combining professional and non-professional actors, this appealing and entertaining film pays attention to details and features well-defined characters. In particular, the presence of César Troncoso in the lead role contributes to its authenticity. The film won six prizes at the Gramado Festival and became one of the most popular titles of the year.

Another road was explored in Carlos Ameglio's **The Rind** (*La Cáscara*), a strange and original comedy that combined dark humour with fantasy. Mixing genres, from old mystery and science fiction films, fantastic literature and comics, it presents a character study of a low-key advertising executive. He is confronted with the sudden death of his partner, and has to deal with an urgent publicity campaign for an anti-flu medicine. Searching for the 'big idea' that his late friend never revealed, he becomes involved in an absurd detective story. Ameglio, a well-known director of commercials, took great risks in attempting something different with his first film. The result is well crafted, frequently ironic and occasionally nonsensical and profits from the impressive central performance by Juan Manuel Alari.

More dramatic events, such as the Condor Plan, which covered the secret collaboration of military regimes in the region, are brought to light in Esteban Schroeder's *Kill Them All*, inspired by true events. It follows the investigation of Julia Gudari, a tenacious lawyer, into the kidnapping in Uruguay of Humberto Berríos, a sinister Chilean chemist wanted by international authorities in connection with crimes committed by the Pinochet regime. Afraid that her own father, General Gudari, is involved in the case, she looks into her own past. This Uruguayan-Chilean-Argentine co-production, with its attractive cast lead by Uruguayan actress Roxana Blanco (*Alma Mater*), Chilean María Izquierdo and Argentine Darío Grandinetti (*Talk to Her*), received the Audience Award at the Biarritz Film Festival and will be released in March 2008.

Carnival tradition

Documentary film production has also been on the rise in recent years, as proved by the success of **La Matinée**, directed by newcomer Sebastián Bednarik, who spent a year following 'murga', a typical choral group in the famous Uruguayan Carnival. Using special singing techniques, and popular tunes, the murgas usually satirise political and real events. The special distinction of the murga in *La Matinée*, is that it was formed by old carnival singers and musicians – a kind of *Buena Vista Social Club* in the

Sebastián Bednarik's **La Matinee**

Uruguayan carnival tradition. With a mixture of testimonies, amusing moments, emotion and great music, the film rescues these forgotten artists and pays homage to their cultural tradition.

More austere and reflexive is **Close to the Clouds** (*Cerca de las nubes*), directed by Aldo Garay (*La espera*), who, in a similar style to Spanish filmmaker Mercedes Alvarez's *The Sky Turns*, explores the life of a group of old people, the last inhabitants in a remote village.

While new productions, such as the political comedy **Polvo Nuestro Que Estás en Los Cielos**, which marks the comeback of Beatriz Flores Silva (*In This Tricky Life*), are expected soon, the most important news is that the Parliament will finally aprove the Cinema and Audiovisual Law and create a Production Fund of $1.2 million. This is an important step to consolidating a creative movement that has given enough proof of its strength and vitality, and its determination to keep going.

Enrique Fernández and César Charlone's **The Pope's Toilet**

The year's best films
The Pope's Toilet (Enrique Fernández and César Charlone)
The Rind (Carlos Ameglio)
La Matinée (Sebastián Bednarik)
Dog Pound (Manuel Nieto)
Close to the Clouds (Aldo Garay)

Quote of the year
'This film is about the need that we all have to pursue a dream, in order to go on, specially in Latin America.' CÉSAR CHARLONE, *co-director of* The Pope's Toilet

Directory
All Tel/Fax numbers begin (+598)
Asociación de Productores y Realizadores de Cine y Video del Uruguay (ASOPROD), Maldonado 1792, Montevideo. Tel: 418 7998. info@asoprod.org.uy. www.asoprod.org.uy.
Cinemateca Uruguaya, Lorenzo Carnelli 1311, 11200 Montevideo. Tel: 418 2460. Fax: 419 4572. cinemuy@chasque.net. www.cinemateca.org.uy.
Fondo Para el Fomento y Desarrollo de la Producción Audiovisual Nacional (FONA), Palacio Municipal, Piso 1°, Montevideo. Tel: 902 3775. fona@prensa.imm.gub.uy. www.montevideo. gub.uy/cultura/c_fona.htm.
Instituto Nacional del Audiovisual (INA), Reconquista 535, 8° Piso, 11100 Montevideo. Tel/Fax: 915 7489/916 2632. ina@mec.gub.uy. www.mec.gub.uy/ina.

JORGE JELLINEK has been a film critic and journalist for over twenty years, contributing to newspapers, magazines and radio. He writes for the Pan-American weekly, *Tiempos del Mundo* and is vice-president of the Uruguayan Critics' Association.

Uzbekistan Gulnara Abikeyeva

N inety-nine percent of cinemas in Uzbekistan show nationally produced films. On average, 40–45 full-length feature films are produced each year, 12–15 of which are sponsored by the national production studio Uzbekfilm, with the remaining thirty made privately.

The majority of films are made on video. This type of production is called 'Khon-Takhta', which translates as 'the vegetables' cutting board' – fast and cheap film production. Such a film costs less than $30,000, with $1–$1.5 charged for each cinema ticket. Only 25,000 or so people need to watch the film for it to break even. Of course, 'Khon-Takhta' films are relatively simplistic, playing up to the generic conventions of melodrama or comedy, and often feature famous Uzbek musicians; there is even a category of popular 'Khon-Takhta' actors. With a population of 26.5 million, virtually any of these films brings in a profit within two weeks of release. However, the real successes remain in cinemas for months.

The majority of Uzbek cinemas have the equipment to show films made on video, while the interest in foreign films is minimal. Only 1% of cinemas show Indian and American films. As a rule, Uzbeks prefer to watch these films at home. An acquaintance from Tashkent told me that when she went to see *Pirates of the Caribbean III*, there were only three people there, and only because she had taken her two granddaughters.

Professional cinematographers, who received their education in Moscow in the All-Union National Institute of Cinematography (VGIK) during the Soviet era, or in the local film school in Tashkent, try to keep their technical and

aesthetic standards high. Only the films that are produced by the national production studio Uzbekfilm are presented at film festivals and on the international circuit.

Elkin Tuichiev's **Chashma**

The most prominent Uzbek film of the past two years is **Chashma**, directed by Elkin Tuichiev, and nominated for Moscow Film Festival's 'Perspectives' competition. A psychological drama, it tells the story of a girl who visits her aunt the day before her wedding to fulfil the traditional custom of purification: to wash her face with water from the mountains. But on her way, she meets people that live in the mountain village, and realises that 'happiness' is not as wonderful as she imagined it to be. It's a simplistic script, which shows the pain and fear Tuichiev feels for the Uzbek nation. Tuichiev is a member of the younger generation of Uzbek filmmakers, who are producing films at 'Studio 5'. Both he and his friend Aiub Shakhobiddinov shot *A Tulip in the Snow* in 2004, which was shown at the Cannes Film Festival. In 2007 Shakhobiddinov made the thought-provoking social drama, **The Yurt** (*Iurta*). The central hero is sickened with what he sees as a society that only brings him pain and suffering.

Aiub Shakhobiddinov's **The Yurt**

When his son grows up, he runs away to the city. On his own, the father finds understanding and support from a deaf woman, whereas the errant son descends into drug addiction.

Another 2006 film, **Motherland** (*Rodina*), directed by Zulfikar Musakov, tells the story of an old Uzbek, now a citizen of the US, who decides, against his son's advice, to return to his motherland. He immediately travels to a village to take revenge on the person who made him and his wife leave Uzbekistan by force during Stalinist times, because they were

Bakhodir Yuldashev's **Shima**

considered enemies of the state. Instead, he meets a blind old man. On his way back to the US, the father dies, but his son now realises where his motherland is. Clearly a pro-Uzbek film, it is produced professionally and with a degree of political sensitivity.

18 Square (*18 Kvadrat*), directed by Djakhongir Kasymov, is an action film about soldiers that work on Uzbekistan's borders, protecting the country from terrorists. **Shima**, directed by Bakhodyr Iuldashev, is a psychological drama about a journalist in a search of his father. Together with a group of people, he is taken hostage by a mad soldier who believes World War II is still raging.

Directed by Kamara Kamalova, **A Path Under the Sky** (*Doroga Pod Nebesami*) is a tender love story. It received the National Prize of Uzbekistan in 2007. **Murravat**, directed by Bako Sadykov, revolves around a 14-year old girl who used to be an athlete, but has become handicapped since an accident. She lives in the rehabilitation centre for athletes, where she writes her first novel.

The year's best films
Chashma (Elkin Tuichiev)
A Path Under the Sky (Kamara Kamalova)
Motherland (Zulfikar Mysakov)
The Yurt (Aiub Shakhobiddinov)

Quote of the year
'Can a symphony orchestra perform in a restaurant? Individual musicians can perform in the restaurant, but not the entire orchestra. We do not want Uzbek filmmaking to be solely of the 'Khon-Takhta' type. Government spending has to be used for the art of Uzbek filmmaking and not for commercial purposes only.' *Filmmaker* SHUKHRAT MAKHMUDOV

GULNARA ABIKEYEVA is a Director of the Centre of Central Asian Cinematography, and Artistic Director of International Film Festival 'Eurasia'. She has written three books on Kazakh and Central Asian cinema.

Venezuela Martha Escalona Zerpa

The last two years have seen a great development in Venezuelan cinema. The government, with the approval of the Law of National Cinematography in August 2005, has developed an impressive structure for film and television production, distribution and exhibition, which has previously never existed. According to Juan Carlos Lossada, director of CNAC (Centre for National Cinematography), more than $54 million has been invested in Venezuelan film institutions, as well as regional projects, such as Telesur TV station.

Two new film institutions

In 2006, two organisations key to the development of the Venezuelan film industry – the National Film Distributor, Amazonia Films, and Villa del Cine – were established. Amazonia Films is an institute under the Ministry of Culture and its goal is to promote and distribute films to national and international audiences. Initially, Amazonia Films aims to produce 24 film and television productions in 2008, among which ten will be targeted at children and teenagers, featuring the participation of 14 other countries. There will also be seven international co-productions.

Villa del Cine is the Venezuelan Cinecittà, a four-hectare village for filming and post-production, located in the city of Guarenas, near Caracas. It has two studios for shooting and a building equipped with high-technology post-production equipment. Its main purpose is to 'foster film and audiovisual production under principles of inclusion, democratisation and national sovereignty,' according to Director Lorena Almarza. Another important purpose is to attract and encourage co-productions

with foreign studios, directors and actors. For instance, Danny Glover is shooting a movie financed by Villa del Cine about Francois Dominique Toussant-Louverture, Haitian independence leader. Sean Penn showed interest in participating in co-productions at Villa del Cine during his visit in August 2007. Villa del Cine plans to produce twenty films for 2008. Two of them will be historical, one about Venezuelan *caudillo* Cipriano Castro, and the other about the heroine of the independence, Luisa Cáceres de Arismedi.

Venezuelan releases

In 2006, eleven Venezuelan films were screened, with a total box office revenue of $2.5 million. Among them is the CNAC-funded documentary **To Play and To Fight** (*Tocar y Luchar*) by Alberto Arvelo, which looks at youth orchestras, in which more than 240,000 children and teenagers from Venezuela and other Latin American countries participate. It won the audience award at three film festivals and also the Best Documentary prize at the 2006 Merida Film Festival. **Francisco de Miranda** by Diego Risquez, the first Villa del Cine production, depicts the life of the titular Venezuelan revolutionary.

Daniela Alvarado and Marlene de Andrade in **A Virgin Grandmother**

CNAC estimates that twenty local productions will have been screened in Venezuela by the end of 2007. The most successful films were **13 Seconds** (*13 Segundos*), **My Life for Sharon** (*Mi vida por Sharon*) and **A Virgin Grandmother**. *13 Seconds* by Freddy Fadel is a controversial independent film that deals with pregnancy and abortion through five separate stories. It was the first Venezuelan film ever to appear in the year's top ten box office successes. Following it were two comedies: *My Life for Sharon*, by veteran filmmaker Carlos Azpúrua, is about the life of a former Venezuelan Oil Industry (PDVSA) engineer whose most important possession, his van called Sharon, gets stolen on Christmas Day; and *A Virgin Grandmother*, by Olegario Barrera, tells of the adventures of Antonieta, an 85-year-old grandmother who finds herself in the body of a 20-year-old girl.

Both comedies received bad reviews, yet these had no effect on the audiences who turned out en masse to watch them. It is not by chance that the most sought-after movies in 2007 have been non-political or do not address the traditionally exploited topics of criminality, poverty and violence. It would appear that the public feels the need for a politically neutral, entertaining film experience, but one they can still identify with socially and culturally.

The Venezuelan government, the main funding body, is very keen to promote popular social, historical and nationalist films. Critics of this new trend call for a continuation of a pluralist, critical and realistic cinema that is, above all, ideologically independent.

Thanks to Amazonia Films' diligence, Venezuelan cinema found itself on display at the Marché du Film, at the 60th Cannes Film Festival. Eight Venezuelan films were shown, including *Francisco de Miranda*.

Mariana Rondón's **Postales de Leningrado** has been chosen as the Venezuelan entry at the 2008 Academy Awards. This is a drama about guerrilla activity in the 1960s whose

Director Olegario Barrera

title derives from the link between some Venezuelan activists and the then Soviet government. The film was supported by the PDVSA, Telesur TV and CNAC. It also represents Venezuela at the 16th International Cultural Festival from Latin America in Biarritz.

The year's best films
Francisco de Miranda (Diego Risquez)
To Play and To Fight (Alberto Arvelo)
13 Seconds (Freddy Fadel)
My Life for Sharon (Carlos Azpúrua)
A Virgin Grandmother (Olegario Barrera)

Quote of the year
'Villa del Cine is a process to become aware of the importance of filmmaking in politics … Nowadays the State has all the right and power to make the movies that will foster its political leanings.' CARLOS AZPÚRUA, *director*

Directory
Centro Nacional Autónomo de Cinematografia (CNAC), Avenida Diego Cisneros, Piso 2, 1071 Caracas. comunicación@cnac.org. ve. www.cnac.org.ve.
Consejo Nacional de la Cultura (CONAC), Centro Simón Bolivar, Piso 15, Caracas. www.conac.org.ve.

MARTHA ESCALONA ZERPA is a Berlin-based freelance film critic and freelance journalist.

Other Countries

BENIN

The tiny cinematic output of Benin – a dozen films since the mid-1970s – has hitherto been dominated by two Paris-based exiles. The actor-turned-director, Jean Odoutan, has made four features, most of which are comedies set in the immigrant community in Paris, where he now lives. Idrissou Mora-Kpaï, who received his film training in Germany, has directed two intriguing pseudo-documentaries about return trips to a homeland he left at the age of nineteen.

In 2007, another two Paris-based Benin filmmakers appeared on the scene. Sanvi Panou, best known as the founder of Cinémas d'ailleurs, a much-respected cinema devoted to independent work from the third world, directed **The Amazonian Candidate** (*L'Amazone Candidate*); a sympathetic documentary study of the lawyer Marie-Élise Gbedo, as she attempts to become Benin's president. The film offers real insight into the rituals of political campaigning in a tiny country that remains committed to democracy.

Sylvestre Amoussou, another ex-actor who has already made a number of fictional shorts, directed **Africa Paradise** (*Africa paradis*), a fascinating comic fantasy set twenty-five years into the future. The economic growth of Africa has outstripped that of a declining Europe so much that the whites have become the clandestine immigrants in a prosperous, and sometimes prejudiced, black African community. The role-reversal provokes fascinating insights into the hollowness of conventional assumptions, as well as some wonderfully humorous moments. – *Roy Armes*

BURKINA FASO

Burkina Faso, the centre of francophone African filmmaking, is also the home of one of Africa's greatest filmmakers, Idrissa Ouedraogo. He has spent his career constantly seeking to reinvent both himself and his film style, without ever quite repeating the world acclaim that greeted his first three 'country' films, **Yam daabo**, **Yaaba** and **Tilai**, in the late 1980s. The action of his ninth and latest film, **Kato Kato**, is aptly captured by the film's French title, 'Misfortunes Never Come Singly'. Ali is a schoolteacher plagued by ill-fortune. As well as his daughter's illness and his own financial problems, he kills a woman in a car accident. But, like all Ouedraogo's protagonists, he strives desperately to make things right.

Other recent Burkinabè films include Issa Traoré de Brahima's **The World is a Ballet** (*Le monde est un ballet*), about a singing star driven mad by the death of her husband on their honeymoon, and newcomer Tahirou Tasséré Ouedraogo's **Djanta**, the tale of an educated young woman's attempt to avoid an arranged marriage and her struggles for women's liberation in a patriarchal society.

But the real novelty of the last year is the attempt by newspaper head and popular novelist, Boubakar Diallo, to industrialise audiovisual production, following the Nigerian pattern and using high-definition video. Since 2003, Diallo has poured out a stream of short fictions, television serials and feature-length works, all in the formats of popular commercial drama: thrillers, detective stories, village dramas and African westerns. This is a first for Francophone West Africa, and at least one of the feature-length works, *Code Phénix* (2005), has been transferred to 35mm film and was

shown in competition at the major African film festival, FESPACO, in Ougadouga in 2007.
– *Roy Armes*

CAMEROON

For the past thirty years, Cameroon has averaged one film a year, mostly with French dialogue because of the country's ethnic and linguistic diversity. But in 2006 three new Cameroonian directors made their appearance. Jude Ntsimenkou's **Urban Jungle** deals with the impact of drug gangs on the immigrant community in the Paris suburbs. Both Ghislain Fotso's powerful AIDS drama, **The Broken Dream** (*Le Rêve brisé*), and Cyrille Masso's **Just Say No** (*Confidences*) are set in Cameroon. In the latter, the narrator tells of the poverty in which he grew up, with an unemployed father and sick younger sister, and also of the unhappy outcome of his efforts to put things right.

The major news was the return, after a hiatus of ten years, of Jean-Pierre Bekolo. A maverick director, Bekolo's first features, **Quartier Mozart** and **Aristotle's Plot** (*Le Complot d'Aristote*), set the pattern for a new style of experimental and semi-autobiographical work so characteristic of many of the younger African filmmakers, such as Mahamet Saleh Haroun and Abderrahmane Sissako. **Bloody Women** (*Les Saignantes*) is in the same vein as Bekolo's previous work, mixing sexuality and magic, fantasy and horror, in a narrative that never aspires to be coherent. – *Roy Armes*

CHAD

The film output of Chad is tiny, just five features, all made during the past decade by two filmmakers. Both Issa Serge Coelo and Mahamet-Saleh Haroun were born after independence, completed their film training in Europe and now live in exile in Paris. Coelo, the more directly political of the two, has followed his courageous study of civil war in

Africa, *Daresalam*, with a new feature, **Tartina City**, which looks at the grim heritage of imprisonment and torture stemming from the military dictatorships that have plagued Chad for decades. *Tartine City* draws an ambiguous portrait of the brutal governor, Koulboul, who seeks in torture the pleasures denied him with women as a result of his impotence. The film is uncompromising in its presentation of torture, but these scenes are inter-cut with conventional action-film footage featuring one of the victims, as well as documentary and fantasy sequences. Coelo's work is extremely ambitious in seeking to find narrative patterns and stylistic forms to depict a subject matter that, because of its violence, is almost un-filmable.

Mahamat-Saleh Haroun's **Daratt**

While Coelo is an uneven filmmaker whose approach sometimes appears clumsy, the internationally distributed Haroun is, by contrast, the epitome of a polished stylist. His early work is an eclectic mix of varied subject matter and diverse formats, with each of his three feature films displaying a distinctive stylistic approach. After the ambiguous mixture of documentary and fiction in *Bye Bye Africa* and the gently nuanced approach to childhood dreams in *Abouna*, Haroun's new feature, **Daratt**, is almost deadpan. His subject is also violence, but he approaches it obliquely, reducing the on-screen action to a minimum. The underlying tensions in the story of a young man sent by his grandfather to avenge his father's murder are always evident, but emotion restrained. Unable to shoot Nassara when he first meets him, Atim is instead drawn into his family and becomes his apprentice. In turn, Nassara gradually becomes a surrogate father. The film's ending points towards possible acceptance and reconciliation. Haroun's strength is his ability to depict precisely the unspoken ties that bind people, often against their will. With *Daratt*, he seals his reputation as one of the leading filmmakers of his generation. – *Roy Armes*

COSTA RICA

2007 has been a transformative year for the Costa Rican film industry. For the first time the government, the private sector and film producers joined together to develop a strategy that aims to attract foreign capital through the creation of a film commission and to foster local production through Ibermedia, the most important pan-regional film fund in Iberoamérica. Costa Rica also recently joined the DOCTV IB, which seeks to encourage cultural and economic exchange amongst Ibero-American countries.

In terms of film production, Daniel Ross and Julio Molina's feature-length documentary, **Dear Camilo** (*Querido Camilo*), tells the story of their old schoolmate, Camilo Mejia, who became the first deserter of the Iraq war. Mejia, a Costa Rican, spent a year in prison, following which he became a pacifist. The film is one of 15 documentaries made for public television across Iberoamérica/Latin America.

In Ishtar Yasin's feature, **The Road** (*El camino*), two boys flee Nicaragua and travel along one of the main migrant routes into Costa Rica, in search of their mother. The film dissolves the boundary between fiction and documentary, dealing with issues such as child abuse, while refusing to negate Nicaraguan values and traditions.

Four films are planned for release in 2008. **The King of Cha-Cha-Cha** (*El rey del cha-cha-cha*) by Isabel Martinez and Vicente Ferraz

presents an account of Paco Jarquín, the notorious tenth commander of the Sandinista revolution, played by renowned Mexican actor, Damián Alcázar; Jarquín abandoned his revolutionary ideals and embarked on a life of anonymity. Miguel Gomez's **The Red Sky** (*El cielo rojo*) focuses on a young group's passage from adolescence to adulthood and the pain it entails. **Three Marias** (*Tres Marías*) by Francisco Gonzalez is an urban drama centring on three women faced with drugs, violence and prostitution in contemporary San José. Cesar Caro's **Third World** (*Tercer mundo*) presents three stories that take place in Chile, Bolivia and Costa Rica, and offer a deeper reflection on the countries' identities. Other productions loom on the horizon, including the adaptation of Hilda Hidalgo's novel, **About Love and Other Evils** (*Del amor y otros demonios*) scheduled for February 2008. If all of these films are completed on time, 2008 will be a record year for Costa Rican cinema, which has produced less than 15 fiction films in the last century.

By **MARIA LOURDES CORTÉS** who teaches film at the Universidad de Costa Rica and directs the Film and Television School of the Veritas University and the Cinergia audiovisual foundation. The most recent of her numerous books on Costa Rican and Central American cinema is *La pantalla rota. Cien años de cine en Centroamérica* (2005).

CYPRUS

Filmmaking in Cyprus, although minimal, has been aided and encouraged over the past few years by the Ministry of Culture. However, with a budget of only €600,000 for each production, approved and allocated by a special committee, most feature filmmakers are forced to look elsewhere for additional funding. Most applicants turn to the Greek Film Centre in Athens, as well as ERT, the Greek national television channel. Andreas Pantzis' **Evagora's Vow** and Christos Siopahas'

Akamas, *directed by Panikos Chrissanthou*

Red Thursday were both funded this way. In all, during the period 2003-2007, 61 projects (feature films, shorts and script development) were approved.

Three Cypriot films were completed in the last two years: **Akamas** (*Akamas, mia istoria agapis*) by Panikos Chrissanthou, **Honey and Wine** by Marinos Kartikkis and **Hi I'm Erica** by Yiannis Ioannou, which is awaiting release. *Akamas* deals with religious and racial prejudice. It centres on the relationship between a Turkish Cypriot boy and a Greek Cypriot girl, commencing during the so-called 'innocent' years on the island and continuing through the insurgence against British rule, finally reaching the conflict that broke out between the two indigenous communities. Chrissanthou, who began his career in documentary (*Our Wall*), bypasses political problems, focusing instead on the human side of his story, as the couples' attempts to live in peace. Excepting the ingenious use of a narrator-poet, the film suffers from unconvincing dialogue and too narrow a narrative focus to do anything but offer a superficial presentation of events.

The relationship between two women of different ages is at the centre of *Honey and Wine*. A middle-aged nurse living alone, with only the memories of her dead son to keep her company, gradually opens up to a young actress who lives in the house opposite. Kartikkis has created a low-key, atmospheric

film, subtly observing the women in their daily routine and adopting a naturalistic style to record their behaviour towards each other.

A number of significant short films were also produced, some of which represented Cyprus at various international festivals. These included Ioakim Mylonas' Pharmacon (Venice Film Festival), **In the Name of the Sparrow** (*Gia to onoma tou spourgitiou*) by Kyros Papavassiliou (Cannes Film Festival) and Johnny Kevorkian's **Fractured**. *– Ninos-Fenek Mikelidis*

DUBAI

Dubai Studio City (DSC), a member of TECOM Investments, was launched in February 2005 as an ultra-modern, fully integrated facility. Spread across 22 million square feet, it houses sound stages, boutique studios, film, TV and audio production facilities, warehouses and production support spaces. There will also be a business centre, hospitality facilities, residential and cinema complexes, theatres and performance areas, as well as academies for film, TV, radio, animation and interactive gaming. 90% of the DSC infrastructure was in place by the middle of 2007, with the rest expected to be completed by 2008. Overall, the DSC will accelerate the growth of film production and broadcast industries in Dubai.

Following a decree issued by the Dubai Executive Council in May 2007, DSC's Location Approval Services (LAS) serves as a single window for film production permits and visas, expediting and facilitating all aspects of filming in Dubai and the United Arab Emirates. So far this year, the LAS has supported 18 film projects, with several more scheduled before the end of the year. Recent productions include Izidore Musallam's *Kef Al Hal*, featuring Hisham Abdul Rahman, and Stephen Gaghan's acclaimed political thriller, *Syriana*.

Dubai, like many other locations previously not included on the filmmaking map, can now boast indigenous talent whose skills are more essential than ever in attracting international business. The Indian film, *Partner*, directed by David Dhawan and starring Salman Khan was handled by Pink House Productions, while Final Cut Productions were responsible for *Anadaleeb Al Dokki*, an Egyptian production directed by Wael Esham and starring Mohamed Henedi.

The Dubai government's ongoing support for the development of the film industry has contributed to Dubai's profile as a compelling destination for the global film and entertainment industry. With the state-of-the-art Dubai Studio City fully functional and a wealth of locations only a stone's throw away, film production is guaranteed to increase.
– *Ian Haydn Smith*

FIJI

Since 2005, when Fiji submitted Vilsoni Hereniko's *The Land Has Eyes* as their official entry for the Best Foreign Language Film prize at the Academy Awards, little has happened in terms of local production.

The American action thriller, *Boot Camp*, directed by Christian Duguay, was shot here in 2006. Thanks, among other factors, to Fiji's appealing tax incentives, Dean and Harrison Zanuck, scions of a renowned Hollywood dynasty, have announced plans to produce a series of medium-budget movies here.

The Fiji Audio Visual Commission (www.fijiaudiovisual.com), which supports all film and TV projects, has announced that the Fiji Film Festival will be held in early 2009. After consulting with various Asian and European festival organisers, chairman Richard Broadbridge said that 'we have the capacity to organise this locally'. He hopes that the festival will serve as a tool for the development of the audiovisual industry in Fiji and will hopefully boost the number of tourists who visit the country.

The TFL Kula Film Awards, a filmmaking competition open to schools and supported by the local TV network, has announced that the best short films from the competition will be made available online (www.tfl.kulafilmawards.com.fj). The hope is to use the competition to encourage new talent. Hopefully, some of these gifted English-speaking filmmakers will soon find their way to stardom, either at home or abroad. – *Lorenzo Codelli*

GUATEMALA

Since 2003, Guatemalan cinema has experienced a gradual increase in filmmaking activity, with the production of one film a year. Casa Comal, responsible for producing Elías Jiménez's *The House in Front* in 2003 and Rafael Rosal's *The Crosses, Next Town* in 2005, were once again behind Jiménez's new film, **Vip, the other House** (*Vip, la otra casa*), the follow-up to his debut, which also dealt with political corruption. It was shot inside one of the most dangerous prisons in the country, with five professional actors, two cameras and the support of the police and the prison inmates. It tells the story of Juan Ramos, sub-general of the nation, who is arrested and, while attempting to prove his innocence on charges of corruption and murder, interned in the most violent sector of the prison, Jiménez's film deals with the problematic issue of civil violence, which is more rife now than during the country's conflict. There are more violent killings today than there were during the civil war in the 1980s and 1990s.

The most important event in Guatemalan cinema this year, not to mention Central America as a whole, is Julio Hernández Cordón's success in winning two awards at the San Sebastián Film Festival, for **Gasoline** (*Gasolina*). Of particular importance is the Film in Progress award, which allows Hernández Cordón to complete post-production on the film, opening the gateway to other festivals. *Gasoline* is a road movie with no destination. Three adolescents steal gasoline in order to drive around at night. When their friendship is put to the test, they have no choice but to face the reality of their situation. The film highlights the lack of any driving force or goals for contemporary youth; all that matters is the ride, the sense of movement – fed by the gasoline – and not the destination.

This rebirth of a national cinema, which has previously had no legal or financial framework supporting it, has led to the recent establishment of the Guatemalan Audio-visual and Cinematography Association (AGAcine), the first step to the construction of a real audiovisual industry. – *Maria Lourdes Cortés*

IVORY COAST

Henri Duparc, who died on 18 April 2006, was a leading figure in Ivoirian, indeed in African, filmmaking. The Ivory Coast's film culture began with a small group of students studying at the Paris film school, IDHEC. Duparc was a part of this group – along with Désiré Écaré and Bassori Timité – playing a leading role in Écaré's celebrated *Concerto for an Exile*. But on his return home, Duparc founded his own production company and made a mixture of short fictions and documentaries for the local market. When, in 1972, he directed his first 35mm feature, *The Family*, he was well aware of the need to find a way of weaning African audiences away from their customary diet of imported Western films. His first two features drew large audiences in Abidjan but gained little critical attention.

His international break-through came in 1988 with the comedy, *Bal poussière*. This tale of a spirited young woman, Binta, forced against her will to marry an older man who already has five wives, set the pattern for Duparc's subsequent career in its mockery of traditional African attitudes and assumptions, particularly with regard to women. The husband's plan is clear: a night for each wife (no problem there) and Sunday for the one who behaves best. But Binta creates havoc among the wives,

exploiting her youth and beauty, finally eloping with a young lover. Duparc's subsequent three features –*The Sixth Finger*, *Rue Princesse* and *Coffee Coloured* – all followed a similar pattern and delighted African audiences, who enjoyed seeing male pretension and the accompanying false sense of superiority deflated by spirited young women. Duparc possessed a keen insight into African sexual mores and a great sense of humour. At his death he left a completed, but unreleased, seventh feature, *Caramel*. – *Roy Armes*

KYRGYZSTAN

Even with the incendiary political climate in Kyrgyzstan, Kyrgyz directors have been working hard to enable the strategic development of a national cinema. The manifesto representing their aims consists of twelve points, describing in detail the route by which a national cinema can be achieved, from the lack of support for filmmaking in Kyrgyz legislation and the necessary development of a financial structure to fund Kyrgyz filmmaking, to an infrastructure that can properly market and distribute Kyrgyz films. The programme sets out plans that extend until 2010 and, although there is currently no state funding of films, it is proposed that an average of five films be produced each year, with the support of the government.

Talgat Asyrankulov and Gaziz Nasyrov's **The Birds of Paradise**

2006 saw the release of Talgat Asyrankulov and Gaziz Nasyrov's domestic success, **The Birds of Paradise** (*Zyma Kystary*). Co-produced by Kazakhstan and Kyrgyzstan, the film tells the story of a group of young people involuntarily carrying drugs across the border between Kyrgyzstan and Tajikistan.

Ernest Abdyzhaparov's **Light Breath** (*Boz Salkyn*) was one of the most successful Kyrgyz films on record. A lyrical melodrama, with elements of comedy, it tells the story of a young bride-to-be who is kidnapped, but soon finds true love. It was awarded two prizes at international festivals: the Grand Prix in the 'Central Asian' section of the Eurasia Film Festival in Kazakhstan, and the prize for the best distribution, as well as being nominated for the Grand Prize at the Cottbus Film Festival of Young Eastern European Cinema.

One of the most remarkable films of recent years was directed by Gennadiyi Bazarov. **Metamorphosis** (*Metamorphozy*) takes place in a small restaurant, away from the city. With their eyes covered, people enter into a variation of Russian Roulette, whereby each participant has to choose a drink on the table in front of them. Only fate will decide whether the glass they have chosen contains wine or potassium cyanide. The stakes are raised when a woman visiting the restaurant, who placed bets on a previous game, decides to become a participant. A documentary approach to the representation of contemporary Kyrgysztan adds to the power of the film.

The future of cinema in Kyrgyzstan lies in the graduates of the film school that opened last year. The first 15 students produced nine short films. Kyrgyzstan also hosted two international film festivals: Kinostan (a seminar-based programme) and the Festival of the Shanghai Cooperation Organisation (Kazakhstan, Kyrgyzstan, Tajikistan, Uzbekistan, Russia and China).

Future films include Aktan Arym Kubat's **Light**, Marat Sarulu's psychological drama, **Song of the Southern Seas**, Marat Alykulov's youth drama, **Adep Akhlak**, and a portmanteau film, **Sem' Novel o Revolutsii**, featuring the work of seven directors, focusing on the March 2005 revolution. – *Gulnara Gabikeyev*

MALTA

The unspoiled coastline and diverse architecture of Malta, Gozo and Comino have doubled on screen for everything from ancient Rome to the Port of Charleston, North Carolina. The islands continued to attract international film and television productions in 2006–07, many drawn in by the Malta Film Commission, the government-funded body charged with attracting visiting productions and facilitating their work on the island. The Commission has revised its audiovisual financial-incentives scheme to constitute a cash rebate of up to 22% on EU-eligible expenditure in Malta by qualifying productions.

Visiting productions in 2006 included the one-off British TV drama *What We Did on Our Holiday*, starring Pauline Collins, in which a British family experiences a revelatory excursion on the island. *Roman Mysteries*, a British TV series in which Maltese locations

stood in for Rome, Pompeii and Ostia, shot for 54 days in 2006. The following year, *Roman Mysteries II* spent 15 days on scenes set in ancient Rome.

Overall, 2007 was busier than the previous year, with more than 175 shooting days in its first ten months. It included a three-week stay by Giacomo Campeotto and his crew for the Danish family adventure sequel, **The Lost Treasure of the Knights Templar III: The Mystery of the Snake Crown** (*Tempelriddernes skat III: mysteriet om slangekronen*), in which the four young heroes of the popular feature series travel to Malta. In January, the UK/Germany co-production feature **Eichmann**, directed by Robert Young and starring Franka Potente and Stephen Fry, used Malta to double for Israel. Jérôme Salle's $39 million graphic-novel adaptation, **Largo Winch**, an adventure story set in the Balkans, was on Malta for 30 days in 2007, and the Russian feature **Man of East** (*Chelovek vostoka*), directed by Oleg Pogodin, used Malta as 'itself' for seven weeks.

Eichmann, *directed by Robert Young*

The water tanks at Malta's Mediterranean Film Studios continued to host commercials and examples of the genre that has been the facility's staple for decades – naval and submarine dramas – with the German TV series *The Sinking of the Gusfoff*.

Indigenous production is still almost non-existent, but a local documentary did appear in Maltese cinemas late in 2007. **Heroes in the Sky – The Pilots Who Saved the**

Mediterranean, written, produced and directed by Engelbert Grech, told the story of British, Commonwealth and American WWII fighter aces who defended Malta, then 'the most bombed place on earth', and 'shot down Hitler's hopes of conquering North Africa', through interviews with veteran pilots and historians, archive footage and CGI sequences.

By **DANIEL ROSENTHAL** who was Editor of *International Film Guide* from 2002 to 2006. He is the author of *100 Shakespeare Films* (2007) and is currently writing *The NT Story*, a history of the National Theatre of Great Britain.

MAURITANIA

Mauritania's film output of just 14 films in 35 years is essentially the work of two filmmakers, both exiles living in Paris, but a generation apart, in terms of age and approach. Med Hondo is one of the great survivors of French cinema, whose first pioneering anti-colonial feature, *Soleil O*, dates from 1971. Since then he has produced a further seven feature-length fiction films and documentaries. He is reportedly actively engaged on a new feature, *Premier des noirs: Toussaint Louverture*, about the eighteenth-century Haitian leader.

Nothing could be further from Hondo's openly committed, left-wing stance than the nuanced approach of his younger compatriot, Abderrahmane Sissako, though the latter learned his filmmaking at the Soviet film school in Moscow. Both have won the top African film festival prize, the Étalon de Yennega at FESPACO, Hondo with *Sarraounia* in 1987 and Sissako with *Heremakono* in 2003. Sissako's style is, in general, more poetic than polemical. However, his latest, internationally shown feature, **Bamako**, is the most overt expression to date of his political beliefs. Like all his films, *Bamako* is intensely autobiographical – it was shot in the house that belonged to his late father. But at its

Abderrahmane Sissako's **Bamako**

core is an international trial, which rigorously examines the injustices inflicted by the West on Africa. Full of impassioned argument and shot in quasi-documentary style, it is set in the courtyard of the house, where ordinary life goes on unaltered: families eat, children go to school, couples meet and break up, and a wife finds that her singing career destroys her marriage. A unique tension is set up between the rhetoric of accusation and everyday African reality. Despite his engagement with the question of Africa's future, Sissako is incapable of constructing a simple linear narrative. As such, the film includes a startling spaghetti western pastiche involving the American actor Danny Glover, Israeli filmmaker Elia Suleiman and Congolese director, Zeka Laplaine. The sequence was, Sissako tells us, intended as a metaphor for the involvement of Africans themselves in the processes that continue to hold back the development of the continent.
– *Roy Armes*

NAMIBIA

The most notable local production in recent years has been Charles Burnett's **Namibia: Struggle for Liberation**, a controversial feature film about Sam Nujoma, the first president of Namibia. Shockwaves were sent through the local film industry when it became apparent that the Namibian government had allocated all the resources of the Film and Video Fund to the film. The Filmmakers Association of Namibia (FAN) reacted by distancing itself from the fund, which comes

under the auspices of the Pan African Centre for Namibia (Pacon).

It was revealed in the Namibian National Assembly during 2006 that the government made the decision to allocate an additional $7 million of taxpayers' money to keep the project afloat, on top of the initial $2 million grant. In a country that faces many dire socio-economic challenges, such a production budget has been regarded as outrageous. The feature eventually cost over $12 million. Many filmmakers felt that this amount should have been used to assist the entire film industry and not just one project.

Over almost three hours, the film details the epic struggle to free the country from South African occupation. It received its world premiere at the 2007 Los Angeles International Film Festival to decidedly mixed reviews. Despite the presence of American actors Carl Lumbly and Danny Glover, the film has been described as a formless, flaccid saga that shows too much attention to facts and too little to dramatics. A bland, state-approved production, Nujoma is apparently unhappy with the depiction of indigenous people and the way certain dialects have been used. In general it is felt that the film lacks authenticity.

A shorter version is being prepared for international markets in order to recoup on the investment. It will be a tough film to market as

Charles Burnett

a large portion of the dialogue is in Afrikaans, Oshiwambo, Otjiherero and German.

Elsewhere, international productions – including documentaries, commercials, feature films and television series – shot in Namibia are reported to have increased from an annual rate of 80 in 1999 and 83 in 2000, to over 100 in 2007.

For local filmmakers the problem of finance and funding, as well as a lack of government incentives, remains a big issue for Namibian producers trying to make a living. The film industry is currently divided into the service industry based in Swakopmund and the local industry based in Windhoek.

During 2007, the Namibian government allocated $90,000 to the Film and Video Fund. However, most of this money will be invested in the new television soap series, 'The Ties That Bind', for the Namibian Broadcasting Corporation. The soap is produced by Optimedia, one of the production companies involved in the Sam Nujoma feature film. – *Martin P. Botha*

NEPAL

The Nepali film industry, which was in a catastrophic state during the period of insurgency, had significantly recovered by late 2006. Filmmaking has dramatically increased, while some innovative experiments have been introduced.

Like many of the arts, the film industry stabilised shortly after the Maoist Communist Party of Nepal (CPN) legitimised itself in mainstream politics. There is still much for the industry to regain, however, in order for it to return to the level of success it achieved prior to the appearance of the CPN.

Last year, the former rebels invested in more than a half dozen films, with only one, Badri Adhikari's **The Voice** (*Aawaj*), showing any traction with local audiences.

Narayan Puri, whose previous film, **The Fire** (*Aago*) was released during the political strife and was heavily censored, returned with a political film, **Alpaviram**, based on the insurgency and counter insurgency between the government and the rebels. It features popular actors Sunil Pokhrel and Bijaya Lama, and ultimately the film attempts to deliver a message of peace.

Recent films have been made in many of the local dialects, including Bhojpuri, Newari, Gurung, Tamang, Magar, and Tharu. Most of these films were shown only to the specific regional groups they were made for. However, they gained more publicity following the first Film Festival of Indigenous Nationalities, organised in Kathmandu in June 2007. Altogether, 17 films were screened in the festival, among them **Kripa** in Gurung, **Minj** in Newari, and **Bhagyake Rekha** in Bhojpuri.

Of the more widely seen films, Narayan Puri's **The Guts** (*Himmat*) featured popular actress, Rekha Thapa, and the first *Indian Pop Idol* winner, Abhijit Sawant. Puri is believed to be

Actor Rajesh Hamal

following that film's success with a sequel featuring the Nepalese singing sensation of the new series of *Indian Pop Idol*, Prashant Tamang.

Meanwhile the government censored Dinesh Karki's **Aahankar**, concerned that it may fuel racial conflict between various ethnic groups. Karki's response was clear: 'We all are Nepali, though we might belong to Madhesi, Pahadi or Himali.' Although released uncut, it is the first Nepalese film to be given an adults-only rating.

Film production in Nepal has finally started to make moves towards digital technology. **Kagbeni**, dealing with youths who leave for foreign countries, will be released shortly. Music-video director Bhusan Dahal has attracted reasonable attention for the technology used to make the film.

2007 saw some interesting documentaries, the best of which were **We, the People of Remote Corner** (*Hami Kunaka Manchhe*), based on Nepal's slowly developing communities, and **Forgive! Forget Not!** (*Chaama Deu! Tara Nabirsa*), based on the story of journalist Bhairaja Ghimire, who was arrested, tortured and detained by soldiers for fifteen months.

By **PRABESH SUBEDI** who is a reporter with *Kantipur Daily*, Nepal's largest-selling newspaper. He is also the editor of the e-magazine *Filmnepal.com*.

PANAMA

As unbelievable as it may seem, Panamanian cinema has not seen a domestic feature film since the middle of last century, when Carlos and Rosendo Ochoa directed *When the Illusion Dies* in 1949. Sadly, that film has not survived. However, the country has been the setting for several North American super-productions, including the next James Bond film. With its estimated budget of $100 million, it will bring income and experience to the country.

For the last two years, the producers' association, Asocine, has been attempting to introduce a law for the promotion and development of the movie and audiovisual industry. Asocine has also approached Ibermedia, the most important Latin American filmmaking fund, and Doctv-Latin America, which promotes documentary filmmaking in the region.

This has enabled a series of projects to materialise. **Family** is the first feature documentary by the talented producer, Enrique Castro Ríos. Having cut his teeth on short films, here he tackles the issues surrounding the enlargement of the Panama Canal and its consequences for one family. It is illustrated by a journey along the canal. By means of this trip, the documentary looks into the concept of development: what is understood by the term and whether it is actually at the service of people or whether people are merely pawns in the notion of development.

A full-length feature film is finally in production. With support from Ibermedia, producer Luis Franco is preparing **The Sigh of the Ugly One**, starring the actor, singer and current Minister of Tourism, Ruben Blades, which is set on an island where all the men are cripples and whose mayor, a swindler and crook, exercises control over every aspect of the islanders' lives. Each year, the villagers choose their carnival queen, except for this year, when the daughter of the mayor decides it is her turn.

Other productions include **The King of the Angels**, by Eduardo Verdumen, and **Treasure in Panama**, by Luis Palomo and Javier Arias. There is also the documentary **Of Employees and Bosses**, by Abner Benain.

In a country previously regarded as little more than a location for Hollywood films, these projects already foresee the growth of a real industry, hopefully soon to appear on international screens. – *Maria Lourdes Cortés*

PARAGUAY

Things seem to be moving faster in Paraguayan cinema, after a long 'siesta' that made this country one of the few in South America without a thriving system of film production. At least five new titles, both fiction and documentaries, were released in the last two years, and many other projects are in different stages of development.

The positive reception of Paraguayan films at international festivals, where they have won important prizes, is also a good omen. This special moment comes after a period of two decades, especially after the recovery of democracy, when many individual efforts were made to develop a sustained system of audiovisual production, and quite a lot of videos were made, but only a few had any real impact on the public and critics.

It seems that a new generation is taking advantage of digital technologies that make it easier to produce with low budgets, and are using them to express themselves in elaborate and risky works that are catching the attention of critics and festival programmers. This is precisely the case with **Paraguayan Hammock** (*Hamaca paraguaya*), directed by newcomer María Paz Encina, which made a strong impact on the international festival circuit, receiving numerous awards, starting with the FIPRESCI Prize in the 'Un Certain Regard' section at Cannes in 2006. It was also a big domestic success, with 50,000 tickets sold, quite a record for a local title. It was justly considered one of the most interesting films produced in many years.

With its rigorous, austere and distant style, it seemed more related to independent Argentine filmmakers, like Lisandro Alonso (*La Libertad, Los muertos*), than previous Paraguayan films. The connection with independent Argentine cinema is strengthened by the participation of well-known producer Lita Stantic and photographer Willi Behnisch who designed its unusual images.

Paz Encina's **Paraguayan Hammock**

Although one can find various influences, from Becket to Asian cinema, it is also profoundly Paraguayan in its cultural and historical references. The story is quite simple and diaphanous: an old couple, who live in the forest, are waiting for their son to come back. The year is 1935, and he is fighting in the Chaco War, a cruel conflict between Paraguay and Bolivia, in the selvatic region.

These old and poor farmers, Cándida (Georgina Genes) and Ramón (Ramón del Río), are also permanently waiting for the rain to come, for the sultry weather to freshen, for their dog to stop barking, and for something to change in their monotonous lives. While they are waiting, they talk (in guaraní language) do domestic chores, and sit in their hammock. Nothing really happens, as their son might be already dead, the distant thunder may not bring the desired rain, and the dog will not stop barking. The metaphor about Paraguayan society is as clear as it is imposing, and transcends the minimal story, to reflect a hope, the passing of time, and the futility of human actions. Using non-professional actors, a static camera, long takes and very slow rhythm, it challenges the viewer, and might seem a bit over controlled, but the general impression is surprising and rewarding.

More conventional, but no less interesting, is the political thriller **Gunter's Winter** (*El invierno de Gunter*), also by a female director, Galia Gimenez, who had already made other video productions: *Réquiem por un soldado* (literally: 'Requiem for a soldier'), a romantic drama about two old ex-fighters who remember their experience during the war against Bolivia (1932-35), and *María Escobar*, an engaging story about a young woman who migrates from the countryside to the capital, Asunción.

Set in the 1970s, and based on a novel by Juan Manuel Marcos, her new work presents the drama of Gunter, a Paraguayan with German origins, who works for the World Bank, and has to come back to try to help his niece, Dolores, who has been detained by the regime of the dictator, General Alfredo Stroessner. It is one of the first direct references in Paraguayan cinema to the time of the strongman who reigned over the country for more than four decades (1954–1989).

Documentary production has also increased in recent years, giving the sense that, through these materials, Paraguayans are finally discovering their own reality. This is the case with **Red Land** (*Tierra roja*), directed by Ramiro Gómez, who with sensibility and using an almost anthropological approach, explores the difficulties of the everyday lives of some indigenous families. The film received a prize as Best Documentary at the Mar del Plata Film Festival in 2007.

The passion for cinema is at the heart of **Profesión cinero**, directed by Hugo Gamarra, who presents the story of Tito Vero, a projectionist who for decades toured with his truck all over the country, bringing magic and entertainment to the people in remote villages. Gamarra has directed *El portón de los sueños*, about the famous writer Augusto Roa Bastos, and is a well-known promoter of film culture in Paraguay, creating the Cinematheque Foundation and directing, since its creation sixteen years ago, the International Film Festival of Paraguay.

Other recent productions made on video are: *Carimea*, a drama directed by Ray Armele, and starring Ana Imizcoz, about a woman with mental problems who is accused of a

horrible crime; *Acople*, an ironic portrait of young and disoriented couples in the streets of Asunción during a Saturday night, using hand-held 'Dogme-style' camerawork, by creative filmmakers Augusto Netto and Rafael Cohan (*Rechts-Links*); *Detrás del sol, más cielo* (literally: 'Behind the Sun, More Sky'), directed by Argentine Gastón Gularte and presents the struggle of young people trying to construct a future and find love in the frontier between Paraguay and argentinean province of Misiones; *Cenizas* (*Ashes*), a documentary by Virginia Ferreira and Eduardo Mora about the last steam train still active in the world; and *El amigo Dunor*, a co-production with Brazil, directed by José Eduardo Alcazar, which presents the story of a French writer involved in the production of a film that is being shot in the selvatic frontier with Paraguay.

All this intense activity is going on with little support from the government, and while a Cinema and Audiovisual Law that will create an official institute and a fund for film production is still being debated in Parliament. With a little market, and only 500,000 tickets sold each year, it is almost impossible to finance a 35mm film without foreign co-producers. But there is no doubt that these difficulties will not stop this new generation of filmmakers, who with talent and determination have demonstrated that they are here to stay. – *Alfredo Friedlander and Jorge Jellinek*

PUERTO RICO

Thanks to the government-backed Puerto Rico Film Fund, the wheels of the local film industry are rolling once again. The Fund, which grants interest-free production loans of as much as 80% of a film's budget, to a maximum of $1.2 million, has been instrumental in increasing local production to six films per year over the past two years. The most successful project supported by the Fund to date has been writer-producer Pedro Muñiz's *Cayo*, which was released in October 2005. **Liars and Thieves** (*Ladrones y mentiro-*

sos), the next released film supported by the Fund, opened locally in early 2006. Co-directed by Ricardo Méndez Matta and his wife and co-writer, Poli Marichal, the $1.47 million drama starred Cuban-American actor Steven Bauer.

Another Fund-supported project released in 2006 was the first official Hispano-Boricua (Spain-Puerto Rico) co-production, **Water with Salt** (*Agua con sal*). Directed by Spaniard Pedro Pérez Rosado, it was co-produced by local producer John E. Viguié's production company, Viguié Films.

Other films released in 2006 include Santo Domingo-born writer-director César Rodríguez's **Noise** (*Ruido*), a film about a young girl confronted by a sexual predator, which garnered awards and glowing reviews on the festival circuit; the television movie **The Clown** (*El Clown*), a clever and original satire on success in the advertising world, which enjoyed a brief theatrical release; and **Nearly Nearly** (*Casi casi*), a small, independently produced teen comedy, directed by Jaime Vallés.

Sadly, despite the sudden increase in their numbers, Puerto Rican films are experiencing a tough time attracting audiences. This trend continued into 2007, with a number of locally produced theatrical releases struggling at the box office.

2007 kicked off with the release of Puerto Rico's first film shot and exhibited in the new High Definition format. Titled **The Runaway Slave** (*El Cimarrón*), writer-producer Iván Gonzalo Ortiz's historical drama, directed by his son Iván Dariel Ortiz, tells the story of a young African couple kidnapped and sold into slavery in 19th-century Puerto Rico.

Soon after, Puerto Rican actress-turned-producer Roselyn Sánchez's **Yellow** hit local screens. Starring Sánchez herself as a struggling young ballerina-turned-stripper, the film unfortunately failed to generate much sizzle at the local box office.

Veteran writer-director-actor Jacobo Morales, followed with the release of **Angel**, his first political thriller. Morales's 1989 film, *What Happened to Santiago*, was nominated for Best Foreign Language Film at the 1990 Academy Awards. *Angel* focuses on the tragic results of police corruption and political persecution in Puerto Rico.

In the fall of 2007, Puerto Rican director Diego de la Texera released **Meteor** (*Meteoro*). The $2.5 million feature film is the first official Carioca-Boricua (Brazil-Puerto Rico) co-production. Set in the 1960s, the film tells the story of a group of workers on the Brasilia-Fortaleza road, abandoned in the middle of the desert by the government following a military coup.

As the end of the year approaches, several films are already scheduled for theatrical release in 2008. The most promising appears to be director Carlos Ruiz Ruiz and co-director Marie Pérez Rivera's **Lovesickness** (*Maldeamores*), a three-part story 'about love of all kinds and ages set in the household backyard of Puerto Rico', which Puerto Rican-born actor Benicio del Toro executive produced. Following a two-week qualifying run – to packed houses – in two cinemas, the film was selected as Puerto Rico's official submission to the 2008 Academy Awards.

Other soon-to-be-released local projects include **Manuela and Manuel** (*Manuela y Manuel*), helmed by Puerto Rican director Raúl Marchand and written by Chilean-born screenwriter José Ignacio Valenzuela. This gender-reversal farce deals with the misadventures of Manuela, a transvestite who reinvents himself as Manuel when his best friend needs him to pass himself off as her fiancée.

Party Time, a teen comedy with lavish pop musical numbers written and directed by local film critic Juan Fernández Paris, deals with the 1980s high-school rivalry between 'Cocolos' (fans of Puerto Rican urban music) and 'Rockeros' (fans of US rock music).

Kabo and Platón (*Kabo y Platón*), directed by Edmundo H. Rodríquez from a screenplay by award-winning Puerto Rican novelist Mayra Santos-Febres, is a coming-of-age urban drama about two teenagers struggling to become Puerto Rico's next rap superstars.

Some 25 short films are currently in development, including two anthology projects: Studio 51's **Voices of Childhood** (*Voces de la niñez*) and **Ten on Music** (*Diez en la música*).

Steven Soderbergh's **The Argentine**, which traces the life of Che Guevara during the Cuban revolution and stars Benicio del Toro in the title role, recently completed filming on the island.

Puerto Rico Cinemafest, the island's 19-year-old international film festival, the Caguas-based Film Foundation's 5-year-old international festival for short films, Cine Fiesta, and Puerto Rico Horror Film Fest, the Island's first film festival focusing exclusively on the horror genre, all enjoyed successful runs this fall.

The Puerto Rico Film Fund's next call for submissions runs through January 2008 and will ensure a steady supply of local production for the near future.

By **RAUL RÍOS-DÍAZ**, a Puerto Rican filmmaker and writer. He heads the production company ALT165 and is the author of *Dominio de la Imagen: Hacia una industria de cine en Puerto Rico* (2000).

RWANDA

2007 saw the creation of the Amani Great Lakes Film Festival (AGLFF). Like the Rwanda Film Festival, which marked its third edition this year, the AGLFF seeks to promote peace in the politically turbulent central African region. The festival is presented by Urungano Youth and Media, a local non-governmental organisation funded by the German Development Agency.

Similar to the Rwanda Cinema Centre, which trains young people in filmmaking, the AGLFF will run courses on filmmaking for the young.

Among the films released in 2007, Gilbert Ndahayo's 30-minute **Behind the Convent** was particularly impressive. It is the emotional story of the Roman Catholic nuns who witnessed Ndahayo's parents, younger sister and two hundred other people massacred during the 1994 genocide. **Scars of Silver**, another film Ndahayo made in 2007, is based on stories of domestic violence and the abuse of a young girl, Nadine, who had managed to survive the genocide, but it remains unclear if she will survive the evil that awaits her. Jacques Rutabingwa followed a similar theme with his earlier work, **Isugi**, about another young girl who survived the genocide, but who is sexually abused by her adoptive father.

Michael Caton-Jones directed **Shooting Dogs** in Rwanda, about refugees who are abandoned by the United Nations, and are eventually murdered by the extremist militias in Kigali. **Shake Hands with the Devil**, directed by Peter Raymont, is about the man who was tasked by the UN with ensuring that peace was maintained in Rwanda, Canadian Lieutenant General Roméo Dallaire. But unsupported by UN headquarters in New York, Dallaire and his handful of soldiers were incapable of stopping the genocide. After ten years of mental torture, reliving the horrors daily and more than once attempting suicide, Dallaire wrote a book, detailing the journey he made to the killing fields that haunt him. – *Ogova Ondego*

SENEGAL

Once the leading innovator of film production in Francophone West Africa, Senegal has been far less prominent of late, with production down to just a couple of films a year and few new directors making an international impact. The multi-talented Moussa Sene Absa was unable to recapture the excitement of his previous production, *Madame Brouette*, in his new film **Teranga Blues**, which deals with the familiar tale of a young man returning home from France under police escort and entering a life of crime. The latest debuts, Cheikh Ndiaye's **Wrestling Grounds** (*L'appel des arenas*), about a convert to Senegalese wrestling ('lambb' in Wolof), and Masaër Dieng's **Bul déconné**, co-directed with Frenchman Marc Picavez and dealing with a mature student's conflict with the examination system, had a muted reception.

The major event in Senegalese cinema in 2007 was, of course, the death on 9 June of Ousmane Sembene, often called 'the father of African cinema'. Sembene lacked the academic background of most Francophone West African filmmakers – he dropped out of school at thirteen, working in a succession of manual jobs – but compensated for this with his powerful intellect and passionate political commitment. His creative talents first found expression in the French-language novel and he continued publishing until well into the 1990s, producing ten novels and collections of stories, many of them translated into English. He turned to filmmaking at the age of 38, in the hope of reaching a wider African audience, and through studying in Moscow with Mark Donskoi and Sergei Gerassimov, found the filmic equivalent of the realist style of his best writing, such as the novel *God's Bits of Wood* (1960). He announced his presence on the film scene with the short film *Borom Sarret* in 1963 and went on to create a series of eight varied and powerful features, ranging from the black comedy *The Money Order* to the historical study of Wolof resistance, *Ceddo*. If there seemed some slackening with 1999's *Faat-Kine*, he was on something near to his best form with his final feature, *Moolade*, in 2002.
– *Roy Armes*

SRI LANKA

Film in Sri Lanka has always been a subsidised industry, initially under the patronage of

a powerful cartel of film importers and distributors, who also controlled exhibition chains and financed a limited number of local productions. The situation improved when the government finally stepped in to nationalise import and distribution. Imports were curtailed, providing more screen time for the local films, while funding was made available through the state-owned People's Bank. However, with the onset of economic de-regulation in the late 1970s and an escalation of violence in the early 1980s, the Sri Lankan film industry lay in ruins and has never quite recovered.

On a more positive note, in recent years, young filmmakers have followed the path of pioneering filmmaker, Lester James Peries, as well as taking advantage of the widespread availability of new formats, finally creating something of a Sri Lankan film culture. The pinnacle came in 2005, when Vimukthi Jayasundera, a Paris-trained 27-year-old, won the Camera d'Or at Cannes for *The Forsaken Land*.

In the last two years, three films attracted praise and a significant local audience. Veteran (at 89 he is the most senior and honoured filmmaker of South Asia) Lester James Peries' **A Tribute to Mother** (*Ammavarunay*) is, like all his films, a beautifully crafted work of Bressonian understatement. Alluding to the brutality of war and its debilitating impact on familial relationships, Peries tells the story of a mother with two sons: one is a Buddhist monk, the other a soldier fighting in the war. She worries about her soldier son, while the priest worries about her.

Sunil Ariyaratne's **Uppalavanna** features a young Buddhist nun in a remote jungle retreat who happens upon a seriously wounded man seeking refuge in this sanctuary. Against the strict rules of abstinence and celibacy, she nurses him back to health, thus committing a criminal offence by protecting and harbouring a terrorist. Ariyaratne, a university don, poet and a veteran of eighteen films, overly sentimentalises her story, although this probably accounts for its success.

Impurities (*Sankara*) marks the directorial debut of Prasanna Jayakody and is almost abstract in its treatment of the conflict experienced by a young priest, painting a series of murals in a distant village temple. The least accessible of the three films, it nevertheless won two major awards in Cairo and Dacca.

All three films draw inspiration from Buddhist ethics and precepts of non-violence, reflection and impermanence. However, their combined success can only be the starting point for Sri Lankan film. The future remains bleak, as Lester James Peries notes: 'Having worked for over half-a-century in the Sri Lankan Cinema, it is my personal view that it never really was a stable industry nor was it a viable commercial proposition for the prospective entrepreneur. Caught at various periods between public-sector (government) control and private-sector monopoly, the industry drifted towards its doom. If there were any significant milestones, they were entirely due to the efforts of individual directors.'

By **TISSA ABEYSEKARA**, a filmmaker, writer, actor, academic and one time policymaker for film in Sri Lanka, as the Chairman, National Film Corporation between 1999 and 2001.

TAJIKISTAN

In the decade following the 1992-96 Civil War, during which most of the equipment belonging to Tajikfilm was destroyed, the Tajikistan film industry has been in a state of upheaval. Most practitioners left the country, resulting in an immigrant cinema of directors like Djamshed Usmonov and Bakhtiar Khudoinazarov. Only recently has the industry been finding its feet.

To Get to Heaven First You Have to Die (*Bihisht faqat baroi murdagon*) was directed by Djamshed Usmonov and screened in the 'Un Certain Regard' section at the 2006 Cannes

Jamshed Usmonov's **To Get to Heaven First You Have to Die**

Film Festival. The story focuses on 20-year-old Kamal, who is unable to have sexual intercourse, even with his wife. After finding out from his doctor that he has no physical problems, he embarks on a quest to find a new wife. Accurately reflecting the mood of the country – men's lack of confidence, the dependence of women, high levels of poverty and crime – *To Get to Heaven First You Have to Die* marks out Usmonov as an important director.

2006 also saw the production of two full-length features: **The Waiting** (*Owora*), directed by Gulandom Mukhabbatova and Daler Rakhmatov, and **Waiting Calendar** (*Kalendar Ozhidania*), directed by Safarbek Soliev. *The Waiting* focuses on the father of seven-year-old Abdullo, who travels to Russia, like thousands of other Tajiks, so he can earn money to send home. Abdullo is brought up by his grandmother and blind grandfather. When it is time for his circumcision, there is not enough money to pay for the celebratory feast. His father's friend arrives with money for the family, pretending it came from Abdullo's father, who is actually in prison. *Waiting Calendar* takes place over the course of one day in a mountainous village, where Samad-akha is finally reunited with his neighbour, Victor, who left for his homeland, Russia, many years before.

No full-length films were made in Tajikistan in 2007. However, director Mohsen Makhmalbaf, who has previously lived in Tajikistan, is helping to organise a masterclass for young Tajik cinematographers, and is allocating grants from the Makhmalbaf Film House for short films by new directors. He is also a founder and president of the international film festival Didor, which is organised in Tajikistan once every two years. – *Gulnara Abikeyeva*

TANZANIA

In a recent study commissioned by ComMattersKenya the country's audiovisual sector was revealed to be a series of fragmentary sectors that failed to speak with each other. Any form of criticism had yet to take hold, rooted as society was in the Ujamaa political system of the late Julius Kambarage Nyerere, the founding president of the Tanzanian nation. Without critical voices, it is difficult, if not impossible, for art to thrive.

Tanzania also has a history of institutions that are created then disappear without a trace: the Tanzania Film Commission vanished after the Ministry of Culture merged with Education, and the Tanzania Broadcasting Commission merged with the Tanzania Independent Communications Regulatory Authority.

Over the past two years, two new cinemas have opened: one in Dar es Salaam (Century Cinemax, Milimani City, with three screens) and the other in Arusha (Arusha Cinemac with two screens), adding to the three-screen New World Cinema established in Dar es Salaam in October 2003. All the country's cinemas are owned by one company, with the average cinema ticket costing $4.62 as opposed to Kenya's $4.33 and Uganda's $6. Despite the fact that Tanzania has one of the most up-to-date copyright laws in the world, copyright infringement is a subject that unsettles the Tanzanian audiovisual sector, and pirate DVDs and videos are readily available on the market in Kenya for approximately 50 cents. Tanzania not only lacks experienced producers, it has no coherent distribution network, so filmmakers are forced to adopt Nigeria's direct-to-video production model. **Kizunguzungu** is a 35-minute film about the elements that contribute to the spread of HIV/AIDS in Africa. Although set in Dar es Salaam and scripted, directed and produced by Mwangaza Paul Kang'anga, it could be any contemporary African society, where the rich – or those perceived to be the best educated and therefore the most informed – become the 'role models' and set the socio-cultural agenda for the poor. – *Ogova Ondego*

UGANDA

Although film production in Uganda has been minimal in the last two years, two local films are worthy of mention. Cindy Evelyne Magara's **Fate** was made in 2006 and was followed a year later by **Divizionz**, directed by Deddac. *Fate* is the story of a successful city woman who lives in a society that dictates how women should lead their lives. *Divizionz* looks at the lives of people who try to survive in central Kampala, where the lack of amenities is only rivalled by high levels of crime and anti-social behaviour.

Also of interest was the controversial **Murder in the City: Doctor Kiyingi**, directed by Haj Ashraf Simwogerere, which mirrored the events in the murder case of a prominent Kampala city lawyer, Robinah Kiyingi, whose husband was arrested and charged only to be acquitted shortly after. Detractors argued that the film sought to influence a case that was still ongoing. A judge finally ruled that it could be released.

The Academy Award triumph of American actor Forest Whitaker, who won the Best Actor Award for his portrayal of the late Ugandan president Idi Amin in **The Last King of Scotland**, set Uganda abuzz. Yet one of the most important film events has been the study undertaken by the local film shacks, or *Bibandas*. More than 2,000 function as cinemas in Uganda. The study – 'Survey of Content and Audiences of Video Halls in

Forest Whitaker as Idi Amin in **The Last King of Scotland**

Uganda 2005' – was conducted by Katerina Marshfield and Michiel van Oosterhout, with funding from the United States embassy. It not only shows that Ugandans are willing to pay more money to watch local films, but identifies the shacks as a largely untapped distribution network of 'infotainment' to underprivileged communities.

The shacks are equipped with wooden benches, one or more television screens and a video or DVD recorder or player. Many shacks also offer satellite broadcasts. The entry fee per head is between 10 and 30 cents compared to $5-7 per show at the cinemas. An average shack seats 100–500 viewers with 4-7 shows a day. Kampala, with 400 shacks each taking in an average 198 customers, caters to 79,000 customers and generates at least $9,028 every day. The programmes are comprised of generic films, ranging from action and martial arts to science fiction, love stories, adventure, war, comedy, music programmes and occasionally 'blue' movies.

The main purpose of the study was to identify and analyse what films were being shown, the demographic watching them and the circumstances in which they were being shown, in order to assess the potential of the shacks as venues for the dissemination of quality information and education, and to design a plan to develop them as such. This crucial research is a starting point for promoting the screening of local films in the video halls as well as for making more 'real life' and educational productions from all over the world widely available. – *Ogova Ondego*

ZIMBABWE

Since the last entry on Zimbabwe, the political situation in the country has become even worse. In addition to the prolonged political crisis, 80% of Zimbabweans are said to be unemployed and are experiencing severe hardships with runaway inflation, as well as critical shortages of food, medicine and fuel.

Not surprisingly, the local industry has suffered. However, the year should be remembered for a feature by director Tawanda Gunda Mupengo and producer Dorothy Meck. **Tanyaradzwa** tells the story of an intelligent, outgoing girl from a rich, loving family. Life seems perfect until one night, during dinner, her nine-month secret is revealed, with the birth of a boy. Feeling betrayed, her parents take their frustrations out on each other. Unable to bear the guilt of destroying her family, Tanya flees in order to find the baby's father. Family, loyalty and social morality are the issues in this kaleidoscopic journey of a naïve and desperate young mother.

Another feature, Anopa Makaka's **Evil in our midst**, is a searing indictment of child sexual abuse and the impunity of the wealthy and powerful. Visiting the shops on her birthday, a 13-year-old is kidnapped and taken to the home of a powerful businessman, who has a predilection for under-age girls. Brutally raped, the girl is left for dead, but survives, and with the loving attention of her parents, slowly

Tawanda Gunda Mupengo's **Tanyaradzwa**

recovers. Elisa's father, faced with police apathy, decides to take drastic measures.

None of these features examines the current political crisis in Zimbabwe. Short films also tend to ignore the harsh socio-political realities of the country and focus instead on domestic and metaphysical issues. **At the Water** (*Pamvura*), made by a women's film cooperative, was initiated by producer and well-known writer, Tsisti Dangarembga. It tells the story of a young mother who thinks the drowning of her son is more than just chance. In the end the film turns out to be a story of superstition, faith, and the clash of unknown forces. Tawanda Gunda's **Spell My Name** (*Peretera Maneta*) depicts the journey of a sophisticated young woman whose city life contrasts greatly with her new job in a rural school. She discovers friendship in places she never expected – with her students. The short was produced by Tsitsi Dangarembga, who appears to work within the Zimbabwean film industry with few problems.

Return to Zimbabwe is a personal documentary by South African filmmaker, Xoliswa Sithole, about her return to the country she grew up in. A complex journey back in time, it includes her memories of her uncle, Edison Sithole, who was one of the first Black Doctors of Law, a liberator and nationalist, who was abducted and killed during the Zimbabwean struggle. One of the most important issues to come out of Sithole's discussions with people was the fact that ZANU PF as a party had failed to transform from a liberation to a progressive party and as a result many young people felt marginalised and joined the MDC instead. – *Martin P. Botha*

World Box Office Survey 2006

ARGENTINA

		Admissions
1.	Ice Age: The Meltdown	2,540,000
2.	The Chronicles of Narnia	2,060,000
3.	The Da Vinci Code	1,600,000
4.	Pirates of the Caribbean: Dead Man's Chest	1,580,000
5.	Cars	1,200,000
6.	Baneros 3 – Iodopoderosos	1,100,000
7.	Over the Hedge	1,000,000
8.	The Hairy Tooth Fairy	950,000
9.	X-Men: The Last Stand	790,000
10.	The Departed	700,000

Population	39 million
Total box office	$85 million
Admissions	35 million
Screens	850
Average cinema ticket price	$2.4

Source: INCAA/SICA

AUSTRALIA

		AUS$
1.	Pirates of the Caribbean: Dead Man's Chest	38,051,375
2.	The Da Vinci Code	27,052,375
3.	Ice Age: The Meltdown	24,566,473
4.	Casino Royale	21,771,132
5.	The Chronicles of Narnia	21,244,281
6.	Cars	17,663,541
7.	Borat	17,271,217
8.	X-Men: The Last Stand	16,593,952
9.	The Devil Wears Prada	16,556,903
10.	Over the Hedge	16,313,606

Population	20.6 million
Total box office	$685 million
Local films' market share	4.6%
Admissions	83.6 million
Sites/screens	464/1,964
Average cinema ticket price	$8.2

Source: AFC, MPDAA, Australian Bureau of Statistics

AUSTRIA

		$
1.	Ice Age: The Meltdown	1,197,007
2.	Pirates of the Caribbean: Dead Man's Chest	882,087
3.	Harry Potter and the Goblet of Fire	743,110
4.	The Da Vinci Code	739,318
5.	Perfume – The Story of a Murderer	598,028
6.	Casino Royale	527,667
7.	Zwerge – Der Wald ist nicht genug	461,783
8.	Over the Hedge	410,031
9.	The Chronicles of Narnia	409,917
10.	The Devil Wears Prada	406,912

Population	8.2 million
Total box office	$149.1 million
Local films' market share	2.1%
Admissions	17.3 million
Sites/screens	177/580
Average cinema ticket price	$8.6

Source: Austrian Cinema Association

BOLIVIA

		Admissions
1.	Ice Age: The Meltdown	161,350
2.	Who Killed the White Llama?	150,000
3.	The Da Vinci Code	102,758
4.	Superman Returns	59,939
5.	Pirates of the Caribbean: Dead Man's Chest	52,428
6.	X-Men: The Last Stand	42,128
7.	Eragon	38,521
8.	Happy Feet	40,194
9.	Cars	35,427
10.	Casino Royale	28,461

Population	9.3 million
Total box ofice	$4 million
Local film's market share	19.1%
Admissions	1.5 million
Sites/screens	19/43
Average cinema ticket price	$ 2.22

Source: Manfer Films

BOSNIA AND HERZEGOVINA

		Admissions
1.	Grbavica	179,483
2.	Border Post	60,000
3.	The Da Vinci Code	29,896
4.	Nafaka	25,151
5.	Borat	23,561
6.	We Are Not Angels	18,196
7.	Pirates of the Caribbean: Dead Man's Chest	16,387
8.	Skies Above the Landscape	15,000
9.	Casino Royale	12,772
10.	The Chronicles of Narnia	10,760

Population	3 million
Sites	30
Average cinema ticket price	$4.75

Source: Cinemateque of Bosnia & Herzegovina

BULGARIA

		Admissions
1.	The Da Vinci Code	144,019
2.	Pirates of the Caribbean: Dead Man's Chest	144,524
3.	Ice Age: The Meltdown	84,465
4.	Casino Royale	41,144
5.	Mission: Impossible III	49,860

6. The Departed	40,376
7. Garfield: A Tail of Two Kitties	49,363
8. The Devil Wears Prada	38,017
9. X-Men: The Last Stand	42,577
10. Crank	37,140

Population	7.6 million
Total box office	$8.1 million
Local film's market share	1 %
Admissions	2.5 million
Sites/screens	66/132
Avgerage cinema ticket price	$3.30

Source: Geopoly

CHINA

	$m
1. Curse of the Golden Flower	37.3
2. The Banquet	17.3
3. TheDa Vinci Code	14.0
4. King Kong	13.6
5. Fearless	13.4
6. Rob-B-Hood	12.9
7. Mission: Impossible III	10.9
8. Poseidon	9.1
9. Battle of Wits	8.9
10. Superman Returns	8.3

Population	1.3 billion
Total box office	$348.9m
Local film's market share	55.03%
Admissions	87.3 million
Screens	3,089

Source: Film Bureau of State Administration of Radio, Film and TV

COLOMBIA

	Admissions
1. Ice Age: The Meltdown	1,253,408
2. A Ton of Luck	1,198,172
3. The Chronicles of Narnia	1,013,611
4. The Da Vinci Code	874,539
5. Superman Returns	679,023
6. Pirates of the Caribbean: Dead Man's Chest	670,203
7. X-Men: The Last Stand	634,785
8. Cars	601,839
9. Karmma, el peso de tus actos	412,884
10. Poseidon	380,870

Population	42.8 million
Total box office	$132.432 millions
Local film's market share	14%
Admissions	20.2 million
Sites/screens	126/439
Average ticket price	US$3.00

Source: Proimágenes en Movimiento.

CROATIA

	$m
1. Borat	$795,100
2. What is a Man Without a Moustache?	$694,805
3. The Da Vinci Code	$691,495
4. Pirates of the Caribbean: Dead Man's Chest	$627,917

5. Casino Royale	$452,594
6. Ice Age: The Meltdown	$374,017
7. Hoodwinked!	$256,851
8. The Devil Wears Prada	$254,151
9. Over the Hedge	$248,578
10. Memoirs of a Geisha	$242,750

Population	4.38 million
Total box office	$12,670,678
Local film's market share	9%
Admissions	2,796,757
Sites/creens	79/95
Average cinema ticket price	$4,53

Source: Continental Film, Zagreb; Continental Film, Zagreb; Republic of Croatia's Central Bureau of Statistics

CZECH REPUBLIC

	Admissions
1. Holiday Makers	788,125
2. Rafters	692,447
3. Ice Age: The Meltdown	674, 005
4. Taming Crocodiles	608,865
5. Pirates of the Caribbean: Dead Man's Chest	572,579
6. The Da Vinci Code	527,167
7. Cars	311,047
8. Beauty in Trouble	296, 685
9. The Chronicles of Narnia	290, 786
10. Harry Potter and the Goblet of Fire	239,675

Population	10.2 million
Total box office	$10,80 mil
Local film's market share	23%
Average cinema ticket price	$4.2

Source: Czech Film Centre

EGYPT

	$
1. The Yacoubian Building	3,449.458
2. Chic	3,068.083
3. Incidental Case	3,018.974
4. One of the People	2,818.060
5. She Made Me a Criminal	2,545.832
6. On the Crime Edge	1,862.347
7. Haha and Tofaha	1,696.901
8. Love and Infatuation	1,647.432
9. Wija	1,406.411
10. 1/8 Dozen of Villains	1,364.912

Population	75 million
Total box office	$45.4 million
Local film's market share	80%
Admissions	25 million
Sites/screens	173/271
Average cinema ticket price	$3.51

Source: United Motion Pictures, Cairo

ESTONIA

	Admissions
1. Ice Age: The Meltdown	129,614
2. Pirates of the Caribbean: Dead Man's Chest	104,765
3. Borat	68,133

4. The Da Vinci Code	62,095
5. Lotte from Gadgetville	56,041
6. Open Season	52,458
7. Casino Royal	49,715
8. Garfield: A Tail of Two Kitties	45,895
9. Ruudi	42,379
10. Cars	37,006

Population	1.35 million
Total box office	$8.5 million
Local film's market share	7%
Admissions	1.59 million
Sites/screens	12/67
Average cinema ticket price	$5.4

Source: Estonian Film Foundation, Estonian Bank

FINLAND

	Admissions
1. Matti: Hell is for Heroes	461,665
2. Pirates of the Caribbean: Dead Man's Chest	458,833
3. Casino Royale	368,621
4. The Da Vinci Code	365,276
5. Ice Age: The Meltdown	272,104
6. Cars	232,049
7. Kummelin Jackpot	229,511
8. FC Venus	223,590
9. Chicken Little	126,743
10. The Devil Wears Prada	116,518

Population	5.2 million
Total box office	$69.9
Local film's market share	24%
Admissions	6.7 million
Screens	330
Average cinema ticket price:	$10.39

Source: Finnish Film Foundation

GERMANY

	$
1. Ice Age: The Meltdown	8.7
2. Pirates of the Caribbean: Dead Man's Chest	7.1
3. The Da Vinci Code	5.6
4. Perfume – The Story of a Murderer	5.4
5. Casino Royale	4.6
6. Germany – A Summer's Tale	4.0
7. Seven Dwarfs	3.5
8. Over the Hedge	3.4
9. The Devil Wears Prada	2.9
10. Cars	2.2

Population	82.3 million
Total box office	$1.185 billion
Local film's market share	25.8%
Admissions	136.7 million
Average cinema ticket price	$8.67

Source: Filmförderungsanstalt FFA (German Federal Board)

HONG KONG

	$m
1. Pirates of the Caribbean: Dead Man's Chest	4.6
2. The Da Vinci Code	4.4

3. The Chronicles of Narnia	3.9
4. Mission: Impossible III	3.9
5. Fearless	3.8
6. Superman Returns	3.2
7. Rob-B-Hood	3
8. X-Men: The Last Stand	2.6
9. Eight Below	2.3
10. Casino Royale	2.1

Population	6.9 million
Total box office	$116.6 million
Local film's market share	31%
Admissions	16.82 million
Sites/screens	47/182
Average ticket price	$6.80

Sources: MPIA, City Entertainment

HUNGARY

	Admissions
1. Ice Age: The Meltdown	614,576
2. The Da Vinci Code	538,221
3. Pirates of the Caribbean: Dead Man's Chest	532,966
4. Children of Glory	451,654
5. Over the Hedge	347,319
6. Glass Tiger 2	304,021
7. Cars	263,897
8. Garfield: A Tail of Two Kitties	241,130
9. The Break Up	238,941
10. You, Me and Dupree	182,016

Population	10.07 million
Total box office	$50,295,324.59
Local films' market share	13.6%
Admissions	10,486,401
Sites/screens	218/439
Average cinema ticket price	$4.79454

Source: National Film Office

IRELAND

	Euros
1. Pirates of the Caribbean: Dead Man's Chest	3,915,525
2. Casino Royale	3,793,239
3. The Wind That Shakes the Barley	3,701,417
4. Walk the Line	3,671,740
5. The Da Vinci Code	3,603,752
6. Borat	3,562,176
7. Ice Age: The Meltdown	2,376,991
8. The Departed	2,124,547
9. The Devil Wears Prada	1,982,946
10. Superman Returns	1,853,664

Population	4.25 million
Total box office	€108.2m
Local films' market share	5%
Admissions	17.9 million
Sites/screens	72/424
Average cinema ticket price	€7.28

Source: Nielsen EDI/Carlton Screen Advertising

ITALY

		$m
1.	The Da Vinci Code	41.3
2.	Pirates of the Caribbean: Dead Man's Chest	28.5
3.	Ice Age: The Meltdown	26.8
4.	My Best Enemy	26.7
5.	Christmas in New York	26.0
6.	The Devil Wears Prada	20.5
7.	Cars	18.8
8.	Night Before Finals	17.9
9.	I Love You in Every Language of the World	13.7
10.	Match Point	13.3

Population	59.1 million
Total box office	$886.8m
Local films' market share	23%
Admissions	104.2 million
Screens	3,794
Average cinema ticket price	$8,2

Sources: Istat, European Cinema Yearbook, Cinetel/Agis.

JAPAN

		$m
1.	Harry Potter and the Goblet of Fire	94.8
2.	Pirates Of The Caribbean: Dead Man's Chest	86.4
3.	The Da Vinci Code	78.0
4.	Tales From Earthsea	65.9
5.	Umizaru 2: Test of Trust	61.2
6.	The Chronicles Of Narnia	59.1
7.	Suite Hotel	52.4
8.	Japan Sinks	46.0
9.	Death Note: The Last Name	44.8
10.	Yamato	43.9

Population	127,768,000
Total box office	$1,749,431,000
Local films' market share	53.2%
Admissions	164,585,000
Screens	3062
Average cinema ticket price	10.62

Source: Motion Picture Producers Association of Japan

LATVIA

		Admissions
1.	The Da Vinci Code	97,450
2.	Pirates of the Caribbean: Dead Man's Chest	91,206
3.	Ice Age: The Meltdown	81,125
4.	Casino Royale	62,432
5.	Daywatch	49,757
6.	Open Season	46,472
7.	Borat	44,326
8.	Garfield: A Tail of Two Kitties	42,882
9.	Cars	42,003
10.	The Devil Wears Prada	34,946

Population	2,294,590
Total box office	$9,144,781
Local films' market share	5.7%
Admissions	2,060,444
Average cinema ticket price	$4,44

Source: Baltic Films' Facts & Figures 2006

MEXICO

		Admissions
1.	Ice Age: The Meltdown	9,300,000
2.	Pirates of the Carribean: Dead Man's Chest	5,700,000
3.	The Da Vinci Code	5,400,000
4.	X-Men: The Last Stand	5,100,000
5.	Superman Returns	4,200,000
6.	Cars	4,200,000
7.	Una Película de Huevos	4,000,000
8.	Over the Hedge	3,900,000
9.	Mission: Impossible III	2,600,000
10.	Poseidon	2,500,000

Population	106,000,000
Total box office	$6.1 million
Local films' market share	7%
Admissions	164.6
Screens	3,762
Average cinema ticket price	$4.5

Source: IMCINE

NEW ZEALAND

		$m
1.	King Kong	6.66
2.	The Chronicles of Narnia	6.25
3.	Pirates of the Caribbean: Dead Man's Chest	5.20
4.	The Da Vinci Code	3.85
5.	Ice Age: The Meltdown	3.56
6.	Casino Royale	3.05
7.	Sione's Wedding (New Zealand)	3.00
8.	Cars	2.50
9.	Over the Hedge	2.42
10.	X-Men: The Last Stand	2.20

Population	4.143 million
Total box office	$US108.25million
Local films' market share	4.8%
Admissions	15.3 million
Screens	378
Average cinema ticket price	$US7.06

Source: Motion Picture Distributors Association of New Zealand

PORTUGAL

		Admissions
1.	The Da Vinci Code	756,770
2.	Pirates of the Caribbean: Dead Man's Chest	638,114
3.	Ice Age: The Meltdown	493,374
4.	Over the Hedge	422,251
5.	Casino Royale	375,162
6.	Miami Vice	307,788
7.	Mission: Impossible III	298,428
8.	You, Me and Dupree	289,038
9.	Inside Man	279,424
10.	Filme da Treta	278,421

Population	10.7 million
Total box office	$ 96,332,363
Local films' market share	2.2%
Admissions	16,367,429
Average cinema ticket price	$5.88

Source: ICA

PUERTO RICO

		$
1.	Ice Age: The Meltdown	2,803,736
2.	X-Men: The Last Stand	2,335,661
3.	Pirates of the Caribbean: Dead Man's Chest	2,078,938
4.	Big Momma's House 2	1,948,418
5.	Click	1,646,280
6.	The Fast and the Furious: Tokyo Drift	1,618,591
7.	Little Man	1,617,389
8.	The Da Vinci Code	1,614,543
9.	Superman Returns	1,510,899
10.	Over the Hedge	1,234,654

Population	3,927,188
Total box office	$ 69,554,716
Admissions	11,869,670
Average cinema ticket price	$4.85

Source: Puerto Rico Film Commission

ROMANIA

		Admissions
1.	The Da Vinci Code	149,463
2.	Ice Age: The Meltdown	116,136
3.	Pirates of the Caribbean: Dead Man's Chest	87,373
4.	The Devil Wears Prada	64,075
5.	Chronicles of Narnia	61,039
6.	Casino Royale	57,043
7.	The Departed	43,397
8.	Failure to Launch	42,837
9.	The Pink Panther	42,408
10.	Mission: Impossible III	42,065

Population	22,607,620
Total box office	11,832,495 $
Local films' market share	3.4%
Admissions	2,776,516
Screens	108
Average cinema ticket price	$4,26

Source: Statistic Report of Romanian Cinematography

SOUTH AFRICA

		$
1.	Casino Royale	3, 387,288
2.	Ice Age: The Meltdown	3,230,083
3.	Pirates of the Caribbean: Dead Man's Chest	2,370,805
4.	The Da Vinci Code	1,834,643
5.	Happy Feet	1,777,701
6.	The Devil Wears Prada	1,708,734
7.	Big Momma's House 2	1,689,157
8.	Over the Hedge	1,689,036
9.	Cars	1,622,911
10.	Mission: Impossible III	1,557,037

Population	47 million
Total Box Office	R582,610,057
Local films' market share	2.52%
Admissions	29,749,489
Sites/screens	130/743
Average cinema ticket price	US$2.79-5.88

Source: Ster-Kinekor

SERBIA

		Admissions
1.	Ivko's Fete	617,607
2.	The Da Vinci Code	118,688
3.	We Are Not Angels 3	114,390
4.	Border Post	101,461
5.	Harry Potter and the Goblet of Fire	100,039
6.	Ice Age: The Meltdown	98,035
7.	Seven and a Half	58,868
8.	Memoirs of a Geisha	56,739
9.	King Kong	45,979
10.	Casino Royale	37,772

Population	7.6 million
Total box office	$5,195,199
Admissions	1,628,589
Local films' market share	57%
Sites/screens	1,40/156
Average cinema ticket price	$3.19

Sources: Film Distributors Association of Serbia

SLOVENIA

		Admissions
1.	Pirates of the Caribbean: Dead Man's Chest	138,862
2.	The Da Vinci Code	137,662
3.	Ice Age: The Meltdown	105,723
4.	Borat	103,599
5.	Garfield: A Tail of Two Kitties	100,064
6.	Casino Royal	84,354
7.	Chicken Little	84.315
8.	Cars	62,313
9.	Memoirs of a Geisha	48,441
10.	Open Season	48,311

Population	2.0 million
Total box office	$14.1 million
Admissions	2.675 million
Sites/screens	104
Average cinema ticket price	$7.34

Source: Slovenian Film Fund

SOUTH KOREA

		$
1.	Pirates of the Caribbean: Dead Man's Chest	39,222,763
2.	The Da Vinci Code	37,590,293
3.	Ice Age: The Meltdown	27,163,367
4.	Alatriste	23,198,672
5.	Cars	17,699,029
6.	Memoirs of a Geisha	16,568,661
7.	Volver	14,239,294
8.	X-Men: The Last Stand	13,537,18
9.	Superman Returns	12,872,61
10.	The Departed	11,880,89

Population	48,991,947
Total Box office	$1,004,937,989
Local films' market share	63.8%
Admissions	153,413,510
Sites/screens	319/1,867
Average cinema ticket price	$7.6

Source: Korean Film Council

SPAIN

	$
1. Pirates of the Caribbean: Dead Man's Chest	39,222,763
2. The Da Vinci Code	37,590,293
3. Ice Age: The Meltdown	27,163,367
4. Alatriste	23,198,672
5. Cars	17,699,029
6. Memoirs of a Geisha	16,568,661
7. Volver	14,239,294
8. X-Men: The Last Stand	13,537,18
9. Superman Returns	12,872,61
10. The Departed	11,880,89

Population	44,873,567
Total box office	$895,247,108.46
Local films' market share	15.43%
Admissions	121,654,481
Sites/screens	936/4,299
Average cinema ticket price	$7.50

Sources: Spanish Ministry of Culture, Spanish National Statistics Institute

SWEDEN

	Admissions
1. Pirates of the Caribbean: Dead Man´s Chest	1,134,745
2. The Da Vinci Code	654,437
3. Ice Age: The Meltdown	648,735
4. Casino Royale	618,860
5. The Chronicles of Narnia	580,330
6. Chicken Little	505,595
7. Heartbreak Hotel	462,820
8. Borat	410,185
9. Cars	359,511
10. The Devil Wears Prada	322,444

Population	9,113,257
Total box office	1,199,931,768
Local film´s market share	18.8 %.
Admissions	15,293,118
Sites/screens	784/1171
Avg cinema ticket price	$11,71

Source: The Swedish Film Institute

TURKEY

	Admissions
1. Valley of the Wolves: Iraq	4,260,000
2. The Class of Chaos Three and a Half	2,100,000
3. The Magician	1,700,000
4. The Exam	1,150,000
5. The Da Vinci Code	1,050,000
6. Pirates of the Caribbean: Dead Man's Chest	1,005,000
7. Keloglan vs. the Black Prince	1,000,000
8. Ice Age: The Meltdown	950,000
9. Who Killed Shadows?	650,000
10. Ice Cream, I Scream	500,000

Population	70 million
Total box office	$200,000,000
Local films market share	52%
Admissions	34,850,000
Average cinema ticket price	$6

Source: Antrakt-Sinema magazine

UK

	$m
1. Pirates of the Caribbean: Dead Man's Chest	102.5
2. Casino Royale	87.9
3. The Da Vinci Code	59.8
4. Ice Age: The Meltdown	58.2
5. Borat	46.7
6. X-Men: The Last Stand	37.6
7. Cars	32.1
8. Superman Returns	31.7
9. Mission: Impossible III	30.5
10. The Devil Wears Prada	27.4

Population	60,600,000
Total box office	$1.5 billion
Local films' market share	19%
Admissions	156.6 million
Sites/screens	3,440/697
Average cinema ticket price	$9.59

Source: Film Distributors' Association/UK Film Council

USA

	$m
1. Pirates of the Caribbean: Dead Man's Chest	423.3
2. Night at the Museum	250.9
3. Cars	244.1
4. X-Men: The Last Stand	234.4
5. The Da Vinci Code	217.5
6. Superman Returns	200.1
7. Happy Feet	198.0
8. Ice Age: The Meltdown	195.3
9. Casino Royale	167.4
10. The Pursuit of Happyness	163.5

Population	299,398,484
Total box office	$9.49 billion
Admissions	1.45 billion
Screens	39,668
Average cinema ticket price	$6.55

Sources: Motion Picture Association of America Worldwide Market Research, U.S. Census Bureau, Variety, MPAA

VENEZUELA

	$
1. Ice Age: The Meltdown	2,968,213
2. The Da Vinci Code	2,496,130
3. Pirates of the Caribbean: Dead Man's Chest	2,226,246
4. X-Men: The Last Stand	1,763,340
5. Cars	1,451,967
6. Mission: Impossible III	1,378,816
7. Poseidon	1,299,625
8. Over The Hedge	1,043,075
9. Monster House	1,024,782
10. The Chronicles of Narnia	997,216

Population	27 million
Total box office	US$65,800,374.55
Local films' market share	3.85%
Admissions	20,188,794
Average cinema ticket price	3.26%

Source: Centro Nacional Autónomo de Cinematografía

WORLDWIDE TOP 25

		$m
1.	Pirates of the Caribbean: Dead Man's Chest	1,060.6
2.	The Da Vinci Code	757.2
3.	Ice Age: The Meltdown	636.3
4.	Casino Royale	588.0
5.	Night at the Museum	571.1
6.	X-Men: The Last Stand	455.3
7.	Cars	454.8
8.	Mission: Impossible III	395.5
9.	Superman Returns	389.6
10.	Happy Feet	379.0
11.	The Pursuit of Happyness	330.6
12.	Over the Hedge	329.6
13.	The Devil Wears Prada	324.4
14.	The Departed	277.3
15.	Borat	260.4
16.	Eragon	245.2
17.	The Holiday	199.9
18.	Open Season	185.9
19.	The Break-Up	185.7
20.	Poseidon	179.7
21.	Deja Vu	175.0
22.	Flushed Away	168.5
23	Click	167.6
24.	Inside Man	161.8
25.	The Pink Panther	158.2

Source: worldwideboxoffice.com

Film Festivals Calendar

Festival News

Edinburgh International Film Festival moves to June

The Edinburgh International Film Festival (EIFF) devotes itself to discovering and promoting the very best in international cinema. It embraces, celebrates and debates changes and developments in the global film industry.

EIFF offers a diverse programme of films drawn from every corner of the earth and from every facet of the artisitic imagination. It has always been a talking-shop for film fans and industry figures alike; a unique launch-pad for new films, as well as a place where contacts are made and deals are done.

Shifting the EIFF after 61 years in an August slot was not a decision to be taken lightly. The move to June has been discussed for a long time, and we're enormously excited to be taking the plunge at last. Edinburgh in August is a cultural phenomenon on a world scale, but so many arts festivals on top of one other is somewhat self-defeating: why not spread the cultural wealth throughout the year? With its own slot in the calendar and an entire city to play with, EIFF has the opportunity to assert

EIFF Artistic Director Hannah McGill in conversation with Judd Apatow

itself as an internationally significant, stand-alone film event, building on the programmes and events it presents and the audiences who get so much out of them. The June slot places us at the start of the season; we'll kick off Edinburgh's culture-packed summer with an event that visitors and delegates from the UK and abroad can feel part of. June is a better time slot for industry guests, a better time slot in relation to other international film events, and – most importantly – a beautiful time of year in a breathtaking city.

HANNAH McGILL is Artistic Director of the Edinburgh International Film Festival.

11th Méliès d'Or Award (2006-2007)
European Federation of Fantastic Film Festivals
Awarded at the 13th Lund International Fantastic Film Festival

AFFILIATED MEMBERS

SABAUDIA, Italy
FANTAFESTIVAL

LUND, Sweden
FANTASTISK FILM FESTIVAL

SITGES, Spain
FESTIVAL INTERNACIONAL
DE CINEMA DE CATALUNYA

LUXEMBOURG, Luxembourg
CYNÉNYGMA - LUXEMBOURG
INTERNATIONAL FILM FESTIVAL

LEEDS, United Kingdom
LEEDS INTERNATIONAL FILM FESTIVAL

PORTO, Portugal
FANTASPORTO

BRUSSELS, Belgium
BRUSSELS INTERNATIONAL FESTIVAL
OF FANTASTIC FILM

AMSTERDAM, Netherlands
AMSTERDAM FANTASTIC FILM FESTIVAL

NEUCHÂTEL, Switzerland
NEUCHÂTEL INTERNATIONAL FANTASTIC
FILM FESTIVAL

ESPOO, Finland
ESPOO CINÉ INTERNATIONAL FILM FESTIVAL

ADHERENT MEMBERS

NATFILM FESTIVAL, Denmark

FRIGHTFEST, United Kingdom

RAVENNA NIGHTMARE FILM FESTIVAL, Italy

SEMANA DE CINE FANTASTICO Y DE TERROR
DE SAN SEBASTIAN, Spain

SCIENCEPLUSFICTION, Italy

UTOPIALES FESTIVAL INTERNATIONAL DE
SCIENCE-FICTION, NANTES, France

SEMANA INTERNACIONAL DE CINE
FANTASTICO DE MALAGA, Spain

RIGA INT'L FANTASY FILM FESTIVAL, Latvia

DEAD BY DAWN HORROR FILM FESTIVAL,
United Kingdom

HORRORTHON DUBLIN, IRELAND

SUPPORTING MEMBERS

FANTASIA, Canada

PUCHON, South Korea

SCREAMFEST, USA

FANTASTIC FEST, USA

Sponsor of the Méliès Competition

MEDIA

Princess
directed by Anders Morgenthaler
World Sales : Trust Films Sales 2 ApS (natjat@trust-film.dk)

SPECIAL MENTIONS: *Grimm Love* directed by Martin Weisz (world sales: Lightning Entertainment)
Renaissance directed by Christian Volckman (world sales: Odyssey Entertainment)
MÉLIÈS D'OR SHORT MOVIE AWARD: *Sniffer* by Bobbie Piers (world sales: Dream Factory)

EFFFF, Romain Roll
8 rue de la Comtesse de Flandre, 1020 • Brussels, Belgium
tel : +352-621-169922 • fax : +352-26897898
e-mail: info@melies.org • www.melies.org

Leading Festivals

American Film Market
November 5–12, 2008

The business of independent motion picture production and distribution – a truly collaborative process – reaches its peak every year at the American Film Market. Over 8,000 leaders in motion picture production and distribution – acquisition and development executives, agents, attorneys, directors, financiers, film commissioners, producers and writers – converge in Santa Monica for eight days of screenings, deal-making and hospitality. The AFM plays a vital role in global production and finance. Each year, hundreds of films are financed, packaged, licensed, and green lit, sealing over $800 million in business for both completed films and those in pre-production. With the AFM – AFI FEST alliance, attendees capitalise on the only festival-market combination in North America. *Inquiries to*: 10850 Wilshire Blvd, 9th Floor, Los Angeles, CA 90024-4311, USA. Tel: (1 310) 446 1000. Fax: 446 1600. e: afm@ifta-online.org. Web: www.americanfilmmarket.com.

Amiens International Film Festival
November 7–16, 2008

Discovery of new talents, new cinematography and reassessment of film masters. A competitive festival in northern France for shorts, features, animation and documentaries. Also retrospectives, tributes and the 'Le monde comme il va' series, which includes works from Africa, Latin America and Asia. 'Europe, Europes', an expanding section for more than ten years, presents new works from Young European Talents (Shorts, Documentaries and Animation). *Inquiries to*: Amiens International Film Festival, MCA, Place Léon Gontier, 80000 Amiens, France. Tel: (33 3) 2271 3570. Fax: 2292 5304. e: contact@filmfestamiens.org. Web: www.filmfestamiens.org.

Amsterdam–International Documentary Film Festival (IDFA)
November 20–30, 2008

The world's largest documentary festival, built up over two decades, IDFA screens 250 films – in 2006 272 films were shown, of which 127 were premieres – and sells more than 131,000 tickets. The programme offers creative documentaries, organises numerous debates and special events and includes numerous awards. IDFA has two markets: the FORUM, a market for international co-financing, and Docs for Sale, which stimulates the sales and distribution of creative documentaries. *Inquiries to*: International Documentary Film Festival-Amsterdam, Kleine-Gartmanplantsoen 10, 1017 RR Amsterdam, Netherlands. Tel: (31 20) 627 3329. Fax: 638 5388. e: info@idfa.nl. Web: www.idfa.nl.

AWARDS 2006
VPRO Joris Ivens Award for the best documentary film longer than 60 minutes: **The Monastery-Mr Vig & the Nun** (Denmark), Pernille Rose Grønkjær.
Joris Ivens Special Jury Award: **Tender's Heat Wild Wild Beach** (Russia), Alexander Rastorguev, Vitaly Mansky and Susanna Baranzhieva.
Silver Wolf Award for the best documentary film shorter than 60 minutes: **Enemies of Happiness** (Denmark), Eva Mulvad.
First Appearance Award for the best documentary debut: **We Are Together** (UK), Paul Taylor.

Austin Film Festival
October 16–23, 2008

Celebrating its fifteenth year, an internationally recognised Film Festival and Screenwriters' Conference – one of the select few in the US accredited by the Academy of Motion Picture Arts and Sciences. It brings together a broad range of established and up-and-coming writers, directors and industry professionals for screenings, panels and high-profile networking. *Inquiries to*: Austin Film Festival, 1145 W 5th St, Ste 210, Austin, TX 78703, USA. Tel: (1 512) 478 4795. Fax: 478 6205. e: info@austinfilm.com. Web: www.austinfilmfestival.com.

AWARDS 2007
Film Jury
Narrative Feature: **Shotgun Stories** (USA), Jeff Nichols.
Documentary Feature: **Children of the War** (UK/USA), Alexandre Fuchs.
Narrative Short: **Deface** (USA), John Arlotto.
Narrative Student Short: **Salt Kiss** (Brazil), Fellipe Barbosa.
Documentary Short: **Absolute Zero** (Australia), Alan Woodruff.
Animated Short: **Over the Hill** (UK), Peter Baynton.

Bergen International Film Festival
October 15–22, 2008

Norway's beautiful capital of the fjords launches the 9th BIFF in 2008. The festival, which is the largest of the Norwegian film festivals in content, has a main International Competition of about 15 films, as well as an International Documentary Competition. The documentary section makes BIFF one of the Nordic countries' biggest annual documentary events. The festival has sidebars with international arthouse films, a Norwegian shorts Competition as well as premieres of the upcoming Christmas theatrical releases, through extensive collaboration with Norway's distributors. Also hosts seminars and other events. *Inquiries to*: Bergen International Film Festival, Georgernes verft 12, NO-5011 Bergen, Norway. Tel: (47) 5530 0840. Fax: 5530 0841. e: biff@biff.no. Web: www.biff.no.

Berlin – Internationale Filmfestspiele Berlin
February 7–17, 2008

Interest in the Berlinale 2007 among visitors from both the film industry and the general public has been greater than ever: more than 19,000 accredited visitors from 127 countries, including 4,000 journalists, attended the 57th Berlin International Film Festival. Approximately 430,000 cinemagoers have attended the festival, including roughly 200,000 audience tickets. The newly added Cubix cinema screens at Alexanderplatz were extremely well received by audiences. Altogether, 373 films were shown in 1,190 screenings. Besides the 'regular sections' – Competition, Panorama, Forum, Generation and Perspektive Deutsches Kino – events in the special Magnum in Motion series, the newly positioned Short Film Competition, as well as the Eat, Drink, See Movies - Culinary Cinema events were almost completely booked out. Under Jury President Paul Schrader, Hiam Abbass, Mario Adorf, Gael García Bernal, Willem Dafoe, Nansun Shi and Molly Malene Stensgaard brought glamour, passion and expertise to the Berlinale 2007. *Inquiries to*: Internationale Filmfestspiele Berlin, Potsdamer Str 5, D-10785 Berlin, Germany. Tel: (49 30) 259 200. Fax: 2592 0299. e: info@berlinale.de. Web: www.berlinale.de.

AWARDS 2007
Golden Bear: **Tuya's Marriage** (People's Republic of China), Wang Quan'an.
Jury Grand Prix: **The Other** (Argentina/France/Germany), Ariel Rotter.
Best Director: **Beaufort** (Israel), Joseph Cedar.
Best Actor: Julio Chavez for **The Other** (Argentina/France/Germany), Ariel Rotter.
Best Actress: Nina Hoss for **Yella** (Germany), Christian Petzold.
Best Short: **Contract** (Netherlands), Hanro Smitsman.

The Berlin International Film Festival

Bermuda International Film Festival
March 28–April 5, 2008

Features the best of independent film from around the world in three competition categories: features, documentaries and shorts. Q&A sessions with directors, and the festival's popular lunchtime 'Chats with...' sessions give filmgoers and filmmakers a chance to mix. A competition victory earns each film's director an invitation to sit on the festival jury the following year. AMPAS recognises the festival as a qualifying event for the Short Films Academy Awards. Submission deadline: October 1. *Inquiries to*: Bermuda International Film Festival, Broadway House, PO Box 2963, Hamilton HM MX, Bermuda. Tel: (441) 293 3456. Fax: 293 7769. e: info@biff.bm. Web: www.biff.bm.

AWARDS 2007
Best Narrative Feature: Shared between **Cashback** (UK), Sean Ellis and **Sweet Mud** (Germany/Israel/Japan), Dror Shaul.
Best Documentary Feature: **The Cats of Mirikitani** (USA), Linda Hattendorf.
Bermuda Shorts Award: **I Want to Be a Pilot** (Kenya/Spain), Diego Quemada-Diez.
Audience Choice: **A Sunday in Kigali** (Canada), Robert Favreau.

Report 2007
Bermuda International Film Festival celebrated its tenth edition screening 85 films from 32 countries to enthusiastic audiences. The festival jury was chaired by Carrie Fisher and Richard Dreyfuss and included acclaimed documentarian Stanley Nelson and award-winning actor Ben Newmark. Bermuda's Earl Cameron, whose acting career spans 50 years, was our special guest. Lively 'Chats With...' panel discussions, great parties and Late Nites gave filmmakers and filmgoers lots of opportunities to mix and mingle.
- **Aideen Ratteray Pryse,** Festival Director.

Bilbao International Documentary and Short Film Festival
November 21–29, 2008

Long-running competitive festival for shorts and documentaries, heading for its 50th edition in 2008. Featuring over 2,600 films from over 75 countries in 2007, with over 90 films selected for the International Competition, which encompasses three categories for fiction, documentary and animation. The number of countries, geographical areas and cultures participating once again underlined the truly universal character of the competition. *Inquiries to*: Bilbao International Documentary and Short Film Festival, Colón de Larreátegui, 37-4° Derecha, 48009 Bilbao, Spain. Tel: (34 94) 424 8698. Fax: 424 5624. e: info@zinebi.com. Web: www.zinebi.com.

Brisbane International Film Festival
July 31–August 10, 2008

Queensland's premier film event, the Brisbane International Film Festival (BIFF), is in its seventeenth year. Presented annually by the Pacific Film and Television Commission, it provides a focus on film culture in Queensland by showcasing the best and most interesting world cinema. Screening more than 100 films, the diverse programme includes features, documentaries, shorts, films from the Asia-Pacific, experimental work, Australian films, animation and Cine Sparks – the Australian Film Festival for Young People. Each year the Festival draws film enthusiasts to view the entertaining mix of local and international films, retrospectives and colourful events that capture the imagination and embrace the vibrant art of film making. *Inquiries to*: Brisbane International Film Festival,

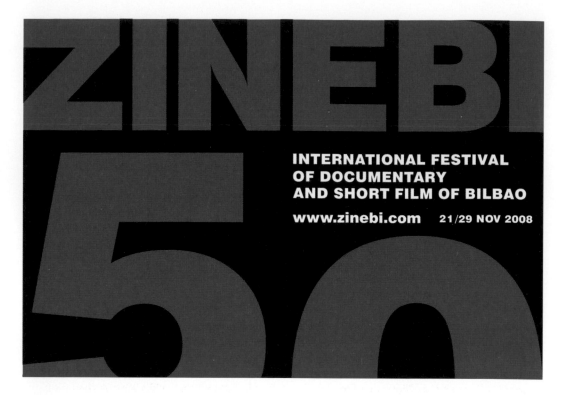

GPO Box 909, Brisbane, QLD, 4001, Australia. Tel: (61 7) 3007 3003. Fax: 3007 3030. e: biff@ biff.com.au. Web: www.biff.com.au.

Report 2007

In 2007, the Festival enjoyed 28 sell-out cinema sessions, seven of which were Australian films. Fifty-five international and national guests attended, including legendary film contributor and 2007 Chauvel award recipient David Stratton. The powerful Australian love story, *Unfinished Sky*, received the highest audience vote while Australian dramas *The Home Song Stories* and *The Jammed*, as well as Filipino comedy, *The Bet Collector* and American Indie film, *Quinceanera*, received top recognition from jury members. – **Catherine Miller,** Public Relations Co-ordinator.

Buenos Aires International Independent Film Festival (BAFICI)
April 8-20, 2008

The Buenos Aires International Independent Film Festival was created in 1999. Sections include the two Official Competitions, for features and shorts. 'Argentina – Brand-New Novelties' has, since 2001, highlighted the increasing production of independent films in Argentina, complemented by the 'Work in Progress' section. BAFICI also programmes sections dedicated to outstanding directors. *Inquiries to*: Buenos Aires Festival Internacional de Cine Independiente, Saenz Peña 832, 6 Piso, 1035 Capital Federal, Buenos Aires, Argentina. Tel: (54 11) 4328 3454. e: produccion@bafilmfest.com. www. bafici.gov.ar

BUFF
March 11–15, 2008

In 2008, BUFF will celebrate its 25th anniversary. It will commemorate the occasion with a series of special events. Since 1995, BUFF has been The Official Swedish Children and Young People's Film Festival, in co-operation with the Swedish Film Institute. BUFF shows about 100 films in the following sections: Competition, Short

Film Competition, Panorama, New Nordic, Documentary, School Cinema Project, and Short Films. BUFF 2008 will also focus on young people by screening their own films and organising discussions. BUFF:FF Financing Forum, organised for the first time in 2007, has proven to be a great success. For BUFF 2008 we will organize the second edition of BUFF:FF. It is an important niche within the festival, expanding the arena to more professionals. *Inquiries to*: BUFF – Filmfestival, PO Box 4277, SE 203 14 Malmö, Sweden. Tel: (46 40) 239211. Fax: 305322. e: info@buff.se. Web: www.buff.se or www.financingforum.eu.

AWARDS 2007
City of Malmö Film Award: **Kidz in Da Hood** (Sweden), Ylva Gustavsson and Catti Edfeldt.
Swedish Church Award: **The Substitute** (Denmark), Ole Bornedal.
Youth Jury Award: **The Substitute** (Denmark), Ole Bornedal.
County Council of Skåne Shortfilm Award: **Chess** (Sweden), Pernilla Hindsefelt.
Sydsvenskan and BUFF Achievement Award: Ulf Malmros, Sweden.

Cairo International Film Festival
Late November–early December 2008

The festival is organised by the General Union of Arab Artists with competitions for feature films, feature digital films and Arab films.
Inquiries to: Cairo International Film Festival, 17 Kasr el Nile St, Cairo, Egypt. Tel: (20 2) 2392 3962. e: info@cairofilmfest.com. Web: www.cairofilmfest.com.

The red carpet at the Cannes International Film Festival

Cannes
May 14–25, 2008

Cannes remains the world's top festival, attracting key films, personalities and industry personnel. The official selection includes the Competition, films out of competition, 'Un Certain Regard', Cinéfondation and Cannes Classics (created 2004). The Marché du Film, with facilities improved and extended since 2000 (Riviera-Producers network, Short Film Corner) is part of the official organisation.
Inquiries to: Festival de Cannes, 3, rue Amélie 75007 Paris, France. Tel: (33 1) 5359 6100. Fax: 5359 6110. e: festival@festival-cannes.fr. Web: www.festival-cannes.org.

AWARDS 2007
Palme d'Or: **4 Months, 3 Weeks & 2 Days** (Romania), Cristian Mungiu.
60th Anniversary Award: **Paranoid Park** (France/USA), Gus van Sant.
Grand Prix: **The Mourning Forest** (France/Japan), Naomi Kawase.

Best Director: Julian Schnabel, **The Diving Bell and the Butterfly** (France).
Best Actor: Konstantin Lavronenko, **The Banishment** (Russia).
Best Actress: Jeon do Yeon, **Secret Sunshine** (South Korea).
Best Screenplay: Fatih Akin, **The Edge of Heaven** (Germany/Turkey).
Jury Prize: **Persepolis** (France), Marjane Satrapi and Vincent Paronnaud and **Silent Light** (France/Mexico/Netherlands), Carlos Reygadas.
Caméra d'Or: **Meduzot** (France/Israel), Etgar Keret and Shira Geffen.

Cartagena
March 2008

Ibero-Latin American films, including features, shorts, documentaries, tributes to Latin American directors and a film and TV market. *Inquiries to*: Victor Nieto Nuñez, Director, Cartagena International Film Festival, Centro, Calle San Juan de Dios, Baluarte San Francisco Javier, Cartagena, Colombia. Tel: (57 95) 664 2345. e: info@festicinecartagena.com. Web: www.festicinecartagena.com.

Chicago International Film Festival
October 2–15, 2008

The Chicago International Film Festival is among the oldest competitive events in North America. It spotlights the latest work by established international directors and newcomers, showcasing over a hundred feature and more than forty short films during the festival. It bestows its highest honour, the Gold Hugo, on the best feature in the International Competition, with separate prizes for documentaries, student films and shorts. Chicago is one of two US sites to award the FIPRESCI prize for first- and second-time directors, judged by top international critics. *Inquiries to*: Chicago International Film Festival, 30 E Adams St, Suite 800, Chicago, IL 60603, USA. Tel: (1 312) 683 0121. Fax: 683 0122. e: info@chicagofilmfestival.com. Web: www. chicagofilmfestival.com.

Cinema Tout Ecran

Cinéma Tout Ecran
October 27–November 2, 2008

Cinéma Tout Ecran looks beyond audiovisual boundaries and focuses on the artistic quality of works made for television or cinema, the unique skills of the filmmaker and the representation of life through fiction. With its selection orientated towards the artistic quality and the talent of the filmmaker, the festival presents an official competition made up of feature films for television and cinema and an international short films selection, makes a point of letting the public discover the best of international series and wishes to promote the

research and support of new films and writers. *Inquiries to*: Adrian Stiefel, Head of Media Relations, Cinéma Tout Ecran, International Film & Television Festival, Maison des Arts du Grütli, 16 rue Génèral Dufour, CP 5759 CH-1211 Geneva 11, Switzerland. Tel: (41 22) 800 1554. Fax: 329 3747. e: info@cinema-tout-ecran.ch. Web: www.cinema-tout-ecran.ch.

Clermont-Ferrand Short Film Festival
January 30–February 7, 2009

International, National and 'Lab' competitions for 35mm films and digital works on DigiBeta and Beta SP, all completed after January 1, 2008, of 40 minutes or less. All the entries will be listed in the Market catalogue. Many other side programmes (retrospectives and panoramas). *Inquiries to*: Clermont-Ferrand Short Film Festival, La Jetée, 6 place Michel-de L'Hospital 63058 Clermont-Ferrand Cedex 1, France. Tel: (33 473) 916 573. Fax: 921 193. e: info@clermont-filmfest.com. Web: www.clermont-filmfest.com.

AWARDS 2007
Grand Prix International: **The Last Dog in Rwanda** (Sweden), Jens Assur.
National: **Mozart of the Pickpockets** (France), Philippe Pollet-Villard.
Lab: **Monkey Love** (Japan/Singapore), Royston Tan.
Audience Prize International: **Tanghi Argentini** (Belgium), Guido Thys.
National: **Mozart of the Pickpockets** (France), Philippe Pollet-Villard.
Lab: **Birds** (France), Pleix.

Starz Denver Film Festival
November 13–23, 2008

The Starz Denver Film Festival presents approximately 200 films from around the world and plays host to more than 150 filmmakers. It includes new international features, cutting-edge independent fiction and non-fiction works, shorts and a variety of special programmes. It also pays tribute to established film artists with retrospective

screenings of their works. Entry fee: $40 ($20 for students). The Denver Film Society also programmes the Starz FilmCenter, Colorado's only cinematheque, daily throughout the year, and produces the Starz First Look Student Film Festival in April. *Inquiries to*: Denver Film Society at the Starz FilmCenter, 900 Auraria Parkway, Denver, Colorado 80204, USA. Tel: (1 303) 595 3456. Fax: 595 0956. e: dfs@denverfilm.org. Web: www.denverfilm.org.

AWARDS 2006
Mayor's Lifetime Achievement Award: Anthony Minghella.
John Cassavetes Award: Tim Robbins.
Stan Brakhage Vision Award: George Kuchar.
Emerging Filmmaker Award: **The Last Romantic** (USA) Aaron Nee and Adam Nee.
The Maysles Brothers Documentary Award: **Kurt Cobain About a a Son** (USA), AJ Schnack.
Krzysztof Kieslowski Award for Best Feature Film: **Beauty in Trouble** (Czech Republic), Jan Hrebejk.

Starz People's Choice Award (Feature):
The Lives of Others (Germany),
Florian Henckel von Donnersmarck.
Starz People's Choice Award (Documentary):
The Trials of Darryl Hunt (USA),
Ricki Stern and Annie Sundberg.
Starz People's Choice Award (Short):
Tie: **A Painful Glimpse Into My Creative
Process** (USA), Chel White and **Big Girl**
(Canada), Renuka Jeyapalan.

Report 2006

The 29th Starz Denver Film Festival
showcased more than 200 films from
around the world with some 200 filmmakers
introducing their works to Rocky Mountain
audiences. Special guests included Anthony
Minghella and Michael Apted (Great Britain),
Tim Robbins, Bob Rafelson, David Strathairn
and Scott Wilson (USA), Vilmos Zsigmond
(Hungary), Wu Tian Ming (China), Allan King
and Sylvie Moreau (Canada), and Florian
Henckel von Donnersmarck (Germany), among
many others. The 2006 Denver festival broke
both attendance and box office records with
more than 40,000 film lovers attending the
ten-day celebration. **– Ron Henderson,** Artistic
Director.

Dubai International Film Festival
December 2008

The festival seeks to celebrate true excellence
in Arab cinema, while also screening films
from across the world, which reflect Dubai's
cosmopolitan and multi-cultural character. The
festival will run for six full days, consisting of
twelve distinct programming sections, featuring a total of approximately 85 films. The Arab
Film Competition was launched at DIFF 2006
with the aim of giving recognition to Arab filmmakers both regionally and internationally. The
competition gives over $300,000 in cash prizes
to the recipients of the 'Muhr Award', carefully
selected by a prestigious international jury.
Inquiries to: Dubai Media City, PO Box 53777,
Dubai, United Arab Emirates. Tel: (971 4) 391
3378. e: diffinfo @dubaimediacity.ae. Web:
www.dubaifilmfest.com.

Edinburgh International Film Festival
June 18–29, 2008

The world's longest continually running film
festival, Edinburgh is also one of the most
accessible. The emphasis is on new films,
innovation and excellence worldwide, UK
films and young directors, retrospectives and
seminars. There's an offbeat sparkle to the mix
of local audiences and visitors. Edinburgh also
encapsulates Film UK, a focus for all matters
concerning UK film. *Inquiries to*: Edinburgh
International Film Festival, 88 Lothian Rd,
Edinburgh EH3 9BZ, Scotland. Tel: (44 131) 228
4051. Fax: 229 5501. e: info@edfilmfest.org.uk.
Web: www.edfilmfest.org.uk.

AWARDS 2007
*Michael Powell Award for Best New British
Feature*: **Control** (UK), Anton Corbijn.
Skillset New Director's Award:
XXY (Argentina/France/Spain), Lucia Puenzo.
Standard Life Audience Award:
We Are Together (UK), Paul Taylor.
*UK Film Council Kodak Award for Best
British Short Film*: **The One and Only Herb
McGwyer Plays Wallis Island** (UK),
James Griffiths.
Special Mention: **Dog Altogether** (UK),
Paddy Considine.
*McLaren Award for Best New British
Animation in Partnership with BBC Film
Network*: **Over the Hill** (UK), Peter Baynton.
European Film Academy Short Film - Prix UIP:
Soft (UK), Simon Ellis.
Special Mention: **Final Journey** (Germany),
Lars Zimmermann and **Ottica Zero** (UK),
Maja Borg.
*Short Scottish Documentary Award Supported
by Baillie Gifford*: **Breadmakers** (UK),
Yasmin Fedda.
Special Mention: **How to Save a Fish From
Drowning** (UK), Kelly Neal.
*PPG Award for Best Performance in a British
Feature Film*: Sam Riley for **Control**, (UK).
Sky Movies Best Documentary Award:
Billy the Kid (USA), Jennifer Venditti.

Espoo Ciné International Film Festival
August 19–24, 2008

Espoo Ciné has established itself as the annual showcase of contemporary European,
primarily long feature, cinema in Finland. The
traditional section should appeal to every
movie buff in Finland, and the growing fantasy
selection should attract those hungry for
stimulation of the imagination. It is a member
of the European Fantastic Film Festivals Federation and organises the Méliès d'Or fantastic
film competition final this year. Also US indies,
new films from other continents, the best of

contemporary Finnish cinema, outdoor screenings, retrospectives, sneak previews, seminars
and distinguished guests. *Inquiries to*: Espoo
Ciné, PO Box 95, FI-02101 Espoo, Finland.
Tel: (358 9) 466 599. Fax: 466 458. e: office@
espoocine.fi. Web: www.espoocine.fi.

Fajr International Film Festival
February 1–11, 2008
Iranian International Market for Films and TV Programmes
February 2–6, 2008

Apart from the International Competition, the
programmes include 'Festival of Festivals'
(a selection of outstanding films presented
at other international festivals), 'Special
Screenings' (documentary or narrative films
that introduce cinema or cultural developments
in specific geographical regions) and
retrospectives. The newly created Competition
of Spiritual Cinema emphasises cinema's
role as a rich medium for the expression of
religious faith. Another new addition is the
Competition of Asian Cinema, organised with

February 1-11. 2008

FARABI
CINEMA FOUNDATION

#19, Delbar St., Toos St.,
Valiye Asr Ave.,
Tehran 19617, Iran
Tel: +9821 22741250-1
+9821 22735090
Fax: +9821 22734801
E-mail: office@fajrfestival.ir

the aim of promoting film art and industry in Asian countries. Festival Director: Majid Shah-Hosseini. During the festival, the Farabi Cinema Foundation also organises the Iranian International Market for Films and TV Programmes. *Inquiries to*: Fajr International Film Festival, 2nd Floor, 19 Delbar Alley, Toos St, Valiye Asr Ave, Tehran 19617-44973, Iran. Tel: (98 21) 2273 5090/4801. Fax: 2273 4801. e: office@fajrfestival.ir. Web: www.fajrfestival.ir.

AWARDS 2007

Best Short Film: **The Circle** (Iran), Shahram Mokri.
Best Technical or Artistic Achievement: **River Queen** (New Zealand/UK), Vincent Ward.
Best Player: **The Lives of Others** (Germany), Florian Henckel von Donnersmarck.
Best Direction: **Mainline** (Iran), Rakhshan Bani-Etemad.
Special Jury Prize: **Sophie Scholl - The Final Days** (Germany), Marc Rothemund.
Best Film: **The Lives of Others** (Germany), Florian Henckel von Donnersmarck.
Best Spiritual Film: **Barefoot in Heaven** (Iran), Habibollah Kasesaz.
Best Asian Film: **Hi-Bil: Days of Fire** (Japan), Banmei Takahashi.

Report 2007

Some 200 recent and classic films were viewed by over 50,000 spectators in a score of screening halls across Tehran at the 25th Fajr International Film Festiva. The festival highlights included a Mario Monicelli retrospective, literary film adaptations and Cinema of Resistance. The new programmes include the competitions of Spiritual Films and Asian Films. The festival Jury comprised Bijaya Jena (India), Majid Majidi (Iran), Tevfik Ismailov (Azerbaijan) and Tsitsi Dangarembga (Zimbabwe). – **Mohammad SG Nadjafi,** Festival Manager.

Fantasporto

February 29–March 8, 2008

The 28th edition of the Oporto International Film Festival takes place in theatres of Oporto,

mostly at the Rivoli – Teatro Municipal, Teatro Sá da Bandeira and ten Warner Lusomundo Theatres (a total of about 5,000 seats). Apart from the Competitive Sections (Fantasy, Director's Week, Orient Express), the festival will also include the Sections 'Panorama of the Portuguese Cinema', 'Anima-te' for younger audiences, 'Première' for previews and vintage features and a 'Love Connection' section. The retrospectives include Alejandro Jodorowsky, Fernando Lopes, Danish films and Gore Cinema. Director: Mário Dorminsky. *Inquiries to*: Fantasporto, Rua Anibal Cunha 84, Sala 1.6, 4050-048 Porto, Portugal. Tel: (35 1) 222 076 050 Fax: 222 076 059. e: info@fantasporto. online.pt. Web: www.fantasporto.com.

AWARDS 2007
Fantasy Section
Film: **Pan's Labyrinth** (Mexico, Spain, USA), Guillermo del Toro.
Special Jury Award: **Historias del Desencanto** (Mexico), Alejandro Valle.
Director: Bong Joon-Ho, **The Host** (South Korea).
Actor: Sergi Lopez, **Pan's Labyrinth** (Mexico/Spain/USA).
Actress: Ariadna Gil, **Ausentes** (Spain), Daniel Calparsoro.
Screenplay: James Moran, **Severance** (UK), Christopher Smith.
Best Visual Effects: Danny & Oxide Pang, **Re-Cycle**, (Hong Kong/Taiwan/Thailand).
Best Short: **The Listening Dead** (USA), Phil Mucci.
Special Mention of the Jury:
The Bothersome Man (Norway), Jens Lien.
Director's Week

Film: **Un Franco, 14 Pesetas** (Spain), Carlos Iglesias.
Director: Carlos Iglesias, **Un Franco, 14 Pesetas** (Spain).
Special Jury Award: **Suicidio Encomendado** (Portugal), Artur Serra Araújo.
Actor: Jung-Woo Ha, **Time** (South Korea).
Actress: Isabella Leong, **Isabella** (Hong Kong).
Screenplay: Kim Fupz Aakeson, **Pure Hearts** (Denmark).
Orient Express Competitive Section
Film: **Isabella** (Hong Kong), Ho Cheung Pang.
Special Jury Award: **The Promise** (Hong Kong/Japan/South Korea), Chen Kaige.
Méliès d'Argent: **Renaissance** (France/Luxembourg/UK), Christian Volkman.
Méliès d'Argent Short Film: **Finkle's Odyssey** (UK), Barney Clay.
Critics Jury Award: **Paprika** (Japan), Satoshi Kon.
Audience Award: **Taxidermia** (Austria/France/Hungary), Gyorgy Pálfi.

Report 2007
Celebrating the 25th anniversary of *ET*, the festival received Henry Thomas as its guest. Over 300 international and Portuguese guests connected with the films screened appeared at the festival, including Rosanna Arquete. Guillermo del Toro's *Pan´s Labyrinth* closed the festival. 100,000 people attended the 27th edition of Fantasporto. **– Áurea Ribeiro.**

Far East Film Festival
April 18–26, 2008

Annual themed event which, since 1998, has focused on Eastern Asian cinema. *Inquiries*

Actress Kim Hye-soo, left, with film director Choi Dong at the 2007 Far East Film Festival

to: Centro Espressioni Cinematografiche, Via Villalta 24, 33100 Udine, Italy. Tel: (39 04) 3229 9545. Fax: 3222 9815. e: fareastfilm@cecudine.org, Web: www.fareastfilm.com.

AWARDS 2007
Audience Award First Prize: **No Mercy for the Rude** (South Korea), Park Chul-hee.
Audience Award Second Prize: **After This Our Exile** (Hong Kong), Patrick Tam.
Audience Award Third Prize: **Memories of Matsuko** (Japan), Nakashima Tetsuya.

Report 2007
The ninth edition of Far East Film attracted an audience of 50,000. Over 1,000 accredited guests from more than 25 countries attended, plus 200 journalists and numerous representatives from international film festivals. Audience participation increased, breaking the previous record for the highest number of votes recorded for the Audience Award. The award went to Korean director Park Chul-hee's noir masterpiece, *No Mercy For The Rude*. Patrick Tam, with his latest work, *After This Our Exile*, was awarded second place.

Following closely was the Japanese fantasy, *Memories of Matsuko*, by Tetsuya Nakashima. – **Chui-Yee,** Executive Manager.

Festival Des 3 Continents
November 25–December 2, 2008

The only annual competitive (with fiction and documentary) festival in the world for films originating solely from Africa, Asia, Latin and Black America. It's one of the few festivals where genuine discoveries may still be made. From Hou Hsiao-hsien or Abbas Kiarostami in the 1980s, to Darejan Omirbaev and Jia Zhangke more recently, unknown great authors have been shown and acknowledged in Nantes. For 29 years, F3C has also charted the film history of the southern countries through retrospectives (genres, countries, actors and actresses), showing more than 1,200 films and bringing to light large pieces of an unrecognised part of the world's cinematographic heritage. *Inquiries to*: Guillaume Marion, General Delegate, Festival des 3 Continents, BP 43302, 44033 Nantes Cedex 1, France. Tel: (33 2) 4069 7414. Fax: 4073 5522. e: festival@3continents.com. Web: www.3continents.com.

Filmfest Hamburg
September 25–October 10, 2008

Under the direction of Albert Wiederspiel, the renowned film festival takes place every year in the autumn. Around 130 international films are screened as German or world premieres in the following sections: Agenda, KinderFilmfest Hamburg (Children's Filmfest

10th ANNIVERSARY　　　www.fareastfilm.com

udine FAR EAST *film* 10

april 18th - 26th 2008 *udine* ITALY

Hamburg), TV Movies in Cinema, Eurovisuell, Voilà!, Vitrina, Nordlichter and Deluxe. The many facets of the programme range from cinematically highbrow arthouse films to innovative mainstream cinema. The Douglas Sirk Prize honours outstanding contributions to film culture and business. There are more than 30,000 admissions and about 1,000 industry professionals attend. Filmfest Hamburg also sees itself as a platform for cultural exchange and dialogue: in the past years, the festival has, among others, shed light more on productions from Asia (from Iran to Japan and Korea) and Europe (from the UK and Scandinavia to France, Spain and Eastern Europe). *Inquiries to*: Filmfest Hamburg, Steintorweg 4, D-20099 Hamburg, Germany. Tel: (49 40) 3991 9000. Fax: 3991 90010. e: info@filmfesthamburg.de. Web: www. filmfesthamburg.de.

Flanders International Film Festival (Ghent)

October 7–18, 2008

Belgium's most prominent annual film event, which attracts attendance of 100,000 plus, is selected by *Variety* as one of the 50 'must attend' festivals due to its unique focus on film music. This competitive festival awards grants worth up to $120,000 and screens around 150 features and 50 shorts, most without a Benelux distributor. Besides the official competition focusing on the impact of music on film, the festival includes the following sections: Festival Previews (World, European, Benelux or Belgian premieres), World Cinema (films from all over the world,

mainly without a distributor), retrospectives, film music concerts, seminars and a tribute to an important international film maker. The festival's Joseph Plateau Awards are the highest honours in Benelux. Presented for the first time in 2001, the festival also hands out the World Soundtrack Awards, judged by some 270 international composers. Every year in October, the Ghent Film Festival is the meeting point for film music composers and fans worldwide. *Inquiries to*: Flanders International Film Festival-Ghent, 40B Leeuwstraat, B-9000 Ghent, Belgium. Tel: (32 9) 242 8060. Fax: 221 9074. e: info@ filmfestival.be. Web: www.filmfestival.be. and www.worldsoundtrackawards.com.

AWARDS 2007

Impact of Music on Film Competition
Grand Prix for Best Film: **The Counterfeiters** (Austria/Germany), Stefan Ruzowitzky.
Georges Delerue Prize for Best Music: Benny Andersson, **You the Living** (France).
SABAM Award for Best Screenplay: Tamara Jenkins, **The Savages** (USA).
Robert Wise Award for Best Director: Saverio Constanzo, **In Memory of Me** (Italy).
Special Jury Mention: Sasson Gabai and Ronit Elkabetz for their contribution to **The Band's Visit** (France/Israel).
Xplore! Award: **Once** (Ireland), John Carney.
National Lottery Award for the Best Belgian Short: **Personal Spectator**, Emmanuel Jespers (Belgium).
Special Mention: **Zoë** (Belgium), Dorothée van den Berghe.
Ace Award for Flemish Student Shorts: **Juliette** (Belgium), Nathalie Teirlinck.

Special Mention: **Yves** (Belgium), Joost Jansen.
Prix UIP/Ghent: **Raak** (Netherlands), Hanro Smitsman.
Prime Audience Award: **Blindsight** (UK), Lucy Walker.
Canvas Audience Award: **Auf der Andere Selte** (Germany/Turkey), Fatih Akin.

Fort Lauderdale International Film Festival
October 17–November 9, 2008

FLIFF features more than 200 films from 40 countries during the world's longest film event, with screenings in Miami, Palm Beach and Fort Lauderdale. Awards include Best Film, Best Foreign-Language Film, Best American Indie, Best Director, Actor, Screenplay, Best Florida Film and Kodak Student prizes for Narrative (over 20 minutes), Short Narrative (20 minutes or under), Documentary and Experimental. The Festival has a fun party side, too, with a Beach Party, Sunday Brunch Cruise, Champagne Starlight Sail, a Fashion Show aboard a 300-passenger luxury barge, and a gala featuring South Florida's top restaurants. The Sundance Channel Festival Cafe has daily and nightly parties. Attendance topped 65,000 in 2006. The deadlines for entries are as follows: July 1 (Professional Early Deadline 1st Call), August 15 (Final Professional Deadline), Sept 15 (Student Deadline for catalogue) and Sept 30 (Final Deadline). *Inquiries to*: The Fort Lauderdale International Film Festival, 1314 East Las Olas Blvd, Suite 007, Fort Lauderdale, FL 33301, USA. Tel: (1 954) 760 9898. Fax: 760 9099. e: info@fliff.com. Web: www.fliff.com.

Fribourg Film Festival
March 1–8, 2008

Features, shorts and documentaries from Asia, Africa and Latin America unspool at this Swiss event, with a competitive section. *Inquiries to*: Fribourg International Film Festival, Ancienne Gare, Case Postale 550, CH-1701 Fribourg, Switzerland. Tel: (41 26) 347 4200. Fax: 347 4201. e: info@fiff.ch. Web: www.fiff.ch.

AWARDS 2007
Grand Prix Le Regard d'Or: **Alice's House** (Brazil), Chico Teixeira.
Special Jury Award: **Roma Wa la n'Touma** (Algeria/France/Germany), Tariq Teguia.
Swiss Oikocredit Award: **Love Conquers All** (Malaysia), Tan Chui Mui.
Swiss Oikocredit Award: **Love Conquers All** (Malaysia), Tan Chui Mui.
Ecumenical Jury Award: **Le Cercle des Noyés** (Belgium/France), Pierre-Yves Vandeweerd.
FIPRESCI Jury Award: **Le Cercle des Noyés** (Belgium/France), Pierre-Yves Vandeweerd.
IFFS Jury 'Don Quijote Award': **Le Cercle des Noyés** (Belgium/France), Pierre-Yves Vandeweerd.

Report 2007
Alongside the competition, panoramas and retrospectives are organised by film experts and offer the possibility of looking deeper into a film topic, genre or period. In 2007, the FIFF showed particular interest in the cinema from South Africa with a panorama entitled 'Beyond Freedom: The Identity of South African Film-makers', prepared by Freddy Ogterop who, for 40 years, was in charge of the video archives of the Western Cape Provincial Library. The programming was at the crossroads between productions with a foreign orientation and those designed for a domestic audience. Through the panorama 'Images of Urban Life', the FIFF proposed recent films from four continents, including Europe, all of which dealt with the topic of city life. **- Joana Borrego,** Press Officer.

Giffoni
July 18–26, 2008

Located in Giffoni Valle Piana, a small town about 40 minutes from Naples, the Giffoni International Film Festival for Children and Young People was founded in 1971 by Claudio Gubitosi to promote films for youthful audiences and families. Now includes five competitive sections: Kidz (animated and fiction feature-length films and short films that tell fantastic stories, juried by 250 children aged six to nine); First Screens (fiction features and animated shorts, mainly fantasy and adventure, juried by 500 children aged 9 to 12); Free 2 Fly sees 400 teenagers (aged 12 to 14) assessing features and shorts about the pre-adolescent world; Y GEN has 350 jurors (aged 15 to 19) and takes a curious look at cinema for young people. Troubled Gaze has 100 jurors (from 19 years old) and is the section which explores the re-lationship between kids and parents. *Inquiries to*: Giffoni Film Festival, Cittadella del Cinema, Via Aldo Moro 4, 84095 Giffoni Valle Piana, Salerno, Italy. Tel: (39 089) 802 3001. Fax: 802 3210. e: info@giffoniff.it. Web: www.giffoniff.it.

AWARDS 2007

Free 2 Fly-Golden Gryphon: **Michou D'Auber** (France), Thomas Gilou.
Free 2 Fly-Silver Gryphon: **A Recaptured Glance** (Italy), Marco Ottavio Graziano).
Free 2 Fly-Jury Grand Prix Bronze Gryphon: **Michou D'Auber** (France), Thomas Gilou.
Y Gen-Golden Gryphon: **Keith** (USA), Todd Kessler.
Y Gen-Silver Gryphon: **Little Man** (Denmark), Esben Toennesen.
Y Gen-Jury Grand Prix-Bronze Gryphon: **Eagle vs Shark** (New Zealand), Taika Waititi.
First Screens-Golden Gryphon: **Kidz in da Hood** (Sweden), Ylva Gustavsson and Catti Edfeldt.
First Screens-Silver Gryphon: **Filiz in Flight** (Germany) Sylke Rene Meyer.
Kidz-Golden Gryphon: **Mid Road Gang** (Thailand,) Somkiat Vithuranich and Pantham Thongsang.
Kidz-Silver Gryphon: **For All the Marbles** (Canada), Kris Booth.

Gijón International Film Festival
November 20–29, 2008

One of Spain's oldest festivals (45th edition in 2007), Gijón is now at the peak of its popularity. Having firmly established itself as a barometer of new film trends worldwide, it draws a large and enthusiastic public. Gijón has built on its niche as a festival for young people, programming innovative and independent films made by and for the young, including retrospectives, panoramas, exhibitions and concerts. Alongside the lively Official Section, sidebars celebrate directors who have forged new paths in filmmaking. Last year's winners: **Longing** (Germany), Valeska Grisebach (International Jury) and **Offside** (Iran), Jafar Panahi (Young Jury). *Inquiries to*: Gijón International Film Festival, PO Box 76, 33201 Gijon, Spain. Tel: (34 98) 518 2940. Fax: 518 2944. e: info@gijonfilmfestival. com. Web: www.gijonfilmfestival.com.

Le Giornate del Cinema Muto
October 4–11, 2008

The world's first and largest festival dedicated to silent cinema. After eight years in the nearby historic town of Sacile, in 2007 the festival moved back to its original venue, Pordenone, and to the rebuilt Verdi Theatre. The festival sees an annual invasion by international archivists, historians, scholars, collectors and enthusiasts, along with cinema students chosen to attend the internationally recognised 'Collegium'. The Film Fair features books, CD-ROMs and DVDs, and provides a valued meeting place for authors and publishers. Festival Director: David Robinson. *Inquiries to*: Le Giornate del Cinema Muto, c/o La Cineteca del Friuli, Palazzo Gurisatti, via Bini 50, 33013 Gemona (UD), Italy. Tel: (39 04) 3298 0458. Fax: 3297 0542. e: info.gcm@cinetecadelfriuli. org. Web: www.cinetecadelfriuli.org/gcm/.

Report 2007
Highlights of the 26th edition included a tribute to the silent films of poet-director Rene Clair, and 'The Other Weimar', featuring German films and directors of the 1920s unjustly forgot-ten and excluded from the traditional canon of 'classics'. G. W. Pabst's masterpiece *Pandora's Box*, starring the incomparable Louise Brooks, was presented with a newly commissioned score by Paul Lewis. Other orchestral shows included Antonio Coppola's score for Clair's *Paris Qui Dort* and the late John Lanchbery's for DW Griffith's *Orphans of the Storm*, shown in the context of the Giornate's 12-year 'Griffith Project'. A remarkable historical rediscovery

was a programme of films of 'The Bible Lands' filmed in 1897 and recently rediscovered, in the form of near-perfect negatives, by Lobster Films of Paris. This year's guests of honour were Academy Award-winning animator John Canemaker, and the famous child star from silent films, Jean Darling, the infant heroine of Our Gang. – **David Robinson,** Festival Director.

goEast Festival of Central and Eastern European Film in Wiesbaden
April 9–15, 2008

Established in 2001 for audiences interested in Eastern European film, with a mix of current productions and historical series, a competition for feature and documentary films, an academic symposium, a students' programme and related events. Member of FIAPF; hosts FIPRESCI Jury. Deadline: end-Dec. Inquiries to: Deutsches Filminstitut – DIF, Schaumainkai 41, D-60596 Frankfurt, Germany. Tel: (49 69) 9612 20651. Fax: 9612 20669. e: kopf@filmfestival-goeast.de. Web: www.filmfestival-goeast.de.

AWARDS 2007
The Škoda Award for the Best Film:
Euphoria (Russia), Ivan Vyrypaev.
The Hertie Documentary Award:
How To Do It (Poland), Marcel Łoziński.
Award of the City of Wiesbaden for Best Director and FIPRESCI-Prize: **The Trap** (Germany/Hungary/Serbia), Srdan Golubović.
Award of the Federal Foreign Office: **Armin** (Bosnia and Herzegovina/Croatia/Germany), Ognjen Sviličić.

Report 2007
At the 7th goEast Film Festival, held during seven days in March/April 2007, and visited by around 9,000 spectators, 150 full-length and short films were screened, accompanied by

film talks, panel discussions, and an extensive sidebar programme. The high points of the festival were the Symposium, 'The Yearning for Spirituality – Film and Religion in Eastern Europe', the 'Promotional Prize for Joint Film Production by Young German and Eastern/ South Eastern European Filmmakers' of the Robert Bosch Stiftung, the Portrait of Fatmir Koçi from Albania and the Homage to Miloš Forman. – **Karin Schyle,** Festival Management.

Göteborg International Film Festival
End January–early February 2008

Now in its 31st year, Göteborg International Film Festival is one of Europe's key film events. With a large international programme and a special focus on Nordic films, including the Nordic Competition, GIFF is Scandinavia's most important film festival. International seminars, master classes and the market place Nordic Film Market attract buyers and festival programmers to the newest Scandinavian films. The 30th jubilee, in 2007, introduced a new international competition – The Ingmar Bergman International Debut Award (TIBIDA). Some 1,800 professionals attend and more than 120,000 tickets are sold to 450 films from around 70 countries. Inquiries to: Göteborg International Film Festival, Olof Palmes Plats, S- 413 04 Göteborg, Sweden. Tel: (46 31) 339 3000. Fax: 410 063. e: goteborg@filmfestival. org. Web: www.filmfestival.org.

AWARDS 2007
Best Nordic Film: **Darling** (Sweden), Johan Kling.
Winner of TIBIDA: **Red Road** (UK), Andrea Arnold.

A papier-mache tribute to Ingmar Bergman at the Göteborg Festival

Haugesund – Norwegian International Film Festival
August 15–22, 2008

Located in Haugesund, on the West Coast of Norway, the festival is Norway's major event for film and cinema. The Norwegian and Scandinavian film industry is represented by over 1,500 participants, as well as several hundred international buyers, producers and directors. The New Nordic Films market runs at the end of the period. The Amanda Awards (the Norwegian 'Oscar') take place the day before the festival starts. Festival Director: Gunnar Johan Løvvik. Programme Director: Håkon Skogrand. Honorary President: Liv Ullmann. *Inquiries to*: PO Box 145, N-5501 Haugesund, Norway. Tel: (47 52) 743 370. Fax: 743 371. e: info@filmfestivalen.no. Web: www.filmfestivalen.no.

AWARDS 2007
Film Critics Award: **You the Living** (Sweden), Roy Andersson.
The Ray of Sunshine: **Gone With the Woman**, (Norway), Petter Næss.
Audience Award: **The Unknown**, (Italy), Giuseppe Tornatore.
Andreas Award: **You the Living** (Sweden), Roy Andersson.

Helsinki International Film Festival – Love & Anarchy
September 18–20, 2008

The largest film festival in Finland, with over 45,000 admissions during the festival's 11 days. Organised annually since 1988, the festival has found its place as the top venue for the new and the alternative in cinema and popular culture. The festival has a memorable subtitle, 'Love & Anarchy', adopted from a 1970s Lina Wertmüller film. It has become a trademark for cutting-edge films over the years: films that offer something different and explore new frontiers. The festival is non-competitive. Submission deadline: June 30. *Inquiries to*: Helsinki Film Festival, Mannerheimintie 22-24, PO Box 889, FI-00101 Helsinki, Finland. Tel: (358 9) 6843 5230. Fax: 6843 5232. e:office@hiff.fi. Web: www.hiff.fi

Drinking to 40 years of the Hof International Film Festival: Film director Aki Kaurismäki (left) and festival director Heinz Badewitz

Hof International Film Festival
October 21–26, 2008

The Hof International Film Festival – often nicknamed 'The German Telluride' – was founded in the northern Bavarian town of Hof in 1968 by current festival director Heinz Badewitz and several up-and-coming filmmakers of the day (Wim Wenders, Volker Schlöndorff, Werner Herzog and Rainer-Werner Fassbinder among them). It has since gone on to become one of the most important

film festivals in Germany, concentrating both on German films by the new filmmakers and independent movies from abroad. The retrospective has so far overseen the careers of directors as varied as Monte Hellman, Mike Leigh, Lee Grant, John Sayles, Brian de Palma, Peter Jackson, Roger Corman, John Cassavetes, Costa-Gavras and Wayne Wang. *Inquiries to*: Hof International Film Festival, Altstadt 8, D-95028 Hof, Germany. Fax: (49) 9281 18816 e: info@hofer-filmtage.de. Web: www.hofer-filmtage.de.

Hong Kong International Film Festival
March 17–April 6, 2008

The Hong Kong International Film Festival Society is a non-profit, non-government organisation which develops, promotes and encourages creativity in the art of film through the presentation of the annual Hong Kong International Film Festival (HKIFF). The Society is also committed to organising regular programmes and other activities throughout the year, in order to promote the art and business of filmmaking, with an international

dimension and outlook. From 2007, the Society will be responsible for three flagship events, including the Hong Kong International Film Festival (HKIFF), the Hong Kong - Asia Film Financing Forum (HAF) and Asia Film Awards (AFA). *Inquiries to*: Hong Kong International Film Festival Society Office, 7/F United Chinese Bank Building, 31-37 Des Voeux Road Central, Hong Kong. Tel: (852) 2970 3300. Fax: 2970 3011. e: info@hkiff.org.hk. Web: www. hkiff.org.hk.

Huelva Latin American Film Festival
November 2008

The 33rd Huelva Latin American Film Festival continued to champion outstanding films from both shores of the Atlantic. It is one of the most important Latin American cultural events, where the work of upcoming and established filmmakers is made available to an international audience. Huelva aims to open a European film market for new, talented, Latin American filmmakers. The best film is awarded a prize known as the Golden Colombus. *Inquiries to*: Casa Colon, Plaza del Punto s/n, 21003 Huelva,

Spain. Tel: (34 95) 921 0170/0299. Fax: 921 0173. e: prensa@festicinehuelva.com. Web: www.festicinehuelva.com.

IFP Market
September 14–20, 2008

If you are seeking financing, sales, completion funding or production partners, IFP Market is the place to access industry executives through screenings, business and pitch meetings, targeted networking and social events. An essential networking opportunity, the IFP Market attracts hundreds of financiers, buyers, distributors, broadcasters, development executives, agents, managers and festival programmers from the US and abroad. *Inquiries to*: IFP Market and Conference, 104 West 29th St, 12th Floor, New York, NY 10001, USA. Tel: (1 212) 465 8200. Fax: 465 8525. e: jhe@ifp.org. Web: www.ifp. org.

International Film Festival India
Late November 2008

Annual, government-funded event recognised by FIAPF and held in Goa under the aegis of India's Ministry of Information and Broadcasting. Comprehensive 'Cinema of the World' section, foreign and Indian retrospectives and a film market, plus a valuable panorama of the year's best Indian films, subtitled in English. *Inquiries to*: The Director, International Film Festival of India, Sirifort Auditoriums, August Kranti Marg, New Delhi 110049, India. Tel: (91 11) 2649 9356. Fax: 2649 9357). e: ddiffi.dff@ nic.in. Web: www.iffi.nic.in.

Istanbul International Film Festival
April 5–20, 2008

The only film festival that takes place in a city where two continents meet, the Istanbul International Film Festival boasted its largest attendance with 150,000 attendees. Now in its 27th year, this dynamic event focuses on features dealing with the arts and the artist in its main competition, the Golden Tulip, retrospectives, selections from world festivals, with other thematic sections such as 'The World of Animation', 'Mined Zone', 'Documentary Time', 'Human Rights in Cinema' now with the Film Award of the Council of Europe – FACE, 'Women's Films', 'Young Masters' and a comprehensive showcase of Turkish cinema. *Inquiries to*: Ms Azize Tan, Istanbul Foundation for Culture and Arts, Istiklal Caddesi 146, Beyoglu 34435, Istanbul, Turkey. Tel: (90 212) 334 0700 exts. 720 & 721. Fax: 334 0702. e: film.fest@iksv. org. Web: www.iksv.org/film.

AWARDS 2007
International Competition
Golden Tulip: **Reprise** (Norway), Joachim Trier.
Special Prize of the Jury: **Delirious** (USA), Tom DiCillo.
FIPRESCI Prize: **The Art of Crying** (Denmark), Peter Schønau Fog.
People's Choice Awards: **Half Moon** (Iran), Bahman Ghobadi.
National Competition
Special Prize of the Jury: **International**, Sırrı Süreyya Önder & Muharrem Gülmez.
FIPRESCI Prize: **Destiny**, Zeki Demirkubuz.
FACE Award: **The Court** (Mali), Abderrahmane Sissako.

From the closing ceremony of the festival, with Gus Van Sant and Sakir Eczacibasi, Chairman Istanbul Film Festival

Best Turkish Film of the Year: **Climates**, Nuri Bilge Ceylan
Best Turkish Director of the Year: Zeki Demirkubuz, **Destiny**.
People's Choice Awards: **Climates**, Nuri Bilge Ceylan.

Report 2007

The 26th edition of the Istanbul Film Festival saw record attendances thanks to a total of 237 films in the programme, including a special section on new Russian film, a new section concentrating on films from the Caucasus to the Mediterranean, retrospectives on Hayao Miyazaki and Gus Van Sant, a specially curated section on R. W. Fassbinder and tributes to Pier Paolo Pasolini and Bob Fosse. Highlights included master classes and panel discussions by Gus Van Sant, Tsai Ming-liang, Park Chan-wook and guests such as Irm Hermann, Paul Schrader, Ferzan Özpetek, Bahman Ghobadi, Ninetto Davoli, Tom DiCillo, amongst many others. The jury of the International Golden Tulip competition this year was composed of Michael Radford (President), Zeki Demirkubuz, Dagur Kari, Udo Kier, Tilbe Saran and Katriel Schory. **– Yusuf Pinhas.**

Jerusalem International Film Festival
July 10–19, 2008

Celebrating its 25th anniversary this year, the Jerusalem International Film Festival offers over 70,000 people the chance to increase their awareness of contemporary world cinema. The Opening Gala event attracts over 7,000 spectators, under the stars, in the shadow of the Ancient City walls. The festival continues to receive warm praise worldwide for its intimate atmosphere, unique setting and its effort to promote the appreciation and distribution of quality films in Israel. The pro-gramme presents over 200 films across a wide spectrum of themes and categories, including: Best of International Cinema; Israeli Cinema; Documentaries; Animation; Jewish Themes; Human Rights; Retrospectives; Avant Garde; Restorations; Television; Special Tributes; and Classics. The festival presents several prizes and awards: Wim van Leer In Spirit of Freedom (International Competition), Mayor's Award for Jewish Experience (International Competition), Wolgin Awards for Israeli Cinema, Awards for Best Israeli Screenplay, Best Actor and Best Actress. *Inquiries to*: Jerusalem Film Festival, Hebron Road 11, Jerusalem 91083, Israel. Tel: (972 2) 565 4333. Fax: 565 4334. e: festival@ jer-cin.org.il. Web: www.jff.org.il.

Karlovy Vary International Film Festival
July 4–12, 2008

Founded in 1946, Karlovy Vary is one of the most important film events in Central and Eastern Europe. It includes Official Selection - Competition, Documentary Films in Competition, East of the West - Films in Competition and other programme sections which give the unique chance to see new film production from all around the world. Film entry deadline: April 18, 2008. *Inquiries to*: Film Servis Festival Karlovy Vary, Panská 1, CZ 110 00 Prague 1, Czech Republic. Tel: (420 2) 2141 1011. Fax: 2141 1033. e: festival@kviff. com. Web: www.kviff.com.

AWARDS 2007

Grand Prix- Crystal Globe: **Jar City** (Germany/Iceland), Baltasar Kormákur.
Special Jury Prize: **Lucky Miles** (Australia), Michael James Rowland.
Best Director: Bård Breien
The Art of Negative Thinking (Norway).
Best Actress: Elvira Mínguez **Pudor** (Spain).
Best Actor: Sergey Puskepalis **Simple Things** (Russia).
Special Jury Mention: Leonid Bronevoy for his role in **Simple Things** (Russia) and Zdeněk Svěrák for the screenplay of **Empties** (Czech Republic/Denmark/UK).
Best Documentary Film Under 30 Minutes: **Artel** (Russia), Sergey Loznitsa.
Special Mention: **Theodore** (Latvia), Laila Pakalnina.
Best Documentary Film Over 30 Minutes: **Lost Holiday** (Czech Republic), Lucie Králová.
Special Mention: **The Mosquito Problem and Other Stories** (Bulgaria), Andrey Paounov.
East of the West: **Armin** (Bosnia and Herzegovina/Croatia/Germany), Ognjen Sviličić.
Special Mention: **The Class** (Estonia), Ilmar Raag.
Audience Award: **Empties** (Czech Republic/Denmark/UK), Jan Svěrák.
Special Crystal Globe for Outstanding Artistic Contribution to World Cinema: Danny DeVito (USA) Břetislav Pojar (Czech Republic).

Report 2007

135,759 spectators saw 250 new films from 58 countries during the 42nd Karlovy Vary IFF in July. Editor-in-chief of *Variety* Peter Bart was the President of the Grand Jury. Apart from the regular sections, this year's festival presented Shochiku Nouvelle Vague, New Hollywood and Focus on New Italian Directors programmes.
– Andrea Szczukova, Head of Film Industry Office.

La Rochelle International Film Festival
June 27–July 7, 2008

The non-competitive festival features more than 200 new releases, tributes to and retrospectives of directors or actors (2007 featured Anastasia Lapsui and Markku Lehmuskallio from Finland, Jean-Paul Rappeneau from France, Ulrich Seidl from Austria and Isao Takahata from Japan); retrospectives devoted to the work of past filmmakers; 'Here and There', a selection of unreleased films from all over the world; 'From Yesterday till Today', premieres of rare films restored and re-edited; 'Carpets, Cushions and Video', video works projected on the ceiling above supine spectators; Films for Children. The festival ends with an all-night programme of five films, followed by breakfast in cafés overlooking the old port. *Inquiries to*: La Rochelle International Film Festival, 16 rue Saint Sabin, 75011 Paris, France. Tel: (33 1) 4806 1666. Fax: 4806 1540. e: info@festival-larochelle.org. Web: www.festival-larochelle. org. Director: Mrs Prune Engler; Artistic Director: Mrs Sylvie Pras.

Las Palmas de Gran Canaria International Film Festival
February 29–March 8, 2008

To See: Official Section (competitive); Informative Section; Hot Spots (this year: Malaysia, Romania, Philippines); Naomi Kawase (retrospective); Facing the Mirror (Autobiographical Filmmaking); Direct Cinema; New Mexican Filmmakers; JH Hermosillo; 'Newest ' USA III; Déjà Vu (Sembene, Yang, Bergman, Antonioni); Déjà Vu (Paulino Viota); The 'Freakest' Night; Dolly Shot (Travelling: arts, cinema and the act of watching films); **To Think:** Maps of the World (A workshop on personal footage travelling); Books (On Kawase, Direct Cinema and Autobiographical Filmmaking); **To Produce:** Euroforo (European

Co-production Meetings). *Inquiries to*: León y Castillo, 322, 4ª Planta, 35007 Las Palmas de Gran Canaria. Tel: (34 928) 446 833/644. Fax: 446 651. e: laspalmascine@hotmail.com. Web: www.festivalcinelaspalmas.com.

Leeds International Film Festival
November 2008

Presented by Leeds City Council, the Leeds International Film Festival is the largest regional Film Festival in the United Kingdom. In addition, Leeds Film curates a year-round exhibition with partner organisations in the city, education programmes and delivers the Leeds Young People's Film Festival. *Inquiries to*: Leeds International Film Festival, The Town Hall, The Headrow, Leeds, LS1 3AD, UK. Tel: (44 113) 247 8398. Fax: 247 8494. e: filmfestival@leeds.gov.uk. Web: www. leedsfilm.com.

AWARDS 2006
Golden Owl Award: **I Don't Care if Tomorrow Never Comes** (Belgium), Guillaume Malandrin.
Audience Award for Best Feature: **The Last King of Scotland** (UK), Kevin Macdonald.
Louis Le Prince Short Fiction Film Award: **Bhai – Bhai** (France/Canada), Olivier Klein.
World Animation Award: **Dreams and Desires – Family Ties** (UK), Joanna Quinn.
Silver Méliès Feature Competition: **Isolation** (UK/Ireland), Billy O'Brien.
Silver Méliès Short Competition: **Home Video** (UK), Ed Boase.
Yorkshire Film Award: **Private Life** (UK), Abbe Robinson.
Audience Award, Documentary Film: **Death of Two Sons** (USA), Micah Schaffer.

Locarno International Film Festival
August 6–16, 2008

The Locarno International Film Festival, one of the world's top cinematic all-feature events, traditionally aims to promote personal filmmaking of artistic merit, to provide a showcase for major new films of the year from around the world and to take stock, in its competitive section, of the new perspectives of filmmaking expression, concentrating especially on such new film directors and industries as command international attention. In fact, the Festival, with its ongoing process of cultural inquiry, has contributed to revealing or confirming directors who are currently enjoying a very wide recognition. Moreover, the Locarno Festival has established itself in recent years as an important industry showcase for auteur filmmaking, a perfect networking opportunity for distributors, buyers and producers from around the world with over 3,700 film professionals and 1,100 journalists attending – together with 190,000 cinema-goers. *Inquiries to*: Festival Internazionale del Film Locarno, Via Ciseri 23, CH-6601 Locarno, Switzerland. Artistic Director: Frédéric Maire. Tel: (41 91) 756 2121. Fax: 756 2149. e: info@pardo.ch. Web: www.pardo.ch.

AWARDS 2007
International Competition
Golden Leopard: **The Rebirth** (Japan), Masahiro Kobayashi.
Special Jury Prize: **Memories** 'Jeonju Digital Project 2007' (South Korea), Pedro Costa, Harun Farocki and Eugène Green.
Prize for the Best Direction: **Capitaine Achab** (France/Sweden), Philippe Ramos.
Actress Leopard: Marian Alvarez, **Lo Mejor de Mi** (Spain).
Actor Leopards: Michel Piccoli, **Sous les Toits de Paris** (France) and Michele Venitucci, **Fuori Dale Corde** (Italy/Switzerland).
Special Mention: Cho Sang-Yoon, cinematographer **Boys of Tomorrow** by Noh Dong-Seok (South Korea).
Filmmakers of the Present Competition
CP Company Golden Leopard: **Tejút (Milky Way)** (Hungary/Germany), Benedek Fliegauf.
Ciné Cinéma Special Jury Prize: **Imatra** (Italy), Corso Salani.
Special Mention: **Tussenstand** (Netherlands), Mijke de Jong.
Leopard for the Best First Feature: **Tagliare le Parti in Grigio** (Italy), Vittorio Rifranti.
Prix du Public UBS (Audience Award): **Death at a Funeral** (UK/USA), Frank Oz.

Locarno International Film Festival

Report 2007

186,000 spectators attended the 60th anniversary of the Locarno Film Festival to enjoy the 170 films presented. The 60th edition was also marked by the presence of film icons such as Spanish actress Carmen Maura and French actor Michel Piccoli, who both received an Excellence Award. Anthony Hopkins presented his film *Slipstream* in the International Competition and filmmaker Hou Hsiao-Hsien received the Leopard of Honour. The Open Air Venue on the Piazza Grande was thrilled by Robert Rodriguez and Rose McGowan, who presented *Planet Terror*, and Frank Oz charmed audiences with his *Death at a Funeral*. Other important guests included Nobel Prize winner Dario Fo, Carole Laure, Christian Slater, Denis Lavant, Anna Mouglalis, Maya Sansa and Peter Lohmeyer, as well as directors Marco Bellocchio, Mike Leigh, István Szabó, Paulo Rocha, Gaston Kaboré, Marco Tullio Giordana, Fredi M. Murer and the producer Lita Stantic, Prize Raimondo Rezzonico.
– **Frédéric Maire,** Festival Director.

The Times BFI London International Film Festival

Mid October–early November 2008

The UK's largest and most prestigious festival, sponsored by *The Times* newspaper and presented at the National Film Theatre, in the West End, and at cinemas throughout the capital. The programme comprises around 200 features and documentaries, as well as a showcase for shorts. There is a British section and a very strong international selection from Asia, Africa, Europe, Latin America, US independents and experimental and avant-garde work. More than 1,600 UK and international press and industry representatives attend and there is a buyers/sellers liaison office. *Inquiries to*: Sarah Lutton, London Film Festival, BFI Southbank, Belvedere Road, South Bank, London SE1 8XT, UK. Tel: (44 20) 7815 1322. Fax: 7633 0786. e: sarah.lutton@bfi.org.uk. Web: www.lff.org.uk.

AWARDS 2006

The Sutherland Trophy Winner: Andrea Arnold, **Red Road** (Denmark/UK).
9th FIPRESCI International Critics Award Winner: Javier Rebollo, **Lola** (France/Spain).
The Alfred Dunhill UK Film Talent Award Winner: Mark Herbert, **This is England**.
The Times BFI London Film Festival Grierson Award: **Thin** (USA), Lauren Greenfield.
The 11th Annual Satyajit Ray Award Winner:
The Lives of Others (Germany),
Florian Henckel von Donnersmarck.
TCM Short Film Award Winner:
Silence is Golden, Chris Shepherd.

Málaga Film Festival

April 4–2, 2008

983 accredited journalists attended the festival (21% more than last year). There were four Audiovisual Markets: Málaga Screenings (Spanish Film Market); TV Market (Market for Spanish Fiction and Animation Productions for Television); Mercadoc (European and Latin-American Documentary Market); and Art TV (Visual Art Market). Mercadoc was represented by 426 accredited people and 97 buyers from 32 countries. 444 documentary programmes were presented in the Videoteca. The President of the Jury was Antonio Isasi-Isasmendi and the winner of the 'Biznaga de Oro' was Félix Viscarret's *Bajo las Estrellas*. There were 23 feature film premieres: Official Section and ZonaZine. 27 documentary premieres, 25 short films, 25 video-clips, 8 Latin American films and 60 feature films between the different cycles. Salomon Castiel has been Málaga Film Festival's director from its first edition.

Inquiries to: Málaga Festival, Calle Carcer 6, 29012 Malaga, Spain. Tel: (34 95) 222 8242. Fax: 222 7760. e: info@festivaldemalaga.com. Web: www.festivalmalaga.com.

Mannheim-Heidelberg
October 2008

The Newcomers' Festival: for young independent filmmakers from all over the world. Presents around 40 new features in two main sections, International Competition and International Discoveries. The Newcomers' Market & Industry Screenings: reserved for international buyers and distributors. The Mannheim Meetings: part one is one of only four worldwide co-production meetings for producers (alongside Rotterdam, New York and Pusan) and runs in parallel to the main event; part two is the unique European Sales & Distribution Meetings for theatrical distributors and sales agents. The Distribution Market takes place during the festival. More than 60,000 filmgoers and 1,000 film professionals attend. *Inquiries to*: Dr Michael Koetz, International Filmfestival Mannheim-Heidelberg, Collini-Center, Galerie, D-68161 Mannheim, Germany. Tel: (49 621) 102 943. Fax: 291 564. e: ifmh@mannheim-filmfestival. com. Web: www.mannheim-filmfestival.com.

AWARDS 2006
Main Award of Mannheim-Heidelberg: **The Only One** (Belgium), Geoffrey Enthoven. *Rainer Werner Fassbinder Prize of Mannheim-Heidelberg*: **Sons** (Norway), Erik Richter Strand. *Special Award of the Jury*: **Stealth** (Switzerland), Lionel Baier and **Thicker than**

Laureates at the 55th International Filmfestival Mannheim-Heidelberg 2006 – photo by Norbert Bach

Water (Iceland), Árni Ólafur Ásgeirsson. *Special Mention Camerawork*: Florent Herry (Turkey), **Times and Winds**. *Special Mention Actor*: Jesper Aholt (Denmark), **The Art of Crying**. *Special Mention*: **Iraq in Fragments** (USA), James Longley. *Best Short Film*: **Something in O** (Belgium), Marc Schaus. *Audience Award*: **The Art of Crying** (Denmark), Peter Schønau Fog. *International Film Critics Prize*: **A Summer Day** (France), Franck Guérin. *Ecumenic Film Prize*: **Tressette-A story of an Island** (Croatia), Drazen Zarkovic and Pavo Marinkovic. *Recommendations of the Jury of Cinema Owners*: **The Art of Crying** (Denmark), Peter Schønau Fog, **The Only One** (Belgium), Geoffrey Enthoven and **The Last Day** (Sweden), Magnus Hedberg.

Mar del Plata International Film Festival
November/December 2008

The festival was first held in 1954, but because of a 26-year hiatus it is only celebrating its 23rd edition in 2008, when it will be held later than its usual March slot. Held annually since 1996. The festival's new President is acclaimed filmmaker José Martínez Suárez. It is the only A-grade film festival in Latin America with an Official Competition, usually comprising around 15 movies, generally two from Argentina. Other sections include Latin American Films, Out of Competition, Point of View, Near Darkness, Soundsystem, Heterodoxy, Documentary Frame, Argentine Showcase, Memory in Motion and The Inner Look. *Inquiries to*: Mar del Plata International Film Festival, 319 Lima, 1073 Cap Fed, Argentina. Tel: (54 11) 4383 5115. e: info@ mardelplatafilmfest.com. Web: www.mardelplatafilmfest.com.

Melbourne International Film Festival
July 22–August 10, 2008

MIFF is widely regarded as the most significant film event in Australia. It has the largest and most diverse programme of screenings and special events in the country, in addition to the largest audience. There is also growing international regard for MIFF as a film market place, with a steady increase in sales agents attending. The longest-running festival in the southern hemisphere showing more than 400 features, shorts, documentaries and new media works, presented in five venues. *Inquiries to*: PO Box 2206, Fitzroy Mail Centre 3065, Melbourne, Victoria, Australia. Tel: (61 3) 9417 2011. Fax: 9417 3804. e: miff@melbournefilmfestival.com.au. Web: www.melbournefilmfestival.com.au.

Middle East International Film Festival
October 10–19, 2008

MEIFF is a cultural event dedicated to presenting a diverse slate of international films and programmes and introducing filmmakers from around the world to the resources of the region. Presented by the Abu Dhabi Authority for Culture and Heritage (ADACH), MEIFF is committed to nurturing relationships and providing opportunities to those looking to invest in the future of film. It hosts the Film Financing Circle (FFC), which has become a significant annual conference on the subject of international co-productions. Showcases films in a number of categories, including films from the Middle East, Bollywood and beyond. The Black Pearl Awards feature Jury prizes in fiction, documentary and short film categories. *Inquiries to*: MEIFF, PO Box 127662, Abu Dhabi, UAE. Tel: (971 2) 631 8461. Fax: 631 3894. e: contact@meiff.com. Web: www.meiff.com.

AWARDS 2007
Incircle Pearl Awards: Shared first prize to **Love Marriage** (USA), Soman Chainani and **Keep Smiling** (Georgia), Rusuhan Chkonia. Second prize to **Battling for Palestine** (USA), Keyvan Mashayekh.
Hayah Film Competition Student Award: **Ramadan** (UAE), Fatima Al Shamsi.
Hayah Film Competition Amateur Award: **Celebrate Life** (UAE), Kamil Roxas.
Hayah Film Competition Professional Award: **For No One** (UAE), Ziad Oakes.

Audience Choice Best Short Film: **Tanghi Argentini** (Belgium), Guy Thuys.
Audience Choice Best Documentary: **Hear and Now** (USA), Irene Taylor Brodsky.
Audience Award Best Fiction Feature: **Persepolis** (France), Marjane Satrapi and Vincent Parannaud.
Best Actor: Carl Markovics for **The Counterfeiters** (Austria/Germany).
Best Actress: Nadine Labaki, Yasmine Al Masri, Joanna Moukarzel, Gisele Aouad and Sihame Haddad for **Caramel** (France/Lebanon).
Black Pearl for New Emerging Director of Short Film: Elizabeth Marre and Olivier Pont for **Manon on the Pavement** (France).
Black Pearl for New Director of Fiction: Michael James Rowland for **Lucky Miles** (Australia).
Black Pearl for Best Animation Short: **I Met the Walrus** (Canada), Josh Raskin.
Black Pearl for Best Short Film: **Bawke** (Norway), Hisham Zaman.
Black Pearl for Best Documentary: **We are Together** (UK), Paul Taylor.
Black Pearl Grand Jury Prize: **Ben X** (Belgium), Nic Balthazar and Peter Bouckaert.
UAE Filmmakers of the Year: Hani Al Shibani and Fedel Al Muheiry for **Jumma and the Sea**.

Mill Valley Film Festival
October 2–12, 2008

Known as a filmmakers' festival, Mill Valley offers a high-profile, prestigious, non-competitive and welcoming environment perfect for celebrating the best in independent and world cinema, set in the beautiful Marin County, just north of San Francisco. Celebrating its 31st year in 2008, the festival includes the innovative Vfest, Children's Film Fest, celebrity tributes, seminars and special events. *Inquiries to*: Mill Valley Film Festival/ California Film Institute, 1001 Lootens Place, Suite 220, San Rafael, CA 94901, USA. Tel: (1 415) 383 5256. Fax: 383 8606. e: zelton@cafilm.org. Web: www.mvff.com.

Report 2007
The 30th Mill Valley Film Festival attendance exceeded 40,000. High-profile actors and

filmmakers were in abundance this year, including Sean Penn and Emile Hirsch presenting a preview screening of *Into the Wild*. The Opening Night featured Academy Award-winning director Ang Lee, present for a Tribute and the screening of his new film *Lust, Caution*, accompanied by his leading lady, Tang Wei. Also in attendance were actress Laura Linney and director Tamara Jenkins with *The Savages*, Michael Schroeder with *Man in the Chair*, Tony Gilroy with *Michael Clayton*, Todd Haynes with *I'm Not There*, Alison Eastwood with her directorial debut, *Rails and Ties* and Ben Affleck and lead actress Amy Ryan with his directorial debut, *Gone Baby Gone*. Other Tribute/Spotlight events featured a Tribute to director Terry George and the screening of his new film, *Reservation Road*, and a Spotlight on the career of actress Jennifer Jason Leigh, along with a screening of Noah Baumbach's *Margot at the Wedding*, with both actress and director in attendance. The Festival closed with Marc Forster's *The Kite Runner*, with the novel's author Khaled Hosseini, screenwriter David Benioff and the film's lead actor, Khalid Abdulla, in attendance. **– Simone Nelson,** Marketing & Communications Manager.

Montreal World Film Festival
August 21–September 1, 2008

The goal of the festival is to encourage cultural diversity and understanding between nations, to foster the cinema of all continents by stimulating the development of quality cinema, to promote filmmakers and innovative works, to discover and encourage new talents, and to promote meetings between cinema professionals from around the world. Apart from the 'Official Competition' and the 'First Films Competition', the festival presents 'Hors Concours' (World Greats), a 'Focus on World Cinema' and 'Documentaries of the World', plus tributes to established filmmakers and a section dedicated to Canadian student films. *Inquiries to*: Montreal World Film Festival 1432 de Bleury St, Montreal, Quebec, Canada H3A 2J1. Tel: (1 514) 848 3883 Fax: 848 3886. e: commandites@ffm-montreal.org. Web: www.ffm-montreal.org.

Moscow International Film Festival
June 2008

The large competition remains international in scope and genres, covering Europe and the CIS, South East Asia, Latin and North America. A new competitive section, Perspectives, started in 2004. The Media-Forum (panorama and competition) is devoted to experimental films and video art. *Inquiries to*: Moscow International Film Festival, 10/1 Khokhlovsky Per, Moscow 109028, Russia. Tel: (7 095) 917 2486. Fax: 916 0107. e: info@miff.ru. Web: www.moscowfilmfestival.ru.

Napa Sonoma Wine Country Film Festival
July 16–August 28, 2008

World cinema, culture and conscience gather in the heart of Northern California's premium wine region, Napa and Sonoma Valleys. The festival is gently paced, mainly non-competitive and accepts features, documentaries, shorts, and animation. All genres are welcome. Programme categories are: World Cinema, US Cinema, EcoCinema (environment), Slow Food on Food, Latin Cinema, Arts in Film and Cinema of Conscience (social issues). Many of the films are shown outdoors. *Inquiries to*: PO Box 303, Glen Ellen, CA 95442, USA. Tel: (1 707) 935 3456. e: wcfilmfest@aol.com. Web: www.wcff.us.

AWARDS 2007
Best of the Fest: **Scandalous** (Spain), Alvaro Begines.
Best First Feature: **De Bares** (Spain), Mario Iglesias.
Best US Cinema: **Mo**, Brian Scott Lederman.
Best Eco Cinema: **We Feed the World** (Netherlands), Erwin Wagenhofer and **Power of Community** (USA), Faith Morgan.
Best Cine Latino: **Maroa** (Venezuela), Solveig Hoogesteij.

Report 2007
At the 21st annual Napa Sonoma Wine Country Film Festival, more than 5,000 film lovers

enjoyed 123 films from around the world, at ten venues scattered through wine country, 45 miles north of the Golden Gate Bridge. Highlights included a spotlight on Spanish cinema and open-air screenings in three spectacular locations. Javier Bardem's *Invisibles* picked up the WCFF Humanitarian Film Award and in the 'World Cinema' section the winner was *Driving With My Wife's Lover* by Korean director Taisik Kim. With over 25 ecological films, *Movie Maker* magazine's Best Environment film went to *Ripe with Change* by Emiko Omori.
– Justine Ashton, Executive Director

Netherlands Film Festival, Utrecht
September 24–October 3, 2008

Since 1981, Holland's only event presenting an overview of the year's entire output of Dutch filmmaking. The festival opens the new cultural season with Dutch retrospectives, seminars, talk shows and premieres of many new Dutch films. Dutch features, shorts, documentaries and TV dramas compete for local cinema's grand prix, the Golden Calf, in 18 categories. The Holland Film Meeting, the sidebar for international and national film professionals, includes a Market Programme and the Netherlands Production Platform for Dutch and European producers. *Inquiries to*: Netherlands Film Festival, PO Box 1581, 3500 BN Utrecht, Netherlands. Tel: (31 30) 230 3800. Fax: 230 3801. e: info@filmfestival.nl. Web: www. filmfestival.nl.

Nordic Film Days Lubeck
October 29–November 2, 2008

Held in the charming medieval town of Lubeck, north of Hamburg, the festival spotlights Scandinavian and Baltic cinema, enabling members of the trade, critics and other filmgoers to see the best new productions. It also features a large documentary section. Attendance exceeds 20,000 for more than 130 screenings. *Inquiries to*: Helga Brandt, Nordische Filmtage Lubeck, Schildstrasse 12, D-23539 Lubeck, Germany. Tel: (49 451) 122 1742. Fax: 122 1799. e: info@filmtage.luebeck. de. Web: www.filmtage.luebeck.de.

AWARDS 2007
NDR Film Prize: **The Art of Negative Thinking** (Norway), Bård Breien.
Baltic Film: **To Love Someone** (Sweden), Åke Sandgren.
Audience Prize: **Suddenly** (Sweden), Johan Brisinger.
Interfilm Church Prize: **To Love Someone** (Sweden), Åke Sandgren.
Documentary Film Prize: **Asylum** (Finland), Jenni Linko.
Children's and Youth Film Prize: **Hoppet** (Sweden), Petter Næss.
Children's Jury: **Mystery of the Wolf** (Finland), Raimo O Niemi.

Visions du Réel, International Film Festival in Nyon
April 17–23, 2008

Since 1994, Visions du Réel, International Film Festival in Nyon (a few miles from Geneva), aims to promote independent films and audiovisual productions classified as creative documentaries, where filmmakers deliver their own personal vision of today's world in all its aspects (social issues, intimate portraits, enquiries, journey diaries, experimental movies...). All these films are treated as a specific and committed form of cinema. The works (irrespective of length or format) are divided into six sections: Competition International; Regards Neufs (international competition for first films); Tendances; Investigations; Helvétiques; Ateliers; Séances Spéciales. Since 2002, Visions du Réel has also organised its own official international market (Doc Outlook), reserved to qualified industry players, with video library, panel discussions and unofficial networking meetings. Entry deadline: mid-

January (regulations and entry form available each autumn on festival website). *Inquiries to*: Visions du Réel, 18 rue Juste Olivier, CH-1260 Nyon 1, Switzerland. Tel: (41 22) 365 4455. Fax: 365 4450. e: docnyon@visionsdureel.ch. Web: www.visionsdureel.ch.

Visions du Réel

AWARDS 2007
International Competition
Grand Prix Visions du Réel: **Söhne** (Germany), Volker Köpp.
Prix SRG SSR Idée Suisse: **Scenes de Chasse Au Sanglier** (Belgium/France), Claudio Pazienza.
Audience Prize: **Heimatklange** (Switzerland), Stefan Schwietert.
Inter-religious Jury Prize: **Welcome Europa** (France), Bruno Ulmer.
Prize of the Société des Hôteliers de la Côte: **Cabale A Kaboul** (Belgium), Dan Alexe.
Prize of the DDC: **Manufactured Landscapes** (Canada) Jennifer Baichwal.
Regards Neufs
Prix de l'Etat de Vaud: **Akhmeteli 4** (Georgia), Artchil Khetagouri and **Das leben Ist Ein**

Langer Tag (Germany), Svenja Klüh.
Cinéma Suisse
Prix Télévision Suisse Romande: **Le Theatre des Operations** (France/Switzerland), Benoît Rossel.
Prix Suissimage/Société Suisse des Auteurs SSA: **Retour A Goree** (Switzerland), Pierre-Yves Borgeaud.
From All Sections
Prix 'Regards Sur le Crime': **Le Cote Obscur de la Dame Blance** (Canada), Patricio Henriquez.

Prix John Templeton Foundation:
State Legislature (USA), Frederick Wiseman.

Report 2007

Already 13 years! And Visions du Réel – the festival and Doc Outlook-International Market – is a milestone in the landscape of independent creative cinema. In Nyon, the 'cinéma du réel' means an amazing diversity of inspiration, commitment and visual writing by people dealing with the realities of the world and forging a channel between documentary and fiction. Two international competitions, many first releases, debates, and a catalogue in three languages featuring original texts. Two main films received awards in 2007: *Söhne* by the German master Volker Koepp and *Scenes de Chasse au Sanglier* by the Italian/Belgium essayist, Claudio Pazienza. Over 80 filmmakers and 640 professionals accredited. Nyon, a charming little city by Lake Geneva, is one of the most appreciated international festivals.
– Jean Perret, Festival Director.

Oberhausen International Short Film Festival

May 1–6, 2008

The Oberhausen festival is known for its open attitude towards short formats, always on the look out for unusual, surprising, experimental works. The traditional competitions – International, German, Children's Shorts and Music Video – provided an extensive overview of current international short film and video production. The 2007 thematic programme KINOMUSEUM looked at artist film and videos between the cinema and the museum. Oberhausen also continued its PODIUM series of lively and very well-attended discussions. Retrospectives of artists Guy Ben-Ner, Marjoleine Boonstra, Kanai Katsu and Ken Kobland rounded off the programmes. Closing date for entries to the 2008 edition will be 1 February 2008, entry forms and regulations can be downloaded at www.kurzfilmtage. de from October 2007. Festival Director: Dr Lars Henrik Gass. *Inquiries to*: Oberhausen International Short Film Festival, Grillostrasse

34, D-46045 Oberhausen, Germany. Tel: (49 208) 825 2652. Fax: 825 5413. e: info@ kurzfilmtage.de. Web: www.kurzfilmtage.de.

AWARDS 2007

International Competition
Grand Prize of the City of Oberhausen:
On the Third Planet From the Sun, (Russia), Pavel Medvedev.
Two Principal Prizes: **Metamorphosis** (Ireland), Clare Langan and **The Terrace** (Vietnam), Hà Phong Nguyen.
ARTE Prize for a European Short Film:
Dad (UK), Daniel Mulloy.
German Competition
Prize for the Best Contribution, ex aequo:
Vali Asr (Germany/Iran), Norman Richter,
Mammal (Germany), Astrid Rieger and
Three Notes (Germany), Jeannette Gaussi.

Odense International Film Festival

August 19–24, 2008

Denmark's only international short film festival invites the best international short films with original and imaginative content. Besides screenings of more than 200 National and International short films and Danish documentaries, Odense Film Festival offers a number of exciting retrospective programmes and the opportunity to view all competition films in the Video Bar. The festival hosts a range of seminars for film professionals, librarians and teachers. It educates children and youths in the field of alternative film experiences and is a meeting place for international film directors and other film professionals in the field of short films and documentaries. Odense Film Festival invites all directors with a film in competition to participate in the festival. *Inquiries to*: Odense Film Festival, Odense Slot, Nørregade 36-38, DK-5100 Odense C, Denmark. Tel: (45) 6551 2823. Fax: 6591 0144. e: filmfestival@odense. dk. Web: www.filmfestival.dk.

AWARDS 2007

International Grand Prix: **Tower Block** (Germany), Nikos Chryssos.

Most Surprising Film: **Coco-Nuts** (Norway),
Charlotte Bloom.
Most Imaginative Film: **Far West, Carlitopolis
& The Professor Nieto Show** (France),
Louis Nieto.
International Special Mention:
The Tube With a Hat (Romania), Radu Jude.
International Special Mention:
I Met the Walrus (Canada), Josh Raskin.
International Special Mention: **Marilena from
the P7** (Romania), Cristian Nemescu.
National Grand Prix: **Someone Like You**
Nanna Frank Møller.
Best Danish Documentary: **On the Road to
Paradise** Suvi Andrea Helminen.
Best Danish Short Fiction: **Sporenstrengs**
Helene Moltke-Leth.
National Special Mention: **Solo**
Kasper Torsting.
National Special Mention: **The Earth beneath
My Feet** Michael Noer.
National Special Mention: **Music is a Monster**
Jytte Rex.
Danish Animation Award - Best in Competition:
Tyger (Brazil), Guilherme Marcondes.
Danish Animation Award - Talent Award: **The
Shadow in Sarah** (Denmark), Karla Nielsen.
International Prize of the Youth Jury: **Ela** (UK),
Silvana Aguirre Zegarra.
National Prize of the Youth Jury: **Disappeared**
(Denmark), Kaspar Munk.
Special Mention of the Youth Jury: **Solo**
(Denmark), Kasper Torsting.
Video Clip Cup: 1st Prize: **Mr Silence**
(Denmark), Johan Holst Støving & Jack
Røygaard.
Video Clip Cup: 2nd Prize: **To Find Silence**
(Denmark), Kasper Jørgensen & Jesper Weile.
Video Clip Cup: 3rd Prize: **Distortion**
(Denmark), Ursula Lundgreen & Trine Lai.
Audience Award: **Solo** (Denmark), Kasper
Torsting.

Oulu International Children's Film Festival
November 17–23, 2008

Annual festival with competition for full-length
feature films for children, it screens recent ti-

tles and retrospectives. Oulu is set in northern Finland, on the coast of the Gulf of Bothnia. *Inquiries to*: Oulu International Children's Film Festival, Hallituskatu 7, FI-90100 Oulu, Finland. Tel: (358 8) 881 1293. Fax: 881 1290. e: oek@ oufilmcenter.inet.fi. Web: www.ouka.fi/lef.

AWARDS 2007

Star Boy Award: **The Substitute** (Denmark), Ole Bornedal.

Palm Springs
January 2009

Palm Springs, celebrating its 20th edition in 2009, is one of the largest film festivals in the US, hosting 120,000 attendees for a line-up of over 250 films at the 2007 event. Special sections of the festival include Cine Latino, New Voices/New Visions, Gala Screenings, Awards Buzz (Best Foreign Language Academy Award submissions), World Cinema Now and the True Stories documentary section. The Festival includes a Black Tie Awards Gala (2007 honourees included Alejandro González Iñárritu, Brad Pitt, Kate Winslet, Cate Blanchett, Philip Glass, Jennifer Hudson, Todd Field, Guillermo del Toro and Sydney Pollack). *Inquiries to*: Darryl MacDonald, 1700 E Tahquitz Canyon Way, Suite 3, Palm Springs, CA 92262, USA. Tel: (1 760) 322 2930. Fax: 322 4087. e: info@psfilmfest.org. Web: www.psfilmfest.org.

AWARDS 2007

Best Film: **The Lives of Others** (Germany), Florian Henckel von Donnersmarck.
New Voices/New Visions Award: **It's Winter** (Israel), Rafi Pitts.
Best Documentary: **Blindsight** (UK), Lucy Walker.
John Schlesinger Award: **Outsourced** (USA), John Jeffcoat.

Pesaro
June 21–29, 2008

The Mostra Internazionale del Nuovo Cinema or Pesaro Film Festival was founded in Pesaro in 1965 by Bruno Torri and Lino Miccichè. Since 2000, Giovanni Spagnoletti has directed the Festival. The Pesaro Film Festival is synonymous with discoveries, with showcasing emerging cinematographers, with re-readings, with 'Special Events'. *Inquiries to*: Mostra Internazionale del Nuovo Cinema (Pesaro Film Festival), Via Villafranca 20, 00185 Rome, Italy. Tel: (39 06) 445 6643/491 156. Fax: 491 163. e: pesarofilmfest@mclink.it. Web: www.pesarofilmfest.it.

Portland International Film Festival
February 7–23, 2008

Portland International Film Festival will be an invitational event presenting more than 100 films from 30 plus countries to 35,000 people from throughout the Northwest. Along with new international features, documentaries and shorts, the festival will feature showcases

The Lives of Others *director Florian Henckel Von Donnersmarck at the Portland International Film Festival – photo by Jason E. Kaplan*

surveying Hispanic film and literature, Pacific Rim cinema and many of the year's foreign-language Academy Award submissions. *Inquiries to*: Northwest Film Center, 1219 SW Park Ave, Portland, OR 97205, USA. Tel: (1 503) 221 1156. Fax: 294 0874. e: info@nwfilm.org. Web: www.nwfilm.org.

Pusan International Film Festival (PIFF)
Early October 2008

Established in 1996 in Busan, Korea, PIFF is known as the most energetic film festival in the world and has become the largest film festival in Asia. This world-class event has been promoting Asian and Korean cinema worldwide, as well as introducing films from over 60 countries, many of which are premieres. Also, retrospectives, special programmes in focus, seminars and other related events are presented annually. In addition, its project market – Pusan Promotion Plan (PPP) – has been a platform for moving Asian film projects forward in the international marketplace, along with its own talent campus, Asian Film Academy (AFA), offering various filmmaking programmes for young talent from all over Asia. *Inquiries to*: 3rd Floor, 1-143, Shinmunno 2-Ga, Jongro-Gu, Seoul, 110-062, Korea. Tel: (82 2) 3675 5097. Fax: 3675 5098. e: publicity@piff.org. Web: www.piff.org.

Raindance
September 24–October 5, 2008

Raindance is the largest independent film festival in the UK and aims to reflect the cultural, visual and narrative diversity of international independent filmmaking, specialising in first-time filmmakers. The festival screens around 100 feature films and 200 shorts as well as hosting a broad range of masterclasses and workshops. *Inquiries to*: Jesse Vile, Festival Producer, Raindance Film Festival, 81 Berwick St, London, W1F 8TW, UK. Tel: (44 20) 7287 3833. Fax: 7139 2243. e: festival@raindance.co.uk. Web: www. raindance.co.uk/festival.

Report 2007
The 15th Raindance Film Festival screened over 70 films, 100 shorts and held over 50 events. Keeping in with its rock and roll rep, Iggy Pop and Mick Jones were on the jury, with Jones presenting a special screening of *Performance*, followed by a Q&A session. Other events included sessions with Ken Loach, Tim Bevan, Michael Madsen, Anthony Dod Mantle and John Sinclair, and Live!Ammunition!, a pitching event held at BAFTA with a panel that included Iain Smith, Ewan McGregor and Mike Figgis. *Tarnation* director Jonathan Caouette documented the festival and showed the finished film on closing night. 2007's retrospective honoured Jean-Luc Godard. Gus Van Sant's *Paranoid Park* closed the festival.
– **Jesse Vile,** Festival Producer.

Rome International Film Festival
October 2008

Rome is not just a great city, but a city of cinema par excellence and provides not just a festival but a real feast for film lovers and a great event for all those who work for cinema, show cinema and tell us stories through cinema. The third edition will be held in Rome Auditorium, along with screenings at film theatres and events held in spots that symbolise the city, from the Via Veneto to Piazza del Popolo, from Cinecittà to 'Greater Rome'. The festival has now established itself as a truly unique occasion with audiences flocking to the events, exhibitions, encounters and screenings proof of a great passion and curiosity for culture. *Inquiries to*: Rome International Film Festival, Via Flaminia 330, 00196 Rome, Italy. Tel: (39 06) 4546 83900. e: pressoffice@romacinemafest.org. Web: www. romacinemafest.org.

AWARDS 2007
Alice in the City Official Awards
Alice in the City K12 Prize for Best Film:
Canvas (USA), Joseph Greco.
Alice in the City Young Adult Prize for Best Film: **Meet Mr Daddy** (South Korea),

Kwang Su Park.
Cinema 2007 - Competition Official Awards
Special Jury Award - AAMS: **Hafez**
(Iran/Japan), Abolfaz Jalili.
Marco Aurelio Award Best Actress - BNL-BNP
Paribas Group: Jiang Wenli for **And the Spring**
Comes (China).
Marco Aurelio Award Best Actor- Lazio Region:
Rade Šerbedžija for **Fugitive Pieces**
(Canada/Greece).
Marco Aurelio Award Best Film - Rome
Chamber of Commerce, Industry, Handicrafts
and Agriculture: **Juno** (USA), Jason Reitman.

International Film Festival Rotterdam
January 23–February 3, 2008

With its adventurous, original and distinctive programming, Rotterdam highlights new
directors and new directions in contemporary
world cinema, exemplified by its Tiger Awards
Competition for first and second feature films;
the annual showcase of films from developing countries that have been supported by the
festival's Hubert Bals Fund; the CineMart, the
international co-production market developed
to nurture the financing and production of new
cinema; as well as the Exploding Cinema programme exploring those 'cutting edges' where
cinema crosses over into other art forms and
new media. *Inquiries to*: International Film
Festival Rotterdam, PO Box 21696, 3001 AR
Rotterdam, Netherlands. Tel: (31 10) 890 9090.
Fax: 890 9091. e: tiger@filmfestivalrotterdam.
com. Web: www.filmfestivalrotterdam.com.

AWARDS 2007
Feature Awards
VPRO Tiger Awards: **The Unpolished**
(Germany), Pia Marais, **Love Conquers All**
(Malaysia), Tan Chui Mui, **AFR** (Denmark),
Morten Hartz Kaplers and **Bog of Beasts**
(Brazil), Claudio Assis.
Movies that Matter Award: **The Mark of Cain**
(UK), Marc Munden.
MovieSquad Award: **Reprise** (Norway),
Joachim Trier.
KPN Audience Award: **The Lives of Others**
(Germany), Florian Henckel von Donnersmarck.

The Rotterdam International Film Festival

FIPRESCI Award: **Me** (Spain), Rafa Cortes.
KNF Award (Association of Dutch Film Critics):
Operation Filmmaker (USA), Nina Davenport.
NETPAC Award (Network for the Promotion
of Asian Cinema): **Fourteen** (Japan), Hirosue
Hiromasa.
Short Awards
Tiger Awards for Short Film: **Video Game**
(India), Vipin Vijay, **Hinterland** (France),
Geoffrey Boulangé and **The Flag** (Turkey),
Köken Ergun.
Prix UIP Rotterdam (Short Film Nominee for
the European Film Awards): **Amin** (France/
Germany/The Netherlands), David Dusa.
Cinemart Awards
Prins Claus Film Fund Grant: **Independencia**
(Philippines), Raya Martin.
Arte France Cinema Awards: **A Rational**
Solution (Sweden), Jörgen Bergmark and
Pieds Nus Sur Les Limaces (France),
Fabienne Berthaud.

Report 2007
At the 37th edition, more than 200 features
and 400 shorts kept 367,000 cinephiles
spellbound. Industry professionals were given
an enjoyable, convenient and ultra-efficient
tool in the form of the festival circuit's first
fully-digitised Video Library. Less conventional
'festival activities' were investigated in the
provocative section, 'Happy Endings, When
Festivals Are Over', which ranged from an
indoor soccer competition with filmmakers
to interactive scenario readings. Highlights
from Johnnie To's dazzlingly cool body
of work complemented those from the

socially committed visionary Abderrahmane Sissako, making 2007's Filmmakers in Focus programme an absolute must see. Meanwhile, Norwegian Artist in Focus Knut Asdam peppered the city with films, installations and supersized video projections. In the end, a jury led by Piers Handling (director of the Toronto IFF) bestowed the prestigious Tiger Awards on filmmakers from Germany, Malaysia, Denmark and Brazil, while the hotly contested Audience Award went to Mark Munden's controversial film *The Mark of Cain*.

San Francisco International Film Festival
April 24–May 8, 2008

The oldest film festival in the Americas, in its 51st year, San Francisco continues to grow in importance and popularity. It presents more than 200 international features and shorts. Special awards include the Skyy Prize ($10,000 cash for an emerging director), The Golden Gate Awards and the FIPRESCI Prize. *Inquiries to*: San Francisco International Film Festival, Programming Dept, San Francisco Film Society, 39 Mesa St, Suite 110, The Presidio, San Francisco, CA 94129, USA. Tel: (1 415) 561 5014. Fax: 561 5099. e: gga@sffs.org. Web: www.sffs.org.

AWARDS 2007
SKYY Prize: **The Violin** (Mexico), Francisco Vargas Quevedo.
FIPRESCI Prize: **Parting Shot** (France), Jeanne Waltz.
Chris Holter Humour in Film Award: **The Silly Age** (Cuba/Spain/Venezuela), Pavel Giroud.
Golden Gate Awards
Documentary Feature: **Souvenirs** (Israel), Shahar Cohen and Halil Efrat.
Bay Area Documentary Feature: **The Key of G** (USA), Robert Arnold.
Documentary Short: **Sari's Mother** (USA), James Longley.
Bay Area Documentary Short: **Outsider: The Life and Art of Judith Scott** (USA), Betsy Bayha.
Narrative Short: **The Tube with a Hat** (Romania), Radu Jude.

Bay Area Non-Documentary Short: **Muse of Cinema** (USA), Kerry Laitala.
Animated Short: **Never Like the First Time!** (Sweden), Jonas Odell.
New Visions: **Dear Bill Gates** (USA), Sarah J. Christman.
Work for Kids and Families: **The Fan and the Flower** (USA), Bill Plympton.
Youth Work: **Focus** (USA), Edward Elliott.

San Sebastián International Film Festival
September 20–29, 2008

Held in an elegant Basque seaside city known for its superb gastronomy and beautiful beaches, the Donostia-San Sebastián Festival remains Spain's most important event in terms of glamour, competition, facilities, partying, number of films and attendance (more than 1,600 production and distribution firms, government agencies and festival representatives from 40 countries, and accredited professionals and more than 1,100 journalists from 39 countries). Events include the Official Competitive section, Zabaltegi, with its €90,000 cash award, Altadis-New Directors, Horizontes Latinos and meticulous retrospectives. In partnership with the Rencontres Cinémas Amérique Latine in Toulouse, the Films in Progress industry platform aims to aid the completion of six Latin American and two Spanish projects. Cinema in Motion 3 is a rendezvous at which to discover projects by moviemakers from Magreb and Portuguese-speaking African countries, presented only to professionals in partnership with Amiens Film Festival, Fribourg Film Festival and Tarifa African Film Festival. *Inquiries to*: San Sebastián International Film Festival, Apartado de Correos 397, 20080 Donostia, San Sebastián 20080, Spain. Tel: (34 943) 481 212. Fax: 481 218. e: ssiff@sansebastianfestival.com. Web: www.sansebastianfestival.com.

AWARDS 2006
Golden Shell for Best Film: **Half Moon** (Austria/France/Iran/Iraq), Bahman Ghobadi and

Mon Fils à Moi (France), Martian Fougeron.
Special Jury Award: **El Camino de San Diego**
(Argentina), Carlos Sorín.
Silver Shell for Best Director: Tom DiCillo,
Delirious (USA).
Silver Shell for Best Actress: Nathalie Baye,
Mon Fils à Moi (France).
Silver Shell for Best Actor: Juan Diego,
Vete de Mi (Spain).
Jury Award for Best Photography: Nigel Bluck,
Half Moon (Austria/France/Iran/Iraq).
Jury Award for Best Screenplay: **Delirious**
(USA), Tom DiCillo.

Santa Barbara International Film Festival
Late January–early February 2008

Given its knack for predicting Academy Award
winners, a proximal distance to Los Angeles
and timing close to the big event, the 23rd
Annual Santa Barbara International Film Festival (SBIFF) in 2008 will once again establish
itself as the pre-eminent Academy Award
film festival. *Inquiries to*: SBIFF, 1528 Chapala
Street 203, Santa Barbara, CA 93101, USA. Tel:
(1 805) 963 0023. Fax: 962 2524. e:info@sb-
filmfestival.org. Web: www.sbfilmfestival.org.

Sarasota Film Festival
April 4–12, 2008

Ten days of independent film, symposiums
and events in a beautiful location; hospitable,
inquisitive audiences plus a well-organised and
publicised programme. *Inquiries to*: Sarasota
Film Festival, 332 Cocoanut Avenue, Sarasota,
Florida 34236, USA. Tel: (1 941) 364 9514. Fax:
364 8411. e: jennifer@sarasotafilmfestival.com.
Web: www.sarasotafilmfestival.com.

Seattle International Film Festival
May 22–June 15, 2008

The largest festival in the US, SIFF presents
more than 270 features, 50 documentaries
and 100 shorts annually. There are cash prizes
for the juried New Directors Showcase, New
American Cinema Competition, Documentary
Competition and Short Films in the categories
of: Live Action, Documentary and Animation.
Festival sections include: Alternate Cinema,
Face the Music, FutureWave, Planet Cinema,
Contemporary World Cinema, Emerging
Masters, Tributes and Archival Films. *Inquiries
to*: Seattle International Film Festival, 400
Ninth Avenue North, Seattle, WA 98109, USA.
Tel: (1 206) 464 5830. Fax: 264 7919. e: info@
seattlefilm.org. Web: www.seattlefilm.org.

AWARDS 2007
New Directors Showcase
Grand Jury Prize: **Sons** (Norway), Eric Richter
Strand.
Special Jury Prize: Valerie Donzelli in **7 Years**
(France), Jean-Pascal Hattu.
Heineken Red Star Award: **Fish Dreams**
(Brazil), Kyrill Mikhanovsky.
New American Cinema Award
Grand Jury Prize: **Shotgun Stories** (USA),
Jeff Nichols.
Special Jury Prize: **Lovely by Surprise** (USA),
Kirt Gunn.
Documentary Competition
Grand Jury Prize: **Out of Time** (Austria),
Harald Friedl.
Special Jury Prize: **Angels in the Dust** (USA),
Louise Hogarth.
Short Awards
Grand Jury Prize: **Wigald** (Germany),
Timon Modersohn.
Special Jury Prize: **Look Sharp** (Australia),
Amy Gebhardt and **Pick Up** (France),
Manuel Shapira.
Documentary
Grand Jury Prize: **Chocolate Country**
(Dominican Republic/USA), Robin Blotnick.
Special Jury Prize: **Freeheld** (USA), Cynthia
Wade.
Animation
Grand Jury Prize: **Everything Will Be OK**
(USA), Don Hertzfeldt.
Special Jury Prize: **The Girl Who Swallowed
Bees** (Australia), Paul McDermott.
Golden Space Needle Audience Awards
Best Film: **Outsourced** (USA), John Jeffcoat.
Best Documentary: **For the Bible Tells Me So**
(USA), Daniel Karslake.
Best Short Film: **Pierre**, Dan Brown (USA)

Best Director: Daniel Waters, **Sex & Death 101** (USA).
Best Actor: Daniel Brühl, **Salvador** (Spain).
Best Actress: Marion Cotillard, **La Vie en Rose** (France).

Report 2007

At the 33rd edition of SIFF, Anthony Hopkins was honoured with a Lifetime Achievement Award. Lisa Gerrard and Julien Temple were on hand for 'Conversations With…'. 160,000 filmgoers enjoyed 405 films in 25 days at seven venues. Over 300 guests, including filmmakers, industry and press were in attendance. A new live score was performed by Kinski, the 'Czar of Noir', Eddie Muller, introduced two classic rarities and there was a focus on the brilliant new German Cinema. With seven Gala screenings, the 33rd Festival was a huge success.
– **Carl Spence,** Artistic Director.

Seville Film Festival
November 2008

Seville Film Festival is established as one of the best showcases for European filmmaking showing more than 160 of the most prestigious long feature films, documentaries and short films produced, not only in the European Union, but also in other countries such as Turkey, the Balkan countries, Norway, Russia, Switzerland, Israel and Palestine. It also includes seminars, lectures, exhibitions and public presentations. *Inquiries to*: Seville Film Festival, Pabellón de Portugal, Avenida Cid 1, 41004 Seville, Spain. Tel: (34 954) 297 833. Fax: 297 844. e: prensa@festivaldesevilla.com. Web: www.festivaldesevilla.com

Shanghai International Film Festival
June 14–22, 2008

Shanghai International Film Festival (SIFF) main sections include Jin Jue Award International Film Competition, Asia New Talent Award Competition, Film Market, China Film Pitch and Catch (CFPC), International Film Panorama, Film Forum, Opening Ceremony, Closing and Awards Ceremony. *Inquiries to*: Shanghai International Film Festival, 11F STV Mansions, 298 Wei Hai Road, Shanghai 200041, China. Tel: (86 21) 6253 71158. Fax: 6255 2000. Web: www.siff.com.

AWARDS 2007
Jin Jue Awards
Best Feature Film: **According to the Plan** (Germany), Franziska Meletzky.
Jury Grand Prix: **The New Man** (Finland/Sweden), Klaus Haro.
Best Director: Tian Zhuangzhuang, **The Go Master** (China).
Best Actor: Juan Jose Ballesta, **Doghead** (Spain).
Best Actress: Corinna Harfouch, Dagmar Manzel, Kirsten Block and Christine Schorn, **According to the Plan** (Germany).
Best Screenplay: Shemi Zarhin, **Aviva My Love** (Israel).
Best Cinematography: Wang Yu, **The Go Master** (China).
Best Music: Isao Tomita, **Love and Honour** (Japan).
Special Award of the 10th Shanghai International Film Festival: **The Knot** (China), Yin Li.
Asian New Talent Awards
Best Feature Film: **Bliss** (China), Sheng Zhiming.
Best Director: Golam Rabbany Biplob, **On the Wings of Dreams** (Bangladesh).

Report 2007
As China's best film festival, SIFF plays a pivotal role in opening up China's film industry to the rest of the world. In 2007, 16 out of nearly 1,000 entries were selected to compete for the Jin Jue Award, while over 200 films screened in the panorama section, with a total number of 300,000 moviegoers. China's Film Pitch and Catch (CFPC), via the newly-initiated film market, successfully inspired the industry to cover new ground with 20 projects finding their partners. Besides, the Co-Production programme is the most popular way of film collaboration between China and the world.
– **Royal Chen,** Advertising & Promotion.

Sheffield Doc/Fest
November 5–9, 2008

For five days, Sheffield Doc/Fest brings the international documentary family together to celebrate the art and business of documentary making. Combining a film festival, industry sessions and market activity, the festival offers pitching opportunities, controversial discussion panels and in-depth filmmaker masterclasses, as well as a wealth of inspirational documentary films from across the globe. Around 100 documentary films are screened, mainly from a call for entries made in March. Around 50 debates, discussions, case studies, interviews and masterclasses are presented and there are a number of well-attended social and networking events. The MeetMarket takes place over two days of the festival. It is a highly effective initiative: pre-scheduled one-on-one meetings where TV commissioning editors, executive producers, distributors and other financiers meet with independent producers and filmmakers to discuss documentary projects in development that are seeking international financing. The film programme is also open to the public. *Inquiries to*: Sheffield Doc/Fest, The Workstation, 15 Paternoster Row, Sheffield, S1 2BX, UK. Tel: (44 114) 276 5141. e: info@sidf.co.uk. Web: www.sheffdocfest.co.uk.

Singapore International Film Festival
April 4–14, 2008

Founded in 1987, SIFF is one of the leading festivals in Southeast Asia. Some 300 films from more than 40 countries are shown to 40,000 viewers through the main, fringe and special programmes and retrospectives. Fringe screenings are free and begin a week before the main programme. The festival's Asian focus and film selection attract programmers from all over the world. The Silver Screen Awards honour the best in Asian cinema, including the NETPAC prize, co-ordinated by the Network for Promotion of Asian Cinema. Since 2003, the festival has begun to highlight the emerging cinema of the Middle East. Selection deadline is 31 January 2008. *Inquiries to*: Singapore International Film Festival, 44B North Canal Rd, Singapore 059300, Singapore. Tel: (65) 738 7567. Fax: 738 7578. e: filmfest@pacific.net.sg. Web: www.filmfest.org.sg

Sitges International Film Festival of Catalonia
October 2008

Taking place in a pleasant town on the Catalan coast, Sitges focuses on fantasy films and is considered one of Europe's leading specialised festivals. The one official category, 'Fantàstic', brings together the year's best genre productions. Other wide-reaching categories include 'Noves Visions' (contemporary cinema with a language of its own), 'Orient Express' (Asian genre films), 'Anima't' (animation), 'Seven Chances' (seven discoveries made by film critics), 'Midnight X-Treme' (midnight sessions for horror fans) and 'Audiovisual Català' (Catalan productions) including Tributes to cinema personalities and Retrospectives. *Inquiries to*: Sitges Festival Internacional de Cinema de Catalunya, Calle Davallada 12, 3rd Floor, CP:08870 Sitges, Barcelona, Spain. Tel: (34 93) 894 9990.

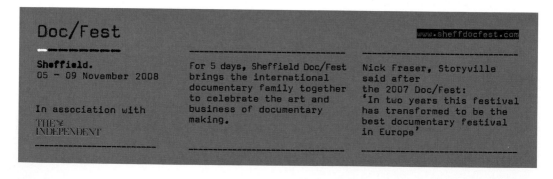

Doc/Fest   www.sheffdocfest.com

Sheffield.
05 - 09 November 2008

In association with
THE
INDEPENDENT

For 5 days, Sheffield Doc/Fest brings the international documentary family together to celebrate the art and business of documentary making.

Nick Fraser, Storyville said after the 2007 Doc/Fest: 'In two years this festival has transformed to be the best documentary festival in Europe'

Guillermo del Toro and the cast of **Pan's Labyrinth** *at the SITGES International Film Festival*

Fax: 894 8996. e: festival@cinemasitges.com.
Web: www.cinemasitges.com

Solothurn Film Festival
January 19–25, 2009

Being the most important forum for Swiss film making, Solothurn is a popular rendezvous. For 42 years the Solothurn Film Festival has been the place to see the results of Swiss film production, to make discoveries, and the place where opinions are formed. It offers a selective survey of all forms of the most up-to-date creative film and video production. A selection of films and videos by Swiss authors and foreign authors residing in Switzerland are on the programme, but also co-productions between Switzerland and other countries. A retrospective of prominent filmmakers or actors refreshes our memories of our domestic cinematographic history. Young talent can be discovered in the film-school section, extraordinary productions can be enjoyed in other special sections with international participation. The screenings are accompanied by a variety of daily round-table discussions, film branch meetings and seminars. The annual presentation of the Swiss Film Prize in the categories best

fiction film, best documentary film, best short film, best animation film, best performance in a leading role and best performance in a supporting role guarantees an atmosphere of suspense and the appearance of well-known faces. *Inquiries to*: Solothurn Film Festival, Postfach 1564, CH-4502 Solothurn, Switzerland. Tel: (41 32) 625 8080. Fax: 623 6410. e: info@solothurnerfilmtage.ch. Web: www.solothurnerfilmtage.ch.

Report 2007
The 42nd Solothurn Film Festival, held in January 2007, hosted more than 44,000 spectators who enjoyed 297 films. For the second time, music clips were presented in the 'Sound & Stories' section. A representative cross-section of music video productions in Switzerland from the past two years was scheduled, covering a wealth of different genres and styles. The retrospective was devoted to cinematographer Renato Berta, who has worked with numerous big-name directors, such as Louis Malle, Alain Resnais, Manoel de Oliveira, Amos Gitai and Robert Guédiguian. – **Ivo Kummer,** Festival Director.

Winners of the Swiss Film Award 2007 at the Solothurn Festival

Stockholm International Film Festival
November 15–25, 2008

The Stockholm International Film Festival is a member of the European Coordination of Film Festivals and welcomes 89,000 visitors, more than 500 accredited media and business representatives and over a hundred international guests every year. Since 2006, Stockholm International Film Festival also

44th Solothurn Film Festival
January 19 – 25 2009   www.solothurnfilmfestival.ch

offers distribution over the Internet through VOD, video on demand. The first titles to be released are *Hamilton* by Matthew Porterfield, *The Last Communist* by Amir Muhammad, *Empty* by Veiko Õunpuu, *Your Life in 65 Minutes* by Maria Ripoll and *The Hawk is Dying* by Julian Goldberger. *Inquiries to*: Stockholm International Film Festival, PO Box 3136, S-103 62 Stockholm, Sweden. Tel: (46 8) 677 5000. Fax: (46 8) 200 590. e: info@stockholmfilmfestival.se. Web: www. stockholmfilmfestival.se.

AWARDS 2006
Film: **Sherrybaby** (USA), Laurie Collyer.
Best Directorial debut: Daniel Sánchez Arévalo, **Darkbluealmostblack** (Spain).
Short Film: **Adults Only** (Malaysia), Joon Han Yeo
Actress: Maggie Gyllenhaal, **Sherrybaby** (USA).
Actor: Ryan Gosling, **Half Nelson** (USA).
Screenplay: Beatrix Christian, **Jindabyne** (USA).
Cinematography: Anthony Dod Mantle, **The Last King of Scotland** (UK).
Lifetime Achievement: Lasse Hallstöm.
Visionary Award: Darren Aronofsky.
Audience Award: **Little Miss Sunshine** (USA), Jonathan Dayton and Valerie Faris.
FIPRESCI Award for Best Film: **Jindabyne** (Australia), Ray Lawrence.
Northern Light: **URO** (Norway), Stefan Faldbakken.
Ifestival: Lars Emil Árnason, **United Short Film** (Iceland).

Sundance Film Festival
January 15–25, 2009

Long known as a celebration of the new and unexpected, the Sundance Film Festival puts forward the best in independent film from the US and around the world. For ten days in January audiences in darkened theatres will discover the 125 feature films and 80 shorts. The critically acclaimed Independent Feature Film Competition and the World Cinema Competition present features and documentaries from the US and around the world, and competition films are combined with nightly premieres of works by veteran film artists. There are also archival gems by early independent filmmakers, animation of every kind, cutting-edge experimental works, midnight cult films, and a jam-packed schedule of panel discussions. *Inquiries to*: Geoffrey Gilmore, Director, Festival Programming Department, Sundance Institute, 8530 Wilshire Blvd, 3rd Floor, Beverly Hills, CA 90211-3114, USA. Tel: (1 310) 360 1981. Fax: 360 1969. e: institute@sundance.org. Web: www.sundance.org.

AWARDS 2007
Grand Jury Prize (Documentary): **Send a Bullet** (USA), Jason Kohn.
Grand Jury Prize (Dramatic): **Padre Nuestro** (USA), Christopher Zalla.
Audience Award (Documentary): **Hear and Now** (USA), Irene Taylor Brodsky.
Audience Award (Dramatic): **Grace is Gone** (USA), James C. Strouse.
World Grand Jury Prize (Documentary): **Enemies of Happiness** (Denmark), Eva Mulvad and Anja Al Erhayem
World Grand Jury Prize (Dramatic): **Sweet Mud** (Israel), Dror Shaul.
World Audience Award (Documentary): **In the Shadow of the Moon** (UK), David Sington.
World Audience Award (Dramatic): **Once** (Ireland), John Carney.

Tampere Film Festival
March 5–9, 2008

Besides the International and Finnish Short Film competitions, the festival screens a wide variety of films. In 2008 there will be a special focus on Palestine, South Korea and Russia. The Canon of Short Film continues to present the best short films. Videotivoli is our event for films made by kids for kids. The festival also features seminars, exhibitions, concerts and club nights. *Inquiries to*: Tampere Film Festival, PO Box 305, FI-33101 Tampere, Finland. Tel: (358 3) 223 5681. Fax: 223 0121. e: office@tamperefilmfestival.fi. Web: www. tamperefilmfestival.fi.

Report 2007

134 festival screenings entertained over 30,000 visitors and 1,000 accredited professionals. A clear audience favourite was the Aki Kaurismäki Retrospective. Likewise, the Carte Blanche screenings curated by Aki Kaurismäki proved very popular. Other sold-out screenings included Karabasz & Kieślowski, Focus on Black Africa, Sami people and culture; New Shorts, Europe in Shorts XII; A Woman's Touch of Humour; Michel Gondry Retrospective; and both Prix UIP screenlngs. The documentaries of Jonas Mekas, the main guest at the festival, were also highly popular. The Grand Prix was awarded to Michaela Kezele for her film **Milan**, the first time a German director has won. The prize for Best Fiction was awarded to the film **Ynglinge** (*First Flush*) directed by the Dane Mikkel Munch-Fals. The best documentary award went to **Zone of Initial Dilution** by French filmmaker, Antoine Boutet. **Tyger** by the Brazilian Guilherme Marcondes was awarded Best Animation. Prix UIP Tampere was awarded to Joanna Quinn for her animation **Dreams and Desires – Family Ties**. The fiction **Graceland**, directed by Anocha Suwichakornpong from Thailand, was awarded a Diploma of Merit. The members of the jury in 2007 were Anke Lindenkamp (Germany), Nakai Matema (Zimbabwe), Pertti Paltila (Finland), Jean-Gabriel Périot (France) and Lulu Ratna (Indonesia). **– Katariina Pasuri,** Festival Organiser.

Telluride Film Festival
August 29–September 1, 2008

Each Labor Day weekend, Telluride triples in size. The programme is kept a secret until the opening day, when anxious audiences learn about the 25 plus new narrative and documentary features with directors, actors and writers present, a dozen restorations, including silent films with live scores, short film programmes, special events and tributes. There are surprise sneak previews, intimate conversations, seminars in the park and a lively student programme, all book-ended by the Opening Night Feed and the Labor Day Picnic. Screened in nine venues including the Abel Gance Outdoor Cinema, the festival presentations meet the highest technical standards using top projectionists. A new venue in 2007 was the Backlot, dedicated to documentaries about cinema. Telluride is a non-competitive festival. *Inquiries to*: The Telluride Film Festival, 800 Jones Street, Berkeley, CA 94710 USA. Tel: (1 510) 665 9494. Fax: 665 9589. e: mail@telluridefilmfestival.org. Web: www.telluridefilmfestival.org.

Thessaloniki International Film Festival
November 14–23, 2008
Thessaloniki Documentary Festival
March 7–16, 2008

Now in its 49th year, the oldest and one of the most important film events in south eastern Europe targets a new generation of filmmakers as well as independent films by established directors. At the 2007 festival, the International Competition (for first or second features) awarded the Golden Alexander (€37,000), to Shangjun Cai's *Red Dawn* (China) and the Silver Alexander (€22,000), to Spiros Stathoulopoulos' *PVC - 1* (Colombia). Other sections include: Greek Film Panorama, retrospectives, Balkan Survey, the thematic section – Focus, and a new section, Independence Days. There are also masterclasses, galas and exhibitions. Furthermore, the festival has set up the Industry Centre as an umbrella service for film professionals, including the Balkan Script Development Fund, Crossroads Co-production Forum, Agora Film Market and Salonica Studio Student Workshops. The Thessaloniki Documentary Festival – Images of the 21st Century is Greece's major annual non-fiction film event. Its sections include 'Views of the World' (subjects of social interest), 'Portraits - Human Journeys' (highlighting the human contribution to cultural, social and historical developments) and 'Recording of Memory' (facts and testimony of social and historic origin). The festival also hosts the International Documentary Market. *Inquiries to*: Thessaloniki International Film Festival, 9 Alexandras Ave, 114 73 Athens, Greece. Tel: (30 210) 870 6000. Fax: 644 8143. e: info@filmfestival.gr. Web: www.filmfestival. gr. Director: Despina Mouzaki. *Inquiries to*: Thessaloniki Documentary Festival (address and Tel/Fax numbers as above). Artistic Director: Dimitri Eipides. e: eipides-newhorizons@filmfestival.gr.

Tokyo International Film Festival
Late October 2008

A major competitive international event, with a cash prize of $50,000 awarded for the Tokyo Sakura Grand Prix and $20,000 for the Special Jury Prize. Other sections include: 'Special Screenings' showing works that have not yet been released, 'Winds of Asia-Middle East', and 'Japanese Eyes' which focuses on the new appeal of Japanese films. *Inquiries to*: Tokyo International Film Festival, 5F Tsukiji Yasuda Building, 2-15-14 Tsukiji Chuo-ku, Tokyo 104-0045, Japan. Tel: (81 3) 3524 1081. e: tokyo@tiff.net. Web: www.tiff-jp.net.

Torino Film Festival
Late November 2008

Dubbed second only to Venice on the crowded Italian festival circuit, and known for its discoveries as well as for its unique retrospectives, Torino constitutes a meeting point for contemporary international cinema. The festival pays particular attention to emerging cinemas and filmmakers, promoting awareness of new directors whose work is marked by strong formal and stylistic features. Its programme includes competitive sections for international features, Italian documentaries and Italian shorts, as well as spotlights and premieres. *Inquiries to*: Torino Film Festival, Via Montebello 15, 10124 Torino, Italy. Tel: (39 011) 813 8811. Fax: 813 8890. e: info@torinofilmfest. org. Web: www.torinofilmfest.org.

Toronto International Film Festival
September 4–13, 2008

The Toronto International Film Festival is one of the most successful public festivals in the

world. For ten days every September, the Festival becomes a must for filmmakers, industry professionals, media and the public alike. It remains committed to supporting Canadian filmmakers and has been a platform for Canada's artists. *Inquiries to*: Toronto International Film Festival, 2 Carlton St, 16th Floor, Toronto, Ontario, M5B 1J3, Canada. Tel: (1 416) 967 7371. Fax: 967 3595. e: customerrelations@ torfilmfest.ca. Web: www.tiffg.ca.

AWARDS 2007

Artistic Innovation Award: **Encarnacion** (Argentina), Anahí Berneri.
Cadillac People's Choice Award: **Eastern Promises** (Canada/UK), David Cronenberg.
Diesel Discovery Award: **Cochochi** (Canada/Mexico/UK), Israel Cárdenas and Laura Amelia Guzmán.
Prize of the International Critics (Fipresci Prize): **La Zona** (Mexico/Spain), Rodrigo Plá.
Toronto City Award for Best Canadian Feature Film: **My Winnipeg**, Guy Maddin.
Citytv Award for Best Canadian First Feature Film: **Continental, Un Film Sans Fusil**,

Stéphane Lafleur.
Award for Best Canadian Short Film: **Pool**, Chris Chong Chan Fui.

Report 2007

The 32nd annual Toronto International Film Festival showcased 349 films from 55 countries on 29 screens across downtown Toronto. Highlights were abundant. It was a strong year for Canadian films. Two Canadian titles, **Fugitive Pieces** and **Emotional Arithmetic**, opened and closed the festival respectively. Other Canadian titles included Guy Maddin's **My Winnipeg** and David Cronenberg's **Eastern Promises**. There was also a strong line-up of international titles, including **Lust, Caution**, **Brick Lane** and **La Zona**. Political films figured heavily at the festival and included titles such as **Man from Plains** and Phil Donahue and Ellen Spiro's **Body on War**. Approximately 500 international guests attended the festival, including Lauren Bacall, Werner Herzog, Eddie Vedder, Amitabh Bachchan, Wayne Wang, and Woody Allen.
– **Naoko Kumagai,** Publicity Manager.

Tribeca Film Festival
April 23–May 4, 2008

The Tribeca Film Festival was founded in 2002 by Robert De Niro, Jane Rosenthal and Craig Hatkoff, following the attacks on the World Trade Center, in an attempt to revitalise lower Manhattan, both economically and spiritually. The Festival's mission is to assist filmmakers to reach the broadest possible audience and to promote New York City as a major filmmaking centre. In just six years, the festival has attracted over five million attendees from the US and abroad and created more than $325 million in economic activity for New York City. The Festival is anchored in Tribeca with additional venues throughout Manhattan. It includes film screenings, special events, concerts, a family street fair, and *Tribeca Talks* panel discussions. *Inquiries to*: Peter Scarlet, 375 Greenwich St, New York, NY 10013, USA. Tel: (1 212) 941 2400. Fax: 941 3939. e: festival@tribecafilmfestival.org. Web: www.tribecafilmfestival.org.

AWARDS 2007
Best Narrative Feature: **My Father My Lord** (Israel), David Volach.
Best New Narrative Filmmaker:
Enrique Begne, **Two Embraces** (Mexico).
Best Screenplay: **Making Of** (Morocco/Tunisia), Nouri Bouzid.
Best Documentary Feature: **Taxi to the Darkside** (Armenia), Vardan Hovhannisyan.
Best New Documentary Filmmakers: Vardan Hovhannisyan (Armenia), **A Story of People in War & Peace**.
Best Actress in a Narrative Feature: Marina Hands, **Lady Chatterley** (Belgium/France).
Best Actor in a Narrative Feature: Lotfi Ebdelli, **Making Of** (Morocco/Tunisia).
'Made In NY' - Narrative: **The Education of Charlie Banks** (USA), Fred Durst.
'Made In NY' Special Jury Recognition-Narrative: **The Killing of John Lennon** (UK), Andrew Piddington.
'NY Loves Film' - Documentary:
A Walk into the Sea: Danny Williams and the Warhol Factory (USA), Esther Robinson.
Cadillac Award (Audience Award):

2007 Tribeca Film Festival attendees outside Tribeca Cinemas

We Are Together (UK), Paul Taylor.
Special Jury Prize for Best Narrative Short:
Super Powers (USA), J. Anderson Mitchell and Jeremy Kipp Walker.
Best Narrative Short: **The Last Dog in Rwanda** (Sweden), Jens Assur.
Best Documentary Short: **A Son's Sacrifice** (USA), Yoni Brook.
Student Visionary Award: **Someone Else's War** (Philippines/USA), Lee Wang.
Student Visionary Award: **Good Luck Nedim** (Slovenia), Marko Santic.
Tribeca All Access Creative Promise Award - Documentary: Dee Rees, **Eventual Salvation**.
Tribeca All Access Creative Promise Award - Narrative: Ben Rekhi, **Waste**.
Tribeca All Access Creative Promise Award - Screenwriting:
Marilyn Fu, **The Sisterhood of Night**.
2007 Tribeca/Sloan Screenplay Development Program Grant:
David Freeman, **A First Class Man**.
L'Oréal Paris Women of Worth Vision Award:
Cherien Dabis, **Amreeka**.

Report 2007
The Sixth Annual Tribeca Film Festival showcased 157 features and 88 short films from 47 countries. The festival included such notable events as three outdoor drive-in movies along the Hudson River, panel discussions featuring a diverse selection of individuals from the entertainment world, including Ludacris, Debra Messing, Tiki Barber and Eva Mendes, performances of DJ Spooky's *Rebirth of a Nation* and the premiere of HBO's film *The Gates* about Christo and

Jeanne-Claude's art installation in Central Park. – **John Kendzierski.**

Tromsø International Film Festival
January 13–18, 2009

The world's northernmost film festival is also Norway's best attended. Tromsø is known for presenting the best of current international art-house cinema, screening more than 150 titles, including a feature competition and several exciting sidebars. 'Films from the North' presents new shorts and docs from arctic Scandinavia, Canada and Russia. *Inquiries to*: Tromsø International Film Festival, PO Box 285, N-9253 Tromsø, Norway. Tel: (47) 7775 3090. Fax: 7775 3099. e: info @tiff.no. Web: www.tiff.no.

AWARDS 2007
Norwegian Peace Film Award: **The Cats of Mirikitani** (US), Linda Hattendorf.
Aurora Prize: **Chronicle of an Escape** (Argentina), Israel Adrián Caetano.
FIPRESCI Prize: **Still Life** (China), Zhang Ke Jia.
Don Quijote: **Longind** (Germany), Valeska Grisebach.
Tromsø Palm: **Prirechnyy** (Norway), Tone Grøttjord and **Tommy** (Norway), Ole Giæver.
Audience Award: **USA Vs Al-Arian** (Norway), Line Halvorsen.

Report 2007
At the 17th annual Tromsø International Film Festival the Norwegian Peace Film Award went to Linda Hattendorf for her film **The Cats of Mirikitani**. The director was one of the festival's many international guests. At the 'Blue Screen' seminar, directors Asif Kapadia (UK), Matthias Glasner (Germany) and Nils Gaup (Norway) discussed their new films. The opening film, **Winterland**, directed by Hisham Zaman, was the first film from Filmcamp, the new film production centre in Northern Norway. **– Martha Otte,** Festival Director.

Umeå International Film Festival
September 15–21, 2008

Umeå International Film Festival screens over 30 features and 100 shorts in different programmes. The largest film festival in Northern Scandinavia, it is a gateway for distribution in the Nordic countries. National and international competitions are complemented by the panorama section, short films, Swedish and Nordic features and documentaries, seminars, workshops, film debates and a host of international guests. The popular long film night was this year combined with a Thai theme, showcasing the best of new Thai cinema. Artistic Director: Thom Palmen. *Inquiries to*: Umeå International Film Festival, Box 43, S-901 02 Umeå, Sweden. Tel: (46 90) 133 388. Fax: 777 961. e: info@ filmfest.se. Web: www.filmfest.se.

AWARDS 2007
International Competition-Grand Prix: **A Parting Shot**, Jeanne Waltz.
Films from the North/Filmblicken: **Situation Frank**, Patrik Eklund.
Swedish Church of Umeå Award: **Processen**, Jonas Selberg Augustsén

Report 2007
At the 22nd International Film Festival in Umeå, around 12,000 spectators watched

19TH
TROMSØ INTERNATIONAL FILM FESTIVAL
NORWAY, JANUARY 13-18 2009

A celebration of art cinema in the polar night | **www.tiff.no**

107 films from both Northern Scandinavia and the rest of the world. Highlights included the national premieres of Swedish director Roy Andersson's new film, and two long film nights (gay and lesbian, and Thai themed). The festival jury, consisting of four members from different European countries, awarded the Grand Prix to Jeanne Waltz's **A Parting Shot**, the Filmblicken award went to regionally produced **Situation Frank**, the newly founded film prize of the Swedish church in Umeå went to Jonas Selberg Augustsén's **Processen**. – **Thom Palmen,** Artistic Director.

Valencia International Film Festival – Mediterranean Cinema
October 2008

The Valencia Mostra/Cinema del Mediterrani aims to promote greater understanding among people and cultures in the Mediterranean area, stressing its historical roots by showing high-quality films which contribute to a better critical awareness of each country's film industry and art. *Inquiries to*: Valencia Mostra/Cinema del Mediterrani, Plaza de la Almoina 4, Puertas 1,2 and 3, 46003 Valencia, Spain. Tel: (34 96) 392 1506. Fax: 391 5156. e: festival@mostravalencia.com. Web: www.mostravalencia.org.

Valladolid International Film Festival
October 24–November 1, 2008

One of Spain's key events, the festival spotlights the latest work by established directors and newcomers. Competitive for features, shorts and documentaries. Also offers retrospectives, a selection of recent Spanish productions and a congress of new Spanish directors. *Inquiries to*: Valladolid International Film Festival Office, Teatro Calderón, Calle Leopoldo Cano, s/n 4ª Planta, 47003 Valladolid, Spain. Tel: (34 983) 426 460. Fax: 426 461. e:festvalladolid@seminci.com. Web: www.seminci.com.

AWARDS 2007
International Jury Awards
Prix UIP Valladolid: **A Kiss For The World** (France), Cyril Paris.
Golden Spike for Short Film: **Sleeping Betty** (Canada), Claude Cloutier and **Toyland** (Germany), Jochen Alexander Freydank.
Silver Spike for Short Film: **If I Should Die Faraway** (Mexico), Roberto Canales.
Best Director of Photography Award to: **14 Kilometres** (Spain), Gerardo Olivares.
Actress: Jowita Budnik, **Saviour's Square** (Poland), Krzysztof Krauze and Joanna Kos-Krauze.
Actor: Karl Markovics, **The Counterfeiters** (Austria/Germany), Stefan Ruzowitzky.
Pilar Miró Prize for Best New Director: Eran Kolirin, **The Band's Visit** (France/Israel).
Golden Spike for Feature Film: **14 Kilometres** (Spain), Gerardo Olivares.
Silver Spike for Feature Film: **Saviour's Square** (Poland), Krzysztof Krauze and Joanna Kos-Krauze

Vancouver International Film Festival
September 25–October 10, 2008

Now in its 27th year, this festival has grown into an event of considerable stature. Approximately 150,000 people attend more than 300

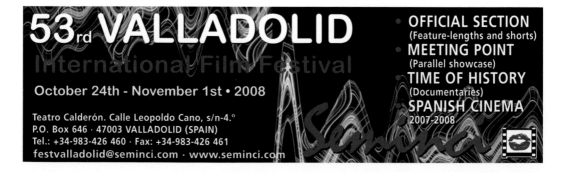

films from around the world. Vancouver also hosts an Annual Film & Television Trade Forum. *Inquiries to*: Alan Franey, 1181 Seymour St, Vancouver, British Columbia, Canada V6B 3M7. Tel: (1 604) 685 0260. Fax: 688 8221. e: viff@ viff.org. Web: www.viff.org.

AWARDS 2007

Audience Awards
Roger's People's Choice for Most Popular International Film: **Persepolis** (France/Iran), Marjane Satrapi and Vincent Paronnaud.
Vancity's Award for the Most Popular Canadian Feature: **She's A Boy I Knew**, Gwen Haworth.
Runner-up: **The Union: The Business Behind Getting High**, Brett Harvey.
People's Choice Award for Most Popular International Non-fiction Film: **Garbage Warrior**, (UK), Oliver Hodge.
Juried Awards
Kyoto Planet 'Climate for Change' Award: **The Planet** (Sweden), Michael Stenberg, Johan Soderberg and Linus Torell.
National Film Board Award for Best Canadian Documentary Feature ($2,500CDN): **Up the Yangtze**, Yung Chang.
Dragons and Tigers Award for Young Cinema: Tie: **Fujian Blue** (China), Robin Weng and **Mid-Afternoon Barks** (China), Zhang Yuedong.
Citytv Western Canada Feature Film Award: **Normal**, Carl Bessai.
Most Promising Director of a Canadian Short Film: **The Windfisherman**, Anna McRoberts.
Women in Film and Television Vancouver's Artistic Merit Award: Gwen Haworth, **She's a Boy I Knew**.

Report 2007

The 26th annual Vancouver International Film Festival broke the $1 million box office mark for the first time. For the past decade, the number of films screened and the size of the audiences in attendance have ranked us among the top five festivals on the continent. This edition of the festival introduced our new Climate for Change series of documentaries and fiction features including award-nominees *4 Elements* (Jiska Rickels, Netherlands), *About Water* (Udo Maurer, Austria), *Bing Ai* (Feng

Yan, China), *Casting a Glance* (James Benning, USA), *Garbage Warrior* (Oliver Hodge, UK), *The Green Chain* (Mark Leiren-Young, Canada), *Keepers of Eden* (Yoram Porath, USA), *Khadak* (Peter Brosens and Jessica Woodworth, Belgium), *Man on Land* (Ariane Michel, France), *The Unforeseen* (Laura Dunn, USA) and winner *The Planet* (Michael Stenberg, Johan Soderberg and Linus Torell, Sweden). We were also very pleased to receive special guest Joan Chen, who appeared in four films screening at the festival. *Lust, Caution*; *Home Song Stories*; *Hollywood Chinese*; and *The Sun Also Rises*. VIFF is renowned for screening the largest contingent of Asian films outside of Asia, in our Dragons and Tigers series.
– Ellie O'Day.

Venice International Film Festival

August 27–September 6, 2008

Under Marco Müller's directorship, the 76-year-old Mostra Internazionale d'Arte Cinematografica is gradually overcoming problems such as its old-fashioned facilities on Lido Island, a vanishing market and heavy political interference. Retrospectives, tributes and parties galore, plus exquisite art exhibitions around downtown Venice, make a visit here essential, especially if you need to meet Italian business partners. Zhang Yimou was president of the 2007 all-directors jury. Tim Burton received a Golden Lion Lifetime Achievement award, alongside Bernardo Bertolucci, who was awarded a special Golden Lion for the Mostra's 75th anniversary. *Inquiries to*: La Biennale di Venezia, San Marco, 1364, Ca' Lolin, 30124 Venice, Italy. Tel (39 041) 521 8711. Fax: 521 8810. e: ufficiostampa@labiennale.org. Web: www.labiennale.org/en/cinema.

AWARDS 2006

Golden Lion for Best Film: **Still Life** (China), Jia Zhangke.
Grand Jury Prize: **Dry Season** (Chad), Mahamat-Saleh Haroun.
Best Direction: Alain Resnais for the film **Coeurs – Private Fears in Public Places**, (France).

Palazzo del Cinema, the main facility and screening theatre of the Venice Festival - photo by Giorgio Zucchiatti

Coppa Volpi for Best Actor: Ben Affleck
Coppa Volpi for Best Actress: Helen Mirren

Report 2006

The Venice Film Festival kicked off in 1932 and celebrated its 75th anniversary in 2007.
The line-up included the Venezia 64 section, whose films competed for the Golden Lion, the Out of Competition, Orizzonti, and Corto Cortissimo sections. A special section dedicated to the 'Secret History of Italian Cinema' featured Spaghetti Westerns, hosted by Quentin Tarantino. **– Festival Press Office.**

Victoria Independent Film & Video Festival

February 1–10, 2008

Vancouver Island's biggest and longest-running film festival screens 190 films at four downtown venues. From the mainstream to the original, the festival offers up the finest contemporary international cinema. It has a strong interest in putting programmers, media and industry professionals together with emerging filmmakers and is dedicated to raising awareness of film and its artistic insights. Set amongst the beautiful historic architecture of Victoria, it offers a film forum, new media event, discussions, family day, and lectures. *Trigger Points Pacific* offers 50 openings for producers to meet with 25 top industry acquisition executives in thirty-minute meetings to make projects happen. Online registration and information at www.victoriafilmfestival.com.

Inquiries to: Victoria Independent Film & Video Festival, 808 View St, Victoria, British Columbia, V8W 1K2, Canada. Tel: (1 250) 389 0444. Fax: 389 0406. e: festival@vifvf.com. Web: www.victoriafilmfestival.com.

AWARDS 2007

Star!TV Award for Best Feature: **Away From Her** (Canada), Sarah Polley.
CHUM TV Award for Best Canadian Feature: **Fido**, Andrew Currie.
Best Documentary Award: **Store** (USA), Cami Kidder.
Cineplex Entertainment Award for Best Short Animation: **Startle Pattern** (USA), Eric Patrick.
Best Short Awards: **Hairlady** (USA), David Birdsell and **Saddest Boy in the World** (Canada), Jamie Travis.
Audience Favourite Award: **Being Cariboo** (British Columbia, Canada), Leanne Allison and Diana Wilson.
Best Documentary Award: **Air Guitar Nation** (USA), Alexandra Lipsitz.
InVision Award for Best Student Film: **Skinheads** (Canada), Michael Vass.

Report 2007

Over 1,200 entries, more than ever before, were juried down to a critically acclaimed selection of 54 feature films and 142 shorts. The best-attended films included *Away From Her*, *Fido*, *Ten Canoes*, *Iraq in Fragments* and *Orchestra Seats* (later released as *Avenue Montaigne*). Guests at the Festival included 14-time Grammy winner David Foster, *Away From Her* leading man Gordon Pinsent and the *Flags of Our Father* actor Barry Pepper. A new music lounge became the meeting place of film-goers and featured local musicians, including an appearance by 54/40's Neil Osborne. Attendance climbed to 16,500. **– Kathy Kay,** Festival Director.

VIENNALE –
Vienna International Film Festival
October 17–29, 2008

The VIENNALE is Austria's most important international film event, as well as being one of the oldest and best-known festivals in the German-speaking world. It takes place every October in beautiful cinemas in Vienna's historic centre, providing a festival with an international orientation and a distinctive urban flair. A high percentage of the approximately 89,000 visitors to the festival consists of a decidedly young audience. In its main programme, the VIENNALE shows a carefully picked selection of new films from all over the globe, as well as new films from Austria. The choice of films offers a cross-section of bold filmmaking that stands apart from the aesthetics of mainstream conventionality and is politically relevant. Aside from its focus on the newest feature films of every genre and structural form imaginable, the festival gives particular attention to documentary films, international short films, as well as experimental works and crossover films. The VIENNALE receives regular international acclaim for its yearly organisation of a large-scale historic retrospective in collaboration with the Austrian Film Museum, its numerous special programmes, as well as for its tributes and homages dedicated to prominent personalities and institutions in international filmmaking. *Inquiries to*: Siebensterngasse 2, 1070 Vienna, Austria. Tel: (43 1) 526 5947. Fax: 523 4172. e: office@viennale.at. Web: www.viennale.at.

Report 2006
12 days, 313 screenings, 119 guests from all over the world, extraordinarily high interest in the documentary film programme and the short films, great attendance at the Peter Whitehead Tribute and the Retrospective Demy/Varda, as well as a repeatedly filled Uranie rooftop at the VIENNALE Zentrale, with a lot of discussions and party nights – this was the VIENNALE 2006! 'The festival is not dominated by the million-dollar deals of Cannes or the workaholic attitude of Berlin,

VIENNALE
VIENNA INTERNATIONAL FILM FESTIVAL

PHOTO: JEM COHEN, A TALE OF TWO CITIES, DER VIENNALE-07 TRAILER, USA 2007

17.–29. OKTOBER 2008
www.viennale.at

but by metropolitan coolness.' (Helmut Merker, *Westdeutscher Rundfunk*). 'It is the more challenging films from the international fest circuit that shine in Vienna, screening to the art-savvy audiences of Austria's cultural centre.' (Anthony Kaufman, *Indiewire*). 'The VIENNALE is the world's only festival, where a Straub film requires an additional screening.' (Jonathan Rosenbaum, *Chicago Reader*).
– **Martina Schwaiger,** Marketing.

Wellington International Film Festival
July 18–August 3, 2008

The Wellington International Film Festival launched its 36th annual programme of over 150 feature programmes from over 30 countries in 2007. The festival provides a non-competitive New Zealand premiere showcase and welcomes many international filmmakers and musicians. The festival shares its programme, brimming with animation, arthouse, documentaries and retrospective programmes, with its 39-year-old sibling, the Auckland International Film Festival. Festival Director: Bill Gosden. *Inquiries to*: Wellington Film Festival, Box 9544, Marion Square, Wellington 6141, New Zealand. Tel: (64 4) 385 0162. Fax: 801 7304. e: festival@nzff.co.nz. Web: www.nzff.co.nz.

WorldFest–Houston
April 11–20, 2008

The 41st Annual WorldFest-Houston International Film Festival will screen around 60 feature film premieres, with an emphasis on American and International Independent feature films, and a spotlight on award-winning short and documentary films. There are special sidebars of Foreign, Children and Family Film Sections. Many filmmakers are in attendance to introduce their films. All 35mm & DVD films are screened at the AMC Dunvale Studio 30 Theatre, the Indie Film Festival for the New Millennium. WorldFest will continue with its annual Short Film Showcase, a special review of 80 new short and student films. Deadline: mid-December. *Inquiries to*:

WorldFest–Houston, PO Box 56566, Houston, TX 77256-6566, USA. Tel: (1 713) 965 9955. Fax: 965 9960. e: mail@worldfest.org. Web: www.worldfest.org.

Zlín International Film Festival for Children and Youth
June 1–8, 2008

The largest and oldest festival of its kind worldwide, presenting fresh and quality films for young movie-goers. Outside the competition section, feature films, animation and documentaries are complemented by a supporting programme focused on topics for children and teens. This year's Days of British Cinema will be introduced with many classics and some of the latest British films aimed at young people. Two other strands of the festival are Zlin Dog (The International Student Film Festival) and The Rainbow Marble (a competition of TV and radio commercials targeted at children). *Inquiries to*: FILMFEST SRO, Filmova 174, CZ-76179 Zlin, Czech Republic. Tel: (420 5) 7759 2275. Fax: 7759 2442. e: festival@zlinfest.cz.

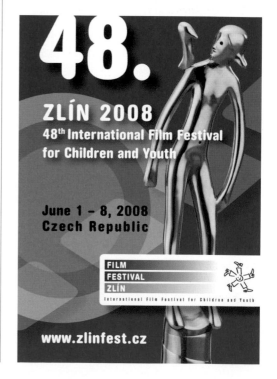

ZLÍN 2008
48th International Film Festival for Children and Youth

June 1 – 8, 2008
Czech Republic

FILM FESTIVAL ZLÍN
International Film Festival for Children and Youth

www.zlinfest.cz

Other Festivals and Markets

ALCINE - Alcalá de Henares/Comunidad de Madrid Film Festival, Plaza del Empecinado 1, 28801 Alcalá de Henares, Madrid, Spain. Tel: (34 91) 879 7380. e: festival@alcine.org. Web: www. alcine.org. *(Competition for Spanish short films, European short films and New Spanish directors' full-length films. Several international sidebars and music sections - Nov 7-15, 2008.)*

Almería International Short Film Festival, Diputación de Almería, Departamento de Cultura y Juventud, Calle Navarro Rodrigo 17, 04071 Almeria, Spain. Tel: (34 950) 211 100 e: coordinador@almeriaencorto.net. Web: www. almeriaencorto.net. *(Competition for international shorts - May.)*

Ambulante, e: info@ambulante.com.mxe. Web: www.ambulante.com.mx. *(Travelling documentary film festival bringing documentary films to places where they are rarely seen - see website for dates and venues in 2008.)*

Angelus Awards Student Film Festival, 7201 Sunset Blvd., Hollywood, CA 90046, USA. Tel: (1 323) 874 6635. e: info@angelus.org. Web: www. angelus.org. *(International competition honouring college-level student films of uncommon artistic calibre that reflect compassion and respect for the human condition. All genres: drama, comedy, animation, documentary and narrative. Entry forms available online. Screening and awards ceremony held at the Directors' Guild of America, Hollywood - Oct.)*

Anima: Brussels Animation Film Festival, Folioscope, Avenue de Stalingrad 52, B-1000 Brussels, Belgium. Tel: (32 2) 534 4125. e: info@folioscope.be. Web: www.anima2008. be. *(Showcase for the newest, most interesting animation - Feb 1-9, 2008.)*

Ann Arbor Film Festival, PO Box 8232, Ann Arbor, MI 48107, USA. Tel: (1 734) 995 5356.

e: info@aafilmfest.org. Web: www.aafilmfest. org. *(Cutting-edge, art-inspired films within genres of experimental, animation, narrative and documentary from all over the world - March 25-30, 2008.)*

Annecy/International Animated Film Festival and International Animated Film Market (MIFA), CITA, 18 Avenue du Trésum, BP 399, 74013 Annecy Cedex, France. Tel: (33 4) 5010 0900. e: info@annecy.org. Web: www. annecy.org. *(Long-established international and competitive festival with a useful sales/ distribution market (MIFA) - Festival: June 9-14, 2008; MIFA: June 11-13, 2008.)*

Arab Film Festival, 300 Brannan St, Ste 508, San Francisco, CA 94107, USA. Tel (1 415) 564 1100. e: info@aff.org. Web: www.aff.org. *(Showcases works by independent filmmakers that provide insightful and innovative perspectives on Arab people, culture, art, history and politics - late Oct- early Nov.)*

Aspen Shortsfest & Filmfest, 110 E Hallam, Ste 102, Aspen, CO 81611, USA. Tel: (1 970) 925 6882. e: filmfest@aspenfilm.org. Web: www.aspenfilm.org. *(Shortsfest: Short subject competition - April 2-6, 2008; Filmfest: Feature- length invitational - Sept 24-28, 2008.)*

Atlantic Film Festival, PO Box 36139, Suite 220, 5600 Sackville St, Halifax, NS, B3J 3S9, Canada. Tel: (1 902) 422 3456. e: festival@atlanticfilm. com. Web: www.atlanticfilm.com. *(Film and video features, shorts, documentaries and animation; also includes industry workshops and panels - Sept.)*

Auckland International Film Festival, PO Box 9544, Marion Sq, Wellington 6037, New Zealand. Tel: (64 4) 385 0162. e: festival@nzff.co.nz. Web: www.nzff.co.nz. *(The festival provides a non- competitive New Zealand premiere showcase* and welcomes many international filmmakers and musicians. Twinned with the Wellington Film Festival - July.)

Augsburg Children's Film Festival, Filmbüro Augsburg, Schroeckstrasse 8, 86152 Augsburg, Germany. Tel: (49 821) 153 078. e: filmbuero@t-online.de. Web: www. filmtage-augsburg.de. (International features for children - March.)

Banff Mountain Film Festival, Mountain Culture at The Banff Centre, Box 1020, 107 Tunnel Mountain Drive, Banff, AB, T1L 1H5, Canada. Tel: (1 403) 762 6675.e: banffmountainfilms@banffcentre.ca. Web: www.banffmountainfestivals.ca. (International competition for films and videos related to mountains and the spirit of adventure - Oct 25-Nov 2, 2008.)

Big Sky Documentary Film Festival, 131 South Higgins Ave, Suite 201, Missoula, Montana 59802, USA. Tel: (1 406) 541 3456. e: director@bigskyfilmfest.org. Web: www.bigskyfilmfest.org. (Screening over 100 films from over 30 countries the festival also includes panel discussions, Q&A sessions with dozens of filmmakers, as well as VIP events, receptions and parties - Feb 14-28, 2008.)

Bite the Mango Film Festival, National Media Museum, Bradford, BD1 1NQ, UK. Festival Director: Addy Rutter. Tel: (44 1274) 203311. e: addy.rutter@nationalmediamuseum.org.uk. Web: www.bitethemango.org.uk. (A cultural celebration of world cinema that draws its influences from South Asia, Africa, the Far East and Central America highlighting different cultures through the medium of film. Includes the Golden Mango Award, screentalk interviews, masterclasses and retrospectives. Open for Entries Jan - Sept 20-27, 2008.)

Bogotá Film Festival, Residencias Tequendama, Centro Internacional Tequendama, Bogotá, Colombia. Tel: (57 1) 341 7562. e: direccion@bogocine.com. Web: www.bogocine.com. (Celebrating our 25th Anniversary in 2008 with an International competitive section, National

competitive section and sidebars. Germany is the 'Guest of Honour' Country - Oct 1-9, 2008.)

Boston Film Festival, 9B Hamilton Place, Boston, MA 02108, USA. Tel: (1 617) 523 8388. e: info@bostonfilmfestival.org. Web: www.bostonfilmfestival.org. (Approximately 50 films, including studio releases, American independents, documentaries and shorts - Sept.)

Bradford Animation Festival, National Media Museum, Bradford, BD1 1NQ, UK. Tel: (44 1274) 203364. e: deb.singleton@nationalmediamuseum.org.uk. Web: www.baf.org.uk. (Industry-based animation festival; masterclasses, seminars, workshops and screenings with some of animation's top names. Home to the BAF Awards which open for entries in Feb - Nov 12-15, 2008.)

Bradford International Film Festival, National Media Museum, Bradford, BD1 1NQ, UK. Festival Director: Tony Earnshaw. Tel: (44 1274) 203320. e: tony.earnshaw@nationalmediamuseum.org.uk. Web: www.bradfordfilmfestival.org.uk. (Includes the BIFF Lifetime Achievement Award, the BIFF Fellowship Award, Shine Short Film Award, director showcase, Screentalk interviews and masterclasses, retrospectives, Film & Music Conference and the Widescreen Weekend - Feb 29-March 15, 2008.)

Britdoc, Keble College, Oxford, OX1 3PG, UK. Tel: (44 20) 7033 2564. e: festival@britdoc.org. Web: www.britdoc.org. (Britdoc is an international documentary film festival. Founded in 2006 by the Channel 4 British Documentary Film Foundation, it is a bespoke festival designed to connect filmmakers, funders and distributors. Hosting inspirational talent, featuring award-winning docs and pitching the most ambitious projects. It is a place to come and be inspired by the best documentary filmmaking in the world, and to come and do business with the most interesting talent in the world. The festival also presents the UK's only International Pitching Forum. Festival director: Beadie Finzi - July 23-25, 2008.)

British Silent Cinema, Broadway, 14-18 Broad St, Nottingham, NG1 3AL, UK. Tel: (44 115) 952

6600. e: laraine@broadway.org.uk. Web: www. britishsilentcinema.co.uk. *(Screenings and presentations - April 3-6, 2008.)*

Brussels International Festival of Fantastic Film, 8 Rue de la Comtesse de Flandre 1020 Brussels, Belgium. Tel: (32 2) 201 1713. e: info@ bifff.org. Web: www.bifff.org. *(Competitive international and European selection for shorts and features. Special side events include the International Body Painting contest - March 27-April 8, 2008.)*

CPH:Dox-Copenhagen International Documentary Film Festival, Stockholmsgade 43, DK-2100 Copenhagn Ø, Denmark. Tel: (45) 3393 0734/36. e: info@cphdox.dk. Web: www. cphdox.dk. *(The largest documentary film festival in Scandinavia presents a selection of more than 130 documentary films from around the world - Nov 7-16, 2008.)*

Camerimage, Rynek Nowomiejski 28, 87-100 Torun, Poland. Tel: (48 56) 621 0019. e: office@camerimage.pl. Web: www. camerimage.pl. *(Competition, Special Screenings, William Fraker Retrospective, Student Festival, World Panorama Retrospective, seminars, workshops, press conferences, exhibitions - late Nov-early Dec.)*

Cartoons on the Bay, Rai Trade, Via Umberto Novaro 18, 00195 Rome, Italy. Tel: (39 06) 3749 8315. e: cartoonsbay@raitrade.it. Web: www. cartoonsbay.com. *(International Festival and Conference on television animation - April.)*

Chicago International Children's Film Festival, Facets Mulimedia, 1517 W Fullerton, Chicago, IL 60614, USA. Tel: (1 773) 281 9075. e: kidsfest@ facets.org. Web: www.cicff.org. *(Largest and oldest festival of children's films in US - Oct 23-Nov 2, 2008.)*

Chicago Latino Film Festival, International Latino Cultural Center of Chicago, c/o Columbia College Chicago, 600 S Michigan Ave, Chicago, IL 60605-1996, USA. Tel: (1 312) 431 1330. e: info@latinoculturalcenter.org. Web: www. latinoculturalcenter.org. *(ILCC promotes awareness of Latino culture through the arts, including this festival - April 14-16, 2008.)*

Cinanima, Rua 62, 251, Apartado 743, 4500-366 Espinho, Portugal. Tel: (351 2) 2733 1350. e: cinanima@mail.telepac.pt. Web: www.cinanima. pt. *(International animated films - Nov.)*

Cinekid, Korte Leidsedwarstraat 12, 1017 RC Amsterdam, Netherlands. Tel: (31 20) 531 7890. e: info@cinekid.nl. Web: www.cinekid.nl. *(International film, TV and new media festival for children and young people - Oct 11-26, 2008.)*

Cinéma du Réel, Bibliothèque Publique d'Information, 25 rue du Renard, 75197 Paris Cedex 04, France. Tel: (33 1) 4478 4516. Web: www.cinereel.org. *(International documentary film festival for the public and professionals showcasing the work of experienced authors as well as new talents, the history of documentary cinema as well as contemporary works - March 7-18, 2008.)*

Cinéma Italien Rencontres D'Annecy, Bonlieu Scène Nationale, 1 rue Jean Jaures, BP 294, 74007 Annecy Cedex, France. Tel: (33 450) 334 406. e: com@annecycinemaitalien.com. Web: www.annecycinemaitalien.com. *(Feature films from Italy, with tributes and retrospectives. Competitive - late Sept-early Oct.)*

Cinema Jove International Film Festival, Calle La Safor 10, Despacho 5, 46015 Valencia, Spain. Tel: (34 96) 331 1047. e: cinemajove@gva.es. Web: www.cinemajovefilmfest.com. Festival Director: Rafael Maluenda. *(Aims to promote the work of young filmmakers and has a feature and short film international competition, as well as a short film market. Deadline for submission: March 26, 2008; June 21-28, 2008.)*

Cinéma Mediterranéen Montpellier, 78 Avenue du Pirée, 34000 Montpellier, France. Tel: (33 4) 9913 7373. e:info@cinemed.tm.fr. Web: www. cinemed.tm.fr. *(Competitive festival for fiction works by directors from the Mediterranean Basin, the Black Sea states, Portugal or Armenia.*

Categories: Feature, Short, Documentary, Panorama. Formats: 16mm, 35mm. Preview on VHS and DVD - Oct.)

Cinemagic World Screen Festival for Young People, 49 Botanic Avenue, Belfast, BT7 1JL, Northern Ireland. Tel: (44 28) 9031 1900. e: info@cinemagic.org.uk. Web: www.cinemagic.org.uk. *(Children's films in competition, screenings, masterclasses and industry discussions - Nov 15-Dec 3, 2008.)*

Cinequest, PO Box 720040, San Jose, CA 95172-0040, USA. Tel: (1 408) 995 5033. e: info@cinequest.org. Web: www.cinequest.org. *(Maverick films, filmmakers and technologies. Competition for features, documentaries and shorts, plus tributes, seminars, entertainment - Feb 27-March 9, 2008.)*

CineVegas Film Festival, 4300 W Sunset Rd, Ste E-3 Henderson, NV 89014, USA. Tel: (1 702) 992 7979.e: info@cinevegas.com. Web: www.cinevegas.com. *(Highlights the most exciting offerings from up-and-coming filmmakers and visionary veterans. Celebrating its tenth anniversary in 2008, the Festival combines the glamour and energy of world premiere films and the intensity of in-depth celebrity tributes set against the backdrop of Sin City. Robin Greenspun serves as the Festival's President, Trevor Groth serves as Artistic Director and Dennis Hopper serves as the Chairman of the Creative Advisory Board - June 12-21, 2008.)*

Cleveland International Film Festival, 2510 Market Ave, Cleveland, OH 44113-3434, USA. Tel: (1 216) 623 3456. e: cfs@clevelandfilm.org. Web: www.clevelandfilm.org. *(International 'World Tour' programme with specials such as family films, American independents and lesbian and gay films - March 6-16, 2008.)*

Cognac International Thriller Film Festival, 3, Allées de la Corderie, BP 18, 16100 Cognac, France. Tel: (33 1) 4134 2033. e: festival@cognac.fr. Web: www.festival.cognac.fr. *(International thrillers and 'films noir'; competitive for features and French-speaking shorts - June.)*

Corona Cork Film Festival, Emmet House, Emmet Place, Cork, Republic of Ireland. Tel: (353 21) 427 1711 e: info@corkfilmfest.org. Web: www.corkfilmfest.org. *(Features, documentaries, competitive shorts, animation, retrospectives, special programmes. Deadline: July - Oct.)*

Cottbus Film Festival - Festival of East European Cinema, Werner-Seelenbinder-Ring 44/45, D-03048 Cottbus, Germany. Tel: (49 355) 431 070. e: info@filmfestival-cottbus.de. Web: www.film-festivalcottbus. *(Festival of East European films: features and shorts (competitive), children's and youth film, spectrum, national hits, focus 2008: new cinema from the Baltics - Nov 11-15, 2008.)*

Crossing Europe Film Festival Linz, Graben 30, 4020 Linz, Austria. Tel: (43 732) 785700. info@crossingeurope.at. Web: www.crossingeurope.at. *(Celebrating its fifth year in 2008, the anniversary event is celebrated in cooperation with Upper Austria's capital Linz, the European Capital in 2009. With the European Competition and the European Panorama, the festival offers Austrian premieres of feature films and documentaries that have been highly acclaimed and distinguished with awards at international festivals - but all too rarely find their way into our cinemas. The festival grants a central place to the diversity and richness of the cultural distinctiveness of young European cinema. Apart from the competitions a great choice of festival specials is on the programme: tributes to outstanding film directors; film evenings centring on music and youth cultures, and more - April 22-27, 2008.)*

Dead by Dawn International Horror Film Festival, 88 Lothian Rd, Edinburgh, EH3 9BZ, UK. Tel: (44) 01383 410281. e: info@deadbydawn.co.uk. Web: www.deadbydawn.co.uk. *(Featuring great cult and classic favourites, new independent and mainstream features and short movies - April 24-27, 2008.)*

Deauville Festival of American Film, Le Public Système Cinéma, 40, rue Anatole France, 92594 Levallois-Perret Cedex, France. Tel: (33 1) 4134 2033. e: jlasserre@le-public-systeme.fr. Web:

www.festival-deauville.com. *(Showcase for US features and independent films - Sept 5-14, 2008.)*

Deauville Festival of Asian Film, Le Public Système Cinéma, 40, rue Anatole France, 92594 Levallois-Perret Cedex, France. Tel: (33 1) 4134 2033. e: jlasserre@le-public-systeme.fr. Web: www.festival-deauville.com. *(Showcase for Asian feature films - March 12-16, 2008.)*

Divercine, Lorenzo Carnelli 1311, 11200 Montevideo, Uruguay. Tel: (59 82) 419 5795. e: cinemuy@chasque.net. Web: www.cinemateca. org.uy. *(Children's festival - July.)*

DocsBarcelona, Calle Provenca 175, Atic 2, 08036 Barcelona, Spain. Tel: (34 93) 452 4618. e: info@docsbarcelona.com. Web: www. docsbarcelona.com. *(The festival screens documentaries from all around the world, divided into four very different thematic sections, each programmed by an international expert. The documentaries are either premieres in Spain or films whose particular cinematic or thematic interest means that they deserve a second chance on the big screen - Jan 31-Feb 3, 2008.)*

Dokville, Film-und Medienfestival GmbH, Schlosstrasse 84, 70176 Stuttgart, Germany. Tel: (49 711) 925 460. Web: www.festival-gmbh.de. *(June 5-6, 2008.)*

Duisburg Film Week, Am König Heinrich Platz, D-47049 Duisburg, Germany. Tel: (49 203) 283 4187. e: info@duisburger-filmwoche. de. Web: www.duisburger-filmwoche.de. *(German-language documentaries from Germany, Switzerland and Austria - early Nov.)*

Durban International Film Festival, Centre for Creative Arts, University of KwaZulu-Natal, Durban 4041, South Africa. Tel: (27 31) 260 1145. e: diff@ ukzn.ac.za. Web: www.cca.ukzn.ac.za. *(South African and international cinema showcasing feature films and a selection of topical documentaries and short films - late June-early July.)*

EcoVision Festival, Via Francesco Bentivegna 51, 90139 Palermo, Italy. e: danieleottobre@ ecovisionfestival.com. Web: www. ecovisionfestival.com. *(International festival exploring the environment and the effects of globalisation - June 5-10, 2008.)*

Edmonton International Film Festival, Edmonton International Film Society, Suite 201, 10816A-82 Avenue, Edmonton, Alberta, T6E 2B3, Canada. Tel: (1 780) 423 0844. e: info@edmontonfilmfest.com. Web: www. edmontonfilmfest.com. *(Feature films, documentaries and shorts - Sept 26-Oct 4, 2008.)*

Emden International Film Festival, An der Berufschule 3, 26721 Emden, Germany. Tel: (49) 4921 9155-0. e: filmfest@vhs-emden.de. Web: http://filmfest.icserver13.de. *(Focus on North Western European films, particularly Germany and the UK - June 4-11, 2008.)*

European Independent Film Festival (ÉCU), 108 Rue Damremont, Paris 75018, France. e: info@ecufilmfestival.com. Web: www. ecufilmfestival.com. *(ÉCU has become Europe's premier event for independent filmmakers and their audiences. It has established itself firmly as the place to be for filmmakers wanting recognition of their storytelling skills as they compete for the right to be acknowledged as one of Europe's best independent filmmakers. The festival will be held at the Bibliotheque Nationale de Francois Mitterrand in Paris and will feature approximately a hundred films in 16 categories - March 14-16, 2008.)*

European Short Film Biennale, Film-und Medienfestival GmbH, Schlosstrasse 84, 70176 Stuttgart, Germany. Tel: (49 711) 925 460. e: kurzfilmbiennale@festival-gmbh.de. Web: www. kurzfilmbiennale.de. *(July.)*

FanTasia International Film Festival, 460 Rue St Catherine, Suite 915, Montreal, Quebec, H3B 1V6, Canada. Tel: (1 514) 876 1760. e: info@ fantasiafestival.com. Web: www. fantasiafestival. com. *(Showcases the most exciting, innovative and individualistic examples of contemporary international genre cinema - July 3-21, 2008.)*

Festival Dei Popoli, Borgo Pinti 82 Rosso, 50121 Firenze, Italy. Tel: (39 055) 244 778. e: festivaldeipopoli@festivaldeipopoli.191. it. Web: www.festivaldeipopoli.org. *(Partly competitive and open to documentaries on social, anthropological, historical and political issues - latc Nov.)*

Festival du Cinema International en Abitibi-Temscamingue, 215 Mercier Avenue, Rouyn-Noranda, Quebec J9X 5WB, Canada. Tel: (1 819) 762 6212. e: info@festivalcinema.ca. Web: www. festivalcinema.ca. *(International shorts, medium- and full-length features; animation, documentary and fiction - late Oct/early Nov.)*

Festival International du Film Francophone de Namur, 175, Rue des Brasseurs, 5000 Namur, Belgium Tel: (32 81) 241 236. e: info@fiff.be. Web: www.fiff.be. *(late Sept-early Oct.)*

Festival Premiers Plans, 54 rue Beaubourg, 75003 Paris, France. Tel: (33 1) 4271 5370. e: paris@premiersplans.org. Web: www. premiersplans.org. *(Competitive festival for European debut features, shorts and student works - Jan 16-25, 2009.)*

Festroia, Avenida Luisa Dodi 61-65, 2900-461 Setúbal, Portugal. Tel: (351 265) 525 908. e: info@festroia.pt. Web: www.festroia.pt. *(Held in Setúbal, near Lisbon. Official section for countries producing fewer than 30 features per year - June.)*

Filmfest Dresden, Alaunstrasse 62, D-01099, Dresden, Germany. Tel: (49 351) 829 470. e: info@filmfest-dresden.de. Web: www.filmfest-dresden.de. *(Filmfest Dresden is an international short film festival. Founded in 1989, it hosts the best-funded short film competitions across Europe. The festival also organises workshops and seminars for young filmmakers. Furthermore, it presents short-film programmes at international festivals and has initiated numerous international film-exchange programmes. In 2008, Filmfest Dresden will celebrate its 20th anniversary. Festival director: Robin Mallick - April 15-20, 2008.)*

Filmfest München, Sonnenstr 21, D-80331, Munich, Germany. Tel: (49 89) 381 9040. e: info@filmfest-muenchen.de. Web: www.filmfest-muenchen.de. *(International screenings and retrospectives - June 20-28, 2008.)*

Filmfestival Max Ophüls Prize, Mainzerstrasse 8, 66111 Saarbruecken, Germany. Tel: (49 681) 906 8910. Web: www.max-ophüls-preis.de. *(Competitive event only for young directors from German-speaking countries who have not produced more than three feature films and the entered film must be produced the year before - Jan 14-20, 2008.)*

Florida Film Festival, Enzian Theatre, 1300 South Orlando Ave, Maitland, Florida 32751, USA. Tel: (1 407) 644 6579. e: filmfest@gate.net. Web: www.floridafilmfestival.com. *(Showcases the best independent and foreign films: narrative, documentary, features, shorts, animation, midnight movies plus educational forums, glamorous parties and other special events - March 28-April 6, 2008.)*

Focus on Asia Fukuoka International Film Festival, 1-8-1, Chuo-ku Tenzin, Fukuoka 810 8620, Japan. Tel: (81 92) 733 5170. e: info@focus-on-asia.com. Web: www.focus-on-asia. com. *(Dedicated to promoting Asian film. Non-competitive - Sept.)*

Fredrikstad Animation Festival, Box 1405, N-1602 Fredrikstad, Norway. Tel: (47) 4024 9364. e: mail@animationfestival.no. Web: www. animationfestival.no. *(Nordic, Baltic and international animation. Competitive - Nov.)*

Full Frame Documentary Film Festival, 324 Blackwell Street, Suite 500, Washington Bldg, Bay 5, Durham, NC 27701, USA. Tel: (1 919) 687 4100. e: info@fullframefest.org. Web: www.fullframefest.org. *(Showcases over 100 documentaries from around the world - April 3-6, 2008.)*

Future Film Festival, Via del Pratello 21/2, 40122 Bologna, Italy. Tel: (39 051) 296 0672. e: info@futurefilmfestival.org. Web: www. futurefilmfestival.org. *(Jan 15-20, 2008.)*

Galway Film Fleadh, Cluain Mhuire, Monivea Road, Galway, Ireland. Tel: (353 91) 751 655. e: gafleadh@iol.ie. Web: www.galwayfilmfleadh. com. *(Documentary features, independent features, short films, Irish films and World Cinema - July 8-13, 2008.)*

Gerardmer International Fantasy Film Festival, Le Public Système Cinéma, 40, rue Anatole France, 92594 Levallois-Perret Cedex, France. Tel: (33 1) 4134 2109. e: presse@gerardmer-fantasticart.com. Web: www.gerardmer-fantasticart.com. *(International fantasy, sci-fi, psychological thriller and horror films, with competition for features and French-language shorts - late Jan-early Feb.)*

Guadalajara International Film Festival, Calle Cenit 1158, Colonia Jardines del Bosque, Guadalajara, Jalisco, Mexico. Tel: (52 33) 3121 7461. e: info@festivalcinedgl.udg.mx. Web: www.guadalajaracinemafest.com. *(Mexican and Ibero-American recent quality film productions, increasing the awareness of the world film industry by screening the work of noteworthy Ibero-American film directors and presenting other remarkable and innovative films by up-and-coming filmmakers - March.)*

Haifa International Film Festival, 142 Hanassi Ave, Haifa 34 633, Israel. Tel: (972 4) 8353 515. e: film@haifaff.co.il. Web: www.haifaff.co.il. *(Premieres the best and most recent international productions: feature films, documentaries, animation, short films, retrospectives and tributes - late Sept- early Oct.)*

Hawaii International Film Festival, 680 Iwilei Rd, Suite 100, Honolulu, Hawaii 96813, USA. Tel: (1 808) 528 3456. e: info@hiff.org. Web: www. hiff.org. *(Seeks to promote cultural understanding between Asia, Pacific and North America through film - Oct.)*

Heartland Film Festival, 200 S Meridian, Suite 220, Indianapolis, Indiana 46225-0176, USA. Tel: (1 317) 464 9405. e: info@ trulymovingpictures. org. Web: www.heartlandfilmfestival.org. *(Established in 1991 to honour filmmakers whose work celebrates the best of the human spirit. Call for entries begins March - Oct 16-24, 2008.)*

Holland Animation Film Festival, Hoogt 4, 3512 GW Utrecht, Netherlands. Tel: (31 30) 233 1733. e: info@haff.nl. Web: www.haff.awn. nl. *(International competitions for independent and applied animation; special programmes, retrospectives, student films, exhibitions - Nov 5-9, 2008.)*

Hot Docs Canadian International Documentary Festival, 110 Spadina Avenue, Suite 333, Toronto, Ontario, M5V 2K4, Canada. Tel: (1 416) 203 2155. e: info@hotdocs.ca. Web: www.hotdocs.ca. *(North America's largest documentary festival presents a selection of more than 100 cutting-edge documentaries from Canada and around the world. Through its industry programmes, the Festival also provides a full range of professional development, market and networking opportunities for documentary professionals - April 17-27, 2008.).*

Huesca Film Festival, Avenida del Parque 1,2, 22002 Huesca, Spain. Tel: (34 974) 212 582. e: info@huesca-filmfestival.com. Web: www. huesca-filmfestival.com. *(Well-established competitive shorts festival in country town, with features sidebars - June.)*

Hull International Short Film Festival, Suite 4 Danish Buildings, 44-46 High St, Hull, UK. Tel: (44) 01482 381512. e:office@hullfilm.co.uk. Web: www.hullfilm.co.uk. *(Dedicated to showcasing the best short films from across the world with numerous competitions, masterclasses, an industry weekend and special programmes. It runs over five days and showcases more than 250 films - April 15-20, 2008.)*

Hungarian Film Week, Magyar Filmunió, Városligeti, Fasor 38, 1068 Budapest, Hungary. Tel: (36 1) 351 7760. e: filmhu@forum.film.hu. Web: www.hungarianfilm.com. *(Competitive national festival showcasing Hungarian features, documentaries and short films from the previous year - Jan 29-Feb 5, 2008.)*

Il Cinema Ritrovato, Mostra Internazionale del Cinema Libero, Cineteca del Comune di Bologna, Via Riva di Reno 72, 40122 Bologna, Italy. Tel:

(39 051) 219 4814. e: cinetecamanifestazioni1@ comune.bologna.it. Web: www. cinetecadibologna.it. *(International festival providing a selection of unknown, little-known, rediscovered, and restored films dedicated to cinema history. Selection made among the best film restorations from all over the world - June 28-July 5, 2008.)*

Imago - International Young Film & Video Festival, Apartado 324 Avenida Eugénio de Andrade, Bloco D, 6230-909 Fundão, Portugal. Tel: (351) 275 771 607. e: info@imagofilmfest. com. Web: www.imagofilmfest.com. *(Oct.)*

Independent Film Days, Filmbuero Augsburg, Schroeckstrasse 8, 86152 Augsburg, Germany. Tel: (49 821) 153 078. e: filmbuero@t-online.de. Web: www.filmtage-augsburg.de. *(International event for documentary and independent features, with retrospectives, national focus and student symposium - Nov.)*

International Cinematographers Film Festival 'Manaki Brothers', 8 Mart 4, 1000 Skopje, Republic of Macedonia. Tel: (389 2) 3211 811. e: info@manaki.com.mk. Web: www.manaki.com. mk. *(Held in remembrance of Yanaki and Milton Manaki, the first cameramen of the Balkans - Sept.)*

International Documentary Festival of Marseille (FID Marseille), 14 Allée Léon Gambetta, 13001 Marseille, France. Tel: (33 4) 9504 4490 e: welcome@fidmarseille.org. Web: www.fidmarseille.org. *(The best international documentaries - early July.)*

International Documentary Film Festival Munich, Landwehrstrasse 79, D 80336 Munich, Germany. Tel: (49 89) 5139 9788. Web: www. dokfest-muenchen.de. *(Feature-length creative documentaries; competitive; submission deadline 10th Jan - May 1-7, 2008.)*

International Film Festival Bangladesh, Eastern Commercial Complex, Suite 7/9, 73 Kakrail, Dhaka-1000, Bangladesh. Tel: (88 2) 936 0982. e: info@iffb.us. Web: www.iffb.us. *(Competitive section for Asian cinema. Also non-competitive sections, including 'Retrospective', 'Cinema of the World', 'Children's Film' and 'Bangladesh Panorama' – Jan.)

International Film Festival Innsbruck, Museumstrasse 31, A-6020 Innsbruck, Austria. Tel: (43 512) 5785 0014. e: info@iffi.at. Web: www.iffi.at. Director: Helmut Groschup. (Films about Africa, Latin America and Asia. International competition, Public Award, Francophone Award and Doc Award - June 3-0, 2000.)

International Film Festival of Uruguay, Lorenzo Carnelli 1311, 11200 Montevideo, Uruguay. Tel: (59 82) 419 5795. e: cinemuy@chasque.net. Web: www.cinemateca.org.uy. (Presents independent and documentary films - late March-early April.)

International Film Forum 'Arsenals', International Centre of Cinema, Marstalu 14, Riga, LV-1050, Latvia Tel: (371) 6721 0114. e: arsenals@arsenals.lv. Web: www.arsenals. lv. (Biannual competitive festival with $10,000 international competition and latest releases from Latvia, Lithuania and Estonia in features, documentary, shorts and animation - Sept 12-21, 2008.)

International Leipzig Festival for Documentary and Animated Film, Grosse Fleischergasse 11, 04109 Leipzig, Germany. Tel: (49 341) 308 640. e: info@dok-leipzig.de. Web: www.dok-leipzig.de. (Screens the best, most exciting, moving and artistically outstanding animated and documentary films. Competitive - Oct 27-Nov 2, 2008.)

International Week of Fantastic Film, University of Malaga, Vicerrectorado de Cultura y Relaciones Institucionales, Pabellón de Gobierno, 3A Planta, 29071 Malaga, Spain. Tel: (34 9) 5213 4192. e: fantastico@uma.es. Web: www.fantastico.uma. es. (Films produced worldwide of Fantastic, Horror and Thriller genre - Nov.)

International Women's Film Festival, Maison des Arts, Palace Salvador Allende, 94000 Créteil, France. Tel: (33 1) 4980 3898. e: filmsfemmes@ wanadoo.com. Web: www.filmsdefemmes.com. (Features, shorts and animation made by women - March 14-23, 2008.)

Inverness Film Festival, Bishops Rd, Inverness, IV3 5SA. Tel: (44 1463) 234234. e: info@invernessfilmfestival.com. Web: www. invernessfilmfestival.com. Directors: Matt Lloyd & Paul Taylor. (International features, documentaries and shorts plus workshops - Nov.)

Israel Film Festival, Israfest Foundation, 6404 Wilshire Blvd, Suite 1240, Los Angeles, CA 90048, USA. Tel: (1 323) 966 4166. e: info@israelfilmfestival.com. Web: www. israelfilmfestival.com. (US showcase for Israeli features, shorts, documentaries and TV dramas - 2008 dates: March in LA; Oct in NY; May in Miami.)

Jameson Dublin International Film Festival, 13 Merrion Sq, Dublin 2, Ireland. Tel: (353 1) 635 0290. e: info@dubliniff.com. Web: www.dubliniff. com. (Founded in 2002 and aimed squarely at the cinema-going public. Non-competitive, largely composed of new international feature films (120 in 2005, including ten Irish productions or co-productions. Daily Talking Pictures events offer lunchtime panel discussions on a variety of filmmaking topics - Feb 15-24, 2008.)

Jihlava International Documentary Film Festival, Jana Masaryka 16, PO Box 33, 586 01 Jihlava, Czech Republic. Tel: (420 7) 7410 1656. Web: www.dokument-festival.cz. (The biggest festival of creative documentary in Central and Eastern Europe. It shows work from around the world, screenings are followed by after-film talks and the programme features an accompanying programme of workshops, panel discussions, theatre, authors' readings, concerts, and exhibitions. Alongside systematically mapping the domestic and world documentary scenes it also focuses on the distribution of films (www. Doc-Air.com portal) and publishing activities - Oct 24-29, 2008.)

JumpCuts, 808 View St, Victoria, BC, Canada, V8W 1K2. Tel: (1 250) 389 0444. e: director@

vifvf.com. *(Participants come play with cameras, computers and their creativity. JumpCuts is a youth oriented festival of hands-on workshops and film screenings.Romp through the world of CGI, Virtual DJ, Stunts, Game Mods, Music, Acting, Editing and so much more - June 5-7, 2008.)*

Kidfilm/USA Film Festival, 6116 N Central Expressway, Suite 105, Dallas, Texas 75206, USA. Tel: (1 214) 821 6300. e: usafilmfestival@ aol.com. Web: www.usafilmfestival.com. *(Non-competitive; oldest and largest family film festival in the US. Accepts US and international shorts and features - Jan 7-20, 2008.)*

Kracow Film Festival, Morawskiego 5 Pok 434, 30-102 Krakow, Poland. Tel: (48 12) 294 6945. e: info@cff.pl. Web: www.cff.pl. *(Poland's oldest international film festival showcasing documentary, animated and short fiction films - May 30-5 June, 2008.)*

Lisbon International Documentary Film Festival, Rua dos Bacalhoeiros, 125, 4°, 1100-068 Lisbon, Portugal. Tel: (351 21) 887 1639. e: doclisboa@doclisboa.org. Web: www.doclisboa.org. *(National and International documentaries - Oct.)*

London Lesbian & Gay Film Festival, BFI Southbank, Belvedere Rd, London SE1 8XT, UK. Tel: (44 20) 7815 1323. e: anna.dunwoody@bfi. org.uk. Web: www.llgff.org.uk. *(Films of special interest to lesbian and gay audiences - March 27-April 10, 2008.)*

Lucas International Children's Film Festival, c/o Deutsches Filmmuseum, Schaumainkai 41, 60596 Frankfurt/Main, Germany. Tel: (49 69) 9612 20670. e: lucas@deutsches-filmmuseum. de. Web: www.lucasfilmfestival.de. *(Germany's oldest children's film festival.An FIAPF A-festival. Competition for new international productions for children aged from five to twelve - end Sept.)*

Margaret Mead Film & Video Festival, American Museum of Natural History, 79th St at Central Park W, New York, NY 10024-5192, USA. Tel: (1 212) 769 5000. e: meadfest@amnh.org.

Web: www.amnh.org/mead. *(The longest-running showcase for International documentaries in the United States - Nov.)*

Marrakech International Film Festival, Le Public Système Cinéma, 40, rue Anatole France, 92594 Levallois-Perret Cedex, France. Tel: (33 1) 4134 2030. e: ffifm@lafondation.ma. Web: www.festival-marrakech.com. *(Showcase for International feature films - Dec.)*

Message to Man Film Festival, Karavannaya 12, 191011, St Petersburg, Russia. Tel: (7 901) 372 1264. e: info@message-to-man.spb.ru. Web: www.message-to-man.spb.ru. *(International documentary, short and animated films - June.)*

Miami International Film Festival, Miami Dade College, 300 NE 2nd St, Room 5521, Miami, Florida 33132, USA. Tel: (1 305) 237 3456. e: info@miamifilmfestival.com. Web: www. miamifilmfestival.com. *(Celebrating its 25th year, the festival shows the best of world cinema with a special focus on Ibero-American films - Feb 28-March 9, 2008.)*

Midnight Sun Film Festival, Kansanopistontie 5, 99600 Sodankylä, Finland. Tel: (358 16) 614 525. e: office@msfilmfestival.fi. Web: www. msfilmfestival.fi. *(International and silent films, plus award-winners from Cannes, Berlin, Locarno and Stockholm - June.)*

Minneapolis/St Paul International Film Festival, Minnesota Film Arts, 309 Oak St Ave SE, Minneapolis, MN 55414, USA. Tel: (1 612) 331 7563. e: jim@mnfilmarts.org. Web: www. mspfilmfest.org. *(Presents over 150 films from more than 50 countries - April 10-26, 2008.)*

Mipdoc, 11 rue du Colonel Pierre Avia, BP 572, 75726 Paris Cedex 15, France. Tel: (33 1) 4190 4580. e: info.miptv@reedmidem.com. Web: www.miptv.com. *(Specialist international screening marketplace and conference for documentaries - April 5-6, 2008.)*

Montreal International Festival of New Cinema, 3805 Boulevard St-Laurent, Montreal,

Quebec, Canada H2W 1X9. Tel: (1 514) 282 0004. e: info@nouveaucinema.ca. Web: www. nouveaucinema.ca. *(Highlights the development of new trends in cinema and new media, providing a showcase for new, original works, particularly in the fields of independent cinema and digital creation - Oct.)*

Mumbai International Film Festival, Rajkamal Studio, SS Rao Road, Parel, Mumbai 400 012, India. Tel: (91 22) 2413 6571. e: info@iff-mumbai. org. Web: www.iff mumbai.org. *(The only independent film festival in India, organised by Mumbai Academy of the Moving Image, whose chairman is renowned filmmaker Shyam Benegal. Full-length feature films only. Sections: Global Vision, with a FIPRESCI award, Retro, Tribute, Focus on Filmmaker, Focus on One Country, Film India Worldwide & Competition for Indian Films, judged by an international jury - March 6-13, 2008.)*

Munich International Festival of Film Schools, Sonnenstrasse 21, D-80331 Munich, Germany. Tel: (49 89) 3819 040. e: info@filmfest-muenchen.de. Web: www.filmfest-muenchen. de. *(Competition for the best student films from around the world - Nov.)*

NatFilm Festival, Store Kannikestraede 6, 1169 Copenhagen, Denmark. Tel: (45) 3312 0005. e: info@natfilm.dk. Web: www.natfilm.dk. Programmer: Kim Foss. *(Off-beat international retrospectives and tributes - March 28-April 69, 2008.)*

New Directors/New Films, Film Society of Lincoln Center, 70 Lincoln Center Plaza, New York, NY 10023, USA. Tel: (1 212) 875 5610. e: festival@filmlinc.com. Web: www.filmlinc.com. *(One of the premier international showcases for the work of emerging filmmakers; co-sponsored by the Department of Film, the Museum of Modern Art and the Film Society of Lincoln Center - March 21-April 1, 2008.)*

New York Film Festival, Film Society of Lincoln Center, 70 Lincoln Center Plaza, New York, NY 10023-6595, USA. Tel: (1 212) 875 5610. e:

festival@filmlinc.com. Web: www.filmlinc.com. *(Highlights the best of American and international cinema - late Sept-early Oct.)*

Nordic Film Festival, 75 rue General Leclerc, 76000 Rouen, France. Tel: (33 232) 767 322. e: festival.cinema.nordique@wanadoo.fr. Web: www.festival-cinema-nordique.asso.fr. *(Competitive festival of Nordic cinema, including retrospectives - March 5-16, 2008.)*

Nordic Film Forum Scanorama, Ozostrasse 1, Vilnius 08200, Lithuania. Tel: (370 5) 276 0367. e: info@kino.lt . Web: www.scanorama.lt. *(Feature and documentary films from Nordic, Central, Eastern and Western Europe - Nov.)*

Officinema, Cineteca del Comune di Bologna, Via Riva di Reno 72, 40122 Bologna, Italy. Tel: (39) 051 219 4814. e: cinetecamanifestazioni1@ comune.bologna.it. Web: www. cinetecadibologna.it. *(Competition for final projects from European schools - Feb 20-24, 2008.)*

Open Air Filmfest Weiterstadt, PO Box 1164, D-64320 Weiterstadt, Germany. Tel: (49 61) 501 2185. e: filmfest@weiterstadt.de. Web: www. filmfest-weiterstadt.de. *(Mainly short films of all genres, formats and lengths; deadline for entries May 15 - Aug 14-18, 2008.)*

Palm Beach International Film Festival, 289 Via Naranjas, Royal Palm Plaza, Suite 48, Boca Raton, Florida 33432, USA. Tel: (1 561) 362 0003. e: info@pbifilmfest.org. Web: www.pbifilmfest. org. *(American and international independent features, shorts, documentaries and large format. Competitive - April 10-17, 2008.)*

Palm Springs International Festival of Short Films & Film Market, 1700 E Tahquitz Canyon Way, Suite 3, Palm Springs, CA 92262, USA. Tel: (1 760) 322 2930. e: info@psfilmfest.org. Web: www.psfilmfest.org. *(Competitive shorts festival and market. Student, animation, documentary, live action and international competition with Audience and Juried Awards. Seminars and workshops - Aug.)*

Philadelphia Film Festival, Philadelphia Film Society, 4th Floor, 234 Market St, Philadelphia, PA 19106, USA. Tel: (1 267) 765 9700. e: info@phillyfests.com. Web: www.phillyfests.com. *(International and US features, documentaries, animation and shorts - April 3-15, 2008.)*

Prix Italia, Via Monte Santo 52, 00195 Rome, Italy. Tel: (39 06) 372 8708. e: prixitalia@rai.it. Web: www.prixitalia.rai.it. *(Prix Italia is the oldest and most prestigious International Radio, Television and Web competition. It awards prizes for quality productions in the fields of drama, documentaries, the performing arts (television) and music (radio); open only to 90 member organisations - Sept.)*

RAI Trade Screenings, Via Umberto Novaro 18, 00195 Rome, Italy. Tel: (39 06) 374981. e: info@raitrade.it. Web: www.raitrade.rai.it. *(International programming buyers view RAI productions for broadcast, video and other rights - April.)*

Ravenna Nightmare Film Festival, Via Mura di Porta Serrata 13, 48100 Ravenna, Italy. Tel: (39 05) 4468 4242. e: ravenna@melies.org. Web: www.ravennanightmare.it. *(The festival was founded in 2003 and its dates are round Halloween weekend. The festival is definitely the place to be for horror in Italy. The main event of the festival is the International Competition for features, which usually admits around 10-12 feature films, all of which are national premieres; while the European Competition for short films screens around 15 films. Added to this are a number of Special Events out of competition; various retrospectives from year to year - and last but not least parties, music, and literature events featuring important writers of the horror genre. Among our previous guests: Dario Argento, Brian Yuzna, Marco Muller, and our special supporter Valerio Evangelisti – Oct 29-Nov 2, 2008.)*

Reykjavik International Film Festival, Fríkirkjuvegi 1, 101 Reykjavík, Iceland. Tel: (354) 411 7055. Web: www.filmfest.is. *(National and international filmmakers compete for creative awards. The festival was conceived to promote Icelandic Cinema culture and nurture a diverse and fruitful film industry - Sept 25-Oct 9, 2008.)*

St Louis International Film Festival, Centene Centre for Arts and Education, 3547 Olive St, St Louis, MO 63103-1014, USA. Tel: (1 314) 289 4150. e: mailroom@cinemastlouis.org. Web: www.cinemastlouis.org. *(Showcases US and international independent films, documentaries and shorts. Competitive - Nov 13-23, 2008.)*

St Petersburg Festival of Festivals, 10 Kamennostrovsky Ave, St Petersburg 197101, Russia. Tel: (7 812) 237 0072. e: info@filmfest.ru. Web: www.filmfest.ru. *(Non-competitive, showcasing the best films from around the world - June 23-29, 2008.)*

San Fernando Valley International Film Festival, 5504 Cleon Ave, North Hollywood, CA 91601, USA. Tel: (1 818) 623 9122. e: festival@viffi.org. Web: www.viffi.org. *(Competition for films and screenplays; showcase for filmmakers and writers who believe in entertainment that should not contain gratuitous violence or profanity - May 30-June 8, 2008.)*

San Francisco International Asian American Film Festival, c/o NAATA, 145 9th St, Suite 350, San Francisco, CA 94103, USA. Tel: (1 415) 863 0814. e: festival@naatanet. Web: www.naatanet.org. *(Screens over 130 films and videos by Asian-American and Asian artists - March.)*

San Francisco International LGBT Film Festival, Frameline, 145 9th St, Suite 300, San Francisco, CA 94103, USA. Tel: (1 415) 703 8650. e: info@frameline.org. Web: www.frameline.org. *(Focus on gay, lesbian, bisexual and transgender themes - June 19-25, 2008.)*

San Sebastián Horror and Fantasy Film Festival, Donostia Kultura, Plaza de la Constitucion 1, 20003 Donostia-San Sebastian, Spain. Tel: (34 943) 481 197. e: cinema_cinema@donostia.org. Web: www.sansebastianhorrorfestival.com. *(Cult, cutting-edge, horror-fantasy festival; short film and feature competition - Oct 31-Nov 8, 2008.)*

San Sebastián Human Rights Film Festival, Donostia Kultura, Plaza de la Constitucion 1, 20003 Donostia-San Sebastián, Spain. Tel: (34 943) 481 471. e: cinederechoshumanos@donostia.org. Web: www.cineyderechoshumanos.com. *(Short films and features about human rights - April 18-25, 2008.)*

São Paulo International Film Festival, Rua Antonio Carlos 288, 01309-010 São Paulo, Brazil. Tel: (55 11) 3141 0413. e: info@mostra.org. Web: www.mostra.org. *(Competitive event for new filmmakers and international panorama - Oct 17-31, 2008.)*

Sarajevo Film Festival, Hamdije Kresevljakovica 13, 71000 Sarajevo, Bosnia and Herzegovina. Tel: (387 33) 209 411. e: programmes@sff.ba. Web: www.sff.ba. *(The festival presents a wide selection of both competitive and non-competitive films with a focus on Southeast Europe and its filmmakers, who compete in Feature, Short and Documentary film sections - Aug 15-23, 2008.)*

Scienceplusfiction, Via Economo 12/9, 34123 Trieste, Italy. Tel: (39 04) 0322 0551. e: info@scienceplusfiction.org. Web: www.scienceplusfiction.org. *(Focus on sci-fi, fantasy and fantastic cinema - Nov.)*

Short Shorts Film Festival & Asia, 2F Hirakawacho Urban Bldg, 2-4-8 Hirakawacho, Chiyoda-ku, Tokyo 102-0093, Japan. Tel: (81 3) 5214 3005. e: look@shortshorts.org. Web: www.shortshorts.org. *(SSFF & ASIA has been an Academy Awards accredited short film festival since 2004 and its Grand Prix winner will be eligible to receive an Academy Award nomination. Supporting the Japanese and International film community, the festival presents over 90 short films and invites filmmakers from all over the world, creating great opportunity for cultural exchange - June 5-15, 2008.)*

Siberian International Festival - Spirit of Fire, Festival Committee, 1 Mosfilmovskaya St, Moscow, 119992 Russia. Tel: (7 095) 143 9484. e: festival@spiritoffire.ru. Web: www.spiritoffire. ru. *(Showcases 15 films directed by young talents; all formats eligible - late Feb.)*

Silent Film Days in Tromsø, PO Box 285, N-9253 Tromsø, Norway. Tel: (47) 7775 3090. e: info @tiff.no. Web: www.tiff.no. *(The venue for the festival is Tromsø's old cinema which opened in 1916 and was originally built for silent films. All films are screened with live music composed and performed by international musicians - Sept 4-7, 2008.)*

Silverdocs: AFI/Discovery Channel Documentary Film Festival, 8633 Colesville Rd, Silver Spring, Maryland 20910, USA. e: info@silverdocs.com. Web: www.silverdocs.com. *(An international festival showcasing over 100 films from over 45 countries which celebrate the creative vision of independent filmmakers and the power of documentary to expand our world view - June 16-23, 2008.)*

Sofia International Film Festival, 1 Bulgaria Sq, Sofia 1463, Bulgaria. Tel: (359 2) 9166 029. e: office@sofiaiff.com. Web: www.sofiaiff.com. *(Showcases new Bulgarian and Balkan films to international audiences - March 6-16, 2008.)*

Stuttgart Festival of Animated Film, Film-und Medienfestival GmbH, Schlosstrasse 84, 70176 Stuttgart, Germany. Tel: (49 711) 925 460. e: itfs@festival-gmbh.de. Web: www.itfs.de. *(One of the largest events for animated film worldwide. The festival showcases a diverse range of animated film starting with artistic short films, through TV series and children's films and rounded off with feature-length animation. The festival focuses particularly on supporting talented young filmmakers with a special sponsorship award and the Young Animation competition - May 1-8, 2008.)*

Sunny Side of the Doc, Résidence le Gabut Bâtiment E, 16 rue de l'Aimable Nanette, 17000 La Rochelle, France. Tel: (33 1) 7735 5300. e: info@sunnysideofthedoc.com. Web: www.sunnysideofthedoc.com. *(International documentary market - June 24-27, 2008.)*

Sydney Film Festival, PO Box 96, Strawberry Hills, NSW 2012, Australia. Tel: (61 2) 9318 0999. e: info@sydneyfilmfestival.org. Web: www. sydneyfilmfestival.org. *(Broad-based event screening new Australian and international features and shorts. The Festival has Australia's only FIAPF-accredited Official Competition in which twelve films from around the world will be selected to compete for a cash prize of $60,000 - June.)*

Tallinn Black Nights Film Festival, Gonsiori 21, 10147 Tallinn, Estonia. Tel: (372) 631 4640. e: poff@poff.ee. Web: www.poff.ee. *(Emphasis on European films - late Nov-early Dec.)*

Taormina International Film Festival, Corso Umberto 19, 98039 Taormina Messina, Italy. Tel: (39 094) 221 142. e: press@taorminafilmfest. it or festival@taorminafilmfest.it. Web: www. taorminafilmfest.it. *(Films by English-language directors. Restorations. Silver Ribbons awarded by Italian film critics. Deadline for submissions 15 May - June.)*

Tel-Aviv International Student Film Festival, Film & TV Dept, Room 20, Tel Aviv University, Ramat Aviv 69978, Israel. Tel: (972 3) 640 9936. e: filmfest@post.tau.ac.il. Web: www.taufilmfest. com. *(Workshops, retrospectives, tributes, premieres; biennial - June.)*

Tempo Documentary Festival, Box 2068, SE-103 12, Stockholm, Sweden. Tel: (46 8) 545 10333. e: info@tempofestival.se. *(New and creative documentary films - Nov.)*

Trieste Film Festival, Via Donota 1, 34121 Trieste, Italy. Tel: (39 040) 347 6076. e: info@ alpeadriacinema.it. Web: www.alpeadriacinema. it. *(Central and Eastern European Cinema - Jan.)*

True/False Film Festival, PO Box 1102, Columbia, Missouri 65205-1102, USA. Tel: (1 573) 442 8783. e: info@truefalse.org. Web: www. truefalse.org. *(International documentary festival held at six venues - Feb 28-March 2, 2008.)*

Tudela First Film Festival, Centro Cultural Castel Ruiz, Plaza Mercadal 7, 31500, Tudela, Navarra, Spain. Tel: (34 948) 825 868. sac010@tudela.es. Web: www.tudela.es. *(Early Nov.)*

Uppsala International Short Film Festival, PO Box 1746, SE-751 47 Uppsala, Sweden. Tel: (46 18) 120 025. e: info@shortfilmfestival.com. Web: www.shortfilmfestival.com. *(Sweden's only international shorts festival. Competitive - Oct.)*

USA Film Festival, 6116 N Central Expressway, Suite 105, Dallas, Texas 75206, USA. Tel: (1 214) 821 6300. e: usafilmfestival@aol.com. Web: www.usafilmfestival.com. *(Non-competitive for US and international features. Academy-qualifying National Short Film/Video competition with cash awards - April 24-May 1, 2008.)*

Utopiales – Festival International de Science-Fiction de Nantes, 10 Bis, Blvd de Stalingrad, 44000 Nantes, France. Tel: (33 2) 4035 3082. e: marie.masson@congres-nantes.fr. Web: www. utopiales.org. *(Multimedia science-fiction festival - Nov.)*

Valdivia International Film Festival, Dirección Vicente Perez Rosales 787E, Valdivia, Chile. Tel: (56 63) 249 073. e: info@ficv.cl. Web: www.ficv. cl/f14. *(International feature contest, plus Chilean and international shorts, documentaries and animation - early Oct.)*

Viewfinders International Film Festival for Youth, PO Box 36139, Halifax, NS, B3J 3S9, Canada. Tel: (1 902) 422 6965. e: festival@ atlanticfilm.com. Web: www.atlanticfilm.com. *(Family-oriented films and videos from all over the world - April 22-26, 2008.)*

Vila do Conde, Praça Vasco da Gama 4480-840, Vila do Conde, Portugal. Tel: (351 252) 248 400. e: geral@cm-viladoconde.pt. Web: www.

cm-viladoconde.pt. *(National and International shorts competitions. Special programme and retrospectives - July 5-13, 2008.)*

Warsaw International Film Festival, PO Box 816, 00-950 Warsaw 1, Poland. Tel: (48 22) 621 4647. e: kontakty@wff.pl. Web: www.wff.pl. *(Key event in Poland. Fiction and documentary features. New Films' and New Directors' competition - Oct.)*

Washington, DC International Film Festival (Filmfest DC), PO Box 21396, Washington, DC 20009, USA. Tel: (1 202) 628 3456. e: filmfestdc@filmfestdc.org. Web: www.filmfestdc.org. *(Celebrates the best in world cinema from over 30 countries - April 24-May 4, 2008.)*

ZagrebDox, Factum Centre for Drama Art, Nova Ves 18/3, 10 000 Zagreb, Croatia. Tel: (385 1) 485 4821. e: info@zagrebdox.net. Web: www. zagrebdox.net. *(International and competitive documentary film festival - Feb 25-March 2, 2008.)*

Zurich Film Festival, Spoundation Motion Picture GmbH, Bederstrasse 51, 8002 Zurich, Switzerland. Tel: (41 44) 286 6000. e: info@zurichfilmfestival.org. Web: www. zurichfilmfestival.org. *(Over the course of eleven days, in the city with Europe's highest concentration of cinemas, the festival presents film premieres from all over the world, offers cinematic treats to a fascinated national and international audience and facilitates direct on-the-spot exchange with the filmmakers. With numerous events and parties complementing the cinema program, the festival offers an ideal platform for networking and exchanging ideas - Sept 25-5 Oct, 2008.)*

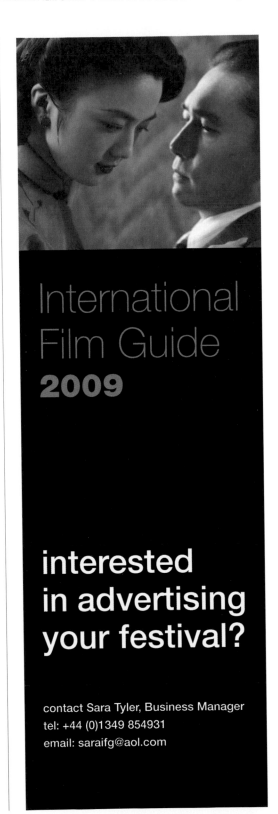

Index to Advertisers

15-19 October 2008

FRANKFURTER BUCHMESSE
GUEST OF HONOUR >TURKEY<

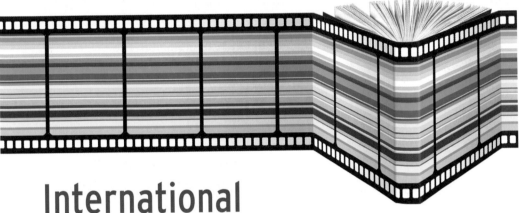

International Agents Centre for Adaptations & Screenplay

Your market place
for film rights from
15 to 19 October 2008
(Forum, Level 0)

ACCREDITATION AND INFORMATION:
Katharina Werdnik | werdnik@book-fair.com
www.book-fair.com